MODERN ASPECTS OF THE LAWS OF NAVAL WARFARE AND MARITIME NEUTRALITY

A PUBLICATION OF THE GRADUATE INSTITUTE OF INTERNATIONAL STUDIES, GENEVA

Also published in this series:

The United States and the Politicization of the World Bank
Bartram S. Brown

Trade Negotiations in the OECD
David J. Blair

World Financial Markets after 1992
Hans Genberg and Alexander K. Swoboda

Succession Between International Organisations
Patrick R. Myers

Ten Years of Turbulence: The Chinese Cultural Revolution
Barbara Barnouin and Yu Changgen

The Islamic Movement in Egypt: Perceptions of International Relations 1967–81
Walid M. Abdelnasser

Namibia and Southern Africa: Regional Dynamics of Decolonization 1945–90
Ronald Dreyer

The International Organization of Hunger
Peter Uvin

Citizenship East and West
Edited by André Liebich and Daniel Warner with Jasna Dragović

Introduction to the Law of Treaties
Paul Reuter

The Imperiled Red Cross and the Palestine-Eretz-Yisrael Conflict 1945–1952
Dominique-D. Junod

Ideology and Economic Reform Under Deng Xiaoping, 1978–1993
Wei-Wei Zhang

Chinese Foreign Policy During the Cultural Revolution
Barbara Barnouin and Yu Changgen

MODERN ASPECTS OF THE LAWS OF NAVAL WARFARE AND MARITIME NEUTRALITY

George P. Politakis

Routledge
Taylor & Francis Group
LONDON AND NEW YORK

First published in 1998 by
Kegan Paul International Limited

This edition published 2015 by Routledge
2 Park Square, Milton Park, Abingdon, Oxon OX14 4RN
711 Third Avenue, New York, NY 10017, USA

Routledge is an imprint of the Taylor & Francis Group, an informa business

Set in Palatino
by Intype London Ltd

British Library Cataloguing in Publication Data
Politakis, George P.
Modern aspects of the laws of naval warfare and maritime neutrality.
(A publication of the Graduate Institute of International Studies, Geneva)
I. Maritime law 2. Neutrality 3. War, Maritime (International law)
I. Title II. Graduate Institute of International Studies 341.7'56'6

ISBN 0–7103–0589–3

Library of Congress Cataloging in Publication Data
Politakis, George P. 1962–
Modern aspects of the laws of naval warfare and maritime neutrality / George Politakis.
p. cm. – (A publication of the Graduate Institute of International Studies, Geneva)
Includes bibliographical references.
ISBN 0–7103–0589–3 (alk. paper)
1. War, Maritime (International law) 2. Neutrality. I. Title. II. Series: Publications de l'Institut universitaire de hautes études internationales, Genève.
KZ6563.P65 1998
341.6'4–dc21 97–50129
CIP

ISBN 13 : 978-0-7103-0589-3 (hbk)

CONTENTS

PART TWO
Belligerent Interference with Neutral Property at Sea

Στούς γονείς μου

To my parents

ABBREVIATIONS

ACDA	United States Arms Control and Disarmament Agency
AFDI	*Annuaire Français de Droit International*
AJIL	*American Journal of International Law*
Ann.AAPSS	*Annals of the American Academy of Political and Social Science*
Ann.IDI	*Annuaire de l'Institut de Droit International*
APSR	*American Political Science Review*
ASDI	*Annuaire Suisse de Droit International*
BYIL	*British Yearbook of International Law*
CIRPÉS	Centre Interdisciplinaire de Recherches sur la Paix et d'Études Stratégiques
CYIL	*Canadian Yearbook of International Law*
GRIP	Groupe de Recherche et d'Information sur la Paix
GST	*Grotius Society Transactions*
GYIL	*German Yearbook of International Law*
HILJ	*Harvard International Law Journal*
ICJ	International Court of Justice
ICLQ	*International and Comparative Law Quarterly*
ICRC	International Committee of the Red Cross
IISS	International Institute for Strategic Studies
IJIL	*Indian Journal of International Law*
ILC	International Law Commission
ILM	*International Legal Materials*
Int.Con.	*International Conciliation*
Int.Sec.	*International Security*
It.YIL	*Italian Yearbook of International Law*
IYHR	*Israel Yearbook on Human Rights*
JCSS	Jaffee Center for Strategic Studies

KCA	*Keesing's Contemporary Archives*
KRWE	*Keesing's Record of World Events (formerly KCA)*
MLR	*Military Law Review*
NILR	*Netherlands International Law Review*
NYIL	*Netherlands Yearbook of International Law*
Ocean Ybk	*Ocean Yearbook*
ODIL	*Ocean Development and International Law*
PCIJ	Permanent Court of International Justice
Proc.APS	*Proceedings of the Academy of Political Science*
Proc.ASIL	*Proceedings of the American Society of International Law*
PYIL	*Polish Yearbook of International Law*
RADIC	*Revue Africaine de Droit International et Comparé*
RBDI	*Revue Belge de Droit International*
RCADI	*Recueil des Cours de l'Académie de Droit International*
RDC	*Revue de Droit Contemporain*
RDILC	*Revue de Droit International et de Législation Comparée*
REDI	*Revue Égyptienne de Droit International*
Rep.ILA	*Reports of the International Law Association*
RGDIP	*Revue Générale de Droit International Public*
RHDI	*Revue Hellénique de Droit International*
RICR	*Revue Internationale de la Croix-Rouge*
RSDIE	*Revue Suisse de Droit International et de Droit Européen (formerly ASDI)*
RUSI	Royal United Services Institution
SDLR	*San Diego Law Review*
SFDI	Société Française pour le Droit International
UNDY	*United Nations Disarmament Yearbook*
UNGA	United Nations General Assembly
UNIDIR	United Nations Institute for Disarmament Research
UNSC	United Nations Security Council
UNTS	*United Nations Treaty Series*
USNIP	*United States Naval Institute Proceedings*
USNWC	United States Naval War College
VJIL	*Virginia Journal of International Law*
Ybk.ILC	*Yearbook of the International Law Commission*
Ybk.SIPRI	*Yearbook of the Stockholm International Peace Research Institute*

YJIL	*Yale Journal of International Law*
YLJ	*Yale Law Journal*
ZaöRV	*Zeitschrift für Ausländischess Öffentliches Recht und Völkerrecht*

PREFACE

My first contact with the exciting subjects of international humanitarian law and the international law of the sea was made in 1986 during a postgraduate programme at the University of London. My first real experience came in March of the following year when I found myself conscript petty officer in the Hellenic Navy aboard an ageing destroyer at a time of crisis with neighbouring Turkey over long-disputed continental shelf rights of the Aegean islands. It was during that 32-day cruise on battle stations, amidst low-flight passes of 'unlockable' aircraft, hasty tests of freshly installed missile launchers, false alarms about suspect submarine contacts, and all kinds of nerve-testing incidents with rival forces that I discovered in the Commander's quarters a book with a blue cover which looked somewhat relevant. Its title: *The Law of War and Neutrality at Sea*, by Robert W. Tucker. To this otherwise unimportant experience I essentially owe the fortunate choice of my thesis topic – not an inappreciable fact by any token, as every doctoral student can confirm.

This study is a revised version of a thesis submitted in October 1994 for the degree of Doctor of Philosophy at the Graduate Institute of International Studies. In its present form it covers developments up to the end of December 1996. This work began in the autumn of 1988 with all those discouraging symptoms that mark any doctoral enterprise: an effort of unknown duration, unclear demands, and unforseeable conclusion. Today, the completion of this endeavour appears at last attained. The pleasant duty of addressing a few acknowledgements which preface my thesis are perhaps the only stressless moment this work had to offer. For, contrary to the place that the text traditionally reserves to them, in reality they symbolize relief at the 'end', but also because after some years of more or less exhausting and solitary strain, the need is sincerely felt to devote a word to those who extended a helping hand, shared the difficulties and believed in the outcome.

To all those who honoured me with their confidence and provided me with their admirable insight, I wish to express my profound gratitude. My mind turns in particular to my teacher, Professor Georges Abi-Saab, whom I thank for his scrupulous guidance throughout this academic adventure, his inspiring tutorship, his friendly support. I can only modestly hope that the present writing will not frustrate his affection for theoretical analysis and logical reasoning, or his preoccupation with balance and measure in legal expression. Highest thanks must also go to Professor Lucius Caflisch, of the Graduate Institute, to Professor Natalino Ronzitti, of the University of Pisa, and to Professor Theodor Meron, of the New York University, whose supervision and advice in the preparation of this thesis were invaluable. Further, I wish to extend my gratitude to Ms. Louise Doswald-Beck, of the ICRC Legal Department, and to Professor Peter Haggenmacher, of the Graduate Institute, for having provided valuable material as well as for the brief, yet enlightening, conversations of which I made the most.

My dear friend and colleague John Packer, currently with the OSCE's High Commissioner on National Minorities, can be assured of my appreciation for his thorough and competent editing of the manuscript. Among the various library services I made use of for the purposes of my research, my special thanks go to the most cooperative staff of the UN library, in particular Werner Simon for his adept and generous assistance, and to Ms. Martine Basset of the Institute's library for her kind help in locating sources unavailable in Geneva. The Military library at Basel, as well as the ETH's Central library at Zurich, proved equally useful.

Financial support for this work was initially received from the Greek State Scholarship Foundation (IKY) which funded the first three and a half years of my doctoral studies, and later from the Graduate Institute and the Faculty of Law of the University of Geneva by means of assistantship and lecturership posts, respectively. To all three institutions I remain greatly indebted. The final acknowledgement is sincerely devoted to my wife for all her understanding and encouragement. I submit the work that follows with the timid hope that it may contribute to the ongoing discussion concerning the modernization of the laws of naval warfare and maritime neutrality, and the personal resolve that this first essay in the fascinating world of legal research will not remain the only one.

F/B Mediterranean Sky, Ionian Sea,
December 1996

Qui mare teneat, eum necesse esse rerum potiri

He who commands the sea has command of everything

Cicero, *Letters to Atticus*, bk.X, sect.8
(transl. by E.O. Winstedt, The Loeb Classical Library, 1960 at p. 303)

INTRODUCTION

The Role of Sea Power in Modern Strategy Before embarking upon the study of the legal parameters of modern naval warfare, it would be pertinent to address as briefly as possible the continued relevance of the sea element in the power struggle among nations.[1] Supremacy at sea has proven historically to be a *sine qua non* of world leadership. The fascinating trail from the Athenian thalassocracy of the classical times to the Pax Britannica of the nineteenth century, passing through the Portuguese and the Dutch predominance in the sixteenth and the seventeenth centuries, confirms that the open seas always provided the milieu for the rise of new hegemonies or the demise of old.[2]

Modern analysts speak of the 'maritimization' of world trade as an irreversible feature of global economy. Seaborne trade represents three-quarters of world trade in tonnage, and 66 per cent of world trade in value.[3] Crude oil and petroleum products

[1]Among the essential readings on modern naval strategy, see MARTIN, L.W., *The Sea in Modern Strategy*, 1967; MASSON, P., *De la mer et de sa stratégie*, 1986; COUTAU-BÉGARIE, H. (ed.), *L'évolution de la pensée navale*, 1990; Id., *La puissance maritime: Castex et la stratégie navale*, 1985, pp. 35–76; BØRRESEN, J., 'The Seapower of the Coastal State', 17 *Journal of Strategic Studies* (March 1994), p. 148*ff.*; TILL, G., 'Maritime Power and the Twenty-First Century', 17 *Journal of Strategic Studies* (March 1994), p. 176*ff.*

[2]As a study set out to demonstrate recently, 'seapower is a condition of active participation in global politics. It is a type of resource whose absence predisposes states to a passive role as consumers of world order . . . Over the entire experience of the modern world since 1500 it has proved decisive in facilitating global coordination and it will remain decisive as long as it continues to do that'; see MODELSKI, G. and THOMPSON, W.R., *Seapower in Global Politics, 1494–1993*, 1988 at pp. 11, 13.

[3]See VIGARIÉ, A., *Economie maritime et géostratégie des oceans*, 1990 at p. 14. No less than 95 per cent of all trade that crosses frontiers is waterborne, including

make up almost 40 per cent of the total volume.[4] Those statistics reaffirm, if there is need, the undiminished importance of economic warfare in the context of naval strategy. In addition, the growing resource-related uses of the sea, which have given rise to what the jurist has called the 'creeping jurisdiction' of coastal states,[5] have rendered the idea of maintaining naval forces extremely popular. At the beginning of this century there were some twenty-two navies plying the world's oceans, while current publications list over 150 nations with navies and/or coastguards.

Modern navies must be able to respond to a great diversity of tasks. Present-day naval missions are often systematized under four headings: nuclear deterrence, sea control/sea denial, power projection and naval presence.[6] Nuclear submarines have transformed the depths of the oceans into the most secure, quasi-undetectable hide-out of ballistic missiles. Sea control denotes the traditional operations aiming at assuming command of maritime communication lanes (e.g. engage a naval battle, enforce a blockade, etc.), whereas sea denial pertains to naval action of a more defensive character such as minelaying or submarine warfare against enemy commerce *(guerre de course)*. By power projection, one implies profiting from supremacy at sea to the advantage of campaigns against the shore; naval or aerial bombardment and amphibious landing operations may best illustrate this type of mission. Lastly, presence means the various forms of naval diplomacy in time of crisis or, as James Cable has memorably put it, 'the use or threat of limited naval force, otherwise than as an act of war, in order to secure advantage, or to avert loss, either in the furtherance of an international

---

inland. A third of world production of iron ore is carried by sea. In 1986, some 3,362 million tonnes were carried by sea, some eight times the amount carried in 1946.

[4]See GROVE, E., *The Future of Sea Power*, 1990, pp. 31–45.

[5]It should be noted that off-shore oil production equals 20 per cent of world's total, while seabed exploitation covers half of world's tin and iron ore needs. As regards the fishing industry, it has known an unprecedented expansion in recent years with global fish catches more than tripled.

[6]See, for instance, TRIPIER, M., 'Les missions navales', 48 *Stratégique* (1990), p. 27*ff*. The special attributes of naval power (versatility, controllability, mobility, projection ability, access potential, symbolism and endurance) are examined in BOOTH, K., *Law, Force and Diplomacy at Sea*, 1985, p. 187*ff*. See also MOTTE, M., 'Au péril de la mer, typologie de la conflictualité maritime', *Trimestre du Monde* (1996/3), p. 89*ff*.

dispute or else against foreign nationals within the territory or the jurisdiction of their own state'.[7]

The Influence of the New Law of the Sea The far-reaching changes in the law of the sea in the last forty years represent one of the primary factors calling for urgent modernization of the traditional law of sea warfare. Significant developments in matters of coastal jurisdiction, however, would tend to affect the geographical scope of application of a revised code of naval operations rather than its normative content. Under the 1958 and 1982 treaty arrangements, but also under the established customary practice of the last twenty years, a number of concepts have undergone considerable modification while new institutions have also been created. The coastal state is now allowed to claim sovereignty over a 12-mile territorial sea belt. It has also been attributed new zones of jurisdiction such as the continental shelf, and more recently the exclusive economic zone. International straits follow today a novel typology, while a liberal right of transit passage has come to supersede in most cases the classical right of innocent passage.

Despite the fact that these conventional undertakings were generally intended to regulate only the peacetime uses of the oceans, it remains undeniable that an updated legal instrument on naval operations should necessarily accord with developments in the peacetime law of the sea and to a certain extent even integrate some of its concepts.[8] This is all the more true since contemporary naval conflicts are most likely to occur ostensibly in time of peace and, therefore, the codified law of the sea provisions would still apply. In this perspective, the theatre of naval operations would be most probably affected.

What needs to be carefully examined is whether the inviolability of neutral waters, confined to a 3-mile territorial sea as it was, should now envelop the entire coastal jurisdiction which currently may stretch out as far as 200 miles. A rule to this effect would severely diminish the area for hostile operations

[7]See CABLE, J., *Gunboat Diplomacy*, 1971 at p. 21.

[8]For an overview of the conventional and customary principles which regulate the military uses of the seas in the current context, see VUKAS, B., 'L'utilisation pacifique de la mer, dénucléarisation et désarmement' in DUPUY, R.-J. and VIGNES, D. (eds), *Traité du nouveau droit de la mer*, 1985, pp. 1047–93, and WANG, J.C.F., *Handbook on Ocean Politics and Law*, 1992, pp. 367–90.

since no belligerent warships or submarines could lawfully operate within 200 miles of the coast, but also no ground mines or other devices could be laid on the continental shelf of the neutral state which, it should be recalled, can exceptionally reach as far out as 350 miles. Equally important would be the question of the limits of belligerent rights within international straits where third states normally enjoy the right of transit passage. It is clear that to accord to neutral shipping, but also to aircraft and submersibles, the right of free transit passage would pose a security problem of extreme delicacy to the belligerent bordering the strait. The inverse proposition, that is to say, a belligerent right of transit passage through an international strait controlled by neutral riparians, raises less difficulty, but yet is not free of legal controversy.[9]

As far as the continental shelf and the exclusive economic zone are concerned, mention has already been made of the view ascribing a progressive 'territorialization' of the continental shelf or the exclusive economic zone (EEZ).[10] As the law now stands, however, it is evident that coastal states do not enjoy therein full sovereignty, but only sovereign rights for the purpose of exploring and exploiting natural resources. The argument has been advanced, therefore, that third states can lawfully exercise in the EEZ all the activities associated with the freedom of the high seas provided that they are not likely to hamper or otherwise interfere with the resource-related rights of the coastal state. Under such interpretation maritime powers have claimed the liberty to engage in various military activities such as naval exercises, weapons testing, or the deployment of underwater monitoring systems without the permission of the coastal state.

[9]For some apposite remarks regarding the impact of the new law of the sea on the theatre of naval warfare, see RONZITTI, N., 'The Crisis of the Traditional Law Regulating International Armed Conflicts at Sea and the Need for its Revision' in RONZITTI, N. (ed.), *The Law of Naval Warfare*, 1988, pp. 13–22, and LOWE, A.V., 'The Commander's Handbook on the Law of Naval Operations and the Contemporary Law of the Sea' in ROBERTSON, H.B. (ed.), *The Law of Naval Operations*, USNWC, 64 *International Law Studies* (1991), pp. 109–47.

[10]The so-called 'creeping jurisdiction' of the coastal state has also attracted other names, not always elegant, such as 'propertization', 'parcellation' or 'ocean enclosure'. The 200-mile exclusive economic zone has placed about 32 per cent of the oceans under some form of national administration. This is considered a direct challenge to the mobility of blue-water navies, given the fact that a carrier task force, for example, is said to require an area of 200 square miles when deployed for action. On the repercussions of expanding coastal zones on the strategic interests of naval powers, see BOOTH, *op. cit., supra* n.6, p. 137*ff*.

Accordingly, in the case of an armed conflict at sea, belligerent naval forces might assert the right to stop and search merchant shipping or lay minefields within the EEZ of a third state. Dormant mines and torpedoes or anti-submarine sonar arrays might thus be emplaced on the continental shelf of a neutral. Apart from the fact that both the continental shelf and the EEZ pertain to the regime of the high seas (except for the limited resource-oriented coastal rights), it has also been pointed out that, if the opposite view was to prevail, neutrals would often be faced with the extremely onerous, if not impossible, task of policing a 200-mile zone in order to honour their obligation to prevent as much as possible any hostile action within their jurisdiction.

With reference to international straits, here again it would by no means be easy to transplant the upshot of long negotiations concerned with the regulation of international intercourse by sea to the sphere of naval warfare and maritime neutrality. To begin with, there is the problem concerning the customary character of the transit passage provisions of the 1982 Law of the Sea Convention. It is still being debated whether the right of transit passage already reflects international customary law, or whether is simply a treaty arrangement only binding between the parties to that Convention. Regardless of the answer to that controversy, it is not so much the concept of transit passage as such that is problematic, but rather the precise rights and duties that such 'continuous and expeditious passage' would involve for the transiting force and the bordering state. For it is one thing to say that ships passing through straits must respect IMO-designated sea lanes and traffic separation schemes, and quite another to decide whether warships should be permitted under the 'normal mode of navigation' clause to launch and recover aircraft, sail in formation, or operate acoustic and electronic surveillance devices.[11]

[11]To give another example, the fact that vessels in transit must comply with international conventions relating to maritime pollution is not at all relevant as to whether a belligerent warship or aircraft may engage in regular crossings for the purpose of monitoring maritime traffic and relaying information concerning suspect vessels. Should belligerent forces when in transit enjoy a practically unlimited freedom of action? But then, would not even defensive action against a suspected submarine contact or an unidentified approaching aircraft be tantamount to using neutral waters as a base of naval operations? Or, should defensive action be understood as involving preventive action as well? Would accompanying the transit passage, for instance, with extensive use of depth charges for fear of enemy submarines possibly lurking within the strait be

In the case of the littoral state at war which has to tolerate the transit passage of neutrals, should it nevertheless be empowered under certain conditions to react against the abusive, provocative or potentially threatening presence of foreign navies? If so, would this differ from exacting an element of 'innocence' and thus relegate transit passage to innocent passage? What about a belligerent claim to curtail navigational rights through the strait by notifying a zonal interdiction? Should the legality of such a measure depend on the exact nature of the declared zone, that is to say whether an exclusion zone or a defensive sea area is involved? The US-Iranian showdown at the closing stage of the Iran-Iraq War in respect of the unobstructed passage of non-belligerent warships and merchantmen through the Hormuz bottleneck has raised some of these legal queries in a most graphic way.[12]

If anything, it is clear that no scholar can pretend at present to be able to offer definitive answers to the questions highlighted above. All suggestions are legitimate and equally defendable hypotheses. The problem does not relate here to deciding among conflicting interpretations of an otherwise binding text, but much more perplexingly to foreseeing the emerging shape of the law of naval warfare on the basis of tentative analogies drawn in the context of the peacetime law of the sea. The mere transposition, however, of notions and rules elaborated within the framework of the peacetime law of the sea is likely to lead to unworkable 'solutions' and militarily unbalanced arrangements. There is little reason in the assertion that compromises worked out in the context of the clash of certain concrete interests such as the freedom of the high seas, the expansion of coastal jurisdiction, the pursuit of equitable development, or the protection of the marine environment and the safety of navigation, may also fit the context of sea warfare where the essential balance to be struck is between the military exigencies of the belligerents

compatible with the general obligation to respect neutral territory and abstain from any hostile action therein? It should be remembered that without the right of transit passage, 116 international straits would have become overlapped by territorial seas to be governed by innocent passage provisions; see BOOTH, *op. cit., supra* n.6, p. 97*ff*.

[12]For comments on the transit passage regime in time of conflict, see ALEXANDER, L.M., 'International Straits' in ROBERTSON, H.B. (ed.), *The Law of Naval Operations*, USNWC, 64 *International Law Studies* (1991), pp. 91–108, and MAYAMA, A., 'The Influence of the Straits Transit Regime on the Law of Neutrality at Sea', 26 *ODIL* (1995), p. 1*ff*.

and the legitimate concerns, commercial and otherwise, of neutrals.

The nature and scale of interests involved are profoundly heterogeneous in the two cases. This implies that different rationales may only produce different legal rules. The 400-Article UN Convention on the Law of the Sea, in force since November 1994, can offer dim guidance at best as to the normative substance of modern rules governing armed conflict at sea. Subtle academic constructions based on interpretation or analogy cannot transform what was developed from start to finish as a code for peacetime uses of the seas into ready-made principles applicable in time of war. The need remains, therefore, for a new law-making effort with the specific aim of drafting clear-cut rules for the conduct of hostilities at sea.

The Charter Dimension Updating the almost one century old Hague law implies, before anything else, harmonization with the UN Charter. To say that a modern 'restatement' of the law of sea warfare must be drafted in full consonance with the letter and the spirit of the constitutional instrument of the post-1945 world order is of course to force an open door. The exact interplay, however, between the Charter principles in general and the codificatory work at the beginning of the century concerning the laws of war poses serious difficulties. Three schools of thought have been debating the issue.

For some, the law on use of force as embodied in the UN Charter has had a catalytic effect on traditional legal prescriptions, so that today *all* questions concerning the conduct of military operations should be referred to the rules on the use of force announced in the UN Charter.[13] Other scholars maintain that the much-acclaimed prohibition of resort to force in Article 2§4, or *jus ad bellum*, is basically unconnected with the laws of war properly so-called, or *jus in bello*, and therefore the traditional laws remain unaltered by the Charter limitations on the use of force. A third view attempts a middle-ground solution arguing that, while remaining independent, the *jus ad bellum* and the *jus in bello* may still exact concurrent obligations on states involved in an international armed conflict. It has thus

[13]See, for instance, LOWE, *op. cit.*, *supra* n.9 at pp. 133, 141.

been suggested that a state's use of force in order to be lawful must comply with the old rules governing hostilities, but it would also have to satisfy the requirement of proportionality laid down by the self-defence principle of the Charter.[14]

One may easily imagine the delicate situations to which the continued application of the self-defence logic would lead. Both *ratione materiae* and *ratione temporis*, the self-defence test would be totally inappropriate in order to resolve the question of lawfulness of any single hostile action which might occur long after the first shots were fired – which is often the case. The principle enshrined in Article 51 of the Charter is conceptually too narrow to 'replace' all the rules governing hostilities. Squeezing the entire *jus in bello* at sea through the self-defence threshold is thought to prove damaging for both bodies of law. As Michael Bothe has rightly put it, 'once an armed conflict has started because aggression has occurred, it is not possible to ask the question, whether there is an armed attack or a situation of self-defence, for each individual shot fired. Within the framework of an armed conflict, the legal yardstick for the individual act of violence is the law of war only, not the *ius contra bellum*.'[15] The question calls for essentially different comments if one turns to the

[14]See, for instance, GREENWOOD, C., 'The Effects of the United Nations Charter on the Law of Naval Warfare', Introductory Report presented in September 1991 at Bergen for the purpose of the Round Table of Experts (copy on file with author) at p. 32. In the words of another scholar, 'les droits des belligérants envers les neutres doivent être rapportés au critère de la légitime défense . . . On sait que celui-ci doit être exercé dans les limites de la nécessité et de la proportionnalité. Il s'ensuit que les droits de belligérance ne peuvent être définis *in abstracto*, mais doivent être rapportés à la situation'; see RONZITTI, N., 'Le droit humanitaire applicable aux conflits armés en mer', 242 *RCADI* (1993) at pp. 138–9. See also RONZITTI, *op. cit., supra* n.9 at pp. 2–10. Note also that for a group of international lawyers and naval experts who have recently debated this matter, 'the rights of belligerents are affected by the restraints of the law of self-defense and that this will affect the rights of belligerents to make full use of all the methods of naval warfare that the traditional law automatically allowed once a state of war existed . . . The majority thought that the requirements of the law of self-defense, namely, necessity and proportionality, would limit the extent to which such measures would be taken, and thus have a restraining influence on the effect of the war'; see DOSWALD-BECK, *op. cit., infra* n.19 at p. 197.

[15]See BOTHE, M., 'Neutrality in Naval Warfare – What Is Left of Traditional International Law?' in DELISSEN, A.J.M. and TANJA, G.J. (eds), *Humanitarian Law of Armed Conflict – Challenges Ahead, Essays in Honour of Frits Kalshoven*, 1991 at p. 393.

implications of the Charter, *except for self-defence,* for the laws of naval warfare.

The Dearth of Legal Landmarks Sea warfare gives the impression of being somehow condemned to operate in a legal vacuum. At least, this is how certain states would attempt to describe the deep-rooted inability to articulate or apply a consistent body of rules in cases of armed conflict at sea. It should be made clear, however, that there is nothing innate about this penury of binding legal instruments. It is more political calculation than any systemic difficulty which can explain the fact that throughout our century the law of naval warfare has remained undecipherable. Every now and then it was the law of reprisals that was given prevalence, or the ever-changing 'modern' conditions which made respect for established law implausible. Later, it was the crumbling effect of two World Wars to which the irrevocable erosion of traditional principles was attributed. Whatever the reason invoked, legal constraint was minimized to the greatest benefit of those states aspiring each time to rule the waves. Indeed, the most powerful navies have customarily preferred to mould the law through unilateral practice rather than by international negotiation. National interests were thought best protected by drafting manuals – far from annoying, often inescapable, compromises in multilateral fora.

The dormant state of the law has other explanations as well. For several decades all efforts focused on the so-called peaceful uses of the oceans, that is to say the codification and progressive development of the far too numerous issues of the law of the sea. Scholars and government officials have been more interested in tackling fresh matters of coastal jurisdiction, maritime delimitation, or environmental protection than unburrying and modernizing the Hague legacy on naval warfare. What is more, the momentum was also missing. International naval armed conflicts since 1945 have been limited in number, duration or intensity. In that sense, the 1982 Falkland Islands conflict and, much more so, the 1980–8 Iran-Iraq War acted as catalysts. The Tanker War, by far the biggest chapter written on lawlessness at sea since the two World Wars, emphasized the queries and hardened the dilemmas.

The Need for a Unified Approach The greatest fallacy that legal theory has to fight against is the persistent belief that naval warfare follows its own set of legal rules, and that, therefore, no attempt should be made to transpose principles however well established in land or aerial warfare to the maritime context. Under modern conditions, the air, land and sea elements in military campaigns are inseparably interconnected. Most of the time, operations are not only combined efforts of ground, naval and air forces, but also within the context of what one might regard as a 'naval action' there may be involvement of air power. Is an amphibious landing manoeuvre to be considered a naval or a ground operation? Are the aircraft stationed or operating from a carrier to be deemed engaged in naval or air missions? What about the ship-based helicopters fitted out for anti-submarine protection of warships, or the helicopters offering minesweeping capability? Is missile warfare governed by different legal rules in case of air- or ground-launched missiles in contrast to missiles delivered by warships or submarines?

These are only a few of the open questions which tend to affirm the weakness of the proposition of an autonomous character of the laws of war applicable to armed conflict at sea. It is indeed difficult to imagine what could be the logical rationale that might necessitate distinct legal principles to apply to perfidy in land and naval warfare, if not a long-pursued policy of preserving the greatest freedom of action for maritime power. The same may apply to all the fundamentals of humanitarian law – from the scope of the principle of distinction to war crimes, and from the concept of unnecessary suffering to reprisals. There is urgent need for a trans-sectorial approach in matters of war laws which would address the legal problems of sea warfare along common humanitarian values and standards.[16]

No one could of course deny or underestimate the particular characteristics prevailing in the maritime context concerning the belligerent treatment of private property. There can be no doubt that notions like that of prize, contraband or continuous voyage have known a special development in the domain of naval warfare. Being a branch with some well-established attributes

[16] On this, see the remarks of ROUCOUNAS, E., 'Some Issues Relating to War Crimes in Air and Sea Warfare', 24 *IYHR* (1994), p. 223*ff*.

unknown to land or aerial warfare, therefore, naval warfare, it might be argued, should preserve its singularity in a separate body of legal rules. Although apparently sound, this view is open to two criticisms. First, it overlooks the fact that the laws of maritime neutrality have themselves also been affected by the expanding use of air power. As a matter of fact, military aircraft, whether fixed-wing or helicopter, have been increasingly assigned the role previously reserved to surface combatants in matters of contraband control, that is boarding and search or diversion to port. In this respect, it becomes evident that a solitary or airtight treatment of maritime practices would be impracticable since it would by necessity have to respond to, and be harmonized with, parallel rules of aerial warfare. The second objection would concern the risk of creating the impression that certain naval warfare tactics are somehow exempt from cardinal principles of humanitarian law. Such a proposition might easily lead to far-reaching if not alarming consequences. To cite but one conspicuous example, does the fact that under certain circumstances enemy or neutral merchant vessels can be seized and even destroyed alienate anything of the civilian character of merchant crewmen?

The Role of Doctrine In view of the dearth of legal sources on the subject, doctrinal works are most often confined to a narrative discourse on state practice and a review of the relevant literature. This makes scholar writings in matters of naval warfare look at times stuffed with technicalities and somewhat poor in legal analysis. However, this remark is specious since no one can be expected to comment, interpret or systematize rules which are simply non-existent. The few conventional texts have been 'honoured' with considerable disrespect and have long since been outdated. As for custom, one has to distinguish between state practice as it arose in the context of both World Wars and state practice arising in regional, limited conflicts. The former, although extremely rich, could hardly be formative of international custom, unless of course one is ready to accept that retaliatory action and *opinio juris* are not mutually exclusive. The latter, on the other hand, is too disparate. International jurisprudence is minimal, such that authors have practically nothing to quarrel over but a few lines from the Dönitz judgment of the Nuremberg Tribunal, while the ICJ pronouncements in the Corfu Channel and the Nicaragua cases have not touched upon truly controversial matters of the law of sea warfare.

Yet, over the past quarter of a century, doctrine has attempted to theorize experience. It was in 1970 that Daniel O'Connell first referred to principles associated with the concept of limited warfare. His idea was based on empirical observation and consisted in the argument that modern naval operations in pursuit of limited objectives tended to remain confined to the territorial waters of the opposing states. The theorem not only appeared consistent in practice (one should think for instance of the Korean or the Vietnam Wars, as well as the Indo-Pakistani or the Arab-Israeli conflicts), but also commended itself as a sound adaptation of the laws of armed conflict to the UN Charter principles. A number of authorities subsequently endorsed that approach and reference was increasingly made to the emerging law of limited naval warfare. Today, the concept inspires less certainty among scholars.

For one thing, the Falkland Islands conflict, and even more so the Gulf Tanker War, could hardly be characterized as 'limited' in scale or geographical scope of operations, or in terms of the means and methods employed. There seems to be no doubt that the South Atlantic conflict occasioned moderate escalation only because it was rapidly brought to an end (and yet, the UK did not refrain from adding a nuclear dimension to the war by deploying nuclear-powered, and possibly nuclear-armed, submarines). Likewise, restraint in the Iran-Iraq War, if any, was imposed by the limits in military assets as such, rather than by any sense of legal obligation (one could easily have foreseen, for instance, the implications that a submarine warfare capability in the hands of the Iraqis, or a modern air force on the Iranian side, might have had). Also sizeable in certain respects, the 1990–1 multinational naval interdiction campaign against Iraq involved warships operating as far as the Gulf of Oman and the Red Sea. And then, there is the extremely delicate question of subjectivity that the word 'limited' conveys in itself. It is obvious that what strikes distant third powers as a 'limited' campaign may well appear differently in the eyes of the fighting actors or in those of their most affected regional neighbours.

It is true, of course, that powerful navies would still adhere to a notion of graduated escalation, or that, in all probability, they would abstain from resorting to non-conventional weapons (e.g. nuclear mines or torpedoes). It is also true that any expansion of the theatre of operations which might appear excessive, or any hostile action which would not qualify as imperative by military standards, would be avoided for risk of causing political prejudice (the discussion surrounding the decision to sink the *General Belgrano*, or the US massive naval deployment in the final year of the Iran-Iraq War, would be relevant in that respect although the problem is further complicated by parallel considerations of necessity and proportionality under the concept of self-defence). Yet, this is far from proving that a whole set of rules applicable in case of limited naval warfare stands by itself as an independent body of law. Besides, from a teleological point of view, it is difficult to see what would be the 'gain' of disposing a 'pair' of legal settings varying in content, if not ultimate confusion. At a time when the laws of naval warfare are still to be explored in general, it would be ill-advised to embark on theoretical constructions about limited naval warfare in particular.

The need for 'bright-line rules', that is to say, rules which demarcate the bounds of legally permissible conduct in specific terms, can hardly be overstressed. And from this perspective, legal principles should refer as little as possible to value-laden notions. This last remark concerning the normative vagueness of often proposed models is best illustrated by the idea of reasonableness advanced in recent writings with regard to the legality of the exclusion zone device. As analysed in greater detail in Chapter 1, the idea of 'reasonable use', to name but one example, may well have proved a clause of extreme convenience in the context of the law of the sea conventions, but it can offer scarcely any guidance as to the legitimacy of certain methods of sea warfare. In fact, making the lawful or unlawful character of war tactics conditional upon the reasonable or unreasonable manner in which these tactics are prosecuted is an arbitrary, empty and evidently dangerous proposition. Designed to afford flexibility in the administration of law where needed, reasonableness cannot create new law by itself. It would seem to stand for the exact opposite of what is lacking in modern laws of war at sea: authoritativeness and precision.

The Round Table of Experts and Recent National Manuals One cannot escape noting the striking resemblance, indeed a remarkable coincidence, between the current context and the situation prevailing one hundred years ago. Very reminiscent of the efforts devoted to the problems of the laws of war and neutrality at sea during the final decade of the last century, the 1990s have also been experiencing a growing consciousness of the unresolved issues. Almost a century after some celebrated works in the field, by Joseph-Louis-Elzéar Ortolan (1864), Ernest Nys (1881), Charles Dupuis (1899) or Richard Kleen (1900), to name but a few, literature manifests a marked return to long-unappreciated thematology. The naval aspects of the Falkland Islands War, the Iran-Iraq War, or the ongoing UN sanctions enforcement operations continue to stimulate copious debate and scholarly writing, while the Hague Academy decided to include in its 1993 programme a course on the subject. One century after the first collegiate reflections of the Institut de Droit International on the subject of maritime neutrality, the eminent society renews its interest in the question. Ambitious initiatives are launched from different quarters and met with zealous responses.

Perhaps the most promising among the recent academic undertakings is the initiative launched in 1987 by the International Institute of Humanitarian Law of San Remo, and carried on ever since in cooperation with a number of other bodies, with a view to studying the present law of armed conflict at sea and eventually drafting a document probably in the form of a 'code of conduct' for modern naval operations. Since the first meeting, held in June 1987 at San Remo,[17] a so-called 'Round Table of Experts' has been organized on a yearly basis, gathering a large circle of academics, naval experts and government officials, all attending in a personal capacity. On average, 37 participants representing some 18 countries have been involved in the work of these annual meetings. At the second meeting, held in Madrid in September 1988, it was decided that for the most effective advancement of the study, the Round Table of Experts should proceed by identifying selected topics

[17]The papers presented at the San Remo meeting were published in 14 *Syracuse Journal of International Law and Commerce* (1988) *Special Issue*, pp. 571–878. For background information on the Round Table of Experts, see also 'Developments in the Law of Naval Warfare: Custom or Codification?', 83 *Proc.ASIL* (1989), pp. 145–52.

of the laws of naval warfare to be discussed in each annual session on the basis of analytical reports prepared and distributed in advance. Under that procedure, which came to be known as the *Madrid Plan of Action*, several aspects of the law of sea warfare were identified, such as the legal rules governing naval targeting, the modern function of neutrality law and the influence of Charter principles.[18]

By March 1994, the group of experts had drafted a preliminary document, entitled 'Harmonised Document on International Humanitarian Law Applicable to Armed Conflicts at Sea', accompanied with a lengthy commentary. Both those documents, with only minor amendments, were finally adopted at the Livorno session of June 1994 as the *San Remo Manual on International Law Applicable to Armed Conflicts at Sea*.[19] It is difficult to overstate the importance of that ambitious 'restatement' which recalls in some respects the Institut de Droit International's *Oxford Manual* of 1913. It remains to be seen, however, if and to what extent the *San Remo Manual* will incite, as its drafters aspire, further national and international action along its

[18]Through 1993 the Round Table of Experts had debated the following subjects: the notion of military objective and the principle of distinction in the naval context were considered at the Bochum meeting of November 1989, William Fenrick acting as rapporteur; the questions relating to means and methods of naval combat were discussed at the Toulon meeting of October 1990 on the basis of a report prepared by G.J.F. van Hegelsom; at the Bergen meeting of September 1991, the participants had before them two reports, one by W. Heintschel von Heinegg on the right of visit, search and capture, and another by Christopher Greenwood on the effects of the UN Charter on the present law of armed conflict at sea; at the Ottawa meeting of 1992, discussions focused on the theatre of naval operations as influenced by the new law of the sea, Horace Robertson acting as rapporteur; finally, the Geneva session of September 1993 was devoted to the problem of protection of victims of naval war, on the basis of an introductory report by Louise Doswald-Beck, the admissibility and implications of non-belligerency, commented upon by Dietrich Schindler, and the problem of environmental protection in naval operations, Salah El-Din Amer and K.S. Carter having submitted background papers. The proceedings of the first two meetings convened under the so-called Madrid Plan of Action have been published by VON HEINEGG, H.W. (ed.), *The Military Objective and the Principle of Distinction in the Law of Naval Warfare – Report, Commentaries and Proceedings of the Round Table of Experts on International Humanitarian Law Applicable to Armed Conflicts at Sea, Bochum, November 1989*, 1991, and VON HEINEGG, H.W. (ed.), *Methods and Means of Combat in Naval Warfare – Report and Commentaries of the Round Table of Experts on International Humanitarian Law Applicable to Armed Conflicts at Sea, Toulon, October 1990*, 1992.

[19]For a brief commentary on the final document, see DOSWALD-BECK, L., 'The San Remo Manual of International Law Applicable to Armed Conflicts at Sea', 89 *AJIL* (1995), p. 192*ff*.

premises. It can only be hoped that such reinvigorated scholarly engagement will eventually prove pregnant of seminal ideas and perhaps achieve at the inter-governmental level a major codification effort in matters of the law of naval warfare. To celebrate the centennial of the Second Hague Peace Conference with a similarly able undertaking is, no doubt, a noble objective to pursue, although it may appear to defy realism for many.[20]

There have also been some significant developments at the national level. In the last seven years some states from among the most influential naval powers have revised their military manuals so as to incorporate the present state of customary law of sea warfare as perceived, or solicited, by them. The United States led that development by publishing in 1987 the *Commander's Handbook on the Law of Naval Operations* (NWP 9), and two years later an *Annotated Supplement* to this manual (NWP 9-Rev.A) containing extensive background analysis in support of some innovative rules purporting to reflect current principles of international law. In August 1992, Germany issued its tri-service manual entitled *ZDv 15/2 Humanitarian Law in Armed Conflicts – Handbook,* two chapters of which are devoted to the laws of naval warfare and maritime neutrality. Yet other states are in the process of finalizing their own instructions by inviting comments or hosting review meetings on their draft manuals. The United Kingdom, Italy and Canada are known to be currently working on such draft manuals. It is obvious that the states involved in this exercise hold a particular interest in adopting essentially harmonious, if not uniform, rules, but also in profiting as much as possible from the ongoing scholarly discussion.

Certainly, the importance of the revised national manuals should not be underestimated. All the more so since they contain the most recent understandings of the law in force by some of the strongest 'western' naval powers. The only caveat, however, should concern any facile or precipitous approach that would fail to distinguish between the undeniably instrumental character of those documents in general and the international validity of specific rules as announced therein. None of these

[20]It will be recalled that GA Resolution 44/23 of 17 November 1989 establishing the Decade of International Law, referred to 'the possibility of holding a third international peace conference or other suitable international conference at the end of the decade'. On this, see the apposite remarks of ALDRICH, G.H., 'Towards a Third (Hague) Peace Conference? – The Laws of War', 43 *NILR* (1996), p. 221*ff*.

texts may be attributed the quality of an authoritative statement of the existing law. No doubt, it is right to foresee that a certain formulation as it now appears in the *US Commander's Handbook*, for instance, may well serve as a model, or even be literally transcribed in several other national manuals. For the moment, however, it would be no less accurate to regard the US regulations as only pertinent, but yet not conclusive, solely for the assessment of US practice.[21]

The Challenge and Paradox of Modern Military Technology Legal discourse in the field of armed conflict has to grapple with unfathomable technicality. The humanitarian law expert is increasingly asked to be conversant with the secrets of advanced electronics, the cutting edge of missile technology and the like. It is natural, of course, that a modern debate on the current state of the law should be addressing practices, theories and ideas in the light of present-day tactics, imposed by novel weapons and fitted on evolving platforms. Modern technology, however, claims the character of a controlling factor in the process of exploring the present law of sea warfare. Several important questions are raised in his respect. Can technological innovation alone create the law? Should the law have an interest in taming technology? It so happens that throughout this century war law and military technology have turned their backs on each other and evolved in unrelated fashions. Not only has law demonstrated an astonishing incapacity to articulate sound principles for novel, often revolutionary, armaments, but also progress in weapons technology seems to have been pursued unconstrained by any legal susceptibility.[22]

[21]See the apposite remarks of POST, H.H.G., 'Some Curiosities in the Sources of the Law of Armed Conflict Conceived in a General International Legal Perspective', 25 *NYIL* (1994), pp. 97–101. *Cf.* REISMAN, W.M. and LEITZAU, W.K., 'Moving International Law from Theory to Practice: The Role of Military Manuals in Effectuating the Law of Armed Conflict' in ROBERTSON, H.B. (ed.), *The Law of Naval Operations*, USNWC, 64 *International Law Studies* (1991), p. 1*ff.*

[22]Military technology at its current pace of development represents an ever-growing challenge for the law which seems to be stricken by chronic unresponsiveness. Understandably enough, the continued invocation of legal instruments which address most often obsolete means or methods of warfare while remaining silent on most current ones can only give rise to scornful comments about the utility of drafting such instruments in the first place. On the role of the technological factor in the evolution of international law in general, see BOURQUIN, M., 'Pouvoir scientifique et droit international', 70 *RCADI* (1947), p. 335*ff.*

The quest for legal rules which can keep pace with technological development should not, however, be pursued too far. There can be no doubt that any modern undertaking to update the law must take into account the phenomenal advancement of military technology. Its effectiveness will largely depend on how far the realities of the day will eventually be reflected in the adopted rules, yet military technology can never 'dictate' the law.[23] After all, legal discourse is hardly relevant on the operational or the technical level; it only comes into play on the normative or institutional level. Law should at best be expected to provide controlling principles, or set standards which, while giving due regard to the military realities of the day, would remain operative beyond them.

So much for the challenge. The paradox of technological progress also relates to the inverse relationship which seems to exist between technological innovation and the tenacity of humanitarian law. The jurist might somewhat naïvely assume that the phenomenal developments in weapons' 'smartness' and accuracy, in identification and the like, would enormously facilitate respect for the law and would even consequently lead to the adoption of more stringent humanitarian constraints. Ironically enough, however, modern combatants need to act more and more in anticipation of whatever presumably hostile, since probably lethal, which means that doubt appears to be no longer permissible and that humanitarian concerns would have in all

[23]As it was tellingly stated by Herbert Arthur Smith in 1938, 'les changements dus à un progrès d'ordre matériel ne pourront qu'effectuer une adaptation du droit aux conditions nouvelles sans être capables de modifier ces principes eux-mêmes. Par exemple, l'introduction des moyens modernes de communication ne change point les principes du droit civil sur la diffamation: le caractère diffamatoire s'apprécie selon les mêmes principes, qu'il s'agisse d'une communication par lettre ou par télégramme'; see SMITH, H.A., 'Le développement moderne des lois de la guerre maritime', 63 RCADI (1938) at p. 610. For him it would be essential, when addressing the problem of modernization of the law, 'de distinguer les changements qui résultent des inventions d'ordre technique de ceux inspirés par la marche de la pensée humaine. Il faut adapter les lois aux idées contemporaines; tandis qu'il faut au contraire adapter les inventions modernes au régime des lois', *ibid.* And elsewhere: 'il faut rejeter absolument la doctrine que les nouvelles armes font les nouvelles lois, doctrine hérétique qui mine les fondations de tout droit. Défendre l'emploi des inventions nouvelles, c'est impossible; mais notre tâche est de les ramener sous l'empire des lois', *ibid.* at p. 687.

cases to surrender to operational 'certainties'. [24] The evolution of military technology at its current hectic pace can thus be seen as 'eroding' the laws of war in a twofold manner: first, by constantly accentuating their inaptness to cope with present-day conditions, and second, by envisaging a combat environment in which cardinal humanitarian requisites can be paid faint attention at best.

The Shape of Things to Come The hard questions that modern weaponry poses for law are best illustrated at present by the continuing discussion about directed energy devices. Directed energy relates to the technology used in laser weapon systems, high-powered microwave devices or particle beams. The military application of that technology consists in the production and emission of a beam of concentrated electromagnetic energy or atomic particles, such as an anti-personnel weapon capable of inflicting temporary or permanent blindness and severe skin burns. The growing consciousness about laser weapons is due to the fact that no effective countermeasures are in development, which would, of course, turn the extensive use of laser devices by a ruthless belligerent into a dreadful possibility.[25]

[24]Missiles of high precision and lethal capacity, although most suitable to offer the principle of distinction the often claimed surgical accuracy, have given shape to a technological environment which calls for split-second decisions at the most, leaving no place for doubt or second thoughts as humanitarian law would seem to envisage. It is a platitude to say that the emphasis in modern naval warfare is moved from absorbing damage to avoiding it. By a way of indication of the tremendous threat posed by modern anti-ship missiles (often with sea-skimming capacity combined with high speed), it has been calculated that the target ship may have only 30 seconds or less warning of the attack to carry out defensive action (since even if the missile employs radar homing which a ship's electronic support measures can detect, this may only be used for the last few kilometres of flight). Furthermore, many anti-ship missiles also have a salvo-firing capability whereby several can be programmed to reach targets simultaneously to enhance their ability to penetrate defences. The tragic incident of the downing of an Iranian civil airliner by one of the most sophisticated US warships best illustrates that paradox. As it was written in relation to the *Vincennes* episode, 'it was said that only 189 seconds were available for command decision on the *Vincennes*. Investment in Aegis cruisers has been justified based on a small fraction of that interval being long in tactical real time'; see ECKHART, M., 'The *Vincennes* Incident', 116 *USNIP* (March 1990) at p. 32.

[25]In the words of one expert, 'there is no cheap, effective, and acceptable eye protection available, and it seems unlikely that such protective means will become available in the near or even not so near future, as the necessary technology does not seem to exist at present. The side that uses mass-deployed and frequency-agile low-energy weapons will have the upper hand for a very

As expected, states engaged in the research and development of military laser technology are ready to defend the anti-personnel use of guided-energy weapons asserting that blindness is not any more cruel than other injuries suffered in battle.[26] On the other hand, those arguing for the illegality of anti-personnel use of laser weapons are seeking to demonstrate that such use would fall foul of the prohibition to cause unnecessary suffering, but also would run counter to the dictates of public conscience better known as the *Martens clause*.[27] As far as the unnecessary

---

long time to come, whether such weapons are used for purposes of attack or defence'; see ANDERBERG, B., 'Protection and Countermeasures Against Laser Weapons', 17 *Military Technology* (May 1993) at p. 30. British warships have carried since the Falklands War 'laser dazzle guns', the only low-energy laser weapon known to be in operational service. A few US tanks experimentally fitted with laser devices were deployed during the 1991 Gulf campaign, while the US Army is currently testing a prototype 'laser rifle'. In February 1994, on the occasion of the first preparatory meeting for the Review Conference on the 1980 Inhumane Weapons Convention, the President of the ICRC, Cornelio Sommaruga, issued a statement in favour of a total ban on anti-personnel landmines and blinding weapons. As regards the latter, the statement read: 'moreover, the Convention should take a stand against the invention of new even more terrifying weapons such as lasers that can destroy the eyesight of a victim. Blindness is considered the most incapacitating and dreaded form of disability. Against lasers there is no defence and there is no cure for the damage they cause. From a humanitarian point of view, we believe . . . that blinding as a method of warfare has to be outlawed now.'

[26]In a Memorandum dated 29 September 1988 on the use of lasers as anti-personnel weapons, the US Judge Advocate General concluded that 'the use of a laser as an antipersonnel weapon would not cause unnecessary suffering when compared to other wounding mechanisms to which a soldier might be exposed on the modern battlefield, and hence would not violate any international law obligation of the United States'. The Memorandum on the use of lasers as anti-personnel weapons is reproduced in DOSWALD-BECK, L. (ed.), *Blinding Weapons – Reports of the Meetings of Experts Convened by the International Committee of the Red Cross on Battlefield Laser Weapons 1989–1991*, 1993, pp. 367–71. It was further argued that 'proposals to conclude that the use of a laser to intentionally blind would result in unnecessary suffering would lead to a contradiction in the law in that a soldier legally could be blinded ancillary to the lawful use of a laser rangefinder or target acquisition lasers against matériel targets, but could not be attacked individually'. In the same vein, Horace Robertson commenting on the US Army Memorandum considered that 'there is no reason to believe that burns caused by lasers or other directed-energy weapons are any more horrible than burns caused by napalm bombs, flame-throwers or other incendiary weapons'; see ROBERTSON, H.B., 'Modern Technology and the Law of Armed Conflict at Sea' in ROBERTSON, H.B. (ed.), The Law of Naval Operations, USNWC, 64 *International Law Studies* (1991) at p. 377.

[27]For that line of reasoning, see DOSWALD-BECK, L., 'Obstacles to Regulating New Weaponry: Battlefield Laser Weapons' in FOX, H. and MEYER, M.A. (eds), *Effecting Compliance*, 1993, p. 107*ff*., and GREENWOOD, C., 'Battlefield Laser Weapons in the Context of the Law on Conventional Weapons' in DOSWALD-BECK, *op. cit., supra* n.26, p. 71*ff*.

suffering principle is concerned, the question comes down to comparing permanent blindness to other types of wounds involving the death risk, which resembles more a metaphysical quandary.[28] As regards the dictates of public conscience, it would be next to impossible to prove that a specific weapon use, with the exception perhaps of nuclear arms, is generally prohibited on these grounds.[29]

What is most disquieting from a juridical point of view is that weapons technology, by reason of its inherent secrecy, its phenomenal pace of development, and above all the enormous interests involved, tends ultimately to create a situation that no humanitarian discourse could ever reverse by itself. In most cases, by the time an international legal concern about the prospective use of a new weapon takes shape, the weapon in question has already taken its place in several national inventories, having been manufactured or exported in great numbers, and sometimes even battle-tested. Under those circumstances, law is often condemned to passivity while the gap separating it from reality is widened. It is in this sense that Louise Doswald-Beck criticizes 'a "wait and see" approach which excludes the possibility of useful preventive work . . . [bearing in mind that] once a weapon is fielded it is exceedingly difficult to withdraw its use, despite international protest, as the experience of chemical weapons has shown'.[30]

[28]It is obvious that any attempt to rank blindness on a scale of 'unnecessary sufferings' or 'superfluous injuries' poses infinite problems and calls for delicate analysis that only specialists in opthalmology and military medicine or psychiatry can perhaps provide. As Christopher Greenwood put it, 'the choice appears to be between traditional battlefield weapons which create a greater risk of death but which may effectively disable a combatant without causing permanent injury or, at least, without causing injuries as serious as loss of sight and laser weapons which reduce the risk of death but which, if they are used effectively will generally cause permanent blindness'; see GREENWOOD, *op. cit., supra* at p. 80. For yet another scholar, the question of newly developed high-precision arms should be addressed in terms of the prohibition of employing arms which render death inevitable and suggested: 'à partir du moment où une arme détruit aussi sûrement ses cibles, son utilisation contre des individus n'est plus une forme de combat: c'est une forme d'exécution pure et simple!'; see DAVID, E., 'Les armes nouvelles à la lumière du *jus in bello*', 26 *RBDI* (1993/1) at p. 171.

[29]As expected, the notion of the dictates of public conscience and the Martens clause were extensively debated in the context of the ICJ Advisory proceedings concerning the legality of the threat or use of nuclear weapons; see Legality of the Threat or Use of Nuclear Weapons, Advisory Opinion of 8 July 1996, *ICJ Reports 1996*, §87, and the Dissenting Opinions of Judges Shahabuddeen and Weeramantry.

[30]See DOSWALD-BECK, *op. cit., supra* n.27 at pp. 120, 115.

Prohibiting Means of Warfare: Grounds for Scepticism Tangible interests of great powers have often slowed down or undermined legal progress in matters of banning new weapons systems. Military staffs and legal experts of technologically advanced states have hardly ever found it difficult to establish the legality of novel weaponry. As Alfred Rubin remarked in respect of the procedures set up by the United States for legal review of new weapons, 'as long as there is a supportable military necessity for using a particular weapons system, a scintilla of military necessity will outweigh the ton of avoidable harm the weapon might cause'.[31] As such, law is essentially kept straitjacketed within a universe which lacks any contact with the modern world. Those concerned with humanitarian law today have no more to content themselves with than had their colleagues of the late nineteenth century, i.e. some extraordinarily polysemous principles like 'unnecessary suffering', 'superfluous injury' or 'the dictates of public conscience' – notions which, in practice, render it easier to 'prove' that the use of a new weapons technology is lawful than to demonstrate its illegality.[32]

As a rule, weapons-developing states abstain from associating themselves with initiatives which could suggest interference with their military research programmes and seek to gain valu-

[31]See RUBIN, A., 'Human Rights and Armed Conflict: Conflicting Views', 67 *Proc.ASIL* (1973) at p. 165. Similarly, in the words of a Red Cross practitioner, 'it is likely that in practice the legal advisers of a country are under a certain pressure to find in favour of the legality of a weapon, especially if such a review is carried out after substantial financial investment into a project and in the context of the desire of the military to field a certain weapon'; see DOSWALD-BECK, *op. cit., supra* n.27 at p. 116.

[32]For critical remarks on what he considers 'one of the most unclear and controversial rules of warfare . . . couched in such vague and uncertain terms as to be barren of practical results', see CASSESE, A., 'Weapons Causing Unnecessary Suffering: Are They Prohibited?', 58 *Rivista di Diritto Internazionale* (1975), p. 12*ff*. According to the same author, these principles may have at best some 'meta-legal value' setting 'a moral and political standard by which world public opinion assesses how belligerent states behave or misbehave'; see CASSESE, A., 'Means of Warfare: The Present and the Emerging Law', 12 *RBDI* (1976) at p. 145. This uncontroverted pattern of calculated stagnancy in the field of war laws has sometimes forced jurists to fatalistic, yet frank, remarks. To quote once more Antonio Cassese, 'in fact, only those weapons have been proscribed which . . . have not been regarded as *decisive* from a military point of view. In deciding whether to prohibit a given weapon account has always been taken of their military effectiveness. And this factor has indeed always overriden humanitarian grounds. Wherever it has turned out that a means of destruction was really effective, States have refrained from outlawing it'; *ibid.* at p. 149.

able time by various techniques such as by withholding scientific information or test results in the name of national security, by promoting the idea that in any event the weapon under development may only become operational in a distant future, or by discrediting any report which might alarm public opinion about the real nature or efficacy of the new weapon. The prospects for effective arms regulation are no brighter even in the rare case whereby prohibitions are announced in an internationally negotiated document. The temptation in this latter case is often to attempt at a later stage – and the 1977 'package deal' offers a most telling example in this respect – to excise some embarrassing clauses from the final compromise in a selective way.[33]

Given the deadlock, then, which any attempt to modernize existing treaty rules is fated to confront, excessive hopes have been placed on the possibility of seeing the long-hoped-for changes brought about via custom. It may be queried, however, whether such a neglected body of law as that of naval warfare can be meaningfully updated by the exclusive means of custom formation.[34] With respect to almost every aspect of present-day warfare at sea, the traditional law can at most offer questions rather than answers. As it turned out, even the 1977 Diplomatic Conference made a mockery of modernization by addressing, for instance, the problems of ruses and perfidy in naval warfare in terms of false colours, or by blatantly ignoring the modern combat environment and keeping all future-oriented legal queries simply frozen. Admittedly, the picture as described above is one of plain pessimism: looking to the past resembles an excursion through anachronisms, while looking ahead obliges a confession of impotence.

[33]Georges Abi-Saab eloquently warned against that risk of 'unpackaging', noticing that this 'is a very risky business, because it may end up with the proverbial baby going down with what some consider the bathwater. Once it starts, no one knows beforehand where the process can or will stop; and the erosion effect can go very far indeed'; see ABI-SAAB, G., 'The 1977 Additional Protocols and General International Law: Some Preliminary Reflexions' in DELISSEN, A.J.M. and TANJA, G.J. (eds), *Humanitarian Law of Armed Conflict – Challenges Ahead, Essays in Honour of Frits Kalshoven*, 1991 at p. 126.

[34]As Natalino Ronzitti remarked, 'customary international law can set up just a few rules but cannot provide the surgical innovation which is needed'; see RONZITTI, *op. cit., supra* n.9 at p. 51.

Uncharted Waters Ahead: Prospects and Fears The task of modernizing the legal rules of armed conflict at sea is an urgent one. It also becomes increasingly complex with so many other related branches of law experiencing momentous change. In fact, the more time passes, the less feasible the prospect for a compehensive revision appears. Today, the juncture seems propitious to such an undertaking. The 1980s, profoundly marked by naval conflicts on a considerable scale such as the Falklands or the Persian Gulf War, provided the challenge and multiplied the questions. Mature reflection followed and keeps advancing, laying valuable groundwork for an eventual codification effort. The end of the Cold War and improved relations between superpowers tend also to favour similar endeavours.

In practical terms, it has occasionally been suggested that it would be highly unrealistic to envisage an international conference embarking upon a re-examination of the totality of problems connected with modern naval warfare. A major obstacle, but certainly not the only one, is the disarmament element that the discussions would inevitably confront with reference to certain naval weapon systems. It has thus been argued that a step-by-step approach would be preferable since it would permit distinction between those sectors which may appear ripe for codification and more contentious ones. One should be reticent, however, about an approach which although pragmatic and commendable at first glance, may well lead to fragmentary results, to incoherent pieces of legislation lacking a common thread.

This is all the more so since as the most debatable legal issues, which happen to be also the most important, will in all probability eschew legal regulation for quite some time. For instance, would it be useful to draft new technical rules for mine warfare in the absence of agreement concerning the fundamental principles of naval targeting, the legality of war zones, or the rights of neutrals, etc.? For, what would be the real contribution of such rules if they were not to address the questions which lie at the very heart of the modern *problématique*, being confined instead to a mere reiteration of most innocuous legal clauses such as the duty of notification? Is it worth agreeing on the modalities of exercise of the right of visit and search while leaving core issues of contraband law, such as the neutral trade in arms, unsettled?

The fear is based on historical experience. Throughout this century, there have been many rules drafted within learned societies, many ill-fated initiatives, inconsequential negotiations, and ultimately unratified documents. There has been dishearteningly little in the form of binding and largely representative treaty commitment, or solidly established custom. While there may be an excess of scholarly interest, it has been counterbalanced by a deficit in effective legal reform. The pessimist would be tempted, therefore, to look at the current situation as much resembling old paradigms of inaction. It is, in fact, difficult to exclude as improbable the 'zero-sum' perspective, that is to say, the possibility that, despite the promising academic efforts or an appearance of growing activism, the momentum will gradually evaporate, the states will continue to interpret the legal obligations incumbent upon them with the same anarchic unilateralism as before, and the law of naval warfare will remain as stagnant and mysterious as ever.

About this Work This study is divided into two parts. The first focuses on certain means and methods of conducting hostilities at sea, whereas the second examines the 'checks and balances' of maritime intercourse between belligerents and neutrals. Both parts are subdivided into three chapters, each studying an aspect which has always elicited polemics and which exemplifies the multiple challenges that a conference aiming at the modernization of the laws of naval warfare will inevitably have to face. The selected topics are certainly not the only sources of controversy in the present-day law of naval operations. Numerous other aspects in the same area of law remain dark.

The legal *problématique*, however, tends to revolve around certain fundamental questions common in almost any of these areas. The contemporary significance of the principle of distinction in naval targeting, for instance, can be explored as much through a legal discussion of the concept of war zones as by looking into submarine warfare. The legal questions related to military applications of modern technology are in essence the same irrespective of whether one wishes to analyse dormant mines, smart missiles or guided-energy weapons. The law of contraband, no less than the law of self-defence and reprisals, can breed reflections on the catalytic influence of the UN Charter on the traditional laws of war.

Accordingly, no effort was made to treat exhaustively the myriad of 'technical' points at issue, but rather to distill the few controlling parameters of prospective law. This point of methodology may also serve as an answer to those who wrongly expect and often judge the jurist on his readiness to provide detailed solutions to problems posed by technology or other extra-legal factors. By way of example, while it is for the law to fix the scale of priorities and to determine the particular humanitarian and other values needing protection in the context of modern mine warfare, it does not lie with the lawyer to sort out the specific operational characteristics modern mines should possess in order to satisfy the conditions for legal permissibility.

In the first chapter, the aim is to explore the notion of war or exclusion zones. The question of legality of the concept of war zones, evocative of World War practices of unrestricted submarine warfare, but also of the recent anti-shipping experience in the Persian Gulf, remains wide open, or an operational necessity for some and a subterfuge for indiscriminate destruction for others. From the days of the *Lusitania* tragedy to the *General Belgrano* incident and later to the downing of the Iranian Airbus, war or exclusion zones have stirred sharp controversy as to their legitimacy. For long defended as a revamped version of the classical blockade, the concept would now appear to borrow more from the logic of anticipatory self-defence. A considerable part of scholarly opinion is favourable to the codification of the practice. According to the most-frequent reasoning, the legal acceptability of the war zone device in its modern cast should be measured by the sole yardstick of reasonableness. As argued *in extenso* in Chapter 1 below, however, similar criteria are spurious since they are least operative during armed conflict. And then, it would be paradoxical to envisage that a practice synonymous to war crime under the 'old law' could be invested international legitimacy under a realistic interpretation of the Charter principles.

The second chapter addresses the legal aspects of mine warfare at sea. The naval mine has always appealed so strongly to seafaring nations, especially to less powerful ones, that it is now deeply rooted in naval strategy and no legal innovation could afford to dispense with its specificities. From the *Petropav-*

losk to the *Samuel Roberts*, and from the Dardanelles disaster to the mined Kuwaiti waters, the 'hidden menace' has not ceased to provoke the same sentiment of helplessness or entrapment to the naval combatant. Here again, the legal enigma consists today in outlining the principles governing the use of underwater mines in the light of accumulated experience and the much criticized Eighth Hague Convention of 1907. With the exception of the duty of notification, the customary character of which was twice reaffirmed in post-1945 jurisprudence, all other rules pertaining to minelaying and minesweeping are still to be defined. Tracing the evolution of the mine weapon since its inception invites gloomy reflections about the *de facto* or 'imposed' legality of certain weapons the cost-effectiveness of which would be such as to dissipate from the outset any doubt which might rightfully be raised as to their lawful character.

The first part ends with a chapter devoted to the use of stratagems in naval combat. The perennial debate about how to differentiate between lawful deception and prohibited perfidy, as old as war itself, has historically assumed a special significance in the context of naval warfare. Apart from the questionable right to fly false colours, the story of the Q-ships or of the secret raiders, and the controversy over 'defensively' armed merchantmen all bear witness to the often deformed connotation of *ruses de guerre* as practised at sea. Regrettably enough, the 1977 First Additional Protocol went only half-way in shedding light on these issues. For, a most welcome definition of perfidious conduct was coupled with a specific disclaimer regarding usages of a dubious customary character in naval warfare. In any event, it would be illusory to believe that the problems of deception in naval warfare are exhausted in the sole practice of flying a false flag, or of erecting a fake funnel. The age of satellite reconnaissance and of ultra-sophisticated electronic warfare carries new challenges which seem to defy the thinking which reigned in the days of camouflage.

The second part starts with a chapter on maritime neutrality – the peculiar collection of 'mays' and 'may nots' which has sought throughout the centuries to reconcile the necessities of warfare with the boons of commerce, to seize the ever ephemeral equilibrium between the military laurels of some and the trade gains of others. Evidently, the principal query relates here to the exact repercussions the adoption of the UN Charter had on the laws of neutrality. According to some learned scholars, an eventual codification effort should not fail to accommodate the notion of 'non-belligerency' or 'benevolent neutrality', that is to say an intermediate status between strict neutrality and co-belligerency. The concept manifested all its eccentricity at the time of the 'destroyers deal' and the Lend-Lease Act in the months that preceded the US entry into the Second World War. Since then, there has not been the slightest indication that the idea that a state can claim neutrality without respecting it has passed into international law. This work argues that institutionalizing non-belligerency would set a regrettable course on a false bearing.

In the fifth chapter, the aim is to penetrate into the notion of contraband and its function under a modern perception of neutral rights and duties. In particular, the study focuses on the core issue of absolute contraband, that is to say the traffic in arms. As the problem proceeds far beyond the narrow confines of sea warfare, it was found necessary to deal with it in a broader context. The private trade in contraband has been contrived as the counterbalance for the onerous duty of abstention incumbent upon the *bona fide* neutral. Today there are so many extra-legal considerations (political, economic, strategic) permeating the sensitive sector of arms exports that a legal analysis of national policies from the sole vantage point of neutrality may seem pointless. It is in this particular area that alignment with the philosophy of the UN Charter would be most meaningful. As argued below, common Article 7 of Hague Conventions V and XIII offers the best example of a treaty provision, now rendered obsolete, which should be brought into line with modern practice and legal theory.

Fanning the flames can no more be excused by invoking a neutral private 'right'. The compulsory licensing system, a standard feature in all industrialized arms exporting countries, divests the arms transfer contract of any 'private' character it might originally have had and shifts full responsibility to the consenting government. The long series of arms exports imbroglios which arose during the eight-year Iran-Iraq War are highly instructive in that connection. Far from attesting the complete liberalization of the right to sell arms through private or public conduits, as some might erroneously conclude (can one truly envisage a retrogression in humanitarian law which would become less demanding than the Hague standards?), the conduct of most of the western world in the final analysis reaffirms the rule according to which neutral status in case of armed conflict unpronounced upon by the UN political organs implies the automatic suspension of *all* arms deliveries to the warring nations. After all, legal discourse on this subject has to build upon two missing links: moral foundations and human rights law.

The sixth and final chapter is an excursus through the various concepts apart from contraband which make up what one calls 'prize law', that is to say the procedural rights of interference with neutral shipping such as visit and search, diversion and capture, but also the legal constructions upon which the eventual condemnation of the seized vessel is justified such as the ideas of continuous voyage, unneutral service or enemy convoying. Iranian operations against non-belligerent shipping and third states' reactions, but also recent UN-mandated naval operations in the Persian Gulf, the Adriatic Sea or around Haiti, are enlightening as to the continuing validity of several of these concepts. The overview of the key elements of traditional prize law is concluded with some observations on the endangered, yet fundamental, distinction in every possible sense between capture and destruction of merchant vessels under modern doctrines of naval targeting.

The subject matter does not lend itself to easy answers. In fact, long neglect has blurred the picture to the point that problems have now assumed an acute, some would even say insurmountable, complexity. Even the few standpoints for which this book firmly argues should only be taken as a confirmation of the very uncertainty reigning in the field. Without pretending to offer an exhaustive analysis, far less to provide answers to all open questions concerning armed conflict at sea, this study only aspires to demonstrate the problematic, if not lamentable, state of the law through the examination of some selected problems. Aside from the main purpose of the book, which is of course to determine the present-day rules governing warfare at sea, and in order to dilute the inevitable technicality inherent in most of the subject matters discussed below, each chapter is followed by some theoretical reflections on a related theme of a more general interest.

Among the topics which are not addressed here, a fleeting mention should at least be made of the crucial environmental parameter of the modern laws of war. At a time when environmental concern and awareness command reconsideration of patterns of behaviour on the global scale, it is to be expected that *jus in bello* will be inevitably affected. However improbable such a prospect may appear to some, academic discussions currently focus on the possibility of a quasi-assimilation of the environment as such to a civilian object, immune therefore from direct belligerent attack.[35] In practice, however, it is difficult to see how ecological conscience would manage to impose on belligerents a level of restraint with regard to human habitat that humanitarianism has so far failed to obtain in respect of civilian population.

A final remark concerns terminology. In recent years it has been argued that the words 'warfare' or 'war' should be banned from the vocabulary of international humanitarian law and be

[35]The issue became extremely topical since the 1991 Gulf War and has been dealt with in copious writings; see ALMOND, H.H., 'War, Weapons and Attacks on the Environment', 31 *Revue de Droit Pénal Militaire et de Droit de la Guerre* (1992), p. 329*ff.*; BOUVIER, A., 'La protection de l'environnement naturel en période de conflit armé', 73 *RICR* (nov.–déc.1991), no.792, p. 599*ff.*; GUPTA, S., 'Iraq's Environmental Warfare in the Persian Gulf', 6 *Georgetown International Environmental Law Review* (1993), p. 251*ff.*; LEIBLER, A., 'Deliberate Wartime Environmental Damage: New Challenges for International Law', 23 *California Western International Law Journal* (1992–93), p. 67*ff.*; LIJNZAAD, L. and TANJA, G.J., 'Protection of the Environment in Times of Armed Conflict: The Iraq-Kuwait War', 40 *NILR* (1993), p. 169*ff.*; JOYNER, C.C. and KIRKHOPE, J.T., 'The Persian Gulf War Oil Spill: Reassessing the Law of Environmental Protection and the Law of Armed Conflict', 24 *Case Western Reserve Journal of International Law* (1992), p. 29*ff.*; ROBERTS, A., 'La destruction de l'environnement pendant la guerre du Golfe de 1991', 74 *RICR* (nov.–déc.1992), no.798, p. 559*ff.*; TARASOFSKY, R.G., 'Legal Protection of the Environment During International Armed Conflict', 24 *NYIL* (1993), p. 17*ff.*; TERRY, J.P., 'The Environment and the Laws of War – The Impact of Desert Storm', 45 *US Naval War College Review* (winter 1992), p. 61*ff.*; 'The Gulf War: Environment as a Weapon', 85 *Proc.ASIL* (1991), pp. 214–29; VON HEINEGG, H.W. and DONNER, M., 'New Developments in the Protection of the Natural Environment in Naval Armed Conflicts', 37 *GYIL* (1994), p. 281*ff.*; BOTHE, M., 'Protection of the Environment in Times of Armed Conflict' in AL-NAUIMI, N. and MEESE, R. (eds), *International Legal Issues Arising under the United Nations Decade of International Law,* 1995, p. 95*ff.*; ZEMMALI, A., 'La protection de l'environnement en période de conflit armé dans les normes humanitaires et l'action du CICR', *ibid.*, p. 105*ff.* See also CARTER, K.S., 'Protection of the Environment and the Law of Naval Warfare', and SALAH EL-DIN AMER, 'The Law of Naval Warfare and the Protection of the Environment', background papers presented at Geneva in September 1993 for the purpose of the Round Table of Experts on International Humanitarian Law Applicable to Armed Conflicts at Sea (copies on file with author).

replaced by expressions such as 'laws of armed conflict', the understanding being that the prohibition of the use of force heralded by the UN Charter should be reflected in legal jargon. Analogous has been the reasoning behind the descriptions 'states non-parties to the conflict' and 'policy of strict impartiality', in contrast to the inelegant, outmoded references to 'neutrals' or 'neutrality'. The question is believed to be one of form, not of substance, and therefore relatively unimportant. That terminological quarrel is in fact meaningless unless one assumes quite erroneously that the mere reference to a war situation involves also an axiological assessment of the legality of the resort to force in question. Yet, war is before anything a question of facts, not value judgments. It is therefore by pragmatism and not by misapprehension or defiance to Charter fundamentals that in this work the traditional phraseology has been freely employed. In any event, as the analysis that follows attempts to demonstrate, there are at present far too numerous and imperative concerns that the law of naval warfare should address in all urgency for it to worry about terminological niceties.

PART ONE

Means and Methods of Naval Warfare

Quid tristes querimoniae,
si non supplicio culpa reciditur?
quid leges sine moribus vanae proficiunt?

Of what avail dismal lamentations,
if wrong is not repressed by penalties?
of what avail are empty laws, if we lack principle?

Horace, *Odes*, bk.III, sect.24, l.35
(transl. by C.E. Bennett, The Loeb Classical Library, 1960 at p. 255)

Chapter One

THE LEGALITY OF WAR ZONES

I Introduction

War zones have long ceased to be a novelty, but they remain a legal enigma. Although existing for almost a century, the issue remains unsettled, feeding prolonged legal speculation. The question of the legality of the war zone device typifies the kind of legal controversies with which a potential codification attempt for the laws of naval warfare will have to cope. The problem arises when an antiquated body of law intersects proliferating state practice which runs contrary to its dictates, when new realities come to upset fundamental principles of humanitarian law.

Of the Concept and Its Evolution Initially, the term was understood as a synonym of the *theatre of naval operations.* The theatre of naval operations can be construed, in a broad sense, as the aggregate of sea tracts where belligerent fleets may be lawfully deployed and hostilities eventually take place; in this sense, 'the outbreak of maritime war automatically converts all the open seas into a war zone'.[1] But it can also be read, more restrictively, as meaning the area of actual or imminent naval engagements. In this latter conception, a war zone is confined to the sea spaces reachable by the range of guns of a belligerent fleet which engages, or approaches, enemy units. War zones have been associated with both the broad as well as the narrow denotations of the theatre of naval operations. The concept at its inception,

[1]GARNER, J.W., 'Some Questions of International Law in the European War – War Zones and Submarine Warfare', 9 *AJIL* (1915) at p. 596.

therefore, was *descriptive of the geographical coordinates of hostilities at sea, either potential or actual.*

Evidently, such demonstrations held true only at the time when naval warfare was visualized as nothing else but capital ships exchanging salvoes. The advent of economic sea warfare and the *enfant terrible* of naval warfare, namely, the submarine, came to alter drastically the notion of naval engagement, and the idea of a war zone was equally affected. What is striking about the First World War, for example, is the impressive inactivity of the belligerent surface fleets, notably of the British 'Grand Fleet' with the exception of the famous Battle of Jutland, in contrast to the stupendous German U-boat campaign which soon came to involve the world's merchant shipping. How can one estimate then, let alone define, the area of actual or imminent naval engagements in such circumstances?

Along the narrower perception of the theatre of naval operations, however, a faint legal implication was also carried; as the naval engagement exclusively concerns belligerent battleships, neutrals should bow to the belligerent aspiration of facing the enemy unobstructed, that is to say at the exclusion of the interfering presence of third ships. The idea of customarily seeing the rough whereabouts of opposing fleets as areas possibly dangerous to neutral shipping had, in the process, given way to the idea of creating a fixed zone, irrespective of the location of naval engagement, for the purpose of defending strategic coastal areas. What was new was the idea of establishing a fixed zone with exact geographical limits. As such, there could be notification so that everyone could be aware of its precise extent. A hybrid notion soon emerged, linking the idea of the vicinity of naval engagements to that of defensive sea areas. The concept of the vicinity of actual or imminent naval engagements gave rise to the notion of localizing the area of conflict so as to spare losses among innocent neutral vessels, whereas the concept of defensive sea areas promoted the idea of proclaiming a zone of fixed bounds. In the event, a war zone connoted a self-limitation upon the area of operations, *a conscious localization of the conflict coupled with an attempt to avoid to the fullest extent any collateral damage inflicted upon innocent neutral vessels.*

The First World War capsized this concept, in the sense that war zones were disconnected from the endeavour to minimize neutral collateral damage, and came to signify instead the manifest commitment to inflict the most devastating harm possible to neutral shipping trading with the enemy. Following the rationale underlying the German war zones established for the purposes of the U-boat campaign, neutral merchant shipping was brought to the very heart of the concept; it became the avowedly direct objective of submarine warfare. Thus, the war zone concept eventually embodied a legal relationship, consisting in *the alleged right of a belligerent to suspend maritime traffic altogether within a designated area, and in the corresponding obligation of a neutral not to sail in these waters or to risk the sinking of its ship.* The Second World War sealed this gradual degeneration of the notion of war zone, from signifying a geographically well defined and limited area for naval operations with particular concern for the safety of non-belligerent merchantmen, to portraying, more often than not, vast sea spaces where shipping could be subject to virtually unwarned attack and indiscriminate destruction.

In the second half of our century, the concept of war zones has displayed persistent affinity to the World Wars' model. In the era of the UN Charter, however, the war zone needed a new rationalization, compatible with the vision of vanishing inter-state violence. With self-defence being the recognized sole instance of permissible resort to armed force in international relations, and anticipatory self-defence being the regrettable travesty of the axiomatic prohibition to use force, war zones came to illustrate the confines where this latter 'necessity' to strike pre-emptively might be practised. Under the strain of positive identification of a closing enemy unit, and in view of the problematic distinction between hostile act and hostile intent, the war zone device gained prominence in modern naval doctrines. The German claim, advanced during the First World War, that because of their extreme vulnerability, the U-boats were forced to sink on sight all enemy merchantmen, instead of visiting and searching their cargoes, has since been rehashed, and is nowadays reflected in the 'persuasion' that present-day hulls are not built to sustain damage and that they should, therefore, forestall a lethal first strike acting upon presumptions. A modern war zone represents essentially one such presumption. The 1982 Anglo-Argentine South Atlantic War exemplified the new connotation of a war zone, as *the geographical concretization of the ambit of anticipatory self-defence,* also known as an exclusion zone; any vessel or aircraft found within a fixed perimeter around the Falkland Islands was presumed hostile and was liable to attack by forces supposedly responding to an imminent threat.

War zones, beyond high-flown expectations or academic constructions, have after all assumed a definite content in practice. What should be traced, therefore, is the core meaning as it was moulded in the hands of legal services, diplomats, war planners and naval officers, throughout this century. This is where the pursuit of theoretical definitions should arrive or rather commence. The element of attack without warning, which, since it is not likely to be preceded by any positive identification attempt, differs little from an indiscriminate attack, is thought to have become inherent in the concepts of zonal interdiction. The analysis that follows is built upon the understanding that a war zone, beyond pretexts, wishful assurances or euchologies, is essentially a free-fire zone which has been historically designed and operated so as to legitimize, or at least to waive responsibility for indiscriminate attack on enemy or neutral merchant ships. Although a number of scholars share Maxwell Jenkins's view that 'clearly an exclusion zone *per se*, must be separately evaluated',[2] modern practices have served to minimize, if not to eliminate, any practical difference between defensive/operational and war/exclusion zones which might have validly existed in the past. The 5 nautical miles defensive 'bubble', for instance, around the US warships deployed in the Persian Gulf in the late 1980s would seem to represent an operational/defensive arrangement. Yet, in the aftermath of the tragic Iranian Airbus incident, who could argue that it was not a veritable exclusion zone in essence? Karl Zemanek has recently written that 'the common denominator of all war zones is the declaring belligerent's claim to suspend in the zone some or all of the rules of naval warfare'.[3] How can law, therefore, come to terms with something decisively beyond its reach, something confessedly lawless? The urgent need for an update of the laws of naval warfare is commonly confessed, but the query remains: at what cost, respecting which fundamentals and serving which teleology?

[2]JENKINS, *op. cit., infra* n.121 at p. 528.
[3]ZEMANEK, *op. cit., infra* n.244 at p. 337.

II The record of lawlessness: from the *Lusitania* to the Iranian Airbus

1 Early examples of coastal defence zones

It is often contended that the 1904–5 Russo-Japanese War enriched twofold the art of naval warfare, in introducing the employment of war zones and large-scale offensive sea mining. This *cliché* has been systematically repeated up to our days, though it holds only partly true. Minelaying was effectively practised during the American Civil War of 1861–5 by the Confederates, yet it was essentially defensive in character. In that respect, therefore, the offensive mine campaign off Port Arthur might be considered to have marked a *première*.[4] But as far as war zones are concerned, one should not rush to false conclusions.

The *defence sea areas*, designated in pursuance to the Imperial Ordinance No. 11 of 23 January 1904, lack even the remotest relevance to the modern strategy of exclusion zones.[5] The freedom of movement of neutral ships was considerably curtailed and strictly regulated, but not in any way excluded. No attack on sight was envisaged for the violators. It was rather a defensive self-blockade,[6] in the sense that Japan attempted to ensure the absolute control over the passage of foreign ships through her sea approaches.[7] The sanction provided for the intruders did not vary from the classical risk of seizure and confiscation associated with blockade measures.[8]

[4]See HOFFMANN, R.F., 'Offensive Mine Warfare: A Forgotten Strategy?', 103 *USNIP* (May 1977), pp. 142–55, and LEVIE, H.S., 'Mine Warfare and International Law', USNWC, 62 *International Law Studies* (1980), pp. 271–9. See also *infra*, chapter 2, note 14 and accompanying text.

[5]See USNWC, 12 *International Law Situations* (1912), pp. 122–6.

[6]A blockade is principally conceived as the maritime siege-like operation having the purpose of capturing an enemy port site and thus being invariably offensive in nature.

[7]The only provision which comes close to the idea of immediate attack is to be found in the *Rules to Be Observed by Vessels Passing the Tokyo Bay, Hakodate and Otaru Strategic Sea Areas*, Article 9 of which reads as follows: 'vessels passing the area at night in violation of article 7, shall do so at the risk of being fired upon by torpedo boats or patrol boats'. Article 7 referred to an exceptional situation and read: 'when necessary, passage of vessels may for a time be prohibited within the area'.

[8]There is a case classically, yet mistakenly, associated with these regulations, namely the case of the French steamship *Quang-Nam*. For the decision of the prize court, see TAKAHASHI, S., *International Law Applied to the Russo-Japanese War*, 1908 at p. 735. The ship seemed to have been captured and confiscated on

The Japanese example was taken over by the United States as soon as they entered the First World War. Several defensive sea areas were proclaimed, the maximum width of which being some 13 n.m. Again minute control over foreign shipping by choking up the access to main ports or strategic localities was the declared goal and its defensive character undisputed.[9]

2 The First World War

A The evolution of the concept of zonal interdiction

The war zone expedient was destined to gain definite prominence with the outbreak of the First World War. Thereafter, the notion of *military, barred* or *danger areas* takes root in naval parlance and typifies the new realities modern strategies had to tackle. So many variant types of naval operations were undertaken or threatened under the guise of imposing a war zone that the concept soon assumed a staggering elasticity and figured as the war's all purpose password. The chain of events has been

grounds of unneutral service rather than war zone running; 'when a ship, though neutral, has engaged in reconnoitring defences and the movements of a squadron for the benefit of the enemy, as this ship did, her confiscation is allowed by international law', *ibid.* at p. 738. The charge was scouting and reporting the positions of the Japanese fleet rather than sailing through defence sea areas without prior permission. See also, *The Industrie, ibid.* at p. 732. George Grafton Wilson, commenting on the Japanese measures a few years later, wrote: 'the practice, nature of regulations, and drift of opinion seem to show that in time of war a belligerent is entitled to take measures for his protection which are not *unreasonable*' (emphasis added); see USNWC, 12 *International Law Situations* (1912) at p. 128.

[9]See 12 *AJIL* (1918) *Suppl.*, pp. 13–22. For the text of an analogous Executive Order establishing defensive sea areas off both entrances of the Panama canal, see 11 *AJIL* (1917) *Suppl.* at p. 168. The only provision which went beyond the threat of seizure concerned approaching defensive sea areas in darkness and read as follows: 'vessels discovered near the limits of the areas at night may be fired upon', *ibid.* at pp. 17, 170. On contiguous zones for defensive purposes, see also USNWC, *International Law Situations* (1939) at p. 59. Referring to those police measures and their evident dissimilarity with subsequent practices, Frederick Goldie correctly points out: 'but today the types of exclusion zones calling for legal analysis involve more complex methods and tactics for enforcement, cover far larger sea areas, and are established for many more diverse ends than was the case with these early and relatively modest and straightforward forerunners'; see GOLDIE, L.F.E., 'Maritime War Zones and Exclusion Zones' in ROBERTSON, H.B. (ed.), *The Law of Naval Operations*, USNWC, 64 *International Law Studies* (1991) at p. 160.

reviewed exhaustively in several works[10] so that only a few highlights are thought to be needed. The transition from the practice of planting upon notification defensive minefields in the proximity of vulnerable coastal sites, to the practice of rendering vast areas dangerous to shipping, of laying huge 'mine barrages' or even of torpedoing passenger liners without notice, was shockingly short.

The Mine Warfare Prelude As from late September 1914, Britain had announced its intention to close several ports on the east coast to Dutch shipping and to protect its sea approaches by mining certain segments of its territorial waters. The British Note of 28 September 1914, makes reference to 'exceptional measures', or 'special measures of control', and advertises that 'any neutral fishing vessel found fishing off the East coast of Great Britain . . . must be treated as under suspicion of being engaged in minelaying', while 'the crews [of trawlers engaged in illicit minelaying or of vessels resisting capture or attempting to escape] being unauthorized combatants will be liable to be treated as war criminals and shot after trial by Court Martial'.[11]

In the first days of October 1914, the Strait of Dover was mined at a point off the Belgian coast. The British Admiralty duly notified the limits of what it came to term a *danger zone*, while it did not omit to say that shipping should not be con-

[10]See FAUCHILLE, P., 'La guerre sous-marine allemande', 25 *RGDIP* (1918), pp. 75–84; GUICHARD, L., *The Naval Blockade 1914–1918*, 1930, p. 46*ff.*; GARNER, J.W., *International Law and the World War*, vol.I (1920), pp. 329–83; TURLINGTON, E., *Neutrality – Its History, Economics and Law*, vol.III (1936), pp. 34–66; GARNER, *op. cit.*, *supra* n.1, p. 594*ff.*; PERRINJAQUET, J., 'La guerre européenne et les relations commerciales des belligérants et des neutres, l'application des théories de la contrebande de guerre et du blocus', 22 *RGDIP* (1915), pp. 127–238; BARNES, W.H., 'Submarine Warfare and International Law', 2 *World Polity* (1960), p. 121*ff.*; TUCKER, *op. cit.*, *infra* n.237, pp. 296–317; MALLISON, *op. cit.*, *infra* n.236, p. 55*ff.* See also SIMS, W.S., *The Victory at Sea*, 1920; JELLICOE, J.R., *The Grand Fleet 1914–1916: Its Creation, Development and Work*, 1919; PARMELEE, M., *Blockade and Sea Power*, 1924; LAURENS, A., *Le blocus et la guerre sous-marine*, 1924; KENWORTHY, J.M. and YOUNG, G., *Freedom of the Seas*, 1928; HOUGH, R., *The Great War at Sea 1914–1918*, 1983, pp. 169*ff.*, 298*ff.*

[11]The Note has been compiled in a Dutch White Book entitled *Diplomatieke Bescheiden Betreffende de Vaart inde Noordzee en het Kanaal in Verband met den Oorlogstoestand*, 1915 at p. 3. In the reply of 7 October 1914, the Dutch government makes mention of the British 'zone dangereuse', or 'zone interdite', and protests 'les intentions du Gouvernement Britannique de se baser uniquement sur une chaîne de simple présomptions pour conclure à la culpabilité de personnes qui pourraient être absolument innocentes'; *ibid.* at p. 4.

sidered less unsafe beyond these limits.[12] Within days, the French Ministry for Marine notified the establishment of a zone dangerous to navigation in the Mediterranean which the French naval forces effectuated by mining the territorial waters of the Austro-Hungarian Kingdom and the channels between the islands along the Dalmatian coast.[13] The action was to offset similar measures taken by the Austro-Hungarian navy in the Adriatic. Shortly after the laying of the British minefield in the Dover Strait off the Belgian coast and the French measures in the Adriatic, the Russian naval authorities gave warning of similar zones dangerous to navigation around the Aaland archipelago at the entrance of the gulf of Riga.[14]

This prelude of mine warfare during the opening stages of the European war calls for three remarks; first, all measures were taken allegedly in order to meet resolutely similar action on the part of the enemy. The war communiqués from the very beginning hinted at the exceptional right of retaliation, a feature which in the course of the four-year war was to bear a sustained recurrence. Reprisals made, therefore, an early entry in a conflict which was destined to be fought not in conformity to a set of rules but in admitted defiance of all rules. Second, the distinction between defensive and offensive operations was relativized and it soon became apparent that these initial danger zones would be modified or spread out in view of new situations. Third, the danger associated with these warning zones, i.e. striking a silent, way-laying mine, made the concept intrinsically linked to indiscriminate warfare.

The Introduction of Free-Fire Zones Before long, however, the concept of danger zones discarded the idea of an ostensibly defensive in character and limited in scope mine campaign and assumed a new significance. Although the intrinsic qualities of blanket exclusion and unsparing destruction remained unaltered, the concept underwent modification in geographic amplitude. On 4 November 1914, the British government declared the entire North Sea to be a *military area*, defined as an

[12]See 11 *AJIL* (1917) *Suppl.* at p. 12. The Channel minefield was extended in May 1916; see 11 *AJIL* (1917) *Suppl.* at p. 34.
[13]*Ibid.* at p. 13.
[14]See 9 *AJIL* (1915) at p. 463. The alleged reason was the threatening presence of German submarines in the Gulf of Finland and the suspected minelaying within Russian coastal waters.

area wherein 'merchant shipping of all kinds, traders of all countries, fishing craft, and all other vessels will be exposed to the gravest dangers from mines which it has been necessary to lay and from warships searching vigilantly by night and day for suspicious craft'. Three months later, on 4 February 1915, Germany published a decree according to which the waters around Great Britain were declared a *war zone*, defining an area where 'all enemy merchant vessels encountered in these waters will be destroyed, even if it may not be possible always to save their crews and passengers'. Moreover, neutral vessels were warned that they 'cannot always be prevented from suffering from the attacks intended for enemy ships'. The British Admiralty proceeded to give a concrete description of the warned off area by drawing a closing line from the northern point of the Hebrides through the Faeroe Islands to Iceland. It so ordered as to compel merchant ships to deviate and sail through the narrow seas of the English Channel. The German response equally provided precise limits for the encirclement of the British Isles, its strategic aim being fairly the converse of the British one, that is to say, keeping the North Sea approaches open while controlling the navigation through the English Channel.

Neutral Reactions The shocking novelty that the free-fire zones purported to impose on the naval war code of conduct was neatly commented upon in the US Note of 10 February 1915, addressed to the German government; 'to *declare* or *exercise* a right to attack and destroy any vessel entering a prescribed area of the high seas without first certainly determining its belligerent nationality and the contraband character of its cargo would be an act so unprecedented in naval warfare that this government is reluctant to believe that the Imperial Government of Germany in this case contemplates it as possible' (emphasis added).[15]

[15]It should be emphasized that in the view of the United States government not only the actual enforcement but even the declaration of contemplated indiscriminate destruction should be held unlawful, or, as it has been pithily expressed, 'a threat to do an illegal act is, according to municipal law, a separate crime in itself, . . . it rather aggravates the offence by showing premeditation and design'; see 9 *AJIL* (1915) at p. 674. For the prolonged diplomatic tug of war between Germany and the United States, see SEYMOUR, C., *American Diplomacy During the World War,* 1934, p. 80*ff.* See also SEYMOUR, C., *American Neutrality 1914–1917*, 1935, p. 27*ff.*, and MAY, E.R., *The World War and American Isolation 1914–1917*, 2nd edn, 1963, p. 113*ff.*

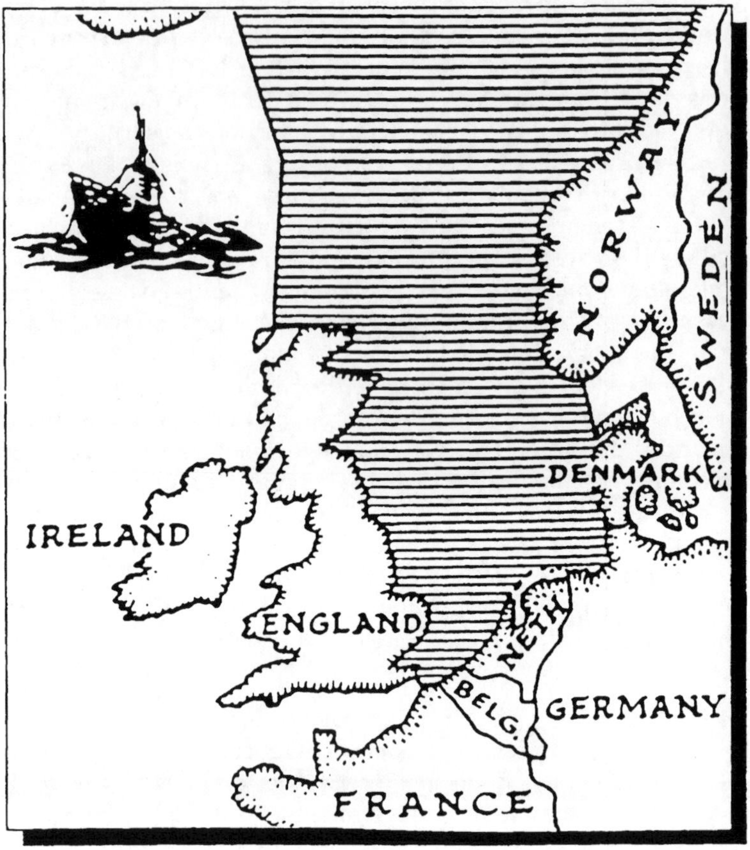

Figure 1 *The British North Sea Military Area, 3 November 1914*
Source: BAILEY, T.A. and RYAN, P.B., *The Lusitania Disaster*, 1975 at p. 30

In the mind of the Dutch Foreign Minister, the only concept to be found in the law of nations and which could bear some resemblance to the British military area or the German war zone, was that of the *sphere of immediate action* of belligerent operations, and suggested that the legality of the new measures should be assessed upon the lines of this latter concept. The Dutch protest of 16 November 1914, against the British proclamation read in part: 'd'après le Droit de Gens seule la sphère d'action immédiate des opérations militaires des belligérants constitue la zone militaire dans laquelle le droit de police d'un belligérant peut s'exercer. Une mer de la superficie de la mer du Nord ne peut être considérée dans toute son étendue comme la sphère d'action immédiate des opérations des belligérants.'[16]

The German government never contested the fact that sinking on sight constituted a new form of maritime war. Its principal contention was that establishing a war zone became a decision essentially forced upon it in the light of Britain's war of famine, or was a justifiable retaliatory act against British illegalities. The German response of 18 February 1915, to the criticisms voiced from across the Atlantic, read as follows:

> in view of this situation the German government see themselves *compelled* after six months of patience and watchful waiting, to meet England's murderous method of conducting maritime war with *drastic counter measures*... [Germany must] in the exigency into which she has *unlawfully been forced*, make her measures effective at all events in order thereby to compel her adversary to conduct maritime warfare in accordance with international law and thus to reestablish the freedom of the seas. (emphasis added)

In other words, the exceptional character of operating a free-fire war zone was openly and repeatedly admitted. It was solely on the grounds of belligerent reprisals that legitimacy was claimed. The major grievances about enemy tactics that Germany sought to redress by resorting to unrestricted submarine warfare concerned the quasi-abolition of the distinction between absolute and conditional contraband, the disregard of the Declarations of Paris and London, the recommended use of false flags,[17] the practice of arming merchantmen and urging them to ram

[16]See the Dutch White Book, *op. cit.*, *supra* n.11 at p. 5. The Dutch memorandum of 12 February 1915, against the German proclamation raised the same objection: 'le Gouvernement Néerlandais n'est pas tenu de veiller à ce que la marine marchande néerlandaise évite de naviguer dans une zone qui, par suite de sa vaste étendue, ne serait pas effectivement la sphère d'action immédiate des opérations de guerre', *ibid.* at p. 9. See also the Dutch Note of 7 February 1917 in another White Book entitled *Diplomatieke Bescheiden Betreffende den Verscherpten Duikbootoorlog*, 1917 at p. 2. The Dutch Notes of 16 November 1914 and of 12 February 1915 appear also in an Orange Book entitled *Recueil de diverses communications du Ministre des affaires étrangères aux États-généraux par rapport à la neutralité des Pays-Bas et au respect du droit des gens*, 1916 at pp. 87, 94. For more, see VANDENBOSCH, A., *The Neutrality of The Netherlands During the World War*, 1927, pp. 191–226.

[17]See the editorial comment, 9 *AJIL* (1915), p. 47*ff*.

German U-boats,[18] the perfidious tactics of Q-ships,[19] and finally the conversion of the entire North Sea into a military area.

Growing Escalation Nothing but exacerbating inhumanities and uncontrollable escalation could result from such a parodic exchange of reprisals and counter-reprisals. Even the practice of the U-boat commanders giving a symbolic few minutes warning before torpedoing merchant vessels was, alas, to last only a few weeks. The atrocious sinking of the *Lusitania* exemplified the measure and the kind of destruction associated with war zones that the world was to witness in the remaining three years of the war. By the Order in Council of 11 March 1915, the British government retained but a minimal contact with the classical law of contraband, declaring that any goods would be seizable as long as they were of presumed hostile destination, ownership or origin. The guidelines for the innovatory long-distance blockade had thereby been laid down.[20] As from October 1915, the *quota system* was first operated as a back-up procedure in order to render the economic blockade of the Central Powers even more stringent. Having departed so distantly from the letter and the spirit of the unratified Declaration of London of 1909, both London and Paris decided to abandon it officially on 7 July 1916. As from February 1917, Germany also renounced all pretexts and unleashed an unrestricted submarine campaign.

[18]On the question whether enemy and neutral merchantmen had the right to be fitted out with weaponry in order to resist forcibly visit and search and to resort to what was called offensive defence, see HIGGINS, A.P., 'Armed Merchant Ships', 8 *AJIL* (1914), pp. 705–22; BELLOT, H.L., 'The Right of a Belligerent Merchantman to Attack', 7 *GST* (1921), pp. 43–57; GARNER, *op. cit., supra* n.10, pp. 384–416. See also *infra*, chapter 3, notes 27–47 and accompanying text.
[19]On this anti-submarine stratagem, see CHATTERTON, *Les bateaux-pièges (Q-ships) contre les sous-marins allemands*, 1928; SMITH, R.W., 'The Q-Ships, Cause and Effect', 79 *USNIP* (May 1953), pp. 533–41; SIMS, *op. cit., supra* n.10, pp. 141–67. See also *infra*, chapter 3, notes 15–21 and accompanying text.
[20]On the Order in Council of 11 March 1915, see GARNER, J.W., 'Some Questions of International Law in the European War', 9 *AJIL* (1915), p. 818*ff*.; MALKIN, H.W., 'Blockade in Modern Conditions', 3 *BYIL* (1922–23), p. 87*ff*. The drafters of the new measures invoked once more the inescapable need to resort to reprisals. A declaration addressed to the US government on 1 March, regarding the intentions of the British and French authorities, read in part: 'her [Germany's] opponents are therefore driven to frame retaliatory measures in order in their turn to prevent commodities of any kind from reaching or leaving Germany'. The Order in Council itself contained a statement denouncing the German war zone as a violation of the laws of war and declaring that 'such attempts on the part of the enemy give to His Majesty an unquestionable right of retaliation'.

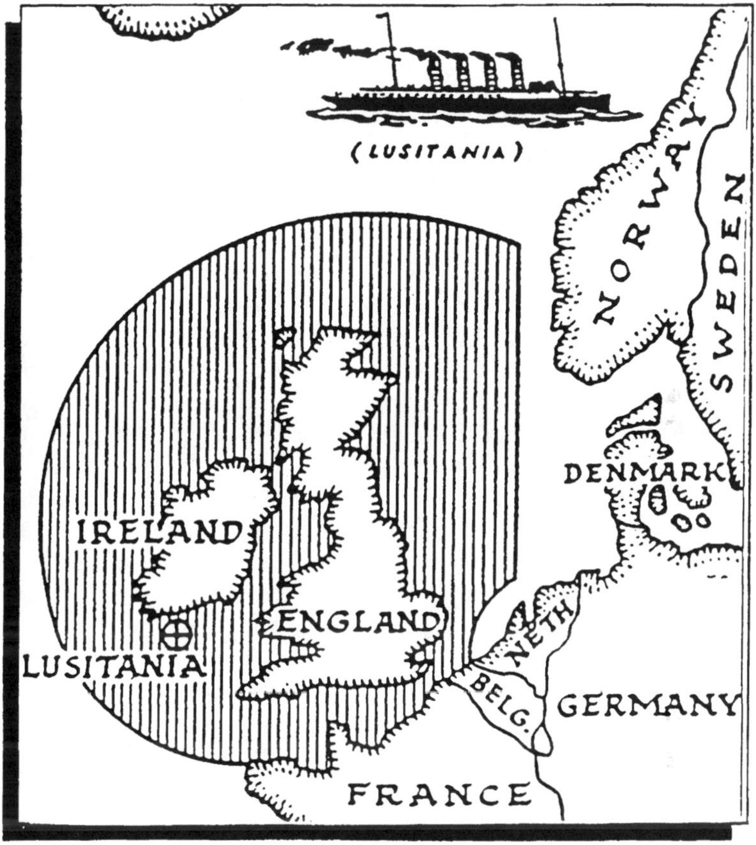

Figure 2 *The German War Zone around the British Isles, 4 February 1915*
Source: BAILEY, T.A. and RYAN, P.B., *The Lusitania Disaster*, 1975 at p. 34

Reducing sweeping war policies to barely laconic communiqués, it announced that 'all sea traffic was to be forthwith opposed by means of mines and submarines'. James Garner's view on the subject suits best to conclude the introductory note on war zones tactics: 'there is a clear distinction between the right of a belligerent to destroy an enemy merchant vessel and the right to destroy the lives of the unoffending non-combatant enemy subjects and neutrals which it may have on board. The former, subject to certain conditions, is lawful; the latter is never justifiable.'[21]

B Modern *guerre de course*: the unrestricted U-boat campaign

The Lusitania Outrage The German submarine warfare policy entered a critical test period right after it became operative in mid-February 1915, and throughout that year. The manifest illegality of unprovoked and indiscriminate attack revealed itself by the appalling surprise sinking of some passenger ships with not infrequently heavy loss of innocent lives. The infamous torpedoing of the trans-Atlantic liner *Lusitania* in early May 1915, in which 1,000 people perished, stands first in a series of strikes which undertook to demonstrate the essentials of a war zone in its cruellest form.[22] The *Arabic* and the *Hesperian*, sunk respectively in August and September of the same year, although of no comparable death toll to that of the *Lusitania*, refuelled the world indignation.[23] In the course of the ensuing long exchange of diplomatic representations, Germany assured the United States government that the U-boat commanders had received new orders to refrain from sinking passenger ships without warning.[24] Facing, however, a tempered but firm Wilsonian diplomacy, the Germans felt they had to give more satisfaction than that. By early October, the German government

[21]GARNER, *op. cit., supra* n.1 at p. 623.

[22]See BAILEY, T.A. and RYAN, P.B., *The Lusitania Disaster*, 1975. For a brief bibliographical note on this incident, see *ibid.* at p. 341. See also the first article of a tetralogy written on the German commercial submarine warfare by PERRIN-JAQUET, J., 'La guerre commerciale sous-marine: Les torpillages du *Lusitania*, de l'*Arabic*, de l'*Ancona* et du *Persia* – Les protestations des États-Unis et les concessions de l'Allemagne', 23 *RGDIP* (1916), pp. 117–203. According to certain accounts, *Lusitania* transported large quantities of rifle ammunition and shrapnel shells consigned to the British government; see GRATTAN, C.H., *Why We Fought*, 1929, pp. 291–6, and BARNES, H.E., *The Genesis of the World War*, 1926, pp. 611–14. Allegations that it carried Canadian troops, or that it had been fitted out with powerful guns, remained even less verified.

[23]On the *Arabic* incident, see 10 *AJIL* (1916) *Suppl.*, pp. 203–29.

[24]What was meant of course here was warning on the spot by the submarine commander. Warning in a far more general sense, if not entirely senseless, could be argued to have been fairly given, once and for all, by simply declaring and notifying a war zone. Besides, in the wake of the *Lusitania* disaster, the Germans argued that American citizens were amply forewarned by a shipping-notice published in the *New York World* of 1 May 1915 or six days before the sinking. The warning was ironically enough placed side by side with Cunard's advertisement of *Lusitania*'s next departure for Liverpool. On this atypical warning, see BAILEY and RYAN, *op. cit., supra* n.22, p. 70*ff.*

had repudiated the sinking of the *Arabic* as an action not conforming with standing naval instructions and announced its intention to indemnify the American citizens killed in the incident. Moreover, it gave reassurances that it would resist from further unwarned attacks against merchant vessels, and that it would carry on its submarine campaign strictly complying to established visit and search procedures.

A short-lived and fragile *modus vivendi* was hence reached after six months of tortuous negotiations whereby American lives were to be respected on board enemy liners, and American merchantmen were to be immune from unexpected submarine attack. No matter the political motives underlying the German retraction, the fact remains that the policy of operating a free-fire zone was seen even in German eyes as precariously justifiable. During the last two months of 1915, the focus shifted to the Mediterranean theatre. The *Ancona* and the *Persia* went down along with several hundreds of their passengers in a new outburst of cruelty.[25] There are two particularly important aspects of these incidents; first, no war zone of whatever description had been declared in the Mediterranean prior to the attacks, and second, responsibility for the acts never seemed a settled question. The first remark may well have signified the eclipse of the concept of war zone as such. The sinking of the *Ancona* and the *Persia* allude to a state of affairs which should not become an adopted policy before February 1917, namely unrestricted submarine warfare. As for the question of responsibility, the German U-boat commanders were instructed to attack and escape without making surface and showing their flag, which of course offered the extreme convenience to the German Admiralty of denying involvement in any inopportune attack.

Stakes Too High The German war cabinet in a memorandum of 10 February 1916, announced that all armed merchant vessels would be assimilated to enemy warships and would be treated accordingly as from 1 March 1916. It soon became apparent, however, that German submariners did not take any trouble to verify the existence or not of inculpatory gunnery on board the vessels they encountered. The *Tubantia* and the *Sussex* incidents

[25]See PERRINJAQUET, *op. cit.*, *supra* n.22, pp. 394–423.

made clear that the German campaign was to be as indiscriminate as ever.[26] In the wake of these attacks, US President Wilson in a memorandum of 20 April 1916, demanded the immediate cessation of the submarine warfare against commercial shipping threatening the rupture of diplomatic relations. Wilhelmstrasse, replying to this quasi-ultimatum refused to renounce and discontinue the submarine warfare, but appeared disposed instead to offer full satisfaction with relation to the *Sussex*.

By the end of 1916, the submarine was acknowledged as the incontestable spearhead of the German war planning. The calculation, though it may have sounded simplistic, was patently clear and realistic. Admiral von Holtzendorff in his memorandum was almost epigrammatic in envisioning Germany's way to victory:

> England was fed and supplied by about 10¾ million tons of British and neutral shipping. The German U-boats, working without restrictions and torpedoing at sight, could be counted upon to destroy 600,000 tons of shipping a month . . . At the end of five months Great Britain would lose 39 per cent of the tonnage employed in carrying her essential supplies, and the loss would be final and irreplaceable . . . I arrive, therefore, at the conclusion that an unrestricted U-boat war started at the proper time, will bring about peace before the harvesting period of the 1917 summer, that is before August 1; the break with America must be accepted; we have no choice but to do so.[27]

Holtzendorff's calculation was practically verified in the spring of 1917. Admiral Jellicoe, the First Sea Lord of the British Admiralty in his memorandum to the government in late April did nothing but present the alarming if not desperate situation.[28] Michelsen,[29] whose military narrative of the events remains one of the most accurate works of reference among German writings, has schematized the U-boat performance throughout the World War by discerning three phases: in what he brands the restricted submarine warfare phase, started on 22 February 1915, and

[26]See PERRINJAQUET, J., 'La guerre commerciale sous-marine', 24 *RGDIP* (1917), pp. 137–243.
[27]Cited in CORBETT, J.S. and NEWBOLT, H., *History of the Great War – Naval Operations*, vol.IV (1928) at p. 345.
[28]*Ibid.* at p. 379.
[29]MICHELSEN, A., *La guerre sous-marine 1914–1918*, 1928.

ended on 24 April 1916, the German Naval Command issued progressively more restrictive orders, these circulated in the aftermath of the *Lusitania*, the *Arabic* or the *Sussex* incidents, which culminated in the near suspension of submarine operations. The second phase, lasted from April 1916 until the autumn of the same year, led to the absolute suspension of the German sub operations. In Michelsen's words, this was the period of sub warfare conducted in accordance with international rules. The third and last phase was the period of unrestricted submarine warfare, inaugurated in January 1917 and carried on unflagging until the end of the war.

C The legal argumentation: the leitmotif of belligerent reprisals

Both belligerents in the long exchange of accusations and their diplomatic correspondence with neutral powers admitted the fresh character of the adopted practices. Britain referred to 'exceptional measures appropriate to the novel condition under which this war is being waged', whereas Germany did not deny that her naval strategies 'constitute new forms of maritime war, as has hitherto been the case with the English measures'. This is not of course to imply, or not exactly so, that they recognized the downright illegality of their respective acts, but it contains at least an outspoken and prompt avowal that the closure of open seas by means of 'blind' (mines) or 'blindfold' (submarines) weapons departed considerably far from modalities until then accepted in law. The sole fact that the defence of such measures was exhausted in the domain of the right to retaliate and the theory of vital interests shows that any argumentation on some other grounds was found barely convincing or simply non-existent. As it has been noted, 'neither party claimed that new weapons and tactics had given rise, as a matter of necessity, to the emergence of a customary norm justifying their prohibited zones. Furthermore, each side argued that the other's reprisal (that is, maritime exclusion zone) was illegal even as a reprisal.'[30]

[30]See GOLDIE, *op.cit.*, *supra* n.9 at p. 161. The alternative of asserting an independent right in *statu nascendi*, even if it was contemplated, was never officially presented as such. The theory that new weapons create new law, and that novel conditions call for new methods of warfare was of course propagated, but this is not necessarily the same as saying that an autonomous right to attack and destroy at will was advocated.

The Germans, in particular, had long demonstrated a hesitation to resort to unrestricted submarine warfare. This hesitation was translated into a half-hearted campaign against neutral merchant shipping. The intermittence of unrestricted submarine warfare and the vacillating orders to submarine officers, the inconsistent position of the German diplomacy regarding reparation for damages and human losses sustained as a result of such warfare, and the plethora of pledges offered time and again in order to pacify the spirits across the Atlantic, all point to the impotence of the German foreign policy to present a case, tenable in law, in the face of the world's opposition. Michelsen makes that point, not sparing any blame against German statesmanship for not having adopted a more resolute stance from the very beginning:

> celle-ci [diplomatie allemande] n'a-t-elle pas très fréquemment présenté, sous une forme lenitive, d'humbles et larmoyantes excuses à l'Amerique, à l'occasion de la guerre sous-marine? N'a-t-elle pas constamment offert de bonnes paroles et des dédommagements aux autres neutres pour les torpillages qu'ils subissaient? Au lieu de se tenir sur le solide terrain du droit, elle a fait considérer de plus en plus par toutes ces tractations, cette guerre comme une chose illégale et interdite.[31]

The overriding German preoccupation was of course how to win the war at sea without excessively irritating the interests of the great American power and so compromising its neutral status. Beyond this very real political apprehension, however, a

[31]See MICHELSEN, *op.cit, supra* n.29 at pp. 51–2. The propriety of enforcing a blockade all around the British Isles by the sole means of the U-boat flotilla is known to have caused the discord between the Minister of Naval Affairs, von Tirpitz, and Admiral von Pohl. For the inner history of that dispute, see TIRPITZ, A. von, *Mémoires du Grand-Amiral von Tirpitz*, 1922, p. 401*ff*. Tirpitz considered the idea of declaring the British Isles blockaded and embarking on submarine warfare as premature and unfortunate. He would favour instead a far more limited blockade operation off the mouth of the River Thames. He advocated a progressive introduction of novel practices which he did not hesitate to qualify as 'brutal' and 'grave'. In expressing his flat disagreement with a plan proposed by Pohl, he wrote in 15 December 1914: 'enfin, je suis porté à croire que celles de nos autorités officielles qui font déjà des objections d'ordre juridique et d'ordre moral à un blocus sous-marin s'éleveront bien plus encore contre cette méthode. Le projet établi par Votre Excellence est de nature à accentuer ces protestations plutôt qu'à les calmer', *ibid.* at p. 403. After citing in chronological order the contradictory and often inexecutable orders communicated to the submarine crews in the first nine months of 1915, Tirpitz concludes: 'voila quelle était l'impression de la flotte. Ordre, contre-ordre, desordre!', *ibid.* at p. 424.

legal impasse was also found; it was simply impossible to find the slightest legal endorsement, either in state practice or in current doctrine, for sinking without warning and without regard for the fate of neutral, non-combatant lives. Wilhelmstrasse, in its official correspondence, never contested the validity of the principles of international law contained in the US diplomatic communications regarding the treatment due to unarmed merchantmen and innocent civilians found on board. There are passages from German or Austro-Hungarian Notes comprising clear and unreserved affirmations of some of the prevailing international customs as they were advocated by the large majority of neutral seafaring nations.[32] As from early 1917, however, a new tendency is traceable which consists in toning down the plea of reprisals, opting instead for absolute necessity. The German declaration of 31 January 1917, for instance, upholds that the new comprehensive arrangement of war zones should be validated as a means of continuation of a struggle fought in order to defend the existence of the German state, and urges the foreign governments to concede the motives and the necessity that dictated such a decision.[33]

[32]See HYDE, C.C., 'Attacks on Unarmed Enemy Merchant Vessels', 11 *Proc.ASIL* (1917) at p. 34; MALLISON, *op. cit., infra* n.236 at p. 63.

[33]The German declaration addressed to the Dutch government read in part as follows: 'le Gouvernement Impérial . . . doit mettre en jeu toutes les armes, afin de continuer la lutte à laquelle il a été contraint pour défendre son existence. Il se voit donc force de supprimer les restrictions apportées jusqu'à présent dans l'emploi de ses moyens de combat sur mer. Dans la ferme confiance que le peuple et le Gouvernement Néerlandais se rendront aux motifs de cette decision et de la nécessité qui la dicte, le Gouvernement Impérial espère que le Gouvernement Néerlandais appréciera le nouvel état de choses'. See the Dutch White Book, *op. cit., supra* n.11 at p. 1. The Austro-Hungarian declaration that was issued the same day and established war zones of identical extent with the German ones, speaks of the need to employ without distinction the most effective arms and concludes by assuring that 'l'Autriche-Hongrie et les Puissances alliées entrent dans cette nouvelle et grave phase de la guerre avec une fermeté dictée par l'amertume de la nécessité'; *ibid.* at p. 4. For a critical appraisal of the German theories of necessity, see DE VISSCHER, Ch., 'Les lois de la guerre et la théorie de la nécessité', 24 *RGDIP* (1917), pp. 74–108. See also SCHWARZENBERGER, G., 'Military Necessity: A Misnomer' in *Mélanges Séfériadès*, 1961 at pp. 20–1; 'the maxim *kriegsraison geht vor kriegsmanier* is nothing less than the assertion of the priority of a primordial concept of sovereignty over duties incumbent on a belligerent under international customary law or treaty obligations. Similarly, the view that military necessity exonerates belligerents from the observance of the laws of war is but an attenuated form of the same anarchist fallacy. It is a more specialised application of another doctrine which is as destructive of international law as it is untenable: the doctrine of an all-overriding right of self-preservation'.

D The conduct of submarine warfare and criminal responsibility

According to Article 228 of the peace treaty of Versailles, the defeated German government should 'hand over to the Allied and Associated powers . . . all persons accused of having committed an act in violation of the laws and customs of war'. The surrender of some 900 war criminals was subsequently demanded by Great Britain, Belgium, France, Italy, Poland and Romania. Admiral von Tirpitz figured prominently among the wanted enemies. Moreover, a fifteen-member Commission on the Responsibility of the Authors of the War and the Enforcement of Penalties was set up for the purpose of inquiring into the war responsibilities and reporting on 'the facts as to breaches of the laws and customs of war committed by the forces of the German Empire and their Allies, on land, on sea, and in the air during the war'. The Report of the Commission, dated 29 March 1919, was adopted unanimously subject to reservations entered by the American and the Japanese representatives.[34] Among the listed crimes was included the 'destruction of merchant ships and passenger vessels without warning and without provision for the safety of passengers and crew'. The whole operation to implement the recommendations of the Commission ended in complete failure, but this in no way decreases the significance of the Commission's conclusion that 'the war was carried on by the Central Empires together with their allies Turkey and Bulgaria, by *barbarous* and *illegitimate* methods in violation of the established laws and customs of war and the elementary laws of humanity' (emphasis added).

3 The Spanish Civil War

On 9 August 1936, the Spanish government declared Spanish Morocco, the Canary islands, Rio de Oro, and two days later, the coasts of Huelva, Cadize, Lugo, Corunna, Ponteverda and the Balearic islands to be *zones of war* subject to blockade measures. Ultimately, the Spanish government proclaimed a war zone concerning all the ports of the peninsula. On 17 November 1936, the insurgent forces under General Franco responded by

[34]For the American reservations, see MARIN, M.A., 'The Evolution and Present Status of the Laws of War', 92 *RCADI* (1957), p. 680*ff*. On the composition and the functioning of the Commission, see WILLIS, J.F., *Prologue to Nuremberg*, 1982, p. 68*ff*.

announcing their intention to close the port of Barcelona to all maritime traffic engaged in transporting logistic support for the loyalist troops.[35] By November 1937, however, the communiqués sounded much more resolutely prohibitive; 'the neutral zones established at Valence and Barcelona are suspended. As from the publication of this notice to mariners vessels which sail into these waters will be attacked.' These were the opening acts of a naval campaign which was launched in Mediterranean waters with unforseen consequences and was destined to project the ambit of a civil strife well beyond ordinary standards.[36] The indiscriminate and unprovoked attacks on merchant shipping that followed were seen to constitute, to use the language of the 1937 Nyon agreement, 'acts contrary to the most elementary dictates of humanity, which should be justly treated as acts of piracy'.[37] Shortly after, the Council of the League of Nations

[35]It is interesting to note that no blockade was officially declared, but rather the intention to destroy the Barcelona port facilities. Foreign vessels were requested to depart the soonest possible in order to spare collateral damage. There was no hint that they would be directly subject to attack. Moreover, in the wake of British diplomatic representations, the nationalists agreed and delimited neutral or security zones for the safe anchorage of foreign vessels off the Barcelona harbour. Later in 1936, the nationalists announced the blockade of the Atlantic coast mainly focused on Bilbao, Santander and Gijon, while towards the end of 1937, they staged another blockade effort in respect of ports along the Mediterranean coast. On the naval operations of evacuation of thousands of foreign nationals from July through October 1936, see FRANK, W.C., 'Multinational Naval Cooperation in the Spanish Civil War, 1936', 47 *US Naval War College Review* (spring 1994), p. 72*ff.*

[36]For an extensive narration of the blockade measures enacted by both parties see ROUSSEAU, Ch., 'La non-intervention en Espagne', 19 *RDILC* (1938), p. 529*ff.* On the legal aspects of the Spanish civil war, see PADELFORD, N.J., 'Foreign Shipping During the Spanish Civil War', 32 *AJIL* (1938), p. 264*ff.*; GARNER, J.W., 'Questions of International Law in the Spanish Civil War', 31 *AJIL* (1937), p. 66*ff.*; JESSUP, P., 'The Spanish Rebellion and International Law', 15 *Foreign Affairs* (1937), p. 260*ff.*; PADELFORD, N.J., 'International Law and the Spanish Civil War', 31 *AJIL* (1937), p. 226*ff.*; SMITH, H.A., 'Some Problems of the Spanish Civil War', 18 *BYIL* (1937), p. 17*ff.*

[37]The Nyon Agreement of 14 September 1937, appears in PADELFORD, N.J., *International Law and Diplomacy in the Spanish Civil Strife*, 1939 at p. 603. See GOLDIE, L.F.E., 'Commentary on the Nyon Agreements' in RONZITTI, N. (ed.), *The Law of Naval Warfare*, 1988, p. 489ff.; KUNIG. P., 'Nyon Agreement' in BERNHARDT, R. (ed.), *Encyclopedia of Public International Law*, instalment 4 (1982), p. 57*ff.* On the question of piracy raised in the context of the Nyon agreement, see LAUTERPACHT, H., 'Insurrection et piraterie', 46 *RGDIP* (1939), p. 513*ff.*; FINCH, G.A., 'Piracy in the Mediterranean', 31 *AJIL* (1937), p. 659*ff*; GENET, R., 'The Charge of Piracy in the Spanish Civil War', 32 *AJIL* (1938), p. 253*ff.*; Anonymous, 'Piracy by Treaty?', 19 *BYIL* (1938), p. 198*ff.* For the discussion on the contemplated abolition of the submarine after the First World War and the abortive Washington conference of 1921, see DOUGLAS, L.H., 'The

declared 'that all attacks of this kind against any merchant vessels are repugnant to the conscience of the civilized nations'.[38]

On 2 February 1938, a meeting of British, French and Italian delegations was convened at the Foreign Office upon the initiative of the British government, and it was decided that the warships composing the International Naval Patrol should be given instructions to attack and if possible destroy within their assigned zones any submerged submarine that they might detect.[39] As of 3 February 1938, the entire western Mediterranean turned into a vast anti-submarine exclusion zone. The new instructions, however, were never tested since no submarine was engaged by the international naval forces after that date.

The fact that the sink-at-sight order exclusively concerned warships and more specifically underwater craft made the occurrence of collateral damage inflicted upon merchant bottoms highly improbable. In any event, the Spanish Civil War witnessed the creation for the first time of a special exclusion zone enforced only against submarines. It was designed as an operational device bearing no connection whatsoever to economic warfare that was set up in the framework of a treaty and aspired to be a collective measure against piracy. If one adds to this description the confusing detail that the whole operation was undertaken in the name of 'non-intervention', the precise character of the campaign becomes even less clear.[40]

Submarine and the Washington Conference of 1921', USNWC, 62 *International Law Studies* (1980), p. 477*ff.*; FRANCOIS, J.P.A., 'L'avenir du sous-marin', 30 *RGDIP* (1923), p. 34*ff.*; ROXBURGH, R.F., 'Submarines at the Washington Conference', 3 *BYIL* (1922–3), p. 150*ff.* See also 'Discussion on the Abolition of Submarines', 11 *GST* (1925), p. 65*ff.*

[38]Resolution of 5 October 1937, cited in PADELFORD, *op. cit., supra* at p. 629.

[39]See ROUSSEAU, *op. cit., supra* n.36 at p. 492. The Nyon agreements had authorized neutral warships to attack submarines assaulting merchant vessels, or upon presumption any submarine suspiciously lurking in the vicinity of a freshly staged attack. Under the amended rules of 1938, however, there was no need even of such a presumption. The Mediterranean having thus been closed to submarines, with the exception of small patches near the coasts reserved for naval exercises, all underwater unidentified contacts might safely be treated as hostile. The naval forces in the western Mediterranean which had been gradually diminished since the end of 1937, were drastically reinforced. Great Britain augmented its presence by deploying forty-five destroyers instead of twenty-seven until then policing the high seas. For specific naval incidents, see FRANK, W.C., 'Misperception and Incidents at Sea: The *Deutschland* and *Leipzig* Crises, 1937', 43 *US Naval War College Review* (spring 1990), p. 31*ff.*

[40]For critical remarks on the so-called policy of non-intervention, see SCELLE, G., 'La guerre civile espagnole et le droit des gens', 46 *RGDIP* (1939), p. 197*ff.*;

4 The Second World War

The overture of the Second World War evidenced something prosaically repetitious: belligerents were prompt to offer hackneyed pledges that they would stick to their international engagements, professing devotion to the rule of law while truly expecting an opportunity to break away and be released from its constraints. History obliged with such an opportunity. The German High Command entered the war adhering scrupulously in all appearances to the London Protocol of 1936 regarding submarine warfare, which besides was incorporated verbatim into Article 74 of the German Prize Ordinance.[41] The arming of British merchant vessels, however, made the dilemma for German submariners a militarily impossible one to face. The German contention was that, from the first day of the war, the British merchant seamen were instructed to report the position of encountered submarines, to use depth charges and gunfire, and, as from 1 October 1939, to ram if possible all German submarines.[42] By 4 October 1939, the German submarine commanders had received orders to attack all enemy armed merchantmen without warning.[43]

ROUSSEAU, Ch., 'La non-intervention en Espagne', 20 *RDILC* (1939), p. 114*ff*.; PADELFORD, N.J., 'The International Non-Intervention Agreement and the Spanish Civil War', 31 *AJIL* (1937), p. 578*ff*.

[41]See 18 *Official Proceedings – International Military Tribunal* at p. 314. Admiral Raeder, interviewed in September 1939, had stated: 'Germany is conducting submarine warfare in accordance with the Prize laws issued on August 28, 1939. These are strictly in accordance with the acknowledged rules of maritime war. The provisions of the London Submarine Protocol are taken over in full in them. The submarines have strict orders to comply with these provisions'; cited in HACKWORTH, G.H., *Digest of International Law,* vol.VI (1943) at p. 484. See also ASSMANN, K., 'Why U-boat Warfare Failed', 28 *Foreign Affairs* (1949–50), p. 659*ff*.

[42]See 18 *Official Proceedings – International Military Tribunal* at pp. 321–2. The British Defence of Merchant Shipping Handbook of 1938 which was invoked during the Nuremberg trials and was classified as document Dönitz-67 read as follows: 'as soon as the Master of a merchant ship realizes that a ship or aircraft in sight is an enemy, it is his first and most important duty to report the nature and position of the enemy by wireless telegraphy', 40 *Official Proceedings – International Military Tribunal* at p. 87.

[43]Three years later, the German submarines were prohibited from aiding or rescuing survivors from torpedoed ships. On the so-called Laconia Order, see MAURER, M. and PASZEK, L.J., 'Origin of the Laconia Order', 109 *Journal of the Royal United Services Institution* (1964), p. 338*ff*. See also BEKKER, C.D., *Swastika at Sea – The Struggle and Destruction of the German Navy 1939–1945*, 1953, pp. 26–34.

A The resumption of economic warfare

The US Combat Area and the Creeping German Danger Zones On 24 November 1939, the German government embarked on what was about to become a new round of galloping escalation. In a Note addressed to several neutral states, Germany warned that the waters around the British Isles and near the French coast could no longer be considered safe for neutral shipping. A few weeks before, the President of the United States had issued a proclamation barring US citizens, ships and aircraft from a *combat area* covering a large area of the Atlantic ocean off the European continent.[44] The German diplomacy thought that duplicating the US combat zone would make the submarine operational area more likely to meet with the acquiescence of third states. What was introduced as a precautionary measure for the safety of US citizens and the protection of American neutrality was readily propagated by the Germans as a tacit consent to the practice of free-fire war zones.[45] Within this broader warning of November 1939, Germany later came to designate several war zones. The first was notified on 6 January 1940 and concerned the waters northeast of Scotland, the Orkneys and the Shetlands. By the end of May 1940, neutral shipping was excluded from a sea strip 60 to 100 miles wide along the French and British coasts. Passenger liners, the Danish '*Malteser*' ships, and merchant ships of those neutrals friendly to Germany (i.e. Italy, Japan, Soviet Union, Spain) were the only ones to be exempted. The graduated deployment of the

[44]Proclamation of 4 November 1939; see 34 *AJIL* (1940) *Suppl.* at p. 58. The prohibited combat area was extended by the proclamations of 10 April 1940 and of 11 June 1940; see 34 *AJIL* (1940) *Suppl.* at pp. 162, 171, and it was again modified on 10 April 1941, see 35 *AJIL* (1941) *Suppl.* at p. 178.

[45]Outside the German camp, many also interpreted the American prohibition as a tacit consent to war zone tactics. Payson Sibley Wild, for instance, evaluating the legal status of war zones in the mid-1940s had this to say: 'in modern practice, however, zones have again been proclaimed by belligerents. Some neutrals, including the United States, *recognized* these danger zones by proclaiming combat areas' (emphasis added); see USNWC, *International Law Developments* (1943) at pp. 57–8. Note also the earlier remarks by George A. Finch: 'I am very glad that the suggestion which has been made in the last few years in the consideration of our Neutrality Law, of forbidding the passage of American vessels to or through war zones, has not been adopted, because *that would be an admission of the legality* of this new and unrecognized method of carrying on a blockade without regard to previously existing rules'; see 31 *Proc.ASIL* (1937) at p. 133.

submarine in its traditional *guerre de course* role, however, was criticized especially among members of the naval staff.[46]

The Proliferation of War Zones It was not until 17 August 1940, that a comprehensive operational zone was notified. The new version was to profess no particular sympathy for passenger liners reviving the horrifying memory of the *Lusitania* incident. The entire combat area indicated in the US proclamation of 4 November 1939, was now branded without any limitation an operational area. In the words of Dr. Kranzbühler, who pleaded the case of Admiral Dönitz before the International Military Tribunal at Nuremberg, 'from this time on the area was fully utilized and the immediate use of arms against craft encountered in it was permitted to all naval and air forces'.[47]

Meanwhile, the British, who had been reconsidering their own methods of war, similarly relaxed restrictions on submarine attacks. On 9 April 1940, the British government ordered that all German merchant vessels should be sunk without warning if found navigating east of 8°E, while in May 1940, the British war cabinet announced that in a limited strategic pocket of the North Sea, the Skagerrak, all German merchant ships would be sunk at day time, and all vessels irrespective of nationality by night.[48] In July 1940, the British Admiralty asked the government to authorize the establishment of a war zone off the coasts of northern Europe and north west Africa suggesting that it should

[46]Raeder, for instance, who had called for a war without restrictions of every possible intensity, held the opinion that no official proclamation of a fixed war zone was even necessary, since the United States had forbidden on their own initiative the access to their citizens; see JOUAN, R., *La marine allemande dans le seconde guerre mondiale d'après les conférences navales du Führer*, 1949, p. 252*ff*.

[47]18 *Official Proceedings – International Military Tribunal* at p. 329. Referring to Admiral Raeder's statements of that time, he argued: 'if therefore in the sea zones mentioned neutral ships and crews sustained losses, at least they cannot complain about not having been warned explicitly and urgently beforehand', *ibid.* To add tellingly: 'this statement in itself has not much meaning in the question of whether areas of operation as such constitute an admissible measure', *ibid.*

[48]The resemblance of these measures to methods of warfare traditionally espoused by Germany was commented by a British officer as follows: 'la répugnance naturelle du Cabinet britannique à adopter les méthodes allemandes de guerre sous-marine avait gêné les premières opérations, troublé les commandants et reduit le tribut qu'aurait dû payer le shipping adverse', GILBERT, 'Les opérations sous-marines de la marine britannique pendant la deuxième guerre mondiale', 208 *Revue Maritime* (1964) at p. 298.

have a width of no less than 300 n.m. The war cabinet decided that as a matter of legal principle the Royal Navy should not endorse a policy of sinking neutral vessels. The area in question, however, was declared a war zone in the following sense: 'any consignment not navicerted, and any ship without a ship navicert, will henceforth be *liable to seizure* by our patrols' (emphasis added).[49]

The aggregate of the German operational areas amounted, according to Allied estimates, to 750,000 square nautical miles while the Germans lowered the figure to 600,000 square nautical miles.[50] The dangerous-to-shipping areas proclaimed by Britain covered about 120,000 square nautical miles.[51] According to other accounts, the British Admiralty as late as 15 February 1944, declared a vast additional area which alone amounted to 150,000 square nautical miles. By far the largest war zone, however, was that declared by the United States in December 1941 in retaliation for the Japanese surprise attack on Pearl Harbor, and which involved more than 30 million square nautical miles of the Pacific Ocean.[52]

[49]See MEDLICOTT, W.N., *The Economic Blockade*, vol.I (1952), p. 433*ff.* Furthermore, Britain, responding to an Italian notice of similar content, declared that all merchant vessels would navigate at their risk and peril within 30 miles from the Italian territory and the Libyan coast.

[50]See 18 *Official Proceedings – International Military Tribunal* at p. 331.

[51]*Ibid.* at p. 336.

[52]*Ibid.* at p. 337. See also the reply to interrogatories put to Admiral Nimitz in the context of the Nuremberg trials and classified as document Dönitz-100, 17 *Official Proceedings – International Military Tribunal*, pp. 378–381. In fact, according to the *Proposed Amendment of Rules for Maritime Warfare*, prepared by the US Naval War College and submitted to the General Board of the US Navy in the spring of 1941, conditional contraband should be abolished and the use of war zones should be adopted instead of traditional blockade operations. Unrestricted warfare would be authorized within such war zones to be enforced by submarines, aircraft and by submarine mines. The General Board, however, categorically rejected all those recommendations, so that until the attack on Pearl Harbor there were no changes in the US Naval Instructions. Provisional orders for unrestricted warfare in the Pacific in the event of a war with Japan were first released in November 1941, while on 7 December, Admiral Stark finally issued the order 'execute against Japan unrestricted air and submarine warfare'. On the origins of the German and American decisions for unrestricted submarine warfare during the Second World War, see the recent work by MANSON, J.M., *Diplomatic Ramifications of Unrestricted Submarine Warfare, 1939–1941*, 1990. Apart from the Pacific Ocean war zone, the United States with the executive order of 11 December 1941, proceeded also to establish several 'naval defensive sea areas' along their coasts; see USNWC, *International Law Developments* (1941) at p. 83*ff.* The order, reminiscent of a similar one issued in 1917, imposed certain shipping restrictions. Vessels should proceed after specific permission had been obtained during daylight, while night sailing was only

B The decline of the plea of reprisals

The Shift in Legal Claim There is a noticeable difference in the way war zones were justified during the two World Wars. In the opening days of the U-boat *guerre de course* in 1915 the German government made exclusive reference to reprisals as an imposed course of conduct due to the allegedly illegal methods of warfare introduced by the Allied forces. In all the communiqués that followed, the invocation of the right of retaliation became an overused *cliché*.[53] The British war cabinet did not seek any less to legitimize analogous war tactics through the doctrine of reprisals.[54]

In striking contrast with the First World War experience, however, the reprisal prayer was distinctly played down in the course of the Second World War. Germany, for her part, attempted to present its operational areas as zones of active and continuous operations, something resembling more the classical concept of the *immediate vicinity of naval engagements* than the blind targeting zones of the First World War. On 24 November 1939, for instance, in its first Note on the subject, the German government emphasized the element of danger for neutral shipping, speaking of unsafe waters due to extensive hostilities: 'to warn anew and more strongly that in view of the fact that the actions are carried on with all the technical means of modern warfare, and in view of the fact that these actions are increasing

---

allowed under authorized supervision. Their identity and destination had to be communicated in advance and they should 'obey any further instructions received from the US Navy or other U.S. authority'. The order, however, kept far from imposing an outright prohibition of navigation and even more so from threatening an unwarned attack against vessels which might attempt to penetrate into the designated areas.

[53]See for example the wording of the following communiqués: 'It [Germany] therefore sees itself forced to military measures aimed at England in retaliation against the English procedure', 4 February 1915; 'the new German method of naval warfare is imposed and justified by the murderous character of the English method of naval warfare, which seeks to condemn the German people to death by starvation', 15 February 1915; 'under these circumstances Germany will meet the illegal measures of her enemies by forcibly preventing after 1 February 1917, in a zone around Great Britain, France, Italy, and in the eastern Mediterranean all navigation', 31 January 1917. The principle of vital interests and the doctrine of necessity or self-preservation were also advanced but were kept in the background at least until the declaration of January 1917.

[54]The announcement of 24 January 1917, for example read as follows: 'In view of the unrestricted warfare carried on by Germany at sea . . . His Majesty's Government gave notice that on and after the 7th proximo the undermentioned area in the North Sea will be rendered dangerous to all shipping'.

in the waters around the British Isles and near the French coast, these waters can no longer be considered safe for neutral shipping'. While on 17 August 1940, the announcement of the total blockade against Britain was accompanied not so much by rhetorical appeals to reprisals as by renewed warnings:

> as the result of the developments which the war has taken during the last weeks England has been brought into the centre of the war activities at sea and in the air. In the sea area surrounding the British Isles constant war action is consequently from now on to be expected . . . the entire sea area around the British Isles has therefore become a *combat one* . . . the German Government most urgently renews its warning to neutral shipping against passing through the *danger zone*. (emphasis added)[55]

Reading these communiqués one gets the impression that Germany in the Second World War ceased to justify its submarine campaign by waving anxiously the reprisals banner, but that it invoked rather confidently, and as a matter of right, a course of action which seemed settled and in which several neutral states had already acquiesced. Admiral Dönitz's counsel in front of the International Military Tribunal at Nuremberg developed all his reasoning upon this very perception: 'these zones . . . were gradually set up where, as a result of mutually increasing attacks and defensive actions at sea and in the air, engagements continually occurred, so that any ship entering this area was operating in the direct presence of the naval forces of both powers'.[56] After recalling the First World War belligerent practices, and the diplomatic developments in the inter-war period relating to the submarine, he concluded in these words:

[55]Another German statement regarding a submarine zone, established in June 1942, referred to a 'zone of operation in which *fighting* may be expected' and warned 'all ships against navigating in this *danger zone*'. Elsewhere in the same communiqué, the German authorities spoke of the 'extension of the *realm of operations* of the German Navy' without the slightest mention been made to the law of reprisals; see USNWC, *International Law Developments* (1941) at pp. 158–9. Reprisals, of course, still remained a valid justification and could not be missing from the official German declarations. The total blockade declaration of August 1940, for instance, after reciting the British violations of the laws of war, announced that 'the Reich Government has now decided to retaliate in kind and to employ armed forces with the same ruthlessness against shipping around England'.

[56]See 18 *Official Proceedings – International Military Tribunal* at p. 328.

'a development, typical for the rules of naval warfare, was confirmed here, namely, that the modern technique of war forcibly leads to the use of war methods which at first are introduced in the guise of reprisals, but which gradually come to be employed without such a justification and recognized as legitimate'.[57] Admittedly, war zone practices in the 1940s did not provoke the same floods of protest among neutrals as was the case twenty-five years earlier. What is more, neutrals, and more specifically the United States, as soon as they entered the war, resorted to indiscriminate, unrestricted destruction much less reluctantly than in the First World War.[58] Is it then that the want of moderation, and the inoperativeness of legal restraints, attest to a possible modification of certain legal rules, sparked in 1914, rooted in the inter-war period, and solidified in 1940?[59]

The Excuse of Reprisals vs. International Custom It can hardly be

[57]*Ibid.* at p. 329. Later in his pleading the same counsel eschewed mentioning reprisals as a possible legal basis for operating war zones; 'I am referring as a legal basis especially to the practice of the First World War, and the statements made by the experts after the First World War, and also to the generally recognized rules about mined areas', *ibid.* at pp. 333–4. While he did not omit to point out that the German measures enjoyed the recognition of third states; 'it was therefore not through arbitrary action that the German operational area, which the Prosecution objects to, grew to such a size; it was only because the German Naval Command was adapting itself to a system which was *recognized* by the other powers also as *justified*' (emphasis added), *ibid.* at p. 336.

[58]In the words of one commentator, 'a fair scrutiny of the last two World Wars makes clear the steady intensification in the inhumanity of the weapons and methods employed by both the aggressors and the victors. In order to defeat Japanese aggression, we were forced, as Admiral Nimitz has stated, to employ a technique of unrestricted submarine warfare not unlike that which 25 years ago was the proximate cause of our entry into World War I'; see STIMSON, H.L., 'The Nuremberg Trial: Landmark in Law', 25 *Foreign Affairs* (1947) at p. 189. For yet another scholar, 'the United States, on December 7, 1941, not only repudiated the long-standing American policy on submarine warfare but adopted the German rationale as well'; see MANSON, *op. cit., supra* n.52 at p. 158. It is not without significance that prominent US naval commanders such as Admirals Thomas Hart and Chester Nimitz issued statements of support for Dönitz concerning the charge of unrestricted submarine warfare. Admiral Hart noted that in waging unrestricted submarine warfare Dönitz did 'what I was ordered to do', while Admiral Nimitz concluded that the 'American practice for unrestricted submarine warfare would be normal in future warfare'; see MANSON, *op. cit., supra* n.52 at p. 182.

[59]As Robert Tucker has noted, the argument of reprisals by the time of the 1939 war was 'a plea that had admittedly taken on a rather perfunctory character and that on occasion was simply omitted altogether'; TUCKER, *op. cit., infra* n.237 at pp. 301–2, and ftn.44.

contested that during the Second World War all naval powers capable of waging unrestricted submarine warfare did so extensively. It is no less undisputed, however, that all timid attempts to justify such demonstrably illegal practice were invariably couched in terms of reprisals, or partly so.[60] The plea of reprisals is in itself an admission of the illicit character of the practice in question, it is an unreserved avowal that, if not for the illegalities committed by the adversary, such practice should be prohibited. Even if one accepts, therefore, that by the mid-1940s the sink-at-sight policy against enemy commerce was a method of warfare enjoying near uniformity, this by no means implies that an international customary rule in *statu nascendi* was to be deduced. The conviction in law that a certain practice is lawful collides head-on with the plea of reprisals. In other words, the invocation of retaliation and the consolidation of an international custom are mutually exclusive legal premises. Thus, if anything was sanctioned by becoming customary, it was the right to resort to reprisals in case of flagrant and continued breach of the laws of war on the part of the enemy and not the creation of free-fire zones. In fact, belligerent reprisals had become such a pandemic feature that virtually no authority challenged their foundation upon an international custom.[61]

5 The Korean War

The Close-In Blockade Economic blockade became once more the rule of the day only five years after the conclusion of the Second World War. The UN-mandated Korean campaign gave rise to naval operations which remained limited only due to the total

[60]As has been written in a recent commentary, 'this raises the question of whether decreased reliance on strong diplomatic protests in World War II as compared to World War I, may arguably be seen as the beginning of an acknowledgment, albeit reluctant, of their decreasing utility and necessity. But, again in World War II, as in World War I, the factors leading to the emergence of a customary international law norm justifying the long-distance blockades were camouflaged by both sides' invocations of reprisal as justification for their actions'; see GOLDIE, *op. cit., supra* n.9 at p. 169.

[61]See HIGGINS, A.P., 'Retaliation in Naval Warfare', 8 *BYIL* (1927), p. 129*ff*. In this sense, estimations like the one which argues that 'as an institution of the law of armed conflict belligerent reprisals have been in decline for most of this century' sound rather curious; see GREENWOOD, C., 'The Twilight of the Law of Belligerent Reprisals', 20 *NYIL* (1989) at p. 69. See also BIERZANEK, R., 'Reprisals in Armed Conflicts', 14 *Syracuse Journal of International Law and Commerce* (1988) Special Issue, p. 829*ff*.

lack of enemy opposition. Yet, the conduct of hostilities at sea, principally led by US naval forces, was not always free of controversy. The central feature of naval operations in Korea was the early established blockade of both the west and east coasts of North Korea.[62]

On 4 July 1950, it was announced that the US President had ordered a naval blockade of the Korean coast. All precautions seemed to have been taken in order to avoid any spillover effect of the operations and to harm strictly the 'aggressors'' sea transport. The northern limits of the blockaded area were so defined as to prevent the likelihood of any incident within the contiguous Chinese or Soviet territorial seas. Moreover, the far off North Korean port city of Rashin was specifically excluded since the Soviet Union enjoyed special rights there and indeed was making regular use of the warm-water port facilities. The North Korean coastal front of a total stretch of about 500 n.m. was to be barred for all merchant vessels, while warships, with the exception of North Korean ones, were allowed to proceed unhindered.

The Task Force 95, bearing the official title *United Nations Blockading and Escort Force*, was divided into two groups which patrolled the west and the east coast respectively. Enemy resistance to the enormous firepower went never beyond minimal harassment by torpedo fast boats, coastal artillery fire or scattered mines throughout the three-year conflict. All sea routes having been effectively blocked, the mission of UN warships soon turned to be not the blockade enforcement but the bombardment of selected targets ashore. Lacking a contestant at sea, the UN fleet guns remained locked on the enemy's logistic routes on land. In Cagle's words, 'in many respects it was a crazy mixed-up blockade where trains and trucks on land were chased by ships at sea'.[63]

[62]See CAGLE, M.W. and MANSON, F.A., *The Sea War in Korea*, 1957, pp. 281–373; FIELD, J.A., *History of U.S. Naval Operations – Korea*, 1962, p. 58*ff*. See also FENRICK, W.J., *Developments in the Law of Naval Warfare Since World War II: the Potential Emergence of a Law of Naval Warfare for Limited Conflicts*, unpublished thesis, 1983, p. 63*ff*.; REES, D., *Korea – The Limited War*, 1964, p. 366*ff*.; VERPLAETSE, J.G., 'The Jus in Bello and Military Operations in Korea 1950–1953', 23 *ZaöRV* (1963), p. 698*ff*.; PRINCE, S., 'The Contribution of the Royal Navy to the United Nations Forces During the Korean War', 17 *Strategic Studies* (June 1994), p. 94*ff*.

[63]CAGLE and MANSON, *op. cit., supra* at p. 283. See also *ibid.* at p. 286. In all, ten nations contributed warships making up the UN Blockading and Escort Force: the United States, Great Britain, Australia, Canada, Colombia, France, Thailand, The Netherlands, New Zealand and the Republic of Korea.

The Fishing Interdiction Campaign Four months after the initiation of hostilities, the UN forces embarked on what was to prove a tactically odd and legally questionable campaign. In fact, in September 1950, the UN Naval Command issued an order prohibiting fishing to North Koreans. The purpose of the operation was not the restriction of fishing as is often falsely maintained. The right of North Korean civilians to engage in coastal fishing for basic nutrition needs was denied altogether, and for once heavily armoured men-of-war of the two largest navies of the western world were found engaging wooden fishing boats. The decision to interdict fishing in North Korean waters was notified by distributing leaflets with the following message: 'you cannot fish from your boats until the Communists are killed or thrown out . . . if you try to fish from your boats until the Communists are completely defeated, you must suffer the consequences'. The official explanation was that the North Korean junks were genuinely used as minelaying vessels, or in order to transport logistical support to the fighting troops.

Attempting to halt all coastal fishing was where UN naval operations came close to indiscriminate attack. Fishing vessels of any size were prohibited from setting sail, and in that respect it could be argued that a special exclusion zone had been enforced. The legality of this practice came particularly into question as entire coastal communities living on fish were brought to starvation, and sooner or later were forced to flee North Korea because their survival was seriously compromised. William Fenrick puts it clearly, yet moderately: 'one aspect which tends to indicate that the U.S. conducted a limited naval campaign by coincidence rather than design is the anti-fishing campaign conducted during the blockade. This campaign appears to be an extension beyond previous economic warfare practices.'[64] In the first year of the war the campaign accounted for some 213 junks and sampans destroyed, 147 damaged and only 9 captured.[65] The fact that the blockading warships appeared at some point engaged in 'overkill' forced the UN Naval Command in early 1952 to launch Operation Junket, ordering the capture and not the destruction of enemy fishing boats for intelligence purposes.

[64]FENRICK, *op. cit., supra* n.62 at p. 70.
[65]CAGLE and MANSON, *op. cit., supra* n.62 at p. 321. For a detailed account on the effects of the starvation campaign, see *ibid.*, p. 353*ff.*

6 The Vietnam War

Coastal Traffic Control and Operation Market Time In spring 1965, the South Vietnamese government, in cooperation with the United States, drafted an official decree instituting an interception zone of 12 n.m. along its coast in order to cut off enemy supply lines passing through its territory. The decree on Sea Surveillance,[66] reflecting meticulously the provisions of the 1958 Geneva Law of the Sea Conventions, referred to South Vietnam's 3-mile territorial sea and the 9-mile contiguous zone as forming a maritime belt where rights of visit and search would be exercised against vessels suspected of carrying war matériel. There was no warning of potential use of lethal force against non-complying ships; suspect vessels would only be subject to board and search and eventually to arrest and disposition.

It is noteworthy that the territorial sea of South Vietnam was declared a 'defensive sea area' which is of course reminiscent of the US legislation enacted in 1917 and again in 1941. Despite the common terminology, the two experiences differed substantially. South Vietnam attempted to fit what were in essence belligerent measures into a peacetime law of the sea framework, namely into the context of the innocent passage regime, customs, fiscal and immigration regulations enforcement, *vérification du pavillon* and hot pursuit. On the contrary, the US defensive arrangements of the two World Wars were far more restrictive keeping all vessels well clear of the coasts and allowing navigation only after clearance and in strict accordance with given instructions.

The 12-mile Vietnamese zone which set the limits of Operation Market Time was in fact a perimeter of intensified watchfulness over coastal traffic, assigning to the Vietnamese and US naval forces the task of a coastguard rather than of 'ready to fire' combatants. During the first seven months of the operation, US ships were reported to have boarded 15,000 junks, while the South Vietnam's navy had for its part searched some 200,000 junks. The scheme of close supervision of coastal traffic, however, hardly produced the expected results. Despite the

[66]Decree No. 81/NG of 27 April 1965; see 4 *ILM* (1965) at p. 461. See also O'CONNELL, D.P., 'International Law and Contemporary Naval Operations', 44 *BYIL* (1970), p. 30*ff*.

thousands of inspected boats, only few hostile cargoes were actually discovered and seized.

In another zonal assignment, the US Naval Command had established as from 1965 the so-called *Yankee* and *Dixie stations* within the Gulf of Tonkin. These were sea pockets where US carriers were stationed to make up for the lack of safe land air bases in South Vietnam.[67] The United States claimed a sanctuary status for these areas, arguing that offensive action could be legitimately launched therefrom but no retaliation should be expected.

7 The Indo-Pakistani Conflict

For their short duration, naval operations during the 1971 war between India and Pakistan were particularly intensive in character.[68] The Indian navy's quantitative (ten to one) and qualitative (one aircraft carrier and several missile boats) superiority assured India's complete sea command from the outset. The Indian fleet was divided into two separate naval commands. The Western Naval Command, directing operations in the Arabian Sea, had as its primary objective to destroy naval targets and military installations at the Karachi port area by launching missile attacks. The Eastern Naval Command, operating in the Gulf of Bengal, was principally assigned the blockade mission of East Pakistan.

The blockade was declared on the morning of 4 December 1971, to take effect the afternoon of the same day. A period of grace of twenty-four hours was given to neutral ships docking at Pakistani ports to leave the area. The blockaded zone was defined by a closing line some 180 miles long, drawn from a point situated between the Matla and Passur rivers to the west and the Burma–East Pakistan international boundary to the east. The aircraft carrier *Vikrant* escorted by several other warships patrolled the zone so as to make escape a difficult enterprise. In the event, six large merchant ships and several small boats were captured, some others were sunk for failing to surrender,

[67]See CAGLE, M.W., 'Task Force 77 in Action off Vietnam', 98 *USNIP* (May 1972), p. 74*ff*., and O'CONNELL, *op. cit., supra*, p. 35*ff*.
[68]See KAOUL, R., 'The Indo-Pakistani War and the Changing Balance of Power in the Indian Ocean', 99 *USNIP* (1973), p. 172*ff*.; ROUSSEAU, Ch., 'Chronique des faits internationaux', 76 *RGDIP* (1972), p. 538*ff*.; LABAYLE, J., 'Chronique maritime', 28 *Revue de Défense Nationale* (1972), p. 327*ff*.

whereas one or two were believed to have run the blockade.[69] Both belligerents had issued lists of contraband.[70] As the fighting came to an early end, no prize courts proceedings were ever instituted, or confiscation of cargoes and ships ever awarded. A United States naval force comprising ten warships, among them the *USS Enterprise,* was ordered to head towards the Gulf of Bengal. There were speculations that the US force might eventually challenge the effectiveness of the Indian blockade but this proved untrue. The Task Force 74 stayed south of Sri Lanka throughout the conflict, being of no concern for India's Eastern Naval Command.[71]

Naval action was far more destructive on the western front. The Western Naval Command, relying principally on the capabilities of the Soviet-built Osa-class boats equipped with Styx missiles, made at least two daring attacks on the heavily defended Karachi harbour, sinking several Pakistani warships, setting an oil storage tank ablaze and inflicting considerable collateral damage to neutral shipping. The British cargo ship *Harmattan* was accidentally hit by missile, killing seven crew members, while a Panamanian freighter was sunk, and a Greek tanker set on fire. Following strong British diplomatic protests, the Indian government announced on 10 December 1971 that neutral shipping would be given until dawn of 12 December to leave Karachi and clear Pakistan's territorial waters.[72] In all, Pakistan lost two out of eight warships, two out of four submarines, two out of eight minesweepers and sixteen gunboats, while India suffered the loss of one frigate. Ten ocean-going merchant vessels flying the flag of Pakistan were captured on the high seas, while Pakistan's navy did not interfere with Indian merchant shipping at all.[73]

[69]Daniel O'Connell claims that 'no blockade was formally gazetted'; see O'CONNELL, D.P., *The Influence of Law on Sea Power,* 1975 at p. 130. Some sources suggest that India had imposed a similar blockade off Karachi, but no such operation seems to have ever been undertaken basically because of the length of west Pakistan coasts; see ROUSSEAU, *op. cit., supra* n. at p. 548.

[70]For the text of these proclamations, see 66 *AJIL* (1972) at p. 386.

[71]For the Indian apprehensions *vis-à-vis* the US policies in South Asia, see PALMER, N.D., 'The New Order in South Asia', 15 *Orbis* (1971–2), pp. 1109–21.

[72]See 18 *KCA* (1971–2) at p. 25057.

[73]In the context of the Algerian insurgency against the French colonial power, the French navy was assigned an interdiction operation off the Algerian coasts aiming at intercepting logistic supplies destined for the revolting FLN. The oddity of this campaign lay with the fact that France although exercising genuine

8 The Arab-Israeli Conflict

The thirty-year state of belligerency between Egypt and Israel had a distinct naval facet: the Suez Canal remained closed from 1948 to 1975 for vessels flying the Star of David and other vessels carrying Israel-bound or Israel-owned cargoes, while the Straits of Tiran and Bab-al-Mandeb were also blocked occasionally against ships leaving or heading to Israeli ports. It may be worth reviewing all these operations insofar as they have been often presented as blockade measures.

The Closure of the Suez Canal As early as 1948, Egypt committed itself to an ardent campaign aimed at paralysing Israel's seaborne commerce by denying the right of free passage through the Suez waterway. The campaign was notably protracted and effective. The first vessel steering for Israel, the Greek freighter *Olympos*, cleared the canal only in November 1975, while merchant vessels and warships flying the Israeli flag had to wait four more years to make the crossing.[74] The legal nature of the Egyptian practices has been for long a matter of controversy. The debate focused on whether the interdiction campaign should be qualified as a blockade operation or rather as ordinary visit and search measures enforced within territorial waters since the 1888 Constantinople Convention, which regulates the navigation through the Suez Canal, stipulates that 'the canal shall never be subject to the exercise of the right of blockade'.

The closure of the Suez Canal was launched in 1948 by means of three military proclamations instituting inspection procedures for vessels calling at the port towns of Alexandria, Port Said and Suez (No.5, 15 May), prescribing the confiscation of arms

belligerent rights of visit and search on the high seas insisted that it was simply enforcing customs regulations within the contiguous zone of her North African colonial territories. On this aspect of the Algerian war of liberation, see LUCCHINI, L., 'Un aspect des mesures de surveillance maritime au cours des opérations d'Algérie', 8 *AFDI* (1962), p. 920*ff*; FRALEIGH, A., 'The Algerian Revolution as a Case Study in International Law' in FALK, R.A. (ed.), *The International Law of Civil War*, 1971, p. 203*ff*.; O'CONNELL, *op. cit., supra* n.66, p. 36*ff*.; ROUSSEAU,Ch., 70 *RGDIP* (1966), p. 1056*ff*.

[74]The merchant vessel *Ashdoud* passed the canal on 30 April 1979, while three Israeli warships sailed through on 29 May of the same year; see LAPIDOTH, R., 'The Reopened Suez Canal in International Law', 4 *Syracuse Journal of International Law and Commerce* (1976), p. 1*ff*. See also LAPIDOTH, R., 'The Suez Canal, the Gulf of Suez, and the 1979 Treaty of Peace Between Egypt and Israel' in *Mélanges Rudolf Bindschedler*, 1980, p. 617*ff*.

and war matériel bound for Palestine (No.13, 6 June), and setting up a prize court to seat at Alexandria (No.38, 8 July).[75] Force was to be used exceptionally in order to force a foreign vessel to submit to visit and search. The Egyptian authorities also practised systematic black-listing of those foreign shipping companies known to have served Israeli commerce in the past.[76] The list of contraband goods was later enlarged so as to include foodstuffs. The campaign resulted in an impressive number of seizures over the years which in turn gave rise to a particularly rich prize jurisprudence. Until 1982, the Alexandria prize court had rendered 581 prize decisions the last being in 1977.[77]

The right of seizure of contraband of war which the Egyptian authorities steadily invoked was not to be confined within certain geographical limits. Article 3 of the military proclamation No.38 of July 1948, as modified by proclamation No.48 of 13 September 1948, defined the maritime prize as 'toute marchandise de quelque nature qu'elle soit... et qui aura été capturée par les autorités navales, par l'Administration des Douanes ou par l'Administration des Garde-Côtes, dans les ports égyptiens, dans les eaux territoriales égyptiennes ou pales-

[75]On these proclamations, see EL TANAMLI, A.M., 'L'exercice par l'Égypte du droit de visite, de recherches et de capture dans le canal de Suez et le golfe d'Akaba', *L'Égypte Contemporain* (April 1955), p. 11*ff.* See also GROSS, L., 'Passage Through the Suez Canal of Israel-Bound Cargo and Israel Ships', 51 *AJIL* (1957), p. 532*ff.*; DINITZ, S., 'The Legal Aspects of the Egyptian Blockade of the Suez Canal', 45 *Georgetown Law Journal* (1956–7), p. 169*ff;* ROUSSOS, G., 'Le principe de la liberté de passage du canal de Suez et l'application des règles du droit de la guerre maritime', 1 *Revue de Droit International pour le Moyen-Orient* (1951–2), p. 151*ff.*; GHOBASHY, O.Z., 'Egypt's Attitude Towards International Law as Expressed in the United Nations – The Egyptian Israeli Dispute on the Freedom of Navigation in the Suez Canal', 11 *REDI* (1955), p. 121*ff.*; MARTIN, P.M., *Le conflit Israelo-Arabe*, 1973, p. 94*ff.* The regulations of 1948 were later consolidated in a Royal Decree of February 1950; see UN Doc. *S/3179*, 15 February 1954.

[76]See UN Doc. *S/3673*, Oct.13, 1956.

[77]For the text of the proclamation establishing the prize court, see 5 *REDI* (1949) at p. 319. The Royal Decree No.32 cf April 1950 amended slightly the proclamation; see 6 *REDI* (1950) at p. 405. For prize decisions, see 5 *REDI* (1949), pp. 139–57; 6 *REDI* (1950), pp. 207–28; 7 *REDI* (1951), pp. 121–35; 13 *REDI* (1957), pp. 131–6; 15 *REDI* (1959), pp. 179–88; 16 *REDI* (1960), pp. 109–13, 118–32. The function of the prize court has been commented in SALWAT, A., 'Le conseil des prises égyptien: Organisation, compétence et procédure', 6 *REDI* (1950), pp. 24–32; TRAPPE, J., 'On the Jurisdiction of the Egyptian Prize Court, 1948–1960', 16 *REDI* (1960), pp. 60–7; ABDEL FATAH, A.M., 'La jurisprudence égyptienne en matière de prise', 38 *REDI* (1982), pp. 119–52; BROWN, T.D., 'World War Prize Law Applied in a Limited War Situation: Egyptian Restrictions on Neutral Shipping with Israel', 50 *Minnesota Law Review* (1966), pp. 849–73.

tiniennes ou en haute mer, durant les opérations militaires en Palestine'. As it turned out, however, Egypt never seized a vessel on the high seas. In only two cases the Alexandria court had to deal with prizes seized off Egyptian ports. The first case related to the interception of an Israeli trawler, the *Doron,* 2 miles off the Egyptian shore, while the second concerned the seizure of a Greek freighter, the *Frankisky,* off the Gaza port.[78]

Egypt in its long campaign attempting to throttle the Israel-related commerce best exploited its unique controlling position over the strategic Suez passage. Egypt tried to, and succeeded in excluding Israel ships from transiting its waters; yet it did not establish any kind of exclusion zone. Egypt denied passage through its territory to commodities bound for Israel; yet it did not enforce a blockade. The Egyptian maritime control measures remained throughout qualitatively different from a classical blockade off enemy shores, and also stood far from a free-fire exclusion zone.

Blockade Measures in the Gulf of Aqaba and the Straits of Tiran

The controversy over Israel's maritime rights in the Gulf of Aqaba sparked off both the 1956 and 1967 Arab-Israeli wars.[79] Here also Egypt tried to take advantage of its favourable position since it controlled the two main islands, Tiran and Sanafir, at the gulf entrance and also the only navigable channels through the straits, that is to say the Enterprise and Grafton passages. As early as 1951, Egypt had enacted legislation requiring vessels transiting the Tiran Strait to file appropriate notification and submit to inspection. Egypt had also designated a 'prohibited zone' in the vicinity of the Strait of Tiran and had demonstrated its determination to intercept any merchant vessel attempting to enter the zone, as illustrated by the *Empire Roach*

[78]See 15 *REDI* (1959) at p. 184, and 6 *REDI* (1950) at p. 207 respectively.

[79]See BLOOMFIELD, L.M., *Egypt, Israel and the Gulf of Aqaba in International Law,* 1957; GROSS, L., 'Passage Through the Strait of Tiran and in the Gulf of Aqaba', 33 *Law and Contemporary Problems* (1968), p. 125*ff.*; ZEIDAN, A.L., 'The Emergence of the Gulf of Aqaba Problem', 35 *REDI* (1979), p. 1*ff.*; WHETTEN, L.L., 'Legal Aspects of the Egyptian Blockade of the Gulf of Aqaba', 45/6 *Revue de Droit International de Sciences Diplomatiques et Politiques* (1967–8), p. 339*ff.*; SALANS, C.F., 'Gulf of Aqaba and Strait of Tiran: Troubled Waters', 94 *USNIP* (Dec.1968), p. 54*ff.*; MARTIN, *op. cit., supra* n.75, p. 104*ff.*

incident.[80] In 1954–5, Egypt, in what allegedly was a move against the illegal traffic of narcotics, issued further regulations concerning navigation through its territorial waters in the Strait of Tiran. Israel, for its part, declared 'the blockade practices in the Suez Canal and in the Gulf of Eilat comprehensively illegal'.[81] Following the 1956 Suez crisis, Israel gained control over the Gulf of Aqaba's entrance chokepoint. Israeli forces withdrew in 1957, to be replaced by a symbolic contigent of UNEF which was stationed at Sharm-el-Sheikh until 1967.[82]

On 23 May 1967, President Nasser announced the blockade of the Israeli port of Eilat in the following terms: 'the armed forces yesterday occupied Sharm-el-Sheikh. It is an affirmation of our rights and our sovereignty over the Gulf of Aqaba. The gulf constitutes Egyptian territorial waters. Under no circumstances will we allow the Israeli flag to pass through the Gulf of Aqaba.'[83] Israel's Prime Minister described the blockade as an act of aggression against its country, while British and US

[80]For details on this incident, see 8 *KCA* (1950–2) at pp. 11597, 11700. In the wake of the incident an agreement was reached providing for different treatment of British ships heading to Aqaba; see BLOOMFIELD, *op. cit., supra* at p. 14. There is some evidence that the campaign was designed to go beyond the narrow confines of a classical blockade. The Egyptian War Minister, for instance, in a statement made on 11 July 1951, alluded to the existence of a war zone by claiming that the *Empire Roach* 'had been sailing in a prohibited zone where Egyptian coastal batteries had instructions to fire on sight'. For these early blockade regulations, see BLOOMFIELD, *op. cit., supra*, p. 7*ff.* It is interesting to note that while the Notice to Mariners of February 1954 urged the approaching ships to 'keep a sharp lookout for signals' made by land stations, the respective Notice to Airmen established a prohibited circle of 20 n.m. radius over the Sharm-el-Sheikh and warned that 'fire will be opened at or on to the contravening aircraft without any previous warning'.

[81]See UN Doc. *S/3168 Add.I,* 29 January 1954 at p. 3. Egyptian enforcement action remained rather rare as the Eilat port facilities for ocean-going vessels and the oil terminal were not constructed until the late 1950s. Until mid-1955 there were only eight minor incidents reported; see BLOOMFIELD, *op. cit., supra* n.79, p. 11*ff.* Western diplomatic circles contemplated at some point a naval solution which would take the form of an Israeli ship attempting to run the blockade under powerful escort of international naval forces in pursuance to a UN resolution. The idea was soon abandoned, however, due to its probably escalatory character; see O'CONNELL, *op. cit., supra* n.69 at p. 111.

[82]For the Israeli position upon withdrawal, see UNGA Doc. *A/3511,* 24 January 1957.

[83]See 16 *KCA* (1967–8) at p. 22065. The Cairo communiqué further specified that the blockade would equally apply to foreign ships carrying strategic goods (including oil) to Eilat. On 24 May 1967, it was announced that the Gulf of Aqaba was effectively sealed off by means of mines, land batteries and sea/air patrolling. Vessels should subject to contraband control, while Israeli ships disregarding orders to turn back would be fired at.

officials condemned the Egyptian action as a clear violation of international law. In the event, the strategic localities of Ras Nasrani and Sharm-el-Sheikh at the mouth of the gulf were captured by a simultaneous air, sea and land assault on the third day of the Six-Day War, without firing a shot, as the Egyptian garrison had evacuated the position beforehand.[84] As from 7 June 1967, therefore, the straits of Tiran had been reopened to international shipping. In pursuance of the terms of the treaty of peace between Egypt and Israel signed at Washington in 1979, the Gulf of Aqaba and the Straits of Tiran will 'remain open to all nations for unimpeded and non-suspendable freedom of navigation and overflight'.[85] The treaty specified that UN forces would be requested to station in the area and ensure the freedom of navigation.[86]

The Interdiction Campaign in the Strait of Bab-al-Mandeb The 15-mile wide strait connects the Red Sea with the Gulf of Aden. The shores controlling the strait belong to Yemen to the east and to Djibouti to the west. The rocky and volcanic island of Perim lies in the very middle of the narrow sea passage. A first incident occurred in 1971 when a fully loaded oil tanker chartered by Israel and bound for Eilat came under fire while proceeding through the strait. The *Coral Sea,* although damaged, managed to reach the Eilat port five days later. A Palestinian group claimed responsibility for the attack. During the Arab-Israeli War of October 1973, Egyptian naval forces presumably enforced blockade measures in the strait against vessels serving Israeli ports. The blockade, although not officially declared, was maintained until mid-December 1973.[87] Some twelve vessels were reported blocked at Eilat port, while another eleven vessels heading to Eilat were forced to reverse course at Bab-

[84]*Ibid.* at p. 22100.

[85]See Article V§2 in 18 *ILM* (1979) at p. 365.

[86]See Article IV§2 and Annex I, Article VI§2(d), *ibid.*, pp. 364, 372. The coastal patrol unit which was subsequently deployed as part of the Multinational Force and Observers (MFO) consisted of four minesweepers provided by Italy. The ships patrol a 60 nautical square mile area between Dahab and Ras Mohammad at the mouth of the Gulf of Aqaba. For more on the MFO, see MACKINLAY, J., *The Peacekeepers – An Assessment of Peacekeeping Operations at the Arab-Israel Interface*, 1989, p. 160*ff*.

[87]The blockade operation is discussed in detail in O'CONNELL, *op. cit., supra* n.69, p. 101*ff*.

al-Mandeb.[88] The blockade was finally lifted after a ceasefire agreement had been reached in November 1973, but it was apparently precipitated by the deployment of the *USS Hancock* in the area.

9 The Falklands/Malvinas Islands Conflict

A The war of zones

If the question of war zones surfaced once again in the 1980s, this is principally due to the short-lived South Atlantic crisis of 1982.[89] In the course of the two month conflict, Britain estab-

[88]See LAPIDOTH, R., *The Red Sea and the Gulf of Aden*, 1982 at p. 136.
[89]Among the copious evaluations of the legal, political and military aspects of the Falklands War, see BARSTON, R.P. and BIRNIE, P.W., 'The Falkland Islands/ Islas Malvinas Conflict: A Question of Zones', 7 *Marine Policy* (1983), p. 14*ff.*; BRING, O.E., 'The Falkland Crisis and International Law', 51 *Nordisk Tidsskrift for International Ret* (1982), p. 129*ff.*; CABLE, J., 'The Falklands Conflict', 108 *USNIP* (Sept.1982), p. 70*ff.*; COOTE, J.O., 'Send Her Victorious . . .', 109 *USNIP* (Jan.1983), p. 34*ff.*; DILLON, G.M., *The Falklands, Politics and War*, 1989; FENRICK, W.J., 'Legal Aspects of the Falklands Naval Conflict', 24 *Revue de Droit Pénal Militaire et de Droit de la Guerre* (1985), p. 241*ff.*; FREEDMAN, L., 'The War of the Falkland Islands, 1982', 61 *Foreign Affairs* (1982), p. 196*ff.*; FRIEDMAN, N., 'The Falklands War: Lessons Learned and Mislearned', 26 *Orbis* (1982–3), p. 907*ff.*; GAVSHON, A. and RICE, D., *The Sinking of the Belgrano*, 1984; GREEN, L.C., 'The Falklands, the Law and the War', 38 *Yearbook of World Affairs* (1984), p. 89*ff.*; GUILMARTIN, J.F., 'The South Atlantic War: Lessons and Analytical Guideposts – A Military Historian's Perspective' in BROWN, J. and SNYDER, W.P. (eds), *The Regionalization of Warfare*, 1985, p. 55*ff.*; HASTINGS, M. and JENKINS, S., *The Battle for the Falklands*, 1983; JUNOD, S.S., *Protection of the Victims of Armed Conflict. Falkland-Malvinas Islands (1982)*, ICRC, 1984; KERR, N., 'The Falklands Campaign', 35 *US Naval War College Review* (1982/6), p. 14*ff.*; LEVIE, H.S., 'The Falklands Crisis and the Laws of War' in COLL, A.R. and AREND, A.C. (eds), *The Falklands War – Lessons for Strategy, Diplomacy and International Law*, 1985, p. 64*ff.*; MURGUIZUR, J.C., 'The South Atlantic Conflict: An Argentinian Point of View', 16 *International Defense Review* (1983), p. 135*ff.*; NOTT, J., 'The Falklands Campaign', 109 *USNIP* (May 1983), p. 118*ff.*; PONTING, C., *The Right to Know – The Inside Story of the* Belgrano *Affair*, 1985; SEGAL, D.R. and GRAVINO, K.S., 'The Empire Strikes Back: Military Professionalism in the South Atlantic War' in BROWN, J. and SNYDER, W.P. (eds), *The Regionalization of Warfare*, 1985, p. 17*ff.*; SCHEINA, R.L., 'The Malvinas Campaign', 109 *USNIP* (May 1983), p. 98*ff.*; The Belgrano Action Group, *The Unnecessary War*, 1988; The *Sunday Times* Insight Team, *The Falklands War – The Full Story*, 1982; TRAIN, H.D., 'An Analysis of the Falkland/Malvinas Islands Campaign', 41 *US Naval War College Review* (winter 1988), p. 33*ff.*; TURNER, S., 'The Unobvious Lessons of the Falklands War', 109 *USNIP* (April 1983), p. 50*ff.*; Several contributors, 'Falklands Postscripts', 109 *USNIP* (June 1983), p. 99*ff.*; WOODWARD, S., *One Hundred Days – The Memoirs of the Falklands Battle Group Commander*, 1992; ZAKHEIM, D.S., 'The South Atlantic Conflict: Strategic, Military, and Technological Lessons' in COLL, A.R. and AREND, A.C. (eds), *The Falklands War –*

lished four different types of war zones in succession. On 7 April, that is to say, five days after the Argentine invasion, the United Kingdom gave notice of its intention to establish, as from 12 April, a *maritime exclusion zone* around the Falkland Islands. This zone would take the form of a circle with a 200 n.m. radius from latitude 51° 40″S and longitude 59° 30″W. The warning was addressed exclusively to the Argentine navy. In fact, neutral shipping, Argentine merchantmen, and even Argentine aircraft were in no way affected by the MEZ declaration: only 'Argentine warships and Argentine naval auxiliaries found within this zone will be treated as hostile and are liable to be attacked by British forces'.[90]

Some two weeks later, and while the British Task Force (T.F.317) was approaching the islands, Britain announced the creation of a defensive area, or *defensive bubble,* surrounding the Task Force and came to define it as follows: 'any approach on the part of Argentine warships including submarines, naval auxiliaries or military aircraft which could amount to a threat to interfere with the mission of the British forces in the South Atlantic, will encounter the appropriate response. All Argentine aircraft including civil aircraft engaging in surveillance of these British forces will be regarded as hostile and are liable to be dealt with accordingly'.[91] Two features sound new in the defensive area declaration of 23 April: first, no specific limits were set, and second, the Argentine air force as well as civil aviation were this time directly concerned.

By 28 April, the time for a *total exclusion zone* had come. The TEZ was to share the same geographical extent with the previous MEZ, but it was fully comprehensive in nature. The British declaration read:

> from the time indicated, the exclusion zone will apply not only to Argentine warships and Argentine naval auxiliaries but also to any other ship, whether naval or merchant vessel, which is operating in support of the illegal occupation of the Falkland islands by Argentine forces. The exclusion zone will also apply to any aircraft, whether mili-

Lessons for Strategy, Diplomacy and International Law, 1985, p. 159*ff.*; ZAKHEIM, D.S., 'The South Atlantic: Evaluating the Lessons' in BROWN, J. and SNYDER, W.P. (eds), *The Regionalization of Warfare,* 1985, p. 37*ff.*

[90]See 53 *BYIL* (1982) at p. 539.

[91]*Ibid.* at pp. 540–41.

> tary or civil, operating in support of the illegal occupation. Any ship and any aircraft, whether military or civil which is found within this zone without due authority from the Ministry of Defence in London will be regarded as operating in support of the illegal occupation and will therefore be regarded as hostile and will be liable to be attacked by the British forces.[92]

In the wake of the most unfortunate moment of the conflict, that is to say, the sinking of the *General Belgrano* while steaming south west and well outside the 200 n.m. exclusion zone, the British felt necessary to broaden their war zone to the maximum and to project it almost to the coastline of the Argentine mainland. Evidently, the intention was to accord a posteriori legitimacy to the widely condemned torpedoing of the *General Belgrano*. It is not by chance that the new policy statement was issued on 7 May, only five days after the *Belgrano* incident:

> because of the proximity of Argentine bases and the distances that hostile forces can cover undetected, particularly at night and in bad weather, Her Majesty's Government warns that any Argentine warship or military aircraft which are found more than 12 nautical miles from the Argentine coast will be regarded as hostile and are liable to be dealt with accordingly.[93]

It should be underlined, however, that the vast extension of the exclusion zone concerned this time only the Argentine warships and military aircraft. Parallel to the operational zones established around the disputed islands, Britain had also created a *terminal control area,* as from 10 May, which had an outer limit of 100 n.m. from Wideawake airfield on Ascension Island. This area called for prior notification of all flights to the island and all overflights. On 22 July, a little more than one month after the Argentine surrender on 14 June, all exclusion zones were lifted. On 23 July, Argentina was notified of a 150 n.m. Maritime

[92] *Ibid.* at p. 542.

[93] *Ibid.* at p. 549. By the end of May, Admiral Woodward had asked that his forces be allowed to operate inside the 12-mile limit, but the permission was not granted; see GAVSHON and RICE, *op. cit., supra* n.89 at p. 130.

Protection Zone which referred to Argentine warships and military aircraft, excluding them from approaching the islands.[94]

Argentina also operated three versions of war zones. Less attention is usually paid to its declarations, however, because they are commonly seen as a tit-for-tat reaction to the British declarations rather than as an autonomous strategy. Moreover, the Argentines had cautiously formulated their announcements so as to make clear that only British vessels and aircraft were concerned. On 8 April, the military government of Buenos Aires identified an area extending 200 n.m. off the mainland and around the Falkland and South Georgia islands as a theatre of operations, and warned that military action could be taken therein if necessary for self-defence. One day after the British TEZ was declared, the Argentines claimed the waters within the circumference of the exclusion zone to be Argentine territorial waters, and warned all British aircraft not to intrude into the zone otherwise they would be attacked. Finally, following the British policy statement of 7 May, Argentina declared on 11 May that the South Atlantic, without further precision, was to be a war zone and gave notice to all British vessels to keep clear.

B The sinking of the *General Belgrano*

The credibility of the TEZ declaration was to be severely tested a few days after it had been issued. The question of war zones, as practised during the Falklands conflict, is ultimately connected with the *Belgrano* incident. The episode underlined, in the most tragic way, just how superfluous and confusing all these variations of zones really were. What could be more telling than the fact that five days after the sinking of the Argentine cruiser the British government practically abolished its war zone strategy. By bringing into play the whole South Atlantic Ocean, up to 12 n.m. off the Argentine coast, the British, one should

[94]See 53 *BYIL* (1982) at p. 557. The MPZ was lifted in early 1990 following a meeting between Argentine and British representatives in Madrid on 14–15 February 1990; see Joint Statement by the British and Argentine delegations, UN Doc. *S/21159*, 21 February 1990 at p. 2. In another development, on 29 October 1986, a *Falkland Islands Interim Conservation and Management Zone* (FICZ) was proclaimed – coming into force in February 1987 – which ran partly coterminous with the 150 n.m. MPZ. For its novel characterisitics and the problems related to it, see SYMMONS, C.R., 'The Maritime Zones Around the Falkland Islands', 37 *ICLQ* (1988), p. 283*ff*. See also CHURCHILL, R.R., 'The Falkland Fishing Zone – Legal Aspects', 12 *Marine Policy* (1988), p. 343*ff*.

not fail to notice, abandoned their war zone tactics. Establishing a vast war zone amounts to no zone. The view here submitted is that, as from the 7 May, it is rather an oxymoron to refer to a 'zone'. To the degree to which the *Belgrano* incident elucidated the depravities of the war zones until then employed, it merits a separate mention.

A Fatal Blow On 2 May 1982, the Argentine cruiser *General Belgrano* was torpedoed and sunk with 1,042 men aboard, while steaming some 36 n.m. outside and south west of the 200 n.m. total exclusion zone. The cruiser was the target of a surprise attack by two torpedoes and sank in 30 minutes. Reports are not unanimous and the estimated number of casualties varies from 330 to 370.[95] The *General Belgrano* had been shadowed for at least 24 hours by the nuclear submarine *HMS Conqueror* before the permission from London was given to attack.[96]

The main argument advanced by the British was that the *General Belgrano* formed the southern arm of a scheduled three-pronged naval assault on the task force. The *Belgrano,* escorted by *Hipolito Bouchard* and *Piedra Buena,* would launch an attack from the south, while the aircaft carrier *Veinticinco de Mayo,* escorted by two destroyers, *Hercules* and *Santissima Trinidad,* would join from the north. Moreover, a submarine was thought to lurk in the area where *HMS Hermes* and *HMS Invincible* were to be attacked.[97] In a White Paper of November 1985, the

[95]On the last moments of the *Belgrano,* see GAVSHON and RICE, *op. cit., supra* n.89, p. 97*ff.* See also The *Sunday Times* Insight Team, *op. cit., supra* n.89, p. 156*ff.*; MIDDLEBROOK, M., *The Fight for the Malvinas – The Argentine Forces in the Falklands War,* 1989, pp. 104–16.

[96]According to the initial official reports the decision to launch a torpedo was clearly one taken by the submarine commander. This allegation later proved incorrect, Mrs. Thatcher having publicly stated that 'the task force clearly is and was under political control'. The *Conqueror* returned to its base on 3 July after a round trip of some 25,000 miles flying the *Jolly Roger,* a disquieting reference to past eras.

[97]See WOODWARD, *op. cit., supra* n.89, pp. 146–64. The Chief naval Judge Advocate of the Royal Navy, Chelton, in a speech delivered in 1983, asserted that the *Belgrano* 'was less than 12 hours steaming from engagement range with the task force and with darkness coming on when she sank', and justified the act on the grounds of the defensive area which was proclaimed on 23 April with reference to any approaching Argentine vessel or aircraft which could amount to a threat for the mission of the British force. It is worth noticing that, according to Argentine accounts, the *Veinticinco de Mayo* on 2 May scheduled an attack, but 'the lack of wind combined with the inability of the *25 de Mayo* to close the enemy frustrated the desired attack'; see SCHEINA, *op. cit., supra* n.89 at

British government reiterated the argument by declaring that 'the Government was satisfied that it was complying with its obligations under the UN Charter and that the warning of 23 April covered the changes to RoE to allow the *25 de Mayo*, the *Belgrano* and other units of the Argentine Navy to be attacked outside the TEZ'.[98] But as the Majority Report of the House of Commons Inquiry on the sinking of the *Belgrano* conceded later, 'it is now clear, that there was, at very least, considerable doubt amongst Ministers as to whether the 23 April warning was fully understood in those terms in Argentina or elsewhere in the world'.[99]

Enforcing Pseudo-Limits One can hardly avoid the conclusion that the principle of fair play was muddled in the case of the *General Belgrano*. As Geoffrey Best has put it with clarity and frankness:

---

pp. 105–6. Yet, a recent research work insists that 'the idea of a pincer movement, implying an aggressive role for the Belgrano, is not supported by the evidence which is now available'; see DILLON, *op. cit., supra* n.89 at p. 208. In any case, it should be noted that even if the aged cruiser was 12-hours away from the Task Force, the real threat, namely the French Super-Etendard bombers carrying the lethal Exocet missiles, were constantly only a few hours flight away but still no major mission was undertaken throughout the conflict to destroy their bases. From several sources it has been asserted, however, that the British government had not excluded even the option of threatening a nuclear strike on Argentine mainland if the Task Force was to suffer great losses. To that effect, a Polaris submarine was deployed within range of Argentina, the designated target being the military complex of Cordoba in northern Argentina; see *The Unnecessary War, op.cit., supra* n., pp. 103–107. On the performance of the Argentine air force, see COLOMBO, J.L., 'Super Etendard Naval Aircraft Operations During the Malvinas War', 37 *US Naval War College Review* (1984), p. 13*ff*.

[98]See *Events Surrounding the Weekend of 1–2 May 1982, Cmnd.9647* (Nov.1985), §17 at p. 6.

[99]See HC Majority Report at para. 6.16 as quoted in DILLON, *op. cit., supra* n.89 at p. 224. Writes Clive Ponting on the significance of the 23 April warning: 'the British Government did not itself regard the 23 April warning as having such a wide interpretation. Why else did it issue further public warnings on 28 April and 7 May and have a major internal debate about the legitimacy of the warning between 30 April and 1 May? The 23 April warning has been used since the event to justify the sinking of the *Belgrano*; at the time it was obviously viewed as much narrower in scope'; see PONTING, *op. cit., supra* n.89 at p. 75. And elsewhere: 'since 1982 the Government have always said that the warning of the 23rd April covered the sinking of the Belgrano. Well . . . if it did why did the Government issue another warning on the 7th May saying exactly what it was they were intending to do and in fact had decided to do five days before? – that is sink Argentine warships outside of territorial waters'; see PONTING, C., 'Was It Illegal to Sink the Belgrano?' in *The Unnecessary War, op.cit., supra* n.89 at p. 78.

> having told the world that the exclusion zone was to stretch 200 miles, it was incumbent on us to stick to it . . . but to make a rule of 200 miles and then without warning to break it was to invite strongest suspicions that our avowed respect for law and limitations was not serious – with what lamentable consequences for the immediate escalation of the conflict, historians will in due course have to assess.[100]

To cite once more the House of Commons Inquiry, as from 23 April the purpose of the exclusion zones became 'unclear and ultimately misleading'.[101]

The understanding was that the British forces would not strike first outside the perimeter of 200 n.m. and there is an abundance of evidence that attests to such an assumption. Hastings and Jenkins, whose war chronicle is possibly the most accurate written so far, narrate in their book:

> Woodward was not happy about the shape of the 200-mile maritime exclusion zone around the Falklands islands, already announced in London, and due to come into effect on the following day, 12 April. The politicians and chiefs of staff had drawn a simple circle. Woodward would have preferred a much wider zone east of the islands to give himself plenty of searoom and to preclude one British nightmare – that of the enemy carrier lying in safety on the 200-mile limit, whence it could launch air attacks against the fleet within comfortable range.[102]

[100]BEST, G., 'The Belgrano Sinking', letter to *The Times*, 11 October 1982 at p. 11. William Fenrick considers that 'the major legal lesson to be derived from the sinking is not one of British duplicity but of the inherent difficulty of drafting rules of engagement for attacking enemy warships in limited conflicts'; see FENRICK, *op. cit.*, *supra* n.89 at p. 258.

[101]See HC Majority Report at para. 6.20.

[102]HASTINGS and JENKINS, *op. cit.*, *supra* n.89 at p. 116. Rear Admiral Woodward's view was that 'exclusion zones may appear politically attractive to those who draw them as nice clean lines on maps and charts. They would seem to be the ideal tool in applying minimum military force to achieve a political aim. You can shoot inside, but not outside – it is all crystal clear. The problem is that it is not actually like that. In practical terms the boundary is not clear-cut – it is very fuzzy and operating a 50-mile across task group within a similar distance of that edge is a military nighmare'; cited in DILLON, *op. cit.*, *supra* n.89 at p. 223. Note also the following commentary: 'what I do find difficult to accept, the restrictions that the British government placed on our own services in the way that they said, if your forces are within the 200 miles then they're open to attack. A plane can come in and sink the *Sheffield* and we'll chase her all the way to the 200 miles and then come back. I think that was not the way that

Ivan Shearer has expressed the view that 'Argentina had every reason to think that if they stayed outside the zone would be immune from attack'.[103] In the mind of yet another scholar, 'politically the incident was damaging to Britain, as the victim was just outside the 200-mile exclusion zone. Although Britain had been very careful not to suggest that this was a combat-inclusive zone it had been widely understood as such.'[104]

Revising the Rules of Engagement What makes this belief an irrefutable truth, however, is the revelation that the war cabinet in London gave the green light for the attack only after it had revised the rules of engagement in force at that time. In other words, until the time of the revision, no British vessel or aircraft was authorized to engage an enemy target outside the 200-mile exclusion zone. The parliamentary Under-Secretary of State for the Armed Forces, Jerry Wiggin during a parliamentary debate

---

wars can or could be fought. I think the fact that they could come in from their land bases, attack our forces and then be safe back again was a nonsense in any military terms at all'; see remarks by E. Ogden, in *The Unnecessary War, op. cit, supra* n.89 at p. 87. On the problem of drafting rules of engagement in general, see SHEARER, I., 'Rules of Engagement and the Implementation of the Law of Naval Warfare', 14 *Syracuse Journal of International Law and Commerce* (1988) Special Issue, p. 767*ff.*, and ROACH, J.A., 'Rules of Engagement', 14 *Syracuse Journal of International Law and Commerce* (1988), p. 865*ff.*

[103]SHEARER, I.A., Comments on the occasion of a symposium held at the University of Kiel on 1–4 December 1982; see DELBRÜCK, J. (ed.), *Das neue Seerecht – Internationale und nationale perspektiven, Veröffentlichungen des instituts für internationales recht an der universität Kiel*, no.89, 1984 at p. 204. While Geoffrey Best, reflecting on the expediency of the 200-mile MEZ the very day of its proclamation, wrote: 'this is a curious proposal. In time of armed conflict at sea, such a limit would restrict action by the Royal Navy to an extent not required by international law'; see BEST, G., 'International Law Would Favour the British Argument', article contributed to *The Times*, 7 April 1982 at p. 4.

[104]FREEDMAN, *op. cit., supra* n.89 at p. 203. Two official documents give further support to the affirmation that the commonly shared understanding in the days before the sinking of the *Belgrano* was that the TEZ outer limits marked the furthermost the British military force was authorized to reach. Both the Argentine peace proposal of 19 April, and the Haig memorandum of agreement of 27 April, referred to the British TEZ and provided that within the first 24 hours from the signature of the proposed agreement the United Kingdom should 'suspend enforcement' of – or 'annul' in the Argentine document – its zone, while Argentina should 'suspend operations in the same area'. If the understanding had been otherwise, one may legitimately infer, the texts would have rather provided for a general ceasefire clause. The eventuality of a strike beyond the 200 n.m. was simply not envisaged. The text of these documents is in GAVSHON and RICE, *op. cit., supra* n.89, appendix 2 at p. 186, and appendix 3 at p. 189.

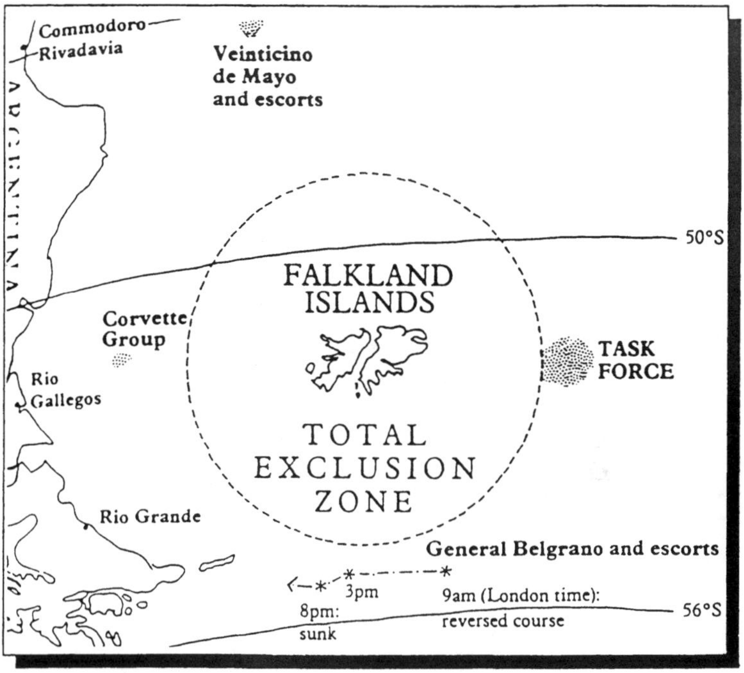

Figure 3 *The Whereabouts of the Argentine and the Royal Navy on 2 May 1982 and the Course of the General Belgrano*
Source: New Statesman, 24 August 1984 at p. 9

in 1983, said: 'the rules of engagement approved by Ministers prior to 2 May did not permit an attack outside the total exclusion zone. The task force commander, worried that *HMS Conqueror* might be unable to follow *Belgrano* over the shallow waters of the Burdwood Bank, sought a change to the rules of engagement to permit an attack outside the zone.'[105]

Yet, even this aspect, which came to be admitted publicly only six months after the conflict had ended, namely, that up to 2 May no first strike was permitted beyond the 200-mile limit, was not without its exception, for, two days before the *Belgrano* incident, the British war cabinet had decided to relax its own largely broadcast rules with regard to the apparently most disturbing enemy vessel, the Argentine aircraft-carrier *Veinticinco de Mayo*. In an annex to a letter addressed to George Foulkes

[105]54 *BYIL* (1983) at p. 546. See also 53 *BYIL* (1982) at p. 558.

MP, dated 19 September 1984, the British Prime Minister Thatcher wrote:

> on 30th April . . . Ministers decided that our forces should be permitted to attack the *25 de Mayo* on the high seas (that is both within and outside the TEZ) in circumstances in which it posed a military threat to the Task Force . . . and Ministers concluded that no further warning was needed. There is no truth in the suggestion that the Foreign Secretary and the Attorney General opposed or dissented from the decision of 30th April. But on 1st May, the day he left for Washington, the Secretary raised the need for a further warning to the Argentine Government.[106]

The *Belgrano* incident brought the British government not far from being accused of perfidy, or even deliberate murder.[107] It may well be long before the exact conditions and calculations underlying the go-ahead order to the submarine commander become firmly established, but the point remains that the fatal torpedoes were launched only three hours before a scheduled

[106] 55 *BYIL* (1984) at p. 593. Francis Pym, the Foreign Secretary, though not dissenting from the decision to sanction the attack, recommended that Argentina should be warned that the *Veinticinco de Mayo* was not to move outside a limit of 12 miles from the coast of the mainland; see DILLON, *op. cit., supra* n. 89 at p. 225, and PONTING, *op. cit., supra* n.89 at p. 82. It so appears, therefore, that the sinking of the *General Belgrano* marked the second occasion on which the British had decided to sidestep their own largely notified rules. The Argentine cruiser was unluckily enough found first. No doubt, the Argentine aircraft-carrier would have shared the same fate, if it had been intercepted – *no matter where* – earlier. As was revealed later, it was only because *HMS Splendid* and *HMS Spartan* lost contact at some point with the *25 de Mayo* and could not find it again that the attack never took place.

[107] See GAVSHON and RICE, *op. cit., supra* n.89 at p. 111; 'the generalized warning to Argentine ships coupled with the creation of a limited TEZ was at best loaded with ambiguity, at worst a deliberate trap for the unwary'. Hastings and Jenkins wonder: 'what was the purpose of declaring geographical limits within which enemy ships would be liable to attack, only to act outside them, even if Britain was within the letter of her legal rights? . . . But it is difficult to believe that, if the British had delayed an attack until they had given warning of an extension of the TEZ, the task force would have been put at serious risk'; see HASTINGS and JENKINS, *op. cit., supra* n.89 at p. 150. For a catalogue of inconsistencies and contradictions in British statements, see *ibid.*, appendix 7, p. 211*ff.* For another list of the embarrassing revelations that the British government was forced reluctantly to accept by March 1984, see PONTING, *op. cit., supra* n.89 at p. 124. See also the writings of a particularly militant (in this respect) labour MP, DALYELL, T., *Thatcher's Torpedo – The Sinking of the Belgrano,* 1983; DALYELL, T., *Thatcher: Patterns of Deceit*, 1986. See also *New Statesman*, 24 August 1984, p. 7*ff.*, and 31 August 1984, p. 8*ff.*

press conference at Lima was to announce peace in the South Atlantic, along the lines of the Peruvian peace plan.[108] Some have gone further to suggest that the unflagging British commitment to a military solution, once the fleet had reached the islands, dictated such an onerous blow as to compel the Argentines to fight.[109] To enter this discussion goes well beyond the purview of the present analysis. The point, however, is that after the *Belgrano* and the *Sheffield*[110] incidents, the comic opera that many had predicted was over, and the margins for a negotiated settlement were virtually eliminated.

The Interplay of Total Exclusion Zone and Anticipatory Self-Defence The *Belgrano* incident assessed by the classical laws of naval warfare, despite the heavy human losses, would pose no legal problem; it involved nothing more than a warship spotted and sunk on sight by an enemy vessel on the high seas.[111] Engaging your enemy's fleet without warning wherever encountered, but outside neutral territorial waters, is, no doubt, the starting proposition of any textbook on the traditional laws of naval warfare. But when an unprovoked attack, even against hostile warships, comes to be appraised with self-defence standards, it may no longer be free of legal objections. The problem with the British proclamations was, above all, that it was alleged to fit in a self-defence framework. Every single episode of the conflict, as well as Operation Corporate in its entirety, was justified by the British exclusively in terms of self-defence. All movements were carefully tailored and all statements studiously framed in order to demonstrate an amazing consistency with

[108]See KINNEY, D., 'Anglo-Argentine Diplomacy and the Falklands Crisis' in COLL and AREND, *op. cit., supra* n.89 at p. 101.

[109]The British Prime Minister has denied of course that the decision to attack the *General Belgrano* was a premeditated act in order to undermine the negotiation process; see 55 *BYIL* (1984) at pp. 595–6. See also *Cmnd.9647* (Nov.1985), §§10–12 at p. 5.

[110]On the *Sheffield* incident, see GAVSHON and RICE, *op. cit., supra* n.89, p. 121*ff*. See also The *Sunday Times* Insight Team, *op.cit., supra* n.89, p. 163*ff*.; MIDDLEBROOK, M., *Operation Corporate – The Falklands War, 1982*, 1985, p. 153*ff*.; PRESTON, A., *Sea Combat off the Falklands*, 1982, p. 61*ff*.; WOODWARD, S., 'It Was a Bit Tight', 118 *USNIP* (March 1992), p. 59*ff*.

[111]For some arguments along these lines, 'it was perfectly reasonable for the authorities ordering the sinking to act on the presumption that the ship was or was intended to become engaged in the operations, and was in any case, as a naval cruiser, a legitimate object of attack'; see GREEN, *op. cit., supra* n.89 at p. 116. See also BURNS, J., *The Land that Lost Its Heroes*, 1987, at pp. 227–30.

the law of self-defence. Recurrent references to the right of self-defence served as a reminder to the world that the UK lived up to its Charter obligations, and that any action taken was first meticulously measured against the legal yardstick of Article 51.[112]

So far, the bone of contention seemed to be whether the UN Charter stipulation of an 'attack' should be restrictively or widely interpreted; in other words, whether the right of self-defence could be exercised in the face of an *imminent,* or only of an *actual,* attack. What we are confronted with in the Falklands context, however, is novel and conceptually unique throughout; the threshold of the legitimate response in self-defence was lowered considerably from *imminent attack,* e.g. a fire control radar of a hostile warship locked on your vessel, to *potential threat.*[113] What is more, it was lowered to *mere presence* coupled with non-threatening activity, e.g. a civil jetliner engaged in reconnaissance and surveillance of the British task force over the mid-Atlantic. Thus, the sinking of the *General Belgrano,* which was resorted to allegedly 'for reasons of self-defence',[114] was undertaken on the grounds of 'indications' and 'signs'. In a letter dated 4 April 1984, Mrs. Thatcher wrote: 'because of the indications that the Belgrano posed a threat to the task force her precise position and course at the time she was sunk were irrelevant'.[115]

The major virtue of operational zones is often claimed to be that they facilitate positive identification, or, to use modern phraseology, that they help to bridge the hiatus between *hostile*

[112]See, for example, the statement of the UK representative, A. Parsons, in the course of the UN Security Council debate of 22 May 1982, in 53 *BYIL* (1982) at pp. 551–3. The British appeared time and again particularly allergic to any suggestion that a state of war existed.

[113]See the revealing wording of the policy statement of 23 April: 'any approach . . . which *could amount to a threat* to interfere'. Gavshon and Rice have commented on this potential threat proviso as follows: 'if this possible threat really meant something merely imaginable sooner or later, then *Conqueror* could have opened fire the previous day, when the cruiser and her escorts were refuelling', *op. cit., supra* n.89 at pp. 143–4. While for another commentator, 'pre-emption being the act of attacking first to forestall hostile action, this precludes taking action against a potential threat – a threat to the mission! – under Article 51'; see GOULD, D., 'Was It Illegal to Sink the *Belgrano*?' in *The Unnecessary War, op.cit., supra* n.89 at p. 71.

[114]See 53 *BYIL* (1982) at p. 550.

[115]See 55 *BYIL* (1984) at p. 590. On the inside story of this reply to Denzil Davies's letter, see PONTING, *op. cit., supra* n.89, p. 125*ff.*

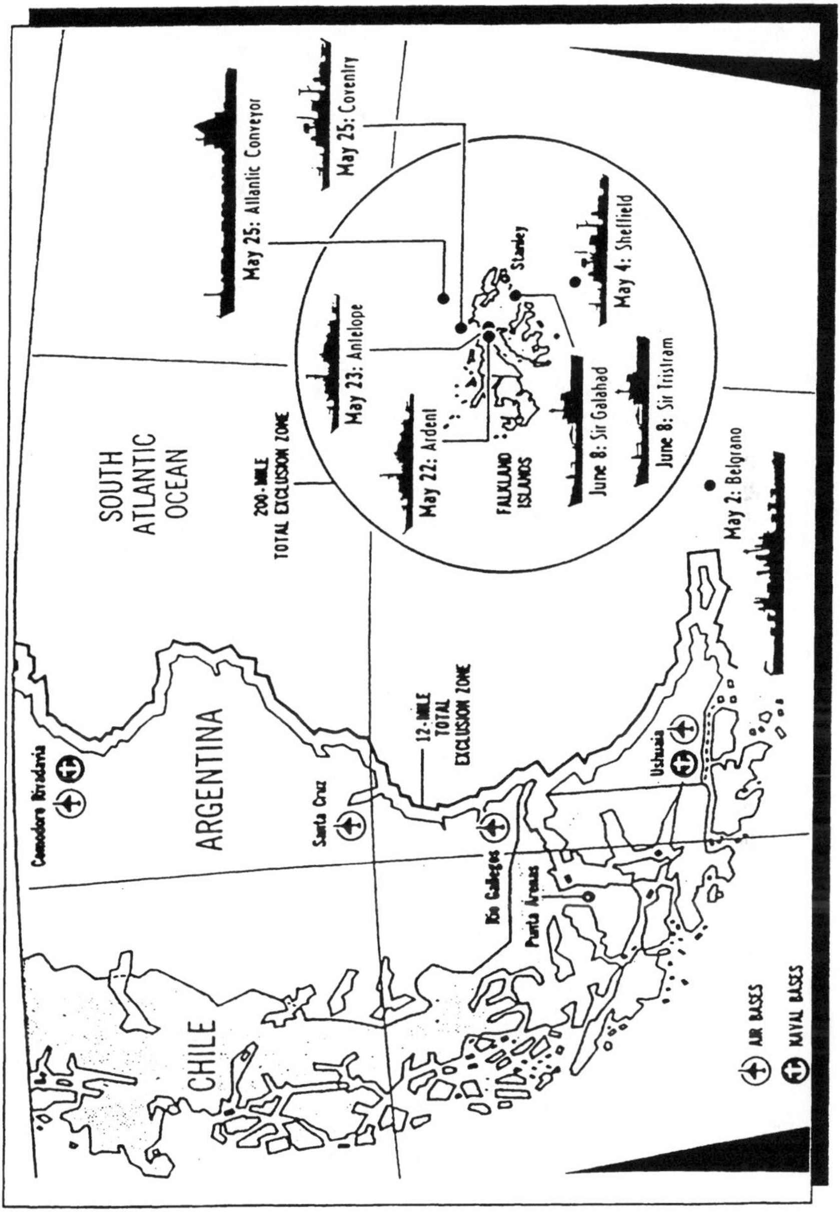

Figure 4 *The Cost of Operation Corporate in Surface Vessels*
Source: COOTE, J.O., 'Send Her Victorious . . .', 109 *USNIP* (Jan.1983) at p. 36

intent and *hostile act*, in the sense that those entering the zone are considered as already staging an attack, and thus the right of self-defence can be exercised without further ado.[116] But what about a warship, as was the case of the *Belgrano*, which not only had not entered the zone but was sailing away from it? What amount, if any, of hostile intent could be presumed in such circumstances?

The broad conclusion is that, in establishing and enforcing these zones, Britain attempted to trace new tracks for the already dubious concept of anticipatory self-defence. In the event, the conceptual clarity and the normative stringency of the right of self-defence were blurred, for, to assert that the *Belgrano* was approaching the task force while some 350 miles away[117] and steering on a course of 280°,[118] or that the *Belgrano* was preparing to launch an attack while at the time of the sinking not 'at action stations' and with most of the perished crewmen crowded in the ship's canteen, is to give the Webster's formula a bold re-reading, or as Lawrence Freedman has commented in that respect, 'any military action which is not self-evidently for defensive purposes, even if it is preemptive, becomes an outrage.'[119] The British zonal arrangements around the Falkland Islands were seen globally as an amalgamation of outright presumptions and preemptive strikes. And this, of course, certifies to the ultimate irrelevance of exclusion zones as offering clear proof of the

[116]See BARSTON and BIRNIE, *op. cit., supra* n.89 at p. 20.

[117]According to the official British account stated by the Defence Minister Nott 'the *General Belgrano* and a group of British warships could have been within striking distance of each other in a matter of some five to six hours, converging from a distance of some 200 nautical miles'. *Cf.* MIDDLEBROOK, *op. cit., supra* n.95 at p. 105.

[118]See 53 *BYIL* (1982) at p. 558. It has now been established that the Argentine cruiser had been steaming on a steady westerly course, not zig-zagging, for at least 6 hours before it was attacked and that its position and reversed course had been communicated to Admiral Northwood twice on 3 May; see PONTING, *op. cit., supra* n.89 at p. 87. Also indicative of its non-hostile posture, the *Belgrano* did not have its sonars switched on; see WOODWARD, *op. cit., supra* n.89 at p. 158.

[119]FREEDMAN, *op. cit., supra* n.89 at p. 209. In the view of another scholar the attack on the *Belgrano* clearly failed to meet the requirements of last resort and proportionality; see BLUTH, C., 'The British Resort to Force in the Falklands/ Malvinas Conflict 1982: International Law and Just War Theory', 24 *Journal of Peace Research* (1987), p. 15*ff.*

willingness to impose self-limitations upon the theatre of war.[120]

The view here submitted is that after the *Belgrano* sinking and the statement of 7 May it is wrong to speak of war zones. Embarrassed by their own entangled strategy and having realized the impractical character of these zones, the British in essence lifted any limitation upon the theatre of naval operations. With the corresponding Argentine statement of 11 May, both belligerents discontinued the operation of war zones and returned to more classical doctrines as to where they would be allowed to engage the enemy.

10 The 1980–8 Gulf War

A Prohibited and targeting areas in the Tanker War

While the South Atlantic War was flaring up, the Iran-Iraq conflict was worryingly unfolding and the world was soon to be forced to familiarize itself with yet another version of war zones. In the course of the eight-year-long war, more than 500 merchant vessels were attacked, and over 200 seamen lost their lives. By some estimates, as many as 30 million tons of shipping were damaged in the Persian Gulf.[121]

[120]As one commentator noted apropos of the TEZ, 'on se trouve ni plus ni moins en présence de la création d'une vraie *presumptio juris et de jure,* d'une présomption irréfragable qui sans doute dépasse toute limite raisonnable du concept de défense . . . comme on le sait, dans le cas aussi bien des représailles que la légitime défense nous nous trouvons en présence d'actes en eux-mêmes contraires au droit des gens. Avoir donc recours à ces deux concepts pour y trouver une justification exceptionnelle du procedé des zones de guerre ne fait que confirmer l'illégalité de celui-ci'; see HALKIOPOULOS, T., 'L'interférence des règles du nouveau droit de la mer et du droit de la guerre' in DUPUY, R.-J. and VIGNES, D. (eds), *Traité du nouveau droit de la mer,* 1985 at pp. 1101–2.

[121]Among the prolific literature on the legal, political, and military parameters of the maritime war in the Gulf, see BILLER, D.P., 'Policing the Persian Gulf: Protecting United States Interests and Freedom of Navigation Through Military Force', 11 *Loyola of Los Angeles International and Comparative Law Journal* (1989), p. 171*ff.*; BOCZEK, B.A., 'Law of Warfare at Sea and Neutrality: Lessons from the Gulf War', 20 *ODIL* (1989), p. 239*ff.*; BOYLE, F.A., 'International Crisis and Neutrality: United States Foreign Policy Toward the Iran-Iraq War', 43 *Mercer Law Review* (1992), p. 523*ff.*; BROWN, J., 'The Superpowers in the Middle East: Lessons from the Persian Gulf', RUSI, *Brassey's Defence Yearbook* (1989), p. 131*ff.*; CIGAR, N., 'The Soviet Navy in the Persian Gulf: Naval Diplomacy in a Combat Zone', 42 *US Naval War College Review* (spring 1989), p. 56*ff.*; Conference Report, 'The Persian/Arabian Gulf Tanker War: International Law or International Chaos?', 19 *ODIL* (1988), p. 299*ff.*; DANZIGER, R., 'The Persian Gulf Tanker

The Iranian Coastal Defence Area On 22 September 1980, Iran notified its intention to halt all maritime commerce destined for Iraq and declared all coastal waters to be zones of war. In the words of the NOTAM no.17/59 of 22 September, 'regarding to the Iraqi aggression we declare Iranian maritime border nearby coast war area. The Iranian government does not give any authorization to the vessels intending to proceed to Iraqi ports', while all other 'vessels after having passed Hormuz Strait will change the route to pass 12 miles south of Abu Musa Island, 12 miles south of Sirri Island, south of Cable Bank Light and 12

War', 111 *USNIP* (1985), p. 160*ff.*; DAVID, E., 'La guerre du Golfe et le droit international', 20 *RBDI* (1987), p. 153*ff.*; DAVIDSON, S., 'United States Protection of Reflagged Kuwaiti Vessels in the Gulf War: The Legal Implications', 4 *International Journal of Estuarine and Coastal Law* (1989), p. 173*ff.*; DE GUTTRY, A. and RONZITTI, N. (eds), *The Iran-Iraq War (1980–1988) and the Law of Naval Warfare*, 1993; DEKKER, I.F. and POST, H.H.G. (eds), *The Gulf War of 1980–1988*, 1992; GEORGE, B. and DAVIS, S., 'Oil, the Gulf War and the Protection of Merchant Shipping', *Brassey's Defence Yearbook* (1988), p. 197*ff.*; JENKINS, M., 'Air Attacks on Neutral Shipping in the Persian Gulf: The Legality of the Iraqi Exclusion Zone and Iranian Reprisals', 8 *Boston College International and Comparative Law Review* (1985), p. 517*ff.*; KARSH, E., *The Iran-Iraq War: A Military Analysis*, IISS, *Adelphi Papers*, no.220, 1987; JOYNER, C.C. (ed.), *The Persian Gulf War – Lessons for Strategy, Law, and Diplomacy*, 1990; KARSH, E., 'Military Lessons of the Iran-Iraq War', 33 *Orbis* (1989), p. 209*ff.*; KING, R., *The Iran-Iraq War: The Political Implications*, IISS, *Adelphi Papers*, no.219, 1987; LECKOW, R., 'The Iran-Iraq Conflict in the Gulf: The Law of War Zones', 37 *ICLQ* (1988), p. 629*ff.*; LEVRAN, A., 'The Iran-Iraq War and the American Naval Intervention', JCSS, *Middle East Military Balance* (1987–8), p. 63*ff.*; LEVRAN, A., 'Strategic Air Attacks in the Iran-Iraq War: The Gulf Campaign', JCSS, *Middle East Military Balance* (1987–8), p. 230*ff.*; MEHR, F., 'Neutrality in the Gulf War', 20 *ODIL* (1989), p. 105*ff.*; NORDQUIST, M.H. and WACHENFELD, M.G., 'Legal Aspects of Reflagging Kuwaiti Tankers and Laying of Mines in the Persian Gulf', 31 *GYIL* (1988), p. 138*ff.*; O'ROURKE, R., 'The Tanker War', 114 *USNIP* (1988), p. 30*ff.*; O'ROURKE, R., 'Gulf Ops', 115 *USNIP* (May 1989), p. 42*ff.*; PEACE, D.L., 'Major Maritime Events in the Persian Gulf Between 1984 and 1991: A Juridical Analysis', 31 *VJIL* (1991), p. 545*ff.*; ROACH, J.A., 'Missiles on Target: Targeting and Defense Zones in the Tanker War', 31 *VJIL* (1991), p. 593*ff.*; RONZITTI, N., 'La guerre du Golfe, le déminage et la circulation des navires', 33 *AFDI* (1987), p. 647*ff.*; RUSSO, F.V., 'Neutrality at Sea in Transition: State Practice in the Gulf War as Emerging International Customary Law', 19 *ODIL* (1988), p. 381*ff.*; SCHILLER, T.S., 'The Gulf War and Shipping: Recent Developments' in PARRITT, B.A.H. (ed.), *Violence at Sea*, 1986, p. 261*ff.*; TAVERNIER, P., 'La guerre du Golfe: Quelques aspects de l'application du droit des conflits armés et du droit humanitaire', 30 *AFDI* (1984), p. 43*ff.*; URQUHART, B., 'The United Nations and the Iraq-Iran War', *Ybk.SIPRI* (1988), p. 507*ff.*; WARBRICK, C., 'The British Position in Regard to the Gulf Conflict', 37 *ICLQ* (1988), p. 420*ff.*; WISWALL, F.L., 'Neutrality, the Rights of Shipping and the Use of Force in the Persian Gulf', 31 *VJIL* (1991), p. 619*ff.*; WOLFRUM, R., 'Reflagging and Escort Operation in the Persian Gulf: An International Law Perspective', 29 *VJIL* (1989), p. 387*ff.*

miles south west of Farsi Island'.[122] At any rate, Iran did not threaten to attack non-complying ships and refrained as a matter of fact up to May 1984 from attacking merchant ships in the Gulf. The measure resembled more a defensive sea area roughly coterminous with Iran's territorial sea limits (though at points reaching out as far as 40 miles from the coast).[123] Another four Notices to Mariners that followed, no.18/59 of 1 October, no.20/59 of 4 November, no.22/59 of 16 November and no.23/59 of 27 January 1981, intended to regulate the clearance procedure to be followed by all inbound vessels.[124]

The Iraqi Exclusion Zone around Kharg Island By way of response, on 7 October 1980, Iraq qualified the Iranian coastal waters north of 29° 03″ as a prohibited zone and made haste to announce its intention to attack all tankers docking at Kharg Island.[125] On 12 August 1982, Iraq formally proclaimed an *exclusion zone* of 50 n.m. around Kharg Island and openly stated that all vessels

[122]For the text of this warning, see DE GUTTRY and RONZITTI, *op. cit., supra* at p. 37. See also 27 *KCA* (1981) at p. 31006.

[123]As regards foreign reactions, it should be noted that the US diffused the Iranian warnings but explicitly stated that such notice is solely for the purpose of advising US mariners and that 'in no way constitutes a legal recognition by the United States of the validity of any foreign rule, regulation, or proclamation so published'; see, for instance, Defense Mapping Agency and Hydrographic Center special warnings no.48 (Sept.1980) and no.67 (Sept. 1985), reprinted in DE GUTTRY and RONZITTI, *op. cit., supra* n.121 at pp. 134, 139.

[124]As a result, all maritime traffic was suspended to and from Iraq. To the end of the war not a single cargo was reported to have been delivered to Iraq by sea; see DANZIGER, *op. cit., supra* n.121 at p. 163. The Iraqi navy consisting in substance of a dozen Soviet-built missile patrol boats retracted early and avoided confrontation. Iraq's main oil facilities situated in the Fao peninsula proved extremely vulnerable. The onshore Mina-al-Bakhr plant as well as the offshore Khor-al-Amaya terminal were promptly destroyed. During heavy fighting in the Khorramshahr area five foreign freighters were sunk or damaged by Iranian shelling. These vessels, although technically the first losses of international shipping, should be reckoned as collateral damage of land hostilities. The evacuation of seventy vessels blocked in the Shatt-el-Arab waterway became a matter of international concern for several months; see 85 *RGDIP* (1981) at p. 178. See also UN Doc. *S/14213*, 10 October 1980; UN Doc. *S/14214*, 12 October 1980, and UN Doc. *S/14221*, 16 October 1980.

[125]See 28 *KCA* (1982) at p. 31850. In the following months only sporadic and often missed attacks on neutral or Iranian vessels were reported. The air attacks were delivered occasionally by French-made Super Frelon helicopters or Soviet Mig-23 fighter bombers while at least four vessels struck Iraqi laid mines.

would be liable to attack.[126] While five days later, Iraqi President Saddam Hussein proclaimed the 'total blockade of the Kharg oil terminal' and warned that 'foreign shipping companies have only themselves to blame if their ships approach'.[127]

With the Iraqi air attacks on neutral vessels carrying on at an irregular pace, apparently due to lack of modern aircraft and sophisticated weaponry, the practices of the two belligerents should be clearly distinguished. The Iranian measures, although not officially named as such, resembled more an effective blockade of the Iraqi coast. As has been observed, 'Iran's measures appear more defensive in purpose, designed to keep out foreign traffic . . . Unlike Iraq's measures, Iran's exclusion zone appears acceptable under international law.'[128] Iraq, on the other hand, while insisting on the blockade character of the Kharg Island campaign, enforced in essence a free-fire war zone, that is to say an unconstrained operation based on simple warning. The measure alluded to the British total exclusion zone established during the Falklands War. In the words of an expert, 'no serious allegation could be advanced by Iraq that the zone is defensive of Iraqi sea approaches or protective of neutral shipping . . . In fact, the Iraqi exclusion zone closely resembles the type of unrestricted warfare Germany conducted in its declared operational zone around the British Isles and in the Atlantic Ocean during World War II.'[129]

Overall, the anti-shipping campaign during the first three years of the war had not gained worrying dimensions. It is not without significance that neither Iran nor any other state whose

[126]According to another source, an Iraqi military spokesman announced of four distinct maritime prohibited areas; see 86 *RGDIP* (1982) at p. 812. The exact limits of these zones, however, were never publicized.

[127]See 28 *KCA* (1982) at p. 31850. For Baghdad the decision was justified because of the severe problem of identification of enemy ships in the Gulf's busy lanes. A few days later, on 19 August, the Turkish freighter *Mar Transporter* was hit and sunk some 130 n.m. away from the exclusion zone.

[128]See LECKOW, *op. cit., supra* n.121 at pp. 638–9. See also MOMTAZ, D., 'Commentary on Iranian Practice' in DE GUTTRY and RONZITTI, *op. cit., supra* n.121 at pp. 20–1.

[129]See JENKINS, *op. cit., supra* n.121 at p. 535. Similarly, another scholar has argued that 'inasmuch as Iraqi attacks occurred inside its declared war zones, they could not have been justified by the traditional law of maritime blockade, since blockade cannot be enforced by unrestricted aircraft attacks on merchant vessels; nor could they have been justified by the new concept of the exclusion zone, since such a concept does not validate attacks on sight on neutral merchant vessels'; see GIOIA, A., 'Commentary on Iraqi Practice' in DE GUTTRY and RONZITTI, *op. cit., supra* n.121 at p. 80.

ships had been hit thought it necessary to file an official protest with the UN Security Council. In fact, the first Iranian letter addressed to the Secretary-General denouncing the Iraqi attacks on foreign vessels and threatening retaliation in kind came only in December 1983.[130] The opening act of the peculiar maritime campaign in the troubled waters of the Persian Gulf ended in October 1983. At that time five French Super-Etendard bombers equipped with air-to-surface AM39 Exocet missiles were delivered on loan to the Iraqi air force,[131] yet another similarity with the South Atlantic War. With the acquisition of such reliable weaponry with battle-tested efficacy, it was only natural that the Iran-Iraq War entered a new phase of escalation and unlawful interference with international shipping.

The Tanker War Under Way On 25 November 1983, the government of Iraq issued a renewed warning to the effect that all shipping in the north of the Gulf would be liable to attack.[132] Iran for its part, acknowledging the improved Iraqi capability to inflict perhaps irreparable harm on its oil industry, attempted to forestall the opening of a new war front by launching diplomatic protests and menacing retaliation. In a letter to the UN Secretary-General, dated 16 December 1983, Iran warned that it 'reserves its right to retaliate against Iraqi shipping, whether direct or indirect, through the Persian Gulf, whenever and however it deems appropriate. In doing so, the Islamic Republic of Iran would be only responding to Iraqi provocations in kind'.[133] On 27 February 1984, an Iraqi military spokesman claimed that Iraqi aircraft launched a major attack on Iranian oil installations at Kharg Island and added that this is 'the beginning of the *blockade* which we have decided to impose on this area' (emphasis added).[134]

[130]See UN Doc. *S/16222*, 16 December 1983.

[131]See 29 *KCA* (1983) at p. 32595. On the characteristics, capabilities as well as the peculiarities of the Exocet missile as against large tankers, see *The Economist*, 30 June 1984 at p. 39. For an assessment of the missile's performance, see DANZIGER, *op. cit., supra* n.121 at pp. 166–7.

[132]See 30 *KCA* (1984) at p. 32689. On 14 February 1984, Iraq made a further announcement threatening to sink any ship approaching the Iranian ports of Bandar Khomeini or Bushire; *ibid.* at p. 33057.

[133]See UN Doc. *S/16222*, 16 December 1983.

[134]See 30 *KCA* (1984) at p. 33057. According to another source, the Iraqi government had announced in early March that 'the siege of Kharg Island had begun';

By the end of May 1984 the waters of northern Persian Gulf were already boiling. In a letter dated 25 May 1984, Iran reaffirmed its diplomatic stand by asserting that it had 'maintained its patience' and 'a policy of restraint' for long towards those who first 'escalated the conflict into attacks on international shipping', and by hinting anew at the law of reprisals as the legal justification for what it might follow; 'if the security of the Persian Gulf is violated, then it is violated for all. We will not permit the Persian Gulf, on which we have more than a thousand kilometers of littoral, to be closed to us and to be used by others against us.'[135] The Iraqi reply came two days later in an interesting statement issued by the Foreign Ministry. The exclusion zone was referred to as either a 'zone of military operations', or a 'blockade of Iranian ports'. The fact that it had been 'strictly delimited' and confined to 'the extreme north eastern part of the Arabian Gulf' and that an ample warning had been given, it was suggested, could suffice to waive responsibility for exposing foreign vessels 'to the dangers of war'.[136] The Iraqi government defended its raids against merchant vessels on two legal grounds, the law of reprisals and the right of self-defence; 'the Iraqi course is meet *like with like* and stems from the right of *legitimate self-defence*' (emphasis added).[137]

The Iraqi anti-ship campaign more often than not paid little attention to the limits of the 50-mile exclusion zone. Vessels were reported to have been hit as far as 70 miles from Kharg Island. In the midst of the Tanker War, the Norwegian Foreign

---

see *The Time*, 12 March 1984 at p. 20. At the time the Kharg Island campaign was launched, as much as 90 per cent of Iranian oil exports were using that terminal rendering it an objective of paramount importance for the Iraqi military planning. For a description of the installations on the island, see *Brassey's Defence Yearbook* (1987) at p. 315. In 1984 alone, Iraq delivered more attacks than it did in the three previous years. Between 1980 and February 1984, 23 Iraqi and 5 Iranian attacks were reported, as compared to 37 Iraqi and 17 Iranian attacks in 1984; see IISS, *Strategic Survey* (1985–6) at p. 126. For a chronology of events and statistics on the attacks, see DANZIGER, *op. cit., supra* n.121, pp. 160–7, and O'ROURKE, *op. cit., supra* n.121, pp. 31–2.

135 See UN Doc. *S/16585*, 25 May 1984.

136 See UN Doc. *S/16590*, 27 May 1984.

137 *Ibid.* Although the statement specified that 'Iraq strikes against vessels . . . in response to Iran's actions against Iraq, since by military force Iran has prevented free navigation in Iraqi territorial waters and Iraqi ports and since Iran insists on continuing its war of aggression against Iraq and refuses to heed to the solutions of the Security Council', it did not offer any explanation as to how direct unprovoked attacks against unarmed ships could be correlated with action in self-defence.

Minister stated that 'it is especially regrettable that attacks have taken place on ships in international waters and *outside the declared zone of war'* (emphasis added).[138] It is true, of course, that the brief note abstains from commenting on the legal validity of attacks within the zone, but, nevertheless, deplores *'all operations* against civilian targets' (emphasis added).[139] In view of the extremely serious threat (oil exports dropped by 50 per cent in the first weeks of May), Iran decided to retaliate in kind. In the absence of vessels trading with Iraq, Iran found it pertinent to direct its attacks against Kuwaiti and Saudi merchantmen. The reprisals were meant to hit the countries supporting the Iraqi war effort. For their part, the Gulf Co-operation Council member states recommended to foreign shipping a 12-mile zone coterminous with their respective territorial seas and promised military protection to all tankers accepting to follow this route.[140]

In 1985, Iraq stepped up its effort in order to disrupt Iranian oil exports through the Gulf. By the end of the year, more than sixty strikes qualified as 'devastating' had been launched against the Kharg Island oil terminal.[141] In a communication addressed to the UN Secretary-General, Iraq re-stated the motives of its campaign. The exclusion zone around Kharg Island was defined as a 'blockade' imposed in retaliation for the continued unlawful Iranian war conduct and 'in order to induce that State to accept peace'. It was further argued that the owners and the crews of neutral ships should be also held responsible for indirectly violating the Iraqi right of free navigation, and, therefore, equally liable to Iraqi reprisals: 'the activity of the said ships is

[138]See UN Doc. *S/16586*, 25 May 1984.

[139]*Ibid.* See also the interventions of the representatives of the UN Security Council member states during a debate on Gulf shipping, 21 *UN Chronicle* (1984), p. 5*ff.*

[140]See *The Economist*, 2 June 1984 at p. 31. In June 1984, the Saudis in what became their first direct military involvement in the war shot down two Iranian Phantoms. The Saudi F-15 fighters, guided by American Awacs radar aircraft, engaged the Iranian planes near a Saudi-owned island 40 miles offshore; see UN Doc. *S/16608*, 8 June 1984; 30 *KCA* (1984) at p. 33059; *The Economist*, 9 June 1984 at p. 44. Besides, on 20 June 1984, US officials announced that Saudi Arabia had set up an *air-defence interception zone* known as the 'Fahd line' which would go beyond Saudi territorial limits. Saudi aircraft guided by US Awacs and refuelled by US tankers would engage any aircraft threatening the Gulf shipping; see *Brassey's Defence Yearbook* (1987) at p. 308.

[141]In what was termed 'the year of the pilot', the Iraqi air force asserted to have flown 20,011 missions, staging 77 destructive raids against Kharg and scoring 124 hits on maritime targets; see *Brassey's Defence Yearbook* (1987) at p. 318.

tantamount . . . to supplying the Iranian military machine and enabling Iran to continue its aggression. Accordingly, the said ships forfeit their neutral character since they violate a right unequivocally conferred by international law [the right of free navigation]'.[142] As for Iran, from the summer of 1985, it intensified maritime inspection operations at the entrance of the Persian Gulf. Freighters were boarded and searched, often diverted to Iranian ports, and cargoes were occasionally confiscated as contraband of war. Most of the countries whose ships had been intercepted acquiesced in the Iranian practice with the notable exception of Kuwait, which claimed the unimpeded freedom of the high seas for its flag vessels.[143]

The Climax of the Anti-Shipping Campaign August 1986 stands as another turning point as far as the theatre of naval operations is concerned. On 12 August, Iraq staged its first attack against the Iranian oil terminal at Sirri Island adding a new dimension to the maritime conflict.[144] Even Larak Island, lying inside the Hormuz Strait, was to be brought within range of Iraqi missiles. Larak is more than 430 n.m. from the nearest Iraqi air base which implies that either a Gulf state allowed Iraqi aircraft to land and refuel on its soil, as Iran often claimed,[145] or that the

[142]See UN Doc. *S/16972*, 20 February 1985.

[143]See UN Doc. *S/17335*, 11 July 1985, and UN Doc. *S/17482*, 20 September 1985. Iran, in rejecting the Kuwaiti complaints, made express reference to the classical Hague law concerning the rights and duties of neutral powers in naval war, and implicitly invoked the continuous voyage doctrine in enforcing the blockade against Iraqi; see UN Doc. *S/17348*, 22 July 1985, and UN Doc. *S/17496*, 25 September 1985. See also *infra*, chapter 6, notes 35–47 and accompanying text.

[144]See 32 *KCA* (1986) at p. 34592. In fact, since December 1984 Iran had completed construction works on a makeshift terminal at Sirri Island. The objective was the supertankers to avoid the risky journey north to Kharg Island by mooring south, presumably out of reach of Iraqi aircraft, and loading oil which would have been previously transported from Kharg aboard small tankers steaming close to the Iranian coastline; see 31 *KCA* (1985) at p. 33560. Besides, Iran seriously envisaged the possibility of abandoning Kharg installations in favour of other smaller terminals like Gavaneh or Lavan, or constructing a new pipeline to safer Iranian ports in the south; see 32 *KCA* (1986) at p. 34514.

[145]See 33 *KRWE* (1987) at p. 35159. See also UN Doc. *S/19971*, 29 June 1988. Saudi Arabia qualified the accusations as 'completely unfounded'; see UN Doc. *S/20007*, 11 July 1988. Protests were also addressed to Kuwait for 'granting air corridor and flight permission to the Iraqi planes'; see UN Doc. *S/20003*, 11 July 1988. Kuwait's reply in UN Doc. *S/20015*, 14 July 1988.

Iraqi air force had acquired air-to-air refuel capacity for its Mirage F-1. The first bombing of Larak installations came on 25 November 1986, and again rumours spread that the aircraft involved in the attack made use of Saudi Arabia's territory.[146] The theatre of naval operations was thus shifted markedly to the south embracing the entire Persian Gulf – an inevitable and predictable development from the very moment the first war zone was declared.

Iraqi air raids intensified in 1987. In September, a total of sixteen vessels were damaged in just one week, while heavy attacks at Kharg, Larak and Sirri islands were also reported.[147] On 14 December 1987, an Iraqi Exocet missile caused the death of twenty-one seamen aboard the Norwegian tanker *Susangerd*.[148] The Iranian Foreign Minister in a letter dated 29 August 1987, emphasized Iran's commitment to resort to retaliatory measures for as long as Iraq continued preying on international shipping: 'retaliation in kind by the Islamic Republic of Iran, as already announced in official statements of policy, can be against any means whereby Iraq equips and strengthens its own war machine'.[149] Among others, the long-promised reprisals took the form of drifting mines scattered along maritime routes in the central Persian Gulf. The unexpected mine threat alerted in particular the western naval forces present in the region which decided to react. Shortly after, the US task force claimed to have neutralized an Iranian ship, the *Iran-Ajr*, while engaged in minelaying 50 miles north east of Bahrain. The United States sought to justify its action under the right of anticipatory self-

[146]See 33 *KRWE* (1987) at p. 35160. An air raid on Sirri Island required a flight of 700 miles, while a similar attack on Larak involved a return trip of over 1,350 miles; see ESHEL, D., 'The Iraqi Air Force – How Effective Is It?', 15 *Military Technology* (Feb.1991), p. 72*ff*.

[147]See 33 *KRWE* (1987) at p. 35599. The high rate of successful hits led to speculation that Indian and French experts had improved the Iraqi air force altitude attack training and planning. Moreover new versions of Mirage F-1 were delivered to Iraq after the return of the first five Super-Etendard to France; see *Brassey's Defence Yearbook* (1987) at p. 315.

[148]Overall, twenty-five incidents were reported in December, the highest level of attacks since 1984; see 34 *KRWE* (1988) at p. 36168.

[149]See UN Doc. *S/19086*, 31 August 1987. Two days later an Iranian gunboat opened fire on a Kuwaiti freighter within the territorial waters of the United Arab Emirates. Kuwait condemned what it called 'Iran's continued acts of piracy'; see UN Doc. *S/19093*, 1 September 1987. For another incident involving a British tanker, see UN Doc. *S/19147*, 22 September 1987.

defence.[150] The fragile US-Iranian relations deteriorated sharply in October 1987. Low-level armed incidents multiplied to the point where the Iranian Foreign Minister estimated that the two countries were approaching 'the brink of another Viet Nam', and held the US administration responsible 'for initiating a full-scale war'.[151]

In March 1988, in the aftermath of a skirmish with Iranian forces, Kuwait threatened for the first time to take retaliatory measures: 'Kuwait reserves the right to retaliate against any act of aggression against its territory or sovereignty.'[152] In April 1988, US forces destroyed by shelling fire the Iranian Sassan and Sirri oil platforms, and engaged several Iranian warships, allegedly 'in response to an attack by the Islamic Republic of Iran against a United States naval vessel'.[153] The incident referred to involved the *USS Samuel B. Roberts* which some days earlier had struck a mine some 60 n.m. east of Bahrain. On the basis of 'conclusive evidence' that the mine had been manufactured in Iran, the US Command ordered the destruction of the Iranian platforms. Despite the evidently retaliatory character of the US action, it was officially justified on grounds of self-defence.[154] Tehran qualified the attack as 'premeditated acts of

[150]See UN Doc. *S/19149*, 22 September 1987, and UN Doc. *S/19153*, 24 September 1987. Iran denied that the *Iran-Ajr* was a minelayer and called the American account of the events a 'total fabrication'. The Iranians also accused the United States of deliberately towing the *Iran-Ajr* into Bahrain's territorial waters and subsequently blowing it up in order to eliminate evidence of its criminal act; see UN Doc. *S/19161*, 29 September 1987. Bahrain denied all allegations that the *Iran-Ajr* was brought and destroyed in its territorial waters; see UN Doc. *S/19169*, 1 October 1987.

[151]See UN Doc. *S/19192*, 9 October 1987. For the destruction of two Iranian platforms at Reshadat after the US flag vessel *Sea Isle City* had been hit by a Silkworm missile, see UN Doc. *S/19219*, 19 October 1987, and UN Doc. *S/19224*, 21 October 1987. See also WYCKOFF, R.C., 'The Navy in 1987', 114 *USNIP* (June 1988) at p. 80. For more on Silkworm missiles fired against Kuwaiti targets, see UN Doc. *S/19210*, 15 October 1987; UN Doc. *S/19215*, 16 October 1987; UN Doc. *S/19227*, 22 October 1987; UN Doc. *S/1932–8*, 8 December 1987. For an early assessment of the US policy in the Gulf War, see JOHANSEN, R.C. and RENNER, M.G., 'Limiting Conflict in the Gulf', 7 *Third World Quarterly* (1985), p. 809*ff*.

[152]See UN Doc. *S/19709*, 30 March 1988. In another letter addressed to the UN Secretary General following a missile attack Kuwait referred to 'the right to take appropriate measures'; see UN Doc. *S/19811*, 20 April 1988.

[153]See UN Doc. *S/19791*, 18 April 1988.

[154]For the operational details of the US action, see PERKINS, J.B., 'Operation Praying Mantis: The Surface View', 115 *USNIP* (May 1989), p. 66*ff*., and LANGSTON, B. and BRINGLE, D., 'Operation Praying Mantis: The Air View', 115 *USNIP* (May 1989), p. 54*ff*. See also POLITAKIS, G., 'From Action Stations

aggression'.[155] On 14 May 1988, Iraqi planes scored five tanker hits killing twenty seamen,[156] among the attacked vessels was the world's largest supertanker, the *Seawise Giant*.

The Decreasing Relevance of Prohibited Zones For the purposes of the present analysis, the Gulf Tanker War has been looked at in three distinct phases, relating to what is considered to have been a downgrading of importance attached by both belligerents to the concept of war zones. In view of the advancing internationalization of the conflict and the widening range of the war events,[157] the question of war zones, it is submitted, progressively lost its importance, so that by 1988 the Kharg Island exclusion zone appeared a remote, if not a long-forgotten memento.

During the initial period (September 1980–October 1983), Iraq threatened, officially declared and started enforcing the 50-mile exclusion zone around Kharg Island. The discussion seemed confined to whether the Exocet missiles were meeting their targets within or outside the zone.

to Action: U.S. Naval Deployment, "Non-Belligerency", and "Defensive Reprisals" in the Final Year of the Iran-Iraq War', 25 *ODIL* (1994), p. 31*ff.*, and *infra*, chapter 2, notes 86–7 and accompanying text.

[155]See UN Doc. *S/19796*, 18 April 1988. On 2 November 1992, Iran filed with the International Court of Justice an application initiating proceedings against the United States in respect of the destruction of the Iranian oil platforms in October 1987 and April 1988. According to the submissions of Tehran, the US action was in clear violation of the 1955 Treaty of Friendship, Commerce and Consular Rights binding upon the two states but also a breach of general international law. See *Oil Platforms (Islamic Republic of Iran v. United States of America), Order of 4 December 1992, ICJ Rep. 1992*, p. 763, *Order of 3 June 1993, ICJ Rep. 1993*, p. 35, *Order of 18 January 1994, ICJ Rep. 1994*, p. 3. On 12 December 1996, the ICJ delivered a judgement by which it rejected the preliminary objection to its jurisdiction raised by the United States. The Court found that it had jurisdiction to deal with the case on the basis of Article XXI, para.2, of the 1955 Treaty; see *ICJ Communiqué* no.96/33 of 12 December 1996.

[156]See 34 *KRWE* (1988) at p. 35938. Iran asserted 'complete co-operation of the American forces stationed in the region' for the attacks; see UN Doc. *S/19885*, 16 May 1988. The United States denied the allegations and affirmed continued neutrality; see UN Doc. *S/19896*, 24 May 1988.

[157]Iran never passed up an opportunity to stigmatize the absence of impartiality in the Gulf policies particularly of Kuwait and the United States. In rejecting UN Security Council Resolution 598 (1987), Iran spoke of the need for 'strict observance of neutrality on the part of all littoral states, particularly Kuwait'; see UN Doc. *S/19301*, 11 August 1987. Moreover, it is extremely interesting to note that in May 1988 Kuwait was accused of 'total disregard for the rules of neutrality' and was reproached to have conducted itself as a 'belligerent nation'; see UN Doc. *S/19865*, 5 May 1988.

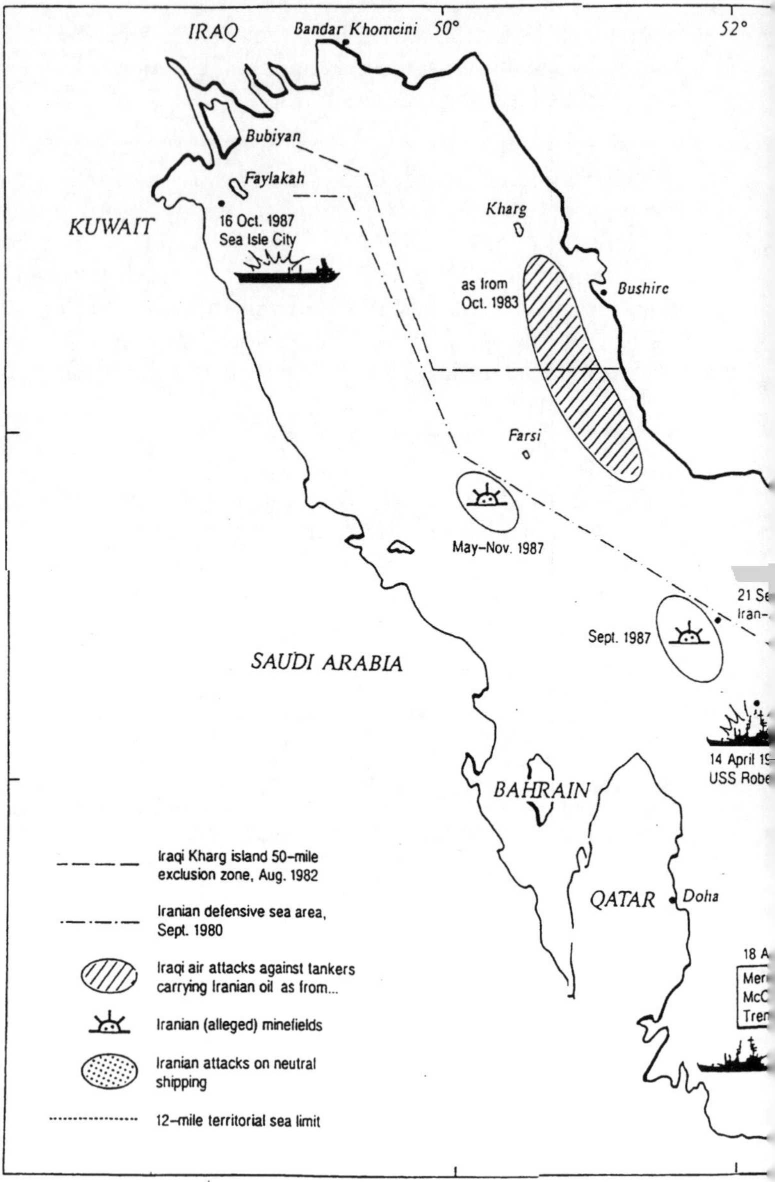

Figure 5 *Major Naval Events in the Closing Year of the Iran-Iraq War*
Source: Author's design

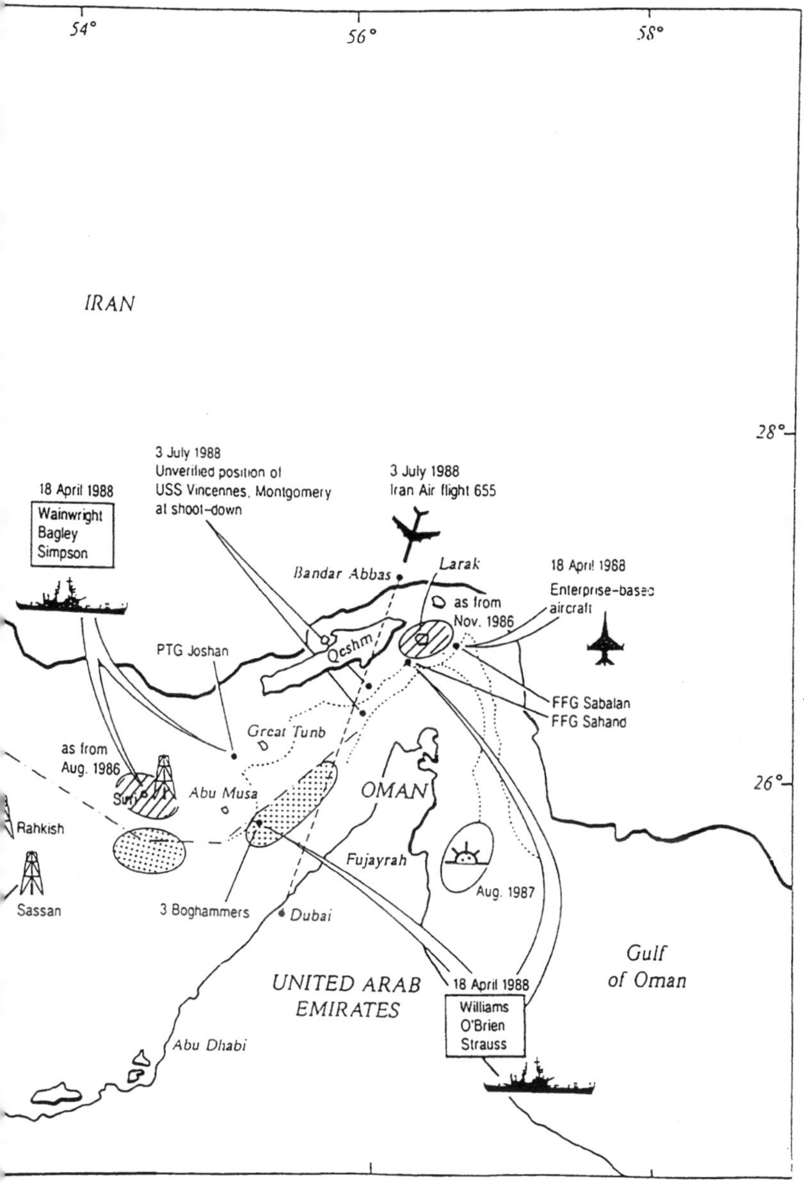
54°
56°
58°
28°
26°
IRAN
3 July 1988
Unverified position of
USS Vincennes, Montgomery
at shoot-down
3 July 1988
Iran Air flight 655
18 April 1988
Wainwright
Bagley
Simpson
Bandar Abbas
Larak
18 April 1988
Enterprise-based
aircraft
as from
Nov. 1986
Qeshm
PTG Joshan
FFG Sabalan
FFG Sahand
Great Tunb
as from
Aug. 1986
Sirri
Abu Musa
OMAN
Rahkish
Fujayrah
Aug. 1987
Sassan
3 Boghammers
Dubai
Gulf
of Oman
UNITED ARAB
EMIRATES
18 April 1988
Williams
O'Brien
Strauss
Abu Dhabi

During the second period (October 1983–August 1986), and particularly during the 1984 Tanker War crescendo, much less attention was paid on the question of the geographical location of the attacks. The Iranians, for their part, set no limits to their endeavour to inflict damage on Kuwaiti or Saudi interests. This is not to suggest that, had they provided for a fixed zone and had they confined their aggressiveness therein, their acts would have attained legitimacy. To the contrary, it is simply to emphasize that the issue has been misleadingly presented as the precisely defined Iraqi zone versus the scattered Iranian reprisals, as if the fixing of the geographical setting in itself would have sufficed to answer the question of the legality of a war zone.[158] The Iraqi campaign, however, continued to seek justification in the argument that a properly declared and widely notified war zone could afford legality for the missile attacks against neutral shipping.[159]

Finally, in the climax of the Gulf War (August 1986–July 1988), war zones seemed to venture on the verge of legal irrelevancy. Belligerent practices substituted the entire Gulf for the relatively modest prohibited zones of the early stages of the conflict. Tankers were now being aimed at, surprisingly, by air-launched missiles or by fast boats, and sea lanes were being freely mined, virtually throughout the 500-mile-long Persian Gulf. As from 1986, therefore, it becomes more and more pointless to speak of attacks within or beyond the limits of war zones, as the latter appear to have been definitely abandoned. Iraq kept on hitting 'large naval targets' as far as Larak Island. Consultation of a

[158]All the more so, as in the words of an analyst, 'despite the big headlines and world-wide condemnation, Iran's attacks have not only been far less frequent that Iraq's but have caused much less damage and fewer casualties. In stark contrast to the results of the Iraqi attacks, no major ship has been sunk by the Iranians and very few crewmen have been killed in their raids'; see DANZIGER, *op. cit., supra* n.121 at p. 164.

[159]See, for instance, UN Doc. *S/16590*, 27 May 1984: 'Iraq has declared a strictly delimited zone in the extreme north-eastern part of the Arabian Gulf a military operations zone and has warned against dispatching vessels to it . . . Iran, on the other hand, has decided to strike at random against vessels . . . far from the theatre of operations.' It has occasionally been argued that Iraq by hitting ships along the Iranian coast could validly claim that it was only enforcing the Iranian war zone. This singular proposition was promptly dismissed by scholars such as Yoram Dinstein who commented: 'if Iraq treats its exclusion zone as a war zone, that is one thing, but for a belligerent to treat an enemy's exclusion zone as its own makes a mockery of the laws of armed conflict'; see 82 *Proc.ASIL* (1988) at p. 608.

map makes it patently clear just how immaterial the 50-mile exclusion zone of 1982 around Kharg Island became over time, and yet the Iraqis declined to replace it with a further enlarged version. It is not without significance that, even upon the cessation of hostilities, neither of the two belligerents found it necessary to officially declare the termination of the war zones in the northern Gulf. This suggests, by all appearances, that the question had long before ceased to bother the legal, political or military minds in both countries. If anything, it proves the inverse proportionality existing between the escalation of hostilities and the operational utility of war zones; the more the war advances, the less the war zone device is employed or respected.

B The US naval intervention and the downing of the Iranian Airbus

The Naval Build-Up Shortly after the reflagging and escort operation of Kuwaiti tankers began in July 1987, the United States massed a naval force of some thirty-five combat ships as well as a little over a dozen support vessels, with a total of some 20,000 men – its biggest war fleet since the Vietnam era. Soon joined by some ten more vessels dispatched by several European nations (mainly minesweepers and support ships), the international armada stood as the largest naval build-up in the Gulf region since the Second World War. In November 1987, there were forty-eight combatants and mine countermeasures vessels of seven different countries deployed in the Gulf and eighteen other vessels in the Arabian Sea.[160] Iran denounced the American naval deployment as a manifestation of an arrogant and expansionist policy destined to provoke further escalation of the conflict. As a letter addressed to the UN Secretary-General, dated 9 April 1987, read: 'the Islamic Republic of Iran believes that United States military presence in the Persian Gulf and the strait of Hormuz, which is aimed at supporting the aggressor régime of Iraq, is the only source of instability and tension that would undoubtedly expand if the United States presence were to continue.'[161]

[160]See 'The Unending War in the Gulf', IISS, *Strategic Survey* (1987–8) at p. 130.
[161]See UN Doc. *S/18794*, 10 April 1987.

The Growing Assertiveness of US Forces In the months that followed the dispatch of the western international armada to the Gulf, the US forces progressively abandoned their deterrence mission, and assumed instead a more assertive role in countering the Iranian threat to international shipping. Iran objected to an almost daily American interference with the free movement of Iranian air forces, varying in form and seriousness from keep-clear warnings to interceptions and outright violations of Iran's airspace. In most cases, Tehran's protests concerned interference by American surface and air forces with Iranian military sea-patrolling aircraft over international waters. The Iranian aircraft were routinely summoned to change course and not approach closer to US warships. Frequently, also, Iranian aircraft were not only requested to change course, but were intercepted or given a chase by US fighters, which at times lasted for as long as 80 minutes.[162] Tehran also contended that now and then American aircraft intruded into the Iranian airspace,[163] and spared no opportunity to express 'its strong protest against such actions by American aircraft which represent nothing but the blatant violation of the sovereignty of an independent nation'.[164]

The Defensive 'Bubble' Around US Warships It will be recalled

[162]See UN Doc. *S/19124*, 11 September 1987 at p. 4; UN Doc. *S/19267*, 13 November 1987 at p. 3; UN Doc. *S/19335*, 11 December 1987 at p. 4; UN Doc. *S/19369*, 22 December 1987 at p. 2; UN Doc. *S/19451*, 26 January 1988 at p. 3; UN Doc. *S/19613*, 14 March 1988; UN Doc. *S/19687*, 25 March 1988 at p. 3; UN Doc. *S/19871*, 9 May 1988; UN Doc. *S/19970*, 29 June 1988 at p. 3; UN Doc. *S/20036*, 19 July 1988; UN Doc. *S/20292*, 23 November 1988 at pp. 6,13; UN Doc. *S/20341*, 20 December 1988; UN Doc. *S/20603*, 25 April 1989 at pp. 6,8–9; UN Doc. *S/21407*, 24 July 1990 at p. 3; UN Doc. *S/21903*, 24 October 1990 at pp. 3–4; UN Doc. *S/21905*, 24 October 1990 at p. 7; UN Doc. *S/22362*, 20 March 1991 at pp. 3–4; UN Doc. *S/24560*, 15 September 1992 at p. 4; UN Doc. *S/24561*, 15 September 1992 at pp. 7–8,10; UN Doc. *S/25327*, 24 February 1993 at p. 3.

[163]See, for instance, UN Doc. *S/19016*, 3 August 1987; UN Doc. *S/19225*, 21 October 1987; UN Doc. *S/19335*, 11 December 1987 at p. 4; UN Doc. *S/19369*, 22 December 1987 at p. 3; UN Doc. *S/19558*, 1 March 1988; UN Doc. *S/19977*, 1 July 1988; UN Doc. *S/19961*, 24 June 1988; UN Doc. *S/19965*, 27 June 1988; UN Doc. *S/20292*, 23 November 1988 at p. 10; UN Doc. *S/20328*, 14 December 1988; UN Doc. *S/20441*, 1 February 1989 at p. 13; UN Doc. *S/20555*, 31 March 1989; UN Doc. *S/20604*, 25 April 1989 at p. 12; UN Doc. *S/21904*, 24 October 1990 at p. 9; UN Doc. *S/21905*, 24 October 1990 at p. 11; UN Doc. *S/24561*, 15 September 1992 at p. 10; UN Doc. *S/24575*, 21 September 1992 at p. 5; UN Doc. *S/24576*, 21 September 1992 at p. 3; UN Doc. *S/24597*, 29 September 1992 at p. 5; UN Doc. *S/24670*, 15 October 1992 at pp. 3,5,9,13.

[164]See UN Doc. *S/19460*, 28 January 1988.

that since January 1984, a protective 'bubble' zone of 5 nautical miles had been established around each surface unit of the US task force operating in the Persian Gulf or the Gulf of Oman, within which all unidentified contacts, or those of unclear intentions, would be presumed hostile and treated accordingly. The Notice to Airmen (NOTAM), published on 20 January 1984, by the ICAO upon a request of the United States, 'requested aircraft *at less than two thousand feet altitude* and not cleared for approach to or departure from a regional airport to avoid approaching *closer than five nautical miles* to United States naval forces'. Aircraft approaching in defiance of the notice and 'whose intentions were unclear to United States naval forces, might be held at risk by their defensive measures' (emphasis added).[165]

The defensive arrangement explains, of course, the regular 'stand-clear' warnings, but it could also give rise to delicate situations. A US warship cruising along the Iranian territorial sea limits presumably would be authorized to take defensive action against an Iranian aircraft flying closer than 5 miles from the ship and yet well within its own sovereign airspace. Few would deny that to interdict a state, even in part, the free and unobstructed use of its airspace would represent an excessive claim, especially on the part of an affirmed neutral. Far from being merely hypothetical, this type of incident did in fact occur.[166] Iran characterized such conduct as unjustifiable and illegal, and 'insistingly demanded that these actions, which are against the sovereignty of the Islamic Republic of Iran, . . . be ended at once'.[167]

[165]See 78 *AJIL* (1984) at p. 884. A similar Notice to Mariners was issued on 21 January 1984; see *ibid.* at p. 885. See also 28 *ILM* (1989) at pp. 910, 942. A week earlier, the US State Department in a Note addressed to the Iranian government had announced that 'the United States has been compelled to adopt prudent defensive measures governing the approach of unidentified ships and aircraft in close proximity to United States military forces'; see 78 *AJIL* (1984) at p. 884. The peculiarity of the 5-mile zone as devised by the US naval forces relates basically to its mobility. The exclusion from navigation or overflight takes here the form of a sphere moving together with the warship, called also *cordon sanitaire*, or 'chastity belt'.

[166]See UN Doc. *S/19840*, 26 April 1988; UN Doc. *S/20349*, 23 December 1988; UN Doc. *S/20292*, 23 November 1988 at p. 8; UN Doc. *S/20441*, 1 February 1989 at pp. 3,8; UN Doc. *S/20452*, 8 February 1989 at pp. 3,5; UN Doc. *S/20603*, 25 April 1989 at p. 3; UN Doc. *S/20604*, 25 April 1989 at pp. 3,10; UN Doc. *S/20776*, 9 August 1989 at p. 5; UN Doc. *S/21904*, 24 October 1990 at p. 3.

[167]See UN Doc. *S/19923*, 3 June 1988. While Iran's Foreign Minister, Ali Akbar Velayati, declared before the UN Security Council: 'The American warships have

In late July 1987, following the inadvertent Iraqi missile attack against *USS Stark*, the United States revised the defensive arrangement for the protection of their warships present in the Gulf. Reference was no longer made to a 5-mile radius, or to any fixed distance from the ships.[168] Accordingly, it would appear that unidentified surface and air contacts might be challenged or engaged at any distance which in the judgment of on-scene commanders would represent a risk. It is worth noting that, according to Iranian reports, aircraft were occasionally summoned from warships cruising some 30 or 40 (and even 66) miles away.[169] Yet, in September 1987, another Notice to Airmen made renewed reference to the 5-mile 'bubble' zone.[170]

Another question raised in the Iranian diplomatic Notes was the interference of US naval units with Iranian passenger planes while on scheduled flights over the Persian Gulf. In a number of communications, Tehran stressed the gravity of the situation and the hazards that irresponsible, or simply careless, conduct might cause to civil aviation. On 26 May 1987, Iran Air flight

on many occasions warned Iranian naval patrol planes as well as search-and-rescue planes and helicopters within the airspace of the Islamic Republic of Iran, preventing Iran from exercising its sovereign right. In violation of the provision of the Chicago Convention concerning the absolute sovereignty of states over their airspace, the American forces have issued warnings to Iranian planes flying over the territory of the Islamic Republic of Iran to keep a 10-mile distance from the American warships stationed near, or even inside, the territorial sea of our country, while such interference cannot occur even over the high seas'; see S/PV.2818, 14 July 1988 at p. 43.

[168]The Notice to Airmen/Notice to Mariners read in part: 'unidentified aircraft whose intentions are unclear or who are approaching US naval vessels may be requested to identify themselves and state their intentions as soon as they are detected. In order to avoid inadvertent confrontation, aircraft (fixed wing and helicopters) including military aircraft may be requested to remain well clear of US vessels. Failures to respond to requests for identification and intentions or to warnings and operating in a threatening manner, could place the aircraft at risk by US defensive measures. Illumination of a US naval vessel with a weapons fire control radar will be viewed with suspicion and could result in immediate US defensive reaction'; see DE GUTTRY and RONZITTI, *op. cit., supra* n.121 at p. 140. It is in this sense that, as an author has suggested, 'it would be misleading to characterize these warning areas as bubbles'; see ROACH, *op. cit., supra* n.121 at p. 610.

[169]See UN Doc. *S/19124*, 11 September 1987 at p. 3.

[170]In the terms of that warning, 'aircraft at altitudes less than 2,000 ft AGL which are not cleared for approach/departure to or from a regional airport are requested to avoid approaching closer than 5nm to US naval forces'; see DE GUTTRY and RONZITTI, *op. cit., supra* n.121 at p. 141. This NOTAM figures in Appendix F of the ICAO Fact-Finding Report on the Airbus incident which contains the US International Notices to Airmen *in effect* on 3 July 1988; see 28 *ILM* (1989) at p. 942.

635 *en route* to Doha, Qatar, while some 160 miles from its destination, was contacted by Bahrain air traffic control authorities and requested to respond to warnings transmitted from US warships on a certain frequency. The US naval forces warned the pilot to divert his aircraft from the standard international civil aviation corridor. As a result, the Iranian liner was diverted from its ordinary course, and on its return flight it had also to choose an alternative route for safety reasons.[171] Iran considered the threat against civil aircraft as 'flagrant violation of the norms and principles of international law', and characterized 'such irresponsible and provocative behaviour [as] a clear indication of foreign interference in the area, designed by the United States to escalate tension in the Persian Gulf'.

Defending the *modus operandi* of its naval forces in the Gulf, the United States invoked the rights of innocent and transit passage as codified in the contemporary law of the sea. To these claims, Iran responded, in the first place, that the provisions on transit passage of the 1982 UN Convention on the Law of the Sea have not as yet passed into customary law and, second, that sailing through the territorial waters of a coastal state loses all its 'innocence' when it creates a danger for or harm to the littoral state. Therefore, American warships, being on military alert, flying their helicopters, transmitting frequent warnings to Iranian patrol-aircraft overflying national territory, shelling Iranian oil platforms and opening fire at Iranian warships could not in any possible way be considered as engaged in innocent passage.[172] Yet, even by peacetime standards, it would be diffi-

[171]See UN Doc. *S/19267*, 13 November 1987. On 27 May 1987, in an almost identical fashion, another Iranian passenger plane in the air for the same round trip was threatened by an American warship; see UN Doc. *S/18889*, 2 June 1987. On 15 July 1987, Iran Air flights 1251 and 1253 to Mecca received several warnings from US warships while crossing the Gulf via air canal G53 toward Bahrain, while on 9 September 1987, two American aircraft intercepted Iran Air flight 7019 on the Tehran-Dubai route; see UN Doc. *S/18988*, 20 July 1987, and UN Doc. *S/19460*, 28 January 1988. In March and May 1989, two more civilian airliners received warnings from US warships over UHF frequencies used by military aircraft only; see UN Doc. *S/21905*, 24 October 1990 at p. 3. A similar incident involving a civilian helicopter occurred in June 1989; see *ibid.* at p. 9. On 11 November 1991, a US warship warned an Iran Air Boeing 727 flying in the international corridor W25 en route to Shiraz Sayri; see UN Doc. *S/25206*, 1 February 1993 at p. 5.

[172]See UN Doc. *S/20525*, 15 March 1989. The interesting question that arises is whether Iran, under the circumstances, would have the right to curtail the movement of foreign warships through the Hormuz bottleneck, or conversely,

cult to reconcile some of the movements of those warships with Article 14§4 of the 1958 Territorial Sea Convention, or with the requirement of 'continuous and expeditious transit' laid down in Articles 38§2 and 39§1(c) of the 1982 LOS Convention.

A Most Tragic Epilogue The issue of war zones was destined to make headlines again in July 1988, on the occasion of the downing of a passenger aircraft by a US cruiser over the strait of Hormuz. On 3 July 1988, Iran Air flight 655 from Bandar Abbas to Dubai was ended minutes after take-off, as the Iranian Airbus exploded in the air after it encountered two surface-to-air missiles fired from the *USS Vincennes*. All 290 passengers and crew aboard, including more than 100 women and children, perished in the tragic incident.[173] According to the US govern-

---

if it should be deemed under an obligation to accord transit passage rights to the imposing western armada. The conventional texts on the law of the sea are of limited value since they are only applicable in peacetime. State practice is scanty on this point, and so are the doctrinal works. A learned author has advanced the proposition that 'granting a right of transit passage when the littoral state is at war appears to be at odds with the latitude of powers that customary international law gives to belligerent states'; see RONZITTI, N., 'Passage Through International Straits in Time of International Armed Conflict' in *International Law at the Time of Its Codification – Essays in Honour of Roberto Ago*, 1987, vol.2 at p. 380. His overall conclusion is that 'the littoral state cannot be obliged to grant transit passage when it is at war. For such a passage would be inconsistent with the right of self-defence and state practice which proves that littoral states are endowed with substantial powers', *ibid.* at p. 383. See also LOWE, V., 'The Impact of the Law of the Sea on Naval Warfare', 14 *Syracuse Journal of International Law and Commerce* (1988) at pp. 670–1. A more recent essay, however, on the so-called right of self-protection or forcible affirmation of rights concludes that a transiting state would have the right to take measures such as formation sailing, the use of anti-submarine or minehunting helicopters and of sonar devices, the deployment of air cover by launching intercepter and early warning aircraft prior to entering the strait, and the operation of successive flights of aircraft in order to deter or repel a possible attack, while the straits state could take no action except when the transiting force is engaged in aggressive acts such as minelaying; see GILL, T.D., 'The Forcible Protection, Affirmation and Exercise of Rights by States under Contemporary International Law', 23 *NYIL* (1992), pp. 162, 164–5.

[173]Iran requested an urgent meeting of the UN Security Council. After a four-day debate, on 20 July 1988, the Security Council unanimously adopted Resolution 616 in which it expressed its 'deep distress at the downing of the aircraft and profound regret over the tragic loss of innocent lives'. Among the non-Iranian passengers, there were 15 citizens of the United Arab Emirates, 19 nationals of India, 6 of Pakistan, 6 of Yugoslavia and one Italian. For some of the first reflections published after the exact conditions of the tragic incident had been elucidated, see LOWENFELD, A.F., 'Looking Back and Looking Ahead', 83 *AJIL* (1989), pp. 336–41, and ENTESSAR, N., 'Superpowers and Persian Gulf

ment, the *Vincennes* was at the time of the incident engaging small Iranian patrol boats, following a skirmish involving an Iranian gunboat and *Vincennes*' helicopter: 'in the course of the United States response to the Iranian atack, the *Vincennes* fired in self-defence at what it believed to be a hostile Iranian military aircraft after sending repeated warnings (to which the aircraft did not respond).'[174]

US President Ronald Reagan qualified the shooting down of the Iranian aircraft as a 'terrible human tragedy', but still nothing less than a 'proper defensive action'.[175] The US argument rested upon the fact that the world's civil aviation and merchant marine companies had been warned, as from 1984, not to fly or sail without promptly identifying themselves when closer than 5 n.m. to US forces operating in the Persian Gulf,

Security: The Iranian Perspective', 10 *Third World Quarterly* (1988), p. 1447*ff.* The most comprehensive legal analysis to date is by LINNAN, D.K., 'Iran Air Flight 655 and Beyond: Free Passage, Mistaken Self-Defense, and State Responsibility', 16 *YJIL* (1991), p. 245*ff.* See also GHARABAGH, M.J., 'Self-Defense in International Law: Legal Aspects of IR655 Tragedy', 7 *Iranian Journal of International Affairs* (spring 1995), p. 119*ff.*

[174]See UN Doc. *S/19989*, 6 July 1988. See also 34 *KRWE* (1988) at p. 36169. Admiral William Crowe, Chairman of the US Joint Chiefs of Staff, in an initial report said that the airliner was flying outside the commercial air corridor and had failed to respond to repeated warnings. Moreover, the plane had been descending and picking up speed when it closed in on the *Vincennes*. Finally, a graphic representation of the events placed the *Vincennes* well within international waters at the time of the shooting down. All these indications have since proved false and it is somewhat ironic that it all occurred aboard such an ultra sophisticated warship as the Aegis-cruiser *Vincennes* – one of the most technologically advanced warships of the US navy. It will be recalled that the much-discussed Aegis system cannot only track every aircraft within 300 miles, but also shoot down as many as 200 incoming enemy aircraft or missiles at once; see *Jane's Weapon Systems 1988–89* at pp. 478–9. See also SANTOS, A., 'Le système d'armes Aegis ou les limites du système d'initiative stratégique', CIRPÉS, 11 *Cahiers d'Études Stratégiques* (1987), p. 93*ff.*; GEDDES, J.P., 'Aegis Protects the Fleet', 16 *International Defense Review* (1983), p. 147*ff.*

[175]The United States has long been thinking about offering *ex gratia* payment to the families of the victims while emphatically denying legal liability for the incident; see LEICH, M.N., 'Denial of Liability: *Ex Gratia* Compensation on a Humanitarian Basis', 83 *AJIL* (1989), p. 319*ff.*; MAIER, H.G., '*Ex Gratia* Payments and the Iranian Airline Tragedy', 83 *AJIL* (1989), p. 325*ff.*; EWING, D.A., 'The Downing of Iran Air Flight 655: Highlighting the Need for International Adjudication of Damages', 13 *Suffolk Transnational Law Journal* (1990), p. 656*ff.* The United States offered to pay US $ 250,000 for a full-time, wage-earning victim and US $ 100,000 for each of the other victims, or less than one-third of the amount that the Iraqi government had paid to the American victims on board the *USS Stark*; see SUCHARITKUL, S., 'Procedure for the Protection of Civil Aircraft in Flight', 16 *Loyola of Los Angeles International and Comparative Law Journal* (Feb.1994) at p. 529.

the Strait of Hormuz and the Gulf of Oman. The misperceived threat was taken in the *Vincennes'* quarterdeck as establishing a clear hostile intent on the part of the unidentified aircraft, and the traditional US standpoint holds action in self-defence permissible not only in response to hostile acts but also in view of a mere hostile intent. The US Secretary of Defence Caspar Weinberger, reporting to the Congress in 1987 on the Persian Gulf security arrangements, had stated that as 'international law recognizes an inherent right to employ proportional force as necessary in self-defence, this right will be exercised in the face of attack or hostile intent indicating imminent attack'.[176]

The USS Stark Precedent In the mind of the *Vincennes'* captain William Rogers, the recollection of another incident must have weighed heavily. In May 1987, the *USS Stark* was hit by an Exocet missile fired by an Iraqi aircraft off Bahrain, the attack resulting in the death of thirty-seven crewmen.[177] In the *Stark* incident it appears that the reaction of the commanding officers was inexcusably delayed, whereas in the Iranian Airbus incident it was unforgivably rash. The *Stark* had been first informed of the Iraqi aircraft's presence when the aircraft was at least 200 n.m. away. The signature of its Cyrano-IV radar was later detected, its flight path was early tracked as being towards the *Stark*, and its radar was found locked on to the *Stark*. Still, the only measures taken to meet the threat were to arm the Chaff launchers and to switch the Phalanx gun on to the stand-by position. No evasive steering, no missiles loaded in the

[176]See 26 *ILM* (1987) at p. 1437. The hostile intent was defined as 'the threat of imminent use of force against friendly forces, for instance, any aircraft or surface ship that maneuvers into a position where it could fire a missile, drop a bomb, or use gunfire on a ship is demonstrating evidence of hostile intent. Also, a radar lock-on to a ship from any weapons system fire control radar that can guide missiles or gunfire is demonstrating hostile intent. This includes lock-on by land-based missile systems that use radar', *ibid.* at p. 1454. As the report concluded, 'the RoE provide authority to the on-scene commander to declare a threat hostile and engage that threat (i.e., a force demonstrating hostile intent or committing a hostile act) with all forces available to him in self-defence of his unit and U.S.-flagged vessels. Only that force which is required to neutralize the threat or prevent a hostile act is authorized', *ibid.*

[177]*Ibid.*, p. 1423*ff.*, and 28 *ILM* (1989), p. 644*ff.* See also VLAHOS, M., 'The *Stark* Report', 114 *USNIP* (1988), pp. 64–7, and 30 *KRWE* (1987) at p. 35597. The passivity of the *Stark*'s skipper and his failure to anticipate the incoming threat 'hurried' him and his first officer into retirement.

launching pad, not even standard warnings to the Iraqi pilot until after the second missile was under way.

In contrast, the *Vincennes,* although operating in much less friendly waters and already in combat action at the time of the incident, lacked any conclusive indication as to the identity and/or the intention of the approaching aircraft. Most important, no fire control radar had been detected as locked on to the *Vincennes.* And yet, the skipper was reported to have 'delayed' his decision for 4 minutes (the whole incident lasted only 7 minutes) so that the lethal missiles should have normally been fired even earlier, despite the doubt as to the nature of the threat. What one might call the *Stark syndrome* was officially put forward in defence of the *Vincennes'* course of action. As the US Chairman of the Joint Chiefs of Staff had stated on 19 August 1988, 'the tragic events of July 3 did not occur in a vacuum as the Secretary explained to you. They happened in an area where 37 American sailors on board the *USS Stark* had been killed by an air attack in May 1987 and where our military has been tested by fire time and again over the last year. The actions of Captain Rogers and the *Vincennes* crew must be judged in that context.'[178]

Iran Air Flight 655: What Really Happened To date, the exact reasons that led *Vincennes'* captain to his fateful decision continue to fuel controversy. However, several aspects of the incident have since been sufficiently elucidated, and as a result much of the initially offered explanation was discredited. Other US warships operating in the same area, such as the frigate *USS John H. Sides,* were reported to have identified the Iranian plane as civilian and at high altitude.[179] On 7 November 1988, the International Civil Aviation Organization's report on its fact-finding investigation verified the critical miscalculations

[178]Cited in DE GUTTRY and RONZITTI, *op. cit., supra* n.121 at p. 206. See also the rather cynical appraisal of a *Vincennes'* officer: 'the *Stark*'s readiness was flawed and 37 sailors died. The *Vincennes*'s readiness was sound, and 17 days later the war ended'; see AGRESTI, M.C., 'The *Vincennes* Incident', 116 *USNIP* (Jan.1990) at p. 24.

[179]This point has since been confirmed by the *Sides*'s captain himself who recalled the stupefaction of his men as they came to identify the aircraft's commercial transponder code at the same time the *Vincennes* fired its missiles; see EVANS, D., 'Vincennes – A Case Study', 119 *USNIP* (Aug.1993) at p. 50.

which led to the decision to fire the missiles.[180] It has now been established that the jetliner was ascending, rather than descending, after permission was given to climb from 12,000 to 14,000 feet, that its transponder had been sending out signals on the appropriate IFF frequency, and that it was flying well within the provided commercial *Amber 59* air corridor.[181]

Immediately after the incident, US Vice President George Bush stressed the responsibility of Iranian authorities for having failed to divert the civilian aircraft from the theatre of ongoing naval engagement.[182] Today, however, it appears certain that neither the airport controllers at Bandar-Abbas nor the perished pilot ever became cognizant of the US naval operations at the heart

[180]The report is reproduced in 28 *ILM* (1989), p. 900*ff*. Selected excerpts appear also in 83 *AJIL* (1989), pp. 332–5. The final report of the US Defense Department, released on 19 August 1988, also admitted that several errors were to be attributed to the *Vincennes*' staff; see 34 *KRWE* (1988) at p. 36170.

[181]According to the US Department of Defense Formal Investigation into the Circumstances Surrounding the Downing of Iran Air Flight 655, also known as the *Fogarty Report*, 'the data from *USS Vincennes*'s tapes, information from *USS Sides* and reliable intelligence information, corroborate the fact that TN 4131 [the unidentified contact] was on a normal commercial air flight plan profile, in the assigned airway, squawking Mode III 6760, on a continuous ascent in altitude from takeoff at Bandar Abbas to shoot down'; reprinted in DE GUTTRY and RONZITTI, *op. cit., supra* n.121 at pp. 205–6. But even if one admits *arguendo gratia* that there was an irregularity concerning the Airbus flight path, or its signals, there was a significant clause in the US standing orders sufficient in itself to refute any claim which might draw thereupon and which read as follows: 'US Navy ship captains *realize* that not all commercial aircraft transmit their proper IFF (Identification Friend or Foe) code or remain in the proper airways and *will take this into account* when they encounter such an aircraft' (emphasis added); see the US Navy Procedure for Communicating with Unidentified Aircraft, 28 *ILM* (1989) at p. 943. The Iranian Airbus was flying, therefore, some 10,000 feet above the highest altitude that, according to the 1987 NOTAM, might under certain circumstances imply a risk. Moreover, no source ever reported that the civil aircraft was flying within, or anywhere close, to a 5-mile perimeter when defensive action was taken. At the point of impact, the Iranian aircraft was some 8 to 9 miles from the *Vincennes*, but the decision to engage the unidentified contact was taken while the aircraft was more than 20 miles away; see *Fogarty Report*, reprinted in DE GUTTRY and RONZITTI, *op. cit., supra* n.121 at pp. 204–5.

[182]See his intervention before the UN Security Council: 'despite these hostilities, Iranian authorities failed to divert Iran Air 655 from the area. They allowed a civilian aircraft loaded with passengers to proceed on a path over a warship engaged in battle. That was irresponsible and a tragic error . . . by allowing a civilian airliner to fly into the area of an engagement between Iranian warships and US forces in the Gulf, Iran must bear a substantial measure of responsibility for what was happened'; see S/PV.2818, 14 July 1988 at pp. 56–7.

of the Hormuz Strait.[183] What is more, it has only recently been revealed that at the time of the shooting down the *USS Vincennes* and the *USS Elmer Montgomery* were inside Iranian territorial waters.[184] Washington has reluctantly come to admit the long-omitted detail, but retorted that both warships were forced there in self-defence. As William Rogers, captain of the *Vincennes*, who has lately acknowledged the presence of his ship in Iran's territorial waters, related: 'when the determination of hostile intent on the part of the Iranian small craft was made, both US ships were in international waters. During the course of the following surface action while maneuvering at high speed both the *Vincennes* and the *Montgomery* exercised their right of self-defense pursuant to international law reflected in Article 51 of the UN Charter and entered Iranian waters'.[185]

[183]According to one commentator, 'it is doubtful that Captain Rezaian [Airbus' pilot] ever heard the warning messages broadcast by the *Vincennes*, or by the frigate *Sides* . . . If he had been monitoring the distress frequencies, the American-educated Captain Rezaian, although fluent in English, might not have known that the warning transmissions were intended for him'; see EVANS, *op. cit., supra* n.179 at p. 49. See also the transcript of the conversation between the pilot and the air traffic control centres of Bandar-Abbas and Dubai where there is not a single mention of any particular military activity in the Gulf waters to which the pilot should be attentive, S/PV.2818, 14 July 1988, pp. 11–15.
[184]See BARRY, J. and CHARLES, R., 'Sea of Lies – Special Report', *Newsweek*, 13 July 1992 at p. 13, and EVANS, *op. cit., supra* n.179 at p. 52.
[185]See ROGERS, W., 'Counterbattery', 119 *USNIP* (Aug.1993) at pp. 57–8. Note also the statement of George Bush during the UN Security Council debate: 'one thing is clear: the *USS Vincennes* acted in self-defence. The tragic accident occurred against a backdrop of repeated, unjustified, unprovoked, and unlawful Iranian attacks against US merchant shipping and armed forces, beginning with the mine attack on the *USS Bridgetown* in July 1987. It occurred in the midst of a naval attack *initiated* by Iranian vessels against a neutral vessel and, subsequently, against the *Vincennes* when it came to the aid of the innocent ship in distress'; see S/PV.2818, 14 July 1988 at p. 56. See also ROGERS, W., *The USS Vincennes and Iran Air Flight 655*, 1992. For some, however, 'the argument of self-defence is untenable. This argument is based on a self-induced error of an impossible scenario – that defensive measures could in any way have been legitimately taken to destroy an unarmed civil aircraft in routine commercial flight'; see SUCHARITKUL, *op. cit., supra* n.175 at p. 535. Note also the statement of Ali Akbar Velayati before the UN Security Council: 'pre-emptive measures before the occurrence of an armed attack cannot be justified as acts of self-defence; rather such measures can be considered only as a blatant breach of the principle of the non-use of force in international relations. Therefore, according to well established principles of international law, the United States criminal act of attacking a civilian airliner can never be justified under the term "self-defence", particularly since the civilian airliner did not even have the potential to launch an attack . . . When the most sophisticated US warship panics over the remote possibility of the existence of an F-14, which in any case could not pose a serious threat to a surface target, and goes on a shooting spree against

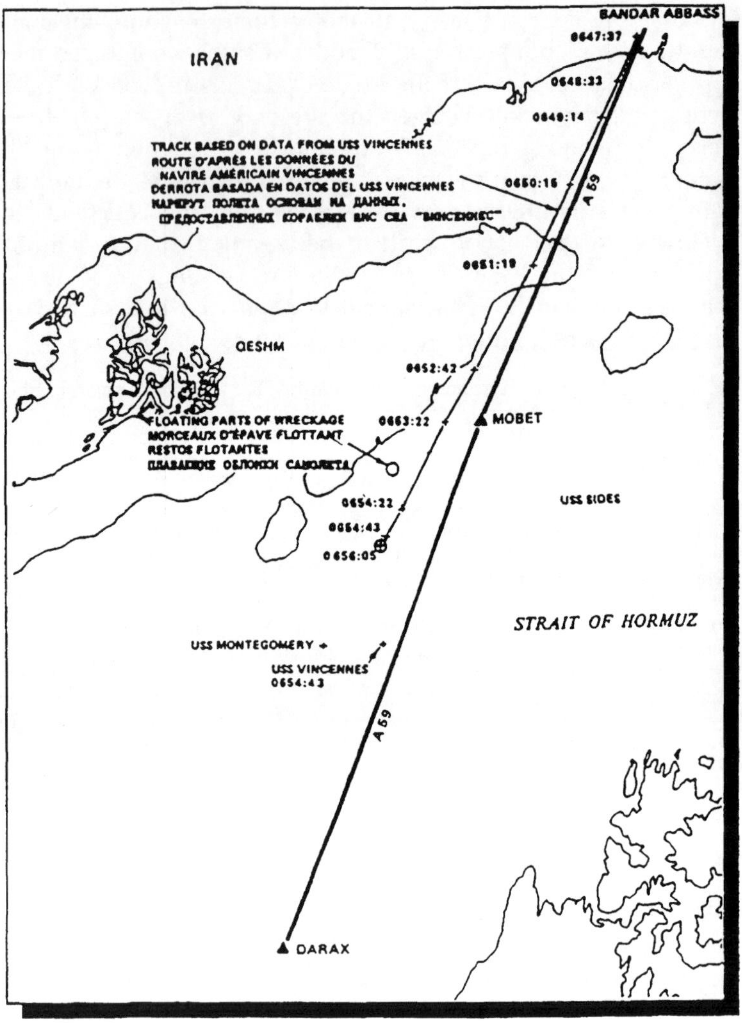

Figure 6 *The Track of Iran Air Flight 655 on 3 July 1988*
Source: Report of the ICAO Fact-finding Investigation of November 1988, as reprinted in 28 *ILM* (1989) at p. 921

Early in the morning of 3 July, Captain Rogers launched his helicopter with a view to flying north and reporting on the Iranian gunboat activity.[186] Despite the standing rules of engagement never to approach the Iranian small craft closer than 4 miles, the helicopter pilot apparently did so and was warned off by machine-gun fire. Upon being informed that his helicopter had taken fire, Captain Rogers turned his ship north, while asking the Commander of the Joint Task Force Middle East in Bahrain permission to engage the boats supposedly for the protection of his helicopter.[187] Soon joined by the *USS Elmer Montgomery*, the *Vincennes* sailed north at full speed giving a chase to the Iranian boats as they fled the scene for safer territorial waters. Minutes after, both warships crossed the 12-mile line into Iranian territorial waters ready to engage boats that had not fired at them.[188] The encounter lasted for 17 minutes

---

an unidentified target, should we not expect less-sophisticated warships to mistake commercial jets smaller than Airbuses for fighter jets probably larger than F-14s?'; see S/PV.2818, 14 July 1988 at pp. 36–7, 37–8.

[186]It should be noted that during the afternoon and evening hours of 2 July, an increased naval activity of the Iranian Revolutionary Guard had been observed, with as many as 13 Iranian craft having been spotted in the strait by the *USS Montgomery*. This irregular force, or *Pasdaran*, had been raiding merchant vessels using armed fast boats (Boghammers and Boston Whalers) which were no threat for the US warships; see CHAPIN, S.R., 'Countering Guerrillas in the Gulf', 114 *USNIP* (Jan.1988), p. 65*ff*.

[187]As David Evans commented, if the pilot 'was in danger, it was because he was not following the rules: to approach no closer than four miles . . . [And yet] the *Vincennes'* helicopter could dash away from danger at 90 knots, three times the speed of the advancing mother ship and, in addition, Captain Rogers already had control of the airspace his helicopter was occupying, some 19 miles distant given the extended range of his antiair warfare weapons'; see EVANS, *op. cit.*, *supra* n.179 at p. 51. Likewise, David Carlson, captain of the *USS Sides*, noted: 'it was a bad move. Why do you want an Aegis cruiser out there shooting up boats? It wasn't the smart thing to do. He was storming off with no plan and, like the Biblical Goliath, he was coming in range of the shepherd boy', *ibid.*

[188]Note also that 'as shown by the *Vincennes'* videotape, the two American warships passed a second Iranian gunboat, this one to starboard of the cruiser. The boat's crew can be seen relaxing topside. Hardly threatening behavior and the Iranians appeared not the least threatened by the passage of the US Navy cruiser'; *ibid.* at p. 52. And elsewhere: 'from the videotape recorded on *Vincennes'* bridge that day, the gunboats, seen as mere specks in the distance, returned fire; they did not initiate shooting. The Iranian gunboats' light weapons were greatly outranged by the heavier ordnance on the *Vincennes*, and the spent shells from the Iranians' weapons fell harmlessly as a brief line of splashes in the water, hundreds of yards short of the *Vincennes*, and fully 45 seconds after the *Vincennes'* first rounds were fired', *ibid.*

during which time the *Vincennes* fired 72 rounds.[189] It was precisely at the time the *Vincennes* mounted its retaliatory action that the Iranian Airbus took off for its scheduled twice-a-week flight – a tragic last voyage.

If these revelations proved to be truthful, it would be difficult to deny the conclusion that the US government bears responsibility for the course of events which surrounded the downing of the Iranian Airbus. First, beyond Captain Rogers' reputed aggressive temperament (the *Vincennes* was accordingly nicknamed *Robocruiser*),[190] one should not forget that he had twice asked and obtained permission from his superiors at Bahrain to open fire against the Iranian boats, which implies that the Command of the Joint Task Force had full knowledge of the often provocative *Vincennes'* manoeuvring but still did not object to the *Vincennes'* and the *Montgomery*'s trespassing of Iran's maritime frontiers.[191] Second, steering within the Iranian territorial sea in the conditions described above had little in common with either self-defence or innocent passage. The *Vincennes* had not been the object of an attack, or under an imminent threat of any sort. Besides, delivering shells at top speed could hardly meet the requirements of 'passage not prejudicial to the security of the coastal state', prescribed in Article 14§4 of the 1958 Territorial Sea Convention, or of 'continuous and expeditious transit', laid down in Articles 38§2 and 39§1(c) of the 1982 Law of the Sea Conven-

[189]See FRIEDMAN, N., 'The *Vincennes* Incident', 115 *USNIP* (May 1989) at p. 74. As a result, two Iranian boats were destroyed and a third was damaged.

[190]See BARRY and CHARLES *op. cit., supra* n.184 at p. 10. On the second day of his first patrol in the Gulf, on 2 June 1988, Rogers had ordered the captain of *USS Sides* to close in on the Iranian frigate *Alborz* engaged in visit and search of a large bulk carrier (the *Vevey*) in a clearly offensive way. *Sides*'s captain protested the escalatory move and higher headquarters at Bahrain detached the *Sides* from the *Vincennes'* control, while ordering the cruiser to steer away from the Iranian warship. Contrary to the often conveyed image of unruly conduct on the part of the Iranian navy, it was later affirmed that 'the conduct of Iranian military forces in the month preceding the incident was pointedly non-threatening. They were direct and professional in their communications, and in each instance left no doubt concerning their intentions'; see CARLSON, D.R., 'The *Vincennes* Incident', 115 *USNIP* (Sept.1989) at p. 87.

[191]According to one account, however, just before the *Vincennes'* helicopter came under fire, the CJTFME (Commander Joint Task Force Middle East) was surprised to see that *Vincennes* was 40 miles north from where he believed he had ordered Rogers to remain, and ordered him to head back toward Abu Musa; see BARRY and CHARLES, *op. cit., supra* n.184 at p. 12.

tion.[192] For certain analysts, however, such as Norman Friedman, 'the loss of Iran Air 655 might be ascribed to the Iranian's continued attacks on US and friendly shipping in the Gulf, in that these attacks created an atmosphere in which it was much better for US forces to shoot than to risk the consequences of not shooting'.[193]

Naval experts, from theorists to electronic warfare specialists, have speculated on the real causes of the IR 655 incident. Some have blamed inexperienced personnel who in a hot combat situation have misread decreasing range figures as decreasing altitude. Others underscored the limited capacity of the human brain as compared to the phenomenal processing speed of modern computers.[194] Still others recalled the human tendency to make available evidence fit a preconceived scenario. Besides all these hypotheses, however, one should call into question the practicality of the 5-mile zone around the US warships

[192]Earlier that eventful morning of 3 July, the *Vincennes* was spotted cruising at full speed through Oman's territorial waters in order to join the scene of a minor skirmish involving Iranian Boghammers, which compelled an Omani Coast Guard officer to signal: 'US Navy warship maneuvers at speeds up to 30 knots are not in accordance with innocent passage. Please leave Omani waters'; see BARRY and CHARLES, *op. cit., supra* n.184 at p. 12. To argue differently would mean that a US warship might lawfully launch lethal missiles at an aircraft 20 miles away (though not positively identified as military), while Iranian patrol boats might not open fire, however symbolic, against a military helicopter threateningly overflying in a mere 2-mile distance and well within Iranian airspace. Iran's Foreign Minister Ali Akbar Velayati, addressing the UN Security Council, made this very point by way of a comment upon US President's recount of events to Congress: 'The President of the United States faults Iranian patrol boats for allegedly taking action against clearly identified military helicopters with hostile intent approaching to within four miles of Iranian airspace and even violating it. But in the same letter, he approves and justifies the shooting down of a commercial plane with 290 passengers aboard at a distance of nine miles, again within Iranian airspace'; see S/PV.2818, 14 July 1988 at p. 27.

[193]See FRIEDMAN, *op. cit., supra* n.189 at p. 76. His argument is all the more striking, however, as he acknowledges that 'almost certainly the airport at Bandar Abbas was entirely unaware that the airliner was being sent over an ongoing surface battle', and that 'it is unknown whether the pilot understood the warning', *ibid.* His note of approval culminates in the startling proposition that 'even had he known that the approaching aircraft was an Airbus, he could not have been sure that it was not intending to attack him, since, like an F-14, it would have made an effective kamikaze', *ibid. Cf.* ECKHART, M., 'The *Vincennes* Incident', 116 *USNIP* (March 1990) at p. 32, SEAQUIST, L., '*Vincennes*: A Case Study', 119 *USNIP* (Oct.1993) at pp. 29–30, and FIELD, M.E., 'The *Vincennes* Incident', 119 *USNIP* (Nov.1993), p. 17*ff.*

[194]On this parameter, see GRUNER, W.P., 'No Time for Decision Making', 116 *USNIP* (Nov.1990), p. 39*ff.*

Figure 7 *The Vincennes Incident: Problems of Identification*
Source: International Herald Tribune, 18 July 1988.

throughout their deployment in the Persian Gulf. The defensive bubble could not and eventually did not prevent the *Stark* incident. It could not and did not avoid similar incidents whereby the Iraqi missiles fortunately missed their target.[195] Conversely, it occasioned the tragic event of July 1988 to the degree to which the fixed zone put an imperative mental strain on the

[195]The destroyer *USS Chandler* and the cruiser *USS Richmond K. Turner* narrowly escaped Iraqi missile attacks in February 1988; see 34 *KRWE* (1988) at p. 36168. It is not without significance that no other country of those contributing to the Gulf armada had declared analogous zones around their naval units. The Italian government, however, instructed vessels to act progressively in response not only to hostile acts *(atti ostili)* but also to hostile intents *(comportamenti ostili)*; see RONZITTI, *op. cit., supra* n.121 at p. 655. Similarly, the British government changed the RoE for its Armilla Patrol in July 1987 'to allow the Royal Navy to react much more positively to a threat, and even to take preemptive action. The Armilla ships would now apparently be allowed in certain circumstances to fire the first shot if Iraqi or Iranian missiles were about to leave their launchers'; see KINLEY, G., 'Legal Principles Governing the Armilla Patrol', *Lloyd's List*, 31 July 1987 at p. 2.

commanding officer to act in defence of its periphery even though the information about the incoming threat might be poor and inconclusive.[196]

In a move that promises to write the epilogue of the Airbus incident, Iran, on 17 May 1989, filed an application with the Hague Court instituting proceedings against the United States for the shooting down of the civil airliner.[197]

11 Exclusion zones and recent UN coercive action

Conceptually similar to maritime war zones, air exclusion zones found further application in the context of two recent conflict situations, that is the 1991 Gulf War and the ongoing civil strife in Bosnia-Herzegovina. Both flight interdiction campaigns were set up in connection with UN enforcement action under chapter VII of the Charter. It should be noted, however, that the no-fly zone over Bosnia was explicitly provided for in Security Council Resolutions 781 (1992) and 816 (1993), while the air exclusion zone over southern and northern Iraq lacks a definite UN mandate. The latter operation is only indirectly linked to Security Council Resolution 706 (1991) which in a preambular paragraph referred in unspecified terms to the 'assistance to all segments of the Iraqi civilian population', and to Resolution 707 (1991) which at para.3(e) authorized UN inspection teams to 'conduct both fixed-wing and helicopter flights throughout Iraq for all relevant purposes, including inspection, surveillance,

[196]As a study concludes, 'the totality of information now available suggests that Captain Rogers "defended" his ship into Iranian territorial waters, and when the air contact appeared, he blew the call'; see EVANS, *op. cit.*, *supra* n.179 at p. 55. As a telling footnote to the recount of events, one might add that several of the *Vincennes'* officers were awarded medals for their professional performance. The air-warfare coordinator officer, for instance, was commended for 'heroic achievement' and his 'ability to maintain his poise and confidence under fire'. Will Rogers retired honourably in August 1991.

[197]More precisely, the dispute before the ICJ concerned the interpretation and application of the 1944 Convention on International Civil Aviation and of the 1971 Convention for the Suppression of Unlawful Acts Against the Safety of Civil Aviation; see 28 *ILM* (1989) at p. 842. For the submitted Iranian contentions, see *ibid.* at p. 845. See also *Aerial Incident of 3 July 1988 (Islamic Republic of Iran v. United States of America), Order of 13 December 1989, ICJ Rep. 1989*, p. 132, *Order of 5 June 1992, ICJ Rep. 1992*, p. 225, and *Order of 18 January 1994, ICJ Rep. 1994*, p. 3. The oral hearings concerning the US-filed preliminary objections to the jurisdiction of the Court and the admissibility of the application were scheduled to open on 12 September 1994, but were deferred *sine die*; see *ICJ Communiqué* no.94/18 of 11 August 1994.

aerial surveys, transportation and logistics, without interference of any kind'. Apart from their exact legal basis, the two operations seem to differ also in enforcement resolve. In the case of Iraq, allied aircraft have promptly responded by using force whenever they felt threatened, whereas NATO planes operating over Bosnia, in a somewhat less menacing environment but against far greater escalation risks, have abstained from opening fire (with one exception) against unauthorized flights. Yet, both exclusion zones have been conceived and are currently enforced more as warning areas rather than free-fire zones.

Operation Southern Watch In the aftermath of Operation Desert Storm and the liberation of Kuwait, measures had to be taken aiming at protecting the Shia and Marsh Arab population in southern Iraq, as well as the Kurds in northern Iraq, from the harsh repression of Baghdad's regime. On 26 August 1992, the United States, France, Russia and the United Kingdom proclaimed a flight ban for all Iraqi military aircraft and helicopters south of the 32nd and north of the 36th parallels.[198] The first serious incident occurred on 27 December 1992, when US F-16 fighters shot down an Iraqi MiG-25. The plane was one of four to cross the 32° parallel, but unlike the others it did not flee the zone when challenged.[199] On 17 January 1993, another Iraqi MiG-23 fighter had been destroyed over northern Iraq.[200]

Both tension and the concern that coalition forces might have exceeded their UN mandate increased. The French government

[198]At the time of the announcement, more than 200 US aircraft were operating in the area, while the UK and France were soon to participate with six Tornado and ten Mirage 2000 jets respectively. The 'no-fly' zones were intended to create a safer environment for the allied reconnaissance aircraft which monitored Iraqi compliance with Security Council Resolution 688 (1991), but they had not been the object of a specific UN authorization. Most Arab states including Syria, Sudan or Yemen condemned the plan, whereas Egypt and Saudi Arabia expressed serious reservations; see 38 *KRWE* (1992) at pp. 39068, 39115, and 52 *Facts on File* (1992) at pp. 614, 625, 641.

[199]Another two Iraqi fighters were chased north on 28 December 1992, the US announcing soon thereafter the redeployment of the carrier *Kitty Hawk* to the Persian Gulf; see 38 *KRWE* (1992) at p. 39247, and 52 *Facts on File* (1992) at p. 967.

[200]See 39 *KRWE* (1993) at pp. 39291–2. Tension mounted sharply in January 1993 when US warships launched forty cruise missiles against the Iraqi nuclear facility at Zafaraniyah, some 20 kilometres south of Baghdad. The missile attack came after several days of intense allied air strikes against Iraqi air defence facilities and radar sites.

openly criticized the United States on such grounds, while Russia urged that an explicit authorization should be delivered from the Security Council. The question finally remained unresolved with more skirmishes between allied planes and Iraqi anti-aircraft batteries being reported in April 1993. In the most serious among the twenty incidents reported that year, surface-to-air missiles were fired in August, for the first time, against US planes.[201] On 14 April 1994, two US warplanes mistakenly shot down two US Army helicopters while flying within northern Iraq's no-fly zone on a humanitarian mission killing all twenty-six UN representatives.[202]

Operation Deny Flight UN Security Council Resolution 781 (1992) imposed an immediate ban on all military flights over Bosnia-Herzegovina with the exception of authorized flights for the needs of UN forces (UNPROFOR). NATO assets were subsequently requested to assist in supervising the implementation of the flight ban. Operation Sky Monitor which began on 16 October 1992 was thus confined to simply monitoring the eventual violations of the no-fly zone (an analogous Operation Maritime Monitor related to trade sanctions against the Federal Republic of Yugoslavia was already in progress in the Adriatic). On 31 March 1993, the UN Security Council passed Resolution 816 authorizing NATO aircraft to 'take all necessary measures in the airspace of the Republic of Bosnia and Herzegovina, in the event of further violations, to ensure compliance with the ban on flights . . . proportionate to the specific circumstances and the nature of the flights'.[203] According to the rules of engagement

[201]See 53 *Facts on File* (1993) at pp. 263, 622.

[202]As the US Defense Secretary William Perry announced later, the fighter planes had fired without prior warning after making what their pilots regarded as positive identification that the helicopters were Russian-manufactured Iraqi craft; see 54 *Facts on File* (1994) at p. 270.

[203]For the various reports of the Secretary-General concerning violations of the ban on flights over Bosnia, see UN Doc. *S/24783*, 9 November 1992; UN Doc. *S/24810*, 13 November 1992; UN Doc. *S/24840*, 24 November 1992; UN Doc. *S/24870*, 30 November 1992; UN Doc. *S/24900*, 7 December 1992 and Add.1–103; UN Doc. *S/25443*, 19 March 1993; UN Doc. *S/25444*, 19 March 1993; UN Doc. *S/1994/5*, 5 January 1994 and Add.1–92. See also UN Doc. *S/1994/4*, 3 January 1994, and UN Doc. *S/1994/63*, 21 January 1994. By 22 December 1994, a total of 3,397 flights in violation of the ban had been observed. See also STARR, B., 'NATO's *Deny Flight* Patrol Hours Mount', 19 *Jane's Defence Weekly* (8 May 1993) at p. 11, and BEAVER, P., 'Bosnia Regularly Breaking No-Fly Zone', 20 *Jane's Defence Weekly* (11 September 1993) at p. 22.

issued by NATO, violators of the ban would be in all cases first warned off and only if the warning was ignored they would be engaged.[204] Operation Deny Flight which began on 12 April 1993, involved some eighty aircraft and as many as 4,000 personnel from ten NATO member states operating from air bases in Italy as well as from the French, British and American carriers present in the Adriatic. By January 1994, over 10,000 sorties had been flown.[205]

Based on the recent UN experience reviewed above, one has to admit that the concept of exclusion or interdiction zones would now seem a regular feature of UN coercive action every time that the suppression of air activity over the targeted state is deemed necessary. However, it would be erroneous to assimilate such no-fly zones with war/exclusion zones of the classical sort related to indiscriminate warfare. At present, there is nothing to support the view that the UN would be ready to sanction a policy which would maintain that any contact within a certain area would be presumed hostile and instantly be fired upon. What is more, the traditional reservations concerning interference with neutral rights seem irrelevant here inasmuch as in the presence of universally binding embargoes no legitimate commercial rights of third states can be said to be affected.

III War zones and the dearth of legal codification

It is a truism to say that the laws of naval warfare have repeatedly escaped the nib of drafters, so that contemplation on the subject more resembles blind-man's buff. The tradition was respected as recently as 1977, during the Diplomatic Conference on the Reaffirmation and Development of International Humani-

[204]See 38 *KRWE* (1992) at p. 39149, and 39 *KRWE* (1993) at pp. 39279, 39375, 39426.

[205]For more, see BOORDA, J.M., 'Loyal Partner – NATO's Forces Support of the United Nations', 39 *NATO's Sixteen Nations* (1994/1) at pp. 10–11. Almost a year after the adoption of Resolution 816 (1993), on 28 February 1994, NATO fighters opened fire for the first time and shot down four Bosnian Serb light attack jets flying over central Bosnia in violation of the UN-imposed flight ban. The air engagement marked the first combat action undertaken by NATO in its forty-five year history. The US F-16 fighters warned the Serb planes to land or exit the airspace immediately or to be engaged. The warnings were given on the international distress frequency that all pilots are supposed to monitor. At the time of the shooting down, the Jastreb aircraft were bombing a munitions factory at Novi Travnik; see 54 *Facts on File* (1994) at pp. 134–5.

tarian Law, when participating delegations saved no opportunity to declare their understanding that nothing in the negotiated protocols would infringe upon traditional usages of war at sea.[206] Under such a grandiose dearth of relevant legal documents then, it merits no amazement that the concept of war zones is omni-absent from conventional texts. Typical as it is of this chronic marginalization of the laws of naval warfare, the case of war zones was, nevertheless, modestly touched upon in some well-intentioned, yet ultimately unfruitful, codification efforts. Most of these intellectual exercises reflect a legal sensitivity to the unprecedented practices inaugurated in the First World War. Regrettably, the feasibility of updating the old law was generally disbelieved in the decades after the Second World War, so that even those early attempts of the inter-war period appear today no less anachronistic than the Hague conventions which they intended to update.

1 The London Declaration of 1909

The ill-fated London Declaration was largely seen, at the time of its adoption, as a faithful representation of the customs and usages pertaining to war at sea.[207] In the preamble, the signatory Powers expressed the view that the rules contained therein 'correspond in substance with the generally recognized principles of international law'. Although the Declaration is not thematically exhaustive, it deals with most of the debatable aspects of the rights and duties of belligerents and neutrals in case of naval

[206]It is not the purpose of this study to address the question of the exact scope of application of part IV of the First Additional Protocol according to article 49§§3,4. On the doctrinal discussion whether the new rules for the protection of the civilian population are applicable to naval warfare, see RAUCH, E., 'The Protocol Additional to the Geneva Conventions for the Protection of Victims of International Armed Conflicts and the United Nations Convention on the Law of the Sea: Repercussions on the Law of Naval Warfare', *Veröffentlichungen des instituts für internationales recht an der universität Kiel*, no.90, 1984. See also RAUCH, E., 'Le droit contemporain de la guerre maritime: Quelques problèmes crées par le Protocole Additionnel I de 1977', 89 *RGDIP* (1985), p. 958*ff*. *Contra* see MEYROWITZ, M., 'Le Protocole Additionnel I aux conventions de Genève de 1949 et le droit de la guerre maritime', 89 *RGDIP* (1985), p. 243*ff*.

[207]See SCOTT, J.B., 'The Declaration of London of February 26, 1909', 8 *AJIL* (1914), p. 274*ff*.; ROOT, E., 'The Real Significance of the Declaration of London', 6 *AJIL* (1912), p. 583*ff*. See also KALSHOVEN, F., 'Commentary on the London Declaration' in RONZITTI, N. (ed.), *The Law of Naval Warfare*, 1988, p. 257*ff*.; DE ZAYAS, A.M., 'London Naval Conference of 1908/1909' in BERNHARDT, R. (ed.), *Encyclopedia of Public International Law*, instalment 3 (1982), p. 249*ff*.

war. The law of blockade, in particular, received a thorough treatment, with the first twenty-one articles devoted thereto. All the principles classically associated with the notion of blockade were endorsed: a blockade should not bar access to neutral ports or coasts (Article 18), it should be impartially enforced (Article 5), and properly declared and notified (Article 9,11). The doctrines of hot pursuit and continuous voyage were not to be part of the law of blockade (Article 17,19). As for the question of effectiveness, the 1909 Declaration merely reiterated the stipulation of the Paris Declaration of 1856.

What should be distilled from the content of the Declaration, however, is that the sanction against neutral merchant vessels was normally not to be sought in measures other than capture and condemnation. The idea of destruction was only envisaged as an exception under circumstances of extreme necessity, and was to be kept within several restraints, while the idea of indiscriminate or unwarned attack was simply never contemplated. According to Article 21, 'a vessel found guilty of breach of blockade is liable to condemnation'. Refusing even to submit to the procedure of visit and search was to beget no more than a right to seize the vessel and confiscate the cargo: 'forcible resistance to the legitimate exercise of the right of stoppage, search and capture, involves in all cases the condemnation of the vessel' (Article 63). The abortive codification effort of 1909 inspired two more intellectual exercises on the subject before the Second World War.

2 The Oxford Manual of 1913

The *Oxford Manual*, adopted by the Institut de Droit International on 9 August 1913, was intended to be the counterpart of the 1880 Land Warfare Manual.[208] The novelty of the rules related to the question of war zones was the notion of the *zone des opérations*. Article 50, under the title 'droits du belligérant dans la zone de ses opérations', envisaged the eventuality of a 'refoulement, même par la force, du navire hors de la zone interdite et le séquestre des appareils'. The same proviso referred to the liability of the vessel to be captured, if it could be estab-

[208]The Manual of naval warfare is reprinted in RONZITTI, N. (ed), *The Law of Naval Warfare*, 1988, p. 277*ff*. It is also to be found in SCOTT, J.B. (ed.), *Resolutions of the Institute of International Law*, 1916, p. 174*ff*.

lished that it had already communicated information to the enemy. It should not escape our attention, however, that none of what the *Oxford Manual* was visualizing departed qualitatively from what were permissible courses of action under classical prize law. It is also worth mentioning that the proposed zone of operations would exclusively concern enemy vessels. True though it was that merchantmen would be kept clear by warning, or even by force, and eventually would be liable to capture owing to their geographic proximity to enemy warships and not because of their cargo or destination, this implied, however, a variation in context rather than in means.

During the deliberations among the members of the Institut, it became clear that the intention was to confine the term *zone des opérations* to the area of active hostilities. Paul Fauchille, for example, acting as Rapporteur, responded to a proposed amendment by saying that, 'les mots employés par la Commission dans l'article 53 zone correspondant . . . *actuelle* indiquent nettement qu'il s'agit uniquement des lieux où se déroulent *en fait* les opérations' (italics in the original).[209] Pietro Verri, in what is probably the most recent commentary on the 1913 Manual, wrongly ascribes to its drafters the intention to regulate 'barred' or 'exclusion' zones of the First World War type.[210] In the light of the preceding remarks one is bound to observe that the World War practice bears no resemblance with the context described in Article 50 of the *Oxford Manual.*

3 The Laws of Naval War of 1920

The laws of naval war presented before the International Law Association in 1920 introduced an air of radicalism. This marked the first codification attempt undertaken in the aftermath of the First World War. The proposed innovations went, not infrequently, beyond the technicalities of conducting hostilities at sea and affected essentially some well-rooted principles. A blockade, for instance, should not have to be restricted to ports and coasts belonging to, or occupied by, the enemy, but it could

[209] 26 *Ann.IDI* (1913) at p. 560. In fact, what was originally Article 67 referred merely to the 'sphère d'action de ses opérations militaires', and was amended on the initiative of Leo Strisower who proposed the words 'action actuelle' in order to limit the 'droit de police' under consideration; *ibid.* at pp. 281, 283.

[210] VERRI, P., 'Commentary on the 1913 Oxford Manual' in RONZITTI, N. (ed.), *The Law of Naval Warfare*, 1988 at pp. 331, 339, and ftn.6 at p. 341.

also close to commerce 'the ports and coasts of contiguous neutral states, insofar as these are capable of use by the enemy for commercial purposes' (Appendix I, Article 1). A blockade should not necessarily have to be maintained by a cordon of warships stationed closely to the coast, but it could be effectively enforced 'at whatever distance from the blockaded area' (Appendix I, Article 2). The doctrines of continuous voyage and hot pursuit were accommodated into the law of blockade (Appendix I, Article 19,20). Anchored contact mines were to be allowed in enforcing a duly declared blockade, 'provided that the mines are laid only in the territorial waters of the enemy within the blockaded area' (Appendix I, Article 22). Finally, although practices like sinking or destroying merchant vessels without adequate provision for the safety of the crew and passengers remained listed under the rubric 'treacherous and barbarous methods of injuring the enemy', a major novelty was introduced: ships caught while attempting to break a blockade, engaged in unneutral service, or resisting visit and search, would be liable not to confiscation, but to *direct attack* and *destruction* (Article 17§6).[211]

As far as the concept of war zones is concerned, the ILA draft laws distinguish between two notions, the *barred zone* and the *area of operations*. A barred zone refers to a portion of the high seas (no clear indication of its limits is given) where belligerent naval forces may assume inspection rights over the passage of neutral ships. The belligerent could exercise control therein, 'provided that he indicates a defined track or tracks for the route or routes of sea-going commerce through such area, and assumes responsibility for the safety of the navigation' (Article 18A). Barred zones would be open to mining – a marked exception to the prohibition of high seas mining – and no compulsory prior notification would be needed in such a case (Article 20).[212] The salient effect these provisions carry is the lack of any requirement of effectiveness which crucially differentiates a barred zone from a blockade. The concept of the area of operations, on the other hand, refers to 'a zone corresponding to the sphere of action of the operations' of a belligerent and the rights

[211]Note, however, that Article 32 and Article 21 of appendix I refer to condemnation in cases of resistance to the exercise of the right of search or attempted blockade running.

[212]*Cf.* the provisions on mining in a blockade operation, appendix I, Article 22.

which he may exercise therein *vis-à-vis* enemy merchant vessels. Naval combatants would have the discretionary power either to impose a radio silence within the zone, or prohibit the entrance altogether (Article 50). The enforcement of such measures would take the form of a threat to sequestrate the wireless equipment or to forcibly drive the enemy vessel out of the forbidden zone, or to capture it.[213]

4 The Harvard Research Draft Convention of 1939

The Harvard Research Draft Convention on Rights and Duties of Neutrals of 1939 does not upset conventional law as much as the ILA draft laws of 1920. The most interesting idea among those upheld by the Advisory Committee with relation to the law of blockade was that of a *blockade zone*. The originality of the new proviso lay not so much in the concept (since, after all, even a blockade in the classical sense results in enforcing a zone) as in the fact that for the very first time a precise limit of 50 n.m. was fixed.[214] Article 69 of the Draft Convention was not drafted in the belief that it codified an existing usage, but rather with the aim of striking a new balance between neutral and belligerent rights.[215] The waters of a blockade zone could be freely mined (Article 83) without prior notification. A blockade zone, however, should never hinder navigation to or from a neutral port, or close an international strait. No other type of zone was to be legally permissible under the Draft Convention that would encroach upon the high seas or impose special prohibition upon the passage of neutral vessels. A belligerent, nonetheless, should be acknowledged the right to 'require neutral vessels in the immediate vicinity of its armed forces not to make use of their radio transmitting apparatus' (Article 70).

In short, neither the 1920 ILA Draft Laws nor the 1939 Harvard Research came to suggest anything that resembled the World War practices. British and German practices alike were largely seen as violations of the existing law that should not be endorsed by future codifications. The commentary which

[213]Article 50 is identical with Article 50 of the *Oxford Manual* of 1913.

[214]A *blockade zone* was defined in Article 1(e) of the Draft Convention as 'that area of water extending fifty miles from a blockaded coast, proclaimed by a belligerent to be such a zone'.

[215]See the commentary on Article 69 in 33 *AJIL* (1939) *Suppl.*, p. 692*ff.*

accompanies the 1939 Draft Convention leaves no room for doubt in that respect: 'no state definitely upheld the legality of war zones or barred areas apart from retaliation; and the neutrals protested against the institution of such zones . . . it is not believed that the World War yielded any substantial evidence in favour of the legality of such belligerent pretensions'.[216]

5 The London Protocol of 1936

Although the Protocol does not purport to regulate specifically the question of war zones, it still represents a vital part of the applicable law.[217] For a considerable number of jurists, the London Protocol has long since rendered defunct, while a few authors have gone as far as saying that the Protocol is 'a monument to naïveté'. It remains undeniable, however, that the Protocol is technically still in force, binding at present some fifty states including the major naval powers of the world with the exception of China. Its significance rests in the hierarchy of values that the Protocol announces, in making the safety of innocent people a prime consideration, and constraining the operational necessities to bow before such an imperative of humanitarian concern.[218] As to its continued legal validity, one should consult the candid language of the Dönitz verdict at Nuremberg. The International Military Tribunal exonerated Admiral Karl Dönitz from the war crimes charges of having launched an unrestricted submarine campaign against British *armed* merchant vessels;

> however, the proclamation of operational zones and the sinking of neutral merchant vessels which enter those zones presents a different question . . . the order of Dönitz to sink neutral ships without warning when found within these zones was, in the opinion of the Tribunal, therefore a violation of the Protocol.

And later in the judgment;

[216]*Ibid.* at p. 705.
[217]See NWOGUGU, E.I., 'Commentary on the 1936 London Procès Verbal' in RONZITTI, N. (ed.), *The Law of Naval Warfare*, 1988, p. 353*ff*.
[218]A principle of analogous content was endorsed by the 1928 Havana Convention on maritime neutrality in Article 1(2). See NELSON, L.D.M., 'Commentary on the 1928 Havana Convention' in RONZITTI, N. (ed.), *The Law of Naval Warfare*, 1988, p. 779*ff*.

the argument of the Defense is that the security of the submarine is, as the first rule of the sea, paramount to rescue and that the development of aircraft made rescue impossible. This may be so, but the Protocol is explicit. If the commander cannot rescue, then under its terms he cannot sink a merchant vessel and should allow it to pass unharmed before his periscope.[219]

6 Recent national navy regulations

The US Commander's Handbook on the Law of Naval Operations
The 1989 US Navy publication is divided in two parts, one examining the law of peacetime naval operations and another focusing on the law of naval warfare. As far as peacetime operations are concerned, a distinction is made between *security zones* and *warning areas*. The security zone gives expression to a claim on the part of some coastal nations of the right to establish, beyond the territorial sea, military security zones of a permanent character and varying breadth in which the activities of foreign warships and military aircraft would be significantly restricted. In that respect, 'the U.S. does not recognize the peacetime validity of any claimed security or military zone seaward of the territorial sea which purports to restrict or regulate the high seas freedoms of navigation and overflight'.[220] In contrast, a warning area may involve only a temporary closure of high seas areas (e.g. for missile testing, gunnery exercises, or other dangerous activities) coupled with a warning to ships and aircraft of other nations that, although they are not required to remain outside the declared zone, they are obliged to refrain from interfering with operations therein. Far from being associated to any notion of exclusion, the right of declaring warning

[219] 22 *Official Proceedings – International Military Tribunal* at pp. 558, 559. The German doctrine of *kriegsraison* was refuted in several post war trials; see DUNBAR, N.C.H., 'Military Necessity in War Crimes Trials', 29 *BYIL* (1952), p. 442*ff.*; RÖLING, B.V.A., 'The Law of War and the National Jurisdiction since 1945', 100 *RCADI* (1960), p. 383*ff.*

[220] See *Commander's Handbook on the Law of Naval Operations* (NWP9-Rev.A) at para.1.5.4. Among the nearly twenty nations claiming a security zone, Saudi Arabia and Egypt claim a 18-mile zone, India, Pakistan or Vietnam lay forward a 24-mile claim, North Korea 50 miles, Indonesia 100 miles, and finally Brazil 200 miles; see the *Annotated Supplement to Commander's Handbook* at p. 1–23.

areas is for the US legally unquestionable and routinely exercised.[221]

Beyond these warning areas properly so-called, however, the *Handbook* makes also reference to *defensive sea areas,* or *maritime control areas,* in connection with the exercise of the right of self-defence at sea under circumstances of exceptional necessity. In this case it would appear that control measures over foreign shipping might well resemble an exclusion zone. In the terms of para.2.4.4.:

> historically, the establishment of such areas extending beyond the territorial sea has been restricted to periods of war or of declared national emergency involving the outbreak of hostilities. International law does not determine the geographic limits of such areas or the degree of control that a coastal or island nation may lawfully exercise over them, beyond laying down the general requirement of reasonableness in relation to the needs of national security and defense.

As regards naval warfare, the only clause alluding to war or exclusion zones is that referring to the *immediate area of naval operations*. Within such an area, 'a belligerent may establish special restrictions upon the activities of neutral vessels and aircraft and may prohibit altogether such vessels and aircraft from entering the area'.[222] The *Handbook* does not contain any precision as to the extent of the immediate area of naval operations other than describing it as an 'area within which hostilities are taking place or belligerent forces are operating'. A caveat is also added to the effect that in enforcing those restrictions in the immediate vicinity of naval operations, a belligerent may not bar access to neutral nations or close an international strait to neutral shipping unless another route of similar convenience remains available to neutral merchantmen.

The German Military Manual In August 1992, the German

[221]See NWP9 at para.2.4.3.1. See also *Annotated Supplement* at p. 2–28.
[222]See NWP9 at para.7.8. The commentary accompanying this provision stressed, however, that 'the belligerent establishment of an immediate area of naval operations should be clearly distinguished from the belligerent practice during the World Wars I and II of establishing operational or war zones'; see *Annotated Supplement* at p. 7–38.

Defence Ministry published a new *Manual on Humanitarian Law in Armed Conflicts*, chapter 10 of which refers to the law of armed conflict at sea. The question of *maritime exclusion zones* is treated under the heading of special provisions concerning means and methods of naval warfare. The German *Manual* defines 'a maritime exclusion zone as a distinct area of sea and the airspace above that area in which a party to the conflict exercises extensive rights of control and prohibits access to ships and aircraft. Its purpose is to facilitate identification of military objectives and defence against hostile acts, but not to attack the war economy of the adversary'.[223] Two types of maritime exclusion zones are also described, the *static* and the *movable* ones, each being subject to different legal conditions. The admissibility of static maritime exclusion zones depends on the fulfilment of the following requirements:

> The establishment of the maritime exclusion zone must be effective. Hence so many units of the air forces and naval forces must be charged with the insurance of the exclusion zone that there is sufficient chance to meet all vessels entering that zone.
>
> The size and duration of as well as the rights claimed in exclusion zones shall, by no means, exceed legitimate national security and defence requirements . . .
>
> The boundaries of exclusion zones, the restrictions to be placed on sea and air traffic within and above these areas and the control measures to be taken shall be determined according to the principles of military necessity and proportionality . . .
>
> The size, the exact boundary lines and the duration of the existence of an exclusion zone shall be announced in public. . . .[224]

As regards movable exclusion zones, the same preconditions of notification and due regard to the principles of proportionality and military necessity apply. Enforcement in this latter case, however, would seem to obey to somewhat more stringent rules to the extent that 'the use of weapons in such zones shall be

[223]See *ZDv 15/2 Humanitäres Völkerrecht in bewaffneten Konflikten – Handbuch* [Humanitarian Law in Armed Conflicts – Manual], August 1992, para.1048 at p. 108.
[224]*Ibid.*, para.1049 at pp. 108–9.

limited to military objectives'.[225] Being couched in such broad terms as the 'legitimate national security requirements', the German *Manual* would appear to endorse, or, at least, not to exclude the legality of war zones in the sense of free-fire zones under exceptional circumstances. As for the apparently more limited movable version of exclusion zones, one might notice that it is tailored as a concept neighbouring that of self-defence, and thus coming closer to the analogous concept of the warning areas within the immediate vicinity of naval operations contained in the *US Commander's Handbook*.

7 Other academic initiatives

The San Remo Manual In June 1994, after six years of periodical meetings and discussions, the Round Table of Experts on the law of naval warfare (also known as the Madrid Plan of Action), at the inception of which lay an initiative of the San Remo Humanitarian Law Institute, adopted a Manual announcing the legal principles applicable to present-day sea warfare. The *San Remo Manual*, as it was finally labelled, apparently wishing to avoid the terminological confusion, eschews any reference to *war*, *barred*, *closed*, *exclusion* or *warning* zones and simply refers to zones. According to the basic principle announced in the *Manual*:

> a belligerent cannot be absolved of its duties under international humanitarian law by establishing zones which might adversely affect the legitimate uses of defined areas of the sea.[226]

[225] *Ibid.*, para.1050 at p. 109. It is obvious that targeting exclusively military objectives presupposes positive identification and thus precludes any idea of indiscriminate attack.

[226] See *San Remo Manual on International Law Applicable to Armed Conflicts at Sea*, Prepared by a Group of International Lawyers and Naval Experts [hereinafter *Manual*], June 1994, at para.105. The accompanying commentary at para.105 reads: 'the fundamental issue addressed by the Round Table was whether or not belligerents establishing zones were entitled to acquire additional rights thereby. Some participants, focusing on the history of the use of zones, particularly during the two World Wars and the Iran-Iraq conflict, argued that State practice supported the view that belligerents could acquire rights by establishing zones and that, indeed, free fire areas could be established in carefully circumscribed areas. After an extended discussion, however, a consensus emerged that the establishment of zones did not and could not create new rights to attack ships and aircraft'; see *Commentary on the Harmonised Document on International Humanitarian Law Applicable to Armed Conflicts at Sea*, March 1994 [hereinafter *Commentary*], para.105.2 at p. 183.

Thus the absolute primacy of international humanitarian law principles over the idea of zonal interdiction is codified as the controlling principle in the matter and would even seem to end all discussion about exclusion zones. Yet, the *Manual* goes on to provide that 'should the belligerent, as an exceptional measure, establish such a zone:

> (a) the same body of law applies both inside and outside the zone;
> (b) the extent, location and duration of the zone and the measures imposed shall not exceed what is strictly required by military necessity and the principle of proportionality;
> (c) due regard shall be given to the rights of neutral States to legitimate uses of the seas;
> (d) necessary safe passage through the zone for neutral vessels and aircraft shall be provided: i) where the geographical extent of the zone significantly impedes free and safe access to the ports and coasts of a neutral State, ii) in other cases where normal navigation routes are affected, except where military requirements do not permit, and
> (e) the commencement, duration, location and extent of the zone, as well as the restrictions imposed, shall be publicly declared and appropriately notified.'[227]

What is most important in that respect is to realize that, fol-

[227]See *Manual* at para.106. The drafters of the *San Remo Manual* illustrated a legally permissible zone as follows: 'a fundamental condition for the establishment of a permissible zone is that a belligerent cannot acquire additional rights through such establishment. A belligerent may, as a matter of policy, decide, for example, not to attack certain ships or aircraft which constitute legitimate military objectives outside a zone while reserving its right to attack such ships or aircraft inside the zone. Such an approach is acceptable provided that the belligerent is merely declining to exercise rights it could exercise outside the zone'; see *Commentary*, para.106.1 at p. 185. As regards the operational attributes of such a zone, the Commentary makes the stereotyped appeal to reasonableness: 'a rule of reason prevails in determining the extent, location and duration of the zone. There must be a proportional and demonstrable nexus between the zone and the self-defence requirements of the State establishing the zone', *ibid.*, para.106.2 at p. 185. In the words of one scholar, deeply involved in the preparation of the *Manual*, 'these provisions can be seen as a compromise between those participants who preferred that such zones be declared illegal and those who believed that more extensive rights should be given to belligerents in such zones . . . this pragmatic proposal is a guide that will help prevent the chaotic and abusive use of zones'; see DOSWALD-BECK, L., 'The San Remo Manual on International Law Applicable to Armed Conflicts at Sea', 89 *AJIL* (1995) at p. 204.

lowing the above prescriptions, a free-fire exclusion zone will always remain beyond the bounds of legal permissibility, since to establish an exclusion zone of the classical cut is, by definition, to claim and enforce radically distinct legal 'rights' inside and outside the zone. Moreover, due regard to the rights of neutrals is unthinkable since belligerents have hitherto created exclusion zones precisely because they refused to take pains to discriminate between enemies and neutrals. In short, the *San Remo Manual* makes it sufficiently clear, though phrased in somewhat convoluted terms, that exclusion zones are and remain illegal. Finally, the *Manual* reaffirms the 'customary belligerent right to control neutral vessels and aircraft in the immediate vicinity of naval operations'.[228]

The ILA Committee on Maritime Neutrality The International Law Association has for many years dealt with questions of *jus in bello* through its Committee on International Medical and Humanitarian Law. The Committee was dissolved in 1988 to be replaced shortly after by another on Maritime Neutrality. The first discussions on the subject were based on a preliminary paper submitted in 1990, while draft reports have been since circulated at the Cairo Conference of 1992, the Geneva Committee meeting of 1993, and the Buenos Aires Conference of 1994. In his latest report, Michael Bothe, states in fairly unequivocal terms that

> the establishment of special zones where a belligerent would have rights in relation to neutral shipping additional to those existing outside any such zone is prohibited. In particular, it is prohibited to declare zones where any neutral ship would be attacked.[229]

In a short note accompanying his proposal, he explains that 'the establishment of special zones (often designated "exclusion zones") is a very controversial subject. In state practice, the establishment of zones where any ship (neutral or other) would be fired upon without prior warning has never been recognized as legal.'[230] Michael Bothe admits, however, that belligerents

[228]See *Manual* at para.108. See also *Commentary,* para.108.1 at pp. 187–8.
[229]See *Report on Neutrality and Naval Warfare* for ILA's Buenos Aires Conference (1994) at para.3.3.
[230]*Ibid.*, commentary on para.3.3.

may, as an exceptional measure, notify zones where neutral shipping would be exposed to risks caused by actual hostilities. In this case, which resembles the concept of immediate vicinity of naval operations, a belligerent should not exceed what is required by military necessity and proportionality with regard to the extent, location and duration of the said zone. As the Rapporteur notes in this respect,

> it may serve a useful purpose clearly to establish and notify where the belligerents intend to conduct hostilities and where commercial navigation would thus be particularly risky. But this device should certainly not be used or rather abused so as to completely bar commercial ships from large sea areas, and in particular from usual sea lanes.[231]

IV War zones in legal thinking: the views of writers

The illegality of declaring and enforcing a free-fire policy within a war zone should normally be seen as rather avowedly manifest. The question presents *prima facie* no labyrinthine complexities. And yet anyone who follows the current literature may have noticed that the doctrine is deeply divided over the issue. On the one hand, there are those who cannot see why they should not continue to profess devotion to sacrosanct legal principles, despite the persistent grave breaches of such principles. On the other hand, there are those who are convinced that after the cataclysm of the two World Wars no rule restricting the *temperamenta belli* should claim sustained validity, unless it is in conformity with current military thinking and heeds to definite operational needs. Chronologically speaking, the doctrinal discussion was heated up in three distinct phases. There has been a first wave of publicists who commented upon the new belligerent practices in the immediate aftermath of the two World Wars. During the 1960s, there was a renewed interest on the subject stimulated in particular by the appearance of some leading works in the field of the laws of war. Besides, the nuclear dimension of the Cold War, the submarine facet of deterrence, the Cuban missile crisis and the Vietnam War made naval diplomacy and strategy a most topical issue. In the last decade, a prolific literature finds its motivation in fresh con-

[231]*Ibid.* See also 65 *Rep.ILA* (1992), Cairo Conference, para.2.8 at p. 170.

tested state practice such as the South Atlantic conflict of 1982 or the 1984–8 Gulf Tanker War which have made exclusion zones the staple of debate for years to come.

Earlier Publicists In early scholarly writings, there is a clear tendency to approve the notion of *defensive sea areas* or *danger zones in the immediate vicinity of active hostilities*, while discarding the idea of war zones associated with unrestricted submarine warfare.[232] For Constantine John Colombos 'any declaration of war zones by a belligerent is unlawful unless . . . it is of such a character as not to imperil the lives of neutral and noncombatant persons.'[233] Herbert Arthur Smith follows the same track: 'from the legal point of view the measures directed towards the total prevention of enemy seaborne trade during the two World Wars must be regarded as outside the ordinary law.'[234]

Revived Interest and Leading Works As of the mid-1950s, the question of the legality of war zones motivated arguments of all sorts ranging from blank condemnation to prompt endorsement. If Castrén stands for the first proposition, Mallison opts for the second, while the middle ground is occupied by writers such as Tucker, or Lauterpacht, in whose view war zones can only be exceptionally legitimized as belligerent reprisals. Erik Castrén's viewpoint is clearly and succinctly stated in the following conclusion: 'we must conclude that the system of war zones is contrary to law both when applied against neutrals and in the relations between belligerents'.[235]

[232]See, for instance, HERSHEY, A.S., 'Should the Right to Establish War Zones on the High Seas be Recognized and What, If Any, Should be the Provisions of International Law on the Subject?', 10 *Proc.ASIL* (1916) at p. 92, and LAWRENCE, T.H., 'Neutrality and War Zones', 1 *GST* (1915) at p. 44.

[233]COLOMBOS, C.J., *The International Law of the Sea*, 6th edn (1967) at p. 531.

[234]SMITH, H.A., *The Law and Custom of the Sea*, 3rd edn (1959) at p. 144. Likewise, Charles Cheney Hyde wrote: 'it may be greatly doubted, however, whether the United States would at the present time be prepared to acknowledge that a belligerent could lawfully establish a danger zone on the high seas surrounding or in proximity to the territory of an enemy, as offensive measure unassociated with the establishment of a blockade'; HYDE, C.C., *International Law*, 2nd edn (1945), vol.3 at p. 1952. *Cf.* HALL, W.E., *A Treatise on International Law*, 8th edn (1924) at p. 642, and MORI, K., *The Submarine in War*, 1931 at pp. 172, 175.

[235]CASTRÉN, E.J.S., *The Present Law of War and Neutrality*, 1954 at p. 316. In the same vein, C.A. Eichelberger considers that the concept of war zones cannot enter the sphere of customary law because the practice was never generally

Diametrically opposite to Castrén's flat rejection, Thomas Mallison holds that the belligerent practices of the protagonists of the First World War have given birth to a specific rule of customary law, according to which both the British long-distance blockade and the German submarine operational area are reasonable and lawful methods for conducting war at sea:

> in summary, the outcome of the decision-making process in the First World War was the development of expectations of uniformity and rightness of the kind usually described as customary law. This customary law upholds as reasonable and lawful both the long-distance surface blockade and the submarine operational area. It should be added that the inter-war period produced no international agreement specifically designed to outlaw submarine operational areas.[236]

In contrast to them both, and in an amazingly balanced work on the laws of naval warfare and maritime neutrality, Robert Tucker emphasizes the inescapable need for evolution of legal

---

accepted. In his words, 'Germany had gone through the routine of World War I, declaring war zones. The United States again acted realistically, forbidding citizens to travel in the danger areas. The action of the Government was like a recognition that a sniper was on the loose and a warning to sensible people to stay away from his sniping-ground. This did not mean that the sniper was being recognized as legal'; see EICHELBERGER, C.A., 'The Law and the Submarine', 77 *USNIP* (July 1951) at p. 696.

[236]MALLISON, W.T., *Submarines in General and Limited Wars*, USNWC, *International Law Series* (1966) at p. 74. Mallison does not enter any reservation to the legality of waging unrestricted submarine warfare. His argumentation revolves around two key words, *realism* in projecting historical experience into the future, and *military efficiency* in overshadowing the principle of humanity: 'it would be highly unrealistic to conclude that the entire practice of naval warfare, both submarine and surface, in the two World Wars is comprised of merely temporary variations from the traditional law conditioned upon the existence of illegality in the conduct of war by the opposing belligerent', *ibid.* at p. 91. And elsewhere: 'it does not seem a realistic way of promoting human values, particularly in the light of the two World Wars, to contend that this use of an efficient military technique is unlawful. It is clear that such contentions have had little impact on the actual process of decision thus far', *ibid.* at p. 93. His analysis as to limited war situations is somewhat more restricted and may be condensed into the following point: in limited wars operational areas remain a remote probability since limited objectives require limited coercive methods, and in that sense the extent of the operational area becomes a relevant factor. Accordingly, the legal appraisal should proceed on a case by case basis. See also MALLISON, S.V. and MALLISON, W.T., 'Naval Targeting: Lawful Objects of Attack' in ROBERTSON, H.B. (ed.), *The Law of Naval Operations*, USNWC, 64 *International Law Studies* (1991), p. 241*ff*.

standards under new realities and the overriding priority of preserving fundamental legal norms. Alhough he admits that state practice clearly favours the adoption of war zones, he is still quite reluctant to abandon the traditional criteria of assessing the legality of blockades: 'there is no warrant for asserting that other criteria used in determining the lawfulness of blockade measures have lost their validity. Blockades, in order to be binding, would still have to be understood in terms of a liability to seizure – not to destruction upon entrance into the forbidden area'.[237] His overall conclusion is summarized in these words:

> despite belligerent practices in two wars the establishment of war zones forms a lawful measure only when taken in response to the persistent misconduct of an enemy. Even then . . . the right to restrict the freedom of movement of neutral vessels implies the belligerent obligation to indicate certain routes by which neutral traffic may pass through the declared war zones with a reasonable assurance of safety.[238]

In his *Legal Controls of International Conflict,* Julius Stone stresses the need for any future legal regulation to take into consideration various operational factors, such as 'the aptness of submarines, aircraft and mines for destroying enemy commerce, their need for surprise and secrecy for effective and safe oper-

[237]TUCKER, R.W., *The Law of War and Neutrality at Sea*, USNWC, 50 *International Law Studies* (1955) at p. 317. Fully aware of the developments which have rendered the close-in blockade of the nineteenth century 'unduly restrictive or more accurately, almost impossible of application under modern conditions', he underlines, nonetheless, that 'while a legal analysis cannot be unmindful of current – and persistent – realities it cannot make so easy an identification of legal right with belligerent practices'; *ibid.* at p. 302.

[238]*Ibid.* at p. 305. In another passage, Tucker attaches much importance to the concept of defensive area or immediate area of naval operations, which, in contrast to that of war zones, he considers to be well-established and permissible; *ibid.* at p. 300. Hersch Lauterpacht, arguing for the main along the same lines as Tucker, sees no justification for a war zone other than the theory of belligerent reprisals; see LAUTERPACHT, H. (ed.), *Oppenheim's International Law,* 7th edn (1952), vol.II, pp. 683–4. Yet, his overall conclusion is couched in somewhat equivocal terms: 'thus viewed, measures regularly and uniformly repeated in successive wars in the form of reprisals and aiming at the economic isolation of the opposing belligerent must be regarded as a development of the latent principle of the law of blockade, namely that the belligerent who possesses the effective command of the sea is entitled to deprive his opponent of the use thereof for the purpose either of navigation by his own vessels or of conveying on neutral vessels such goods as are destined to or originate from him', *ibid.* at pp. 796–7.

ation, the importance in modern war of the industrial economy which such destruction undermines'.[239] His reflections stem from the conviction that war law should be 'law in action rather than on paper', and that international lawyers should face the 'bitter truth' abridged to the caption 'war law ... is no expression of sheer humanity, save as adjusted to the exigencies of military success'.[240]

Finally, for a certain number of scholars, the legality of war zones should be no doubt conditioned, but still addressed in terms of an irreversible reality. Georg Schwarzenberger, for instance, defends the thesis that international customary law has changed due to the 'twilight situation' created by the widely adopted practices during both World Wars. He identifies the causes that rendered such practices necessary as being the bankruptcy of the concept of neutrality and the extinction of genuine private trade, and argues that the only way to maintain the 'continuity between the law that was and such little law as, in future major wars, is likely to be observed in sea warfare' is to admit the idea of the emergence of a new customary rule endorsing the pattern of action followed in the two World Wars.[241]

[239]STONE, J., *Legal Controls of International Conflict*, 1959, pp. 574, 598–607.

[240]*Ibid.* at p. 606. With regard to economic blockade, he maintains that 'the adaptation of the law of blockade to present conditions is not likely to be attained by agreement. In such circumstances, the illicit escape from law via reprisals may well prove to be not only *pro tempore* but also *sine die*', *ibid.* at p. 602.

[241]SCHWARZENBERGER, G., *International Law as Applied by International Courts and Tribunals*, 1968 at p. 653. William Barnes, for his part, suggests that all enemy merchant marine should be considered as appertaining to naval auxiliaries liable to be attacked at sight while war zones should be legalized under two conditions, i.e. every attack should prove that it was really necessary and proportionate (no indiscriminate declaration of a war zone in areas where no feasible military objective might be gained), and second, it should be kept within reasonable limits. He further estimates that ample warning 'should suffice to warn the neutral of the consequences of disregard of a declared war zone', *ibid.* at p. 146. As for the London Protocol, he is 'of the opinion that the Protocol was a monument to naïveté', and interprets the Dönitz judgement as if 'the Tribunal's stand was also indicative of the fact that the London Protocol was dead as international law', *ibid.* at pp. 184, 187. For yet another writer, 'war zones directed against neutral shipping are illegal, but war zones established to limit the enemy in his movements may well be recognized as a legitimate exercise of belligerent rights'; see POWERS, R.D., 'International Law and Open-Ocean Mining', 15 *Judge Advocate General Journal* (1961) at p. 71. Finally, Charles Weiss, writing in 1967, was the first to suggest the adoption of a fixed limit of 200 n.m. the zone: 'within clearly announced and defined war zones, limited by a line extending 200 miles outside the coastline of an area where land

Doctrinal Discussion in the Last Decade In recent years, numerous have been the authors who voiced their support for the notion of war zones. William Fenrick's analysis proposes a number of emerging legal standards:

> if belligerents use exclusion zones, they should publicly declare the existence, location, and duration of the zones, what is excluded from the zone, and the sanctions likely to be imposed on ships or aircraft entering the zone without permission . . . As with blockades, 'paper' zones are insufficient. Belligerents declaring zones should deploy sufficient forces to the zone to make it 'effective' . . . There must be a proportional and demonstrable nexus between the zone and the self-defence requirements of the state establishing the zone . . . Finally, the purpose of the zone is particularly relevant. If the purpose of the zone is to limit a conflict to a confined geographic area, it is probable that it will be considered acceptable.[242]

Francis Russo deduces the international customary character of the war zones from the silence observed by the UN Security Council in its resolutions regarding the Gulf Tanker War.[243] Karl

---

hostilities are in progress, or 200 miles outside the coastline of any territory occupied by a belligerent state, all vessels belligerent or neutral, excepting clearly marked hospital ships and coastal fishing vessels, are subject to sinking upon sight'; see WEISS, C.J., 'Problems of Submarine Warfare under International Law', 22 *Intramural Law Review* (1967) at p. 149. His proposal was grounded on the idea that 'the new law must be realistic and not attempt to control conduct which cannot be controlled; it must not try to prohibit conduct in the context where the belligerent will be faced with the choice between a possible legal sanction and military defeat', *ibid.* at p. 148.

[242]See FENRICK, W.J., 'The Exclusion Zone Device in the Law of Naval Warfare', 24 *CYIL* (1986) at pp. 124–5. Fenrick readily admits how delicate these criteria might prove in practice. He suggests, for instance, that in principle 'all militarily practicable efforts should be made to employ minimum sanctions, such as seizure instead of attack on sight', conceding, nonetheless, that 'sometimes the minimum practicable sanction will be attack on sight', *ibid.* In his opinion, it would be always advisable to turn to reasonableness as the ultimate test of legitimacy, *ibid.* at p. 114. Even more open to discussion appears his argument in favour of a functional-oriented targeting theory. Subscribing to a large interpretation of the Dönitz judgement, and in the light of the Iraqi anti-shipping campaign in the Gulf, he expresses the view that 'neutral merchant ships incorporated into the enemy war effort can also be considered legitimate military objectives and, as such, acceptable targets in an exclusion zone', *ibid.* at p. 121.

[243]RUSSO, *op. cit., supra* n. 121 at p. 396. Similarly, see ROACH, J.A., 'Missiles on Target: The Law of Targeting and the Tanker War', 82 *Proc.ASIL* (1988) at p. 158, and LECKOW, *op. cit., supra* n. 121 at p. 644. This is believed to be a weak argument, for the Security Council was silent on so many aspects of the

Zemanek maintains that an international custom has been crystallized through 'constant practice by all parties involved', and advances two limitations for what he sees as a new belligerent right: the principle of necessity, and some unidentified 'belligerent duties towards the neutrals'. He further supports the view that 'the lawfulness of a war zone depends not on the declaring state's ability to enforce it by effectively blocking entry through surface warships but rather on the probability of danger through continuous combat action which may also be created by submarines or mine fields.'[244]

Several other scholars prefer to point out the practical utility of the concept. Vaughan Lowe, for instance, advocates the usefulness of the exclusion zone device, at least as it was employed in the Falklands context, and considers it a 'reasonable, prudent compromise' and an 'excellent example' of modernizing the laws of war.[245] Following the same train of thought, Louise

---

Iran-Iraq conflict. It is, of course, true that the protests of neutral flag states whose ships had been suffered from unprovoked attacks in the Persian Gulf have been rare and soft-toned. But, as one commentator argued, 'although the belligerents [Iran, Iraq] have not been subjected to the severe and hostile criticism that may have been expected, or that was the experience of the belligerents in World War I, the neutral states' muted outrage may not be due to their tacit acceptance of a new customary rule exposing them to random, raiding attacks. Rather, their relative silence may be attributed to the fact that the very large tanker surplus fleet (and threat of a oil surplus as well) and the favorable conditions of insurance in the 1980s rendered such attacks relatively less unacceptable to the tanker fleets' owners than did such attacks during the World Wars, when they resulted in a great scarcity both of shipping and of the cargoes those sunken ships had carried'; see GOLDIE, *op. cit., supra* n.9 at p. 176. Besides, as Anthony D'Amato has nicely put it in his *Concept of Custom in International Law*, states 'do not issue notes of protest to the actions of other states that they regard as illegal under international law . . . foreign offices which did so would have little time for anyting else'; quoted in GOLDIE, *op. cit., supra* n.9 at p. 180. In a more recent writing, however, Russo concedes that an exclusion zone 'fails to satisfy important humanitarian considerations because it neither conserves values, shortens the conflict, nor promotes target discrimination'; see RUSSO, F.V., 'Targeting Theory in the Law of Armed Conflict at Sea: The Merchant Vessel as Military Objective in the Tanker War' in DEKKER and POST, *op. cit., supra* n.121 at p. 176.

[244]ZEMANEK, K., 'War Zones' in Bernhardt, R. (ed.), *Encyclopedia of Public International Law*, instalment 4 (1982) at p. 338.

[245]LOWE, A.V., 'Some Legal Problems Arising from the Use of the Seas for Military Purposes', 10 *Marine Policy* (1986) at p. 184. See also BARSTON and BIRNIE, *op. cit., supra* n.89 at p. 24. Michael Reisman also considers the war zone device as 'a major contribution to humanitarian conflict, since it tends to localize the conflict by concentrating in one place, rather than spreading out'; see 14 *Syracuse Journal of International Law and Commerce* (1988) Special Issue, at p. 756.

Doswald-Beck argues for some degree of reasonableness (in the sense of restraint) in enforcing a war/exclusion zone. Commenting upon the Falklands TEZ, she finds that 'the fact that it was limited in area and far from major shipping routes meant that it seemed to be generally accepted by States as reasonable by way of military necessity.'[246] G.J.F. van Hegelsom, who prepared the introductory report for the Toulon session of the Round Table of Experts on International Humanitarian Law Applicable to Armed Conflicts at Sea, held in October 1990, attempted to elaborate a framework of legitimacy for exclusion zones and expressed the view that 'the zones envisaged might be the ultimate tool in enhancing the protection of innocent shipping. For this reason, the zones are to be given the benefit of the doubt in international law.'[247] Jane Gilliland urges the international codification of the use of exclusion zones as providing 'realistic and workable' solution to the long-standing impasses in the field of naval warfare and emphasizes their 'benefits and practical necessity'. Using a phraseology no less cryptic than that of the reasonableness standard, she argues for 'properly designed and controlled zones.'[248]

[246]DOSWALD-BECK, L., 'After the Submarine: The Need for a New Law of Naval Armed Conflict', 7 *It.YIL* (1986–7) at p. 267. It remains clear, however, that for her 'any move toward an attitude that one can attack without prior identification is totally impermissible'; see DOSWALD-BECK, L., 'The Principle of Humanity in the Law of the Sea Warfare: The Protection of Civilians and the Hors de Combat', 82 *Proc.ASIL* (1988) at p. 601.

[247]See VAN HEGELSOM, G.J.F., 'Methods and Means of Combat in Naval Warfare – Introductory Report' in VON HEINEGG, H.W. (ed.), *Methods and Means of Combat in Naval Warfare – Report and Commentaries of the Round-Table of Experts on International Humanitarian Law Applicable to Armed Conflicts at Sea*, 1992 at p. 52. See also his comments at the 1987 San Remo Round Table, 14 *Syracuse Journal of International Law and Commerce* (1988) at pp. 592, 752, 784. His propositions took shape in the following tentative conclusion: 'Maritime Operational Zones (MOZs) shall not unduly hamper the freedom of passage of ships and aircraft of States not party to the conflict. The purpose of the MOZs and the measures to be taken by belligerents shall be notified to States not party to the conflict. Opportunity shall be given to innocent ships and aircraft to leave the area. If practicable or practically possible, means of transit through the zone shall be provided. Compliance with the directives of belligerents shall not be considered tantamount to integration in the enemy's war effort'; see VON HEINEGG, *op. cit., supra* at p. 59. For favourable remarks thereupon, see W.J. Fenrick, *ibid.* at p. 78; D.Fleck, *ibid.* at p. 83; W.H. von Heinegg, *ibid.* at p. 107; S. Lyons, *ibid.* at p. 120; I.A. Shearer, *ibid.* at p. 128. *Contra*, see the remarks of O. Bring/M. Jacobsson/F. Rosenius, *ibid.* at p. 64; B. Godet, *ibid.* at pp. 88–89; C. Greenwood, *ibid.* at p. 102.

[248]GILLILAND, J., 'Submarines and Targets: Suggestions for New Codified Rules of Submarine Warfare', 73 *Georgetown Law Journal* (1985) at p. 1005. In Gilliland's

Finally, reference should be made to analysts like Daniel O'Connell who consider that, as far as pre-Charter law is concerned, the question of legality seems categorically settled since the Nuremberg trial of Admiral Dönitz regardless of the ongoing discussion on the utility of exclusion zones, but that in the current context: 'legal evaluation would need to proceed not from the concepts of reprisals or belligerency but from that of self-defence. Provided that publicity is given to the creation of an exclusion zone, and neutral shipping is not put unduly at risk, self-defence can conceivably justify a proclamation that contacts within a zone will be treated as hostile.'[249]

Confronted with the copious testimonies in favour of the war zone device, Maxwell Jenkins ranks among the very few who refuse to see any legality in establishing a war zone and enforcing it by indiscriminate attack inasmuch as:

> recognition of such a claim would entail the abandonment of all legal limitation on the conduct of war, as presumably within a legally recognized war zone, belligerents would have *carte blanche* to operate as they perceive necessary . . . mere notification of an intent to commit an illicit act at a certain place will not suffice to make the act legal.[250]

---

view, 'a method of warfare possible in practice but illegal at codified law, will be used but cannot be controlled. It is clearly better to attempt to codify the practice, and therefore to attempt to control it, than to leave protection of neutrals and belligerents alike to chance and the presumably honorable intentions of belligerents', *ibid.* See also REED, J.J., 'Damn the Torpedoes!: International Standards Regarding the Use of Automatic Submarine Mines', 8 *Fordham International Law Journal* (1984–5) at p. 315, and HARLOW, B.A., 'The Law of Neutrality at Sea for the 80's and Beyond', 3 *UCLA Pacific Basin Law Journal* (1984) at pp. 42, 49–50.

[249]O'CONNELL, D.P., *The International Law of the Sea*, 1984, vol.II at pp. 1110–11. Dieter Fleck, for his part, simply ascertains that contemporary practice 'did not provide convincing answers', and stresses the need for 'the development of detailed rules acceptable by all parties'; see FLECK, D., 'Rules of Engagement for Maritime Forces and the Limitation of the Use of Force under the United Nations Charter', 31 *GYIL* (1988), p. 182*ff.* Drawing mainly upon William Fenrick's analysis, he considers that the question of legality has to be addressed on a case-by-case basis, and that certain parameters such as the location, size or duration of the zone have to be assessed by reference to the principles of proportionality and necessity.

[250]JENKINS, *op. cit., supra* n.121 at p. 534. For another scholar, 'il faut d'abord réaffirmer que la création de telles zones a toujours été contestée par les neutres et qu'elles ne sauraient donc trouver une assise coutumière. En aucun cas, elles ne sauraient justifier la destruction d'un navire sans sommation et sans que des mesures soient prises pour mettre à l'abri l'équipage et les papiers de bord'; see TORRELLI, M., 'La neutralité en question', 96 *RGDIP* (1992) at p. 21.

For Frederick Goldie:

> a maritime exclusion zone which is only enforced sporadically or randomly merely by raiding tactics should not be seen as entitled to recognition as lawful under customary international law . . . [Thus] indiscriminate sinkings of merchant ships by the U-boat arm as the main means of pursuing a raiding logistical strategy cannot claim to fit under justifications which may uphold the legality of the persisting logistical strategies reflected in the Long Distance Blockades by, respectively, the Entente Powers (in World War I) and the United Nations (in World War II).[251]

In a similar vein, Natalino Ronzitti maintains that 'war zones enforced against neutrals . . . are to be regarded as unlawful even according to pre-Charter law', while with reference to the British total exclusion zone around the Falkland Islands he considers that 'the legality of the TEZ was questionable.'[252]

Summing Up As this overview has demonstrated, the doctrine is deeply divided over the question of the legality of declaring and enforcing a war zone. If required to make a quantitative estimation, one should not deny the fact that the writers casting a favourable eye on the concept of war zones outnumber the sceptical ones. There is a marked tendency, no doubt, to legalize the practice of declaring war zones voiced in several quarters and based on a variety of grounds. There is the view that such

[251]See GOLDIE, *op. cit., supra* n.9 at pp. 177–8.
[252]RONZITTI, N., 'The Crisis of the Traditional Law Regulating International Armed Conflicts at Sea and the Need for its Revision' in RONZITTI, N. (ed.), *The Law of Naval Warfare*, 1988 at pp. 10, 40. In his 1993 Hague course, Ronzitti reiterated this position: 'le *dictum* du Tribunal de Nuremberg est clair: ces zones sont illégales dans la mesure où elles concernent les Etats neutres. Le fait que le belligérant ait dû avoir recours à la théorie des représailles pour les justifier est une preuve ultérieure de leur illégalité.' To add: 'à notre avis, la legalité des zones de guerre ou des zones d'exclusion reste un problème de *lege ferenda*. Nous pouvons seulement dire que les exigences de la guerre poussent à une légalisation'; see RONZITTI, N., 'Le droit humanitaire applicable aux conflits armés en mer', 242 *RCADI* (1993) at pp. 100–1. See also GIOIA, A. and RONZITTI, N., 'The Law of Neutrality: Third States' Commercial Rights and Duties' in DEKKER and POST, *op. cit., supra* n.121 at p. 234. Likewise, Michael Bothe, defends the view that 'the practice in the Gulf War can not be alleged as being an accepted application of the very controversial notion of exclusion zones'; see BOTHE, M., 'Neutrality at Sea' in DEKKER and POST, *op. cit., supra* n.121 at p. 211.

practice has long since passed into international custom. It has also been held, more moderately, that although not having yet assumed a customary character, the war zone device would nevertheless sooner or later become admissible, inevitability stemming from irresistible developments in military technology. In a different proposition, some writers have suggested a relativistic approach, advocating an *ex post facto* assessment of the circumstances under which a war zone had been operated, so that its legal character is determined not through the application of a cut-and-dried rule, but rather through a process of weighing the controlling realities of a given conflict situation.

V On the elusive criterion of reasonableness

In what seems to be a fresh reinstatement of the McDougalian spirit, reasonableness is proposed as the preferable criterion to measure the legality of a war zone on a case by case basis. For the apostles of realism, it should be remembered, 'reasonableness is determined by the familiar process of balancing the utility of the conduct causing damage and the gravity of the harm to the injured party.'[253] Most of the scholars who have recently commented on the war zone device, in the light of the Falklands campaign and the 1980–8 Gulf War experiences, seem to follow with amazing consistency Myres McDougal's leitmotif. For William Fenrick, for instance, 'the legitimacy of the TEZ [around the Falkland Islands] must ultimately be determined on the basis of reasonableness.'[254] Ross Leckow reaches a similar conclusion saying that, 'it would appear that the use of war zones can be justified . . . only in limited circumstances where the dictates of reasonableness are respected.'[255] As for Francis Russo, all a war zone needs is to 'be implemented in a manner that is reasonable under the circumstances and satisfies established norms of the law of armed conflict proscribing indiscriminate attack.'[256] Hardly any effort has been made,

[253]McDOUGAL, M.S. and SCHLEI, N.A., 'The Hydrogen Bomb Tests in Perspective: Lawful Measures for Security', 64 *YLJ* (1955) at p. 691. See also McDOUGAL, M.S. and BURKE, W.T., *The Public Order of the Oceans*, 1962 at p. 48, ftn.125.
[254]FENRICK, *op. cit., supra* n.89 at p. 254.
[255]LECKOW, *op. cit., supra* n.121 at p. 644. Similarly, BOCZEK, *op. cit., supra* n.121 at p. 251.
[256]RUSSO, *op. cit., supra* n.121 at p. 396.

however, to elaborate on how this criterion of reasonableness should function in practice. At the most, the parameters of extent and duration have been recommended, without, of course, making the idea of reasonableness any less relativistic.

Reason in English Legal Theory Bearing the load of the Aristotelian concept of right reason,[257] and of Latin jurisprudence *(lex est aliquid rationis)*,[258] the idea of reasonableness was ceded a wide scope of application in English common law. As contrasted to 'closed' legal systems of the Romano-Germanic family, the English legal order is in a constant process of completion through the accretion of case-law.[259] What in the European continent was attained by legislation and enactment, the English tradition reserved primarily for reason and equity, or, to recall the Year Books of the seventeenth century, the common law has remained over the centuries the 'perfection of reason'. The preponderance of the element of reasonableness in the English legal theory explains itself by the fact that it preserves the core quality of this law of precedents which is, as Wolfgang Friedmann has put it, 'the elasticity resulting from this method of social experimenting, of trial and error'.[260] For yet another thinker: 'le droit anglais, dans sa conception originelle et pro-

[257]According to Aristotle, 'of political justice part is natural, that which everywhere has the same force and does not exist by peoples thinking this or that; legal, that which is originally indifferent, but when it has been laid down is not indifferent . . . the things which are just by virtue of convention and expediency are like measures: for wine and corn measures are not everywhere equal . . . similarly the things which are just not by nature but by human enactment are not everywhere the same . . . though there is but one which is everywhere by nature the best'; see *Nichomachean Ethics*, bk.v, ch.vii, 1134–5.

[258]Cicero in *De Republica* writes: 'there is in fact a true law namely right reason which is in accordance with nature, applies to all men and is unchangeable and eternal . . . it will not lay down one rule today at Rome and another at Athens, nor will it be one rule today and another tomorrow. But there will be one law eternal and unchangeable binding at all times and upon all peoples'; see *De Republica, De Officiis*, bk.iii, xxii. For a concise overview of the natural law theories flourished through the ages, see STONE, J., *The Province and Function of Law*, 1950, pp. 215–38. See also VEDROSS, A. and KOECK, H.F., 'Natural Law: The Tradition of Universal Reason and Authority' in MacDONALD, P.St.J. and JOHNSTON, D.M. (eds), *The Structure and Process of International Law: Essays in Legal Philosophy Doctrine and Theory*, 1983, pp. 17–50.

[259]For a discussion on the codificatory and the jurisprudential approaches in law-making, see SCHWARZ-LIEBERMANN von WAHLENDORF, H.A., 'Quelques réflexions sur l'affaire Case v. Code' in his book *Politique, Droit, Raison*, 1982, pp. 70–80, 81–99.

[260]FRIEDMANN, W., *Legal Theory*, 4th edn (1960) at pp. 485, 86.

fonde, est tout entier construit sur la notion de raison, sur la *reasonableness*, sur l'exigence d'être raisonable. L'invocation de la raison expérimentale, d'une raison qui est le fruit de l'expérience, de l'observation, qui compare les phénomènes et qui en tire des conclusions, est véritablement le *life blood*, la vie du droit anglais, de sa structuration, de sa construction'.[261]

The criterion of reasonableness suffers, however, from two blemishes, namely, an intrinsic ambiguity of its meaning, and an unmanageable subjectivism in its application; 's'essayer à donner un sens precis au mot raisonnable c'est vouloir compter ce qui n'est pas nombre et mesurer ce qui n'est pas espace',[262] 'certains pourraient bien se demander s'il y a chose plus deraisonnable que l'utilisation du terme raisonnable'.[263]

Reasonableness and International Law At a later stage, and always through the influence of jurists of a common law tradition, reasonableness sought a place in the law of nations. For John Westlake, to cite but one example, the two main sources of international law would be custom and reason.[264] As for the international jurisprudence, in the Oscar Chinn case, adjudicated by the PCIJ in 1934, Great Britain relied on the principle of reasonableness and argued:

[261]SCHWARZ-LIEBERMANN von WAHLENDORF, H.A., 'Les notions de *right reason* et de *reasonable man* en droit anglais', 23 *Archives de Philosophie du Droit* (1978) at p. 45. For similar reflections on the legal-philosophical affinities of the notion of reasonableness, see RECASÉNS SICHES, L., 'Equity and Logic of the Reasonable' in NEWMAN, R.A. (ed.), *Equity in the World's Legal Systems*, 1973, p. 411*ff*.; RECASÉNS-SICHES, L., 'La logique materielle du raisonnement juridique' in HUBIEN, H. (ed.), *Le raisonnement juridique – Actes du Congres de Bruxelles*, 1971, p. 129*ff*.; PERELMAN, C., 'The Rational and the Reasonable' in *The New Rhetoric and the Humanities*, 1979, p. 121*ff*.; PERELMAN, C., 'L'usage et l'abus des notions confuses', 21 *Logique et Analyse* (1978), p. 3*ff*.; FORIERS, P., 'Le raisonnement pratique: Le raisonnable et ses limites', 33 *Revue Internationale de Philosophie* (1979), p. 323*ff*.

[262]See *Altschuler vs. Coburn, Nebraska* case, quoted in TIXIER, G., 'La règle de reasonableness dans la jurisprudence Anglo-Américaine', 72 *Revue du Droit Public et de la Science Politique en France et à l'étranger* (1956) at p. 281.

[263]SCHWARZ-LIEBERMANN von WAHLENDORF, *op. cit., supra* n.259 at p. 70.

[264]WESTLAKE, J., *International Law*, vol.I, 2nd edn (1910) at pp. 15, 18. On Westlake's theory of sources of international law, see LAUTERPACHT, H., *International Law: Collected Papers*, vol.2 (1975), p. 393*ff*. 'La raison' – writes Alexander Pearce Higgins – 'avec Westlake, devient la norme, l'étalon, l'idéal. Ce n'est pas le vieux droit naturel, mais l'idée d'une approximation vers la justice'; HIGGINS, A.P., 'La contribution de quatre grands juristes britanniques au droit international', 40 *RCADI* (1932) at pp. 35–6.

> an action is permissible in many circumstances if it is *reasonably necessary* to achieve this or that end or to prevent this or that danger, but unlawful if it goes beyond what is reasonable for this purpose. This criterion of reasonableness plays a very large part in English municipal law, but is in no way peculiar to that law. It is to be found described by one term or another, I believe, in almost every system of municipal law and there are many cases where it applies in international law. (emphasis added)[265]

Today the notion of reasonableness is to be found in the form of various clauses in a considerable number of international documents. This has proved a convenient legislative technique for the purpose of sidestepping delicate issues in international negotiations. In the words of Jean Salmon, reasonableness remains a 'notion confuse par excellence . . . il n'en demeure pas moins que le caractère vague et confus de la notion de "raisonnable" rend ici la question d'autant plus aiguë et partant laisse une évidente latitude à l'interprète'.[266]

Reasonableness and the Law of the Sea The enigmatic notion of reasonableness was destined for a remarkable eminence in the maritime context. Insofar as the North American literature is concerned, Philip Jessup's work on maritime jurisdiction ranks among the first to have drawn upon the 'test of reasonableness' in assessing the permissibility of encroachments of national authority upon the high seas.[267] Beyond any shadow of doubt, however, the most vehement of all proponents of reasonableness remains Myres McDougal. His name has been inseparably connected with the US attempt to justify the vast warning zones precluding international use around the Bikini Atoll in the Pacific which were enacted temporarily for the needs of US

[265]Reply by Mr. Beckett, *PCIJ, Series C,* No.75 at p. 304.
[266]SALMON, J.J.A., 'Le concept de raisonnable en droit international public' in *Le droit international: unité et diversité – Mélanges Paul Reuter,* 1981 at pp. 449, 476.
[267]Jessup commented, in particular, on three types of action to which the test of reasonableness would seem applicable, namely, the seizure of foreign vessels within a customs zone adjacent to the territorial waters, the practice of establishing neutrality zones contiguous to the belt of the territorial sea in time of war, and the so-called right of hot pursuit; see JESSUP, P.C., *The Law of Territorial Waters and Maritime Jurisdiction,* 1927 at pp. 95, 105, 258.

testing of thermonuclear weapons.[268] McDougal's contention amounts to saying that 'for all types of controversies the one test that is invariably applied by decision-makers is that simple and ubiquitous, but indispensable, standard of what, considering all relevant policies and all variables in context, is reasonable as between the parties'.[269] The discussion over the legitimization of acts denying the essence of the freedom of the high seas inspired by McDougal's pattern of thinking was relayed by several writers throughout the 1950s and well into the 1960s.[270]

[268]The first US *Danger Zones* for nuclear bomb tests were established in July 1946 and extended over an area of approximately 150,000 square nautical miles. By the mid-1950s the warning areas encompassed no less than 400,000 square nautical miles of open sea. For the needs of the intercontinental ballistic missiles programme of the former Soviet Union safety areas as large as 200,000 square nautical miles were frequently designated in the central Pacific, while the first British H-bomb tests in the spring of 1957 occasioned the creation of a 700,000 square nautical miles warning zone. For an updated analysis of warning zones connected with missile or nuclear bomb testing and other military activities on the high seas, see VAN DYKE, J.M., 'Military Exclusion and Warning Zones on the High Seas', 15 *Marine Policy* (1991), p. 147*ff.*

[269]McDOUGAL and SCHLEI, *op. cit., supra* n.253 at p. 660. As indications of the reasonableness of the US claim, he suggests 'that it is for a purpose much honored in world prescription, that it asserts the least possible degree of authority necessary to the achievement of its purpose, that it is limited both in area and in duration to the minimum consistent with its purpose, that the area which it affects is of relatively slight importance to international trade and fishing, and that it is asserted in a context of crisis which makes its purpose of paramount importance to all who value a free world society', *ibid.* at p. 686. His idea of 'reasonable competence' is couched in terms clearly pointing at the concept of self-defence and state necessity; 'the claim of the United States is in substance a claim to prepare for self-defence . . . it is a claim to take certain *preparatory measures* under conditions . . . of *high necessity.* The conditions of this *grave necessity* and the absence of *reasonable alternatives* are familiar knowledge' (emphasis added), *ibid. Contra,* see MARGOLIS, E., 'The Hydrogen Bomb Experiments and International Law', 64 *YLJ* (1955), pp. 629–47, and VAN DYKE, *op. cit., supra* at p. 168. A few years later, McDougal entered upon the same question to note that 'this formulation does not mean that each state may itself unilaterally decide what is reasonable with respect to its exclusive claims and lawfully impose its decision upon the community. It is not the unilateral claim, but the acceptance by other states, even when manifested in reciprocal tolerances, which creates the expectations of uniformity and rightness in decision which we commonly call international law'; McDOUGAL, M.S. and BURKE, W.T., 'Crisis in the Law of the Sea: Community Perspectives Versus National Egoism', 67 *YLJ* (1958) at p. 565.

[270]GIDEL, G., 'Explosions nucléaires expérimentales et liberté de la haute mer' in *Problèmes fondamentaux du droit international – Mélanges Jean Spiropoulos,* 1957, pp. 173–205; BIERZANEK, R., 'La nature juridique de la haute mer', 65 *RGDIP* (1961), pp. 242–7; FISCHER, G., 'Droit international et expérimentation des armes

During the deliberations of the International Law Commission, which led to the adoption of the draft articles used as the basis of discussion in the 1958 Law of the Sea Conference, Jean-Pierre Adrien François, acting as the Special Rapporteur of the Commission on the subject of the regime of the high seas, sided with McDougal's viewpoint that 'what was most relevant in prior prescriptions from the regime of the high seas was simply the test of reasonableness',[271] and suggested the following statement of principle: 'the freedom of the high seas does not include the right to utilize the high seas in a manner which unreasonably prevents other states from enjoying that freedom. Scientific research and tests of new weapons on the high seas are only permitted subject to this qualification.'[272] After that statement, and the codification of the regime of the high seas that soon followed, we should speak of reasonableness as embodying an *idée fixe* of the international law of the sea.[273] As Daniel O'Connell has pertinently noted:

---

nucléaires', 2 *AFDI* (1956), pp. 309–19; ODA, S., 'The Hydrogen Bomb Tests and International Law', 53 *Die Friedens-Warte* (1956), pp. 126–35. Among the various rejoinders to McDougal's analytical model, see ANDERSON, S.V., 'A Critique of Professor McDougal's Doctrine of Interpretation by Major Purposes', 57 *AJIL* (1963), p. 378*ff.*; FREEMAN, A.V., 'Professor McDougal's Law and Minimum World Public Order', 58 *AJIL* (1964), pp. 711–16; FALK, R.A., 'International Legal Order: Alwyn V. Freeman vs. Myres S. McDougal', 59 *AJIL* (1965), pp. 66–71. In one of the most recent critiques it has been argued that 'the McDougal-Lasswell jurisprudence possesses an uncanny ability to justify in pseudo-legal terms whatever course of behavior the U.S. government deems expedient to its national self-interest under the particular historical conditions'; see BOYLE, F.A., *World Politics and International Law,* 1985 at p. 66. See also DORSEY, G.L., 'The McDougal-Lasswell Proposal to Build a World Public Order', 82 *AJIL* (1988), p. 41*ff.*

[271] *Ybk.ILC* (1956), vol.I, §35 at p. 11.

[272] *Doc.A/CN.4/97* in *Ybk.ILC* (1956), vol.II, §52 at p. 10. When discussing the exploitation rights over the continental shelf, the ILC members had been again facing the problem of best expressing the idea of reasonable use. Terms such as *unreasonable, substantial, d'une manière injustifiée, sensiblement, unfounded, unnecessary and exagerement* were all given consideration in prescribing the obligation not to interfere abusively with navigation or shipping; see *Ybk.ILC* (1953), vol.I, 201 mtg., p. 108*ff.* and 206 mtg., §§50, 53, 56 at pp. 141–2.

[273] The 1982 Law of the Sea Convention is replete with 'reasonable' clauses. Among the nearly 400-article-long text, one can find provisions for *reasonable safety zones* (60§4) or *safety zones of a reasonable breadth* (260), *unreasonable risk* (225) or *unreasonable threat* (226§1c), *reasonable regard* (147§1) and *reasonable manner* (236), *reasonable rules* (255) and *reasonable procedures* (226§1b), *reasonable measures* (79§2, 232) and *reasonable terms* (266§1), *reasonable period of time* (74§2, 83§2, 246§6,253§3, 298§1a), *reasonable time* (annex II, 8 – annex III, 9§1 – annex IX, 5§5) or *reasonable time-limit* (294§2), *equitable and reasonable conditions* (269b), *reasonable bond* (292§1) and *reasonable quantity* (annex III, 2§2), *reasonable oppor-*

> however plausible the concept of reasonable use may be, it is essentially relativistic and hence susceptible of subjective evaluation. From it diametrically opposite inferences can be drawn, as occurred in the case of the debate over nuclear testing at sea. The concept is, therefore, not capable of resolving specific questions: all that it is capable of is the exclusion of their automatic resolution according to rigid rules, and the requirement that resolution be based upon appraisal as distinct from mandate.[274]

During the Cuban missile crisis of 1962, reasonableness was brought once more to the forefront. United States President J.F. Kennedy, ordering on 23 October 1962, the interdiction of the delivery of offensive weapons to Cuba, authorized the Secretary of Defense to make designations 'within a reasonable distance of Cuba, of prohibited or restricted zones and of prescribed routes'.[275] In the heated intellectual debate ensuing the original *'quarantine'* operation against Cuba and concerning the legality of such an operation, reasonableness was commonly appealed to. Thomas Mallison states explicitly that 'it is rather the reasonableness of the claim and the consequent toleration of and acquiescence in it by other states which establishes its lawfulness'.[276] Brunson MacChesney sounds even more categorical: 'what seems factually reasonable is not to be deemed legally objectionable.'[277] Others interpreted the 1958 High Seas Convention as meaning that 'reasonableness of a particular use or uses

tunity (242§2) and *reasonable allowance* (annex III, 17§2c), *reasonable rates of interest* (annex III, 130) and *reasonably attributable revenues* (annex III, 13§§6g,n) as well as many others. On the interrelated concepts of 'reasonable use', 'due regard' and abuse of right in the modern law of the sea, see VAN DYKE, *op. cit., supra* n. 268, pp. 163–5.

[274]O'CONNELL, D.P., *The International Law of the Sea*, vol.I (1982) at p. 58. And yet, in a paper prepared for the Geneva Conference, the US delegation did not hesitate to qualify 'the reasonableness of the area or zone from the standpoint of size, duration, and location' as providing 'objective standards'; reprinted in WHITEMAN, M.M. (ed.), *Digest of International Law*, vol.4 (1965) at p. 550.

[275]WHITEMAN, *op.cit, supra* at p. 524.

[276]MALLISON, W.T., 'Limited Naval Blockade or Quarantine-Interdiction: National and Collective Defense Claims Valid Under International Law', 31 *Georgetown Law Journal* (1962) at p. 345.

[277]MacCHESNEY, B., 'Some Comments on the Quarantine of Cuba', 57 *AJIL* (1963) at p. 595. See also McDOUGAL, M.S., 'The Soviet-Cuban Quarantine and Self-Defense', 57 *AJIL* (1963) at pp. 602–3.

of the high seas is an essential element of the broader determination of permissibility.'[278]

As late as 1986, Judge Schwebel in his dissenting opinion in the Nicaragua case, was ready to argue that 'a belligerent is entitled, under international law, to take *reasonable* measures (*a fortiori* within the internal waters of the opposing belligerent) to restrict shipping, including third flag shipping, from using the ports of its opponent' (emphasis added).[279]

Of Reasonable Necessity There is an interesting correlation between the notions of reasonableness and State necessity. In fact, the inherent characteristics of pervasive ambiguity and capricious subjectivism become more patent in connection with the timidly re-emerging idea of state necessity, now featured as Article 33 of the ILC Draft Articles on State Responsibility. The ambiguity concerning this latter concept pertains to the idea of 'grave and imminent peril', or as one of the most critical voices raised against Article 33 has put it, 'les critères constitutifs de la notion demereunt vagues et imprecis. Tel est le cas de la notion d'intérêt essentiel à sauvegarder et plus encore celle de peril grave et imminent . . . L'intérêt essentiel de l'État victime et la pesée des intérêts en cause repose sur des jugements de valeur qui ne peuvent être apprécies objectivement et où les qualifications unilatérales subjectives et contradictoires s'affronteront nécessairement.'[280] The subjectivism concerns the process of pondering the 'essential interest' in jeopardy of one state against the 'subjective right' to be violated of another. The Commission has pointed out that 'the interest sacrificed on the altar of "necessity" must *obviously be less important* than the interest it is thereby sought to save',[281] but this prescription raises the

[278]CHRISTOL, C.Q. and DAVIS, C.R., 'Maritime Quarantine: The Naval Interdiction of Offensive Weapons and Associated Matériel to Cuba, 1962', 57 *AJIL* (1963) at pp. 539–40.
[279]*Military and Paramilitary Activities in and against Nicaragua (Nicaragua v. United States of America), Merits, Judgment, ICJ Rep. 1986*, §236 at p. 379.
[280]SALMON, J.J.A., 'Faut-il codifier l'état de nécessité en droit international?' in *Mélanges Manfred Lachs*, 1984 at p. 263. Although Roberto Ago devoted a lengthy part of his reports to trying to distinguish the concept of necessity from that of self-preservation and the theory of vital interests, it is difficult to see how these postulates can be meaningfully separated in practice; see *Ybk.ILC* (1980), vol.I, 1612 mtg., §§41–2 at p. 154, 1613 mtg., §§4–7 at pp. 155–6. See also *Doc.A/CN.4/318/ADD.5–7* in *Ybk.ILC* (1980), vol.II, part one, §§7–8 at pp. 16–17.
[281]*Ybk.ILC* (1980), vol.II, part two, §35 at p. 50.

objection whether each state should be allowed to pretend the judge *in rem suam*. In the words of Jean Salmon, 'le caractère flou et fuyant des critères se trouve en quelque sorte aggravé par l'absence en droit international d'un système de contrôle juridictionnel obligatoire de droit commun sur les qualifications unilatérales . . . dès lors les rapports de force domineront nécessairement la problématique du recours à l'exception de l'état de nécessité. On peut croire que la très grande majorité des États se trouveront par consequent du côté des victimes plutôt que du côté des bénéficiaires de la notion.'[282]

Necessity, as a study of the ILC debates reveals, is conceived not only as the *material condition* precluding the international responsibility of a state for an act in violation of standing rules, but also as an *indication of the measure* not to be exceeded in the exercise of such an exceptional power. Roberto Ago, speaking of the limits of the plea of necessity, has suggested that 'the state must not go beyond what was strictly necessary to safeguard that interest: any excess, either in proportion or in time, must be regarded as wrongful. As soon as such action was no longer "necessary" no excuse of necessity could justify it.'[283] Under this construction, therefore, necessity comes decisively close to reasonableness.[284]

Similarly, the notion of military necessity poses intricate legal questions as it may reflect at the same time the rationale lying

[282]SALMON, *op. cit., supra* n.280 at pp. 264–5. *Contra,* see BARBOZA, J., 'Necessity (Revisited) in International Law' in *Mélanges Manfred Lachs,* 1984, pp. 27–43. See also JAGOTA, S.P., 'State Responsibility: Circumstances Precluding Wrongfulness', 16 *NYIL* (1985), pp. 266–71, and RABY, J., 'The State of Necessity and the Use of Force to Protect Nationals', 26 *CYIL* (1988) at p. 261.

[283]*Ybk.ILC* (1980), vol.I, 1612 mtg., §44 at p. 154.

[284]What could be more illustrative of the kinship linking the two notions than the fact that, in the mind of one of the members of the ILC, Article 33 should be supplemented 'by introducing into the text a standard of reasonableness'; C.W. Pinto, in a somewhat curious proposal, suggested that, in order to mitigate the overt subjectivism Article 33 lays bare, the criterion of reasonableness could possibly bestow 'a minimum of objectivity' in the assessment of a situation of grave and imminent peril; see *Ybk.ILC* (1980), vol.I, 1618 mtg., §§4, 6 at p. 178. It is also worth mentioning at this juncture that Lord Stowell in two cases used the terms interchangeably. In the *Christiansberg* he referred to the act under consideration and estimated that if 'it was merely an act of necessity and if that is proved a clear necessity will be a sufficient justification for everything that is done fairly and reasonably under it'. While in the *Gratitudine* he held the view that 'necessity creates the law; it supersedes rules; and whatever is reasonable and just in such cases is likewise to be considered legal'; both cases are cited in WEIDEN, P., 'Necessity in International Law', 24 *GST* (1938) at pp. 119–20.

behind codified rules of the *jus in bello* and the legal exemption from observing those rules.[285] It should be noted, however, that in the view of the Commission, a state of necessity cannot serve under any pretext as an excuse for violations of peremptory legal norms. What is more, the fundamental tenets of humanitarian law were referred to as precluding the admissibility of the justification of necessity.[286] The firmness with which this latter point was emphasized time and again in the Commission's discussions makes it safe to argue that the principle of distinction or the principle of unnecessary suffering as prominent facets of the cornerstone principle of humanity could never be

[285]One notes the strained language of the ILC Report on this very point: 'the principal role of military necessity is not that of a circumstance exceptionally precluding the wrongfulness of an act which, in other circumstances, would not be in conformity with an obligation under international law. Military necessity appears in the first place as the underlying criterion for a whole series of substantive rules of the law of war and neutrality, namely those rules which, by derogation from the principles of the law of peace, confer on a belligerent state the legal faculty of resorting, against the enemy and against neutral states (and against their nationals), to actions which meet the needs of the conduct of hostilities. In relation to those rules, therefore, what is involved is certainly not the effect of necessity as a circumstance precluding the wrongfulness of conduct which the applicable rule does not prohibit but rather the effect of "non-necessity" as a circumstance precluding the lawfulness of conduct which that rule normally allows'; *Ybk.ILC* (1980), vol.II, part two, §27 at pp. 45–6. See also *Ybk.ILC* (1980), vol.II, part one, §49 at pp. 34–5. For the concept of military necessity as integral part of the positive laws of war, see DOWNEY, W.G., 'The Law of War and Military Necessity', 47 *AJIL* (1953), p. 251*ff.*; RAUCH, E., 'Le concept de nécessité militaire dans le droit de la guerre', 19 *Revue de Droit Pénal Militaire et de Droit de la Guerre* (1980), p. 205*ff.*; DINSTEIN, Y., 'Military Necessity' in BERNHARDT, R. (ed.), *Encyclopedia of Public International Law,* instalment 3 (1982), p. 274*ff.*

[286]See *Doc.A/35/10* in *Ybk.ILC* (1980), vol.II, part two, §28 at p. 46. The only concrete example, however, mentioned in the Report is the 'rule categorically condemning the killing of prisoners of war', *ibid.*, §37 at p. 50. See also *Doc.A/CN.4/318/ADD.5–7* in *Ybk.ILC* (1980), vol.II, part one, §54 at p. 37. Similar has been the reasoning with regard to lawful reprisals: 'even where the internationally wrongful act in question would justify a reaction involving the use of force, whatever the subject responsible for applying it, action taken in this guise certainly cannot include, for instance, a breach of obligations of international humanitarian law. Such a step could never be "legitimate" and such conduct would remain wrongful'; see *Ybk.ILC* (1979), vol.II, part two at p. 116. On the notion of belligerent reprisals under the Geneva Protocols, see HAMPSON, F.J., 'Belligerent Reprisals and the 1977 Protocols to the Geneva Conventions of 1949', 37 *ICLQ* (1988), p. 818*ff.*; KALSHOVEN, F., 'The Belligerent Reprisals in the Light of the 1977 Geneva Protocols', *European Seminar on Humanitarian Law,* Krakow, 1979, p. 31*ff.*; NAHLIK, S.E., 'Le problème des représailles à la lumière des travaux de la conférence diplomatique sur le droit humanitaire', 82 *RGDIP* (1978), p. 130*ff.*

disregarded in the name of an overwhelming necessity, however reasonable it may appear to its solicitors.

Final Thoughts If we now turn back to examine the soundness of the argument which makes the legality of a war zone conditional upon its conformity with the dictates of reasonableness, some aspects of the question may seem conclusively clear. First, the notion of reasonableness, no matter how deeply rooted in legal theory and jurisprudential legal systems, continues to embody something mentally unmastered or unseizable. Given the delphic nature of the notion of reasonableness, a host of grave illegalities could claim undeserved legitimacy in the name of cut-and-dried 'reasonableness'. More often than not, it would perform as a chimerical 'open sesame', conducive to confusion if not chaos. Nearly any imaginable practice could be cast, one way or the other, as a profile of reasonableness.[287] Second, the criterion of reasonableness pursues a meaningful function only when it comes to appraise the exercise of *existing* rights, of *established* powers protected by law, or, to draw upon Perelman's distilled scholarship; 'tout droit, tout pouvoir légalement protégé est accordé en vue d'une certaine finalité: le détenteur de ce droit a un pouvoir d'appréciation quant à la manière dont il l'exerce. Mais aucun droit ne peut s'exercer d'une facon déraisonnable car ce qui est déraisonnable n'est pas de droit.'[288] This is exactly where the main objection lies. How can one logically construe the establishment and enforcement of a war zone as involving a *'pouvoir légalement protégé'*? It would be difficult, indeed, to argue that a naval force can, *as a matter of right*, proscribe maritime and air traffic altogether within certain

[287]It suffices to cite one example in this connection. Thomas Mallison, in his contribution to the US Naval War College blue book series, clears the US submarine war zone established in the Second World War (which, it should be remembered, covered the whole Pacific ocean) with disarming effortlessness; 'considering the factual characteristics of the Pacific war, the area of the Pacific Ocean is not an unreasonable extent for the United States submarine operational area. It is therefore not persuasive to argue that the United States operational area is illegal because of its size'; MALLISON, *op. cit.*, *supra* n.236 at p. 88. Having determined so he proceeds to demonstrate the reasonableness of the German zones with even greater ease, in just a footnote; 'it is easier, *a fortiori*, to uphold the reasonableness of the geographic extent of the smaller German operational areas', *ibid.*

[288]PERELMAN, C., 'Le raisonnable et le déraisonnable en droit', 23 *Archives de Philosophie du Droit* (1978) at p. 42.

confines, give notice of this interdiction, and consequently enforce it by attacking and destroying arbitrarily any spotted target.

Perhaps the most pertinent conclusion one may draw is that the idea of reasonableness partakes primarily of the judicial operation of applying the law, and evaluating the degree of rationality, or moderation, with which competing rights are exercised. For Jean Salmon, 'la notion de raisonnable joue un rôle considérable dans le contrôle de l'exercise des droits, compétences ou pouvoirs. L'attribution de ceux-ci est non contestée, c'est leur exercise qui fait l'objet de controverse.'[289] In that perspective reasonableness offers the yardstick against which an *abus de droit* is to be measured; 'c'est en droit (law) que la distinction entre l'usage et l'abus, entre l'usage raisonnable et déraisonnable d'un droit (right), a été mise en évidence par la doctrine et la jurisprudence . . . tout usage déraisonnable d'un pouvoir discrétionnaire sera censuré comme abusif, et ceci dans toutes les branches du droit'.[290] Under certain circumstances reasonableness may be also the determinant consideration for a judicial body to affirm the emergence of a new legal right. Both propositions, however, should be read with caution. The *remedial* or *corrective,* as well as the *legislative* or *creative,* attributes of the notion of reasonableness should depend only on judicial assessment. These are prerogatives which should remain vested with competent judicial organs in order to secure flexibility in the administration of justice. Reasonableness is not a self-materializing concept. It presupposes an authoritative legal reasoning that breathes life into it, and gives a

[289]SALMON, *op. cit., supra* n.266 at p. 452. See also PERELMAN, *op. cit., supra* n.288 at p. 36.

[290]PERELMAN, *op. cit., supra* n.261 at p. 15. And elsewhere; 'every time any legal institution gives to an authority a certain power, even a discretionary power, it is presupposed that this power will not be exercised in an unreasonable manner. There are different ways to denominate this unreasonable exercise of power: you may call it abuse of law, excess or misapplication of power, bad faith, inequity, a ridiculous or arbitrary application of legal regulations, an act contrary to the general principles of law common to all civilized nations. Due process of law cannot permit the exercise of power in an arbitrary and unreasonable manner'; see PERELMAN, *op. cit., supra* n.261 at p. 121. The terms *abusif* and *déraisonnable* are commonly handled as synonymous; see POLITIS, N., 'Le problème des limitations de la souveraineté et la théorie de l'abus des droits dans les rapports internationaux', 6 *RCADI* (1925) at p. 95.

precise material sense in what would otherwise remain a legal chimera.[291]

Reasonableness is no panacea for the moot points of the international law regulating human conflict and use of force. Not only does it offer no concrete guidance whatsoever, but, owing to its open-endedness, it can be precariously deceptive. It can imply anything and nothing. International law chronically suffers from such lax notions, which, although heralding new possibilities for stagnant problems, have come ultimately to multiply the impasses. Employing nebulous concepts with the expectation of clarifying legal principles sounds paradoxical and is certainly not a very fertile exercise. To quote the late Professor Paul Reuter, 'le culte de l'ambivalence et de la contradiction ne prennent pas le praticien et l'homme d'État au dépourvu, mais embarrassent le pédagogue. L'esprit doit-il, une fois de plus, s'humilier et se persuader que c'est une loi générale de la vie de progresser à l'abri de l'ambiguïté?'[292]

VI Concluding remarks

One should feel a certain reticence about offering a single, perhaps oversimplified, aphorism regarding the legality or illegality of war zones. A considerable part of the doctrine sides with the view that 'a dogmatic statement that exclusion zones are legally acceptable or unacceptable would be inaccurate'.[293] True, who could venture to be dogmatic on a point on which law is rather a matter of guesswork?

To evaluate its present legal status one should commence by stating what is readily ascertainable; in the post-1945 era the world has experienced numerous international naval conflicts in most of which states declared and enforced blockade measures and war zones of varying extent, nature and scope. Only few writers have been quick to claim the emergence of an international custom based on those historical precedents. The view has not found many partisans owing to an insurmountable difficulty, that is to say, all one has is a set of very varied

[291]For similar reflections, see HENKIN, L., 'International Law: Politics, Values and Functions – General Course on Public international Law', 216 *RCADI* (1989) at pp. 293–8.

[292]REUTER, P., 'Quelques réflexions sur le vocabulaire du droit international' in *Mélanges Louis Trotabas*, 1970 at p. 434.

[293]FENRICK, *op. cit., supra* n.89 at p. 253.

practices, and at best scanty hints of an *opinio juris*. Besides, as has already been suggested, no custom could emanate from a practice which has been consistently justified purely on grounds of belligerent reprisals.

No Analogy with Classical Blockade Operations As far as the successive remodelling of the war zone device is concerned, it is crucial to dispel the misconception that war zones are nothing but modernized versions of the classical naval blockades. Blockade has been a traditional manifestation of naval power both as a belligerent and a peacetime measure. The aim in wartime conditions is to suspend all maritime communications to and from an enemy coast. Ships are offered the choice to keep clear, or to attempt surreptitiously to creep in the prohibited area, running, in this latter case, the risk of capture and having their cargoes confiscated.[294] In sharp contrast, exclusion zones represent the upshot of a new approach towards the exigencies of sea warfare, inspired by advanced weapon technology, according to which any craft detectable within the prohibited zone should bear full responsibility for being instantly fired upon and destroyed.

Those who view the new strategy as a long-term transformation of the dated law of blockade fail to appreciate the most central dimension of the problem. When speaking of a war zone, we do not refer to just another variety of the old action of blocking access to enemy coasts. We here speak of a notion which, in its fullest and militarily most effective form, 'licenses' the sinking of any target spotted on the radar screens within a

[294]On blockade in general, see FRAUNCES, M.G., 'The International Law of Blockade: New Guiding Principles in Contemporary State Practice', 101 *YLJ* (Jan.1992), p. 893*ff.*; JONES, T.D., 'The International Law of Maritime Blockade – A Measure of Naval Economic Interdiction', 26 *Howard Law Journal* (1983), p. 759*ff.*; LEINER, F.C., 'Maritime Security Zones: Prohibited Yet Perpetuated', 24 *VJIL* (1984), p. 967*ff.*; MALLISON, S.V. and MALLISON, W.T., 'A Survey of the International Law of Naval Blockade', 102 *USNIP* (Feb.1976), p. 44*ff.* Recent UN-authorized naval actions in the Persian Gulf and the Red Sea against Iraq, in the Adriatic against the Federal Republic of Yugoslavia (Serbia and Montenegro), and in the Caribbean against Haiti confirm that close-in blockades are still operationally feasible. For comments on those blockade operations as an atypical form of sanctions under chapter VII of the UN Charter in the post-Cold War era, see POLITAKIS, G.P., 'UN-Mandated Naval Operations and the Notion of Pacific Blockade: Comments on Some Recent Developments', 6 *RADIC* (1994), p. 173*ff.*, and *infra*, chapter 6, notes 52–69 and accompanying text.

predetermined distance. It qualitatively exceeds the broadest conceptions of traditional law and clearly oversteps the limits of legitimate analogies. The idea of gradual transformation, although arguably valid in relation to the concept of long-distance blockade, can hardly be applied to war zones. As long as indiscriminate attack and destruction makes no good substitute for capture, it is believed, the two concepts will remain irreconcilable. War zones venture into a legal vacuum and cannot borrow validity from concepts with which share no parity.

True Attributes, False Excuses Indiscriminate attack and destruction tend to become inherent in the *modus operandi* of establishing a war zone. In this sense, a war zone runs by definition contrary to the most elementary principle of distinction. Seen realistically, a war zone is nothing but a permission to sink whatever is floating (or overflying) once the minimum standard has been ascertained, i.e. that the spotted target does not belong to friendly forces.[295] Such an unqualified equation of what is targetable with what is a legitimate military objective represents certainly the epitaph of the principle of distinction. When it all comes down to such oversimplified courses of action, totally relieved from legal constraints, to wave the neutrality banner seems in vain, a pointless cacophony in an era of dominant lawlessness.

It has sometimes been argued that, to the extent a war zone contributes to the localization of the conflict, it may serve humanitarian values. The observation, however, lacks contact

[295]When all is said and done, one gets the impression once again old wine is served in new bottles. The Germans during both World Wars claimed dire necessity in order to use the most effective of their weapons, notably the submarine, against the Allied hunger blockade. In the event, in view of the extreme vulnerability of the submarine when exposed on the surface, they found it necessary to declare the waters around the British Isles as barred zones reserving the right to sink at sight. The United States, on the other hand, dispatched a naval task force in the Persian Gulf and found it equally necessary due to the missile threat and the vulnerability of surface vessels to declare a 5-nautical-mile defensive bubble around their units. In the former case vessels should bear full responsibility for entering the prohibited zone even if they were unarmed neutral passenger liners. In the latter case aircraft should run the risk of being locked on by a missile fire control radar if they failed to respond to challenges by US warships even if they were civil airliners which – by construction – are not so equipped as to receive messages on military frequencies. The German zone as it turned out associated itself with the *Lusitania* disaster. The US defensive zone in the Gulf led to the Iranian Airbus tragedy.

with reality and recent historical experience. A war zone from the time of its proclamation conveys two inseparable elements, namely, the seeds of *retaliation* and *expansion*. It triggers a spiral of escalation which inevitably leads to an uncontrollable enlargement of the exclusion area. Containment of the ambit of armed conflict effectuated through enforcing a war zone is as yet unheard of.

The outlook defended in the preceding pages could be summarized then as follows: unless one is ready to sidestep entire chapters of the classical *jus in bello*, unless one attaches no significance to the distinction between merchant marine and naval forces, or, unless one envisages the notion of neutrality as *de facto* abolished, the concept of war zones should remain well outside the bounds of legality.

The Subterfuge of Reasonableness As a last-ditch defence then, several jurists boarded the apocryphal idea of *reasonableness*, arguing that, in the absence of concrete legal criteria, a war zone should ultimately be judged on the merits of its compliance with the 'dictates of reasonableness'. Although this eclectic approach making the legality of a war zone dependent on the singular circumstance of a specific situation seems at first glance to evade a cut-and-dried answer, there are good reasons to suspect that, after all, it is an approval of the legitimacy of war zones in disguise; this is so for the simple reason that among the many aspects and peculiarities of a conflict there will always be some which could eventually afford the mask of reasonableness and absolute necessity. In the end, it all comes down to a question of the subjective weighing of considerable in number, controversial in nature, and constantly changing circumstances.

It remains highly doubtful whether, in international law and *a fortiori* in the perplexing domain of the laws of armed conflict, reasonableness can be of any determinant value.[296] Everyone can easily realize the practical consequences of an unconditioned transfusion of such a 'test' into the international laws of war; everything would become permissible in the light of a self-proclaimed, irresistible, but still reasonable necessity. What remains for law so construed then, if not to eulogize unhesi-

[296]See the accurate remarks of NELSON, L.D.M., 'Certain Aspects of the Legal Regime of the High Seas' in *Mélanges Shabtai Rosenne*, 1989, p. 525*ff.*

tantly the untamed necessities of a conflict, or, as Westlake put it, 'law reduced from a controlling to a registering agency'?[297] After all, as Smith wrote in 1938, that 'nobody never knew what was the real content of the laws of war at sea'[298] may well have been a perfectly deliberate and cautiously preserved policy goal.

Another vexing feature is that the pseudo-criterion of reasonableness implies a necessarily *ex post facto* assessment, or better, an *ex post bello* estimation of the merits of wartime practices. The laws of war, no less than any piece of legal prescription in their proper function, should give guidance, setting *ex ante* the limits of tolerable violence between belligerents, so that the question of the legality of a certain method of warfare does not remain idly pending until long after the conclusion of the hostilities, when an answer, if at all achievable, may well be irrelevant or academic.[299] Reasonableness is too blurred a concept and too weak an argument to suffice to overrule time-sanctioned principles of *jus in bello*.

The Charter Dimension Finally, a few thoughts on the continuing

[297]WESTLAKE, *op. cit.*, *supra* n.264 at p. 318; 'but the office of jural law is not to register and consecrate the effects of the laws of nature, but to control them by the introduction of the principle of justice, where an unreflecting submission to the tendencies which in their untamed state they promote would be destructive of society'.

[298]SMITH, H.A., 'Le développement moderne des lois de la guerre maritime', 63 *RCADI* (1938) at p. 607.

[299]One may refer in this connection to Myres McDougal's vision of the function of the laws of war which runs somewhat differently: 'the realistic function of those rules considered as a whole, is, accordingly, not mechanically to dictate specific decision but to guide the attention of decision-makers to significant variable factors in typical recurring contexts of decision, to serve as summary indices to relevant crystallized community expectations and, hence, to permit creative and adaptive, instead of arbitrary and irrational decisions'; McDOUGAL, M.S. and FELICIANO, F.P., 'International Coercion and World Public Order: The General Principles of the Laws of War', 67 *YLJ* (1958) at p. 815. And elsewhere: 'if by law one means to make any operational reference to probable or realistically expected decision, the continued characterization by some commentators of certain pre-1914 prescriptions as law, despite their practically universal nonobservance in two World Wars, may at best be harmless nostalgia'; *ibid.* at p. 811. Yet others oppose such reasoning and argue: 'the traditional view follows the principle of the excluded middle. It argues the law either permits a given action or it does not; there are no gaps in the law wherein the same action is at once allowed and prohibited; even if sparse, the law is a seamless web. As part of a legal system, each rule cannot be met by an equal and opposite rule; exceptions may modify but may not neatly cancel rules'; ANDERSON, *op. cit.*, *supra* n.270 at p. 379.

validity of some core principles of the laws of war, and on the relevance of the Charter law dictates, will conclude this chapter. The principle of distinction, as a mirror image of the cardinal principle of humanity, has always been the vital spark of humanitarian law; can we truly speak of humanitarian law in the absence of imperative considerations of humanity?[300] The concept of war zone for its part, if legitimized, would cause an atrophy, a withering of the principle of distinction and consequently a shrinking of the primordial role of the principle of humanity, or a change in the very physiognomy of humanitarian law. There is no cogent reason, therefore, why the various inroads on these principles in recent history should be elevated to the heights of a rising normativity. The principle of distinction, although severely dimmed in modern practice,[301] has been laboriously refined as recently as 1977 during the Conference on the Reaffirmation and Development of International Humanitarian Law and inspired several articles of the First Additional Protocol.[302] Moreover the need to respect at all times the distinc-

[300]In the words of one of the leading authorities in the field, 'today we talk of the international humanitarian law of armed conflict to indicate that the principle of humanity dominates the modern law of war, humanitarianism in warfare is no longer an ideal exclusive to the Red Cross movement'; DRAPER, G.I.A.D., 'Humanitarianism in the Modern Law of Armed Conflicts' in MEYER, M.A. (ed.), *Armed Conflict and the New Laws: Aspects of the 1977 Geneva Protocols and the 1981 Weapons Convention*, 1989 at p. 4.

[301]See the gloomy remarks by NURICK, L., 'The Distinction Between Combatant and Noncombatant in the Law of War', 39 *AJIL* (1945), pp. 680–97; BEST, G., *Humanity in Warfare*, 1980, pp. 244–62, and HOWARD, M., 'Temperamenta Belli: Can War Be Controlled?' in HOWARD, M. (ed.), *Restraints on War*, 1979, pp. 1–15; LAUTERPACHT, H., 'The Problem of the Revision of the Law of War', 29 *BYIL* (1952), p. 364*ff*. Charles Fenwick in his passionate comments on the subject had this to say: 'the old distinction between combatants and noncombatants is gone. The sooner every man, woman and child old enough to think realizes that he will be a party to the next war, the better. There is no practical distinction today between noncombatants. They must all take to the dug-out, hoping the bomb won't blow up the dug-out. Let's face the facts. War has got beyond the control of law, other than the elementary law of humanity, if that can be discovered among the ruins of devastated cities', 43 *Proc.ASIL* (1949) at p. 110.

[302]See Articles 35§§1,2, 48, 49§3, 50, 51§§2,4–6,8, 52§1, 57, 58. For commentaries, see ROSENBLAD, E., *International Humanitarian Law of Armed Conflict – Some Aspects of the Principle of Distinction and Related Problems*, 1979; BLIX, H., 'Means and Methods of Combat' in *International Dimensions of Humanitarian Law*, 1988, pp. 135–51; BRETTON, P., 'Le problème des méthodes et moyens de guerre ou de combat dans les protocoles additionnels aux conventions de Genève du 12 août 1949', 82 *RGDIP* (1978), pp. 32–81; CASSESE, A., 'Means of Warfare: The Traditional and the New Law' in CASSESE, A. (ed.), *The New Humanitarian Law of Armed Conflict*, 1979, pp. 161–98; DRAPER, G.I.A.D., 'Indiscriminate Attack' in BERNHARDT, R. (ed.), *Encyclopedia of Public International Law*, instalment 3

tion between combatants and non-combatants or between military and civilian objectives has motivated a number of judicial decisions.[303]

The UN Charter was meant to yield a fresh reading of the problems of use of force between states, to set up an as yet unrehearsed prototype in peaceful coexistence.[304] For those, however, who refused to wish the past goodbye, the old doctrines could and still had to be retailored and squeezed into the new scheme of international organization, or, to put it plainly, Article 51 had to be stretched and refashioned. The upshot of such exercise was all the *lusi naturae* which came to carry the names of pre-emptive self-defence, humanitarian intervention, reprisals in self-defence and others. The stereotyped addendum to all these law acrobatics was an idoloclastic reference to realism as the imposing rationale.[305]

(1982), p. 219*ff.* See also SAUNIER, P., 'Les règles fondamentales sur l'usage de méthodes et moyens de combat et les règles du Protocole I de 1977 sur les dommages excessifs causés aux civils' in KALSHOVEN, F. and SANDOZ, Y. (eds), *Implementation of International Humanitarian Law,* 1989, pp. 359–73; WEI, S., 'The Application of Rules Protecting Combatants and Civilians Against the Effects of the Employment of Certain Means and Methods of Warfare', *ibid.,* pp. 375–93; DOSWALD-BECK, L., 'The Civilian in the Crossfire', 24 *Journal of Peace Research* (1987), pp. 251–62; HAMPSON, F., 'Winning by the Rules: Law and Warfare in the 1980s', 11 *Third World Quarterly* (1989), p. 31*ff.*

[303]See BLISHCHENKO, I.P., 'Judicial Decisions as a Source of International Humanitarian Law' in CASSESE, A. (ed.), *The New Humanitarian Law of Armed Conflict,* 1979, pp. 41–51.

[304]On the implications of the UN Charter upon the right to resort to armed force, see FLECK, *op. cit., supra* n.249, pp. 165–86. See also GREENWOOD, C., 'The Concept of War in Modern International Law', 36 *ICLQ* (1987), pp. 283–306.

[305]Note, for example, how identical the argumentation read apropos the Cuban quarantine operation. Christol and Davis invoke a 'realistic interpretation of Article 51 of the U.N. Charter which takes into account the tempo and scientific capabilities of the atomic-space age'; CHRISTOL and DAVIS *op. cit., supra* n.278 at p. 543. For MacChesney 'realism, common sense and the destructive nature of modern weapons demand the retention of this customary right [Article 51] under adequate safeguards'; MacCHESNEY, *op. cit., supra* n.277 at p. 595. Among the opponents of the concept of anticipatory self-defence, see WEHBERG, H., 'L'interdiction du recours àla force. Le principe et les problèmes qui se posent', 78 *RCADI* (1951), pp. 71, 81; HENKIN, L., 'Force, Intervention and Neutrality in Contemporary International Law', 57 *Proc.ASIL* (1963), pp. 150–52; JIMÉNEZ DE ARÉCHAGA, E., 'International Law in the Past Third of a Century', 159 *RCADI* (1978), pp. 95–8; DINSTEIN, Y., *War, Aggression and Self-Defense,* 1988, pp. 174–6. *Contra,* see SCHWEBEL, S.M., 'Aggression, Intervention and Self-Defence in Modern International Law', 136 *RCADI* (1972). Regrettably enough, the International Court of Justice in the latest offered occasion to pronounce on the moot questions of the use of force, reserved judgement on the lawfulness of anticipatory self-defence; see *ICJ Rep. 1986,* §194 at p. 103.

Unless the Charter law is to be read as something more than analects of pious euphemisms and empty promises, it can offer no legitimacy to practices demonstrably unlawful, even under the pre-Charter international legal prescriptions. It would be absurd, to say the least, if the unrestricted, indiscriminate destruction at sea connected with the practice of war zones (which was censured as an act of piracy under the 1922 Washington Treaty and the 1937 Nyon Agreement, and which was treated as a convictable war crime by the Nuremberg Tribunal) came to receive even the dimmest hint of acceptability under a 'realistic' interpretation of the right of self-defence as codified in the UN Charter.

ήπερ ισχυομεν, ταις ναυσί αμύνεσθαι. πλέον γάρ όμως ημείς έχομεν
τού κατά γήν εκ τού ναυτικού εμπειρίας ή κείνοι εκ τού κατ'
ήπειρον ες τα ναυτικά... το δε ναυτικόν τέχνης εστίν, ώσπερ και άλλο
τι, και ούκ ενδέχεται, όταν τύχη, εκ παρέργου μελετάσθαι, αλλά
μάλλον μηδέν εκείνω πάρεργον άλλο γίγνεσθαι.

Our strength lies with our fleet. For we have gained more experience of operations on land from our career on the sea than they of naval operations from their career on land... Seamanship, like any other skill, is a matter of art, and practice in it may not be left to odd times, as a by-work; on the contrary, no other pursuit may be carried on as a by-work to it

Thucydides, *The Peloponnesian War*, bk.I, sect.CXLII
(transl. by C.F. Smith, The Loeb Classical Library, 1962 at p. 247)

Chapter Two

LEGAL ASPECTS OF MINE WARFARE

I Introduction

Damn the torpedoes! Full speed ahead! – yelled out Admiral Farragut at the sight of a group of mines barring his ship's course through the Mobile Bay, and his words have ever since resounded as an apt expression of the peculiar sentiments of alarm, fright, impotence and anger that the detection of naval mines has always aroused to seamen. The fascinating stories of mine blasts in the American Civil War are now more than a century old, yet the questions surrounding mine tactics have not found even today their proper military, far less their legal answers.[1]

The view has often been expresed that 'la mine sous-marine est sans conteste l'arme la plus perfide et la plus odieuse qui ait jamais été inventée par l'homme pour rendre les mers infréquentables',[2] but still no diplomatic eloquence ever came

[1]Among the most influential works, see LEVIE, H.S., *Mine Warfare at Sea*, 1992; Id., 'Mine Warfare and International Law', USNWC, 62 *International Law Studies* (1980), p. 271*ff.*; VON HEINEGG, W.H., 'The International Law of Mine Warfare at Sea', 23 *IYHR* (1993), p. 53*ff.*; DIMITROV, G., 'Possible New Restrictions on the Use of Naval Mines' in GOLDBLAT, J. (ed.), *Maritime Security: The Building of Confidence*, UNIDIR 1992, p. 79*ff.*; GRIFFITHS, M., *The Hidden Menace*, 1981; COWIE, J.S., *Mines, Minelayers and Minelaying*, 1949; BRASSEUR, P., *La guerre de mines*, 1939; REED, J.J., 'Damn the Torpedoes!: International Standards Regarding the Use of Automatic Submarine Mines', 8 *Fordham International Law Journal* (1984–5), p. 286*ff.*; THORPE, A.G.Y., 'Mine Warfare at Sea – Some Legal Aspects of the Future', 18 *ODIL* (1987), p. 255*ff.*; HOFFMANN, R.F., 'Offensive Mine Warfare: A Forgotten Strategy?', 103 *USNIP* (May 1977), p. 142*ff.*; MEACHAM, J.A., 'Four Mining Campaigns: An Historical Analysis of the Decisions of the Commanders', 19 *US Naval War College Review* (June 1967), no.10, p. 75*ff.*; HAMPSHIRE, A.C., *On Hazardous Service*, 1974; MELIA, T.M., *Damn the Torpedoes: A Short History of US Naval Mine Countermeasures, 1775–1991*, 1992.
[2]GENET, R., *Précis de droit maritime pour le temps de guerre*, tome I (1937) at p. 135.

close to pleading for its total ban. Military pragmatism made out of the mine asset a strategy far too inalienable for legal sensibilities to prime. In fact, the earlier the mine's efficacy was battle-proven, the fainter grew the chances for an agreed framework of restraint. As Rolin-Jaequemyns wrote in 1878:

> d'ailleurs, il n'est probablement pas un État maritime qui ne se soit déjà mis en mesure d'employer les torpilles en cas de guerre. Dans ces conditions, il semble difficile d'en proscrire absolument l'emploi . . . Peut-être pourrait-on trouver un élément de solution rationnelle dans une distinction entre l'emploi des torpilles comme moyen de défense des ports, des côtes ou de l'entrée des fleuves, et leur emploi en pleine mer. Le premier usage serait licite, le second prohibé.[3]

The Hidden Menace: Low Cost, High Reliability A sea mine is essentially an explosive charge, weighing up to 2,400 kg contained in a shell and laid underwater with the object of surprising and destroying enemy shipping. The naval mine, much like the self-propelling torpedo or the air-delivered bomb, revolutionized the art of sea warfare by adding a crucial vertical dimension to the theatre of naval operations.[4] Ever since underwater explosives scored their first success in battle during the 1854–6 Crimean War, man has not ceased to explore the military use of sea depths. To date, naval mines have missed no opportunity to demonstrate their continued excellence in spreading sudden destruction and unmanageable hardship to seamen in defiance of all considerations of enemy superiority, technological or other.

Of all the characteristics which make of mine warfare a rewarding strategy, none is more conspicuous than its cost-effectiveness. One of these large piked iron spheres sufficed to

[3]ROLIN-JAEQUEMYNS, G., 'Chronique du droit international – L'année 1877 et les débuts de 1878, au point de vue du droit international', 10 *RDILC* (1878) at p. 27.

[4]Mines and torpedoes were both developed to answer the age-old puzzle of how to hit a ship in its most vulnerable part, that is below the water line. Underwater sabotage originates in ancient times. In the battle of Artemisium in 480 B.C., for instance, Scyllis cut the anchor cables of several Persian ships which wrecked themselves on the rocky coast, while Phoenician divers cut the cables of Alexander the Great's fleet in 333 B.C. off Tyre. As for the Greek fire, a highly inflammable mixture of sulphur, naptha and nitre was invented by Callinicus of Heliopolis in A.D. 668.

sink the 11,000-ton *Petropavlosk*, Admiral Makaroff's flagship in the 1904–5 Russo-Japanese War, while similar terrific blasts sent down another sixteen of their floating fortresses. Likewise, in 1915, twenty-odd mines blew up in just one day two British and one French heavy battleships while attempting to force their passage through the Dardanelles. During the Second World War, one ship was sunk for every thirty or so mines laid. While in February 1991, a batch of musty contact mines of pre-1914 design, laid by the Iraqis off occupied Kuwait, were enough to cripple two multi-million dollar US Navy warships in the course of Operation Desert Storm. In fact, the last three US Navy ships to sustain combat damage were victims of mines.[5]

Beyond and above its military impact, however, in terms of actual sinkings, sea mining has the rather unique faculty to produce a profound psychological effect. As mine traps are laid furtively and remain invisible, the assumed degree of risk is, almost invariably, considerably greater than the real threat.[6] The

[5]Today, as many as 43 countries are believed to stock naval mines of an estimated total of several hundreds of thousands. Only the former Soviet Navy is known to have a mine stock somewhere between 250,000 and 400,000 mines. Advances in technology have now carried sea mining much farther than relying on physical contact by surface ships to initiate detonation. Modern mines, generically dubbed as *influence mines*, are able to detect a signature (acoustic, pressure or magnetic), emanating from the target vessel. Besides, multi-influence mines are fitted to be responsive to two or all three of these complementary functions. Present-day mine warfare has also progressed in mobility. Most often laid in ground containers, modern mines can either be released by sensing an approaching target (rising mine), or guided toward their victims by seabed launchers (rocket mine), or self-propelled (torpedo mine). Some sub-delivered mines can also transit (under direction from the submarine) up to 20 miles before reaching their pre-determined waiting position. Housing ultra-sophisticated signal and data processing equipment, mines have grown 'intelligent' enough to reject simulated ship signatures and can be adapted as against a certain category of ships. Moreover, they can count targets so that a number are allowed to pass before the charge is detonated, or switch off in periods of inactivity. Disguised and buried mines have also been developed so that mine-hunting techniques become less efficient. Wartime mining calls, of course, for careful planning at peacetime, and especially for monitoring of shipping traffic in strategic approaches or through choke points. Modern assessment mines, in essence underwater electronic devices not containing explosive charges, facilitate this task by scanning sea lanes and recording signatures and operating patterns of various possible target vessels.

[6]In the words of some experts, 'the real effect of a minefield derives from the more subtle influence of an exaggerated fear. Minefields work more on the mind than on ships . . . Mines are weapons of calm and persuasive reason, exerting their primary inducements through psychological deterrence rather than by physical destruction'; see GREER, W.L. and BARTHOLOMEW, J., 'The Psychology of Mine Warfare', 112 *USNIP* (Feb.1986) at pp. 60, 62.

most significant aspect of minelaying is precisely these intangible or unquantifiable consequences that the mine's mere presence generates, for it is practically impossible to evaluate in concrete terms factors such as the cargo flow interruption, the losses by diversion of traffic, the costs of overestimated mobilization and mine clearance effort, or the demoralization of crews.[7]

To draw from recent events, in 1987, a handful of Iranian drifting mines had hardly been spotted in the Gulf, when the alarm signal was given and began puzzling great many governments around the world. In hindsight, the hurried deployment of naval forces inside the Persian Gulf was disproportionate to the real risk, and in any event beyond compare with the rather passive reaction to the far more numerous and destructive missile attacks on merchant shipping which had been going on for years. On yet another occasion, the scanty Iraqi minefields off Kuwait beaches, as it was later admitted, were adequate deterrent to frustrate all plans of an amphibious assault on the part of the coalition forces during the 1991 Gulf War.

As yet, no effective remedy has been found for the mine threat, mineclearing becoming an extremely demanding and often hopeless exercise as the description 'unsweepable mine' clearly implies.[8] Perhaps it is precisely because of the naval

[7]These distinct attributes of mine warfare are finely examined in PATTERSON, A., 'Mining: A Naval Strategy', 23 *US Naval War College Review* (May 1971), p. 61*ff*. Moreover, the mine weapon possesses several other qualities. As said before, mines can be engineered to be selective, for instance, as against a specific type or size of target, they do not require continued commitment of forces, and they can also be activated or disactivated at will. On the other hand, they can never create a 100 per cent threat but they can only hope for a high attrition rate. What is more, despite the increasing intelligence stuffed into them, mines cannot react. Although receptive of 'clever' programming, they remain stationary. As much as they wait for their unsuspected victims, they wait also to be swept.

[8]The unremitting effort to develop reliable minesweeping and minehunting techniques, commonly known as mine countermeasures (MCM), proves the extreme complexity of the mine threat in the modern naval combat environment. *Minesweeping* refers to the practice of mine clearance without having located the mines first. Mechanical sweeping, for instance, involves towing a wire sweep that catches moored mines and disposes of them by detonating their charges or by cutting their cables so that they rise to the surface, where they can be destroyed by rifle fire. Influence sweeping is used against mines with magnetic, acoustic or pressure fusing, and requires a towed device that radiates the appropriate signature. *Minehunting*, on the other hand, is the method of finding and recognizing mines by means of sonars so that they can be later disposed of by divers or underwater remotely operated vehicles (ROVs). Apart from typical 'hull-mounted' sonars, towed 'variable depth' sonars are now available for

mine's early felt staggering efficacy that the consideration of its legal specifities has always been given skin-deep attention at best.[9] Mine warfare continues to concretize the harsh reality – that remarkably effective military discoveries can mostly be put to use unaffected by humanitarian concerns. The only legal regulations ever adopted were drafted in equivocal terms, to be interpreted at will, and honoured in disrespect. Throughout the present century matters remained practically stagnant with the exception of the reaffirmation on two occasions of the customary obligation of notification – a rather illusory or euphemistic mechanism of legal control. Indicative of the chronic impotence in the face of the mine challenge, courageous proposals cannot surface even among academics, as the unwillingness of the drafters of the 1994 *San Remo Manual* to forbid the use of free-floating mines amply attests.

II The mine strategy in historical perspective

1 From the Battle of the Kegs to the Port Arthur catastrophe

The Early Days of Underwater Destruction It is customary to trace the origins of the mine weapon as far back as 1585 when the Dutch resisted the siege of Antwerp by sending small boats loaded with gunpowder against large Spanish vessels to be detonated by clock-operated flintlocks. The English made use of similar floating petards in 1628 off La Rochelle with no luck. There is some historical incorrectness, however, in relating both those precedents to the evolution of mining, since no under-

---

minehunting in deeper waters while in the wake of the Persian Gulf mining of the late 1980s, industries are experimenting with laser-radar mine-detection systems. As for the remotely operated vehicles they are increasingly used to identify and destroy ground mines. Equipped with television cameras, sonars and precise propulsion systems, they can approach and position their mine disposal charge (MDC) beside a spotted mine. Among the novelties in mine warfare, however, are the so-called 'guardian' mines intended to deal specifically with MCM vessels or approaching ROVs in order to protect the main minefield. ROVs have been operated in the Falklands, the Red Sea and the Persian Gulf.

[9] Thus, when the question of restraint in mine warfare was first addressed in 1906, the Rapporteur of the Institut de Droit International was driven to admit: 'car s'il existe des philanthropes qui considèrent les torpilles comme quelque chose de diabolique et agissant sournoisement, s'il existe même toute une école de marins qui tiennent le torpille pour une arme vile et déloyale, il n'en est pas moins vrai que de nos jours le service des torpilles et des mines tend à prendre de plus en plus la première place dans la conduite de la guerre navale'; see 21 *Ann.IDI* (1906), Gand Session, at p. 95.

water explosion, which is the essence of modern mine warfare, is part of either technique.[10]

Two American engineers have associated their names with pioneering efforts in developing the naval mine. David Bushnell is credited with the design of a magazine containing 150 lb of gunpowder, intended to be delivered by a one-man submersible craft and to be set off by a clockwork mechanism. Worked out at the time of the American Independence War, Bushnell's machine was first put to the test against the blockading squadron of the English fleet off New York harbour. The egg-shaped submarine was steered successfully alongside the British flagship yet its copper-covered hull proved impenetrable to the magazine's screw and the attempt ended in frustration.

The inventive genius of Robert Fulton was to take up Bushnell's scheme of a submersible manoeuvring beneath the hull of an enemy ship and attaching an explosive charge by means of a spike. After having his plans repeatedly rejected by the French and the Dutch, in 1800 Fulton was eventually granted the permission by Bonaparte to construct and start experimental trials with the *Nautilus*. In August 1801, and while operating at a depth of 25 feet, Fulton's vessel blew up an old schooner, the first successful underwater attack in European waters.[11] It is noteworthy that Fulton's proposals were met with much scepticism not on account of their technical imperfection but rather because detonating explosive charges beneath the sea surface was regarded as a morally unfit and ungentlemanly method of combat.

The next notable event in the evolution of underwater warfare came in 1843 when Colonel Colt succeeded in destroying a moving ship 5 miles from shore by way of an electrically controlled minefield. The mines connected to the circuit, thereafter

[10]On the early developments of mine warfare, see SUETER, M.F., *The Evolution of the Submarine Boat, Mine and Torpedo*, 1907, pp. 262–92, GRIFFITHS, *op. cit., supra* n.1, pp. 26–46, and COWIE, *op. cit., supra* n.1, pp. 7–32.

[11]In the years that followed Fulton's contrivances were funded at times by the British or the American governments. His explosive catamaran, or a drifting wooden structure carrying barrels of gunpowder connected to a clockwork mechanism, was used in 1804 by the British against the French fleet off Boulogne. Between 1810 and 1814, he produced the *harpoon torpedo*, that is to say a case containing a powder load suspended from a float which would be then aimed at a ship by firing a harpoon into its hull. He also worked out blueprints for what would be the first moored contact mine, and for the turtle boat, an iron-plated floating structure for the purpose of towing torpedoes.

named *observation mines,* were seen as the most suitable for harbour protection. As the naval mine was rapidly maturing into a redoubtable weapon of far-reaching implications for established naval doctrines, defensive minelaying was to prove first its deadly merits. During the Crimean War of 1854–6, the Russian ports of Sevastopol, Sveaborg and Kronstadt were protected by means of mechanical contact mines. As a result, two British ships, the *Merlin* and the *Firefly,* suffered severe damage by mines off Kronstadt. The Russian engines were equipped with an original fuse comprising a glass tube filled with chemicals and an overall lead tube the end of which protruded from the mine case. As soon as the external horn was bent upon contact, the glass tube broke triggering a chemical reaction that set off the mine's explosive charge.

The Mine Weapon: The First Battle Test In the American Civil War of 1861–5, the Confederates, lacking a naval force comparable to that of the Federals, found in the employment of contact mines the unfailing solution against large gunboats.[12] Primitive mine factories came up with makeshift devices such as the famous *keg torpedoes* which were soon set adrift most of the Southern waterways to the encounter of Union ironclads. Among the countless mine episodes of the Secession War, perhaps the most arresting was Admiral David Farragut's cruise through the mined entrance of Mobile Bay in August 1864. Caught in surprise by hundreds of keg torpedoes obstructing his passage at the mouth of Mobile Bay and seeing the ironclad *Tecumseh* going down in half a minute with 120 of her crew, Admiral Farragut decided to steer through the minefield. Brushing by the mines, his vessels eventually forced their passage to engage and defeat Admiral Buchanan's flagship, the *CSS Tennessee.*

Unsurprisingly, the major maritime powers showed a prompt interest in the new promising weaponry. Elaborate systems of

[12]Ground mines fired electrically from a distance and the *Davids* (small quasi-submersibles fitted with spar torpedoes) were also used with equal success. The first ship to run into a mine was the *USS Cairo* while going up the Yazoo river in December 1862. Mines of all types accounted for the destruction or damage of 43 Union ships whereas only 9 vessels were sunk by gunfire. On the mine warfare aspects of the American Civil War, see the narrative by PERRY, M.F., *Infernal Machines – The Story of Confederate Submarine and Mine Warfare*, 1965.

mines were deployed by the Austrians in 1866 off the Istrian and Dalmatian coast, and again by the Germans in 1870 for the protection of the Jade, the Elbe and the Weser rivers. The *Herz* horn, invented in 1868, marked a major improvement in the firing mechanism of contact mines. During the Russo-Turkish War of 1877–8, the hopelessly outmatched in tonnage and gun-power Imperial Russian Navy employed mine barriers across the Danube River in order to protect the passage of Russian troops and keep the strength of the Turkish fleet divided.[13] In 1898, the US battleship *Maine* was sunk probably by a mine while anchored at the Spanish harbour of Havana provoking the Spanish-American War.

Although significantly ameliorated in construction, mine had yet to prove its efficacy as an offensive weapon. The Russo-Japanese War of 1904–5 stands as a landmark in this respect. The sinking of Admiral Makaroff's flagship, the *Petropavlosk,* while outside Port Arthur as well as the destruction of Admiral Togo's best assets by drifting mines have long entered the annals of military history announcing the new era in sea warfare. The Russians were the first to suffer casualties due to a field of forty-eight mines laid skilfully off Port Arthur along the normally used path of the Russian fleet. Lured to battle out of Port Arthur, before being driven back by the surprise presence of superior Japanese forces, the Russians were sent right through the planted mines. The 11,000-ton *Petropavlosk* having hit a pair of mines went down in minutes with more than 600 men. The Russian response, a forty mine plant laid some 10 miles off Port Arthur, was destined to neutralize one third of the Japanese battleship squadron, that is the 15,000-ton *Hatsuse* and the 12,500-ton *Yashima,* in a single day. In all, offensive mining

[13]The 10 to 1 naval superiority of the Turks was before long rendered immaterial due to the well thought out Russian mine strategy. The Turkish Danube flotilla was, in effect, kept isolated throughout the war in the upper and lower portions of the river, while the powerful Turkish ironclads remained idle in the Black Sea. Apart from the minefields, the Russian tactics consisted also in small boat attacks against anchored Turkish ships by means of towed or spar torpedoes. The Turks were forced to immobilize most of their warships encircling them with heavy nets and rings of patrolling boats. In the event, at least one ironclad lying at the mouth of the Danube was sunk by a mine in October 1877, while several other ships were sunk or captured. For more, see BRAINARD, A.P., 'Russian Mines on the Danube', 91 *USNIP* (July 1965), p. 51*ff.*, and MITCHELL, D.W., 'Russian Mine Warfare: The Historical Record', 109 *Journal of the Royal United Services Institution* (1964) at p. 33.

showed anything but a modest debut. The Japanese fleet sustained the loss of as many as ten ships, including two battleships, four cruisers, two destroyers, one torpedo boat and one minelayer totalling 40,000 tons, while the total losses of the Russian navy amounted to six warships of 22,000 tons.[14]

2 The First World War

Looking back on the European war of 1914–18, it has to be noted from the outset that all belligerents sought to exploit to the fullest possible degree the methods of underwater warfare. Germany, in waging its First World War, capitalized on expedients which inflicted maximum damage to the British maritime transportation system while evading the superior enemy surface fleet. The use of the naval mine and the submarine torpedo, therefore, imposed itself as the backbone of the German naval planning.

The British Admiralty, on the other hand, in its struggle to keep the Isles well supplied with raw materials relied heavily on extensive mining of the U-boat infested seas. At least until the standardization of the convoy system, no other scheme could bear fruits except the one intending to prevent German U-boats from making it out to the open seas by densely mining the North Sea and the English Channel. Arming decoy ships or ordering merchant vessels to ram when possible surfaced U-boats could not be expected to have much chance in the long run as a reliable anti-submarine strategy. As it turned out, the issue of the war was decided in that silent unspectacular confrontation beneath the waves. The Germans had placed their hopes in the daily reports of sunk tonnage much as the British had reposed their trust in the unreportable U-boat attrition rate resulting from minefields, mined nets and, later, depth charges.

[14]These losses apart, a great number of ships struck mines but suffered only repairable damage, while international merchant shipping had to be watchful for years for freely floating mines in the China Sea. Another hard lesson of the Russo-Japanese conflict was that minelaying forgives no errors. In one case, the Russian steamer *Yenesei* after having placed 389 mines was itself blown up by the 390th. For more, see LAWRENCE, T.J., *War and Neutrality in the Far East*, 2nd edn (1904), p. 93*ff*., and LEROUX, C., *Le droit international pendant la guerre russo-japonaise*, 1911, p. 53*ff*.

Deafening naval guns were to silence. The time had come for lurking mine horns and sneaky periscopes.[15]

Early Mine Operations: The Legal Controversy The opening act of the war at sea was typical of what would become constant anguish for thousands of seamen in the following four years. On the night of 4 August 1914, the German minelayer *Koenigen Louise* laid a minefield 40 miles off Lowestoft on the east coast of England. On the following day the German vessel was intercepted and sunk by the British cruiser *Amphion* before herself going down having struck one of *Koenigen Louise*'s secret devices. A fortnight later, the German cruisers *Maniz* and *Stuttgart* attempted to plant mines off the Humber and the Tyne. Contrary to Germany's unreserved decision to mine the high seas without much regard for the safety of merchant shipping, the British government had been hesitant in the early stages over the appropriateness of unrestricted minelaying. It is true, of course, that the British Admiralty had every reason to be least supportive of anything likely to restrict the freedom of movement of the Grand Fleet. The first limited mining operation was carried out on 2 October 1914, off Ostend while a public notification of a dangerous area for shipping was issued the following day.[16]

In view of its importance sea mining was the first issue to be addressed in the diplomatic tug of war between London and

[15]As a matter of fact, the first instance of mine warfare after the adoption of the 1907 Hague Convention on the use of submarine contact mines was the Italo-Turkish War of 1911–12. In the event, Turkey decided in April 1912 to close all of its ports together with the Dardanelles Straits by means of extended minefields. Neutral losses were not averted in spite of buoys especially marking the safe route to ports. Incidents were reported in the waters of the harbours of Smyrna and Salonica. In May and June 1913, for example, three merchant ships bearing the French, the American and the Italian flag respectively sank off the port of Smyrna; see GENET, *op. cit., supra* n.2 at p. 140. *Cf.* RAPISARDI-MIRABELLI, A., 'La guerre italo-turque et le droit des gens', 15 *RDILC* (1913), 2ème série at p. 115.

[16]Mine operations of the First World War are given a concise review in CLAUDEVILLE, C., 'Importance des mines sous-marines dans les guerres maritimes', 75 *Revue Maritime* (mars 1926), p. 305*ff.*; 76 *Revue Maritime* (avril 1926), p. 507*ff.*; 77 *Revue Maritime* (mai 1926), p. 627*ff.* See also RUGE, F., 'L'évolution de la stratégie de la guerre des mines', *Revue Maritime* (déc.1966), no.238, p. 1412*ff.*; TOUVET, G., *Les mines sous-marines automatiques de contact et la guerre 1914–1918*, 1932; PCHEDECKI, E., *Le droit international maritime et la Grande Guerre*, 1916, pp. 15–28.

Berlin, well before the questions of armed merchantmen and submarine warfare took up the relay. In fact, only a week after the opening of hostilities, the British government claimed that 'the Germans are scattering contact mines indiscriminately about the North Sea in the open sea without regard to the consequences to merchantmen' and went on to declare:

> the waters of the North Sea must therefore be regarded as perilous in the last degree to merchant shipping of all nations. In view of the methods adopted by Germany the British Admiralty must hold themselves fully at liberty to adopt *similar measures* in self-defence which must inevitably increase the dangers to navigation in the North Sea. (emphasis added)[17]

By late September 1914, eight neutral and seven British merchant vessels had run into mines in the North Sea and some sixty seamen were lost. In the British view, this was only the result of the persistence of the 'German naval authorities in laying mines on the high seas on the trade routes, not only to British but to neutral ports, and in furtherance of no definite military

[17]See Foreign Office statement, 11 August 1914, in 11 *AJIL* (1917) *Sp.Suppl.* at p. 4. Although the Memorandum referred to measures in self-defence, it is clear that retaliation in kind is what was genuinely implied. The swiftness with which London expressed its determination to match the German practices gave rise to the following comment on the part of the US State Department: 'If an enemy of His Majesty's Government has, as asserted, endangered neutral commerce by an act in violation of The Hague Convention, which cannot be justified on the ground of military necessity, the Secretary of State perceives no reason for His Majesty's Government adopting a similar course, which would add further dangers to the peaceful navigation of the high seas by vessels of neutral powers'; see Memorandum dated 13 August 1914, *ibid.* at p. 5.

London appeared for a moment irresolute in assessing the legality of the German practices. On 19 August 1914, it was affirmed that 'it is not alleged that they [German minelaying practices] are a breach of any Convention concluded at The Hague to which Germany is a party, but that does not make them less dangerous to merchant shipping', whereas four days later the British Admiralty announced that German 'mines do not conform to the conditions of The Hague Convention; they do not become harmless after a certain number of hours; they are not laid in connection with any definite military scheme such as the closing of a military port or as a distinct operation against a fighting fleet, but appear to be scattered on the chance of catching individual British war or merchant vessels'; see *ibid.* at p. 7. In the same communiqué, the Admiralty reserved 'the utmost liberty of *retaliatory action* against this new form of warfare' which qualifies more accurately the British measures that followed. Similarly, in October 1914, France acting in retaliation for similar measures of the Austro-Hungarian Navy, announced the mining of the enemy territorial waters including those around the Dalmatian islands; *ibid.* at p. 13.

operation. His Majesty's Government have reason to think that fishing vessels, possibly disguised as neutral, are employed for the purpose, and lay these mines under the pretence of following the ordinary avocations of fishing. Mines have been found in several cases as much as 50 miles from the coast.'[18]

In replying to these protests, Germany availed itself of all the imperfections and lacunae to be found in the Hague Convention. In the first place, it invoked the *si omnes* clause arguing that since 'Russia, which is allied with England, has not ratified the Agreement, it is therefore not binding by international law on any of the participants in the present war'.[19] As regards the complaints concerning the minelaying upon the high seas, Berlin countered rightfully that 'the Convention does not stipulate how far from the coast and ports of an enemy mines may be anchored, and there is no established practice in this respect in international law'. Germany flatly denied all allegations that merchant ships were used as minelayers and stressed that mining had been carried out *with all possible precaution* . . . the German Government is satisfied that for its part, in taking the measures required by *military exigency*, it has reduced *as far as possible* risk or injury to neutral shipping,[20] which again tallies with the lax provisions of the 1907 Convention.

On 3 November 1914, the British Admiralty felt it necessary, in adopting what it qualified as 'exceptional measures appropriate to the novel conditions under which this war is being waged', to declare that 'the whole of the North Sea must be considered a military area. Within this area *merchant shipping of all kinds, traders of all countries*, fishing craft, and all other vessels *will be exposed to the gravest dangers from mines* which it has been necessary to lay and from warships searching vigilantly by night

[18]See Memorandum of 26 September 1914, *ibid.* at p. 10. The British government further proceeded to substantiate what it branded a 'flagrant violation of the accepted principles of international law and contrary to the primary dictates of humanity' by referring to the standards laid down in the 1907 Eighth Hague Convention. Contrary to the stipulations of the latter instrument, it was asserted, the Germans 'neglected to take every possible precaution for the safety of neutral shipping . . . the mine zones have not been kept under observation nor has any notification of their locality ever been made . . . [and] mines which they have laid have in numerous instances been found adrift from their moorings without having become harmless', *ibid.* at p. 11.
[19]See the communiqué of 7 November 1914, *ibid.* at p. 17.
[20]*Ibid.* at p. 19.

and day for suspicious craft' (emphasis added).[21] It is not without interest to observe that, unlike what is often assumed, the first exclusion zone of a considerable extent was associated with mine rather than submarine warfare. Three months after the British warning of a 'military area', Berlin declared on 4 February 1915, 'the waters surrounding Great Britain and Ireland, including the whole English Channel to be comprised within the seat of war', and announced its intention to 'prevent by all means at its disposal all navigation by the enemy in those waters'.[22]

As things stood in February 1915, therefore, it appeared that offensive sea mining and the deceptive use of neutral flags were the main legal issues around which the argumentation of both belligerents was passionately revolving. Thus, US Secretary of State Bryan, in his well-intended but fruitless mediation effort of 20 February 1915, focused on these very points of discord and called for mutual concessions. Following his proposals, Germany and Great Britain should agree *inter alia* 'that neither will sow any floating mines, whether upon the high seas or in territorial waters; that neither will plant on the high seas anchored mines except *within cannon range of harbors for defensive purposes only*; and that all mines shall bear the stamp of the Government planting them and be so constructed as to become harmless if separated from their moorings' (emphasis added).[23]

It would be illusory, however, to expect that what was not

[21] *Ibid.* at p. 15.

[22] See 9 *AJIL* (1915) *Sp.Suppl.* at p. 85. For the American note of protest dated 10 February 1915, see *ibid.*, p. 86*ff.* With further reference to the prohibited zone, the German government made known on 16 February 1915, that it would 'obstruct this area of maritime war by mines wherever possible and also endeavor to destroy the merchant vessels of the enemy in any other way'; see the letter from Foreign Minister Von Jagow to US ambassador Gerard, *ibid.* at p. 93. The point was also made that any act of minelaying results inevitably to indiscriminate destruction on a certain scale and that German practice could not be argued to have exceeded the anything but strict standards established by international law – a further hint to the large discretion afforded by international regulations on the matter: 'it is very far indeed from the intention of the German government, acting in obedience to these compelling circumstances, ever to destroy neutral lives and neutral property, but on the other hand they can not be blind to the fact that dangers arise through the action to be carried out against England which menace without discrimination all trade within the area of maritime war. This applies as a matter of course to war mines, which place any ship approaching a mined area in danger, *even if the limits of international law are adhered to most strictly*' (emphasis added), *ibid.*

[23] *Ibid.* at p. 98.

found acceptable during the deliberations of the 1907 Hague Peace Conference could be agreed upon amidst the flames of a swiftly escalating war. Victorious strategies, it is often claimed, best resist appeals for restraint, and so Berlin appeared unwilling to renounce offensive mine warfare considered at the time a most promising method for the dislocation of the seaborne trade of the British Empire. The German response to the American initiative read in part: 'with regard to the sowing of mines, the German Government would be willing to agree as suggested not to use floating mines and to have anchored mines constructed as indicated. Moreover, they agree to put the stamp of the Government on all mines to be planted. On the other hand, it does not appear to them to be feasible for the belligerents wholly to forego the use of anchored mines for offensive purposes.'[24]

The Dardanelles Expedition If the daring Japanese mine masterstroke off Port Arthur stands out as a famous instance of offensive minelaying, the Dardanelles mine catastrophe of 1914 is probably the most classic, though certainly not the first, operation to make history out of defensive minelaying. As it has been observed, 'if ever clear-cut evidence were needed that underwater weaponry now dominated sea warfare and that the big gun was only of secondary importance, the naval opening of the Dardanelles campaign provides it'.[25]

In launching the Dardanelles expedition, British warships were expected to force their passage through the Turkish straits and attack Constantinople so that direct aid could be brought to Russia. Except perhaps for a masterful mining, there was nothing to indicate that the original planning did not have every chance of success. Between November 1914 and February 1915, the Turks, probably with German assistance, had reinforced their defences with ten rows of mines and anti-submarine nets. What was also known as the *Kephez barrier* comprised 350 mines of

[24]See the reply of the German Foreign Ministry dated 28 February 1915, *ibid.* at p. 100.

[25]See HOUGH, R., *The Great War at Sea 1914–1918*, 1983 at pp. 161–2. For a good account on the Dardanelles mine episode, see CORBETT, J.S., *History of the Great War – Naval Operations*, vol.II (1921), p. 184*ff.* See also MEACHAM, *op. cit., supra* n.1, p. 77*ff.*, ASPINALL-OGLANDER, C.F., *History of the Great War – Military Operations, Gallipoli*, vol.I (1929), p. 93*ff.*, and LANGMAID, K., *The Approaches Are Mined!*, 1965, pp. 71–94.

Russian, French and Bulgarian construction. Shore batteries and powerful search lights further protected the minefield. Navigational aids in the narrows were removed and it was formally announced that the straits were closed for navigation. Throughout the first fortnight of March 1915, British minesweepers staged abortive attempts to clear a channel, driven back by coastal artillery fire, while the cruiser *Amethyst* was also badly hit.

Finally, the risky breakthrough attempted on 18 March 1915, was to end in disaster for the Allied forces. Three battleships were lost, the French *Bouvet* with over 630 men of its complement, the *HMS Irresistible* and the *HMS Ocean*, while the *HMS Inflexible* suffered considerable damage. Following such severe losses, no further effort was undertaken to penetrate the mined approaches. In the words of the official historian of the British Admiralty:

> the great attempt to force the Narrows with the fleet had ended in what could only be regarded as a severe defeat. Out of the sixteen capital ships engaged three had gone down and three more, including the only battle cruiser, had been put out of action for an indefinite period. Of the whole Allied battle fleet, therefore, one-third was spent in the one day's operation. At such a rate of loss, with results apparently so meagre, it looked extremely doubtful whether the navy unaided could ever force a passage.[26]

It was against this dismal background of the mighty Royal Navy been overpowered by a few tens of mines that the Gallipoli land campaign was launched with all its unfortunate consequences.

The English Channel Minefields The south east coast of England and the English Channel were mined on numerous occasions for defensive purposes. The waters off the Belgian coast between Ostend and the River Scheldt were also protected by double lines of deep contact mines and mined nets as of May 1916. Despite all sorts of underwater obstructions, however, it could not be claimed with any degree of certainty that the enemy had been deterred altogether from venturing in the Dover Strait area. In a cable addressed to the US Navy Department in October

[26]See CORBETT, *op. cit., supra* at p. 223.

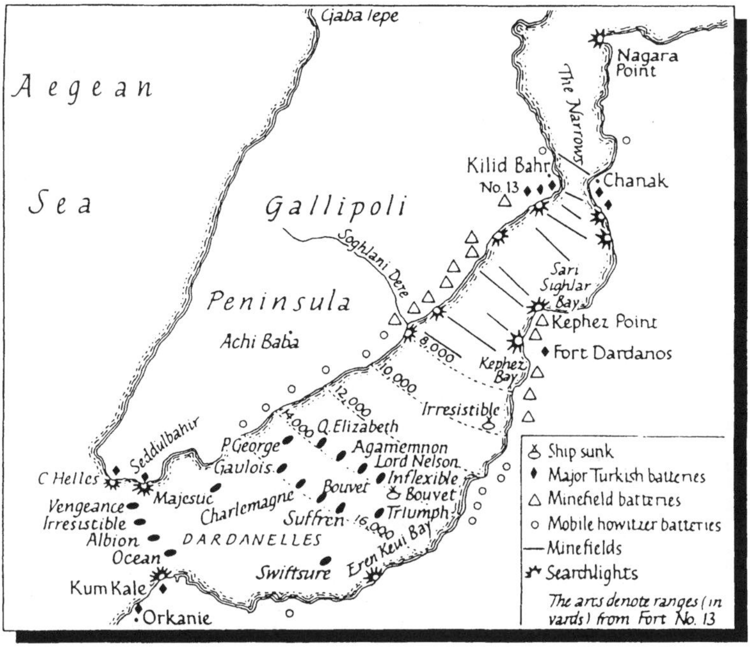

Figure 8 *The Dardanelles, 18 March 1915*
Source: HOUGH, R., *The Great War at Sea 1914–1918*, 1983 at p. 158

1917, the British Admiralty admitted that 'no scheme yet tried has been effective in closing the Dover Straits to submarines but measures are being constantly improved and they are the least always a considerable deterrent'. In November 1917, with the need for a drastic interception campaign in the Channel growing imperative, a Channel Barrage Committee was charged with the task of studying and suggesting the optimal means for blocking submarine access to the open seas through the English Channel.

Operations for what became known as the *Folkestone–Gris Nez barrage* began in late November 1917 and were virtually completed by August 1918. A total of 10,000 mines were planted, while the deep minefield areas were patrolled by five armed vessels and were illuminated by flare-burning crafts. In its original form, the plan envisaged also the construction of large concrete towers every 2 miles, each station controlling a section of the minefield. This project was never rounded off, however, only one tower having been completed before the end of the war. The mine barrier proved an unexpected success since as many as ten U-boats met their fate there. For good reasons, the Channel minefields had more chances against enemy submarines than the ambitious Northern Barrage to be examined below. Ten times shorter in length, in waters between three and six times shallower and washing Allied shores, the Folkestone–Gris Nez barrage contributed considerably in containing the German submarine campaign.

The Northern Barrage With the monthly losses of Allied merchant shipping having reached alarming heights in the first half of 1917, British and American mine warfare experts started examining the feasibility of a plan which would practically seal off the North Sea, and thus progressively clear the Atlantic Ocean of enemy U-boats. The next best thing to destroying the German submarines at their dockyards, which had been dismissed as a militarily unattainable option, was to inhibit their outward journey into the Atlantic. Such an ambitious plan would call, on one hand, for dense mine barriers across the English Channel, and on the other, for a far more demanding 'mine wall' to be erected from the north east coast of Scotland eastwards through the North Sea up to the Norwegian territorial sea limits.

For reasons that engineering, mathematics or hydrography can explain, the British Admiralty had for long taken an unenthusiastic stance arguing that such an operation exceeded by far their available resources. When the first American proposal was presented in this regard in early May 1917, Admiral Sims disapproved it stating that 'bitter and extensive experience has forced the abandonment of any serious attempt at blockading these passages'. American naval authorities, on the contrary, pushed energetically for the realization of the challenging plan, and authorized, as of July 1917, the production of large quantities of the newly invented *antenna mine* which was equipped with an improved firing gear able to double the mine's danger area.

By the time of the Allied Naval Conference of September 1917, the British, still hesitant but now facing the bare truth that 'any increase in the present rate of sinking might bring about

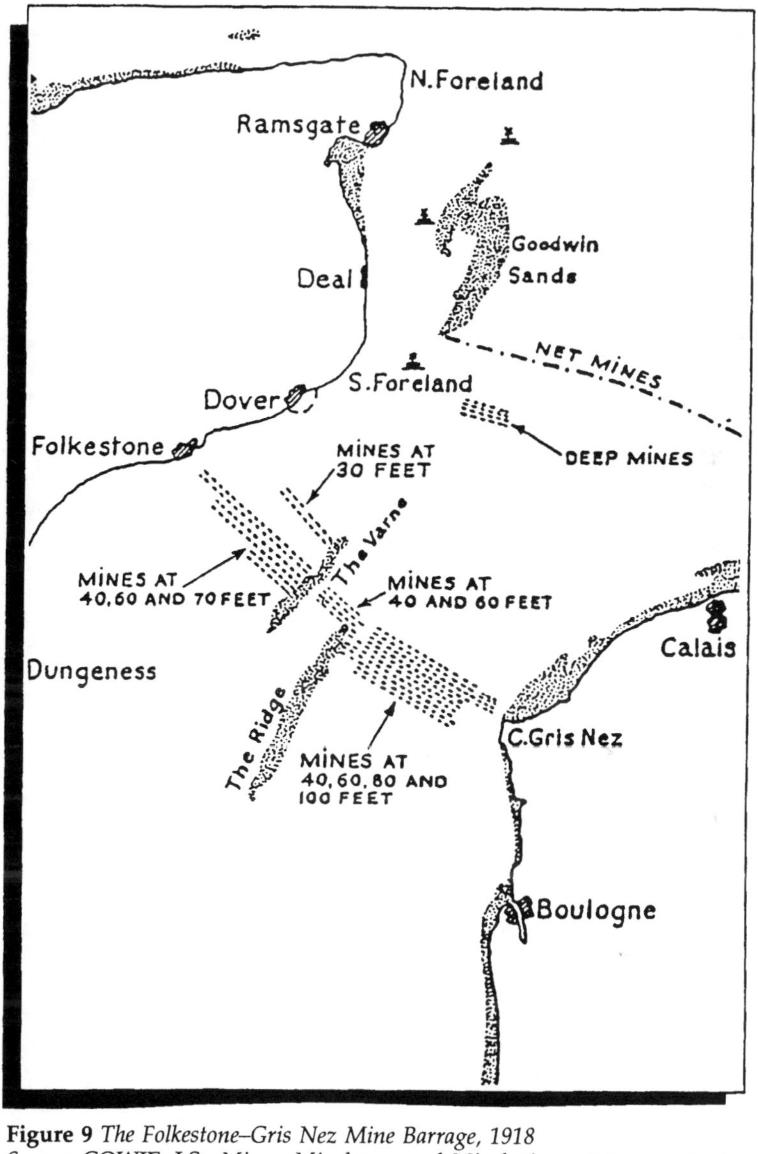

Figure 9 *The Folkestone–Gris Nez Mine Barrage, 1918*
Source: COWIE, J.S., *Mines, Minelayers and Minelaying*, 1949 at p. 73, by permission of Oxford University Press

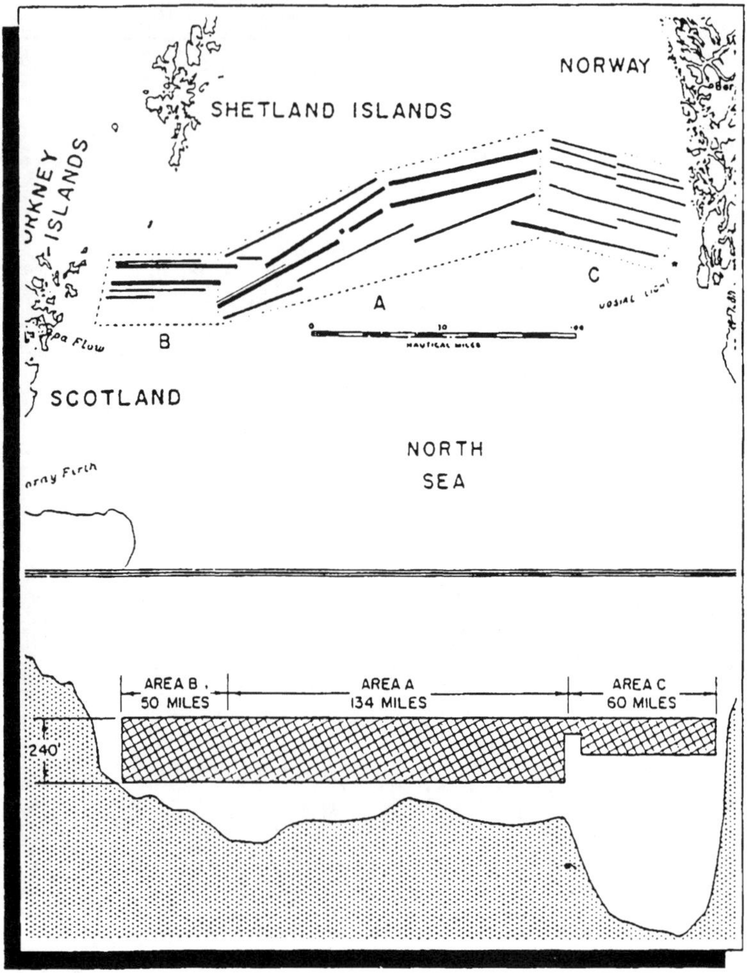

Figure 10 *Location and Vertical Projection of the North Sea Mine Barrage*
Source: DUNCAN, R.C., *America's Use of Sea Mines*, 1962 at p. 59

an unsatisfactory peace', finally consented in the scheme. Yet, the definitive plan was not agreed upon before January 1918.

The projected 250-mile long and between 15 and 35 square nautical mile large minefield, known as the *Northern Barrage*, would be divided into three segments; the central Area A was to be mined by the Americans with antenna mines, and the wing Areas B and C by the British with ordinary contact mines. Primarily designed to deter submarines, the mines were to be moored at depths ranging from 80 to 240 feet while patrol ships would deal with any submarine attempting to run the mine blockade on the surface.[27] There was considerable disagreement, however, as to whether the closing line should extend from mainland to mainland offering no breaks to enemy submarines. The British Admiralty wishing to maintain manoeuvrability around Scapa Flow in the prospect of meeting the German fleet in battle, insisted that a 10-mile corridor east of the Orkney Islands should be left open. For US naval planners, in contrast, nothing short of a sound design would justify the effort, 'the requirements of a sound design [being] the extension of the barrage complete in the vertical plane from coast to coast'.

The British and US minelaying squadrons carried out their first mission on 6 June 1918. Minelaying progressed as scheduled up to the late days of October 1918, and then discontinued until the signing of the armistice on 11 November. At the time of the cessation of hostilities, mining of Area A was about 15 per cent from completion, Area B had not been mined at depth, while Area C was the weakest of all. The eastern extremity of the barrage, starting in neutral Norwegian coastal waters was not mined until 29 September 1918, when Norway announced that certain localities would be closed for general traffic due to minefields. The barrage in its incomplete form accounted for the destruction of at least six submarines, while many more were damaged and discouraged from continuing their operations. It was completely swept and considered safe for navigation by September 1919 – an arduous task involving no less than 100 vessels.[28]

[27]It has been reckoned that in the best case a U-boat venturing through at a level of 50 feet would have one chance in three of passing unharmed, while at depths from 50 to 250 feet it would have two out of three, but due to mine imperfection and technical shortcomings their chances were possibly the double. The mine scheme required an unprecedented exercise in coordination and enhanced industrial capacity. By way of indication, the United States built in less than four months a new 22-building plant which received, stored and loaded 1,500 mines per day, or an aggregate of 73,000 mines, which meant the safe handling of 22 million pounds of TNT. For a detailed account on the North Sea mining operation, see US Navy Department, *The Northern Barrage and Other Mining Activities*, 1920. See also DUNCAN, R.C., *America's Use of Sea Mines*, 1962, p. 47*ff.*, and SIMS, W.S., *The Victory at Sea*, 1920, p. 244*ff.*

[28]For more, see DAVIS, N., 'The Removal of the North Sea Mine Barrage', 37 *National Geographic* (Feb.1920), p. 103*ff.*

Mine Strategy: Further Options and End Results According to US Navy planning, the extensive mine campaign in the North Sea should be complemented with similar action in the Mediterranean. At an Allied Conference, held at Malta in August 1918, consideration had been given to five mine barrage schemes with the aim of sealing off the Adriatic, the Dardanelles, the Aegean and to block off the Tunisia-Sicily passage and the strait of Gibraltar.[29] Had the hostilities not been concluded in November 1918, it is most likely that some or all of these projects would have been carried out in further evidence that mines and torpedoes almost monopolized naval tactics in the First World War. What is more, work on *influence mines,* which was to be popularized in the Second World War, had already been advanced before the end of the First. Magnetic mines of some primitive design were, in fact, laid by the British in 1918 off the Belgian coasts.

The overall number of mines laid by belligerents and neutrals was commensurate with the scale of a World War. Great Britain started the war technologically least prepared and politically not motivated to undertake a mine campaign of any appreciable extent, and yet by the end of the war the British had been laying 7,000 mines per month. Throughout the war British minelaying accounted for an aggregate of 128,000 mines in all theatres of operations, 40 per cent of which were laid offensively in Heligoland, the Kattegat, off the Belgian coast, and in the Mediterranean. The US Navy made an able contribution to the Northern Barrage by laying over 56,000 mines. According to estimates, some 195,000 Allied mines disposed of as many as 150 enemy warships including 48 submarines.

The German mine campaign totalled 43,000 mines laid in various areas around the British Isles, France, Italy, Greece, in the Baltic and the Black Sea, off Tunisia and the Dalmatian coast,

[29]As regards the Adriatic mine scheme, the French, after a first abortive attempt to close the Otranto passage in autumn 1915 by means of 65 crafts carrying mined fishing nets and cruising between Otranto and Brindisi, undertook in summer 1918 a fixed barrage from Otranto across to Corfu Island. Fifty-metre-high mined nets were moored some 10 metres below the surface covering a total distance of 66 km. The anchored obstructions were to be complemented by several Allied destroyers permanently patrolling north and south of the barrage. The Otranto barrage, insufficient in the vertical plane as it was, accounted for the destruction of only one submarine – the UB-53 been sunk there on 3 August 1918. For more, see THOMAZI, A., *La Marine française dans la Grande Guerre (1914–1918) – La guerre navale dans l'Adriatique,* 1925, p. 179*ff.*

and as far as the Pacific Ocean. Moreover, the Atlantic coast of the United States was equally mined in a half-dozen locations with 60 submarine-laid mines which accounted for the destruction or damage of six vessels, including the cruiser *San Diego* and the battleship *Minnesota*. In all, 40 British warships and 225 auxiliaries fell victims of German mines as well as 586 Allied merchantmen representing over 1 million tons.

As regards minesweeping, the Allied Naval Council had taken up thoroughly the question of the removal of mines at the end of the war in a series of meetings between September and November 1918. In the event, it was decided that a Committee of British naval officers, known as the International Mine Clearance Committee should be established for the purpose of collecting and distributing to seafaring nations information regarding the process of mine clearance operations and issuing mine warnings when necessary. Despite all efforts, however, in the first four years after the conclusion of the First World War mines sent to bottom as many as 111 ships.

3 The Second World War

By 1940, mine development had scored new achievements in surprise destruction. Both the British and the Germans had worked out the secrets of the magnetic mine and had elaborated techniques for delivering mines from aircraft and submarines. The laying of mines from the air represented a major innovation since aircraft could drop their mine loads in waters inaccessible to warships, while they could always 're-enter' a minefield for the purpose of inspecting or adding to it. It has been estimated that only in the European theatre of operations, British bombers laid throughout the war 47,000 mines which accounted for 550 ships sunk and 480 damaged.[30] As regards magnetic mines, one of Hitler's dreaded secret weapons, these were first used during

[30]See SPAIGHT, J.M., *Air Power and War Rights*, 3rd edn (1947) at p. 494. Inland waters were often mined too. Traffic through the Kiel Canal, for instance, was interrupted on several occasions and blocked at least once for several months while the Königsberg and the Stettin canals were mined in 1944. Allied aircraft dropped also mines in the Danube River sinking more than 60 tugs and 200 barges; *ibid.* at p. 495. Similarly, the Germans attempted to block the Suez Canal by air-dropped mines. An interesting mine detection technique was used in this latter case. Nets were stretched across sections of the Suez Canal so that holes in the net were a sure sign of a mine below; see BROWN, D.K., 'Damn the Mines', 118 *USNIP* (March 1992) at p. 47.

night raids in the Thames estuary in November 1939, while the first German acoustic mines, set off by the noise of a ship's propulsion plant, were to follow in August 1940.[31]

Mine Activity around the British Isles According to plans worked out in detail many months before the war, the first British mines were to be laid defensively in the waters of the Channel. A barrage across the Dover Strait was, in fact, laid with extreme rapidity as early as September 1939 consisting of some 7,000 mines with a double system of electric sensors on the seabed to reveal the presence of U-boats. By October, the Germans had already lost three of their U-boats refraining thereafter from sending submarines through the Channel in numbers. The *Dover barrage* was soon outflanked, however, as France fell to the hands of Axis forces. Extensive minelaying was undertaken next along the east coast of England and Scotland, from the Pentland Firth to Essex. Operations for the so-called *East coast barrage* commenced in late November 1939 and chiefly aimed at protecting the coastal traffic from the submarine threat.[32]

By October 1939, the British Admiralty had also decided to proceed swiftly with a mine barrage between Scotland and Norway, repeating in essence the Anglo-American undertaking of 1918. Before preparations were completed, however, Norway had been occupied by Germany and containment of the German U-boat fleet within the North Sea did not appear possible any more. Nevertheless, another closing line was still considered lying further to the west and running across vast spaces of the Atlantic ocean itself. Thus, the *Orkneys–Iceland mine barrage* option came to be examined and despite the unfavourable physical conditions the scheme was approved. Minelaying began in July 1940 and proceeded until January 1943 when the strenuous campaign was finally discontinued. More than 140,000 mines were deployed along the Orkneys–Faroes–Iceland–Green-

[31]Mines of the influence type were recovered early enough allowing British experts to work on possible countermeasures. In the event, the degaussing coils were developed as an effective protection against magnetic mines, while the acoustic mine was dealt with by means of vibrating hammers capable of causing its detonation. On the battle of wits around the German influence mine and the contest between German naval scientists and the RMS (Rendering Mines Safe) experts of the British Admiralty, see GRIFFITHS, *op. cit., supra* n.1, pp. 79–111.
[32]See BARNETT, C., *Engage the Enemy More Closely – The Royal Navy in the Second World War*, 1991 at pp. 90–2.

land path resulting in the destruction of several enemy submarines. In addition to these main operations, the Royal Navy laid innumerable small defensive minefields as an anti-invasion measure, or for harbour protection.

As for the Germans, their principal minefield ran some 80 miles north from the Friesian Islands to the latitude of Jutland and aimed at protecting the North Sea naval bases from a direct British attack. The *'West Wall'* as it was called later turned into an extensive system of minefields starting from the Dutch territorial waters and extending for more than 150 miles northward. In the first six months of the war German mines accounted for the loss of 120 enemy merchant ships, or about 400,000 tons of shipping, as well as 15 minesweepers and 2 destroyers.[33]

Mine Defences off the American Continent The United States planted the first defensive controlled minefields while still neutral, in February 1941, off both entrances of the Panama Canal. Several other strategic coastal areas had been mined before December 1941. The electrically controlled minefields were not fired by contact but contact was necessary to notify the control station of a ship's presence. Later in the war these minefields were replaced by ground mines with firing devices so that the station was given notice whenever a steel ship of 1,000 tons or more passed over the line of mines. The US Navy laid also some 20,000 independent mines in numerous defensive minefields all along the Atlantic coast. To the end of the war, no enemy ship had been reported sunk or damaged in those defensive minefields. As regards German mine warfare operations after the US entered the war, it was in May–June 1942 that German submarines laid mines for the first time off St. John's, New Foundland, off Boston, or Delaware and Chesapeake bays. Offensive minelaying was undertaken anew in July 1942 off Santa Lucia in the British West Indies, in June 1943 off Halifax, Nova Scotia, and in October 1943 off the Panama Canal. In total, 338 German mines were scattered along the east coast of the United States accounting for some ten ships sunk or

[33]See RUGE, F., *Der Seekrieg – The German Navy's Story 1939–1945*, 1957 at pp. 63, 67.

damaged. Contrary to German tactics, Japanese submarines kept clear of the US Pacific coast.

The Starvation Campaign against Japan Selective submarine and aerial mining of Japan-controlled waters in the greater south west Pacific theatre, known as the Outer Zone Mining Campaign, was undertaken as early as October 1942 and went on unabated until March 1945. Thirty-two submarines from the US Seventh Fleet based in Australia took extemely long cruises and initiated an attrition campaign against Japanese shipping laying 658 mines in 36 different fields which accounted for the loss or damage of 54 enemy ships. Surface minelayers joined the effort as of early 1943 by laying 2,840 mines in 17 fields, while the aerial offensive followed with heavy bombers of the US, British and Australian air forces dropping influence mines to almost every port in Burma, Malaysia, Thailand, Indochina, South China and Formosa. In total, 3,231 aircraft successfully laid 9,254 mines in 108 target zones, sinking 186 ships and damaging 154.[34]

As Japan began pulling out of its Pacific conquests, a mine blockade of the Japanese inland waters became tactically possible. The Inner Zone Mining Campaign, or Operation Starvation as it was named, left no doubt as to its ultimate objective.[35] From March 1945 through the very last day of the war, US Air Force B-29s Superfortresses, operating from the Mariannas Islands, dropped 12,135 mines into Japanese waters

[34]As a result, Japan's vital seaborne commerce was slowed down significantly. Steel-hulled freighters had to be abandoned and cargoes from Singapore or Bangkok were shipped on board wooden barges. Experienced merchant crews became increasingly difficult to obtain. By the end of March 1945, the Japanese had been forced to operate most of their remaining 2 million tons of shipping in the protected East China Sea, Yellow Sea and the Sea of Japan. The full record of mine warfare in the Pacific theatre is given in JOHNSON, E.A. and KATCHER, D.A., *Mines Against Japan*, 1974.

[35]In 1944, Japan depended on sea traffic for 80 per cent of its oil supplies, 88 per cent of iron ore and 20 per cent of its food supplies. It was estimated that if this latter 20 per cent could be decreased through an economy destroying campaign, it could have actually meant starvation for a considerable part of the Japanese population. According to American planning, with the Japanese industry to a standstill for scarcity of raw materials and most of domestic sea routes heavily mined, 7 million Japanese would starve within a year. For more on the mine blockade against Japan, see LOTT, A.S., *Most Dangerous Sea – A History of Mine Warfare, and an Account of US Navy Mine Warfare Operations in World War II and Korea*, 1959, p. 207*ff*. See also DUNCAN, *op. cit., supra* n.27, p. 145*ff*.

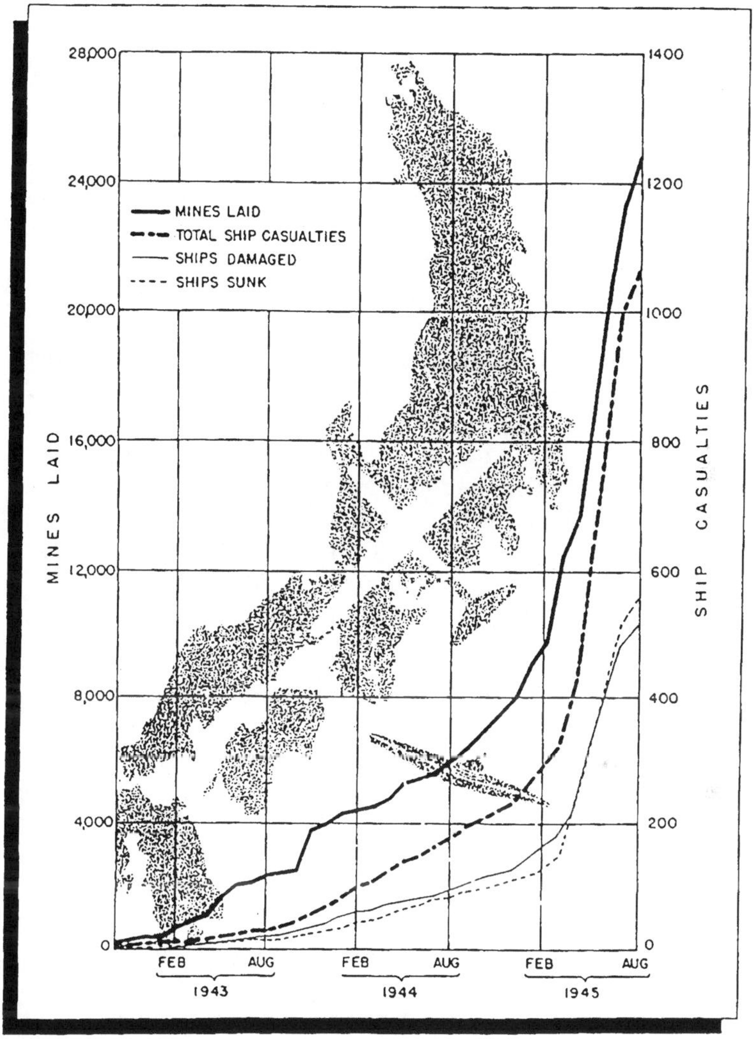

Table 1 *Offensive Mining Against Japan*
Source: JOHNSON, E.A. and KATCHER, D.A., *Mines Against Japan*, 1974 at p. 22

sinking or damaging 670 ships, including 65 warships, a total of 1.4 million tons, or 75 per cent of all the tonnage at Japan's disposal at the start of the operation. All of the mine stocks featured delayed arming and ship-count capability offering to assembly crews as many as 200 possible operation patterns with which to confuse enemy minesweeping efforts. The situation quickly became so desperate that the Japanese either pushed their ships through dangerous areas regardless of risk, or attempted to sweep mined straits using small suicide craft.

The campaign was carried out in five phases. The first phase was planned in support of the Okinawa operation and consisted in mining the Shimonoseki Straits, the naval bases of Kure, Sasebo and the military port of Hiroshima with some 2,030 mines. In early May, the second phase, called the 'Industrial Center Blockade', aimed at destroying the seaborne communication routes between the industrial zones of Japan by mining the ports of Tokyo, Nagoya, Kobe and Osaka. A total of 1,422 mines of all types were used. The third phase was designed to prevent enemy shipping from plying between the Asiatic mainland and Japan by mining the harbours of Honshu and Kyushu with some 1,313 influence mines. As for the fourth and fifth phase, these were meant to deliver the final blow by carrying the blockade to every possible point of the Empire (3,542 and 3,746 mines were dropped respectively).

Weapons that Wait: The Aftermath Given the massive use of mines, it is difficult to exaggerate the importance of hazardous and skilful minesweeping. Operation Overlord, code-name for the Allied invasion of France, for instance, required no less than 385 Allied minesweepers to clear ten approach channels for the thousands of landing craft. In the event, some 40 ships were sunk by mines in the Normandy landings, including 3 destroyers and 26 amphibious vessels.[36] German sea mining obliged the British to maintain a force of 1,000 minesweepers. Similarly, it has been estimated that by the end of the European war, the Germans had more personnel engaged in mine counter-

[36]During the early months of 1944, the Germans had planted huge defensive minefields along the coasts of northern France, Belgium and Holland. Estimating that the invasion would be attempted before the end of May, they had adjusted their mines to scuttle themselves at that time (German mines were fitted with 80-day sterilizing clocks which made them harmless after that period). So, six days before the Allied crossing, thousands of German mines sank themselves. In the three months after D-Day, minesweeping operations accounted for one-tenth of all the mines swept in all theatres from the beginning of the war to 6 June 1944; see BARNETT, *op. cit., supra* n.32 at pp. 829–30.

measures than would be required to man the entire British navy in peacetime.[37]

The United States and Great Britain together laid over 300,000 mines. The British planted 185,000 defensive and 76,000 offensive, while the United States laid nearly 50,000 mines. Allied mines are believed to have caused the destruction of nearly 2,700 enemy ships in all theatres. The Germans, for their part, laid 120,000 mines which accounted for the loss of 281 British warships of all types and 296 merchant vessels. In total, 534 Allied merchant vessels were lost, or, an estimated 7 per cent of all losses of Allied tonnage was inflicted by mines.[38] As for Japan, it used a total of 51,000 mines exclusively for defensive purposes. No more than 15 US naval vessels and as few as 10 merchant ships were lost due to Japanese mines.

Shortly after the end of the war, the International Mine Clearance Board was established to handle European mine clearance. By the end of 1947, 1,900 minesweepers had cleared 125,000 square nautical miles. The Board was finally dissolved in January 1952. Suggestive of the disrespect of the 1907 Eighth Hague Convention, wartime minefields remained active for years after the conclusion of hostilities. By July 1948, no less than 251 ships of all nationalities had hit mines in the Atlantic and the Pacific. In August 1953, the British trawler *Marach* caught a live Second World War mine in her net, while in 1956 eight mines were washed up on Hawaiian beaches.

4 The Korean War

Following the end of the Second World War, naval interest in mine warfare was expected to ebb, most of the Allied minecraft having been scrapped or sold due also to budgetary cuts. By way of illustration, during the Second World War the US Navy's Pacific minesweeping fleet numbered 550 ships, whereas when the Korean War broke out the US minesweeping force in the Far East consisted of only ten vessels. In this respect, the 1950–3

[37]For the unglamorous minesweeping operations in the Second World War, see ELLIOTT, P., *Allied Minesweeping in World War 2*, 1979, and LUND, P. and LUDLAM, H., *Out Sweeps! The Story of the Minesweepers in World War II*, 1978.

[38]As far as mine countermeasures are concerned, 18,000 Allied vessels were degaussed in the years 1939–45, nearly 250,000 depth-charges were dropped, while the Germans laid 30,000 sweep obstructors; see LANGMAID, *op. cit., supra* n.25 at p. 248.

Korean operations came as a timely warning that naval mines should still be considered as reliable weaponry in the post-1945 world. Extensive mining of the shallow coastal waters was all the North Koreans could do to forestall the amphibious assault of UN forces and they did so with success.

In what is the most telling incident of mine warfare operations in Korea, a 50,000-man US invasion force aboard 250 ships was stymied for over a week off Wonsan, on the East Korea Bay of the Sea of Japan, by reason of a dense enemy minefield. The landings at Inchon, Wonsan or Chinnampo involved laborious and often costly engagements on the part of the poor UN minesweeping assets. Without committing anything but junks and sampans and a lot of Russian antiquated contact mines, the North Koreans were able to inflict considerable damage on an enemy fleet which otherwise operated virtually unopposed all around the Korean peninsula.[39]

As already mentioned, the awkward situation of 50,000 troops and 250 warships held up for a week off the port of Wonsan, which had fallen in the meantime into friendly hands, for fear of enemy mines illustrated most compellingly the efficacy of the mine weapon in the Korean context.[40] The Allied Task Force had to make its way to land supported by only six minesweepers – sufficient reason for anxiety if one considers that 100 minesweepers had participated in the amphibious assault against Okinawa, while the Normandy landings had called for some

[39]Only in the last five days of September 1950, two US destroyers, the *Brush* and the *Mansfield*, as well as three minesweepers had struck mines with over 110 casualties. In October, two more minesweepers, the *Pirate* and the *Pledge*, were lost to enemy mines with another 102 casualties. During 1951, three naval vessels were sunk, two US destroyers, the *Walke* and the *Small*, were damaged, and 70 servicemen perished in mine incidents. As from 1952, however, and due to the increased mine-consciousness of Allied seamen, only two ships, the tug *Sarsi* and the destroyer *Barton* ran into mines. Late in the war, the North Koreans devised new techniques in order to spare the fishing craft from minelaying operations. The explosive devices were attached beneath oil drums and logs and set adrift in rivers to be carried down to the sea. On the mine aspects of the Korean War, see CAGLE, M.W. and MANSON, F.A., *The Sea War in Korea*, 1957, pp. 107–64, 193–221, and LOTT, *op. cit., supra* n.35, p. 268*ff*.

[40]On the Wonsan mine episode, see FIELD, J.A., *History of United States Naval Operations – Korea*, 1962, p. 229*ff*., and MEACHAM, *op. cit., supra* n.1, p. 104*ff*. No more than 32 junks were involved in laying some 3,000 mines. Minelaying was carried out with makeshift equipment. Wooden barges were fitted with iron or wooden tracks and carried an average load of 15 mines. The barges were then towed by tugboats and the mines were rolled off their stern at regular intervals.

400 minesweepers. Mine clearance by aerial bombing was also attempted but with no success.[41] When the Wonsan approaches were finally swept on 25 October 1950, only 225 of those mines had been destroyed, while 600 more had broken loose and were later washed up ashore. Mines, for those attracted by statistics, caused 70 per cent of all US naval casualties during the first two years of the war, and sank the only ships lost by the US Navy in Korean waters.[42]

5 The Vietnam War

The US Navy mission throughout the Vietnam War was to reduce the flow of arms to enemy forces. Most of these supplies were believed to enter North Vietnam through the ports of Haiphong, Cam Pha and Hon Gai at which some forty cargo ships called every month. Blocking access to the ports of North Vietnam by initiating a mine campaign had been given serious consideration time and again since early 1966, but it was ruled out for fear of

[41]As the US Navy's Chief of Naval Operations, Admiral Forrest P. Sherman, was forced to declare, 'let's admit it. They caught us with our pants down. Those damn mines cost us eight days' delay in getting the troops ashore and more than two hundred casualties. That's bad enough . . . We've been plenty submarine-conscious and air-conscious. Now we're going to start getting mine-conscious – beginning last week'; quoted in CAGLE and MANSON, *op. cit., supra* n.39 at p. 142. For Admiral Joy, Commander of Naval Forces in the Far East, 'the main lesson of the Wonsan operation is that no so-called subsidiary branch of the naval service, such as mine warfare, should ever be neglected or relegated to a minor role in the future. Wonsan also taught us that we can be denied freedom of movement to an enemy objective through the intelligent use of mines by an alert foe'; see *ibid.* at p. 151. Finally, Admiral Allan Smith, Commander of the amphibious task force, summed up his experience in these words: 'we have lost control of the seas to a nation without a navy, using pre-World War I weapons, laid by vessels that were utilized at the time of the birth of Christ'; quoted in FORTIN, E., 'Those Damn Mines', 118 *USNIP* (July 1992) at p. 32. In yet another mission, the Chinnampo sweep in the Yellow Sea, Allied craft were engaged in the clearance of a 200-mile channel. No lives were lost and no ships were damaged during the Chinnampo operation.

[42]LOTT, *op. cit., supra* n.35 at p. 285. Minesweeping operations accounted for a total of 1,088 mines during the three-year campaign. The only enemy ship to be captured at sea during the war was a minelaying junk manned with North Korean naval officers. It was surprised by the Canadian destroyer *Nootka* in late September 1952 while engaged in planting magnetic mines along Korea's west coast. Except for limited use of magnetic mines, North Korean forces employed mainly contact mines since the virtually unsweepable pressure-magnetic or pressure-acoustic mines were not as yet technically available to them. It has been estimated, however, that had they used even a combination of magnetic-acoustic mines, the task of minesweeping would have been increased 100-fold.

escalatory implications that any foreseeable damage to international shipping, especially Soviet and Polish, might have had.[43] In May 1972, however, in response to a major North Vietnamese offensive reversing the military picture and weakening the prospects of negotiations, the Nixon administration ordered the mining of all North Vietnamese ports with a view to preventing further war supplies been shipped to enemy forces.[44]

In the communiqué addressed to the UN Security Council, the United States notified that:

> the entrances to the ports of North Viet-Nam are being mined, commencing 0900 hours Saigon time, May 9, and the mines are set to activate automatically beginning 1800 hours Saigon time, 11 May. This will permit vessels of other countries presently in North Viet-Namese ports three daylight periods to depart safely. The mines will be so positioned within the internal waters and claimed territorial waters of North Viet-Nam as to prevent access to North Viet-Namese ports and North Viet-Namese naval operations from these ports.[45]

The drafters of these measures took great pains to ensure that the dictates of international law would be strictly observed. Three points bearing the stamp of restraint were particularly emphasized; first, minelaying would be confined to the internal and territorial waters of North Vietnam. No mines were, therefore, to be expected on the high seas. Second, all reassurances

[43]The only concession to the military commanders was made in February 1967 when the mining of rivers and inland waterways of North Vietnam was finally authorized. By mid-April 1967, US aircraft had planted the first five river minefields. Viet Cong forces had equally planted at times some rather crudely fabricated mine devices and other shore-controlled explosives on Long Tao River with a view to disrupting the river communication of the capital of South Vietnam. No fewer than two merchant ships, two US minesweepers and several South Vietnamese minesweepers were lost to these mines. From 1966, therefore, a detachment of 12 US minesweeping boats was charged with keeping the main river channel to Saigon free of mines. For more, see KOLBENSCHLAG, G.R., 'Minesweeping on the Long Tao River', 93 *USNIP* (June 1967), p. 89*ff*.

[44]The Haiphong mining in its legal merits is reviewed in SWAYZE, F.B., 'Traditional Principles of Blockade in Modern Practice: United States Mining of Internal and Territorial Waters of North Vietnam', 29 *Judge Advocate General Journal* (1977), no.2, p. 143*ff*., and LEVIE, *op. cit., supra* n.1, p. 144*ff*. See also LUCKOW, U., 'Victory Over Ignorance and Fear: The U.S. Minelaying Attack on North Vietnam', 35 *US Naval War College Review* (Jan.–Feb.1982), p. 17*ff*., and O'CONNELL, D.P., *The Influence of Law on Sea Power*, 1975, p. 94*ff*.

[45]See UN Doc. *S/10631*, May 9, 1972.

were given that the operation would be amply notified. In addition to public announcement and ordinary notices to mariners, US on-scene naval forces were instructed to warn any approaching vessel of the mine hazards. Third, the mine campaign had a definite military objective which was to interdict further seaborne war supplies to Hanoi, and to deny the use of ports by North Vietnamese forces for launching attacks.[46]

Reports are not unanimous as to the number of merchant vessels concerned by the announcement of the mine blockade.[47] In the course of the interdiction campaign an estimated total of 8,000 acoustic mines was laid by carrier aircraft in coastal waters and some 3,000 in inland waterways.[48] The operation was markedly successful. The flow of war materials was reduced to approximately 10 per cent of its prior level, while political complications were evaded as no ship was sunk or damaged. A protocol annexed to the agreement of 27 January 1973, on Ending the War and Restoring Peace in Vietnam expressly provided for mineclearing of North Vietnamese inland and territorial waters.[49] In the event, as many as eighteen ships were assigned to the task of sweeping the mined areas, a mission which was completed by 18 July 1973.[50] What was uncommon

[46]The concern was that the interception of merchant shipping should not appear as the sole object of the operation. It is for this reason that President Nixon in his announcement of 8 May 1972 referred repeatedly to the objective as being 'to keep the weapons of war out of the hands of the international outlaws of North Viet-Nam'; see *ibid.*, Annex at p. 3.

[47]According to one analyst, 36 vessels were found in Haiphong harbour at the time of the US notice, eight of which departed during the grace period; see SWAYZE, *op. cit., supra* n.44 at p. 163. *Cf.* LUCKOW, *op. cit., supra* n.44 at p. 25. Other estimates refer to 72 ships berthed in Haiphong harbour, over a quarter of which had left the port within three hours; see O'CONNELL, *op. cit., supra* n.44 at p. 95.

[48]See 20 *KCA* (1974) at p. 26335. Some of the mines were set to sterilize themselves in 100 days, others in 200. In their effort to make the mine blockade effective not only against deep-draft vessels but also against junks and sampans, the Americans developed a new type of mine, the *Destructor*, a dual purpose weapon for it was easily convertible from bomb to mine, with increased sensitivity and wide-target spectrum.

[49]See Protocol Concerning the Removal, Permanent Deactivation, or Destruction of Mines in the Territorial Waters, Ports, Harbours, and Waterways of the Democratic Republic of Vietnam, in 12 *ILM* (1973), p. 91*ff.*

[50]Task Force 78 comprised surface as well as airborne assets. The surface minesweeping task group was made up of ten ocean minesweepers, while each of the four airborne mine countermeasures units consisted of 15 helicopters towing sweep gear such as magnetic sleds and acoustic devices. The full account of the minesweeping operation is given in McCAULEY, B., 'Operation End Sweep', 100 *USNIP* (March 1974), p. 19*ff.*

about Operation End Sweep was, first, that it was carried out as a post-war operation, that is in total absence of enemy opposition and with the location, type and settings of all mines known, and secondly, that it marked the first use of helicopters in minesweeping missions.

The legal nature of the Haiphong mining has been a matter of controversy. Washington qualified the action as measure of collective self-defence in full accordance with Article 51 of the UN Charter.[51] The Soviet Union castigated what it branded as 'a most flagrant violation of the universally recognized principle of freedom of navigation'[52] and the 1958 Geneva High Seas Convention. The reactions of other communist countries were couched in like wording. For the People's Republic of China, for instance, the US action 'grossly violates the freedom of international navigation and trade', while elsewhere the mine campaign is described as 'a flagrant blockade of the territorial sea and ports of Viet-Nam'.[53] In the view of the Cuban government, 'the President of the United States has not hesitated to put himself above international law, to violate the rights of freedom of navigation and freedom of trade' by ordering 'the illegal blockade of the Democratic Republic of Viet-Nam, to be achieved by mining the entrances to its ports'.[54]

6 The closure of the Suez Canal

The Suez Canal remained closed to international navigation for eight years following the 1967 Six-Day Arab-Israeli War. In the course of the hostilities, ten merchant vessels and eighty barges

[51]George Bush in his letter to the Security Council wrote: 'as the minimum actions necessary to meet this threat the Republic of Viet-Nam and the United States of America have jointly decided to take the following measures of collective self-defence'; see UN Doc. *S/10631*, 9 May 1972. A number of western scholars subscribed to that view arguing that the Vietnam experience exemplified the feasibility of resorting to mine warfare in a self-defensive posture and in circumstances whereby 'the destruction of shipping as such is neither the purpose of minelaying nor its necessary effect'; see O'CONNELL, *op. cit., supra* n.44 at p. 96.

[52]See UN Doc. *S/10643*, 11 May 1972.

[53]See UN Doc. *S/10644*, 11 May 1972, and UN Doc. *S/10638*, 11 May 1972.

[54]See UN Doc. *S/10642*, 11 May 1972. Mongolia also condemned the mine campaign and called upon the United States to 'observe its commitments assumed under international treaties and respect the right to freedom of international navigation and trade'; see UN Doc. *S/10651*, 12 May 1972. Yugoslavia, for its part, expressed its sharp condemnation without further qualifying the American action; see UN Doc. *S/10640*, 11 May 1972.

were intentionally sunk in the waterway to block passage. Later in 1969–70, extensive minefields were laid in the canal and along its banks. Sixteen ships were thus trapped in the canal at the time of its closure. In January 1974, Egypt and Israel agreed on a military disengagement scheme so that Egypt was to regain control over Suez. Technical assistance was soon thereafter asked from the United States, the United Kingdom and France for clearing the canal of mines, unexploded ordnance, the scuttled vessels and other obstructions.

Operation Nimbus Star, code-name for the minesweeping undertaking, commenced in late April 1974 entailing the use of helicopter-towed sleds as well as surface minesweepers. Most of the mineclearing was carried out by the US Navy, which deployed helicopters and two amphibious assault ships, the *Iwo Jima* and the *Inchon,* while the British committed for their part three of their newest minehunters, the *Maxton,* the *Wilton* and the *Bossington,* as well as a support ship. In July 1974, the *Maxton* became the first vessel to travel the full 103-mile length of the canal since 1967, while in November 1974 four small Egyptian passenger vessels were successfully towed through the waterway from north to south. By April 1975 when British and French minesweepers returned to make a final check, it was estimated that some 42,000 live explosive objects had been removed from the canal, and 750,000 land mines removed from its banks. Ten major wrecks and 120 smaller sunk obstacles including tanks and aircraft had also been cleared.[55]

[55]See 21 *KCA* (1975) at p. 27167. For more, see *The United States Role in Opening the Suez Canal: Hearing Before the Subcommittee on the Near East and South Asia of the Committee on Foreign Affairs House of Representatives,* 8 May 1974. See also Suez Canal Authority, *The Suez Canal: Present Conditions and Future Prospects,* 1975, and BOYD, J.H., 'Nimrod Spar: Clearing the Suez Canal', 102 *USNIP* (Feb.1976), p. 18*ff*.

In reviewing contemporary instances of mine warfare, passing reference should also be made to the civil war in Cambodia. As from January 1975, the forces of the National United Front of Cambodia, better known as the Khmers Rouges, had seized control of the entire length of the Mekong River from the South Vietnamese border to a point 15 miles south east of Phnom-Penh, and proceeded to mine the river in order to prevent all supplies from reaching the capital. As a result, several tugs had been sunk by floating mines and artillery fire. It is noteworthy that, whereas in 1974, a convoy arrived on average every ten days and only two vessels were lost, in the first five weeks of 1975 alone as many as 16 barges were sunk or abandoned. The closing of the Mekong to river convoys, which accounted for 80 per cent of the supplies reaching Phnom-Penh, soon proved of critical importance for the final capture of the city; see 21 *KCA* (1975) at p. 27150.

7 The mining of Nicaraguan ports

In its sustained effort to topple Managua's Sandinista government, the Reagan administration authorized in 1984 a covert mine campaign with the aim of disrupting all seaborne commerce to and from Nicaragua.[56] The move was expected to prevent Soviet shipments of military supplies from reaching Central America, and also to bring Nicaraguan economy to its knees by obstructing coffee exports. In early January 1984, a faction of the Contras, the Nicaraguan Democratic Force, announced that all Nicaraguan ports had been mined and that they should be avoided as danger zones.[57] In March 1984, it was further made known that mines had been laid off the ports of Corinto, Puerto Sandino and El Bluff. The mines were scattered along the sea lanes regularly used by merchant shipping by speedboats operating from a US-manned

[56]Before examining the mine campaign against Nicaragua, brief mention should be made of the mine warfare aspects of the 1982 Falklands War. After invading the islands the Argentines mined the approaches of Port Stanley as well as a few other strategic localities in anticipation of a British landing. The mine deterrent proved in the Falklands context as forceful as ever since it constrained the British commanders to choose a practically undefended landing site whatever other tactical disadvantages this might involve. Thus, the landing of 21 May 1982, at San Carlos, East Falkland, was decided primarily because of the absence of Argentine minefields in the Falkland Sound despite the fact that the British troops would then have to march across the island from west to east over a distance of 65 miles before arriving at Port Stanley. As a war narrative relates, 'the naval staff had become deeply concerned by intelligence reports that Berkeley Sound and possibly Cow Bay were mined . . . [On the contrary] the SBS [Special Boat Squadron] reported that there were no enemy whatever around San Carlos . . . The SBS found no evidence of mines on the shore, nor could they see any minelaying taking place at sea'; see HASTINGS, M. and JENKINS, S., *The Battle for the Falklands*, 1983 at p. 184. On the considerations governing the selection of the landing site, see TRAIN, H.D., 'An Analysis of the Falkland/Malvinas Islands Campaign', 41 *US Naval War College Review* (1988/1) at pp. 41–2. Ten days before the landing, in fact, *HMS Alacrity* undertook the first and only complete 100-mile transit of Falkland Sound in order to reconnoitre the Argentine defences and verify the absence of mines; see CRAIG, C., 'Fighting by the Rules', 37 *US Naval War College Review* (1984/3) at pp. 25–6. It is probably true that Operation Sutton, as the landing was code-named, might well have turned into a disaster had the British opted to land at a mine-protected location.

[57]Already in October 1983, the FDN had threatened to prevent by force Mexican tankers from supplying oil to Nicaragua by mining the port of Corinto. As a result, the US oil company Exxon which accounted for three quarters of all Nicaraguan oil imports decided to suspend its services for reasons of safety; see 30 *KRWE* (1984) at p. 32844.

mother ship stationed outside Nicaragua's 12-mile territorial sea limit.[58]

Operation Sancho was carried out by means of sophisticated bottom influence mines which were activated only by large cargo ships and which were designed to cause noisy explosions rather than sink targeted vessels. Yet, 2 Nicaraguan fishermen were killed and 14 others injured in at least 12 reported explosions involving vessels of Dutch, Panamanian, Soviet, Liberian, Japanese and Nicaraguan registry.[59] Nicaragua, lacking all technical means for mineclearing, turned to countries such as Brazil, the Soviet Union or North Korea for assistance. A French offer to provide minesweepers never materialized. In the event, local fishing boats dragging steel chains astern or fishing nets were used in order to sweep safe channels. On the Pacific coast, at least three fishing vessels were lost during the minesweeping operations.

The US covert mine operation was soon to cause a major political furore domestically but also strong international reactions.[60] Among the countries that voiced their disapproval,

[58]The Contras denied any involvement of US secret services, but, in fact, CIA, as was later confirmed by its Director, had lent a helping hand in both the planning and the execution of the sea mining. The mother ship was believed to be an oil-rig service vessel of Panamanian registry, which had been purchased or leased by the CIA at an estimated cost of US $1.2 million. As for the speedboats, called Q-boats, were operated by unilaterally controlled personnel (known as UCLAs) obtained by contract from Ecuador, Guatemala, El Salvador and other Latin American countries. For more, see 'A Furor Over the Secret War', *Newsweek*, 23 April 1984, p. 8*ff.*; 'Explosion Over Nicaragua', *Time*, 23 April 1984, p. 6*ff.*

[59]A Nicaraguan fishing boat was destroyed by two mines in El Bluff on 25 February 1984. On 1 March, a large Dutch dredger was hit in Corinto. A week later, the *SS Los Caribes*, a Panamanian ship sustained heavy damage. A Soviet ship, the *SS Lugansk*, carrying 250,000 barrels of crude oil struck a mine at Puerto Sardino on 20 March, while on 28 March, the Liberian-flagged *SS Iver Chaser* reported mine damage exceeding US $1.6 million. The last reported incident came on 2 May 1984, the Nicaraguan vessel *SS Pedro Arauz Palacious* been sunk in Corinto. A short account of the events is given in Military and Paramilitary Activities in and against Nicaragua (Nicaragua v. United States of America), Merits, Judgment, *ICJ Reports 1986*, §§76–80 at pp. 46–8. See also REED, *op.cit.*, *supra* n.1 at pp. 316–21, and MARTIN, J.M. and RAMSAY, B.P., 'Sea Mines in Nicaragua', 116 *USNIP* (Sept.1990), pp. 111–16. According to this latter source, no more than 39 mines were planted damaging or destroying 19 vessels registered in eight different countries.

[60]Senator Glenn, for instance, expressed his resentment at what he called 'the hypocritical position of opposing state-sponsored terrorism when it is directed against our friends – and of condoning and even conducting it when it is directed against our real or imagined enemies'; cited in CHURCH, K.J., 'The Briar Patch of Reality: A Legal Analysis of the Mining of Nicaragua's Harbors', 18 *New York University Journal of International Law and Policy* (1985) at p. 169.

Britain characterized the mining as interference with international shipping, and deplored as a matter of principle 'any threats to navigation whenever and wherever they occur'.[61] For France it was a 'blockade undertaken in a time of peace against a small country which presents a serious problem of political ethics'.[62] The Soviet government held Washington 'responsible for this grave crime, an act of bandity and piracy'[63], while the Soviet Representative to the Security Council termed the action an 'attempt to set up a military blockade around Nicaragua', 'a gross transgression of the traditional usages of international navigation and trade' and 'an act of piracy and international terrorism'.[64]

Indicative of the international outcry, the United States were forced to veto on 4 April 1984, a UN Security Council resolution condemning the mining which had obtained the support of thirteen Security Council members.[65] It is not without significance that the US representative in his short intervention did not attempt to defend the legality of the mine campaign, but preferred, instead, to reproach the draft resolution for being unbalanced and unfair:

> the U.S. would have no problem with this draft resolution if it were concerned with all the violence in the region . . . apparently the only crime against the peace that the Security Council is concerned with is mining. Not bombing, as in Sudan; not shelling, as in Costa Rica; not in child

[61]See the statement of the UK Permanent Representative to the Security Council of 4 April 1984 in 56 *BYIL* (1985) at p. 488.

[62]See the statement of French Foreign Minister Claude Cheysson, quoted in CHURCH, *op. cit.*, *supra* n.60 at p. 182. While before the UN Security Council, the French government condemned 'resolument cette escalade dans la violence, ce type d'action nouvelle qui, entravant le libre accès des installations portuaires d'un pays souverain, conduit à une forme de blocus déguisé, foncièrement contraire aux grands principes du droit international'; see the intervention of the French Representative of 2 April 1984 in 30 *AFDI* (1984) at p. 1022.

[63]See 30 *KRWE* (1984) at p. 32845.

[64]See UN Doc. *S/PV.2529*, 4 April 1984, §201 at p. 22. The Dutch government expressed the view that 'violations of international law' such as the mining of Nicaraguan ports 'which has grave implications for the right of free navigation' should come to an end; *ibid.*, §§11–12 at p. 2. As for the Representatives of Vietnam and the German Democratic Republic, they drew an analogy with the 1972 mining of Haiphong and qualified the campaign as an act of aggression and piracy; *ibid.*, §23 at p. 3 and §56 at p. 7. Likewise, Afghanistan held the view that 'the international community should vehemently condemn this brazen act of aggression'; *ibid.*, §161 at p. 18.

[65]See UN Doc. *S/16463*, 4 April 1984.

> sacrifice or gassing, as in the Iran-Iraq War; not infiltrating and subverting, as in El Salvador; not invading, as in Chad; not occupying, pillaging or burning, as in Afghanistan; not Yellow Rain, as against defenseless South-East Asian populations. Only mining. How extraordinary that the prohibitions of the Charter should have been reduced to one simple negative.[66]

On 9 April 1984 Nicaragua filed an application with the International Court of Justice against the US illegal intervention together with a request for provisional measures. A month later, on 10 May, the Court indicated interim measures of protection providing, in the first place, that 'the United States of America should immediately cease and refrain from any action restricting, blocking or endangering access to or from Nicaraguan ports, and, in particular, the laying of mines'.[67]

8 The Red Sea mine mystery

In July 1984, a series of mysterious underwater explosions had been reported by crew members of various merchant vessels while navigating in the Red Sea and heading for the Suez Canal. The first incident involved a Soviet trawler, the *Knud Jesperson*, which alerted the Egyptian coastguard after suffering minor damage from an 'odd blast' on 9 July. A few days later, a Japanese ship signalled another explosion. The incidents reached a climax in the period between 27 July and 2 August 1984, when at least ten vessels were reported damaged. Similar episodes were reported throughout August and September with a total of nineteen ships, for the most cargo ships and oil tankers, flying

[66]See UN Doc. *S/PV.2529*, 4 April 1984, §§240, 244 at p. 26.

[67]See Military and Paramilitary Activities in and against Nicaragua (Nicaragua v. United States of America), Provisional Measures, Order of 10 May 1984, *ICJ Reports 1984*, §41 B(1) at p. 187. This operative paragraph of the Court's decision is all the more important as it was adopted unanimously. For the Court's judgement on the Merits, see *infra* notes 188–192 and accompanying text. In March 1986, the Chaser Shipping Corporation filed a complaint against the United States for damages arising from a mine incident involving one of the company's ships. The complaint was dismissed by the lower courts for lack of access to classified documents relating to covert operations. On 11 January 1988, further hearing was also denied by the US Supreme Court; see 484 U.S. 1004.

the flag of fifteen different countries, sustaining serious damage but no casualties.[68]

Although initially hesitant, Egyptian authorities finally admitted that the explosions were in all probability due to tethered mines which should be expected in three main areas, namely, the waters between the Hamish Islands and the North Yemeni coast, off Ras Shukheir at the entrance of the Gulf of Suez, as well as in the vicinity of the Suez harbour. Muslim fundamentalists of the Islamic Al Jihad organization claimed they had planted 190 mines in the area, whereas Iran and Libya were the preferred suspects within western circles. Be that as it may, it was never conclusively determined the type and origin of the mines, or the identity of the minelayer vessel.[69]

In early August 1984, following the request of Egypt and Saudi Arabia, warships of five western navies undertook surveillance and minesweeping operations in the zones of danger. The United States deployed three ships, eight helicopters and over 1,500 personnel in Operation Intense Look, while Great Britain operated five minehunters and one support ship. France dispatched another four minesweepers and two support vessels, while Italy and the Netherlands participated with further MCM assets. The Soviet Navy marked also its presence with three minehunters, one destroyer, and one helicopter carrier stationed

[68]Still, the traffic through the Suez Canal was slightly affected scoring only a 10 per cent decrease of its normal August total. By mid-August, traffic in the Suez Canal, which had dropped to as low as 42 ships per day at the beginning of the month, was back to normal, about 60 ships per day. For the full story of the Red Sea mine mystery, see TRUVER, S.C., 'Mines of August: An International Whodunit', 111 *USNIP* (May 1985), p. 94*ff*. See also BLANTON, S.L., 'Mines of August: Revisited', 113 *USNIP* (Nov.1987), p. 16*ff*.; ROUSSEAU, C., 'Chronique des faits internationaux', 89 *RGDIP* (1985), p. 132*ff*.; 31 *KRWE* (1985), p. 33371*ff*.; 'Fighting the Mines of August', *Newsweek*, 20 August 1984, p. 28*ff*.; 'The Minesweepers Move in', *Newsweek*, 27 August 1984, p. 12*ff*.; 'On Board the USS Shreveport', *Newsweek*, 3 September 1984, at p. 29.

[69]Diplomatic and shipping sources had at first speculated that Iran might have orchestrated the Red Sea mining in retaliation for Iraqi attacks on ships serving Iranian ports and also to punish Egypt for backing Iraq in the Gulf War. Egyptian high officials later accused directly that Tehran and Tripoli were to blame for the series of explosions and threatened that Egypt would deny use of the canal to all ships from any country proven to be implicated. President Hosni Mubarak, however, subsequently expressed hope that a search for the mines would prove Iran was not involved and declared that all indications would now point at Libya. For some time, in fact, the Libyan freighter *Ghat* gathered all suspicions since she had transited the Suez Canal three days before the first mine incident. The *Ghat* was intercepted by the French coastguard off Marseilles on Aug.18, 1984 and was searched unavailingly for evidence of minelaying gear.

at the south entrance of the Red Sea. At the height of the operation, no fewer than twenty-six ships from six countries were in the Gulf of Suez and Red Sea hunting for evidence which could designate the author of the attacks.[70]

9 The 1980–8 Gulf Tanker War

Operation Earnest Will and the Neglected Mine Threat In a letter dated 29 June 1987, US Senator Nunn, commenting upon the Weinberger Report concerning the Administration's plan to reflag and protect eleven Kuwaiti tankers, expressed the following concern: 'there is one area that did not receive adequate attention in the report: that being the threat from naval mines. Mine warfare would be an indirect form of attack that Iran might favor. U.S. mine countermeasures capabilities are limited. As a consequence, the United States must be prepared well in advance to counter any mining threats.'[71] As it turned out, these words of caution proved particularly relevant. In summer 1987, in fact, sowing floating mines at random along the Gulf sea lanes appeared to Tehran an appealing strategy in a twofold sense; politically, it would enable Iran to cause considerable trouble to international shipping while avoiding retaliation which might have been expected in case of overt attacks. In military terms, sea mining was meant to be an unpleasant surprise for US naval forces present in the Gulf, at the time least prepared to deal with this type of threat.[72]

On 16 May 1987, the Kuwaiti tanker *Marshal Cheykov,* the first of the Soviet ships chartered by Kuwait, was damaged by a mine explosion while navigating in international waters off Kuwait. Following the incident, three Soviet minesweepers were dispatched to the Persian Gulf at the end of the month. On 24 July

[70]Finally, on 17 September 1984, the British contingent deployed in the Red Sea, managed to retrieve a section of an object resembling a mine and containing sophisticated electronic instrumentation. It was later announced that in all likelihood it made part of an unknown type of Soviet-made mine manufactured some time later than 1981. American specialists, for their part, concluded that bottom acoustic mines must have been used with relatively small charges intended to cause inconvenience rather than casualties and wrecks.

[71]See 26 *ILM* (1987) at p. 1474.

[72]American MCM capability at the time depended primarily on 23 minesweeping helicopters, three ocean-going sweepers and 18 reserve ships. None of these assets, however, operated in the Gulf; see 'Oops, We Forgot Minesweepers', *Newsweek*, 10 August 1987, at p. 28.

1987, the reflagged Kuwaiti tanker *Bridgeton* struck a mine while sailing in convoy 120 miles south east of Kuwait, or 18 miles west of Iran's Farsi Island, on its maiden voyage under the American flag.[73] It was under these circumstances that a Staff Report to the Foreign Relations Committee of the US Senate was forced to conclude in November 1987: 'the Iranian tactic revealed a glaring weakness in the American plan to escort the reflagged tankers: the US naval vessels were themselves completely unprotected against mines'.[74]

Calculating the Risk: Multinational Alert In response to the mine crisis, France ordered a task force consisting of an aircraft carrier and two frigates to leave for the Persian Gulf on 29 July 1987. American requests, however, to the UK, France, the Netherlands and West Germany to deploy minesweepers as a matter of urgency were turned down. European policies were destined to shift radically only following a major development in the Iranian mine campaign at the beginning of August. On 10 August 1987, a Panamanian-registered tanker, the *Texaco Caribbean*, carrying ironically enough a full load of Iranian oil, ran into a mine off the Fujairah port, in the Gulf of Oman, in waters which had previously been considered free of all danger. In view of what was perceived as Tehran's clear intention to escalate the clandestine mine warfare, the United Kingdom and France announced their intention to deploy minesweeping squadrons,

[73]The 400,000 deadweight-ton tanker escorted by three US warships, the *Kidd*, the *Crommelin* and the *Fox*, participating in Operation Earnest Will was proceeding at 16 knots unloaded to Kuwait when it was rocked by a blast. The mine's 115-kilogram charge failed to sink the ship ripping a hole through into the 27mm-thick steel hull about 10 metres long by 5 metres wide. Shrapnel went through even the main deck some 25 metres away from the impact. American naval experts later confirmed that the mines used were of the same type as those in four previous minings. They were bottom-moored contact mines of 1908 Russian design, adjusted to be floating a few meters below the surface. There were no casualties and the vessel made its way to Kuwait at reduced speed. The incident's most embarrassing aspect, however, was that although large tankers may survive even several mine explosions, thin skinned warships would only be expected to suffer massive damage and loss of life. It is indicative that *Bridgeton*'s escort warships promptly aligned for the rest of the journey behind the damaged tanker they were supposed to protect and let it clear a safe passage through the unexpected minefield. For more on this incident, see 'SS *Bridgeton*: The First Convoy', 114 *USNIP* (May 1988), p. 52*ff.*, and TRUVER, S.C., 'Weapons that Wait . . . and Wait . . .', 114 *USNIP* (Feb.1988), p. 31*ff.*

[74]Cited in DE GUTTRY, A. and RONZITTI, N. (eds), *The Iran-Iraq War (1980–1988) and the Law of Naval Warfare*, 1993, doc.2.a.37 at p. 294.

while the Italian, Dutch and Belgian governments followed shortly thereafter with similar decisions.[75] In the meantime, a small Swedish-owned supply ship, the *Anita,* hit a mine in the Gulf of Oman and sunk with six of its crew members.[76]

Moreover, Iran stepped up its attacks on merchant shipping by speedboats armed with machine-guns and rocket-propelled grenades. On 18 August 1987, a tanker of Panamanian registry, the *Sea Sierra,* was the first to come under fire outside the Hormuz Strait. A Kuwaiti tanker was attacked in the same area on 31 August, while two Japanese tankers were hit on 2 October of the same year. With the Iranian hit-and-run tactics progressively spreading out of the Gulf, there was also growing concern for the safety of the aircraft carriers and their battle groups stationed in the Arabian Sea. US officials estimated that although no more than 50 contact mines had been laid, Iran had nearly 1,000 more in reserve. Other reports added alarmingly that Iran was also capable of producing influence mines of the magnetic or the acoustic type. The Iranian government praised the mine attacks on merchant shipping still denying any direct involvement. According to an often-quoted statement of Prime Minister Moussavi, this was simply the work of 'an invisible hand against arrogant powers'.

Initially, the European mine countermeasures contingents operated under national command. Operation Cimnel, for instance, launched by the British in September 1987, involved four Hunt-class minehunters together with support ships.[77] The French task group, for its part, consisted of two minesweepers and their escort vessel, while Italy deployed three Lerici-class

[75]As for West Germany, it floated the possibility of sending some ships to the Mediterranean in order to fill the gap left by the two dozen US warships assigned to the Gulf, but excluded the deployment of minesweepers in Middle East waters. Indeed, from October 1987 until June 1988, between three and five German warships were present in the Mediterranean; see GIEGERICH, T., 'The German Contribution to the Protection of Shipping in the Persian Gulf: Staying out for Political or Constitutional Reasons?', 49 *ZaöRV* (1989), p. 1*ff.*

[76]In six previous incidents since May 1987, only big tankers had bumped into mines with no casualties. For a brief account on the mine incidents in summer 1987, see RONZITTI, N., 'La guerre du Golfe, le déminage et la circulation des navires', 33 *AFDI* (1987), p. 647*ff.*, ROUSSEAU, C., 'Chronique des faits internationaux', 92 *RGDIP* (1988), p. 142*ff.*, and 33 *KRWE* (1987), p. 35597*ff.* See also 'The Mines of August', *Newsweek,* 24 August 1987, p. 8*ff.*; 'Here a Mine, There a Mine', *Time,* 24 August 1987, p. 18*ff.*; 'In Deeper in the Gulf', *Newsweek,* 31 August 1987, p. 8*ff.*

[77]See DE GUTTRY and RONZITTI, *op. cit., supra* n.74, doc.2.a.37 at p. 294.

minehunters, three frigates and two support vessels.[78] As regards the Dutch navy, two minehunters of the Alkmaar-class were deployed for an initial period of three months. The Dutch minehunters, it was further announced, would not enter without protection waters where an attack might be expected.[79]

By mid-October 1987, the mine countermeasures forces of the Netherlands and Belgium were united in a single minesweeping squadron.[80] The integrated command structure comprised the tactical command assigned to the commander of the joint task force aboard the Belgian support vessel *De Zinnia*, and the operational command which was left with the Admiral Netherlands Home Fleet in Den Helder. The area of operations was clearly specified as including the international waters (outside the war zones designated by the belligerents) in the Gulf of Oman, the Strait of Hormuz and the southern part of the Persian Gulf, that is no further north than Bahrain.[81]

In late June 1988, the United Kingdom, Belgium and the Netherlands decided to put their MCM assets under unified command, constituting a trilateral task force named Calendar. The British commander of the task force in the Gulf was charged with the tactical command, while the operational control would lie with the Commander-in-Chief of the British Royal Navy in Northwood. The ships of the trilateral force would continue to enjoy the protection of the British frigates of the Armilla Patrol. As regards the area of operations, Calendar was authorized to carry out 'minesweeping operations, if necessary, in the terri-

[78]*Ibid.*, doc.2.b.2 at p. 412, doc.2.a.1 at p. 445, and doc.2.a.5 at pp. 454–5.

[79]It was not clear, however, at that point whether the Dutch warships had received orders to keep clear of belligerent war zones and remain in international waters or whether they would seek protection from other naval forces present in the region; see 19 *NYIL* (1988) at pp. 359–60.

[80]As announced in a press release of 14 September 1987: 'tout en observant sa stricte neutralité . . ., la Belgique participera dans les eaux internationales du Golfe arabo-persique à des opérations purement défensives de déminage, dans le but d'assurer le respect du principe de la libre navigation'; see 22 *RBDI* (1989) at p. 427.

[81]The Dutch-Belgian squadron was to cooperate closely with the British naval force in areas where an aerial or surface threat might be anticipated. In such situation, the Dutch and Belgian vessels should place themselves under the command of the British commander. In the vicinity of Armilla Patrol warships, therefore, Dutch and Belgian minesweepers would enjoy the same protection as British vessels. It was further agreed that British, Dutch and Belgian vessels when sailing together would use their armament in their own but also the common defence; see 20 *NYIL* (1989) at pp. 180–2.

torial waters of the coastal States too, if agreement on this has been reached with the relevant countries'.[82]

The Iran-Ajr Incident On 21 September 1987, American forces managed to intercept a boat in the act of laying mines substantiating their allegations about Iranian responsibility. US surveillance helicopters, in fact, attacked and disabled an Iranian landing vessel, the *Iran-Ajr,* while engaged in minelaying activities in international waters at a point about 50 miles north east of Bahrain, in an area frequently used as an anchorage by merchant ships. Three men were killed in the attack and twenty-six more crew members were taken prisoners, while a number of contact mines together with minelaying gear were found aboard. The seized vessel was later scuttled in deep waters off Bahrain. Shortly after the incident, the US permanent representative to the UN informed the president of the Security Council that the United States had 'exercised its inherent right of self-defence under international law by taking defensive action against a naval vessel of the Islamic Republic of Iran in the Persian Gulf'.[83]

Iran's Foreign Minister Ali Akbar Velayati in a letter addressed to the UN Secretary-General asserted that the *Iran-Ajr* was in reality a cargo vessel under commercial registration, unarmed and carrying a load of victuals at the time it came under attack. He further dismissed the minelaying accusations

[82]*Ibid.* at p. 183. The whole operation was intended to 'serve the purpose of de-escalation in view of the strict neutrality of the participating countries in the conflict between Iraq and Iran'. The mineclearing effort of the European participants under the umbrella of the Western European Union was hailed as the 'culmination of a major pioneering landmark in European naval co-operation'; quoted in VENTURINI, G., 'Commentary on International Organizations' Action' in DE GUTTRY and RONZITTI, *op. cit., supra* n.74 at p. 533. For more, see *ibid.*, pp. 495–519.

[83]See UN Doc. *S/19149*, 22 September 1987. For the initial Iranian reply, see UN Doc. *S/19153*, 24 September 1987. According to the American account of the events, the *Iran-Ajr* had already managed to roll off six mines before being neutralized by helicopter gunfire, while ten additional mines were later discovered on board the vessel. The night of the *Iran-Ajr* incident, in fact, a small survey boat of Panamanian registry hit a mine and sank near Farsi Island, while six days later more mines were spotted between Dubai and the Iranian islands of Abu Musa and Farsi. According to experts, the mines were of Soviet design and probably of North Korean construction. For a detailed description of the incident, see the letter from the US President to the Speaker of the House and the President of the Senate, reprinted in DE GUTTRY and RONZITTI, *op. cit., supra* n.74, doc.2.a.8 at p. 173. See also 'Ambush in the Gulf', *Newsweek*, 5 October 1987, p. 10*ff.*

as a 'total fabrication' which 'has simply been put forward to create disrepute for the Islamic Republic of Iran', and alleged that the US blew up the vessel 'owing to its inability to present evidence and proof for its allegations'.[84] In the days following the *Iran-Ajr* incident, a Panamanian ship, the *Marisa I*, struck a mine and sank with four of its crew members some 50 miles north of where the *Iran-Ajr* had been intercepted. No further incidents were reported, however, during the final months of 1987.

The Samuel Roberts Incident As the Iran-Iraq War drew near to its conclusion, floating mines were to resume taking their toll on ships plying the troubled Gulf waters. On 17 February 1988, a Liberian vessel, the *Prosper World*, hit a mine off Dubai, while on 14 April 1988, the frigate *USS Samuel Roberts* was damaged by a mine while navigating 70 miles east of Bahrain. In a swift reaction, Washington attributed to Iran the full responsibility for the incident. As President Reagan wrote to the Speaker of the House and the President of the Senate on 19 April:

> an examination of the mines remaining in the water established that they were M-08 mines, the same type Iran was caught placing in the water from the *Iran Ajr* on September 21, 1987. They had been freshly laid in an area transited by U.S. convoys. No barnacles or marine growth were on the mines. Most important the mines bore markings of the same type and series as on those laid by the *Iran Ajr*. No doubt exists that Iran laid these mines for the specific purpose of damaging or sinking U.S. or other non-belligerent ships.[85]

[84]See UN Doc. *S/19161*, 29 September 1987. And elsewhere: 'concurrent with this action, the United States claimed that the said vessel was photographed while mining the regional waters. However, subsequently it was claimed that the photographs could not be developed . . . How could this vessel, which was a slow-speed vessel, commercial and unarmed, be used for the purposes of mining?', *ibid.* See also UN Doc. *S/19167*, 30 September 1987 at para.4. On the *Iran-Ajr* incident, note the absorbing remarks of Theodor Meron in 82 *Proc.ASIL* (1988), p. 164*ff.* See also NORDQUIST, M.H. and WACHENFELD, M.G., 'Legal Aspects of Reflagging Kuwaiti Tankers and Laying of Mines in the Persian Gulf', 31 *GYIL* (1988) at pp. 161–4.

[85]See DE GUTTRY and RONZITTI, *op. cit., supra* n.74, doc.2.a.11 at p. 178. In the days that followed, American and French minesweepers discovered and destroyed four mines in the same area; see ROUSSEAU, C., 'Chronique des faits internationaux', 92 *RGDIP* (1988) at p. 714.

On 18 May 1988, in what was termed a 'measured response' to the mining of the *Samuel Roberts*, US naval forces destroyed two Iranian oil platforms at Sirri and Sassan islands.[86] The US government justified the action as a lawful exercise of the inherent right of self-defence under Article 51 of the UN Charter, and laid particular emphasis on the fact that Tehran had been repeatedly given fair warning of the consequences of its unscrupulous minelaying policy. As the US Representative to the UN declared before the Security Council, 'through diplomatic channels, we have informed the Government of the Islamic Republic of Iran on four separate occasions, most recently October 19, 1987, that the United States would not accept Iran's minelaying in international waters or in the waters of neutral states'.[87]

Lessons Relearned Drifting mines continued to be a matter of international concern even after the ceasefire agreement of August 1988. Although mine incidents in the Persian Gulf had virtually ceased, no one could claim with certainty that all mine danger was gone. The Iranian navy announced on 22 September 1988 that it had cleared all mines from the southern Gulf. On 27 October 1988, minesweepers from the UK, the Netherlands and Belgium launched Operation Clearsweep with the aim of sweeping a channel, 1 mile wide by 350 miles long, in order to

[86]See 34 *KRWE* (1988) at p. 36169. Several Iranian naval vessels that attempted to resist the American retaliatory action came also under attack. At the end of fierce fighting, the Iranians had lost two frigates, four armed speedboats, and one missile patrol boat with at least 40 men killed; see 'Iran's Devastating Week', *Newsweek*, 2 May 1988 at p. 11. For a description of Operation Praying Mantis, see PERKINS, J.B., 'Operation Praying Mantis: The Surface View', 115 *USNIP* (May 1989), p. 66*ff.*, and LANGSTON, B. and BRINGLE, D., 'Operation Praying Mantis: The Air View', 115 *USNIP* (May 1989), p. 54*ff.* In November 1992 Iran brought a case against the United States now pending before the ICJ for the destruction of the oil platforms. On 12 December 1996, the ICJ delivered a judgement by which it rejected the preliminary objection to its jurisdiction raised by the United States. The Court found that it had jurisdiction to deal with the case on the basis of Article XXI, para.2, of the 1955 Treaty of Friendship, Commerce and Consular Rights between the United States and Iran; see *ICJ Communiqué* no.96/33 of 12 December 1996. For some preliminary remarks on the US retaliatory action of October 1987 and April 1988, see POLITAKIS, G.P., 'From Action Stations to Action: U.S. Naval Deployment, "Non-Belligerency", and "Defensive Reprisals" in the Final Year of the Iran-Iraq War', 25 *ODIL* (1994), p. 31*ff.* See also *supra*, chapter 1, notes 153–5 and accompanying text.

[87]See UN Doc. *S/19791*, 18 April 1988. See also DE GUTTRY and RONZITTI, *op. cit., supra* n.74, doc.4.a.3 at p. 212, and doc.3.12 at p. 196.

provide a safe passage for international shipping to the northern end of the Gulf.[88]

Iran's – in all probability – mine campaign, as a distinct facet of the so-called Tanker War, had an unquestionable impact on the course of events which marked the final year of the Gulf War. At the time of the suspension of hostilities in August 1988, 547 merchant ships had been attacked with 420 seamen killed and 452 injured. The total losses of shipping companies exceeded an estimated $2 billion.[89] For the most part, these figures are to be attributed to Iraqi missile air strikes, or to the hit-and-run speedboat attacks of the Iranian Revolutionary Guard. Human losses and material damage caused by mines have been astonishingly low, even negligible, as contrasted to the far more destructive Exocet raids.[90] For all the doubt of an approximation, there must have been no more than fifteen mine incidents in all, while the total number of the allegedly Iranian mines must have been in the neighbourhood of 100 to 200. As regards casualties, they would seem to be limited to twenty seamen lost or injured aboard the *Anita*, the *Marissa I* and the *Samuel Roberts*.

Yet, paradoxically, the scattering of a few contact mines proved far more significant than any other event as far as the naval aspects of the Iran-Iraq War are concerned. More than even the deployment of Chinese Silkworm missiles, naval mines were thought likely to bring the flow of oil to an halt and the Gulf shipping to complete disorder. The uneasiness grew so acute that western navies began crowding the Persian Gulf in unprecedented numbers, or as an eloquent overstatement put it, 'there are more minesweepers than mines out there'.[91] Fol-

[88]See 35 *KRWE* (1989) at p. 36570.

[89]See ROUSSEAU, C., 'Chronique des faits internationaux', 93 *RGDIP* (1989) at p. 140.

[90]Compare, for instance, the 10 injured sailors of the mine-struck *USS Samuel Roberts* with the the 37 crewmen killed in the inadvertent missile attack against the *USS Stark*. This is perhaps the reason why statistics on mine attacks have never been published separately. In the words of one analyst, 'even counting some of the unknown attacks as mine-related, however, mining accounted for only a small fraction of all attacks in 1987. The significant attention paid to the mining threat in the middle months of the year by both on-scene naval forces and the western press might thus be seen in part as a reflection of the psychological effect that mines can generate'; see O'ROURKE, R., 'The Tanker War', 114 *USNIP* (May 1988) at p. 30.

[91]See the interview of F.C. Seitz, captain of *SS Bridgeton*, following the mining of his ship, *ibid.* at p. 57.

lowing the first mine reports, the United States dispatched their biggest war fleet since the Vietnam War. Whereas in March 1987, it was only the US and the UK that operated a total of eight warships within the Persian Gulf, in September seven more countries marked their presence with 27 warships, the number increasing to 48 in November of the same year. Critics pointed to flawed naval planning in matters of mine countermeasures. Yet, more than unpreparedness, the mine headache of summer 1987 demonstrated the undiminished efficacy of the mine weapon in modern conditions, and the continued vulnerability of warships to underwater hazards.[92]

10 The 1991 Gulf War against Iraq

Desert Storm and the Mine Deterrent In the months that saw the impressive build-up of naval forces in and around the Persian Gulf during the second half of 1990, it was reported that as many as nine minesweepers, four American and five British, had detected a total of 225 mines of which 133 were destroyed. They were all drifting mines of the obsolescent contact type. It was estimated and mostly feared, however, that the real Iraqi threat concerned bottom influence mines of modern design laid in Kuwaiti territorial waters – all the more so, as the geography and bathymetry of the Persian Gulf make it extremely suitable for mining, especially with moored and ground mines. It is possible, therefore, that the idea of attempting a landing was abandoned precisely because the aniticipated Iraqi minefields off Kuwaiti shores represented an unmanageable tactical difficulty of unpredictable cost.[93]

[92]In a telling footnote concerning the cost-effectiveness of naval mines, the reported transport and repair cost of the frigate *Samuel Roberts* reached US $52.1 million, or roughly one-sixth of what it cost to built her, being out of service for 17 months, whereas the cost of the sea mine that caused the damage was less than US $1,500.

[93]As one naval analyst wrote later, 'it remains to be learned, whether or not the suspected presence of large quantities of Iraqi mines in Kuwaiti waters and around the Shatt-al-Arab had a role in the decision to use amphibious forces for deception purposes only'; see PRESTON, A., 'Naval Aspects of the Gulf Conflict', 15 *Military Technology* (1991/4) at p. 61. See also HUNT, L.M., 'In Stride', 120 *USNIP* (April 1994), p. 59*ff*. According to a US Defense Department draft report, published one year after Desert Storm and which purports to assess the military lessons of the Gulf War, 'Iraq's minelaying ability out-stripped the limited U.S. mineclearing capability, hampering naval operations in the Gulf'; see *International Herald Tribune*, 24 February 1992 at p. 2.

Iraq was known to be in possession of important stocks of mines, mainly of Russian and Italian manufacture, but with a limited surface and aircraft minelaying capability. The Iraqi salvage tug *Aka*, for instance, laid several minefields and then hid inshore or up the Shatt-al-Arab. Although detected by satellite and repeatedly targeted, it was never neutralized. As it turned out, an estimated 1,200 mines were planted by Iraq off Kuwaiti coasts in a semi-circle with a 50-mile radius centred on Kuwait City and reaching from Kuwait's southern border to the entrance of Shatt-al-Arab.[94] It should also be recalled that in view of the mine threat the UN Security Council in its Resolution 686 (1991) had demanded Iraq *inter alia* to 'provide all information and assistance in identifying Iraqi mines, booby traps and other explosives as well as any chemical and biological weapons and material in Kuwait, in areas of Iraq where forces of Member States cooperating with Kuwait pursuant to resolution 678 (1990) are present temporarily, and in the adjacent waters'.

At the time of victory of the coalition forces, the US amphibious assault ship *Tripoli* was withdrawn for repairs, while the Aegis-class cruiser *USS Princeton* was badly damaged and suffered casualties, both vessels having struck Iraqi mines on 17 February 1991 in the northern Gulf.[95] At least one Iraqi warship is known to have also fallen victim of floating mines. After the termination of hostilities, mine countermeasures assets from ten nations engaged in an international effort to restore safe navigation in the upper Persian Gulf. It is noteworthy that the Gulf mineclearing effort occasioned also the first post-Second World War deployment of German and Japanese naval contingents in distant theatres of operations. Beyond the forces deployed by the Western European Union and the United States, Saudi Arabia participated with one MCM vessel while Australia provided diving teams.[96] On 20 July 1991, the conclusion of the mine-

[94]See DE WILDE, J., 'Mine Warfare in the Gulf', 37 *NATO's Sixteen Nations* (1992/1), p. 9*ff*. See also DUVAL, M., 'Les crises du Golfe vues de la mer', 47 *Défense Nationale* (déc.1991) at p. 64, and COLLET, A., 'Mines et progrès technologiques', 47 *Défense Nationale* (oct.1991), p. 159*ff*.

[95]On those incidents, see MARTIN, J.M., 'We Still Haven't Learned', 117 *USNIP* (July 1991), pp. 64–8, and EVANS, F., '*Princeton* Leaves the War', *ibid.*, pp. 70–2.

[96]On the work of Explosive Ordnance Disposal (EOD) teams, see NAGLE, R.J., 'Having a Blast in the Persian Gulf', 118 *USNIP* (Oct.1992), pp. 104–7, and RANKIN, A.G. and SMITH, R.G., 'Australian Divers Clear Mines', 117 *USNIP*

clearing operation was communicated to the United Nations by a joint statement of the WEU, the US and Japan.[97]

III Drafting rules for the mine trap: too long for too little

1 The first academic exercises of learned societies

The Work of the Institut de Droit International, 1906–1913 M.-S. Kebedgy in his first Report for the 1906 Gand Session of the Institut de Droit International on the *Réglementation internationale de l'usage des mines sous-marines et des torpilles automatiques* submitted four main propositions:

(a) It is prohibited to lay secret engines of destruction on the high seas;
(b) Belligerents cannot lay in their territorial waters secret engines of destruction susceptible to drift away;
(c) The same applies to neutrals who would make use of similar engines in order to hinder access to their territory;
(d) Violation of the preceding rules implies the responsibility of the offending state for all consequences of its act.[98]

The tendency was at that point in favour of stringent rules against the abusive use of naval mines. The high seas should remain the unobstructed highway for seafaring nations, while

(July 1991) at p. 74. It is noteworthy that some ships and helicopters were equipped with mine detection devices such as high-resolution sonars most suitable for mine evasion, not mine disposal. On 3 February 1991, using this technique which was first tried in the Iran-Iraq War, the *USS Nicholas* guided the battleship *Missouri* into firing position off the Kuwaiti coast; see FRIEDMAN, N., *Desert Victory*, 1991 at p. 213.

[97]Apart from the mine countermeasures operations against the Iraqi minefields, during Operation Desert Storm naval aircraft conducted also the first US offensive mining action since the Vietnam War. On 18 January 1991, the US Navy laid mines at the mouth of the Khawr Az Zubayr river near the Kuwait-Iraq border to isolate Iraqi port facilities and naval bases. Of the 48 mines dropped, 42 were laid successfully at four locations. Eighteen aircraft were assigned to the minelaying mission, of which one was shot down; see KELSO, F.B., 'Building Blocks of Naval Power', 118 *USNIP* (Nov.1992) at p. 41. Despite the rather insignificant naval action in the ongoing war in former Yugoslavia, mines have nonetheless marked their presence. In the best-known incident, one German passenger ship was sunk in the Danube River apparently by a homemade Croatian mine.

[98]See 21 *Ann.IDI* (1906), Gand Session at p. 99.

the coastal waters of belligerents and neutrals alike should be spared the frightening reality of drifting mines.[99]

The seminal ideas of M.-S. Kebedgy were followed up with valuable observations in the Institut's plenary session. The distinguished society appeared notably concerned with the problem of a mine enforced blockade, the scope of the duty of notification, and the legality of mining international straits. The resolution that was finally adopted read as follows:

> I. Il est interdit de poser en pleine mer des mines fixes ou flottantes.
>
> II. Les belligérants peuvent poser des mines dans leur eaux territoriales ou dans celles de l'ennemi, à l'exception de mines flottantes ou de mines fixes susceptibles de causer, par leur déplacement, un danger pour la navigation en dehors des eaux des belligérants.
>
> III. 1. Il en est de même des Etats neutres qui voudraient placer dans leur eaux des engins pour empêcher la violation de leur neutralité.
>
> 2. Mais les Etats neutres ne peuvent placer de telles mines dans le passage des détroits qui conduisent dans une mer ouverte.
>
> IV. L'obligation de la notification incombe à l'Etat belligérant aussi bien qu'à l'Etat neutre.

[99]The prohibition of open seas mining emerged as the essential point of departure: 'tout le monde est d'accord' – wrote Kebedgy – 'sur l'interdiction de poser des engins secrets en pleine mer. C'est là une règle qui résulte naturellement du principe même de la liberté de la mer, et peut-être se trouvera-t-il des esprits pour objecter que cela va de soi. Nous leur répondrons que si cela va sans dire, cela ira encore mieux en le disant', *ibid.* at p. 96. Yet, as the first attempt to tackle the question, it was only natural that Kebedgy's draft sounded at times excessively ambitious and controversial: overambitious in that it followed Politis's suggestion that 'tous les engins secrets, quelle que soit leur dénomination' should be commonly addressed, thus posing delicate questions concerning submarine torpedoes; *ibid.* at p. 91; controversial in that it denied in certain cases the existence of a general duty of notification incumbent upon the minelaying power: 'faut-il obliger en outre le belligérant qui place des engins secrets dans la limite des eaux littorales, à donner un avertissement? . . . Personnellement, nous pensons que l'avertissement est ici inutile', *ibid.* at p. 97. Kebedgy appeared reluctant to adopt Politis's other proposal that in case a neutral vessel hit accidentally a mine laid by one of the belligerents, 'il faudrait admettre qu'elle [responsabilité] serait encourue *solidairement* par les deux belligérants' (italics in the original); *ibid.* at p. 92.

V. La violation de l'une des règles qui précèdent entraîne la responsabilité de l'Etat fautif.[100]

The discussions remained inconclusive on several points. No doubt, the naval mine represented a sea change for naval warfare in its classical conception calling for a readjustment of legal principles and military doctrines that only needed time and far-sightedness. It may be that the Russo-Japanese experience was, after all, too fresh to digest, and that the technical parameters of the mine weapon not yet exactly known for the eminent jurists to produce already mature rules on the subject.

The members of the Institute addressed the issue anew in the 1908 session at Florence, while in the Paris session of 1910 a fresh Report by Edouard Rolin reanimated academic discussion.[101] Common was the feeling that the Eighth Hague Convention of 1907 left much to be desired by having dealt with the problem of sea mining in a partial and wholly indeterminate way. The 1910 Draft Report set out to reaffirm, therefore, the absolute prohibition of laying mines of every kind (not only contact mines) on the high seas, the equally unreserved interdiction of enforcing a mine-blockade and of mining international straits, as well as the principle that any violation thereof would engage the international responsibility of the state concerned.[102] The draft articles, as amended in the Paris and Madrid

[100]*Ibid.* at pp. 344–5. The discussions at the Gand Session are reviewed in DUPUIS, C., 'L'Institut de droit international – Session de Gand', 14 *RGDIP* (1907), p. 370*ff.*

[101]See 23 *Ann.IDI* (1910), Paris Session, p. 177*ff.*

[102]*Ibid.* at pp. 203–4. Elaborating on Rolin's Report, several members objected, first, that electrically controlled mines being, as they argued, 'des armes intelligentes et pas aveugles comme les mines de contact', should not be prohibited even on the high seas. Second, some contended that there was a contradiction between allowing belligerents to mine freely enemy territorial waters on the one hand, and forbidding the blockade of enemy coasts and ports on the other. The proviso which was finally approved attempted a fine distinction between sea mining off enemy territory 'pour des buts navals et militaires' which would be lawful, and minelaying 'pour établir ou maintenir un blocus de commerce' which would be prohibited. As to mining of straits, the question was left unanswered since, in the majority view, it would necessitate a separate study. Edouard Rolin drafted in 1912 a summary report on this point, recommending a blanket prohibition of minelaying within international straits; see 25 *Ann.IDI* (1912), Christiania Session, p. 412*ff.* Finally, as regards the international responsibility of a state acting in breach of the announced rules, the Institute formulated two important clauses. The first would create a presumption of guilt against the state that laid the minefield, while the second would authorize individuals to institute proceedings for damages against the minelaying state before an

sessions, were subsequently included in the *Manual of Laws of War at Sea* which was adopted in the 1913 session of the Institute at Oxford.[103]

Parallel Discussions of the International Law Association Another society of learned scholars, the International Law Association, had been focusing at the same time on the mine legal puzzle. The stimulus came in the form of a paper presented by von Martitz in the Berlin Conference of 1906, the gist of which could be reduced to the following suggestions: no infringement of the principle of the freedom of the seas is involved in the use of moored mines on the high seas provided that belligerents ensure that neutral vessels are notified of the danger and that they undertake to remove the anchored mines after the termination of hostilities. On the contrary, the use of floating mines has to be specifically prohibited – possibly along the model of the 1868 St. Petersbourg declaration. Blockading an enemy coast by means of mines is permissible only for the purpose of containing naval forces. Finally, belligerents and neutrals are entitled to mine home waters up to a distance of 10 nautical miles following due warning.[104]

A year later, a Committee of the same society, appointed to consider the question of maritime neutrality and presided by Gaston de Leval, circulated a preliminary questionnaire which contained the following two principles: first: 'les belligérants ne pourront se servir, en dehors de leurs eaux territoriales ni pour l'attaque ni pour la défense, d'engins de destruction à déclanchement automatique', and second: 'les belligérants ne pourront se servir, même dans leurs eaux territoriales, d'engins de

international tribunal. The record of the discussions is found in 23 *Ann.IDI* (1910), Paris Session, pp. 429–57, and 24 *Ann.IDI* (1911), Madrid Session, pp. 286–302.

[103]See Articles 20–4 of the *Manuel des lois de la guerre maritime dans les rapports entre belligérants*, 26 *Ann.IDI* (1913), Oxford Session at pp. 646–7. See also the commentary on the respective draft articles by Paul Fauchille, acting as Rapporteur, 25 *Ann.IDI* (1912), Christiania Session, pp. 330–4, and 26 *Ann.IDI* (1913), Oxford Session, pp. 227–33. All the articles referring to neutral rights and duties with regard to minelaying were expressly omitted since the *Oxford Manual* was intended to codify the rules of naval warfare governing the relations between belligerents. Besides, the *Manual* remained silent on the permissibility of laying observation mines, that is to say, electrically fired mines, as well as on matters of international rsponsibility.

[104]See 23 *Rep.ILA* (1906), Berlin Conference, p. 74*ff*.

destruction à déclanchement automatique susceptibles d'être, par la force des éléments, entraînés au-delà de la zone des eaux territoriales.'[105]

2 The 1907 Hague Peace Conference

By the time the Second Peace Conference met at The Hague in June 1907, naval mines had gone through several battle tests with enormous success. The challenges of underwater warfare fascinated some and outraged others.[106] As the political interests started running high, the gap between major seafaring nations and some newly emerging naval powers became deep enough to deprive in advance the Hague Conference of all its chances with regard to the use of contact mines. However imperfect and lacunary, the Eighth Hague Convention remains to date the only binding legal instrument it was ever possible to adopt relating to naval mine warfare.[107]

Rival Interests, Poor Results The problems related to sea mining soon laid bare the chasm separating British from German interests. England appeared to be courting the neutrals' good graces and crusading in defence of the time-honoured principle

[105]See 24 *Rep.II.A* (1907), Portland Conference at p. 258. The Neutrality Committee held also the view that belligerents should not be allowed to mine maritime narrows except for straits falling within belligerent jurisdiction, *ibid.* at p. 257.

[106]As the Chinese delegation declared with reference to drifting mines left behind after the Russo-Japanese war, 'in spite of every precaution being taken, a very considerable number of coasting trade boats, fishing boats, junks and sampans have sunk as a consequence of collisions with these automatic submarine contact mines, and these vessels have been utterly lost with their cargoes without the details of the disasters reaching the western world. It is calculated that from five to six hundred of our countrymen in the pursuit of their peaceful occupations have met a cruel death through these dangerous engines'; see SCOTT, J.B., *The Proceedings of the Hague Peace Conferences – The Conference of 1907*, vol.III (1921) at p. 400.

[107]The negotiation process which eventually led to the adoption of the Eighth Hague Convention Relative to the Laying of Automatic Submarine Contact Mines is traced in various works: HIGGINS, A.P., *The Hague Peace Conferences and Other International Conferences Concerning the Laws and Usages of War*, 1909, p. 328*ff.*; DUPUIS, C., *Le droit de la guerre maritime d'après les conférences de la Haye et de Londres*, 1911, p. 545*ff.*; LÉMONON, E., *La seconde conférence de la paix*, 2ème édn (1912), p. 412*ff.*; ROLIN, A., *Le droit moderne de la guerre*, tome II (1920), p. 91*ff.*; BUSTAMANTE, A.S.de, *La seconde conférence de la paix réunie à La Haye en 1907*, 1909, p. 278*ff.*; LEVIE, *op. cit.*, *supra* n.1, p. 23*ff.*

of the freedom of the seas; 'we are firmly convinced' – said Sir Ernest Satow seeking severe restrictions on the use of naval mines – 'that belligerents have not the right to expose neutrals to the dangers to which only their adversaries should be exposed and also that it is no less the duty of neutrals not to do anything for the preservation of their neutrality which would involve injury to other neutrals'.[108]

The German national security concerns, on the contrary, could not be appeased by anything less than a free hand in minelaying when military necessity would so demand. Admiral Siegel, elaborating on an earlier German proposition that a mines Convention be concluded for a period of five years in anticipation of further revision, expressed the view that 'pending this definitive solution, the German delegation reserves to itself the liberty which it believes necessary for certain military actions, not considering itself bound in any measure by an international conventional rule which limits too narrowly the places where mines may be employed and the duration of their effectiveness'.[109]

Given such antipodal policy objectives, the limited success of the Conference came as no real surprise. In introducing the draft regulations concerning the laying of automatic submarine contact mines to the Conference, the Rapporteur of the First Subcommission of the Third Commission Georgios Streit admitted the limited accomplishments on the subject: 'this tedious work, although inspired from the beginning by the conviction, common to all the members of the Commission, that some decision must be reached, and animated by a spirit of conciliation and accord on all sides had, it is true, but a modest result, which approved by us should constitute the first step in the settlement of the question. But one cannot fail to realize that the problems to be solved in this new and difficult matter are of a very complicated nature'.[110]

[108]See SCOTT, *op. cit., supra* n.106 at p. 383. In yet another remark, he recalled that his country 'has always supported every proposition tending to limit the employment of mines. In England, the employment of mines had been abolished even for defense'; *ibid.* at p. 453.

[109]*Ibid.* at p. 380.

[110]*Ibid.* at p. 272. As for the British delegate, understandably dissatisfied with the turn of the discussions, had this to say in addressing the same plenary meeting: 'having voted for the mines Convention which the Conference has just accepted, the British delegation desires to declare that it cannot regard this arrangement as furnishing a final solution of the question, but only as marking a stage in international legislation on the subject', *ibid.* at p. 274.

In fact, it was the shared understanding of all contracting parties that the Eighth Hague Convention could only serve as a provisional regime for as long as negotiations would take to arrive at a new, less equivocal arrangement. In the pathetic terms of its preamble, the Convention was only agreed upon 'until such time as it is found possible to formulate rules on the subject which shall ensure to the interests involved all the guarantees desirable'. The question at all events should be reopened, as it was expressly provided for in Article 12 of the Convention, six months before the expiration of a seven-year period, by which time the Third Peace Conference was expected to re-examine the matter. The work of the Conference principally focused on the distinct legal prescriptions applicable to moored and to drifting mines.

Anchored (Moored or Fixed) Mines The basic principle to govern the use of anchored mines gave rise to little discussion. It was rather the scope of its geographical application that provoked much disagreement. In fact, everyone appeared to be welcoming a clause forbidding the laying of moored contact mines which would not deactivate themselves as soon as they broke loose from their anchors. The crucial issue was rather how far into the sea one should be allowed to go in planting such minefields. The original British proposal, for instance, would authorize belligerents to make use of fixed contact mines only in their own territorial waters or in those of their enemy.[111] While according to a Colombian proposal, the use of anchored mines should be absolutely prohibited 'except as a means of defense'.[112] In clear

[111]Before fortified military ports, however, belligerents would exceptionally be permitted to lay mines up to a maximum distance of 10 miles from shore batteries with an increased responsibility of duly notifying neutral merchant shipping; see Article 4 of the 'Proposition of the British Delegation', *ibid.*, Annex 9 at p. 662.

[112]Belligerents, therefore, should abstain from laying mines on the high seas or in enemy waters, which would leave them with the sole possibility of using anchored contact mines within home waters and up to the cannon-range distance; see 'Amendment of the Delegation of Colombia to the Draft Regulations based upon the deliberations of the Commission', *ibid.*, Annex 36 at p. 682. For the discussion thereupon, see *ibid.*, p. 451*ff*. Bolivia and Britain promptly supported the Colombian proposal. In the vote that followed, the amendment failed to obtain the absolute majority (16 to 15 with 6 abstentions and 7 absences) and was not submitted to the Conference.

contrast, Germany claimed the right for belligerent navies to mine at will the theatre of naval operations.[113]

With a view to reconciling such diametrically opposed views, the Committee of Examination proceeded to adopt a number of Articles stipulating that it would be forbidden to lay anchored mines beyond a distance of 3 nautical miles from the low water mark (limit to be extended to a distance of 10 miles off military ports), whereas in the sphere of their immediate activity, belligerents would have exceptionally the right to lay anchored mines so constructed as to become harmless within 2 hours at the latest after their deployment. Discussion over these articles was soon stalemated. Most important, by nine votes to seven, the Subcommission decided that the laying of moored contact mines should as a matter of principle and under certain circumstances be permitted outside the 3- and the 10-mile zones.[114]

Although Articles 2 to 5, dealing with the geographical scope of the use of moored mines, continued to stir controversy, they featured in the Draft Regulations brought before the Third Commission of the Conference. It was there, following numerous votes on copious amendments and exchange of irreconcilable views that it was finally decided to omit the three articles altogether. As the Convention did not provide in the end for any geographical limitation, few would deny that the German views ultimately prevailed. Anchored mines, therefore, could be employed practically everywhere, that is where hostilities might be in progress or expected, as much in belligerent territorial waters as on the high seas.

Georgios Streit in his Report to the Conference could only regret that the Convention, in its new emasculated form, would seem to confide restraint to the humanitarian conscience of warring seamen:

> by thus overturning, through the suppression of Articles 2 to 5, the decision which had seemed to obtain unanimous

[113]As Admiral Siegel had expounded, 'belligerents ought to be permitted to place mines also in the war zone; the sea area in which there occurs or has just occurred a naval engagement, or in which such an operation is likely to take place by reason of the presence or the approach of the naval forces of the two belligerents, shall be considered as a war zone'; *ibid.* at p. 531. See also the 'Amendment of the German Delegation to the Proposition of the British Delegation', *ibid.*, Annex 16 at p. 666.

[114]On the much debated Articles 2–5, see the 'Report to the Commission', *ibid.*, Annex A, p. 410*ff.*

> support in the committee and according to which a restriction as to area in the use of anchored mines ought to be expressly set forth in the regulations, there has been no intention to swerve from the conviction that a restriction as to area also is in principle imposed upon the employment of such mines... even without any written stipulation, there will surely not be lacking in the minds of all the knowledge that the principle of the liberty of the seas, with the obligations that it carries for those who make use of this means of communication open to all peoples, is definitively dedicated to humanity.[115]

Unanchored (Drifting or Floating) Mines According to the British draft convention which had been adopted by the Committee of Examination as the basis of discussion, 'the use of unmoored automatic submarine contact mines is forbidden'.[116] Other countries such as Japan and Italy opposed an absolute prohibition, and favoured instead the use of drifting mines so constructed as to turn themselves inert after a certain lapse of time. For Italy, for instance, scattering freely floating mines would seem an expedient method of defence, especially in case of naval pursuit, provided that the activation period of such devices did not exceed 1 hour.[117]

It is noteworthy that the British had argued alternatively for a much shorter period of 5 to 10 minutes within which the drifting mines should scuttle themselves.[118] In view of the firm opposition, however, to such limitation, discussions drew out in an unfruitful consideration of extreme positions. The British proposal of an unconditional prohibition of the use of untethered mines was ultimately put to a vote within the Committee of Examination and was defeated by 11 votes to 4 and 2 abstentions. The same Committee finally accepted the 1-hour time-

[115] *Ibid.* at p. 282.

[116] See Article 1 of the 'Proposition of the British Delegation', *ibid.*, Annex 9 at p. 662.

[117] See Article 1 of the 'Preliminary Motion of the Italian Delegation', *ibid.*, Annex 10 at p. 663, and the statement by Castiglia, *ibid.* at p. 523. See also the 'Amendment of the Japanese Delegation to the British Proposition', *ibid.*, Annex 11 at p. 663, and the declaration of the Japanese representative Keiroku Tsudzuki, *ibid.* at p. 524.

[118] See Captain Ottley's remark, *ibid.* at p. 531. A limit of 10 minutes had received also the support of Dutch Admiral Röell; see *ibid.* at p. 537.

limit of the Italian proposal which subsequently was also endorsed by the Conference.

The Issues of Blockade, Notification and Conversion Three more aspects provoked heated discussion but led eventually to least satisfactory solutions – further proof of the Convention's overall weakness. First, the legal merits of a naval blockade exclusively enforced by mines were treated in an enigmatic fashion. Second, the duty of notification, although generally admitted, was seriously conditioned. Third, as regards the technical modification of existing mine stocks so as to conform with the provisions of the Convention, it was left to the discretion of the signatories to interpret for themselves what 'as soon as possible' could have really meant.

In relation to the so-called mine-blockade, the British had argued that the use of contact mines in order to maintain a commercial blockade ought to be prohibited.[119] For the purpose of avoiding an overlapping with the mandate of the Fourth Commission, it was agreed to abstain from using the term blockade. Instead, a new formula, based upon proposals of Hammarskjöld, Hagerup and Tornielli, proscribed the laying of automatic contact mines off the coasts and ports of the enemy 'with the sole object of intercepting commercial shipping'. The British reply to those who advanced the 'sole object criterion' was that 'here is a clause which leaves to the belligerent a very dangerous mask', or, as Sir Ernest Satow rhetorically asked, 'who could be judge of the purpose for which the mines are laid if not he who laid them?'.[120] Despite the criticisms, however, the empty formula made its way to the final text, transferring all its vagueness to what later became Article 2 of the Eighth Hague Convention.

One would logically expect that in a mines convention which had been negotiated for the purpose of promoting the safety of peaceful shipping, abundant would have been the provisions

[119]See Article 3 of the 'Proposition of the British Delegation', *ibid.*, Annex 9 at p. 662. The British delegation later submitted two amendments which would have proscribed minelaying before an enemy port other than a war port, or a commercial port 'when there is anchored there at least one large fighting unit'; *ibid.*, Annex 25 at p. 673, and Annex 32 at p. 679.

[120]*Ibid.* at pp. 383, 454. France and Colombia raised similar objections, while the German delegate, von Bieberstein, observed that the principle in its new wording introduced a subjective element which might create difficulties in application; *ibid.* at p. 283, and vol.III (1921) at p. 450.

calling for compulsory precautionary measures to be taken by belligerents and neutrals alike in sowing mines at sea. True though it is that the common sentiment was that the best way to reduce risks for merchant vessels would be to prescribe for self-deactivating mines, the duty of notification was marginally addressed and only in moderate terms. The question of notification was taken up in the original British draft which laid down that belligerents should bear the responsibility to give notice to neutrals, but only in the exceptional case that mines were to be planted as far as 10 miles from shore, that is to say, before fortified military ports.[121] For the Dutch delegation, 'the laying of mines in territorial waters should be published', while Brazil suggested that if neutrals were to lay mines in home waters 'a notice thereof should be given'.[122]

It may be noticed that the obligation to notify was, at the outset, couched in absolute terms. Germany, however, striving for more rights than duties, later suggested a qualified clause that read: 'the belligerents undertake especially in case these mines are left to themselves to notify, *as soon as possible*, the danger zones to the public' (emphasis added).[123] It appears that the obscurity of the German formula pleased a great many of the participants so that the Committee of Examination accepted that clause almost verbatim.[124] As if the requirement of warning had not been already shrouded in ambiguity, the Commission unanimously opted for an even more perplexed formulation which made out of the duty of notification a mere wish; 'the belligerents undertake *to do their utmost* to render these mines harmless within a limited time, and, should they cease to be under surveillance, to notify the danger zones *as soon as military exigencies permit*, by a notice addressed to ship-owners, which

[121]See Article 4 of the 'Proposition of the British Delegation', *ibid.*, vol.I (1920), Annex 9 at p. 662.

[122]See Article 5 of the 'Amendments of the Netherland Delegation to the Proposition of the British Delegation', *ibid.*, Annex 12 at p. 664, and the 'Amendment of the Brazilian Delegation to the British Proposition', *ibid.*, Annex 13 at p. 665. While an initial US proposal referred simply to 'due precautions' to be taken for the safety of neutrals; see the 'Amendment of the Delegation of the United States to the Proposition of the British Delegation', *ibid.*, Annex 17 at p. 666.

[123]See Article IV of the 'Proposal of the German Delegation based on the different propositions and amendments already submitted', *ibid.*, Annex 23 at p. 672.

[124]The 'as soon as possible' clause was turned into 'as soon as it can be done'; see Article 6 of the 'Draft Regulations Presented to the Commission', *ibid.*, Annex 31 at p. 678.

must also be communicated to the Governments through the diplomatic channel' (emphasis added).[125]

As already mentioned, Article 1§1 of the Eighth Hague Convention assumed a technical configuration for unanchored mines not yet available in 1907. It was naturally asked, therefore, whether in adopting that instrument states would be bound to produce within a specified period of time mines which would conform to the standards of the Convention. Opinions stood as far apart as ever.[126] Not surprisingly, here again the negotiating parties agreed upon a proviso that scarcely gives any guidance. According to Article 9 of the Draft Regulations which appears as Article 6 in the final text of the Convention, the states which had not yet developed perfected mines, should effect the necessary improvements as soon as possible in order to bring their mine stocks into line with the Convention's requirements.[127]

[125]See Article 3 of the 'Draft Regulations based upon the deliberations of the Commission', *ibid.*, Annex 35 at p. 681. Note also the view of Georgios Streit in his Report to the Conference: 'since it was unanimously recognized that the provision obliging belligerent States to notify the danger zones "as soon as it can be done" was intended to qualify this obligation as the exigencies of war might make necessary, it seemed preferable to express this idea more clearly in the very text of the relulations', *ibid.* at p. 283. Even though it may be argued that by military exigencies it was simply meant the safe completion of the specific minelaying operation in the sense that prior warning would never be possible, it is also plausible to read military necessity in the abstract so that the notification requirement could be far too easily evaded in most cases. On the contrary, the Commission expressed in indubitable terms the respective principle for mine activities of neutrals; 'the neutral Power *must* inform shipowners, by a notice *issued in advance*, where automatic contact mines will be anchored. This notice *must* be communicated *at once* to the Governments through the diplomatic channel' (emphasis added); see Article 4 of the 'Draft Regulations Presented to the Commission', *ibid.*, Annex 31 at p. 681. Apparently it was thought that a prior notice was here preferable since it would induce no risk for the neutral minelaying force.

[126]In the words of the British delegate, for instance, 'only experts in the matter would be able to give an approximate answer, and I am sure that their opinion will coincide with the opinion of my delegation which is that this conversion would take but *a few months*' (emphasis added); *ibid.* at p. 384. In contrast, the Austro-Hungarian delegation 'could not however accept either the period of three years proposed or *any other period fixed in advance* as a measure of this kind contains, independently of individual volition, an element of uncertainty that, as long as it exists, is inconsistent with entering into a formal engagement that perhaps could not be fulfilled' (emphasis added); see the 'Amendment of the Delegation of Austria-Hungary to the Draft Regulations', *ibid.*, Annex 27 at p. 675.

[127]On the drafting of Article 9, see *ibid.*, pp. 423–7. In the Commission the British delegation had proposed an amendment providing that the prohibition of Article 1 should come into force one year after ratification which failed, nonetheless, to obtain the required majority; see *ibid.* at p. 284.

The Final Balance Sheet: Little Effect, Much Disillusionment Far from suggesting the abolition or the limited use of naval mines, as Great Britain had hoped, the Conference participants contented themselves with simply hailing the advent of an impressive new weapon and admitting their incapacity to draw up a substantive legal framework for its use. The Committee of Examination, created by the First Subcommission of the Third Commission, sounded categorical in this respect:

> no one dreams of contesting the legitimacy of these weapons from the view-point of existing law; likewise, no one has thought of forbidding their use completely – especially a use for the purpose of injuring the armed forces of the enemy . . . We must take into account the incontestable fact that submarine mines are a means of warfare the absolute prohibition of which can neither be hoped for nor perhaps desired even in the interest of peace . . . This means that automatic contact mines are an indispensable weapon. Now to ask an absolute prohibition of this weapon would consequently be demanding the impossible; it is necessary to confine ourselves to regulating its use.[128]

Yet, even regulating its use, they never arrived at; despite an apparent consensus on a few key legal principles, these only generated illusory pledges of restraint. Legal constraints, if any, were shrouded in such Delphic equivocation as to end up being nominal.[129]

Academics writing shortly after its adoption had nothing but scornful remarks in respect of the Hague text; 'one of the saddest

[128] *Ibid.*, vol.III (1921), Annex A at pp. 397–8.

[129] The Convention was signed by all the powers participating at the Second Hague Peace Conference except China, Spain, Montenegro, Nicaragua, Portugal, Russia and Sweden. The Dominican Republic and Siam entered reservations to Article 1§1, while France and Germany made reservations regarding the oracular Article 2. Yet, the reservation that best illustrated the flagrant defects of the mines Convention was attached by Great Britain; 'the mere fact that the said Convention does not prohibit a particular act or proceeding must not be held to debar His Britannic Majesty's Government from contesting its legitimacy'. A *si omnes* clause was also inserted to the text, following the usage of the time. According to Article 7, 'the provisions of the present Convention do not apply except between contracting Powers, and then only if all the belligerents are parties to the Convention', which, of course, weakened even more the relevance of the instrument at the time of the First World War (in 1914, the Eighth Convention still lacked the ratifications of Turkey, Serbia, Montenegro and Russia).

and most conspicuous of the failures of humanity', estimated by Thomas J. Lawrence,[130] while for Alexander Pearce Higgins 'the Convention is a wholly unsatisfactory attempt to deal with a question of vital importance to neutrals and has only been accepted by many states for want of a better'.[131] The Convention, wrote Charles Dupuis, 's'arrête à d'insuffisantes velléités; elle se perd en des contradictions déplorables entre des principes justes et des applications qui manquent le but'.[132] For others, however, the mines Convention, which should be further improved at the Third Peace Conference, was 'something where nothing before existed, and at least a milestone on the way to a more complete correction of the evils with which it deals'.[133]

3 The 1920 report of ILA's British Maritime Law Committee

The next instance of ambitious law-making in the field of war laws was the London Naval Conference of December 1909. Its final document, however, entitled *Declaration concerning the Laws of Naval War,* unlike what one might expect, avoided the slightest reference to the question of naval mines. It will be recalled, in this regard, that the Conference was convened upon the initiative of the British government for the purpose of identifying the generally recognized principles of international law to be applied by the International Prize Court the creation of which was envisaged in the Hague Convention XII of 1907, and that, therefore, technical rules on means and methods of war received less attention than issues related to contraband, capture and destruction of prizes, blockade, unneutral service or neutral convoying.[134] After all, the delegates who met in London might

[130]LAWRENCE, T.J., *International Problems and Hague Conferences,* 1908 at p. 121.
[131]HIGGINS, *op. cit., supra* n.107 at p. 344.
[132]DUPUIS, *op. cit., supra* n.107 at p. 587. For yet another publicist, 'cette convention n'est certes pas de celles qui augmenteront la gloire et le renom de la seconde Conférence de la Haye'; see BUSTAMANTE, *op. cit., supra* n.107 at p. 295. While as a recent study concludes, 'the drafting bodies of the Conference failed miserably in their efforts to draft meaningful prohibitions on the use of mines in maritime warfare, particularly to provide any restrictions on their use on the high seas'; see LEVIE, *op. cit., supra* n.1, at p. 52.
[133]STOCKTON, C.H., 'The Use of Submarine Mines and Torpedoes in Time of War', 2 *AJIL* (1908) at p. 284.
[134]In any case, sea mining did not appear among the eight topics of discussion suggested in the original British circular; see the *General Report on the Declaration Presented to the Naval Conference on Behalf of Its Drafting Committee,* in HIGGINS, *op. cit., supra* n.107 at p. 568.

well have thought that no breakthrough could be seriously expected on the subject merely two years after the adoption of the Hague instrument.

In the aftermath of the First World War, the International Law Association delved with keen interest into the chaotic principles and usages of naval warfare on the basis of an outstanding study prepared by a British Committee. The British Maritime Law Committee had in fact been working since 1918 on a draft code of laws of war at sea in the light of the Hague Conferences, the London Declaration, the *Oxford Manual*, and above all the World War experience. A provisionally adopted *Report on the Laws of Naval War* was presented in 1920 to the 29th ILA Conference at Portsmouth.[135] The five articles of section III, relative to the methods of injuring the enemy, dealing with mine warfare announced a certain degree of innovation without always avoiding some of the ambiguities of the Eighth Hague Convention.

The Report attempted to regulate the most controversial of World War practices by introducing the notion of *barred zones*. According to the terms of Article 18A, a belligerent would be permitted to exercise control over the passage of neutral ships within an area of the high seas previously declared and notified to be a barred zone on condition that he would assume responsibility for the safety of navigation therein. Furthermore, a belligerent would have the right to lay mines in those barred zones – a marked exception to the key principle forbidding minelaying on the high seas.[136] Mines could also be placed lawfully on the high seas but this would concern only warships 'being chased or engaged in action' in which case mines should 'become harmless within half an hour of being thrown overboard' (Article 21). The last novelty set forth in the Report of the British Maritime Law Committee was Article 23 according to which 'neutrals are prohibited from placing within their terri-

[135]See 29 *Rep.ILA* (1920), Portsmouth Conference, p. 169*ff*. As the Chairman of the Committee, Sir John MacDonell, had pointed out on that occasion, the Report 'does not profess to be much more than an imperfect statement with some modifications of existing rules. Far from regarding it as final, it is presented as very imperfect and incomplete, and as falling far short of what is needed'; *ibid.* at p. 207.

[136]See Article 20, *ibid.* at p. 173. The prohibition announced in this article, however, would risk to turn almost meaningless as Article 18A refrains from giving any indication as to the maximum extent of barred zones.

torial waters any but controlled mines', that is shore-based electrically fired minefields.

As regards the remaining provisions, these were basically echoing the Hague regulations. Thus, belligerents could place mines in home and enemy territorial waters using either unanchored contact mines designed to be deactivated within an hour from the time of deployment, or moored ones which 'become harmless on their becoming disconnected from their mooring' (Article 22). Belligerents were under an obligation to take 'all precautions for the security of non-combatant or neutral shipping' (Article 23A), and not simply 'every possible precaution' as stipulated in Article 3 of the Hague text. In a similar vein, belligerents 'shall especially arrange that the mines become harmless after a limited lapse of time' (Article 23A), in place of 'do their utmost' as laid down in the 1907 proviso, while they should observe the duty of notification merely 'so far as military exigencies will permit' (Article 23A).[137]

Finally, with reference to blockade, the Report opted for an intermediate solution between Article 2 of the Hague Convention and Article 4 of the IDI Draft Rules of 1910. According to Article 22§3, 'placing mines on the coasts and ports of their opponents except for naval and military purposes' would be forbidden to belligerents, which would seem to follow to the letter the Institut's rule.[138] Insofar as it refrains, however, from explicitly prohibiting a commercial blockade (as the corresponding rule of 1910 does), it comes closer to the shadowy Hague formulation. Still, mines could be used in support of a duly established blockade, the belligerent being in this latter case authorized to lay only anchored contact mines.[139]

A further opportunity to stimulate reflection on mine warfare regulation was missed by the Commission of Jurists, which met at The Hague in 1923 and was composed of representatives of the United States, Great Britain, Italy, France, Japan and the

[137]In contrast, nothing is said in the Report with regard to the neutral duty of notification. It was obviously deemed redundant inasmuch as observation mines posed no threat of indiscriminate attack against peaceful shipping.

[138]Furthermore, it could be argued that the Report rejects implicitly the idea of a mine blockade to the extent that an effective blockade would presuppose 'a force at whatever distance from the blockaded area sufficient actually to prevent access to, or egress from'; see 29 *Rep.ILA* (1920), Portsmouth Conference, Appendix I, Article 2 at p. 191.

[139]*Ibid.*, Article 22 at p. 194.

Netherlands. It will be remembered that the Commission did produce two sets of draft rules on the *Control of Radio in Time of War* and on *Aerial Warfare*, significantly narrowing in so doing its mandate which was set out in the Washington Conference on the Limitation of Armament of 1922 in far more general terms and which read as follows:

(a) Do existing rules of International Law adequately cover new methods of attack or defense resulting from the introduction or development, since the Hague Conference of 1907, of new agencies of warfare?
(b) If not so, what changes in the existing rules ought to be adopted in consequence thereof as a part of the law of nations?[140]

4 The 1939 Harvard research

The 1939 *Draft Convention on Rights and Duties of Neutral States in Naval and Aerial War*, has been a distinguised undertaking with the view to reconsidering established principles in the light of World War events and subsequent developments. The more than 100 annotated Articles of the Harvard Research were not the fruit of any sort of unanimity, but still represent a prodigious effort of dispassionate evaluation and constructive reflection on those legal principles which had been most severely tested during the First World War.

Five Articles concerning the use of naval mines make up the last section of part two of the study which addresses the Rules for surface and submarine vessels.[141] With regard to mine specification, Article 83§2 follows closely the Eighth Hague Convention authorizing the laying of anchored contact mines on condition that they 'become harmless on their becoming

[140]See *Resolution No.1 for a Commission of Jurists to Consider Amendment of Laws of War*, in 16 *AJIL* (1922) *Suppl.* at p. 74. The Dutch delegation had in fact insisted, though unavailingly, that the broadly phrased resolution authorized the Commission to look into many open legal questions such the high seas mining, the creation of war zones, or the arming of merchant vessels with relation to submarine warfare; see VAN DER MANDERE, H.G.J., 'Nouvelles règles du droit de guerre', 2 *Revue de Droit International de Sciences Diplomatiques et Politiques* (1924) at pp. 63–4.

[141]See Articles 83–7 of the *Draft Convention on Rights and Duties of Neutral States in Naval and Aerial War*, 33 *AJIL* (1939) *Suppl.* at pp. 192–3.

disconnected from their moorings', and of unanchored ones as long as 'they are so constructed as to become harmless within half an hour from the time that the belligerent who has laid them has lost control over them'.[142]

In respect of the geographical limits of mine warfare, the Draft Convention breaks fresh ground. A belligerent is, in fact, allowed to mine, apart from its own territorial waters and those of its enemy, the high seas but only in two specific cases; first, 'in the course of actual engagements with or pursuit by warships of its adversary, a belligerent may throw overboard mines which become harmless within half an hour of being thrown overboard' (Article 85).[143] Second, in the context of a blockade operation, a belligerent would also be permitted to lay mines up to a distance of 50 miles off the enemy coast which would constitute the so-called *blockade zone*.[144]

In this latter case, a belligerent should imperatively deploy warships, submarines or aircraft in order to maintain an effective blockade, while secondarily he could also use anchored mines in support of such operation (Article 73). This article avoids any distinction between commercial and military blockades as it had been suggested in previous texts, and it equally steers clear of the problematic 'sole object criterion' of the Hague Conven-

[142]Regrettably enough the drafters of the Harvard Research kept referring exclusively to contact mines failing to realize that other types of mine fusion might sooner or later come out of naval laboratories. It should be noticed, however, that even though in 1939 both the Germans and the British already possessed the secrets of the influence (magnetic) mine, such development was only disclosed in the course of the Second World War.

[143]It should be borne in mind that Article 85 is strictly limited to conditions of actual naval action, particularly anti-submarine warfare. As the commentary explained, the Article 'adds a special provision permitting a practice developed during the World War and now understood to have been adopted as a regular part of naval operations, namely the use of depth charges which may be thrown overboard by a warship seeking to destroy an enemy submarine'; see 33 *AJIL* (1939) *Suppl.* at p. 753.

[144]In Article 1(e), a blockade zone is defined as 'that area of water extending fifty miles from a blockaded coast, proclaimed by a belligerent to be such a zone', while according to Article 69 a blockade zone intended to support the enforcement of a blockade may in no case close international straits. The provisions on blockade zones, although not codifying any existing practice, have been elaborated on the grounds that 'the increase in the range of fire of coastal batteries and the operations of submarines and aircraft, may make almost impossible in many cases the planting of mines and other obstructions within three miles of the enemy's coast'; see *ibid.* at p. 693.

tion.[145] As far as neutrals are concerned, Article 87 stipulates that they could place mines only within the limits of their own territorial waters which, of course, offers greater precision than the respective Hague rule that authorized minelaying 'off their coasts'.[146]

5 Post-1945 developments

In the nine decades since the signature of the 1907 Eighth Hague Convention, naval mine technology has evolved by leaps and bounds. Already the Second World War was fought with influence mines, while advanced mines of today feature an astonishing degree of built-in 'intelligence'. Modern navies equally boast ground dormant torpedoes and homing mines, while sophisticated minehunting has come to complement the traditional minesweeping. Yet, the arm of the law seems impotent to reach further than the obsolete contact mines of the pre-1914 design. Whether laudable or lamentable, the work of the Hague forerunners has not been carried on in recent times. The 1971 Treaty on the Prohibition of the Emplacement of Nuclear Weapons and Other Weapons of Mass Destruction on the Seabed and on the Ocean Floor and in the Subsoil Thereof marks, in fact, the sole exception in that, although not explicitly dealing with mine warfare, it prohibits the deployment of a specific type of naval mines to a specific environment.

A Action within the UN disarmament framework

The 1971 Seabed Treaty It was at the time of the Pardo initiative and the United Nations Seabed Committee that the Soviet Union first raised the question of the demilitarization of the seabed and ocean floor.[147] The United States floated a counter-proposal with a view to preventing therein only the emplacement of

[145]Evidently, it was thought that since a naval force would be at any rate present off the blockaded territory (Article 72), there should be no objection if anchored mines were also used in an auxiliary manner. The commentary on Article 73 remains, however, somewhat laconic as to what exacted the departure, at least in principle, from Article 2 of the Hague Convention; see *ibid.*, p. 715*ff.*

[146]Relevant neutral practice is reviewed in *ibid.*, pp. 755–6. According to the same provision, neutral states would be required to notify the limits of the mined area but it remains unclear whether a prior notice was meant as in Article 4 of the Hague text.

[147]See UN Doc. *A/AC.135/20*, 20 June 1968.

weapons of mass destruction.[148] Negotiations within the eighteen-nation Disarmament Committee began in March 1969 with the submission of a Soviet draft treaty. According to its terms, all military uses of the seabed and ocean floor, beyond a 12-mile coastal zone, should be prohibited.[149] Following a major concession on the part of the Soviet Union, the so-called Seabed Treaty was finally accepted by the United Nations General Assembly in December 1970.[150]

In the terms of Article I§1 of the treaty, parties are bound not to emplant or emplace nuclear weapons or other weapons of mass destruction, as well as structures, launching installations or any other facilities specifically designed for storing, testing or using such weapons on the seabed and the ocean floor and in the subsoil thereof beyond a 12-mile zone contiguous to their coasts.[151] Since the treaty wording was not particularly clear as to the exact object of the prohibition, the sponsoring superpowers were asked to furnish some interpretative explanations. On the basis of such clarifications it was resolved that the treaty prohibits not only bottom nuclear mines but also nuclear mines anchored to the seabed.[152]

[148]See UN Doc. *A/AC.135/24*, 28 June 1968.

[149]See UN Doc. *ENDC/240*, 18 March 1969. The American draft, on the other hand, submitted in May of that year provided for a ban on the emplacement on the seabed of nuclear weapons and other weapons of mass destruction beyond a 3-mile territorial sea limit; see UN Doc. *ENDC/249*, 22 May 1969.

[150]See GA Resolution 2660 (XXV), 7 December 1970. See also UN Doc. *A/PV.1919*, pp. 2–5. Some 104 states voted in favour, two against (El Salvador and Peru), while two others abstained (France and Ecuador). To a number of states the final compromise seemed unsatisfactory for it failed to give full meaning to the declared objective of the reservation of the seabed and ocean floor 'exclusively for peaceful purposes', set forth in the well-known General Assembly Resolution 2340 of 18 December 1967.

[151]See 955 *UNTS* 115, reprinted in 10 *ILM* (1971), p. 145*ff*. The Seabed Treaty came into force in May 1972 and has received, as of November 1995, 90 instruments of ratification or accession. On its main provisions and the long negotiation process, see GORALCZYK, W., 'Legal Problems of the Peaceful Uses of the Sea-Bed and the Ocean Floor: Denuclearization', 5 *PYIL* (1972–3), p. 43*ff*., and MIGLIORINO, L., 'Declarations and Reservations to the 1971 Seabed Treaty', 6 *It.YIL* (1985), p. 106*ff*. See also HIRDMAN, S. and GOLDBLAT, J., 'The Militarization of the Deep Ocean: The Sea-Bed Treaty', *Ybk.SIPRI* (1969–70), p. 154*ff*., and RAMBERG, B., *The Seabed Arms Control Negotiations: A Study of Multilateral Arms Control Conference Diplomacy*, 1978.

[152]See STEIN, E., 'Legal Restraints in Modern Arms Control Agreements', 66 *AJIL* (1972) at p. 266, and TREVES, T., 'Military Installations, Structures, and Devices on the Seabed', 74 *AJIL* (1980), ftn.83 at p. 821. The main significance of underwater nuclear explosions lies upon the fact that they can tackle targets whose position is not exactly known. It has been calculated, for example, that

According to analysts, the very fact that it was jointly agreed that anchored/bottom nuclear mines were outlawed following the terms of the Seabed Treaty confirms the low military interest of such weapons. Bearing this in mind and given the fact that fixed nuclear installations on the ocean floor, as compared to mobile ones, were never favoured by either of the superpowers, it has been pointed out that the treaty in its final form is pregnant of no genuine disarmament.[153] In the words of some experts, the Seabed Treaty 'amounts to the banning of something which does not exist and which, even without the sea-bed treaty, was not likely to develop'.[154] Put it differently, it 'is a "preventative" kind of arms control. The treaty precluded a military option to which no country had yet made a serious commitment'.[155]

---

the shock wave from a mine carrying a nuclear charge of 10 KT and exploding within about 1.2 nautical miles would destroy a submarine found at a depth of 500 ft. Likewise, if an area of 50 square nautical miles was to be covered, twelve 10-KT charges would be needed to destroy a submarine. It has also been argued that powerful nuclear mines could be used to create large flood waves that would devastate enemy coastal areas; see EVENSEN, J., 'The Military Uses of the Deep Ocean Floor and its Subsoil – Present and Future' in SZTUCKI, J. (ed.), *Symposium on the International Regime of the Sea-Bed, Proceedings*, 1970 at p. 543. However attractive these military options may appear, resorting to nuclear bursts would never be without tremendous consequences and most nations seem reluctant to envisage similar scenarios. What is more, navies involved in nuclear minelaying would have to cope with the extremely worrying possibility of such devices being stolen, captured, or otherwise removed by the military forces of another state; see, for instance, the working paper prepared by the UN Secretariat on The Military Uses of the Sea-Bed and the Ocean Floor Beyond the Limits of Present National Jurisdiction, UN Doc. *A/AC.135/28*, 10 July 1968 at p. 4.

[153]It is noteworthy, for instance, that according to the 1989 Naval Warfare Publication of the US Navy, 'this treaty prohibits emplacement of nuclear mines on the seabed and ocean floor or in the subsoil thereof. It does not, however, prohibit the use of nuclear weapons in the water column that are not so affixed to the seabed (e.g. nuclear armed depth charges and torpedoes)'; see *Commander's Handbook on the Law of Naval Operations* (NWP9-Rev.A) at para.10.2.2.1.

[154]HIRDMAN and GOLDBLAT, *op. cit., supra* n.151 at p. 178.

[155]RAMBERG, *op. cit., supra* n.151 at p. 87. The 1979 SALT II treaty extended for the United States and the Soviet Union the ban on military activities in the seabed. It prohibits the development, testing or deployment of fixed ballistic or cruise missile launchers for emplacement on the ocean floor, on the seabed, or on the beds of internal waters, or in the subsoil thereof, or missiles for such launchers; see Article IX§1(b), 18 *ILM* (1979) at pp. 1133, 1153. In the aftermath of the 1991 Gulf War against Iraq, and following the momentous change in East–West relations, the United States announced further arms control measures. In fact, on 27 September 1991, President Bush promulgated new deterrence policy intitiatives including *inter alia* the withdrawal and storing in continental US depots of all US Navy's surface short-range nuclear weapons and thus of all nuclear depth-charges or mines. For comments on this initiative, see STOBBS, E.E., 'Tactical Nuclear Weapons: Do They Have a Role in U.S. Military Strategy?', 13 *Comparative Strategy* (1994), p. 197*ff*.

The 1990–1 Swedish Initiative The latest diplomatic initiative aiming at bringing up to date the Hague instrument of 1907 took the form of a working paper submitted by Sweden to the UN General Assembly's Disarmament Commission in May 1990. Drawing upon a few principles of the Eighth Hague Convention which apparently have preserved their legal validity intact through time, drawing also upon some concepts already adopted in Protocol II on land mines annexed to the 1981 Convention on Certain Conventional Weapons, and finally taking into account the work of the Round Table of Experts within the so-called Madrid Plan of Action, the Draft Protocol on Prohibitions or Restrictions on the Use of Naval Mines sought to accommodate conflicting interests while preserving a modicum of originality.[156]

A naval mine is defined as 'an explosive device laid in the water, on the sea-bed or in the subsoil thereof, with the intention of damaging or sinking ships or deterring shipping from entering a sea area', thus excluding devices attached to the bottom of ships or to harbour installations by frogmen. As a basic rule, Article 4 of the Protocol provides for a clear prohibition of the indiscriminate use of mines, defined as '(a) any detonation of *controlled* mines which is not directed at a military objective; (b) any laying of *independent* mines which may be expected to cause incidental loss of civilian life, injury of civilians, or a combination thereof, which would be excessive in relation to the concrete and direct military advantage anticipated'. Moreover, the Swedish draft lays down two novel principles. First, Article 5§4 stipulates a flat interdiction of the use of drifting or freely-floating mines, and second, Article 5§3 provides for the fitting of all mines with a neutralizing mechanism of a maximum life of five years after the mines are laid.

For the remainder, the document is unfortunately wrapped up in vagueness and couched in stereotyped terms with the hope of being accepted by some major naval Powers. Article 3 of the Hague Convention was reproduced without any variation in Article 7 of the Draft Protocol. The 'every possible precaution' clause was only rehashed some eighty years later to read 'all feasible precautions'. As for the duty of notification, it remains severely qualified by 'military considerations' – the modern sub-

[156]See UN Doc. *A/CN.10/141*, 8 May 1990.

stitute for 'military exigencies' as it appeared in the text of the 1907 Convention. Finally, Articles 8, 9 elaborate on Article 5 of the Hague Convention. What is novel is that the Parties to a conflict would be under an obligation to record all pre-planned minefields and retain such records with a view to facilitating the mineclearing operations to be launched after the cessation of hostilities. Moreover, the Parties may agree to call upon third states or international organizations for the purpose of exchanging information or providing technical and material assistance in clearing the minefields.

Put straight, it seems that most countries would be ready to assume the most burdensome of engagements as long as these refer to a period after the cessation of hostilities when nothing would be at stake any more. Although the rationale seems to be that the thought of post-war obligations would possibly deter a belligerent from initiating an unrestrained mine campaign, one tends to be sceptical about how well-grounded such expectations might be. All the more so, as the Draft Protocol falls short of providing for the consequences that a state would bear if it did not conform to these obligations. It is indeed difficult to imagine who could oppose, whether belligerent or neutral, victor or vanquished, to the idea of ocean routes being swept and rendered safe for international shipping after an armed conflict has come to an end. From that point of view, Article 8 and Article 9 of the Draft Protocol would appear as pseudo-innovations. What is more, recording may be said to have always been practised, since no mining is decided without a concrete military planning. It can also be said that the possibility of international cooperation in matters of minesweeping was implicitly alluded to, or at least not excluded, under Article 5 of the Eighth Hague Convention which provides that the Parties should 'undertake to do their utmost to remove the mines which they have laid'.

In November 1991, Sweden presented a revised version of its working paper containing a few significant amendments, some exacting further restraint while others bearing the earmark of laxity.[157] Suggestive of additional strictness, for example, is the revised Article 5§1 which proposes a neutralizing mechanism

[157]See UN Doc. *A/C.1/46/15*, 6 November, 1991. The Swedish government has since made known that it has the intention to introduce the Draft Protocol at the upcoming Review Conference of the 1980 Inhumane Weapons Convention.

of a two-year limit instead of five. Furthermore, with regard to the duty of notification, the controversial formula 'as soon as military considerations permit' was omitted. As for the basic rule defining indiscriminate mining, the somewhat confusing reference to controlled or independent mines was deleted. Conversely, it is to be regretted that the truly innovatory outright prohibition of drifting mines was repealed in order to be aligned once again with the long-inherited idea of 1-hour self-scuttling limit. At any rate, the Swedish initiative is to be hailed as a creative and rather solitary endeavour, revealing persistent commitment to the need for modernization of some of the most problematic aspects of international humanitarian law and disarmament.

B Recent military manuals

The US Commander's Handbook The legal aspects of mine warfare are discussed in chapter 9 of the 1989 *US Manual,* which deals with conventional weapons and weapons systems. As a general proposition, it is laid down that naval mines are lawful weapons, although with potentially indiscriminate effects.[158] With regard to mining during armed conflict, the *Handbook* follows closely, almost verbatim, the Eighth Hague Convention in its basic principles. Thus, anchored mines 'must become harmless as soon as they have broken their moorings', unanchored ones 'must become harmless within an hour after loss of control over them', notification is required 'as soon as military exigencies permit' and finally 'naval mines may not be emplaced off the coasts and ports of the enemy with the sole objective of intercepting commercial shipping, but may otherwise be employed in the strategic blockade of enemy ports, coasts, and waterways'.[159]

[158]See *Commander's Handbook on the Law of Naval Operations* (NWP9-Rev.A) at para.9.2. In that sense, drifting armed contact mines are given as an example of prohibited devices for being indiscriminate in their effect; see *ibid.* at para.9.1.2.
[159]*Ibid.* at para.9.2.3. See also *Annotated Supplement to Commander's Handbook,* p. 9–6*ff.* Beyond these customary law principles, the *US Manual* breaks little new ground. It announces, for instance, that a belligerent may not employ naval mines 'to impede the transit passage of international straits or archipelagic sea lanes passage', it also prescribes that 'mining of areas of indefinite extent in international waters is prohibited [whereas] reasonably limited barred areas may be established by naval mines', and finally, that the location of minefields must be carefully recorded to facilitate subsequent removal and deactivation, *ibid.*

In relation to peacetime mining, the *Handbook* draws a distinction between *armed* mines, that is mines with all safety devices withdrawn, and *controlled* mines, which have no destructive capability until they are activated by some form of controlled arming order (whereupon they become armed mines).[160] A nation is entitled to use both armed and controlled mines in its own internal waters with or without prior notification. It can also freely mine its territorial sea with armed mines, in which case notification is required, or controlled mines which, since they pose no hazard to navigation until they are armed, may remain unnotified. In respect of high seas mining, however, more stringent requirements, or apparently so, have to be observed. Thus, controlled mines may be emplaced in international waters 'subject only to the requirement that they do not unreasonably interfere with other lawful uses of the oceans' (no obligation for prior notification), whereas 'armed mines may not be emplaced in international waters prior to the outbreak of armed conflict, except under the most demanding requirements of individual or collective self-defence'.[161]

The German Manual Unlike the *US Handbook*, the 1992 German Defence Ministry publication proceeds by looking at the nature of mining operations (defensive or offensive) and not so much at the state of activation of the emplaced mines (live or dormant). Three kinds of minelaying activities are so identified, *protective mining*, i.e. laying mines in friendly territorial or internal waters, *defensive mining*, i.e. laying mines in international waters for the protection of passages and port approaches, and *offensive mining*, i.e. laying mines in hostile territorial and internal waters or in waters predominantly controlled by the adversary.[162]

[160]*Ibid.* at para.9.2.1.
[161]*Ibid.* at para.9.2.2. See also *Annotated Supplement* at p. 9–5. In this latter case, international notice must be provided as well as the anticipated date of their complete removal. It is clear that the legal conditions for high seas mining leave much room for discretion since it may not always be easy to determine what amounts to 'unreasonable interference' or 'most demanding requirements' of self-defence.
[162]See *ZDv 15/2 Humanitäres Völkerrecht in bewaffneten Konflikten – Hanbuch* [Humanitarian Law in Armed Conflicts – Manual], August 1992, para.1039 at p. 106. One may question, however, whether high seas mining is always of a defensive character as the German classification seems to imply.

For the German Navy 'the principles of effective surveillance, risk control and warning' would apply to all three forms of mine warfare, be it prior to or after the beginning of hostilities.[163] Beyond those minimum common requirements, however, the three types of mine operations are subject to distinct legal rules during an armed conflict. Protective mining is permissible without any limitation except the need for notification.[164] Defensive mining is permissible to the extent that shipping lanes of neutral and non-belligerent states are 'kept open to an appropriate extent, if military circumstances so permit'.[165] As for offensive mining, it 'presupposes an armed attack [while] acts of aggression below the threshold of an armed attack do not suffice as a motive'.[166]

As regards neutral rights and duties, the German *Manual* stipulates that 'neutral states are subject to the same safety regulations as are the parties to the conflict', and that 'they must notify the location of the minefields to the governments of maritime states without delay'.[167] In what is perhaps the most controversial provision, neutral warships are accorded the right to engage in minesweeping 'on international shipping routes and on the high seas . . . as necessary to ensure neutral shipping. Such minesweeping activities are no unneutral service to the adversary of the minelaying party to the conflict'.[168]

As a general remark, one may observe that the German *Manual* is innovative in that it does not follow the classic distinction between moored and free-floating mines. Neither does the German *Manual* make the belligerent duty of notification conditional upon any military consideration. Finally, concerning the neutral right of minesweeping on the high seas, attention should be drawn to the fact that the German *Manual* goes considerably,

[163]*Ibid.*, para.1040 at p. 106. Contrary to the *US Commander's Handbook*, prior notice is here required regardless of the fact that not yet activated mines may have been used.

[164]Implicitly this clause would even recognize the legality of mining of an international strait which runs opposite to the corresponding proviso of the *US Commander's Handbook* (para.9.2.3§6).

[165]See para.1042 at p. 107.

[166]*Ibid.* Moreover, it would be unlawful to resort to offensive mining for the 'only purpose of interdicting merchant shipping'. At the time of crisis, only protective mining may be undertaken on the condition that all due regard is paid to the right of innocent passage of foreign ships, and that straits serving international navigation are not in any way affected; see para.1041 at pp. 106–7.

[167]See para.1124 at p. 116.

[168]See para.1148 at p. 119.

and perhaps unreasonably, farther than other sets of rules (e.g. the *San Remo Manual* at para.92) which admit such a right but only in order to remove mines laid in violation of international legal rules (for example unnotified drifting mines along busy commercial shipping lanes).

C Current academic initiatives

Recent Work of the ILA on Maritime Neutrality The latest Report of International Law Association's Maritime Neutrality Committee on Neutrality and Naval Warfare advances an interesting yet questionable proposition with relation to mining of international straits. In fact, the Committee's Rapporteur, Michael Bothe, supports the view that neutral warships do not have the right to remove mines 'within the territorial sea of a belligerent state, except to the extent necessary for the exercise of the right of transit passage or archipelagic sea lanes passage'.[169] As argued in the attached commentary:

> the mining of straits or archipelagic waters for which there exists a right of transit or archipelagic sea lanes passage is, however, considered as an *illegal suspension* of that right against which there would be no defense if the mines could not be taken away. In view of the particular importance of the right of transit passage and the reduced relevance of state sovereignty in these sea areas, it is therefore proposed that an exception should be made to the established rule and that minesweeping to the extent strictly necessary for the exercise of the transit passage should be permitted.[170]

[169]See *Report on Neutrality and Naval Warfare* for ILA's Buenos Aires Conference (1994) at para.6.3.

[170]*Ibid.* This proviso has not as yet received wide acceptance among ILA members and is likely to give rise to further debate. Another alternative would be to recognize, on the one hand, the right of the belligerent state to mine an international strait which is fully or partly subject to its jurisdiction, and on the other, the right of neutral states to engage in mineclearing operations within such strait in order to restore safe transit passage. However balanced this solution may appear, it would be difficult to underestimate the extremely delicate problems that a neutral naval presence within belligerent territorial waters would give rise to. *Cf.* para.5.2.8 of his Report, however, where he admits that 'the coastal state may subject such rights [transit passage] to reasonable defense requirements', which might be of course interpreted as permitting among others the laying of mines. See also 65 *Rep.ILA* (1992), Cairo Conference, para.4.3 at p. 174.

The San Remo Manual The Round Table of Experts produced a substantial set of rules regarding sea mining. The *San Remo Manual* adopted in June 1994 builds upon the principle that 'mines may only be used for legitimate military purposes'[171] which amounts to saying that 'indiscriminate mining practices on the high seas are unlawful'.[172] In respect of anchored and unanchored mines the *Manual* does not depart, except textually, from the familiar rules of the 1907 Eighth Hague Convention. Thus, para.81 prescribes that anchored mines must be so constructed that 'effective neutralization occurs when they have become detached or control over them is otherwise lost'. According to para.82 the use of free-floating mines is prohibited unless a twofold condition is satisfied, that is to say they are directed against a military objective and they are equipped with a one-hour self-scuttling mechanism.[173] In a clause reminiscent of the *US Commander's Handbook*, the *San Remo Manual* makes notification compulsory only as far as armed, or activated mines are concerned: 'the laying of armed mines or the arming of prelaid mines must be notified unless the mines can only detonate against vessels which are military objectives'.[174]

Among the rules betraying a certain degree of progressive development in the field, mention should be made of para.85 which codifies the need for a *période de grâce* to be accorded to neutral ships found in offensively mined belligerent waters; 'mining operations in the internal waters, territorial sea or archipelagic waters of a belligerent State should provide, when the mining is first executed, for free exit of shipping of neutral

[171]See *San Remo Manual on International Law Applicable to Armed Conflicts at Sea*, Prepared by a Group of International Lawyers and Naval Experts, June 1994 [hereinafter *Manual*] at para.80.

[172]See *Commentary on the Harmonised Document on International Humanitarian Law Applicable to Armed Conflicts at Sea*, March 1994 [hereinafter *Commentary*] at para.80.1.

[173]The *Commentary* reveals that the option of prohibiting altogether this category of mines was also considered; 'the majority, however, felt that military necessity still required the use of these mines, for instance in the case of immediate pursuit by opposing forces', *ibid.* at para.82.2.

[174]See *Manual* at para.83. As the *Commentary* explains, 'the present wording reflects the general wish of participants to extend the notification requirement to all types of mines, while at the same time taking into consideration the fact that technology has evolved so that not all mines form a danger to navigation at all times. Therefore, the requirement is limited to the laying of armed mines and the arming of prelaid mines', at para.83.1.

States'.[175] As regards the notion of a mine-enforced blockade, the *San Remo Manual* attempts to formulate a clear principle while avoiding the much-criticized 'sole object criterion' of the Hague Convention. Thus, para.97 reads: 'a blockade may be enforced and maintained by a combination of legitimate methods and means of warfare provided this combination does not result in acts inconsistent with the rules set out in this document'.[176]

Concerning the knotty problem of unobstructed passage through international straits, the *Manual* stipulates that 'transit passage through international straits and passage through waters subject to the right of archipelagic sea lanes passage shall not be impeded unless safe and convenient alternative routes are provided'. Lying half-way between the outright prohibition of international strait mining announced in the *US Manual* and equally espoused in Michael Bothe's ILA Report, and the unqualified right of international strait mining at wartime endorsed in the German *Manual*, para.89 is believed to encapsulate a most balanced view. As the *Commentary* reads: 'the new regimes regarding transit and archipelagic sea lanes passage do not have the effect of rendering the mining of straits and sea lanes unlawful *per se*. In view, however, of the importance of these straits and sea lanes for international navigation, belligerents may not exercise unlimited mining rights in those waters.'

As far as the relations of belligerents with neutrals are concerned, the *Manual* on the one hand prohibits the mining of neutral waters as a corollary of the principle of inviolability of neutral territory,[177] and on the other accepts that 'neutral states do not commit an act inconsistent with the laws of neutrality by clearing mines laid in violation of international

[175]The *Commentary* concedes that the clause 'is new in relation to naval mining. It is, however, considered to have evolved into a customary law obligation. Participants felt that it was timely to formulate a rule which would effectively protect neutral shipping in much the same way as the protection of such shipping under the rules of blockade', *ibid.* at para.85.1.

[176]As the *Commentary* further clarifies, 'this paragraph prohibits the enforcement solely by weapon systems, such as mines, unless they are employed in such a manner as not to endanger legitimate seagoing commerce'. *Cf. Manual* at para.102 concerning blockade measures with the *sole purpose* of starving the civilian population.

[177]*Ibid.* at para.86.

humanitarian law'.[178] With reference to mineclearing operations after the cessation of hostilities, the *San Remo Manual* describes the duties incumbent upon the belligerents as follows: first, belligerents have the obligation to record the locations of their minefields, without necessarily making them public.[179] Second, 'parties to the conflict shall do their utmost to remove or render harmless the mines they have laid, each party removing its own mines'.[180] Third, there is a non-compulsory duty of cooperation between the belligerents themselves and also between the belligerents and competent international organizations (including joint operations) in matters of technical and material assistance necessary to remove minefields.[181]

The Growing Momentum against Land-Mines Naval mines have always been treated distinctively from land-mines.[182] During the 1979–80 Diplomatic Conference on Prohibitions or Restrictions on the Use of Certain Conventional Weapons which May Be Deemed to Be Excessively Injurious or to Have Indiscriminate Effects common was the understanding that any negotiated instrument on the use of mines would not in any way affect sea mining. Hence, Article 1 of Protocol II on Prohibitions or Restrictions on the Use of Mines, Booby Traps and Other Devices makes clear that it 'relates to the use on land of mines laid to interdict beaches, waterway crossings or river crossings, but does not apply to the use of anti-ship mines at sea or in

[178]*Ibid.* at para.92. The *Commentary* adds the important remark that 'the paragraph should be considered as declaratory of international customary law', at para.92.1.

[179]See *Manual* at para.84, and *Commentary* at para.84.2.

[180]See *Manual* at para.90. The *Commentary* specifies that actual physical removal of the mines is not an absolute obligation and that simply deactivating them *in situ* may be sufficient (para.90.1), and also that 'a mere cease fire . . . would not automatically trigger the obligation under this paragraph', at para.90.2.

[181]See *Manual* at para.92. This paragraph is identical with Article 8 of the 1991 Swedish Draft Protocol. The *Commentary* adds that 'while it must be acknowledged that for the moment, these states and organizations may not have the necessary expertise to handle naval mine clearance, such a possibility should not be excluded in the future. The rise of non-governmental organisations that have gained expertise in this field should, when beneficial to the protection of international shipping, be used as a complementary resource whenever mine clearance needs to be undertaken', at para.92.3.

[182]See HOOG, G., 'Mines' in BERNHARDT, R. (ed.), *Encyclopedia of Public International Law,* instalment 3 (1982), p. 283*ff.*

inland waterways'.[183] Consequently, naval mines are not at all concerned by the current growing mobilization for the prohibition of anti-personnel mines through a Review Conference of the 1981 Convention.[184]

In 1992 the United States unilaterally proclaimed a one-year moratorium on exports of anti-personnel mines which was later extended for three more years. In February 1993, France requested that the UN Secretary-General convene a Review Conference of the Convention on Inhumane Weapons. The ICRC,

[183]See Draft Articles for a treaty on the regulation of the use of land mines and other devices, submitted by Australia, Austria, Denmark, France, Germany, Federal Republic of Mexico, the Netherlands, New Zealand, Norway, Spain, United Kingdom – UN Doc. *A/CONF.95/PREP.CONF./L.9*. Article 1 of the proposal, concerning the material scope of Protocol II, met with general approval. One delegation, however, suggested that the inclusion of the use of anti-ship mines at sea or inland waters should be studied. There was also some support for the suggestion that when the proposal (once it would have become law), would undergo review, extension of its application to the use of mines at sea should be considered; see UN Doc. *A/CONF.95/PREP.CONF./10*. On the Second Protocol on land-mines in general, see CARNAHAN, B.M., 'The Law of Land Mine Warfare: Protocol II to the United Nations Convention on Certain Conventional Weapons', 22 *Revue de Droit Pénal Minitaire et de Droit de la Guerre* (1983), p. 119*ff.*, and BRETTON, P., 'La Convention du 10 avril 1981 sur l'interdiction ou la limitation de l'emploi de certaines armes classiques qui peuvent être considérées comme produisant des effets traumatiques excessifs ou comme frappant sans discrimination', 27 *AFDI* (1981), p. 127*ff.*

[184]Land-mines took and continue to take a harrowing toll on innocent populations around the globe and have thus alerted the world public opinion on a scale unequalled by the relatively less shocking sea mining. Among the most recent writings, see CAUDERAY, G.C., 'Les mines antipersonnel', 75 *RICR* (juillet-août 1993) n.802, p. 293*ff.*; WILLIAMS, J., 'Les mines terrestres et les mesures visant à les éliminer', 77 *RICR* (juillet-août 1995) no.814, p. 409*ff.*; PARLOW, A., 'Vers une interdiction mondiale des mines terrestres', *ibid.*, p. 429*ff.*; BONSIGNORE, E., 'Land Mines – No More?', 18 *Military Technology* (April 1994), p. 68*ff.*; PROKOSCH, E., *The Technology of Killing*, 1995, p. 181*ff.* See also *Land Mines and the CCW Review Conference*, UNIDIR Newsletter, no.28/29 (Dec.1994/ May 1995); BOUTROS-GHALI, B., 'Les mines terrestres, un désastre humanitaire', 59 *Politique Étrangère* (1994), p. 1069*ff.*, and *Agenda for Development and International Economic Cooperation – Report of the Secretary-General*, UN Doc. *A/ 48/935*, 6 May 1994, §26. Recent estimates speak of more than 100 million uncleared mines in over 30 countries on the five continents, still waiting for their victims; about 10 million in Afghanistan (where they have already killed or severely maimed 350,000 to 500,000 people), 9 million in Angola, 5–10 million in Iraq, 5–8 million in Cambodia, 2 million in Bosnia, 2–3 in Mozambique, 1 million in Somalia; see ICRC, *Basic Facts – Landmines: Issues and Human Costs*, April 1993 at p. 2. The number of victims is growing at an estimated worldwide rate of 1,000 per month; see BONSIGNORE, *op. cit., supra* at p. 69. It has been calculated that using currently available techniques of mine disposal it would take 4,300 years in order to render safe 20 per cent of Afghan territory; see ICRC declaration on mines of 29 October 1993, reproduced in 76 *RICR* (janvier–février 1994) no.805 at p. 65.

for its part, organized a symposium on anti-personnel mines in April 1993 in order to stress the need for coordinated action and gain further support of governments. The gathering momentum against the uncontrolled use of land-mines incited also the UN General Assembly to take concrete action.[185] In pursuing all these initiatives, however, states as well as international organizations have cautiously avoided any correlation with naval mines. The only exception was a declaration made on 9 November 1993 by the Swedish representative who, in introducing on behalf of thirty-four states the draft resolution that was later adopted as GA Resolution 48/79, stated that naval mines have not been regulated by an international agreement since 1907 and that it was necessary that the Review Conference on Inhumane Weapons should address this aspect as well.

Epilogue: A Thriving Past, Present and Future If the review of international legislative efforts, either diplomatic or academic, for the regulation of sea mining breeds certainty over one thing, this is that the naval mine was never exposed to the threat of

[185]At its forty-eighth session, the General Assembly addressed three items related to mines, i.e. the Convention on Inhumane Weapons and its Second Protocol, a moratorium on the export of anti-personnel mines, and the issue of assistance in mine clearance. With relation to the first subject, the General Assembly adopted Resolution 48/79 on 16 December 1993 in which 'welcomes the request to the Secretary-General to convene at an appropriate time, if possible in 1994, in accordance with article 8, paragraph 3, of the Convention of 10 October 1980, a Conference to review the Convention'. The General Assembly further called upon the maximum number of states to attend the Review Conference and encouraged the creation of a group of governmental experts to prepare and assist the Conference in all possible ways. Acting upon a draft resolution introduced by the United States, the General Assembly also passed Resolution 48/75K on 16 December 1993 by which it 'calls upon States to agree to a moratorium on the export of anti-personnel land-mines that pose grave dangers to civilian populations. As regards assistance in mine clearance the General Assembly adopted Resolution 48/7 on 19 October, 1993 in which welcomes *inter alia* the establishment within the UN Secretariat of a coordinated mine clearance programme and requests the Secretary-General to prepare a comprehensive report on the problems caused by the presence in alarming numbers of mines left over by regional armed conflicts, including the financial aspects of launching mineclearing operations. For the diplomatic developments discussed above, see 'Inhumane Weapons Convention', 18 *UN Disarmament Yearbook* (1993), p. 200*ff*. The first preparatory meeting for the Review Conference was held in Geneva in February 1994. In a press statement on the occasion of the opening of its works on 24 February, the President of the ICRC, Cornelio Sommaruga, set the objective of the undertaking as being 'a worldwide ban on antipersonnel mines [as] the only truly effective solution'. See also 76 *RICR* (mars–avril 1994) no.806, pp. 131–201.

prohibition. Unlike what history has recorded regarding the submarine, in the case of mine warfare there was never raised even the faintest voice in favour of a total prohibition of the use of mines at sea. The most the academic societies pleaded for in their early essays was a proscription of minelaying on the high seas. In like manner, the Colombian amendment submitted to the 1907 Hague Conference was the farthest a national delegation ever reached in supporting the limitation of the use of naval mines.

In all available sources, whether international studies, national policy statements, or scientific monographs, common is the feeling that there should be never question of squarely deleting mine stocks from naval inventories, but only of seeking a moderate orderliness in their wartime utilization. Deadly in efficacy, uncomplicated in fabrication and inexpensive in acquisition, the mine weapon was and remains so popular, especially among the less powerful maritime nations, that no initiative could ever have a chance of putting an end to its use. One cannot help but notice the persistent narrowness in tackling the issue in present-day forums, or the limited disposition to embark on the progressive development of the law governing mine warfare at sea. The only reason which could perhaps explain such attachment to the old law and which impedes any major innovation, is the hard-to-face reality that any significant departure from the traditional rules, however desirable, would necessitate burdensome changes in the mine stocks of the world's navies – a perspective with rather minimal chances to have its day.[186]

IV Mine warfare in international jurisprudence and doctrinal writings

From Corfu to Corinto: Covert Mining and the World Court In a rather unique turn of coincidence, two pronouncements of the International Court of Justice on the extremely sensitive issue

[186]The timeless appeal of the mine weapon to the military is amply confirmed in all specialized writings; see, for instance, SAAR, C.W., 'Offensive Mining as a Soviet Strategy', 90 *USNIP* (Aug.1964), p. 43*ff.*; COWIE, J.S., 'The Role of the US Navy in Mine Warfare', 91 *USNIP* (May 1965), p. 53*ff.*; TAYLOR, J.D., 'Mining: A Well Reasoned and Circumspect Defense', 103 *USNIP* (Nov.1977), p. 41*ff.*; HORNE, C.F., 'New Role for Mine Warfare', 108 *USNIP* (Nov.1982), p. 34*ff.*; McDONALD, W., 'Mine Warfare: A Pillar of Maritime Strategy', 111 *USNIP* (Oct.1985), p. 47*ff.*

of state intervention, and perhaps two of the most important judgments ever delivered, dealt *inter alia* with sea mining. Whether along the Corfu Channel or off the ports of Nicaragua, minelaying and minesweeping occasioned two of the most fortunate moments in the history of the Hague Court. What is common to these cases is that the Court constructed its reasoning upon the principle of warning or notification insofar as minelaying activities were concerned.

In fact, both Albania back in 1949 and the United States in 1986 were found answerable for not having duly warned other nations of the presence of mines. In one of the most renowned passages of the Corfu Channel judgment, the Court said:

> the obligations incumbent upon the Albanian authorities consisted in notifying, for the benefit of shipping in general, the existence of a minefield in Albanian territorial waters and in warning the approaching British warships of the imminent danger to which the minefield exposed them. Such obligations are based, not on the Hague Convention of 1907, No.VIII, which is applicable in time of war, but on certain general and well-recognized principles, namely: elementary considerations of humanity, even more exacting in peace than in war; the principle of the freedom of maritime communication, and every State's obligation not to allow knowingly its territory to be used for acts contrary to the rights of other States.[187]

In 1986, the Hague Court, partly reformulating the 1949 dictum, concluded as follows:

> if a State lays mines in any waters whatever in which the vessels of another State have rights of access or passage, and fails to give any warning or notification whatsoever, in disregard of the security of peaceful shipping, it commits a breach of the principles of humanitarian law underlying the specific provisions of Convention No.VIII of 1907.[188]

While in the eighth operative paragraph the Court resolved:

> By fourteen votes to one, [the Court] *decides* that the United

[187]See Corfu Channel Case, Judgment of April 9th, 1949, *ICJ Reports 1949*, at p. 22.

[188]See Military and Paramilitary Activities in and against Nicaragua (Nicaragua v. United States of America), Merits, Judgment, *ICJ Reports 1986*, §215 at p. 112.

> States of America, by failing to make known the existence and location of the mines laid by it . . . has acted in breach of its obligations under customary international law in this respect.[189]

It is interesting to note that although three judges voted against the sixth operative paragraph which condemns the laying of mines as such, only one of them dissented from the afore-quoted eighth operative paragraph. Judge Jennings, recalling the general principles of law as applied in the Corfu Channel Case, held the view that:

> this law would seem to apply *a fortiori* where a State lays mines in another State's ports or port approaches, and fails to notify shipping. Nor does this conclusion depend upon a construction of Article 51 of the Charter, for even supposing the United States were acting in legitimate self-defence, failure to notify shipping would still make the minelaying unlawful. No doubt that the Court is right, therefore, in finding that the United States has, in this matter, acted unlawfully.[190]

Even Judge Schwebel, in his ardent polemic against the Court's reasoning, admitted that

> if the United States were to be justified in taking blockade-like measures against Nicaraguan ports, as by mining, it could only be so if its mining of Nicaraguan ports were publicly and officially announced by it and if international shipping were duly warned by it about the fact that mines would be or had been laid in specified waters. However, no such announcement was made by the United States in advance of or upon the laying of mines; international shipping was not duly warned by it in a timely, official manner.[191]

As regards the dissenting opinion of Judge Oda, in whose view the notification requirement does not stem from customary international law, one would vainly go over his analysis in search of supporting evidence. The nearest reference to this question is a short observation, which betrays his unsettledness on this

[189]*Ibid.*, §292 at pp. 147–8.
[190]See Dissenting Opinion of Judge Jennings, *ibid.* at p. 536.
[191]See Dissenting Opinion of Judge Schwebel, *ibid.*, §238 at p. 380.

point, and in which Judge Oda concedes that 'this action [mining of ports] did not meet the conditions of necessity and proportionality that may be required as a minimum in resort to the doctrine of self-defence under general and customary international law'.[192]

To recall the Memorial of the United Kingdom in the course of the Corfu Channel proceedings, 'the Hague rules constitute a minimum international standard binding at all times on civilised States . . . this Convention was ratified by twenty-nine States and must be regarded as establishing the general rules of international law governing the laying of mines'.[193] It should not escape our attention that the existence of a general duty of notification was not contested by any of the judges who attached dissenting opinions to the 1949 judgment. Referring to the legality of an unnotified mining activity, Judge Azevedo, for instance, affirmed that 'even in the absence of any convention one could not admit that such an act as secret minelaying in time of peace does not involve the responsibility of the State concerned . . . the community could not continue to exist if an act so definitely characteristic of criminality – whatever may be its conventional definition – were to go unpunished'.[194]

Two more judges objected only as to whether the knowledge of the Albanian government had been conclusively established, and not as to whether Albania would be under the obligation to notify if such knowledge was proved. In the words of Judge Winiarski, 'if that be admitted [that the mines could not have been laid without the cognizance of the Albanian government], then, as Albania did not give notice of the existence of the minefield and did not warn the British warships that were approaching, her responsibility is involved'.[195] For Judge Badawi Pasha, 'since knowledge has not been judicially proved, it is superfluous to consider whether, Albania after learning of the minelaying, was, in the hypothesis that mines were laid on October 20th or 21st, in a position to notify the existence of the minefield in the Medri channel, or at least to warn the British

[192]See Dissenting Opinion of Judge Oda, *ibid.*, §89 at p. 253.
[193]See ICJ Pleadings, Corfu Channel, vol.I, §§64, 70 at pp. 38–9.
[194]See *ICJ Reports 1949* at p. 85.
[195]*Ibid.* at p. 49.

fleet when it was steaming towards the Channel, and whether, by her failure to do so, Albania's responsibility was involved'.[196]

The Views of Writers: Mostly Descriptive, Rarely Insightful Doctrinal analysis of the legal aspects of mine warfare suffers chronically from a certain repetitiousness and lack of constructive suggestions for reform. The anything but numerous studies are often confined to reviewing the drawbacks of the 1907 Eighth Hague Convention, whereas the only true theoretical discussion revolves occasionally around the issue of mining of international straits in time of crisis or armed conflict. Howard Levie, for instance, in his recent work on *Mine Warfare at Sea*, presents an updated overview of state practice, an exhaustive analysis of the negotiating history of the Hague instrument as well as an instructive note on the latest developments of naval mine technology, but fails disappointingly to address the current state of the law of mine warfare or to reflect on required changes. His nearly 200-page monograph rounds off in an one-page conclusion simply to say that 'today the practice of nations is that there is only one geographical limitation on belligerent minelaying – they may not be laid in the territorial sea or inland waters of neutrals'.[197]

Thomas Clingan seems to envisage a different set of rules applicable to situations of undeclared war as contrasted to conditions of formal belligerency. As regards the latter, he holds the opinion that 'the Hague Convention rules continue to be viable in this age of new technology, that they provide reasonable rules of conduct, and that these rules seem to be recognized and followed'.[198] With respect to the former, he considers that the combined effect of the Vietnam or the Gulf War experiences and the ICJ's ruling in the Nicaragua case indicate that some of the

[196] *Ibid.* at pp. 64–5. Finally, even in the argumentation of Judge *ad hoc* Ecer what was called into question was not whether an obligation to notify generally exists, but rather whether such an obligation rested specifically with the Albanian government; 'hence we may conclude that Albania, who was acquainted with the functions of this central agency [the Central Mine Clearance Board], . . . did not consider it to be her duty to notify the discovery of the minefield, seeing that that was the duty of the Central Board in London', *ibid.* at p. 123.

[197] See LEVIE, *op. cit., supra* n.1 at p. 177.

[198] See CLINGAN, T.A., 'Submarine Mines in International Law' in ROBERTSON, H.B. (ed.), *The Law of Naval Operations*, USNWC, 64 *International Law Studies* (1991) at p. 360.

wartime rules (especially the duty of notification or the prohibition of indiscriminate mining) may well be applicable to situations short of war.[199]

For Juden Reed, a customary international law standard relative to the laying of submarine mines should reflect a certain legal priority already imposed by the Hague Convention, namely that 'the right to freedom of the seas is superior to the right of any belligerent to war on the seas', but should also 'acknowledge the totality of naval war in its present state of sophistication, and accommodate the inevitable by recognition of the war zone'.[200] Proceeding from this viewpoint, he formulates the following principles:

> the use of mines is legal, in war, for belligerent purposes. Unanchored mines must have a one hour time limit, and may be used anywhere . . . Anchored mines may be used anywhere, unless used solely to effect a commercial blockade, but unsupervised use on the high seas without the declaration of a war zone cannot be considered legal . . . The use of mines is legal, during peace, for neutral purposes. States laying mines during peacetime may only use anchored mines . . . They must also give notification of their use and location in advance.[201]

Drawing upon the 1972 Vietnam experience, the Persian Gulf events of 1987, and the 1990 Swedish Draft Mine Protocol, G.J.F. van Hegelsom, who prepared the Introductory Report for the Toulon session of the Round Table of Experts, identifies the present-day customary law principles regulating sea mining as follows: the overriding principle is that mines should be directed

[199]For another scholar, advanced mine technology may alter the need for prior notification so that the latter will henceforth be associated with mine-activation rather than mine-emplacement: 'the whole concept of laying a minefield that is, in fact, safe until activated remotely obviates the need to notify the presence of mines as a danger to nonbelligerent shipping as soon as they are laid'; see THORPE, *op. cit., supra* n.1 at p. 272. Addressing separately the legal conditions of the use of mines in war, in peace and during periods of tension *(status mixtus)* – a trichotomy which may seem neat in theory but often unworkable in practice – he concludes that as a common parameter it will always be 'a question of weighing the reasonableness of a state's action in genuine self-defense against the degree of protest that any interference with the freedom of navigation will probably provoke. This protest will depend on whether other states believe that a state mining the seas is really defending its vital interests', *ibid.* at p. 273.

[200]See REED, *op. cit., supra* n.1 at p. 314.

[201]*Ibid.* at pp. 315–16.

at legitimate military objectives, with the important caveat that where this cannot be guaranteed, e.g. on the high seas, the presence of mines shall be notified to states not parties to the conflict. Mines have to be so constructed as to become inactive when control over them is lost. The territorial waters of a neutral state remain inviolable, while those of a belligerent should only be mined after innocent shipping has given the opportunity to leave. Whenever the freedom of passage of neutral states is hampered on the high seas, or through international straits and archipelagic waters, belligerents are under an obligation to provide for safe passage or reasonable alternative routes. Finally, belligerents must put on record the exact location and extent of their minefields and must cooperate at the end of the conflict with a view to removing those fields.[202]

The International Straits Mining Issue Maritime narrows are for obvious reasons attractive locations for sea mining. It is not by coincidence that the first naval mines were used in order to block access to river mouths and harbour approaches. From the First World War Dover Strait minefields and the 1915 Dardanelles campaign to the mining of the Japanese straits in 1945, and from the never-elucidated Red Sea mine mystery to the Iranian threat of closing the Hormuz Strait in the late stages of the Iran-Iraq War, history shows that mines proved the ideal weapon to deny passage through choke-points.

The legal prescriptions for navigation through international waterways, be they naturally formed straits or artificial inter-

[202]His analysis was built upon the premise that 'it is quite clear that, as any other weapon, mines can be used in an indiscriminate way. The argument that mines are inherently indiscriminate, however, should be rejected'; see VAN HEGELSOM, G.J.F., 'Introductory Report – Methods and Means of Combat in Naval Warfare' in VON HEINEGG, H.W. (ed.), *Methods and Means of Combat in Naval Warfare: Report and Commentaries of the Round-Table of Experts on International Humanitarian Law Applicable to Armed Conflicts at Sea, Toulon 19–23 October 1990*, 1992 at p. 19. The introductory report gave rise to commentaries most of which concerned the spatial application of any restrictions on the use of sea mines in the light of the 1982 LOS Convention and in particular the questions of mining within the EEZ or the archipelagic waters of belligerent or neutral coastal states. See, for instance, O. Bring/M. Jacobson/F. Rosenius, *ibid.* at p. 62; A.W. Dahl, *ibid.* at pp. 66, 68; L. Doswald-Beck, *ibid.* at p. 72; D. Fleck, *ibid.* at p. 82; B. Godet, *ibid.* at pp. 86–8; W.H. von Heinegg, *ibid.* at pp. 106–7; P. Huyghe, *ibid.* at pp. 111–13; R. Lagoni, *ibid.* at pp. 116–17; S. Lyons, *ibid.* at p. 119; H.H.G. Post, *ibid.* at p. 124; H.B. Robertson, *ibid.* at pp. 125–6; I.A. Shearer, *ibid.* at p. 128.

oceanic canals, have evolved significantly in the last fifty years, so that today we benefit from an elaborate regime, partly customary and partly conventional, regulating the right of passage through such maritime spaces. The unsuspended right of innocent passage in straits used for international navigation codified in Article 16§4 of the 1958 Geneva Territorial Sea Convention, much like the transit passage framework announced in the 1982 Law of the Sea Convention were of course unknown institutions to the drafters of the 1907 mines Convention. Yet, both instruments are of little help to the naval strategist since they are generally held to be applicable only in peacetime.

As regards international jurisprudence, it has twice come close to giving meaningful, yet not full answers to the question of permissible wartime interference with navigation in international straits. In its 1923 judgment on the *Wimbledon* case, the Permanent Court of International Justice resolved that the mere passage of a contraband-carrying belligerent steamship through the Kiel Canal could not be regarded as compromising the neutrality of Germany being the bordering state. Having assimilated that artificial waterway to a natural maritime strait, the Court proceeded to declare that 'it appears clearly established that Germany not only did not, in consequence of her neutrality, incur the obligation to prohibit the passage of the *Wimbledon* through the Kiel Canal, but, on the contrary, was entitled to permit it. Moreover under Article 380 of the Treaty of Versailles, it was her definite duty to allow it.'[203]

In the Corfu Channel case, on the other hand, the International Court of Justice touched upon the limits of control measures that Albania might lawfully have taken against international shipping in view of the exceptional circumstances of tension – yet no formal belligerency – then existing with neighbouring Greece:

> It is a fact that the two coastal States did not maintain normal relations, that Greece had made territorial claims precisely with regard to a part of Albanian territory bordering on the Channel, that Greece had declared that she considered herself technically in a state of war with Albania, and that Albania, invoking the danger of Greek incursions, had considered it necessary to take certain measures of

[203]See *The S.S. 'Wimbledon'*, PCIJ, Series A, No.1 at p. 30.

> vigilance in this region. The Court is of opinion that Albania, in view of these exceptional circumstances, would have been justified in issuing regulations in respect of the passage of warships through the Strait, but not in prohibiting such passage or in subjecting it to the requirement of special authorization.[204]

There is no doubt that both judgments lay bare at least a presumption of right of free passage in international straits, acknowledging at the same time that this right can be at times curtailed, though not altogether suspended. The pertinence of those judicial precedents, however, remains limited, since in the case of the *Wimbledon*, Germany was at all events bound to keep the Kiel Canal open by virtue of the Paris Peace Treaty, while in the Corfu Channel case the Court's ancillary reference to the Greco-Albanian relations was not evocative of an actual state of war existing between the two countries.

That leaves modern writers no safer option than venturing conjectural analogies for wartime situations. As Natalino Ronzitti has recently observed, 'the status of international straits in time of war has never been completely clarified'.[205] Antithetical doctrinal opinions, therefore, make out of international straits mining, another open question not likely to be resolved soon. For some, coastal states parties to an international armed conflict should never be permitted either to lay mines in that portion of their waters which forms an international strait or even to conduct visit and search therein, since either activity would clearly be hampering transit passage which 'is simply too important to international commerce and communication to permit any activity which limits or threatens its exercise'.[206] Likewise, it has been argued that 'neutral nations cannot suspend, hamper or otherwise impede the right of transit

[204]See Corfu Channel Case, Judgment of April 9th, 1949, *ICJ Rep. 1949* at p. 29.

[205]See RONZITTI, N., 'The Crisis of the Traditional Law Regulating International Armed Conflicts at Sea and the Need for Its Revision' in RONZITTI, N. (ed.), *The Law of Naval Warfare,* 1988 at p. 14. See also MAYAMA, A., 'The Influence of the Straits Transit Regime on the Law of Neutrality at Sea', 26 *ODIL* (1995), p. 1*ff*.

[206]See HARLOW, B.A., 'UNCLOS III and Conflict Management in Straits', 15 *ODIL* (1985) at p. 206. *Contra,* see RONZITTI, N., 'Le droit humanitaire applicable aux conflits armés en mer', 242 *RCADI* (1993) at p. 50.

passage of surface ships, submarines and aircraft of belligerent States through international straits'.[207]

Others would admit that littoral states, when neutrals, 'are allowed to take reasonable measures for protecting their own security, such as compulsory pilotage or even the laying of mines', whereas when parties to the conflict, may expose neutral merchant shipping to all hazards of hostilities, going even as far as 'affecting the very possibility of passage'.[208] In principle, however, passage should not be totally denied in either case. As it has been written, 'it can be expected that sea lanes through archipelagic waters will be mined in any future conflict just as the passage of international straits has been barred by mines in past conflicts and undoubtedly will be again in the future'.[209]

In contrast, the great majority of authors agrees that mining likely to impede the transit pasage through straits used for international navigation would be unlawful during peacetime or in time of crisis. Juden Reed, for instance, considers that 'during peacetime, states laying mines in their territorial waters may do so in defense of sovereignty, but only if such territorial waters are not a strait connecting two open bodies of ocean'.[210] Likewise, Thomas Clingan maintains that 'mining of international straits in peacetime would not be acceptable under customary rules'.[211]

[207]See ALEXANDER, L.M., 'International Straits' in ROBERTSON, H.B. (ed.), *The Law of Naval Operations*, USNWC, 64 *International Law Studies* (1991) at p. 93. See also GILL, T.D., 'The Forcible Protection, Affirmation and Exercise of Rights by States under Contemporary International Law', 23 *NYIL* (1992) at pp. 164–5.

[208]See RONZITTI, *op. cit., supra* n.205 at pp. 19, 23. And elsewhere: 'granting a right of transit passage when the littoral State is at war appears to be at odds with the latitude of powers that customary international law gives to belligerent States . . . For such a passage would be inconsistent with the right of self-defence and State practice which proves that littoral States are endowed with substantial powers'; see RONZITTI, N., 'Passage through International Straits in Time of International Armed Conflict' in *International Law at the Time of Its Codification – Essays in Honour of Roberto Ago*, 1987, vol. 2 at pp. 380, 383. See also RONZITTI, *op. cit., supra* n. 206 at p. 54. Similarly, see LOWE, V., 'The Impact of the Law of the Sea on Naval Warfare', 14 *Syracuse Journal of International Law and Commerce* (1988) at pp. 670–1, and VON HEINEGG, *op. cit., supra* n. 1 at p. 63.

[209]See LEVIE, *op. cit., supra* n.1 at p. 178.

[210]See REED, *op. cit., supra* n.1 at p. 316.

[211]See CLINGAN, *op. cit., supra* n.198 at p. 356.

V Progressing technology and static law: the missing interaction

There is certainly nothing particularly impressive in the development of naval mine warfare in terms of technological evolution. Yet, it offers a telling manifestation of the frequently observed gap separating ageing written law from contemporary uses of a military hardware unknown at the time of legal codification. From this perspective, sea mining invites some comments on the archaic state of the laws of war as compared to the leading edge of today's weapons technology.[212]

The Problem Stated Common is the feeling that contemporary military technology has reduced international humanitarian law to a mere spectator, or almost so, of the phenomenal change the world has experienced since the end of the Second World War. In most cases, legal rules prove mismatched to confront the products of such technology, let alone to contain its evolution. Modern weapons systems are being developed above and beyond the reach of static legal prescriptions. Two main reasons explain the everlasting phenomenon. First, there is no possible way for law to anticipate the trends, nature or the outcome of military research programmes, foresee the consequences and react preventively. Often the jurist is not at all conversant with existing weapons technologies and the legal quandaries to which their use may eventually give rise. Second, the development of hyper-sophisticated means of fighting involves an investment of such a scale as would suffice in itself to dash any belated legal opposition.

Thus, to the extent that an early legal intervention cannot be expected from rules often silent, fragmentary or obsolete, whereas all legal resistance at a later stage can easily be defeated by the powerful web of interests vested in the meantime, technological change in the military field takes often the form of a *fait accompli*. Runaway technology has outpaced legal control to such an extent that the century-old Martens clause remains still today

[212]The evolution of sea warfare through technological innovation from 1851 to date is traced in LAUTENSCHLAGER, K., 'Technology and the Evolution of Naval Warfare', 8 *International Security* (1983), p. 3*ff*. For an overview of the latest trends in naval technology, see PEREZ-LLORCA, J., *Emerging Technology and Defence*, North Atlantic Assembly Papers, 1991, pp. 69–114, and BOSMA, J.T., 'The Alternative Futures of Naval Force', 5 *ODIL* (1978), p. 181*ff*.

the only legal prescription against the perverse applications of military technology. As regards modern legal instruments, Article 36 of the First Additional Protocol stands out as the single future-oriented provision albeit unable in itself to determine the legal or illegal character of the prospective use of new weapons.[213]

States remain extremely reluctant to undertake an international commitment which might compromise in advance the future development and use of new weapons. At the time of negotiating, for instance, Article 36 of the First Geneva Protocol which deals with the study, development, acquisition or adoption of new weapons states were not ready to accept any idea of international control favouring instead a domestic decision with regard to the lawfulness of pursuing the development of newly invented means of warfare.[214] In the words of the Rapporteur of Committee III, 'determination by any State that the employment of a weapon is prohibited or permitted is not binding internationally, but it is hoped that the obligation to make such determinations will ensure that means or methods of warfare will not be adopted without the issue of legality being explored with care'.

Moreover, even the most moderate *ex post facto* intervention of law is not always easy to operate in the field of humanitarian

[213]The problem is far from being limited to the sphere of modern weapons technology. The formidable challenges represented by biomedical or computer technologies are well known, reaffirming the general tendency of technical innovation to become a dominant and uncontrollable force. The legal debate on child-cloning or the limits of interactive computing in essence gives expression to the same concern, that is to say, how to tame new technological applications in order to preserve fundamental human values. For reflections on the relations between law and technology in general, see TRIBE, L.H., *Channeling Technology through Law*, 1973, and LIVINGSTON, D.A., *The Stabilizing Effects of Science and Technology on International Law*, 1967.

[214]See SANDOZ, Y., SWINARSKI, C., ZIMMERMANN, B. (eds), *Commentary on the Additional Protocols of 8 June 1977 to the Geneva Conventions of 12 August 1949*, 1987, pp. 421–8. It will be recalled at this juncture that according to Article 86 *bis* of the Draft Protocol, a 31-member special committee would be created with a view to drawing a list of weapons which would fall under the superfluous injury or unnecessary suffering prohibition. Provision was also made for special conferences to be convened in due course for concluding suitable agreements. All these institutionalized control mechanisms, however, were rejected in plenary meeting, the Conference having adopted instead Resolution 22 on the *Follow-Up Regarding Prohibition or Restriction of Use of Certain Conventional Weapons*. The text of that Resolution is in SCHINDLER, D. and TOMAN, J. (eds), *The Laws of Armed Conflicts – A Collection of Conventions, Resolutions and Other Documents*, 3rd edn, 1988 at pp. 729–30.

law. The negotiations surrounding the proposed ban of certain conventional weapons in 1978–80 best illustrated the difficulties involved. A major obstacle in those negotiations was the unwillingness to pronounce clearly and loudly the illegality of certain types of weapons, despite the general acknowledgement of such illegality, for fear of the implications such a decision would carry with respect to previous large-scale use of those dubious weapons. To give a concrete example, the main reason for certain states opposing a total ban of incendiary weapons such as napalm bombs and flame throwers was not so much their refusal to admit that these weapons should be outlawed for the future as their wish to escape the politically costly conclusion that the extensive employment of such devices in the past was unlawful.

Military Technology and the Deepening Crisis of Humanitarian Conscience The modern world has no doubt departed significantly far from the days when a leading military power convened on its own initiative an international conference with a view to outlawing a new type of piercing ammunition that at the time only itself possessed.[215] Any attempt to find analogous initiatives or experiences in recent years would certainly be surreal. Today, states engaged in the development of the war-winning weapons

[215]Back in 1868, the Imperial Russian government invited states to attend an International Military Commission at St. Petersburg to consider the matter of explosive projectiles convinced that the use of bullets which exploded in contact, despite their definite military utility in some cases, ought to be generally and solemnly renounced. The Imperial War Minister had formulated a proposal to Tsar Alexander II in this sense in which he argued: 'il est hors de doute que les balles explosives peuvent être utiles pour faire sauter les caissons; mais employées contre des êtres vivants pour aggraver les blessures, elles doivent être classées au nombre des moyens barbares qui ne trouvent aucune excuse dans les exigences de la guerre. Si la guerre est un mal inévitable, on doit cependant chercher à en diminuer les cruautés autant que possible, et c'est pourquoi il n'y a pas lieu d'introduire des armes meurtrières qui ne peuvent qu'aggraver les calamités sans avantage pour le but direct de la guerre. L'usage d'une arme doit avoir uniquement pour objet l'affaiblissement des forces militaires de l'ennemi; il suffit de mettre hors de combat un nombre considérable d'hommes, mais ce serait de la barbarie que de vouloir aggraver les souffrances de ceux qui ne peuvent plus prendre part à la lutte. Les parties belligérantes ne doivent tolérer que les calamités qui sont impérieusement nécessitées par la guerre. Toute souffrance et tout dommage qui n'auraient pas pour seul résultat d'affaiblir l'ennemi n'ont aucune raison d'être et ne doivent être admis d'aucune manière'; see MARTENS, G.F. von, *Nouveau Recueil Général de Traités*, vol.18, 1873 at p. 460.

of the twenty-first century invest enormously, test secretly and distrust openly any legal move which would hold them back from their effort. As a telling footnote to the historical parenthesis, one might add that the Russian initiative of the past century came at a time when war was a perfectly admissible phenomenon of inter-state relations, whereas the current stagnancy in regulating new weapons technologies persists at a time when the resort to arms is generally prohibited.[216]

In a recent article, a Red Cross official has identified with vivid displeasure the various tactics weapon-developing countries usually make use of in order to bar the way to a timely and conclusive legal assessment concerning the lawfulness of the use of new weapons. First, she alludes to the routinely denied access to reliable information and pertinently remarks that 'it is obvious that the most effective way of preventing the use of illegal weapons is the establishment in advance of whether a proposed new weapon would violate the law... However, if information is classified until such development, and indeed until general widespread use of a weapon, such preventive assessments become very difficult'.[217] Second, she notes the tendency of the principally concerned states to oppose any international action by abstaining from related discussions, by dismissing unfavourable findings of international fora as unconvincing, or threatening the outcome of critical negotiations in some other field if the focus on the legality of new weapons is not discontinued. Last, she calls into question the credibility of national legal findings in favour of the legality of a specific weapons technology, especially in circumstances where the military-financial establishment of the state involved would be

[216]Most governments pay lip service at best to legal principles of restraint while refusing to check the pace of military research, far less to give up promising new military inventions. As the Prussian delegate had pointedly observed in 1868 before the St. Petersburg Military Commission, 'on voit en effet d'un côté l'Europe et l'Amérique se préoccuper du sort des blessés en temps de guerre et s'imposer de grands sacrifices pour l'alléger; – de l'autre côté, la science moderne, encouragée et soutenue par les gouvernements, se préoccupe constamment d'augmenter le nombre des blessés et d'aggraver les conséquences de la guerre'; see *ibid.* at p. 452.

[217]See DOSWALD-BECK, L., 'Obstacles to Regulating New Weaponry: Battlefield Laser Weapons' in FOX, H. and MEYER, M.A. (eds), *Effecting Compliance*, 1993 at p. 115.

pushing heavily for the production of that weapon, or the political go-ahead signal would have already been given.[218]

Apart from the negative attitude of principally affected powers, legal action is also frustrated by another factor relating to the policy considerations which dictate a state's decision – or better indecision – to commit itself actively to the resolution of an international problem. Governments often demonstrate their unwillingness to respond to new challenges until domestic public opinion gets sufficiently alerted exerting pressure which then becomes politically costly to ignore (concerted international action in matters of global environmental protection is a case in point). Given, however, the lack of information in the defence field, public opinion cannot be expected to grow sufficiently momentous in order to drive government action.

What is more, most countries might still consider it inadvisable to embark on a discussion concerning the prohibition or restriction of the use of weapons that they might never be able to produce or procure, and therefore of little relevance to their immediate interests. Be it then on account of either the stiff opposition of the few directly interested states, or the tardy awareness of some others marginally concerned, the fact remains that humanitarian law is confronted in the sphere of weapons development with established and hardly reversible realities.

Faced with the endemic contradiction between promotion of humanitarian values and incessant technological progress, law has to persist in the hitherto Sisyphean task of holding war technology in check – a concrete way of proving that humanitarian law is a contribution to civilization rather than an alibi for cruelty.[219] In pursuing this objective, it should also be kept

[218]*Ibid.* at pp. 116–17. Her overall conclusion is that states in the forefront of the technological development of weapons bear a primary responsibility 'for it is their research and development today that will fashion the weapons used in the conflicts of tomorrow', and that they should be guided by 'a certain enlightened self-interest' since new weapons can eventually be used against the developer; *ibid.* at p. 121.

[219]For a recent study claiming that 'despite noble rhetoric to the contrary, the laws of war have been formulated deliberately to privilege military necessity at the cost of humanitarian values [and] as a result, the laws of war have facilitated rather than restrained wartime violence', see JOCHNICK, C. and NORMAND, R., 'The Legitimation of Violence: A Critical History of the Laws of War', 35 *HILJ* (1994), p. 49*ff.* For further reflections on what has been alluded to here as the deepening crisis of humanitarian conscience, see VEUTHEY, M., 'Pour une politique humanitaire' in SWINARSKI, C. (ed.), *Studies and Essays on International Humanitarian Law and Red Cross Principles in Honour of Jean Pictet*, 1984, p. 989*ff.*

in mind that the evolution of humanitarian law standards can only be conceived as a mono-directional process, that is to say constantly moving ahead towards higher levels of restraint. As Georges Abi-Saab has observed in outlining the pattern of development of humanitarian law, 'for the protective rules of humanitarian law to remain effective, they have constantly to expand their scope and tighten their requirements in response to the evolution of war technology on the one hand and the ever increasing requirements of civilization on the other'.[220]

Exotic Technology and the Principle of Distinction One of the most interesting aspects of military technology to be explored from a legal perspective is the impact of technological progress on the promotion of the humanitarian principle of distinction. Speaking of technological improvement of a weapons system one logically implies accrued targeting precision, efficacy and reliability. In this sense, one may validly expect that the more weapons technology advances, the less the principle of distinction will have to suffer from indiscriminate methods and means of warfare. Considering the difference in precision between gravity bombs and laser-guided missiles, it is undeniable that modern weaponry serves better the principle of economy of force and also the prevention of collateral damage. If the same military objectives can be taken out by firing a few 'smart' cruise missiles instead of resorting to 'saturation bombing', no one would be opposed to the employment of sophisticated weaponry, and certainly not the innocent civilian population living near, for instance, a military industrial compound under air attack.

Yet, targeting accuracy has not come alone. Lethal capacity has also increased dramatically, or, to put it otherwise, the survival rate has decreased significantly. The technical sophistication of modern weapons systems has thus shaped a combat environment in which acting quickly can be at times more vital than acting consciously. Split-second decisions are most often required which tend to eclipse the very advantages such technological evolution is supposed to offer. The downing of the Iranian Airbus in 1988 by one of the most technologically advanced US warships, apparently carried out under a 'fire first

[220]ABI-SAAB, G., 'The Specificities of Humanitarian Law' in SWINARSKI, *op. cit., supra* at p. 276.

and identify later' state of mind, depicted most graphically this reality. It is no doubt, therefore, one of the greatest ironies of the current state of development of military technology that the more accurate and lethal modern weapons become the more imperative the need for indiscriminate use grows.

VI Concluding remarks

Assessing the legal merits of sea mining by applying current humanitarian law standards leads to a number of baffling imbroglios. Reconciling, for instance, the use of blind weapons such as mines with the commanding principle of distinction can be taken for mere fantasy. As one writer remarked with irony, 'if a mine with a built-in IFF procedure can be developed, which in addition to identifying a ship as friend or foe, will also identify neutral ships and further determine if the neutral vessel is carrying contraband, the problem of mining in international law will be considerably lessened'.[221] Unlike the submarine which only if so ordered could give itself up to unrestricted warfare, the use of the naval mine necessarily causes indiscriminate destruction. For all the electronic sophistication and purported intelligence of modern devices, the naval mine remains an unmanned machinery incapable of second thoughts.

Apart from the uneasy relation with the principle of distinction, the discussion over the legal perplexities of sea mining gets singularly close to that relating to war zones from yet another aspect, that is to say, with regard to the problem of notification. In fact, if notification is the only legal obligation incumbent upon belligerents before they engage in minelaying, it would be as good as saying that the simple announcement of the intention to commit an act, however legally objectionable, may suffice to exonerate the act itself. Warning would thus amount to unqualified authorization, which would mean confounding form with substance. Yet, it is widely held that a general duty of notification is practically the only conclusive legal prescription in the matter of minelaying.

This latter point has been particularly affirmed in the jurispru-

[221]See POWERS, R.D., 'International Law and Open-Ocean Mining', 15 *Judge Advocate General Journal* (1961) at p. 55. Lessened perhaps, but certainly not definitely resolved, for destroying what would otherwise be an ordinary prize is far from free of legal objections.

dence of the International Court of Justice. In the Corfu Channel case, it was precisely the 'grave omission' of the Albanian authorities to warn the approaching vessels of the imminent danger that incurred the international responsibility of Albania – the act of planting the mines not having been clearly attributed to that country. As regards the Nicaragua case, the failure of the United States to make known the existence and location of the mines prompted a separate operative paragraph, the eighth in the Court's decision, which would seem *prima facie* pleonastic in view of a previous paragraph where the mining of Nicaraguan waters as such was already declared an internationally illegal act.[222]

By looking at the voting record, however, one understands the need for separate treatment of the question of notification, since to the mind of two judges, namely Stephen Schwebel and Robert Jennings, the United States had acted in breach of its obligations under customary international law by failing to issue a warning, even though the act of mining *per se* was for the former and might have been for the latter a legitimate exercise of collective self-defence.[223] One can reasonably gather, therefore, that for the International Court of Justice the requirement of notification would remain a customary obligation for the minelaying state even when sea mining is resorted to as an otherwise permissible use of force, that is in the exercise of the right of self-defence.

Yet, sea mining, it is submitted, is by nature unfit to simply repel an armed attack, as Article 51 seems to impel, and inevitably affects third states interests. A simple notification, therefore, does not suffice in itself to determine the legality of compromising the safety of international merchant shipping through the act of mining. Notification is no more than a unilateral declaration of intention which by affirming the existence of one's own rights arbitrarily defines the limits of the rights of others, and which more often than not conceals abusive claims. As the World Court pronounced in 1949, a state is not bound to abstain from exercising its rights, here the right of navigation and the right to engage in peaceful commerce, which

[222]Contrary to the Corfu Channel context, in the Nicaragua case the identity of the minelaying state appeared undisputed. In establishing the facts imputable to the respondent state, pointed out twice that neither before the laying of mines nor subsequently did the American government publicly warn international shipping of the existence of mines; see *ICJ Reports 1986*, §§77, 80 at pp. 46–7, 48.
[223]See Dissenting Opinion of Judge Schwebel, *ibid.*, §§237–8 at pp. 379–80, and Dissenting Opinion of Judge Jennings, *ibid.*, at pp. 536–7.

another state has illegally denied.[224] The much acclaimed criteria of necessity and proportionality, it is submitted, cannot afford much guidance in this respect.

Mine warfare poses a host of arduous dilemmas to the legally minded. The continued legal validity of the Eighth Hague Convention of 1907 would seem to underlie them all. Many do not see how this instrument could have survived a century-long international practice which evolved in persistent defiance of its most pronounced requisites. Doubts have also been raised as to the applicability of a Convention which exclusively relates to contact mines in the age of combined-influence mines, torpedo mines and other modern devices. For others, however, the convention continues to produce its effects among the twenty-seven states that have ratified it thus far, binding for instance the United States, China and major European powers such as France, Germany, the United Kingdom or the Netherlands. Certainly, there have been many violations, but it was more the spirit than the letter which was most often infringed, as the very language of the convention lends itself to abuse. As to the Convention's suitability to modern conditions, the key principles of the Hague text, it is asserted, could be applied with no difficulty to present-day mine designs, for it would be unreasonable to consider that these principles had been tailored to fit a specific type of mine-fusing mechanism only.

Leaving aside the rights and wrongs of the opposing views, it appears irrefutable that the 1907 Convention has functioned only minimally all these years. For one thing, it never overcame the mishaps of its own drafting. At the time of its conclusion, for instance, it provided for something as yet technically unavailable (the 1-hour self-scuttling time-limit), which by the time was developed it no longer responded to the needs of mine warfare. In like manner, the Hague text sounded oracular regarding the legality of a mine blockade. First alluded to in the course of the Spanish-American War of 1898, the question came up again owing to German practices in the First World War, to become once more topical at the time of Operation Starvation against Japan. And yet, the 'sole object' criterion of Article 2 of the Convention would seem to afford a valid legal pretext even to this latter most controversial blockade campaign.

[224]See *ICJ Reports 1949* at p. 30.

The 1907 Eighth Hague Convention courts legal irrelevance for other reasons as well. It is of course a truism to say that if the Hague Convention is to be deemed of continued validity, it has to operate within its proper assumptions. The 1907 instrument was constructed upon the premise that high seas mining would be lawful if only incidental to actual naval engagement of opposing warships, while merchant shipping should be spared to the fullest possible degree. Following considerable modern practice, however, mine warfare appears to have passed at the service of the reverse logic. We are now faced with prevailing economic warfare considerations according to which naval mines are counted upon for an energetic attrition strategy against enemy and neutral merchant shipping alike. It is doubtful, therefore, whether the Hague Convention can be of lasting influence under such circumstances suggestive of a fundamentally altered, if not capsized, perception of legal permissibilities in pursuing war victory.

Mines, originally conceived as naval operations support weapons, seem in our days best suited for covert peacetime operations and acts of economic terrorism. Along the pattern that first the Albanians modelled in the Corfu Channel, and half a century later the Americans followed in Nicaragua, the Iranians in the Persian Gulf, and possibly the Libyans in the Red Sea, minefields are to be activated without previous warning and with no one assuming responsibility – a sort of nefarious sniping at sea for which, of course, the 1907 Convention would be the last to blame.

In the end, the question of the continued validity of the Eighth Hague Convention may prove an insignificant one, for, even if it is considered to be still in force, it does not serve much with its ageing and equivocal provisions. If, on the contrary, it is to be held discarded, we would still have to agree on what has taken its place. Overall, one can hardly escape the conclusion that on the academic quest for balanced rules rests perhaps the only ray of hope in the current context of legal unchartedness, product of long years of misunderstanding, indifference and systematic sophistry. *'Utopie ou calcul?'* – asked rhetorically Albert de La Pradelle back in 1933 – alluding to the motives of the chronic neglect of the codification of the laws of war;[225] some sixty years later, there should be no doubt left as to the right answer.

[225]LA PRADELLE, A.de, 'Utopie ou calcul? Négligera-t-on longtemps encore l'étude des lois de la guerre?', 12 *Revue de Droit International* (1933), p. 511*ff*.

Dolus an virtus, quis in hoste requirat?

Whether deceit or valour, who would ask in warfare?

Virgil, *Aeneid,* bk.II, l.390,
(transl. by H.R. Fairclough, The Loeb Classical Library, 1965 at p. 321)

Chapter Three

RUSES AND PERFIDY AT SEA

I Introduction

R . . . R . . . R . . . R . . . By then it was clear that the approaching merchant vessel with the Dutch colours painted on its hull and the Dutch flag on its mast was alas a disguised man-of-war. While the ambushed ship was trying to send the code message for help, the German flag was hoisted high, the neutral marks were coated and the concealed guns put in action. In the days of the Second World War, the chances of survival for merchant ships and crews against roaming German raiders depended, in fact, on the speed the wireless operator could click the dots and the dashes before the first salvoes landed in his room. On account of such a lethal trap, hundreds of merchantmen went down, innocent lives were lost and chaos ruled the world's oceans. Some called it skill or ingenuity. Others denounced it as lawless savagery. Whatever its merit, this is the unique fashion maritime deception has been recorded in recent times – fertile ground, no doubt, for legal reflection and reform.

Of Strategy, Stratagems and Surprise in War In world military history, hardly a memorable battle was fought, far less won, without large reserves of craftiness, nor has a strategist ever became one of the immortals without having associated his name with some wily war plan. Much as the wooden horse marked the ultimate stratagem of the Greeks in the Trojan War, the decisive blow to the Persian hordes delivered in the Straits of Salamis was also attributable to surprise tactics and cunning manoeuvring. Nothing but astuteness could have promised victory to the modest formation of 310 Greek triremes against

1,200 ships in Xerxes' fleet. Themistocles' brilliant ruse was to lure the enemy to attack in narrow waters by feigning disarray and flight. The Persians rushed in congested lines to the channel, confident that the Greek forces were fleeing the scene, to discover the fatal ploy much too late.[1] *Dolus* and *heuremata bellica* were later to make part of the tactics of the Roman legions,[2] while one of the finest works of Chinese military literature, dating back to the fourth century B.C., suggested that 'all warfare is based on deception. Therefore, when capable, feign incapacity; when active, inactivity. When near, make it appear that you are far away; when far away, that you are near.'[3]

Strategy refers to the elaboration of an orderly scheme for pursuing an end, in this case for conducting hostilities, an arrangement of priorities and alternatives, or a sound choice of tactics, based on a rational evaluation of the enemy's strengths and weaknesses. *Stratagem* is an anti-strategy in that it substitutes the unconventional for the probable, the risky for the reasonable. It is all about how to secure the marginal advantage which may turn a main strategy to glory. It aims to overpower the enemy's defences more by ingenuity and rapidity than by sheer force. *Surprise*, in turn, connotes the effect, the state of mind when faced with the unexpected. It points to the confusion and the irrationality of the enemy's reaction when suddenly confronted with the spectre of defeat.[4] Defined in such idyllic and often misleading terms as techniques and devices intended to 'win war without a trace of blood or tears', ruses of war imply luring the enemy into making a wrong assessment, and numbing his capacity for cool reflection. They may thus consist

[1]See HAMMOND, N.G.L., 'The Battle of Salamis', 76 *Journal of Hellenic Studies* (1956) at pp. 45–8. The appropriateness of the Greeks' recourse to stratagems is confirmed by the following oracle the Pythian priestess of Delphi had once given to the Lacedaemonians: 'Phoebus bids thee not to fight with the sword only/By guile a people holds the Messenian land/And they will be caught by the very devices which they/were first to use'; see Pausanias, *Description of Greece*, bk.IV, ch.XII, §1. While Thucydides in his *History of the Peloponnesian War* puts these words in the mouth of the Spartan Brasidas: 'and these wiles carry with them the greatest glory of all, by which, deceiving most the enemy, a man does most benefit his friends'; see Thucydides, *History of the Peloponnesian War*, bk.V, §9.

[2]Etymologically, the Latin word *dolus* which means the artifice derives from the Greek verb δολοω meaning to deceive, while the noun δολωμα connotes both the stratagem and the bait.

[3]See Sun Tzu, *The Art of War*, translated by Griffith, S.B., 1963 at p. 66.

[4]See ANDREWS, F., 'Surprise in Naval Warfare', 104 *USNIP* (1978), p. 84*ff*.

of operations of *counter-intelligence or disinformation* (e.g. deliberate leaking of inaccurate information, breaking enemy codes or mock movement of forces), operations of *camouflage and dissimulation* (e.g. concealing of warships by netting or paintwork, and use of decoys), and operations of *diversion* (e.g. cover attacks or feint retreats).

In the watershed of the Second World War, for instance, history has recorded no shortage of intrigue and deception. Driving back Rommel's army in North Africa was only made possible through a brilliant diversion scheme using everything from dummy tanks and trucks to fake water pipelines and railway tracks.[5] The crushing defeat of the Japanese fleet at Midway was equally due to a stratagem after the US Naval Intelligence had deciphered *Yamamoto*'s codes of communication. As S. Reit eloquently describes, 'painted canvas in North Africa and wireless fakery in the Pacific', were all it took to turn the fortunes of war to the Allied side.[6] By 1943, the Allies had similarly managed with the assistance of Polish, British and French scientists, to break the German Navy's cipher system known as *Enigma*. Information from the decrypted radio correspondence of the German Navy played a unique role in intercepting the German commerce raiders such as the notorious *Atlantis* and tracking down numerous U-boats during rendezvous with the tankers that supplied them at sea.[7] A most carefully

[5]The gist of the plan was to make the Germans believe that a substantial attack would be mounted in the south whereas the real move was to be attempted in the north possibly earlier than anticipated. For more on the preparation of the deception plan for the battle of El Alamein, or *Operation Bertram*, see the narrative by one of its architects BARKAS, G., *The Camouflage Story – From Aintree to Alamein*, 1952. See also FISHER, D., *The War Magician*, 1983; CRUICKSHANK, C., *Deception in World War II*, 1979, p. 19*ff*.; DEWAR, M., *The Art of Deception in Warfare*, 1989, p. 55*ff*.

[6]See REIT, S., *Masquerade – The Amazing Camouflage Deceptions of World War II*, 1978 at p. 207. See also HOLMES, W.J., *Double-Edged Secrets: U.S. Naval Intelligence Operations in the Pacific during World War II*, 1979, and WHITLOCK, D.L., 'The Silent War against the Japanese Navy', 48 *US Naval War College Review* (autumn 1995), p. 43*ff*.

[7]From June to October 1943, for example, American forces conducted operations against German submarines and supply ships in the vicinity of the Azores almost entirely on the basis of Enigma data. As a result, at least 19 U-boats and all but one of their supply ships (milk cows) were sunk. The German Submarine Command had repeatedly ordered investigations for the fear of leakage, but the possibility of enemy cryptologists having cracked Enigma had been always discarded. For more, see KOZACZUK, W., *Enigma – How the German Machine Cipher Was Broken, and How It Was Read by the Allies in World War Two*, edited

executed diversion plan also formed an essential part of Operation Overlord (the code name for the Allied invasion of France).[8]

In the 1991 Gulf War, to draw from a recent experience, the Iraqi army marked its only, though ephemeral, victory thanks to a simple 'ruse'. In fact, on 6 February 1991, a column of Iraqi tanks drove into, and occupied for little more than 24 hours, the Saudi city of Khafji practically unopposed by the Saudi and American troops stationed in the city. On this day, tanks closed on the city at midday with their turrets reversed and their big guns facing north, a clear surrender signal in accordance with the air-dropped instructions prepared by the coalition forces.[9] Hence, even in this short desert encounter, widely considered

---

and translated by Kasparek, C., 1984, and BROWN, A.C., *Le guerre secrète – Le rempart des mensonges* [Bodyguard of Lies, 1975], French transl.(1981), vol.1, pp. 275–91. See also KAHN, D., *Seizing the Enigma: The Race to Break the German U-boat Codes, 1939–1943*, 1991.

[8]*Fortitude*, as the entire diversion plan was called, was divided into *Fortitude North* for Norway, and *Fortitude South* for the Pas-de-Calais. In order to contain the German forces in Norway, dummy heavy-bomber concentrations were built on Scottish airfields and a great number of vessels were assembled in North English ports as though an Allied attack were imminent. As for the Navy, it concentrated on an enhanced offensive against enemy submarines off the Norwegian coast while two separate naval forces opted for radio deception simulating formations of some 40 warships, each supposedly carrying out training with an assault force and disembarkation exercises. In the south, the intention was to simulate preparations for a massive attack on the Pas-de-Calais, 200 miles east of the chosen landing places. Radio deception was coupled with sham reconnaissance flights and diversionary air bombing and sea mining. *Quicksilver III* stood for the counterfeit display of landing-craft circling the east and south-east coast of England. More than 250 dummy crafts, better known as *Bigbobs*, were in fact stationed in the Thames estuary and elsewhere. Visual or wireless deception apart, highly ingenious electronic decoying was also carried out in support of the invasion of Europe. *Taxable* and *Glimmer* were combined air and sea operations performed on D-day at the eastern end of the English Channel and designed to electronically simulate two big assault convoys approaching the French coast. Three devices would reproduce on German radar-screens the movement of a large number of ships. *Window*, or air-dropped aluminium strips, *Filbert*, or balloons carrying a reflecting mechanism, and *Moonshine*, an apparatus capable of reflecting the pulse of enemy radar in much amplified form. On the fascinating story of deception on the eve of the Normandy landings, see HASWELL, J., *The Intelligence and Deception of the D Day Landings*, 1979, NORMAN, A., *Operation Overlord – Design and Reality*, 1952, p. 124*ff.*, CRUICKSHANK, *op. cit., supra* n.5, p. 85*ff.*, BROWN, *op. cit., supra*, vol.2, p. 65*ff.*, and SHEEN, H.G., 'A Cloak for Overlord', 29 *Military Review* (1950), no.11, p. 20*ff.* On *Operation Mincemeat* – a most intriguing ploy used in connection with the Allied invasion of Sicily – see BROWN, *op. cit., supra*, vol.1, p. 301*ff.*, and DEWAR, *op. cit., supra* n.5, p. 67*ff.*

[9]See *U.S. Department of Defense Report to Congress on the Conduct of the Persian Gulf War – Appendix on the Role of the Law of War* [10 April 1992], reprinted in 31 *ILM* (1992) at pp. 631–2, and *Newsweek*, 11 February 1991 at pp. 11–12.

as the most sophisticated war campaign of all times, there proved to be still room for classical visual deception. Who would have thought, for instance, that the Iraqis would be able to fool the huge 'electronic eye' the allies kept on them by using dummy inflatable tanks (an artifice of British origin dating back to the Second World War) and missile launchers?[10] In turn, the ground offensive of the coalition forces, better known as the 100-Hour Battle, was contrived as part of a large diversion plan which led the Iraqis to believe that a major amphibious landing was imminent on the Kuwaiti shores, while the real strike came from a flanking attack involving some 200,000 troops which had been moved at the last minute and under utmost secrecy 300 miles further to the west.[11]

The Place and Function of Law If legal theory takes an interest in warfare tactics, it is because it has long prescribed that the use of deception should have its limits, and that preserving a modicum of good faith is essential even among warring enemies. To the legally minded, deception qualifies methods of fighting that may range from guileful bravery to treacherous killing. It can partake as much of gallant heroism as of dishonourable criminality. Although the theoretical distinction between lawful means of misleading and illicit treachery has been debated since the days of Thomas Aquinas, the law of nations has since found it arduous to spell out how these expedients should be distinguished in practice.[12]

[10]See 'Decoys: Tanks But No Tanks', *Time*, 4 February 1991 at p. 17.
[11]See *Newsweek*, 18 March 1991 at p. 25. The coalition forces during the Operation Desert Storm also made extensive use of unmanned aerial vehicles (UAVs) for multiple missions including reconnaissance, surveillance, target identification, damage assessment, electronic warfare and deception. In their decoy mission, UAVs were deployed to deceive, confuse and saturate the Iraqi air defences. It has now become known that the high number of aircraft the Iraqi forces claimed to have shot down in the first days of the Gulf War were not unrealistic, but more than 90 per cent of these concerned decoy planes; see 'US UAV Programmes: Where Do We Stand?', 15 *Military Technology* (Oct.1991), no.10 at p. 19.
[12]Among the few scholar works, see FLECK, D., 'Ruses of War and Prohibition of Perfidy', 13 *Revue de Droit Pénal Militaire et de Droit de la Guerre* (1974), pp. 269–314, and BOURDONCLE, R., 'De l'influence des ruses sur l'évolution du droit de la guerre', *Annales de l'Université de Lyon*, 1958, pp. 31–133. In German language, see GIMMERTHAL, M., *Kriegslist und Perfidieverbot im Zusatzprotokoll vom 10. Juni 1977 zu den vier Genfer Rotkreuz-Abkommen von 1949*, 1990; FURRER, H.-P., *Perfidie in der Geschichte und im heutigen Kriegsvölkerrecht*, 1988; ADAM, S., *Kriegslisten und Perfidieverbot in der Geschichte des Kriegsaktionenrechts vor Abschlub der Haager Landkrieg-sordnung von 1899*, 1992.

What is more, a strange tradition in naval manners, if not academic minds, maintains that maritime warfare should heed distinct rules. Yet, given that no such rules have ever been agreed upon, the laws of war at sea continue to be enveloped in mystery. In the words of Blaise de Monluc, a French strategist of the sixteenth century, seamen have been 'peu entraînés à observer la foy'.[13] As if naval tactics were at pains to disengage from the age of pirates and privateers, some singular practices of deception, although clearly condemned in land and air warfare, would still seem tolerated at sea. Of special currency at the time of the *lettres de marque* and booties, the misuse of foreign flags, and the mounting of guns aboard merchantmen could, for some, claim legitimacy even today. Both these practices may, and have, in effect, at times muddled the distinction between belligerent and neutrals, frustrated any hope for orderly fighting, and preserved an almost customary anarchy at sea. Belligerent practices in both World Wars only reaffirmed that the question of ruses and perfidy remains of particular significance in the maritime context.[14]

In 1977 when a move was made to reaffirm and develop certain rules of humanitarian law, the opportunity was seized in order to draft a clear definition of the notion of perfidy. The long-awaited definition, despite certain reservations, is of course worthy of praise. Most analysts have expressed their satisfaction especially in that perfidy is now linked to a tangible legal, and not merely moral, obligation which renders the notion more clear. Be that as it may, there are also some points to deplore such as the clause that perpetuates the discussion over the legality of the deceptive use of foreign flags in maritime war.

II Of Q-ships and secret raiders: World War practices revisited

1 Her Majesty's mystery ships

Concealed Guns as an Anti-Submarine Strategy: Camouflage or Treachery? It is perhaps necessary to recall the context in which appeal was made to the so-called Q-ships. In the early summer of 1915, the German U-boat flotilla was able to sink as many as

[13]Quoted in GARDOT, A., 'Le droit de la guerre dans l'oeuvre des capitaines français du XVIe siècle', 72 *RCADI* (1948) at p. 528.
[14]See, for instance, the monograph of BRUNEAU, J., *La ruse dans la guerre sur mer*, 1938.

eight steamers per day. Although rare, there were instances where submarines surfaced and duly summoned neutral vessels to stop and have their books checked. It was thought, therefore, that a merchant ship with well-concealed, yet moderate, firing power and an adept crew could very possibly destroy an enemy submarine. It would only have to lower its life-boat in an apparent move of compliance, before getting into position and opening fire.[15]

The steamships chosen by the Admiralty for the so-called 'Special Service' were taken away from their ordinary crew so that their concealed armament could be fitted in absolute secrecy. Once placed under their command, the Royal Navy officers were given a free hand to select the type and quantity of armament to be installed aboard the ships. Most commonly three to six relatively small guns were mounted, properly camouflaged, while in some cases torpedo tubes were also provided. A number of easily retractable structures such as telescopic masts, dummy funnels or whale-boats, folding screens, tents, and fake load (timber, machinery or even train wagons), enabled the mystery ships to assume a varying appearance within hours. Less innovative practices included the painting of another company's marks on the smoke-stack, a colour-change of the ship's hull, the unrolling of huge linen cloths carrying neutral colours along the sides of the vessel, or simply the hoisting of a new false flag and the adoption of a well-suited name.

The U-boat hunters were originally scheduled to patrol the English approaches steaming along the traditional commercial

[15]With the battle against the U-boats growing in agony and despair, all types of vessels were given a chance as disguised warships, from ocean liners to schooners, and from three-masted ships to ketches and colliers. Experience showed, however, that old cargo steamers of a medium tonnage were most suitable for the 'bluffing'. The most comprehensive account on the Q-ships strategy is given in CHATTERTON, E.K., *Les bateaux-pièges, Q-ships contre les sous-marins allemands*, French transl., 1928, and HAMPSHIRE, A.C., *On Hazardous Service*, 1974, p. 15*ff*. See also the personal narrative by CAMPBELL, G., *Mes navires mystérieux*, French transl., 1929; SIMS, W.S., *The Victory at Sea*, 1920, pp. 141–67; SMITH, R.W., 'The Q-ship: Cause and Effect', 79 *USNIP* (May 1953), p. 533*ff*. Other deception plans of doubtful legitimacy had already been tested; in August 1914, for example, Admiral Jellicoe had ordered all the trawlers recently armed and enlisted as Royal Navy auxiliaries not to receive the ordinary grey paint of warships but to retain instead their peacetime external marks. In early summer 1915, a large number of these disguised fishing boats was despatched to Dogger Bank with a view to surprising unwary German submarines.

routes which linked England to the American continent. The expansion of the German submarine operations, however, soon forced the Admiralty to redeploy its Q-ships to cover the entire Atlantic. Several trap boats stationed at Malta also operated in the Mediterranean. Throughout the war as many as 180 British merchant ships of all sorts were assigned to the Special Service, in all accounting for only 11 German submarines sunk and approximately 60 others damaged. Compared to the total of 200 submarines lost by the Germans in combat, the contribution of Q-ships is to be judged fairly minimal – they proved a lot more effective in spreading confusion and eliminating the rare eventuality of U-boats conforming to traditional visit and search standards.[16]

The goal of the stratagem was evidently to invite enemy submarines to surface and approach the disguised combatant. As the German Admiralty gave the first orders for a sink-on-sight policy, the Q-ships were instructed to act in such manner as to encourage an attack, eventually giving the impression of vessels disorderly abandoned. According to the standardized technique, following the torpedo launch and irrespective of its fate, 20 to 30 seamen of the vessel's crew were to precipitate to the life-boats simulating great fear and panic. This group – appropriately called the 'panic party' – should be composed of officers and sailors of all ranks so that the attacker would be

[16]The first two 'trap boats' were the British *Victoria* and the French *Marguerite* which were fitted out at about the same time in November 1914, only to end their short career a few months later without scoring any hit. In January 1915, the liner *Antwerp* was converted and started patrol operations in the English Channel equally without being able to intercept any U-boat. The first successful surprise attacks on German U-boats were carried out by British submarines towed by innocent looking merchantmen. It was under these conditions that the submarine C.24, following the trawler *Taranaki*, torpedoed the U.40 off Aberdeen on 23 June 1915, and the submarine C.27 sank the U.23 while taken in tow by *Princess Marie José* on 20 July 1915. It was not until 24 July 1915, that *Prince Charles*, a small coastal steamer of almost 400 tons, engaged and sank a German submarine off Roma island. It was next for the *Baralong* to destroy U.41 on 24 September 1915, and for the *Farnborough* to wreck an uknown submarine on 15 April 1916; on these incidents, see CHATTERTON, *op. cit., supra*, pp. 35*ff*, 50*ff*. In France, no more than four steamers (code-named as *U-ships*), the *Marguerite*, the *Meg*, the *Michel et Renée* and the *Jeanne et Geneviève* were transformed to trap-boats marking no success. The US Navy, for its part, after having entered the war, fitted out just one Q-ship, the *Santee*. Its most striking innovation was a periscope having the resemblance of a cooking-stove pipe which gave the skipper a good view of the outside while remaining well below the deck. As for the Germans, they operated a few *bateaux-pièges* in the Baltic accounting for three allied submarines.

reassured that the victim was desperately deserted.[17] Under those circumstances the submarine would come to the surface, open its conning-tower and proceed with a close observation of the abandoned vessel. In many cases, the latter was even boarded and searched for victuals and documents. During these long moments of waiting, those manning the guns on board the Q-ship had to remain well-hidden and motionless until the submarine had closed to an optimum distance of a few hundred metres offering a good mark for the open-fire signal to be given. At the time of engagement, the Royal Navy ensign was to be hoisted while white cloths were unrolled to cover the until-then false marks on the ship's sides.[18]

The action of mystery ships often trespassed what one might reasonably expect from deception. When the *Baralong* met U.27, for instance, the course of action was nothing short of perfidious. In August 1915, the *Baralong* steered in the direction of the *Nicosian,* at the time sending out distress signals after being summoned by a German submarine. Upon reaching the scene,

[17]As it has been observed, however, 'the panic party would often throw into the lowered boat a packet of what appeared to be the ship's papers. This practice of feigning surrender may have been one of the reasons why the Germans decried the Q-ship program as barbarous and contrary to the rules of civilized warfare'; see HALL, M.T., 'False Colors and Dummy Ships: The Use of Ruse in Naval Warfare', 42 *US Naval War College Review* (1989), no.3 at p. 60. Another major issue, which had been the object of heated controversy during the war, was the generous remuneration awarded by the British Admiralty for every enemy submarine destroyed. As it was admitted later, the sum of £1,000 had been fixed as the 'prize-money' to be distributed among the crew members for every U-boat sunk; see CHATTERTON, *op. cit., supra* n.15 at pp. 16, 25, 32, and CAMPBELL, *op. cit., supra* n.15 at pp. 107, 177.

[18]With a view to relaxing the growing suspicion of U-boat commanders and enticing them to expose more vulnerable parts of their vessels rather than their sole periscope, the idea was later advanced that a Q-ship should steer so that the incoming torpedoes could securely reach their target. Despite the higher risk to the crew, in early 1917 it was considered that, given the increasing use of defensive armament by merchant vessels and the possible leakage of the Q-ships secret to the enemy, this might well be the only method which offered a good chance of ambushing the foe. It was under such conditions that the *Farnborough* on 17 February 1917, attacked and destroyed U.83 south-west of Ireland. For a detailed account on this incident, see CAMPBELL, *op. cit., supra* n.15, p. 158*ff*. The torpedoed *Farnborough* was later towed to the Berehaven port while its captain was decorated with the Victoria Cross for 'courage éclatant, sang-froid, extraordinaire et habileté dans le commandement d'un des navires de Sa Majesté au cours d'un combat'; *ibid.* at p. 177. In a similar incident, on 7 June 1917, the *Pargust,* after it had been torpedoed and while seemingly abandoned, opened fire and sank UC.29. It is worth noting that at the time of engagement the submarine commander was giving orders through a voice-tube to the British seamen in the life-boats; *ibid.* at p. 200.

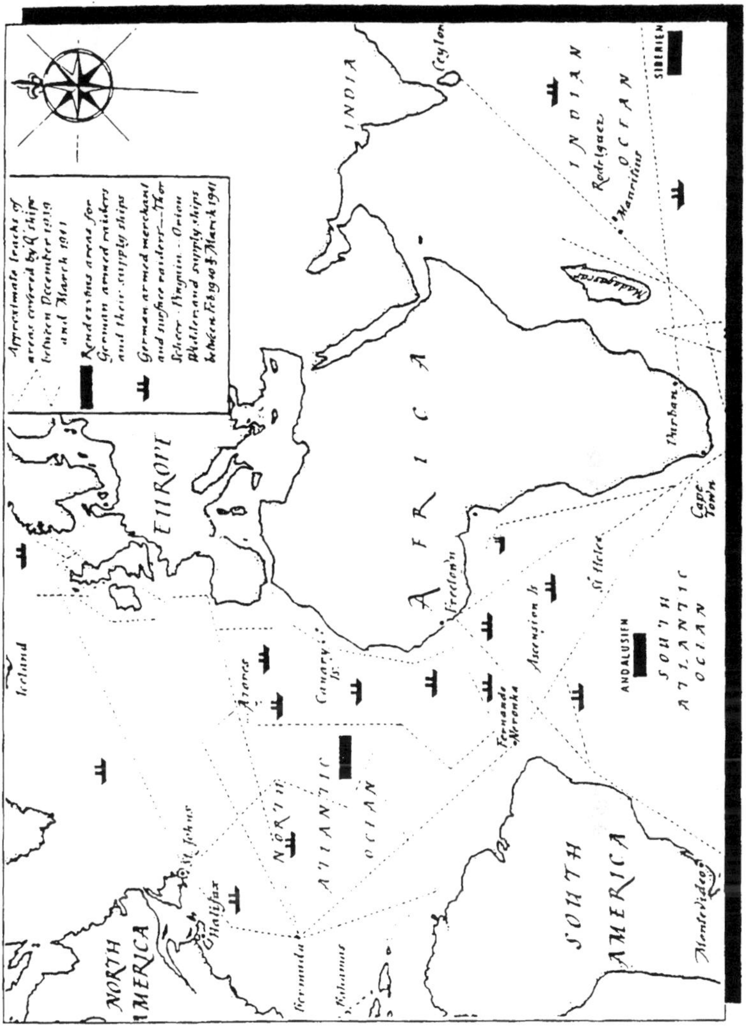

Figure 11 *Areas Covered by the Q-ships*
Source: HAMPSHIRE, A.C., *On Hazardous Service*, 1974 at pp. 26–27

the trap-ship hoisted the American flag and the international code signal 'to save life only'. A few moments later, as the surfaced submarine closed in on the deserted steamship, the skipper of the *Baralong* ordered fire. The German submarine sank within minutes while the few survivors who had taken refuge aboard the *Nicosian* were executed for fear of disclosing the Q-ship secret. The incident aroused a storm of criticism in Germany which demanded that the British captain be prosecuted for murder or turned over to them.[19]

By the time the German *guerre de course* had reached its apogee in April 1917, however, no masquerade appeared good enough to avert defeat. By then, Allied merchant shipping losses were rising to the levels of 875,000 tons per month. Overall, in 1917 as many as 6.1 million tons of shipping were sent to the bottom, while British shipyards were only capable of delivering 1.16 million tons of new vessels, which obliged an Allied force of some 8,000 ships and 2,000 aircraft to be unleashed in the pursuit of some 150 deadly enemy submarines. As for the Q-ship ploy, there was probably not much of a secret left. This is why, as from 1917, the trap-boats had all been designated as HMS vessels and their officers ordered to carry their uniform while in port. The mystery ships could no longer count on surprise attacks. Moreover, with the introduction of the convoy system it would have been rare, and, therefore, highly suspicious for a merchant vessel to cruise alone across the Atlantic ocean.[20]

In the opening hours of the Second World War, the British Admiralty tried vainly to renew the lure of Q-ships. Between October 1939 and March 1940, eight decoy ships of this type had been fitted out in the outmost secrecy. All were equipped

[19]For the German memorandum on the conditions of the incident and the British reply, see 10 *AJIL* (1916) *Suppl.*, p. 80*ff.* In yet another incident, a German submarine, after having intercepted an innocent looking vessel, approached to inspect its prize. On the deck of the abandoned ship only a woman holding a baby in her hands was crying which made the U-boat to come alongside. Once near enough, the woman, a disguised sailor in reality, threw her 'baby' exploding the submarine's tower; see MÉRIGNHAC, A. and LÉMONON, E., *Le droit des gens et la guerre de 1914–1918*, tome II, 1921 at p. 20.

[20]The convoy system functioned so effectively that through to November 1918, 26 million tons of food supplies and 36 million tons of munition made it safely to England. The losses were lessened from 10 per cent to about 1 per cent. Extensive deep-water mining campaigns also contributed to containing the submarine menace. The reverse strategy of that of Q-ships, that is to say warships of the destroyer class disguised as merchant vessels, was also put to the test. The so-called *P.Q-ships* appeared in the middle of 1917 numbering a total of 16 converted vessels. Failing, however, to engage any enemy submarine they were soon placed on other duties. A different class of decoy ships, classified as *P-boats,* was also considered but never employed. The silhouette of these ships was to closely resemble a large submarine steaming on the surface in the anticipation of inviting the approach of an enemy U-boat.

with torpedo tubes and a sufficient complement of depth charges, while some were mounted with as many as nine 4-inch guns. They were never called Q-ships, but rather bore the code name *'freighters'*. None of them were ever reported to have sighted a U-boat.[21]

2 The German commerce raiders

Disguise at the Service of Economic Warfare Lacking control of strategic sea routes and the means for a prolonged presence, the German Navy in both World Wars fell back on the idea of disguising heavily armed merchantmen for the purpose of crippling the British seaborne commerce.[22] The raiders posed as peaceful traders, they could alter their disguise as they wished, make use of wireless distress signals, and navigate for months without the need of supply ships or refuelling. Flying neutral colours, often the Norwegian ones, and adopting different names, they used to summon passing ships to approach, only to launch a surprise attack thereafter, take the crewmen as prisoners and scuttle their prize. The *Möwe*, probably the most famed of the raiders of the First World War, accounted for the destruction of 123,000 tons of merchant shipping in four months, while the *Wolf* on her eventful 444-day cruise

[21]See ROSKILL, S.W., *The War at Sea 1939–1945*, vol.I (1954) at p. 136. According to reports of German U-boat commanders, the British had also armed fishing boats and sailing ships, while on at least one occasion, in February 1942 off Freetown in Sierra-Leone, speed torpedo boats were disguised as life boats; see BOURDONCLE, *op.cit, supra* n.12 at p. 62.

[22]The commerce-destroying effort initially did not call for disguised raiders, the light cruisers *Emden, Breslau, Goeben, Dresden* and *Karlsrühe* being more than adequate match for the slow and defenceless enemy cargo vessels. Their brief career was marked with remarkable exploits but their effect was rather isolated. Although searched for or pursued at times by as many as 70 Allied warships, they were able to score a 230,000 of Allied tonnage sunk. The *Emden* alone paralysed the navigation in the Indian ocean having destroyed 19 vessels before being itself sunk in November 1914. In all, 61 merchant ships were captured by the German cruisers during their *guerre de course* missions. Besides ordinary warships, large ocean liners like the *Kronprinz Wilhelm*, the *Prinz Eitel Friedrich*, the *Kaiser Wilhelm* and the *Cap Trafalgar*, were formally converted to auxiliary cruisers and accounted for 36 merchant ships. The *Kronprinz Wilhel* alone destroyed some 15 Allied merchant ships totalling 60,000 tons. Their greatest handicap, however, was the unaffordable coal consumption and their all too frequent need for replenishment, so that they had to be withdrawn by the end of 1915.

(November 1916 through February 1918) sank 135,000 tons of Allied shipping.[23]

While German 'exploits' during the First World War were significant, it should be noted that during the course of the Second World War only 9 freighters underwent conversion into armed raiders out of a merchant navy composed of 250 vessels between 5,000 and 10,000 tons. Yet the original German war planning provided for converting no less than 26 merchant ships. Three of these ships were put to service by the end of 1939 and three more in the first half of 1940. What the Germans called the 'first wave', comprised the *Atlantis*, the *Orion*, the *Widder*, the *Thor*, the *Pinguin* and the *Komet*. The *Kormoran*, the first ship of the 'second wave', went to sea before the end of 1940 and was followed by the *Stier*, the *Michel*, the *Komet*, the *Thor* and the *Togo*. In the event, the *Hilfskreuzer*, or auxiliary cruisers, were responsible for more than 890,000 tons of shipping destroyed, damaged or captured as prizes during the forty-three-month hunt of their unsuspecting prey. In fact, between 1940 and 1943, these 9 secret raiders sank 130 ships altogether totalling nearly three times the total tonnage of merchant shipping sunk by the German surface warships.[24]

The famed *Atlantis* sank 22 vessels (over twice as much tonnage as the *Graf Spee*) on a 176,000 km, twenty-one-month trip around the world beginning in March 1940. Its 622-day

[23]Operating in the same period, the *Greif*, the *Leopard* and the sailing ship *Seeadler*, took an equally heavy toll on Allied and neutral commerce. The German raiders were also very active in laying mines and in transforming captured vessels into fellow disguised raiders on the high seas. The *Wolf*, for instance, provided a prize crew and armed a few of the vessels it seized such as the *Iltis* and the *Igotz Mendi*. For detailed accounts on the German raiders, see WOODWARD, D., *The Secret Raiders – The Story of the German Armed Merchant Raiders in the Second World War*, 1955; MUGGENTHALER, A.K., *German Raiders of World War II*, 1977; ROSKILL, *op. cit.*, *supra* n.21, vol.I (1954), pp. 279*ff*, 381*ff*., and vol.II (1956), pp. 177*ff*., 265*ff*.; RUGE, F., *Der Seekrieg – The German Navy's Story 1939–1945*, 1957, pp. 174–83. See also the narratives by LUCKNER, F. von, *Le dernier corsaire (1914–1918)*, French transl., 1929, and WITSCHETZKY, F., *Le navire noir – Le croiseur auxiliaire* Wolf *1916–1918*, French transl., 1929.

[24]Famed for their most carefully planned supply arrangements through secret rendezvous with mystery ships, the raiders were able to make very long cruises. The cruise of the *Orion*, for instance, lasted 510 days steaming over 112,000 miles, while the *Komet* returned to Bordeaux after 15 months at sea; see ROSKILL, *op. cit.*, *supra* n.21, vol.I at p. 278. The Italians, for their part, sent out one merchant raider, the *Ramb I*, with no success on its record, while the Japanese later employed three such ships with feeble results at best.

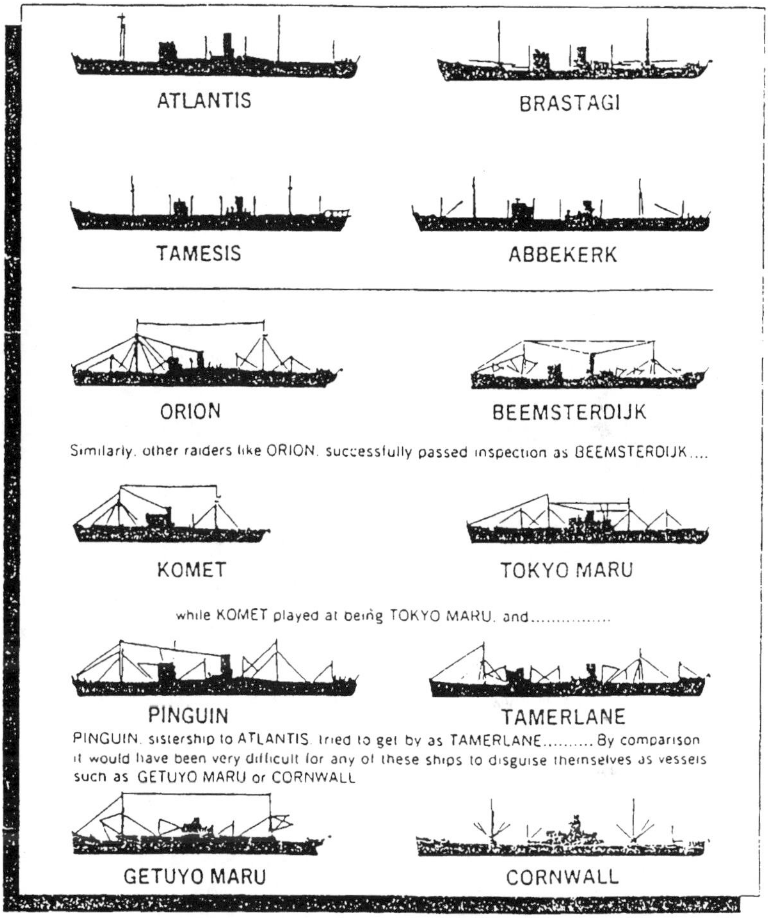

Figure 12 *Some of the Disguises Employed by the German Raiders*
Source: MUGGENTHALER, A.K., *German Raiders of the World War II*, 1977 at p. 18, by permission of IMG Literary

journey remains a telling story in masquerade and well-thought-out tactics. The armament of the *Atlantis* included six 5.9-inch guns concealed behind collapsible bulkheads, one 75 mm gun, six anti-aircraft guns and four torpedo tubes. It carried also 92 mines and a Heinkel seaplane. Its complement neared 350 men. In falsifying its true identity it was at its best. It was first put

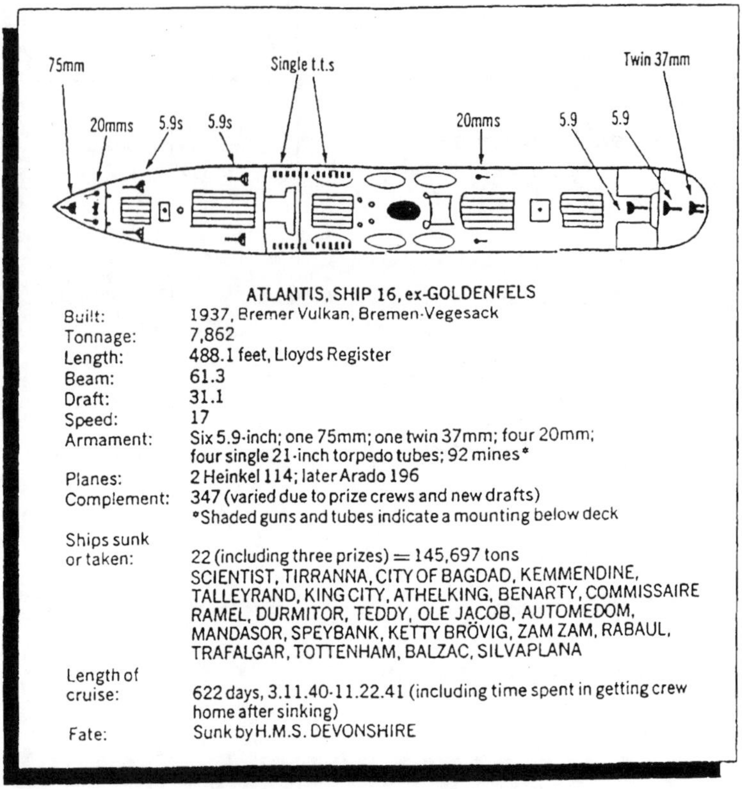

Figure 13 *Portrait of a German Raider: The Atlantis*
Source: MUGGENTHALER, A.K., *German Raiders of the World War II*, 1977 at p. 16 by permission of IMG Literary

to sea and made its way into the North Sea disguised as a Russian auxiliary warship. It later assumed a Norwegian appearance, to roam the South Atlantic and the Indian oceans as the Japanese *Kasii Maru*, the Dutch *Abbekerk*, the British *Antenor* or the Norwegian *Tamesis*. The *Atlantis* was finally destroyed in November 1941 by the British cruiser *Devonshire*.[25]

[25]For more, see MOHR, U., *Atlantis – The Story of a German Surface Raider*, 1955, and WOODWARD, *op. cit., supra* n.23, p. 51*ff.* The *Kormoran*, the biggest of all the armed merchant raiders, gained celebrity for overwhelming the Australian cruiser *Sydney* in its last fight on 19 November 1941. Flying the Dutch flag, it enticed the enemy warship to come comfortably close – a fatal mistake of *Sydney*'s skipper in those days of reigning confusion and sweeping abuse of neutral colours. When the *Kormoran* was finally challenged to show its secret

At home, the feats of the raiders brought honour and pride. Destined to fight alone 'always behind enemy lines', their exemplary discipline, skilful disguise, and their more often than not humane treatment of the captured crewmen became legendary. Survivors were, with few exceptions, sought and rescued. Contrary to the sink-on-sight policy of the U-boats, the disguised auxiliaries had been duly summoning their victims to identify themselves and surrender, sparing, if possible, the prizes since these were often their only chance for mid-ocean food and fuel supply. Their most important impact was the disruption of trade resulting in considerable delays and re-routing. Once the likelihood of a raider was signalled, convoys had to be arranged and several warships to be deployed in escort. In Stephen W. Roskill's words,

> they never approached the U-boat, nor even air attacks and minelaying, in the losses they caused and the difficulties they produced. None the less the cost to the enemy of fitting out and operating such ships cannot have been heavy. As long as their expectation of life was reasonable, and a fair number of unescorted ships could be found, he was probably right in considering that they yielded a sufficient return to justify themselves.[26]

call-sign, it hauled down the Dutch flag and hoisted the German Navy ensign. In the course of the fierce exchange of salvoes that followed, both ships were set ablaze and sunk. All 645 seamen aboard the *Sydney* perished in the incident. On the deadly *Kormoran–Sydney* duel, see GÖSSELN, J. von, 'The Sinking of the Sydney', 79 *USNIP* (March 1953), p. 251*ff.* See also MUGGENTHALER, *op. cit., supra* n.23, p. 185*ff.*, and WOODWARD, *op. cit., supra* n.23, p. 224*ff. Detmers*, commander of the scuttled *Kormoran*, and some 300 of his shipwrecked men were rescued 25 days after the incident. Interned in an Australian POW camp, they feared an unfair trial for having engaged the *Sydney*, but no proceedings were ever initiated.

[26]See ROSKILL, *op. cit., supra* n.21, vol.II at p. 412. After the war, Von Ruckteschell, commander of the *Widder* and later of the *Michel*, as well as ex-submarine officer the Allies had hoped to bring to trial for war crimes after the First World War, was tried by a British Military Court in 1947 at Hamburg and sentenced to 10 years imprisonment; see *Trial of Helmuth von Ruckteschell*, 5–21 May 1947, British Military Court, Hamburg, in United Nations War Crimes Commission, *Law Reports of Trials of War Criminals*, vol.IX, p. 82*ff.* He was convicted on account of his ruthless methods of fighting, or prolonged firing and failure to provide for the safety of the crews of some of his prey. He refused to ask for mercy and welcomed the verdict by saying: 'we both did it on orders and in the belief that we were right, and now we are both wrong'. The question of the legality of the method of attack of the German raiders did not arise in the course of the proceedings. As the Prosecutor pointed out, the accused was not charged with launching any illegal attack, but only with failing to give quarter and

3 Armed merchantmen and the notion of offensive defence

Guns Everywhere: Belligerent Practices and Neutral Reactions

Aside from the practice of concealing guns in merchant ships for eventual surprise attacks (be it to ambush enemy submarines or to raid unwary traders), both World Wars also experienced the progressive arming of belligerent merchantmen arguably for defensive purposes, that is to resist visit and search as some established maritime usage seemed to allow, or *lupum auribus teneo* as Lord Stowell had termed it in the *Catharina Elizabeth* case.[27] For the British, mounting guns on ordinary cargo vessels appeared a reasonable measure of defence against the unwarranted attacks of the German U-boats.[28] For the Germans, the presence of weaponry alone sufficed to preclude any possibility of visit and search in the classical sense and entitled them to assimilate armed belligerent merchantmen to enemy warships.[29] As for the neutrals, the practice of arming merchantmen raised delicate questions: first, whether they should prevent departure of belligerent merchant vessels suspected of making preparations, while in neutral ports, in order to be converted on the high seas, and second, how to deal with armed merchantmen which entered their jurisdiction.[30]

---

rescue survivors of the attacked merchantmen, *ibid.* at p. 87. For the story of the two-month journey of the *Widder* in summer 1940, see ROMAT, E., 'L'heureuse croisière du Raider 21', *Revue Maritime* (Sept.1948), no.29, p. 1109*ff.*

[27]See *The Catharina Elizabeth* (1804), 5 *C. Robinson's Admiralty Reports* at p. 233.

[28]The British view is best defended in HIGGINS, A.P., 'Armed Merchant Ships', 8 *AJIL* (1914), p. 705*ff.* See also GARNER, J.W., *International Law and the World War,* vol.I (1920), p. 384*ff.*; BORCHARD, E. and LAGE, W.P., *Neutrality for the United States,* 2nd edn (1940), p. 83*ff.*; SCOTT, J.B., 'The Status of Armed Merchant Vessels', 9 *AJIL* (1915), p. 188*ff.*; Id., 'The Controversy Between the United States and Germany over the Use of Submarines Against Merchant Vessels', 9 *AJIL* (1915), p. 666*ff.*; Id., 'Armed Merchant Ships', 10 *AJIL* (1916), p. 113*ff.* Note also VIDAUD, J., *Les navires de commerce armés pour leur défense,* 1936; HACKWORTH, G.H., *Digest of International Law,* 1943, vol.VII, p. 488*ff.*; WHITEMAN, M.M., *Digest of International Law,* vol.10 (1968), p. 670*ff.*; SEAMANS, A.B., 'Armed Merchantmen a Factor in Naval Warfare', 30 *Current History* (1929), p. 593*ff.*

[29]It should be noted that already in August 1914 some forty vessels of the British mercantile fleet had received armaments, while the first submarine attack against a merchant vessel, the steamship *Glitra* sunk by U.17, occurred only on 20 October 1914.

[30]The embarrassment for American diplomacy, for instance, began as early as 4 August 1914, when the British *chargé d'affaires* at Washington addressed a communication to the Secretary of State inviting the American government to use due diligence in order to prevent the fitting out of enemy vessels intended to be used for warlike purposes; see 9 *AJIL* (1915) *Sp.Suppl.* at pp. 222–3. In fact, the British were apprehensive that the German Admiralty might be ordering

FIRST WORLD WAR	
Emden	101,182 tons
Möwe, 1st cruise	65,590 tons
2nd cruise	119,600 tons
Wolf	38,391 tons plus
	73,988 tons sunk by the mines which she had laid.

SECOND WORLD WAR	
Atlantis	145,697 tons
Thor, 1st cruise	96,547 tons
2nd cruise	42,791 tons
Pinguin	136,551 tons
Scharnhorst and *Gneisenau* (operating together)	115,622 tons

Table 2 *Tonnage Sunk by the Most Successful Raiders by the Two World Wars*
Source: WOODWARD, D., *The Secret Raiders – The Story of the German Armed Raiders in the Second World War*, 1955 at p. 283

Less than a week after the war broke out, Great Britain felt compelled to inform neutral governments that 'a certain number of British merchant vessels are armed as a precautionary measure adopted solely for the purpose of defence'. London also gave full assurances that defensively armed merchantmen 'will never be used for purposes of attack, that they are merely peaceful traders armed only for defence, that they will never

merchant vessels to rush into neutral ports and procure armaments for eventually converting themselves into vessels of war on the high seas in accordance with their declared policy since the days of the Hague Conference of 1907. Ten days later, however, on 13 August 1914, it was a British freighter, the *Francisco*, that arrived in New York with two guns mounted aft.

fire unless first fired upon, and that they will never under any circumstances attack any vessel'.[31] The German answer to the British pretensions came on 15 October 1914:

> the equipment of British merchant vessels with artillery is for the purpose of making armed resistance against German cruisers. Resistance of this sort is contrary to international law, because in a military sense a merchant vessel is not permitted to defend itself against a war vessel . . . the distinction between the defensive and offensive is irrelevant. The destination of a ship for use of any kind in war is conclusive, and restrictions as to the extent of armament afford no guarantee that ships armed for defensive purposes only will not be used for offensive purposes under certain circumstances.[32]

In a memorandum issued on 19 September 1914, the US Department of State attempted to define general rules to deal with belligerent armed merchant vessels. In this document the general principle was pronounced that 'the presence of an armament and ammunition on board a merchant vessel creates a presumption that the armament is for offensive purposes' although such a presumption could under certain conditions be overcome.[33] In his ill-fated initiative of 18 January 1916, Secretary

[31]See the communications of the British ambassador to the US Secretary of State of 9 August 1914, and 25 August 1914, in 9 *AJIL* (1915) *Sp.Suppl.* at pp. 223, 230. By way of indication, 'by the middle of May 1915, 149 British merchant ships had been fitted with defensive armament, by Feb. 15 of the following year such vessels numbered 991, on April 12, 1,109, and on Sept.18, 1916, the defensively armed merchant squadron counted 1,749 vessels'; see BORCHARD and LAGE, *op. cit., supra* n.28 at p. 94. In France, by 29 September, 1915, all the ships engaged in transporting troops were ordered to receive two guns manned by crews from the Navy. On 19 November 1915, the defensive armament was extended to all the requisitioned vessels, while on 20 December 1915 guns were also to be mounted on several of the passenger liners serving North African ports.

[32]See 9 *AJIL* (1915) *Sp.Suppl.* at p. 238.

[33]*Ibid* at p. 234. Among the indications that the armament would not be used offensively were that the guns carried did not exceed a specified calibre, that they were few in number, not mounted on the forward part of the vessel, or that the quantity of ammunition was small. In practice, whenever an armed merchant ship entered an American port, the custom authorities reported to Washington on the armament of the vessel. The Department of State, in its turn, required from the diplomatic or consular representatives of the flag state formal assurance that the armament would not be used offensively before the ship was cleared. Despite differing views on the need for revision, this procedure remained unaltered throughout the period of American neutrality. For

of State Robert Lansing proposed to belligerents a *modus vivendi* with the view to bringing 'submarine warfare within the general rules of international law and the principles of humanity without destroying its efficiency in the destruction of commerce'. According to the terms of the American compromise:

> it would appear to be a reasonable and reciprocally just arrangement if it could be agreed by the opposing belligerents that submarines should be caused to adhere strictly to the rules of international law in the matter of stopping and searching merchant vessels, determining their belligerent nationality, and removing the crews and passengers to places of safety before sinking the vessels as prizes of war, and that merchant vessels of belligerent nationality should be prohibited and prevented from carrying any armament whatsoever.[34]

The German government in its long memorandum of 10 February 1916, argued that England had proceeded as a matter of officially declared policy since 1913 to arming merchant vessels, that those vessels were instructed to engage hostile submarines with every possible means, and that, in fact, there had been numerous cases where German submarines were accordingly fired upon by enemy steamers sometimes even flying false flags. Under such circumstances, the memorandum concluded: 'enemy merchantmen armed with guns no longer have any right to be considered as peaceable vessels of commerce. Therefore the

interesting remarks on the legal debate within the State Department about devising the best policy *vis-à-vis* armed merchantmen, see BORCHARD, E., 'Armed Merchantmen', 34 *AJIL* (1940), p. 107*ff*., and McDIARMID, A.M., 'The Neutrality Board and Armed Merchantmen, 1914–1917', 69 *AJIL* (1975), p. 374*ff*.

[34] See 10 *AJIL* (1916) *Sp.Suppl.* at p. 312. What was most soundly argued in the American note was the profound change of context so that the arming of merchant vessels would seem no longer justified; 'prior to the year 1915 belligerent operations against enemy commerce on the high seas had been conducted with cruisers carrying heavy armaments. Under these conditions international law appeared to permit a merchant vessel to carry an armament for defensive purposes without losing its character as a private commercial vessel . . . [Today] pirates and sea rovers have been swept from the main trade channels of the seas, and privateering has been abolished. Consequently, the placing of guns on merchantmen at the present day of submarine warfare can be explained only on the ground of a purpose to render merchantmen superior in force to submarines and to prevent warning and visit and search by them. Any armament, therefore, on a merchant vessel would seem to have the character of an offensive armament'; *ibid.* at pp. 311–12. For the British response, see *ibid.*, p. 336*ff*.

German naval forces will receive orders, within a short period paying consideration to the interests of the neutrals, to treat such vessels as belligerents.'[35] In April 1916, the British government, upon the request of the US Department of State, communicated to Washington its standing orders concerning the use of defensive armament by merchant vessels. Given the fact 'that hostile submarines and aircraft have frequently attacked merchant vessels without warning', and since 'British and Allied submarines and aircraft have orders not to approach merchant vessels', the British Admiralty presumed that 'any submarine or aircraft which deliberately approaches or pursues a merchant vessel does so with hostile intention' and that 'in such cases fire may be opened in self defence in order to prevent the hostile craft closing to a range at which resistance to a sudden attack with bomb or torpedo would be impossible'.[36]

[35]*Ibid.* at p. 318. Among the reasons given for such decision was that evidence had been discovered on board Allied merchantmen instructing them how to use their guns preemptively against enemy submarines; see *ibid.*, p. 327*ff.* On the same day, Vienna also announced that 'all merchant ships armed with canon, for whatever purpose, by this very fact lose the character of peaceable vessels' and that 'orders have been given to the Austro-Hungarian naval forces to treat such ships as belligerent vessels'; *ibid.* at p. 314. Berlin and Vienna soon declared that the skippers of such vessels would be treated as unlawful belligerents, or *franc tireurs.* It was on this count that a German martial court in July 1916 tried and sentenced to death Charles Fryatt, captain of the *Brussels,* who had attempted in March 1915 to ram U.33. On this episode, see SCOTT, J.B., 'The Execution of Captain Fryatt', 10 *AJIL* (1916), p. 865*ff.*, and GARNER, *op.cit, supra* n.28, vol.I, p. 407*ff.* On the British pre-war measures to arm merchantmen, such as the so-called 'Cunard agreement' of 1903, see BORCHARD and LAGE, *op. cit., supra* n.28, p. 90*ff.*, and MANSON, J.M., *Diplomatic Ramifications of Unrestricted Submarine Warfare, 1939–1941,* 1990, p. 25*ff.* On whether the *Lusitania* carried guns on its last trip, see *ibid.*, p. 155*ff.*, and VILLARD, O.G., 'The True Story of the Lusitania', *American Mercury* (1935), no.137, p. 41*ff.*

[36]See 11 *AJIL* (1917) *Sp.Suppl.* at p. 227. The French instructions of 29 December 1915 were even more explicit: 'dès qu'un sous-marin naviguant en surface est aperçu, lui présenter l'arrière en lançant la machine à toute vitesse, et, s'il y a de la mer, faire une route telle que le sous-marin, pour se rapprocher, soit obligé de prendre la mer debout, ce qui réduira sa vitesse et paralysera en partie le tir de son artillerie. Commencer le feu dès que le sous-marin sera à bonne portée. Si, ayant pris chasse, on est gagné de vitesse par le sous-marin, ne pas hésiter à virer de bord et à foncer dessus avant qu'il ne soit trop rapproché'; quoted in VIDAUD, *op. cit., supra* n. at p. 53. According to the same orders, 'en cas d'alerte ou de combat, l'officier de marine prenant le commandement, le commandant d'armes doit se considérer dès lors comme étant un *véritable navire de guerre,* et veiller à l'exécution par les troupes de tous les orders donnés par le commandant'; *ibid.* at p. 142. By mid-1916, the arming of the entire French merchant fleet was only frustrated for the want of guns. In February 1917, the French government decided the creation of *Centres d'Armement Militaire des Bâtiments de Commerce (AMBC)* and by 15 March 1917, all merchant ships had

The American compromise formula having thus failed, the US State Department issued on 25 March 1916 a new memorandum in respect of the status of armed merchant vessels which laid down: 'in brief, a neutral government may proceed upon the presumption that an armed merchant vessel of belligerent nationality is armed for aggression, while a belligerent should proceed on the presumption that the vessel is armed for protection. Both of these presumptions may be overcome by evidence – the first by secondary or collateral evidence, since the fact to be established is negative in character; the second by primary and direct evidence, since the fact to be established is positive in character'.[37] Finally, on 2 April 1917, the US President met the challenge and declared war on German U-boats by espousing the Allied rationale for arming merchant vessels:

> because submarines are in effect outlaws when used as the German submarines have been used against merchant shipping, it is impossible to defend ships against their attacks as the law of nations has assumed that merchantmen would defend themselves against privateers or cruisers, visible craft giving chase upon the open sea. It is common prudence in such circumstances, grim necessity indeed, to endeavor to destroy them before they have shown their own intention. They must be dealt with upon sight, if dealt with at all.[38]

The Netherlands appeared to be the sole neutral state which denied British armed merchantmen access to Dutch ports on account of Article 4 of its neutrality proclamation dated 6 August 1914, which prescribed that 'no warships or *ships assimilated* thereto belonging to any of the belligerents shall have

been fitted defensive gear without exception. France also declared ready to furnish similar equipment to any foreign neutral vessel which would make a request. French naval crews, however, were not to be authorized to go aboard neutral ships.

[37]See 10 *AJIL* (1916) *Sp.Suppl.* at p. 369.

[38]See 11 *AJIL* (1917) *Suppl.* at p. 145. What was implicitly admitted in such statements was the inherently unlawful character of arming merchant vessels, the practice becoming exceptionally lawful in retaliation for the German unrestrained submarine warfare. Consider also the following comment: 'it may be confidently anticipated that as a result of the German campaign every passenger ship and freight-carrier in future, even after the close of the war, will be armed. The maritime Powers will never again put their trust in the dictates of humanity, the law of nations, or the Hague Convention'; see HURD, A., *The British Fleet in the Great War*, 1918 at p. 217.

access to the said [Dutch] territory' (emphasis added).[39] For one thing, the Dutch government insisted that merchantmen had been rendered capable of committing war acts by carrying armament which differed little from warships. In a letter dated 31 July 1915, the Dutch Foreign Minister J. Loudon argued that 'a belligerent merchant vessel which fights to escape capture or destruction by an enemy warship commits an act the legitimacy of which is indeed unquestionable, but which is none the less an act of war'.[40] In subsequent communications the Dutch authorities argued that changing their announced policy on the single request of one of the belligerents would be considered a serious violation of their neutral status.[41]

The question of defensive armament of merchantmen arose in the case of *SS Rockingham*, adjudicated by the US-German Mixed Claims Commission on 25 March 1924, whereby it was held that:

> the arming for defensive purposes of a merchantman and the manning of such armament by a naval gun crew, coupled with the routing of such ship by the Navy Depart-

[39]For the long diplomatic correspondence following that decision, see 12 *AJIL* (1918) *Suppl.*, p. 196*ff*. When, for instance, the British steamship *Princess Melita* with a gun mounted aft attempted to enter a Dutch port in March 1917, it was ordered to proceed outside territorial waters and to drop its gun overboard there before it could return to port. The Netherlands apart, only Mexico had adopted a similar rule excluding defensively armed merchant ships from their ports. The Chilean government, on the other hand, announced on 7 July 1915 to the British government that they saw no reason why defensively armed merchantmen should be denied access to Chilean ports provided that the identity, destination and the type of cargo of such vessels would have been communicated in advance; see ALVAREZ, A., *La Grande Guerre européenne et la neutralité du Chili*, 1915 at p. 259.

[40]See Cd.8690, *Correspondence with the Netherlands Government Respecting Defensively Armed British Merchant Vessels*, December 1917 at p. 5. In a similar note on 18 June 1917, it was restated that 'an armed merchant vessel undeniably possesses in its armament not only a means of defence, but a means of attack as well'; *ibid.* at p. 15.

[41]As the note of 4 April 1917 made clear, the Dutch government did 'not hesitate to admit the perfect right of such vessels to arm themselves. But the considerations which in August, 1914, determined the attitude of the Government still hold good. What, however, renders the question far more serious is the fact that it would be a matter of revoking at this moment a rule of neutrality which was established at the very beginning of the war, and was duly notified later to the two belligerent parties. Nothing could be more contrary to the very principle of neutrality than to revoke during the course of a war, and at the demand of one of the belligerents, a rule of neutrality which, owing to the course of events, whatever they may be, proves to be disadvantageous to that belligerent only'; *ibid.* at p. 6.

> ment of the United States for the purpose of avoiding the danger of submarines and the following by the civilian master of the ship of instructions given by the Navy Department for the defence of the ship when in danger of attack by submarines, certainly do not change the juridical status of the ship or convert it from a merchant-ship to a warship or make of it naval material.[42]

During the period of American neutrality in the Second World War, the practice of arming merchantmen continued to incite the same negative reaction in Washington. Installing weaponry on board American merchant vessels 'engaged in commerce with any *belligerent state*' was, in fact, prohibited under section 10 of the 1935 Neutrality Act.[43] While under section 6 of the Neutrality Act of 4 November 1939, it was declared 'unlawful for any American vessel, engaged in commerce with any *foreign state* to be armed, except with small arms and ammunition . . . for the preservation of discipline aboard any such vessel'.[44] Owing to circumstances, however, this latter proviso was repealed on 17 November 1941. As the Joint Resolution read, 'during the unlimited national emergency, proclaimed by the President on May 27, 1941, the President is authorized . . . to arm, or to permit or cause to be armed, any American vessel'.[45] It is not without significance that in the Panama Declaration of 3 October

[42]See WILLIAMS, J.F. and LAUTERPACHT, H. (eds), *Annual Digest of Public International Law Cases*, vol.2 (1933) at p. 408. The *Rockingham* was an American-owned cargo ship which was sunk by a German submarine on 1 May 1917 while bound for Liverpool. It was armed with two 4-inch guns and was manned by a naval gun crew of 13 in addition to its normal civilian complement of 36 seamen.

[43]See 31 *AJIL* (1937) *Suppl.* at p. 154. Access to American ports and territorial waters was also to be denied to any belligerent submarine or armed merchant vessel according to section 8 of this instrument, *ibid.* at pp. 153–4.

[44]See 34 *AJIL* (1940) *Suppl.* at p. 49. It was also stipulated that upon a Presidential proclamation, it would be 'unlawful for any such submarine or armed merchant vessel to enter a port or the territorial waters of the United States or to depart therefrom'; see section 11, *ibid.* at p. 51. In the event, Procl. No.2375 of 4 November 1939 prohibited only *belligerent submarines* to enter American ports; see *ibid.*, p. 56*ff.*

[45]See 36 *AJIL* (1942) *Suppl.* at p. 56. See also the statement of the US Secretary of State soliciting the repeal, 36 *AJIL* (1942), p. 118*ff.* One of the DEMS (Defensively Equipped Merchant Ships), the *Stephen Hopkins*, fitted with a single 4-inch gun and manned by an armed guard of naval reservists overpowered and sank the German raider *Stier* on 27 September 1942, despite the overwhelming superiority of the latter in fire power. The story of this unique action is given in WOODWARD, *op. cit.*, *supra* n.23, p. 272*ff.*

1939, the American republics had resolved that they 'shall not assimilate to warships belligerent armed merchant vessels if they do not carry more than four six-inch guns mounted on the stern, and their lateral decks are not reinforced, and if, in the judgment of the local authorities, there do not exist other circumstances which reveal that the merchant vessels can be used for offensive purposes. They may require of the said vessels, in order to enter their ports, to deposit explosives and munitions in such places as the local authorities may determine'.[46]

After the war, at the time of the trial of the German war criminals, justice was done to the German theory relating to the non-immunity of enemy armed merchantmen. The Nuremberg International Military Tribunal, in fact, espoused the view that belligerent merchantmen armed upon instructions of the public authority, often convoyed with warships, ordered to provide intelligence assistance or to directly engage the enemy, in short, integrated for all practical purposes into the military effort, should be rightfully treated as belligerent men-of-war. Thus, evaluating the nature of the British policy concerning the wartime role of the merchant navy, the Court pronounced that 'in the actual circumstances of this case, the Tribunal is not prepared to hold Dönitz guilty for his conduct of submarine warfare against *British armed merchant ships*' (emphasis added).[47]

4 The deceptive use of foreign flags

The Widespread Abuse of National Flags and Symbols At the risk of an understatement, one has to admit that the use of false flags by belligerents and neutrals alike was extensive in both World Wars. Two well-known examples of these were the *Lusitania* which on her last crossing of the Atlantic was flying the US flag, and the *Emden* which made use of enemy colours for her raid at Penang. Putting the faith of belligerents to a severe test and running counter to legitimate neutral interests, that practice was not left unchallenged.

The first American protest was filed with the British government as soon as it was reported that the latter had explicitly authorized, on 31 January 1915, the use of neutral flags by

[46]See 34 *AJIL* (1940) *Suppl.* at pp. 11–12.
[47]See 22 *Official Records of the International Military Tribunal at Nuremberg* at p. 508.

British merchantmen for the purpose of escaping detection and capture by the German Navy. The Secretary of State William J. Bryan in his letter of 10 February 1915, communicated the concern of his government about any general use of the American flag by British trading vessels in these words:

> the occasional use of the flag of a neutral or an enemy under the stress of immediate pursuit and to deceive an approaching enemy seems to this Government a very different thing from an explicit sanction by a belligerent government for its merchant ships generally to fly the flag of a neutral power within certain portions of the high seas which are presumed to be frequented with hostile warships. The formal declaration of such a policy of general misuse of a neutral's flag jeopardizes the vessels of the neutral visiting those waters in a peculiar degree by raising the presumption that they are of belligerent nationality regardless of the flag which they may carry.[48]

In the British reply, dated 19 February 1915, the practice of navigating under a false flag was defended on the grounds of a long naval tradition:

> Great Britain has always when neutral accorded to the vessels of other States at war liberty to use the British flag as a means of protection against capture, and instances are on record when United States vessels availed themselves of this facility during the American Civil War . . . The British Government have no intention of advising their merchant shipping to use foreign flags as general practice or to resort

[48]See 9 *AJIL* (1915) *Sp.Suppl.* at p. 89. Similar had been the reaction of the Dutch government. As Foreign Minister J. Loudon stressed in his letter of 15 February 1915, to the British ambassador at The Hague 'le fait de se servir du pavillon d'un Etat sans le consentement de celui-ci est toujours un abus. En temps de guerre cet abus prend un caractère dont la gravité ne saurait être méconnue par les puissances signataires de la Déclaration de Paris: il compromet le pavillon neutre, il jette un doute sur les navires neutres battant leur propre pavillon, il les expose à être pris eux-mêmes pour des navires ennemis et à en subir de périlleuses conséquences'; see *Recueil de diverses communications du Ministre des Affaires étrangères aux États-Généraux par rapport à la neutralité des Pays-Bas et au respect du droit des gens,* Sept.1916 at p. 101.

> to them otherwise than for escaping capture or destruction.[49]

The question of false flags was taken up again by the US government in the context of the Neutrality Debate preceding the Second World War. The Neutrality Act of 1935 was silent on the issue, whereas the Act of 4 November 1939 under section 14 proscribed the deceptive use of the American flag in these words: 'it shall be unlawful for any vessel belonging to or operating under the jurisdiction of any foreign state to use the flag of the United States, or to make use of any distinctive signs or markings, indicating that the same is an American vessel'.[50]

5 Of phantom fleets and dazzle-painting

Deceiving by Optical Illusion: Decoys and Camouflage Tactics Aside from all the legally controversial methods examined above, deception at sea can also take inoffensive or 'passive' forms, such as dummy craft not able in themselves to engage the enemy, and camouflage, which of course are far less open to question. The creation in 1914 of the *Special Coastal Squadron,* or *S.C. Squadron,* which also stood for *Scare Crow Squadron,* is attributed to Winston Churchill, then First Lord of the British Admiralty. The promising plan, consisting in masquerading a dozen merchant ships so they assumed the silhouette of existing British warships, was first advanced in his note of 21 October 1914, when he wrote:

> it is necessary to construct without delay a dummy fleet. Ten merchant vessels, either German prizes or British ships, should be selected at once. They are then to be mocked up to represent fast battleships of the First and Second Battle Squadrons. The actual size need not correspond exactly as it is notoriously difficult to judge the size of vessels at sea, and frequently even destroyers are mistaken for cruisers.

[49]See 9 *AJIL* (1915) *Sp.Suppl.* at p. 97. On 20 February, 1915, Washington eventually devised a frame of agreement on the most contentious issues of high seas mining, submarine attacks and abuse of neutral flags. According to this proposal, Germany and Great Britain would be bound to 'require their respective merchant vessels not to use neutral flags for the purpose of disguise or ruse de guerre'; *ibid.* at p. 98. Yet, both belligerents appeared reluctant to proceed along these lines.

[50]See 34 *AJIL* (1940) *Suppl.* at p. 53.

> Even when the enemy knows that we have such a fleet its presence will tend to mystify and confuse his plans, and baffle and distract the enterprise of his submarines. He will always be in doubt as to which is the real and which is the dummy fleet.[51]

The thirteen duplicate cruisers, officially known as the Tenth Battle Squadron, were then dispatched in the Mediterranean, off the Turkish straits, or across the Atlantic. Their sole mission was to confuse the enemy with regard to the real number and position of the operating units of the British fleet, inducing spy agents to false reports and facilitating surprise attacks on the German *Hoch See Flotte*.[52] Although an original concept, these vessels proved impractical, especially because of their extremely slow speed. These units of the phantom fleet were later reconverted to oilers or water-carriers for the fighting fleet.

This stratagem was undertaken anew in the Second World War with equally poor results. Only three vessels, the destroyers *Revenge* and *Resolution* and the carrier *Hermes* were duplicated this time. The dummy ships, known collectively as *Force W*, or *Fleet Tenders A, B* and *C*, sailed for the first time in their new garb in December 1939, and, until May 1941 when their decommission was approved, they lay idly at their berths in the Forth. The Luftwaffe, probably aware of their existence, seemed uninterested in attacking these targets. Finally, the fake '*R* and *R*' were reconverted into food-carrying ships, while the replica of

[51]Quoted in HAMPSHIRE, A.C., *The Phantom Fleet*, 1960 at pp. 32–3. In fact, average-sized merchant vessels from 4,000 to 9,000 tons had to impersonate super-dreadnoughts ranging from 20,000 to 27,000 tons. Alteration work began in November 1914 and in less than a month the first two dummy battleships, the *City of Oxford* and the *Michigan*, were ready. Fake superstructures of wood and canvas were built, guns and gun turrets, bridges, masts and funnels were added in order to reproduce most faithfully the outline of the real men-of-war. More tricky yet was the problem of how to give the replicas the warships' distinctive oval look from above so as to appear authentic from the air as well.

[52]On the pseudo-cruisers scheme, see LE MASSON, H., 'L'escadre des épouvantails', *Revue Maritime* (Oct. 1937), p. 487*ff.*, and BRÉDAT, J., 'Le camouflage à la mer', 71 *Science et Vie* (janvier 1947), no.352, p. 43*ff.* Three units of the dummy fleet were sent to the Mediterranean to participate in the Gallipoli campaign feigning support to troop transport operations. One of these, the fake battle cruiser *Tiger* was torpedoed and sunk by the German submarine U.21 in the Aegean Sea. The dummy battle cruiser *Queen Mary* was sent out to the Atlantic *en route* for America its role being to patrol off the American coast and discourage the two German merchant raiders, the *Kronprinz Wilhelm* and the *Prinz Eitel Friedrich* from attempting to leave neutral ports. Both auxiliary cruisers were eventually interned for the duration of hostilities by the US naval authorities.

the *Hermes* sank accidentally while in its first and last convoy mission.[53]

A great variety of other *trompe l'oeil* tricks falling under the general purview of camouflage were attempted. Dazzle-painting, for instance, involved making the ordinary grey hulls of warships look like strange patchworks of curves, whirls, stripes and angular slashes, aimed at reducing visibility and misleading enemy submarines as to the vessel's true course and speed. Despite initial reticence, the principle of dazzle-painting was progressively adopted so that by the end of June 1918 as many as 195 British warships and 2,112 British merchantmen had undergone the face-lift.[54] By painting false waterlines or waves on bows, it was thought they could equally produce speed distortion thus rendering the tracking and aiming of a moving ship inaccurate.[55] An often recounted episode concerned the auxiliary cruiser *Prinz Eitel Friedrich* and the successful ruse it employed during the Falklands Battle in December 1914. The German ship was capable of fleeing the scene and escaping the British warship that pursued her merely by exposing alternatively her sides, one painted black and the other white.[56]

[53]The Germans, for their part, had been experimenting with other forms of decoy craft. What they called a *Wasseresel*, or 'water donkey', for instance, consisted of a full-scale decoy conning tower of a submarine, packed with explosives and towed by a submerged U-boat. This simulation was designed to deceive Allied warships and invite mistaken attacks on the fake submarines. The *Wasseresels* were apparently never engaged in war action; see REIT, *op. cit., supra* n.6 at p. 199.

[54]For more on dazzle-painting during the First World War, see HARTCUP, G., *Camouflage – A History of Concealment and Deception in War*, 1979, p. 40*ff*.

[55]Camouflage at sea was to reach a new climax of sophistication with the Second World War. Air attacks posed naval camouflagers with added difficulties and required fresh ingenuity. A most imaginative experiment, for example, involved painting the outline of a light cruiser on the hull of a large heavy cruiser. The Japanese carrier *Zuiho* displayed a painted contour of a light cruiser with three-dimensional shadows on its flight deck with the hope of deceiving attacking planes; see REIT, *op. cit., supra* n.6 at p. 197, and HARTCUP, *op. cit., supra*, p. 117*ff*.

[56]Cited in MÉRIGNHAC and LÉMONON, *op. cit., supra* n.19, tome II (1921) at p. 15. *Cf.* BRUNEAU, *op. cit., supra* n.14 at p. 72. In yet another development, just prior to the Armistice of 1918 and with the Germans fully aware of the Q-ship device, the British Admiralty introduced the *double enders*, or vessels designed with their fore and aft parts indistinguishable by use of dummy bridges, masts or funnels. Apparently abandoning the idea of decoy ships in the sense of ambushing the enemy U-boats, these vessels only sought to make a torpedo attack more troublesome.

III The perennial debate on how to tell a ruse from perfidy

1 From ancient practices to medieval chivalry

Fides etiam hosti servanda: The Roman Tradition The condemnation of disloyal chicanery in fighting can be traced back to the early history of human civilization. As a common standard with primitive societies, and despite the all too frequent recourse to derailed brutality, treachery was generally deemed inappropriate as a means to overpower the adversary. Chivalric instincts were not alien to primitive tribes; 'the warrior will withhold his hand until the enemy is equally armed . . . declarations of war may sometimes have this motive'.[57] Among the Greeks, treacherous stratagems were condemned as uncivilized.[58] Cutting off the enemy's water supply, or making use of poisoned weapons should always be avoided, while individuals caught in the act of spying were put to death without trial.[59]

Many of the Hellenic ideas concerning dubious methods of fighting later inspired the Roman *jus belli*. Breach of faith and, in particular, treason, was considered grossly criminal and impious, as the maxim *fides etiam hosti servanda* implies, while 'they [Romans] rarely resorted to ambuscades and underhand stratagems'.[60] As the Roman Senate declared: *non fraude neque*

[57]See WRIGHT, Q., *A Study of War*, 2nd edn (1965) at p. 94. The author acknowledges, however, that 'the rules of primitive war do not ordinarily manifest much fairness to the enemy. Attacks are from ambush or at night when the victims are at every disadvantage.'

[58]As Thucydides wrote, for instance, 'it is more dishonourable, at least to men in dignity, to amplify their estate by specious fraud, than by open violence. For the latter assails with a certain right of power given us by fortune, but the other, with the treachery of a wicked conscience'; see Thucydides, *op. cit., supra* n., bk.IV, §86. While Xenophon, in a passage of his *Anabasis*, considers that 'it is just that those who violate their oaths should suffer death'; see Xenophon, *The Anabasis*, bk.II, ch.5, §41.

[59]See PHILLIPSON, C., *The International Law and Custom of Ancient Greece and Rome*, vol.II (1911) at pp. 221, 299. For a number of other ancient societies, however, unremitting cruelty and indiscriminate slaughter were regular practice. In resorting to what he calls 'the usual oriental savagery, the Assyrians, the Phoenicians, and the Egyptians were given to treachery, inhuman passion, destruction of every thing and every living being in their way, whether or not the victims took part in the wars against them'; see *ibid.* at p. 203. Similarly in ancient China and among the Hebrews or the Carthaginians unrestrained ferocity obtained.

[60]*Ibid.*, p. 231*ff*. The ritual of declaring war through the elaborate procedures of the *ius fetiale* is also thought to owe its existence to chivalric sentiments. According to the customary practice, the fetials proceeded to the frontiers of the hostile people for the *pater patratus*, head of the college, to make a solemn

occultis, sed palam et armatum, populum Romanum hostes suos ulcisci.[61]

A primordial rule of warfare among Hindus allowed fighting only between forces of the same nature; 'thus, if any army consisted of elephants, horses, chariots and footmen, it was incumbent on each category to give combat to the opposing like category ... the principle of like matching and fighting the like was based on grounds of chivalry and fairness particularly when armies had several different categories and the employment of the mounted soldier against the unmounted was an obvious act of cruelty to the latter'.[62]

Honourable Conduct and Medieval Warfare Modern prescriptions on perfidy, however, are considered to originate more in the medieval notion of chivalry, the once cardinal principle in the code of conduct of warring nobles of feudal Europe, synonymous with brave and high-minded knighthood.[63] Among the

declaration of war, throwing at the same time a spear, pointed with steel and dipped in blood. It is interesting to note that etymologically the word *fetiales* most likely derives from *fides*, 'on the ground of their guardianship of the public good faith as manifested in the relationships between States'; see *ibid.* at p. 317. See also HEURGON, J., 'La guerre romaine aux 4e-3e siècles et la *Fides Romana*' in Brisson, J.-P. (ed.), *Problèmes de la guerre à Rome*, 1969, p. 23*ff.*

[61]See Tacitus, *The Annals*, bk.II, ch.lxxxviii.

[62]See SINGH, N., 'Armed Conflicts and Humanitarian Laws of Ancient India' in SWINARSKI, C. (ed.), *Studies and Essays on International Humanitarian Law and Red Cross Principles in Honour of Jean Pictet*, 1984 at p. 532. According to the ancient Indian laws, as affirmed in the epic Sanskrit poems of Mahābhārata and Rāmāyana, all tactics of fooling the enemy were regarded as improper. Giving notice to the enemy before engaging in battle was an imperative formality to respect. Night attacks or the use of concealed weapons, for instance, were contrary to the pious tradition of warfare; see *ibid.* at p. 535. Hindu warriors were equally invited to refrain from attacking a retreating enemy, and spare combatants in distress, unprepared for combat, or willing to surrender, clear manifestations that fraudulent and compassionless conduct was incompatible with priestly doctrine of honour. For relevant excerpts from the Sanskrit texts, see 'Les lois de la guerre chez les anciens hindous', 33*RICR* (Nov.1951), no.395, p. 869*ff.* Yet, 'in some cases the blackest treachery was practised, but this was contrary to the Dharma [moral duty] of pious kings'; see ARMOUR, W.S., 'Customs of Warfare in Ancient India', 8 *GST* (1922) at p. 73. See also MOUTON, M.W., 'History of the Laws and Customs of War up to the Middle Ages', 12 *RICR* (Oct.1959) *Suppl.*, p. 188*ff.*

[63]On the influence that chivalry exerted on the customs of war, see the illuminating account of WARD, R., *An Enquiry into the Foundation and History of the Law of Nations in Europe, from the Time of the Greeks and Romans, to the Age of Grotius*, 1795, vol.II, pp. 155–230.

sanctities of the *jus armorum* was the respect for the given word and the usage of freeing a captured nobleman on parole. According to the law of ransom, the captor was expected temporarily to release his prisoner to go home on parole and raise the agreed sum. The captive, on the other hand, should declare himself ready to assume all dishonour and humiliation if he broke his promise (known as the anathema clause). The most common form of *deshonnoirement* was the symbolic public exhibition of the unfaithful prisoner's arms reversed, or *subversio armorum*. A related social ritual of the professional soldier was the oath on the honour of knighthood, which amounted to a promise weighing heavier than any obligation under the law of contract.[64]

The medieval perception of chivalry, however, was not always confined to an orderly code of knightly loyalty, honour and Christian gratitude. Profit, through the practice of taking men for ransom, was one of the most extensive practices of professional armies in the Middle Ages. As one of the most renowned experts on that age has commented, 'one cannot, indeed, help wondering whether the law of arms would have meant anything, if it had not been for the financial stakes at issue in battle . . . [In fact, the effectiveness of those rules] was due to their appeal to two most potent human motives, pride

[64]So profound was the respect of oaths by soldiers, writes Robert Ward, 'that when they lay under any of these restrictions, they appeared every where with little chains attached to their arms or habits, to shew all the world that they were *slaves* to their words; nor were they taken off till their promise had been performed, which sometimes extended to a term of four or five years'; *ibid.* at p. 174. Courtesy in combat and fidelity to his word were the knight's most cherished ideals; 'it was beneath the honourable enmity of a knight to invade an enemy unawares; he scorned to take advantage of him, even in the heat of combat; much less could he deliberately make an attack which all the rules of courtesy would have forbidden. When driven therefore to open war, it was a necessary consequence to inform his enemy of it, and the intention was denounced in the most solemn manner by an officer whose function was generally considered as sacred and inviolable. Hence arose the modern *declaration of war by heralds and poursuivants*; a ceremony which seemed to spring from magnanimity alone'; *ibid.* at pp. 206–207. A further manifestation of the regularity sought in chivalric *jus belli* is the practice often followed in case of a siege. When confronted with an outnumbered entrenched garrison an offer to surrender should be considered 'provided no army came to its relief within a fixed period; and in case it did, the besiegers were bound to wait for it, give it battle, and the place was to remain with the victor'; *ibid.* at p. 226.

and profit.'[65] It is within this atypical setting of discrepant properties, varying from virtue to immorality, and from cruelty to sentimentalism, that the true meaning of chivalry should be explored.[66]

2 Early writings and the first codifications

The Limits of Lawful Deception and International Law Classics

Christian morals and chivalric ideals of the High Middle Ages solicited philosophical analysis of all the questions related to the recourse to arms. Parallel to the dominant discussion of just and unjust causes for going to war, it was natural to debate on just and unjust means and methods of conducting a war. Thomas Aquinas (1225–74) was the first among the scholastics of the thirteenth century to draw the distinction in clear terms between lawful deception in the sense of covertness, and unlawful perfidy always involving a breach of faith owed to the enemy; 'on peut induire quelqu'un en erreur d'une double manière, d'abord en lui disant une chose fausse et en ne gardant pas une promesse faite, ensuite en ne lui faisant pas connaître ouvertement ce que l'on se propose de faire ni ce que l'on pense; la première manière est absolument condamnée, la seconde est licite'.[67]

[65]See KEEN, M.H., *The Laws of War in the Late Middle Ages*, 1965 at pp. 244, 246. Moreover, chivalrous conduct did not always imply humane treatment and sparing defenceless civilians. Barbaric methods of torture were often exercised against peasants or the humble of the vanquished fiefdom in order to extort money. In the words of Ernest Nys, 'les règles que la chevalerie établit ne protègent que les égaux; le code d'honneur qu'elle formule ne s'étend point aux inférieurs . . . dès qu'il s'agit d'autres que de nobles et de chevaliers, de cruelles passions viennent prendre la place d'une magnanimité trop vantée'; see NYS, E., *Les origines du droit international*, 1894 at p. 191. While for Thomas Alfred Walker, 'the tale of the war-practice of the Golden Age of Chivalry is the tale of tinsel splendour and cold-blooded brutality'; see WALKER, T.A., *A History of the Law of Nations*, vol.I (1899) at p. 130.

[66]As G.I.A.D. Draper pertinently observed, 'dans sa forme finale et achevée, la chevalerie réunissait trois éléments distincts qui s'interprénétraient, à savoir: la guerre, la religion et l'amour charnel . . . Si l'on ne perd pas de vue ces éléments, il me semble qu'on peut comprendre les oppositions, délicatesse, grossièreté, compassion, cruauté, idéalisme, dépravation, équité, férocité, dévouement, avidité, amour romanesque, luxure, bonne foi, perfidie, démence, atrocités de la guerre, courage, brutalité envers les êtres sans défense qui sont les aspects réels de la chevalerie'; see DRAPER, G.I.A.D., 'L'évolution de droit de la guerre – Influences du christianisme et de la chevalerie', 47 *RICR* (Jan.1965), no.553 at p. 7.

[67]Quoted in NYS, *op. cit.*, *supra* n.65 at p. 218.

Among the theologians of the 'Spanish Age' (1500–1648), Francisco Suárez (1548–1617) reintroduced Aquinas's teaching which was to inspire the customs of war in the sixteenth century. What should be prohibited was the breach of the combatant's word of honour, while there should be nothing reproachable in the simple fact of keeping war plans secret from the enemy. In his *Work on the Three Theological Virtues Faith, Hope and Charity* he maintains that 'stratagems in war are permissible insofar as relates to the prudent concealment of one's plans; but not with respect to the telling of lies . . . breaking faith plighted with the enemy is not permissible since it involves patent injustice, and consequently, if the enemy suffers loss for this reason, full reparation should be made'.[68] Yet, it was in Alberico Gentili's (1552–1608) *De jure belli libri tres* that the question of craftiness

[68]See SUAREZ, F., *De triplici virtute theologica, fide, spe, et charitata*, Disp.XIII, On War, section VII, para.23. According to this criterion certain stratagems would no longer be permitted; to simulate death, to be dressed in the enemy's uniform, or to use women as human shields for advancing soldiers. On the other hand permissible ruses would include the false announcement of the death of a general, the use of horrible clamours in order to terrify the horses of the enemy, and even the use of traps. Pierino Belli (1502–75) and Balthasar Ayala (1548–84), for their part, drew upon the imposing wealth of Roman law in order to refine principles of the *jus gentium*. For the former, 'the law of nations requires that pledges be not violated, and that agreements made even with the enemy be carried out . . . With wit and arms, war should be waged against the enemy, and with wiles too, if they involve no wrong or treachery (for there is no room for valour and glory)'; see BELLI, P., *De re militari et bello tractatus*, part II, ch.XIV. For the latter, 'indeed stratagems bring as a rule very great praise and glory to a general', but 'whenever a transaction is entered into a just and lawful enemy, . . . terms and agreements relating to the war and hostilities ought not to be perfidiously upset, even when they have been entered into by private persons, for it is a serious thing to break faith'; see AYALA, B., *De jure et officiis bellicis et disciplina militari libri III*, bk.I, ch.VIII, para.3, and ch.VI, para.2. While he goes on to say that 'in war, even though you have a perjured, treaty-breaking foe to deal with, and one who has once and again and repeatedly played you false, yet you may not break you faith in return . . . [since] it was always held a deep disgrace to requite perfidy with perfidy'; *ibid.*, ch.VI, para.21. As for Niccolò Machiavelli (1469–1527), 'encore qu'il soit détestable d'user de la fraude en toute action, néanmoins, dans la conduite de la guerre, c'est chose louable et glorieuse. Celui qui vainc l'ennemi par la ruse est tout à fait l'égal de celui qui vainc par la force . . . [mais] non pas la ruse qui te fait rompre la foi donnée et les engagements conclus: celle-là peut te donner, en l'occasion, l'état et le trône, mais ne t'acquerra jamais de gloire'; quoted in BENOIST, C., 'L'influence des idées de Machiavel', 9 *RCADI* (1925) at p. 279. For a fine selection of doctrinal views on good faith from the sixteenth through to the eighteenth centuries, see the essay by O'CONNOR, J.F., *Good Faith in International Law*, 1991, pp. 45–79.

in war probably received the most thorough treatment; 'in waging war there is one principle which pervades all parts of it; namely, craft and stratagem . . . our only precaution must be not to allow every kind of craft and every cunning device; for evil is not lawful, but an enemy should be dealt with according to law. And the law is never evil, but it is the practice of the good and the fair.'[69]

As for the compelling reference to the legacy of Hugo Grotius (1583–1645), 'war is never to be undertaken except to assert rights, and, when undertaken, is never to be carried on except within the limits of rights and of good faith'.[70] His feeling on the means of injuring the enemy is that 'if you take account only of the law of nature, in case it is permissible to kill a person, it makes no difference whether you kill him by the sword or by poison. By the law of nature, I repeat, for it is indeed more noble to kill in such a way that he who is killed may have a chance to defend himself.'[71] As a study on that period has concluded, 'l'analyse des cas licites et des ruses prohibées, si on la pousse, fait apparaître que le critérium n'est autre que celui de la foy à la parole donnée, voire à une convention tacite entre les combattants. Le respect de cette foy

[69]See GENTILI, A., *De jure belli libri tres*, bk.II, ch.III. He approves of lying to the enemy in these words: 'and if it is not unjust to feign flight, to pretend fear, to seem to depart, and to do other things of that kind, why should it be unjust to deceive an enemy by words? For what difference does it make whether you feign in words or in act, whether you indicate with tongue or hands or feet, that something will happen which you know will not take place; that you will do what you surely know that you will not do?'; *ibid.*, bk.II, ch.V. He holds, however, that 'the wording of our agreements with our enemies should be free from every kind of trickery'; *ibid.*, bk.II, ch.IV. By way of example, he mentions the Romans who cut in parts all the ships of Antiochus, because the king was bound by a treaty to surrender the half of his ships, or the Greeks who owing ships, delivered them without helms, oars, or sails, alleging that these were ships all the same.

[70]See GROTIUS, H., *De jure belli ac pacis*, Prolegomena at para.25.

[71]*Ibid.*, bk.III, ch.IV, section XV, n.1. And elsewhere: 'ruses which do not involve breach of faith are held to be permissible; permissible, again, is even the inciting of another to treachery. In truth the law of nations begins to wink at these frequent minor wrongs, just as municipal laws at harlotry and usury'; *ibid.*, bk.III, ch.V, section IV. See also bk.III, ch.IV, section XVIII. Richard Zouche (1589–1660), writing in 1650, approves also of falsehood in war as long as it refers to 'assertions, not to promises; for a promise confers a right on him to whom the promise is made, and this holds good even between enemies'; see ZOUCHE, R., *Juris et judicii fecialis, sive, juris inter gentes, et quaestionum de eodem explicatio*, part II, section X, para 4.

commande la solution de bien d'autres problèmes du droit de la guerre'.[72]

Turning now to the international law writers of the post-Westphalia period (1648–1815), Christian Wolff (1679–1754) suggests that:

> deceit is allowable in war, whether it consists in pretence, or falsehood without the plighted word, or in concealment. For if those things to which the belligerent has a right can be obtained in war without force, he must refrain from force in obtaining them . . . Stratagems are unexpected acts of war dependent upon cunning. Therefore, when acts of war are allowable, stratagems also are allowable, and since acts of war may consist both in force and in deceit, stratagems can consist both in force and in deceit.[73]

For Emmerich de Vattel (1714–67) the principle of economy of force would plead in favour of stratagems just as much as the notion of chivalry would argue against them. Thus, though suggesting that 'comme l'humanité nous oblige à préférer les moyens les plus doux dans la pursuite de nos droits, si par une

[72]See GARDOT, *op. cit., supra* n.13 at p. 465.

[73]See WOLF, C., *Jus gentium methodo scientifica pertractatum*, §§857, 858. To the mutual interest of belligerents, however, faith should be preserved; 'since the things which are promised to an enemy as an enemy, nay, even to a robber and a brigand as robber and brigand, are to be performed, and since he who keeps his promises keeps faith, with an enemy, nay, even with a robber and a brigand, good faith is to be observed. Whereas if it is allowable to break a pledge given to an enemy, promises made to an enemy are turned into mere illusions; and it is to the interest of each of the belligerent parties that this should not happen', *ibid.*, §800. In the view of Samuel Pufendorf (1632–94), 'whilst I am exercising my proper right, I am not always obliged to hinder another from taking up a false opinion, in other respects, harmless . . . as to the other instance, of deceiving an enemy, by counterfeiting flight, clothes, colours, sails, arms, and the like, this practice is allowable beyond dispute'; see PUFENDORF, S., *De jure naturae et gentium libri octo*, bk.IV, ch.I, para.12, and bk.VIII, ch.VI, para.6. In the interest of making the return to peace possible, however, craftiness should not exceed certain limits; 'what prevents us from inflicting damage upon one by cunning and without any peril to ourselves, whom we may hurt by open violence? The reason why some have spurned this manner of injuring an enemy is not because they believed that it violated some right, but because among more hardy spirits glory only attaches to those acts against an enemy, which show a certain vigour and dash on the part of mind and body. But what is said about deceiving an enemy should in no wise be extended to any pacts entered into with the enemy about concluding peace, or about an armistice. For since the law of nature commands that peace be maintained as far as possible, and that any violence offered it be healed, it is also understood to enjoin the use of the means without which that end cannot be attained'; *ibid.*, bk.IV, ch.I, para.19.

ruse de guerre, une feinte exempte de perfidie, on peut s'emparer d'une place forte, surprendre l'ennemi et le réduire, il vaut mieux, il est réellement plus louable, de réussir de cette manière que par un siége meurtrier ou par une bataille sanglante', he admits all the same that 'il faut avouer que, quand on peut vaincre un ennemi à force ouverte, en bataille rangée, on doit se flatter bien plus sûrement de l'avoir dompté et réduit à demander la paix, que si on a obtenu l'avantage par surprise'.[74]

In the post-1815 period, most of the literature of the century reflects the belief that guileful means of combat are permissible as long as they do not involve a breach of faith. In his *Précis du Droit des Gens,* George Frédéric de Martens (1845–1909) argues that 'ni la loi naturelle ni l'usage ne défendent, dans la généralité, l'emploi de stratagèmes pour tromper l'ennemi, en tant que ces ruses servent au but de la guerre, et que l'on n'a pas promis expressément ou tacitement de le traiter de bonne foi'.[75] Using similar reasoning Pasquale Fiore (1837–1914) affirms that:

> généralement la loi naturelle n'empêche pas le stratagème dans la guerre, pourvu que cependant il ne constitue pas une violation de la foi jurée à l'ennemi et n'emporte pas l'assassinat ou la provocation à l'assassinat . . . Les deux parties combattantes doivent être fidèles à observer leurs devoirs, et si la feinte leur est permise pour induire en erreur la partie opposée et obtenir la victoire, elles ne doivent pas pour cela se croire autorisées à violer les principes de la moralité et de la loyauté, en justifiant leur conduite sous le prétexte d'user de stratagèmes de guerre.[76]

[74]See VATTEL, E. de, *Le droit des gens, ou principes de la loi naturelle appliqués à la conduite et aux affaires des nations et des souverains,* ed. of 1820, tome 2, §178 at pp. 633–4, 636.

[75]See DE MARTENS, G.F., *Précis du droit des gens moderne de l'Europe fondé sur les traités et l'usage,* 3ème édn (1831), tome 2, §274 at pp. 184–5.

[76]See FIORE, P., *Nouveau droit international public suivant les besoins de la civilisation moderne,* tome 2 (1869) at pp. 281–2. For Carlos Testa, during a war 'a-t-on recours à des moyens qui compensent l'inégalité. On donne à ces moyens le nom de stratagèmes de guerre; souvent, ils peuvent amener des résultats qui épargnent bien des existences et évitent la dévastation; ce sont les embuscades, les surprises, les fausses retraites, les nouvelles répandues pour abattre le courage de l'ennemi. Mais dans l'emploi de ces moyens indirects pour obtenir un avantage sur l'ennemi, il ne doit pas y avoir de procédés incompatibles avec l'honneur, la loyauté et la dignité de celui qui les met en pratique. La guerre doit être une lutte entre des forces subordonnées seulement à l'habileté et à la valeur. On n'y doit, par conséquent, pratiquer aucune perfidie ou infamie'; see TESTA, C., *Le droit public international maritime,* 1886 at p. 143. Antoine Pillet, for

The Lieber Code and the Hague Regulations The nineteenth century also saw the first undertakings to codify the distinction between permissible ruses and prohibited treachery. According to Article 15 of the *Instructions for the U.S. Government of Armies in the Field*, drafted by Dr. Francis Lieber in 1863, 'men who take up arms against one another in public war do not cease on this account to be moral beings, responsible to one another and to God', and, therefore, a ruse permits 'such deception as does not involve the breaking of good faith either positively pledged, regarding agreements entered into during the war, or supposed by the modern law of war to exist'.[77] As regards perfidy, it is referred to as 'an act of bad faith, of infamy or fiendishness' (Article 117).

At the turn of the century, the cornerstone principle of all humanitarian law, i.e. that the right of belligerents to adopt means of injuring the enemy is not unlimited, was codified in the celebrated Article 22 of the Hague Regulations respecting the laws and customs of war on land annexed to the Hague Convention II of 1899 and IV of 1907. This principle stipulated broad restrictions on the permissible means and methods of warfare inspired by the mixed sentiments of humanity, ethics and honour. In what relates to the latter, Article 23(b) declared 'especially forbidden to kill or wound treacherously individuals belonging to the hostile nation or army', while para.(f) of the same Article proscribed the 'improper use of a flag of truce, of the national flag or of the military insignia and uniform of the enemy, as well as the distinctive badges of the Geneva Convention'. Article 24, on the other hand, endorsed the use of 'ruses of war and the employment of measures necessary for obtaining information about the enemy'. Neither treachery nor ruse, however, were defined in the Hague Regulations.

3 The new definition of perfidy: law of deception or deception of law?

At first glance it is reassuring to note that, due to the labours of the *Diplomatic Conference on the Reaffirmation and Development*

his part, stresses that 'l'emploi de la ruse dans la guerre maritime ne doit comporter aucune atteinte à la foi que se doivent les ennemis, et à la signification que donne à certains usages des traditions bien établies'; see PILLET, A., *Les lois actuelles de la guerre*, 2ème édn (1901) at p. 116.

[77] See SCHINDLER, D. and TOMAN, J. (eds), *The Law of Armed Conflicts*, 3rd edn (1988) at p. 6. See also Articles 16, 101.

of International Humanitarian Law Applicable in Armed Conflicts, we now enjoy a brand new definition of perfidy embodied in Article 37 of the 1977 First Additional Protocol.[78] This is all the more so since the previous attempt of a definition dates, as mentioned above, as far back as the Lieber Code itself, while Article 23 of the Hague Regulations on treacherous killing failed to define perfidy as such. Upon second reading, however, the new definition does not appear to live up to expectations. For many, it fell short of articulating an all-embracing prohibition of perfidy. Indeed, its scope, as it was ultimately formulated, is even narrower than that of the corresponding prohibition in the Hague Regulations.[79] Moreover, in what would seem the incurable taboo of all humanitarian law-making, some of the most controversial usages in naval warfare escaped revision of any kind.

Delving into the ICRC reports which preceded the Diplomatic Conference offers no little ground for scepticism. The first texts which the Red Cross Conference of Government Experts drafted in the early 1970s were indicative not so much of bad draftmanship as of the inherent difficulty of speaking out with clarity on the limits of permissible deception. At an initial stage, the

[78]Article 37 reads as follows:
1. It is prohibited to kill, injure or capture an adversary by resort to perfidy. Acts inviting the confidence of an adversary to lead him to believe that he is entitled to, or is obliged to accord, protection under the rules of international law applicable in armed conflict, with intent to betray that confidence, shall constitute perfidy. The following acts are examples of perfidy:

(a) the feigning of an intent to negotiate under a flag of truce or of a surrender;
(b) the feigning of an incapacitation by wounds or sickness;
(c) the feigning of civilian, non-combatant status; and
(d) the feigning of protected status by the use of signs, emblems or uniforms of the United Nations or of neutral or other States not Parties to the conflict.

2. Ruses of war are not prohibited. Such ruses are acts which are intended to mislead an adversary or to induce him to act recklessly but which infringe no rule of international law applicable in armed conflict and which are not perfidious because they do not invite the confidence of an adversary with respect to protection under that law. The following are examples of such ruses: the use of camouflage, decoys, mock operations and misinformation.

[79]Article 37, wrote Knut Ipsen, 'shows that States have not been prepared to outlaw perfidy as such. This limited prohibition, therefore, may be taken as an example of the low ethical standards which characterize present practice in the conduct of hostilities within armed conflicts'; see IPSEN, K., 'Perfidy' in BERNHARDT, R. (ed.), *Encyclopedia of Public International Law*, instalment 4 (1982) at p. 132.

ICRC attempted a teleological approach in the sense that practices which, on account of their gravity 'would close the road to peace', should not be resorted to.[80] In another study on the *Rules Relative to Behaviour of Combatants*, submitted to the Conference in January 1971, the ICRC opted for an 'illustrative listing' of instances constituting legitimate ruses of war or prohibited perfidy in order to better juxtapose the two notions. In so doing, the drafters of the report indicated *inter alia* that 'it is likewise permissible to have recourse to the forces of nature against the antagonist: fire, flood, avalanches'.[81]

What in 1972 stood as Article 31 of the Draft Additional Protocol defined as perfidious those 'unlawful acts betraying an enemy's confidence', which, of course, differs little from declaring that unlawful acts are . . . unlawful. The ICRC commentary on Article 31 read as follows: 'a ruse is licit, if only because it is the only way to wage war while avoiding bloodshed'.[82] The commentary seems to hold the legality of a stratagem dependent on the humanitarian merits of its outcome, or a calculation of the comparative cost in human lives had the surprise tactics not been adopted, which is again misleading, given that some of the most renowned, though blood-soaked, military victories have been won by perfectly legitimate

[80]In the terms of a 1969 report, for instance, 'it is no longer so much a matter of obtaining a spirit of chivalry on the battlefield or an ideal of loyalty, as of denouncing everything that can make a return to peace more difficult'; see Extract from the Report of the ICRC to the 21st International Conference of the Red Cross, Istanbul 1969, in *Conference of Government Experts*, Geneva, 24 May–12 June 1971 (1st session), vol.IV *(Rules Relative to Behaviour of Combatants)*, documentary annex I at pp. 06–07. In the same document it was further asked rhetorically: 'would it not be advisable to reaffirm specifically the prohibition of every type of perfidious means, which bar the way to a cease fire and consequently to the diminution of useless suffering or violate the basic laws of humanity?' Even though the effort for a comprehensive prohibition of perfidy may be understandable, this criterion of finality would be far too conjectural and even arbitrary in application and, therefore, would offer no guidance.

[81]*Ibid.* at p. 13. Such a proposition, however, calls for two remarks. First, it is difficult to see how setting forests ablaze, for instance, or destroying water barrages, might be construed as a legitimate ruse *stricto sensu*, that is, an act which is intended to mislead an adversary. Second, acting in a likely manner would in all probability run counter to the elementary principles of distinction and unnecessary suffering. Turning to real cases, this provision could arguably have offered an unmerited justification to instances of enviromental warfare such as the massive use of incendiary bombs by US troops in Vietnam, or the 1991 blowing up of Kuwait oil wells by the receding Iraqi army.

[82]See *Conference of Government Experts*, Geneva, 3 May–3 June 1972 (2nd session), II Commentary, part one at p. 63.

resourceful manoeuvring. The brief note contained yet other abstract propositions of little practical significance such as that a ruse 'cannot make licit that which is not, nor can it excuse unjustified breaches of commitments', or that acts 'which use the instruments of peace and humanity for war and attack' should be censored as perfidious.

A judicious review of the negotiating history of Article 37 reveals several interesting aspects and inspires some points of reflection.[83] With the exception of two brief mentions of an inscrutable 'law governing the uses of neutral flags in warfare at sea',[84] the means and methods of armed conflict at sea, as might be affected by perfidious tactics, passed virtually unnoticed at the Diplomatic Conference.[85] Article 37, in its final wording, was based on the ICRC draft Article 35 as amended basically by a joint proposal by Canada, Ireland and Britain.[86] The import of perfidy was thus shifted as to denote 'acts inviting the confidence of the adversary with intent to betray that confidence', but only to the extent that the adversary is led to believe 'that he is entitled to, or is obliged to accord, protection under international law'. What was principally intended was to correlate perfidy more to a verifiable legal obligation than to a loose moral commitment.[87]

[83]Two main sources facilitate the reading of the relevant provisions of the First Additional Protocol: a summarized record of the proceedings of the Diplomatic Conference is offered in LEVIE, H.S., *Protection of War Victims: Protocol 1 to the 1949 Geneva Conventions*, vol.II (1980), pp. 290–327, while Article 37 is given a lengthy commentary in SANDOZ, Y., SWINARSKI, C., ZIMMERMANN, B., *Commentary on the Additional Protocols of 8 June 1977 to the Geneva Conventions of 12 August 1949*, 1987, p. 429*ff*.
[84]See *CDDH/III/338* and *CDDH/III/236/Rev.1*, para.18 in Official Records, vol.XV at pp. 426, 382.
[85]Much of the proposed amendments and the deliberations within the Working Group of the Third Committee concerned exclusively the correlation between the feigning of a non-combatant status as a form of perfidy and the guerrilla tactics of fighting in civilian clothing. On the delicate questions of ruse and perfidy arising in the context of guerrilla warfare, see *Conference of Government Experts*, Geneva, 24 May–12 June 1971 (1st session), vol.VI *(Rules Applicable in Guerrilla Warfare)* at pp. 34–5.
[86]See *CDDH/III/233*, 25 February 1975 in Official Records, vol.III at p. 164.
[87]In the words of the American delegate Reed who actively supported the tripartite amendment, 'experience showed that there was no uniform standard of morality in the world in general, and still less in time of war . . . the notion of perfidy should relate perfidy solely to legal obligations recognized in international law . . . the text in the amendment sets forth a uniform standard that is capable of universal application and would not be difficult to explain to combatants'; see *CDDH/III/SR.28* in Official Records, vol.XIV at p. 264. A key

As for the deceptive use of foreign emblems, draft Article 37 was couched in absolute terms; 'it is forbidden to make use of the enemy or neutral flags, military insignia and uniforms in order to shield, favour or impede military operations'. Given the large ambit of the term operations, it is thought that false flags or uniforms were to be prohibited at all times.[88] The original ICRC text was consequently divided in two paragraphs providing separately for the use of neutral and enemy national marks.[89] Finally, on 10 April 1975, the Working Group drew up a third paragraph to the effect that nothing in the provisions on perfidy shall affect 'the existing generally recognized rules of international law applicable to the use of flags in the conduct of armed conflict at sea', which now features as Article 39§3 of the First Geneva Protocol.[90] It is necessary to note at this point that the use of false flags in naval warfare received no special mention in the Draft Additional Protocols presented by the ICRC in 1973. It was only during the 1971 session of the Conference of Government Experts that reference was made to 'the rule in naval warfare, where it is possible to make use of the enemy flag, on condition that it is lowered before the first cannon shot', without elaborating any further than stating that 'this matter may call for further study with a view to formulating, if possible, a more precise rule'.[91]

suggestion of the ICRC text which was retained and re-emphasized in the course of the drafting sessions was the need for perfidious animus, that is to say, the criminal intention to break with the trust evinced by the enemy, or a premeditated disloyalty. On 28 May 1976, the Working Group reported to the Third Committee as follows: 'in order to be perfidy, an act must be done "with intent to betray" the confidence created. This was intended to mean that the requisite intent would be an intent to kill, injure or capture by means of the betrayal of confidence. Thus, acts such as feigning death, which are intended merely to save one's life would not be perfidy, whereas feigning death in order to kill an enemy once he turned his back would be perfidy'; see *CDDH/III/338* in Official Records, vol.XV at p. 426.

[88]*Cf.* the Report of Committee III, *CDDH/215/Rev.1*, para.38 in Official Records, vol.XV at pp. 270–1.

[89]See the Venezuelan proposal, *CDDH/III/239*, 3 March 1975 in Official Records, vol.III at p. 167. While the US delegation favoured an amendment to the effect that the use of enemy flags should be prohibited only 'while engaging in attacks'; see *CDDH/III/240*, 3 March 1975 in Official Records, vol.III at p. 168.

[90]See *CDDH/215/Rev.1* in Official Records, vol.XV at p. 300.

[91]See *Conference of Government Experts*, Geneva, 24 May–12 June 1971 (1st session), vol.IV *(Rules Relative to Behaviour of Combatants)* at p. 16. Before that, the 1969 Report of the ICRC to the 21st International Conference of the Red Cross at Istanbul referred to 'a custom in maritime warfare whereby the enemy flag may be flown before combat'; see documentary annex I, *ibid.* at p. 07. While the UN

It is generally understood that Article 39§3 was drafted in a cautious attempt to respect the peculiarities of the laws and customs of naval warfare. Some commentators, however, contend that Article 39(3) preserves 'the *lawfulness* of the rule according to which a ship may use false colours before opening fire (this means that the use of false colours is a *legitimate* ruse of war in sea warfare)'.[92] According to its terms, the contracting parties no doubt agreed that neither the provisos on perfidy nor those on national emblems shall affect the existing generally recognized rules of international law, *if any,* applicable to the use of flags in the conduct of armed conflict at sea. Yet, as this analysis wishes to submit, given the negotiating history of Articles 37 and 39, and in the light of state practice and literature to be reviewed below, there are no generally recognized customary principles concerning the use of false flags, neutral or enemy, in naval warfare. As it now stands, therefore, Article 39§3 is rather an empty formula which adds practically nothing definite to the ongoing academic discussion concerning the permissible *ruses de guerre* at sea.[93]

Articles 37 and 39§3 do not lend themselves to an easy assessment. The Geneva Conference made considerable strides in clarifying the notions of treachery and ruse, first spelled out in the Hague Regulations of 1907. Since it is no more than a casual truism to say that deception never ceased to serve military planning, it was positive to find fresh interest animating

Secretary-General, reporting to the General Assembly on the *Respect for Human Rights in Armed Conflicts* (Doc-.A/8052), echoed the ICRC report and made renewed reference to a 'custom in maritime warfare whereby the enemy flag may be flown before combat'; see documentary annex II, *ibid.* at p. 09. Although in all three instances the mention of a *custom* is made in rather conclusive terms, two observations can still be made: first, it appears that there is something of a mechanical reiteration of what was said in 1969 without being truly based on a thorough study of practice and doctrine. Second, the customary practice here alluded to seems to be confined in the use of enemy flags and then only by warships. Even following these texts, therefore, the question still remains unsettled as to the right of merchant vessels to fly a belligerent, and even more so, a neutral flag.

[92]See RONZITTI, N., 'The Crisis of the Traditional Law Regulating International Armed Conflicts at Sea and the Need for its Revision' in RONZITTI, N. (ed.), *The Law of Naval Warfare,* 1988 at p. 32.

[93]In this sense, what Michael Bothe wrote in 1982 describes with precision the current state of the law: 'the legality of the use of enemy flags at sea is controversial... Article 39(3) of Protocol I leaves this question open'; see BOTHE, M., 'Flags and Uniforms in War' in BERNHARDT, R. (ed.), *Encyclopedia of Public International Law,* instalment 3 (1982) at p. 174.

the debate. Yet, valid questions can still be asked as to whether the issue was truly considered in a new light, and whether the rules as now codified afford satisfactory solutions to contemporary war practices. Two remarks point to the erroneous construction or reading of the idea of perfidy. First, the perfidious intent clause, although necessary for the understanding of the concept, leaves much room for guesswork. To insist upon the need to verify such an intention would, therefore, render the task of substantiating perfidy a hopeless exercise. Second, despite the effort of the Third Committee to link perfidy to a breach of faith related exclusively to a *legal* obligation, it is difficult to overlook the fact that *moral* blame is, above all else, innate to the notion of perfidy.[94]

Although the desire to enhance the clarity and operability of the concept is understandable, one should not overstate the dichotomy between moral and legal obligations, for it is clear that morality pervades international humanitarian law. Indeed, morality forms the grand repository of inspiration for international humanitarian principles. Moreover, establishing a meaningful distinction between ruses of war and perfidy in complete detachment from moral analysis is somewhat illusory. Who could argue, for instance, that the principle of superfluous injury and unnecessary suffering can be satisfactorily approached by applying exclusively medical terms, without inevitably referring to moral criteria? Perfidy contains a nuance of moral denunciation which, although hard to handle *in concreto*, lies at the very heart of its meaning and no effort would seem able to transform it to a simply technical concept. From this viewpoint at least, it is believed that the 1973 ICRC draft article would comport better than Article 37 with the intrinsic moral significance of the concepts of ruse and perfidy.[95]

[94]A ruse of war, wrote René Bourdoncle, 'sous quelque forme qu'elle se manifeste, est condamnable lorsqu' elle rejoint la perfidie. En d'autres termes, sa *nature morale* est susceptible d'influer sur sa licéité et cette idée n'a cessé d'inspirer la doctrine'; see BOURDONCLE, *op. cit., supra* n.12 at p. 32.

[95]The ICRC commentary on draft Article 35 read: 'like ruses, perfidy involves simulation; but in addition it aims at creating falsely a situation in which the adversary feels obliged by a *legal* or *moral* rule to abstain from any hostile act or to neglect to take precautions which would be in fact necessary, thereby putting himself at a disadvantage' (emphasis added); ICRC, *Draft Additional Protocols to the Geneva Conventions of Aug.12, 1949 – Commentary,* October 1973 at p. 43.

A last remark concerns the value of Article 37 as a meaningful yardstick of evaluation of modern war tactics. In this respect, most people would agree that the present proviso on ruses and perfidy offers poor guidance. With the exception of self-evident and never contested cases such as the perfidious use of protective emblems, Article 37 would be of limited help if applied to the electronic battlefield of today. As for Article 39§3, it begets only consternation that the discussions were destined merely to drag on the sterile quarrel over the legitimacy of flying false flags. Negotiating a clause dealing with the deceptive use of enemy or neutral flags in the era of over-the-horizon targeting calls for two thoughts; first, that international law lags at times aberrantly behind reality, partakes at times more of a cynical political calculation than an unavoidable truth of life. Second, in a modern situation of armed conflict at sea, law would have to operate in the shadow of derision and ineffectiveness, at least as far as naval deception is concerned.

4 Recent national naval instructions

The US Naval Warfare Publication The closing chapter of the *US Commander's Handbook* on the Law of Naval Operations, chapter 12, deals with the legal aspects of deception during armed conflict in general. As a general proposition, it is provided that 'stratagems and ruses of war permitted in armed conflict include such deceptions as camouflage, deceptive lighting, dummy ships and other armament, decoys, simulated forces, feigned attacks and withdrawals, ambushes, false intelligence information, electronic deceptions, and utilization of enemy codes, passwords and countersigns'.[96] As for the definition of perfidy,

[96]See *Commander's Handbook on the Law of Naval Operations* (NWP9-Rev.A) at para.12.1.1. The *Annotated Supplement to Commander's Handbook* adds to the list of examples of permissible deceptions the use of 'traps; mock operations; feigned retreats or flights; surprise attacks; simulation of quiet and inactivity; use of small units to simulate large units; use of dummy aircraft, vehicles, airfields, weapons and mines to create a fictitious force; moving landmarks and route markers; pretending to communicate with forces or reinforcements which do not exist; deceptive supply movements; and allowing false messages to fall into enemy hands', at p. 12–1. The *Commander's Handbook* has been further commented upon in ROACH, J.A., 'Ruses and Perfidy: Deception duirng Armed Conflict', 23 *University of Toledo Law Review* (winter 1992), p. 395*ff.*

it is modelled along the terms of Article 37§1 of the Geneva Protocol.[97]

With respect to the false flags rule, the *Handbook* reaffirms the continued validity of the customary usage in these words: 'under the customary international law of naval warfare, it is permissible for a belligerent warship to fly false colors and disguise its outward appearance in other ways in order to deceive the enemy into believing the vessel is of neutral nationality or is other than a warship. However, it is unlawful for a warship to go into action without first showing her true colors. Use of neutral flags, insignia, or uniforms during an actual armed engagement at sea is, therefore, forbidden.'[98] The *Handbook* then proceeds to examine the deceitful use of certain signs and emblems stipulating, for instance, that the:

> misuse of protective signs, signals, and symbols in order to injure, kill, or capture the enemy constitutes an act of perfidy. Such acts are prohibited because they undermine the effectiveness of protective signs, signals and symbols and thereby jeopardize the safety of noncombatants and the immuntity of protected structures and activities. For example, using an ambulance or medical aircraft marked with the red cross or red crescent to carry armed combatants, weapons, or ammunition with which to attack or elude enemy forces is prohibited. Similarly, use of the white flag to gain a military advantage over the enemy is unlawful.[99]

[97]See para.12.1.2. It is noteworthy also that in chapter 5 of the *Handbook* concerning the principles and sources of the law of armed conflict, the following principle is included: 'dishonorable (treacherous) means, dishonorable expedients, and dishonorable conduct during armed conflict are forbidden', at para.5.2(3).

[98]See para.12.3.1. See also *Annotated Supplement* at p. 12–6. And elsewhere: 'naval surface and subsurface forces may fly enemy colors and display enemy markings to deceive the enemy. Warships must, however, display their true colors prior to an actual armed engagement'; see para.12.5.1. See also *Annotated Supplement* at p. 12–7.

[99]See para.12.2. Likewise, feigning shipwreck, wounds or non-combatant status in general with the intention to overpower the enemy is branded a perfidious conduct; 'a surprise attack by a person feigning shipwreck, sickness, or wounds undermines the protected status of those rendered incapable of combat. Similarly, attacking enemy forces while posing as a civilian puts all civilians at hazard. Such acts of perfidy are punishable as war crimes'; see para.12.7. Moreover, it would be unlawful to feign distress through the false use of internationally recognized signals such as SOS and MAYDAY; see para.12.6. It

Concerning armed merchant vessels, the US naval instructions provide that enemy merchant vessels may lawfully be attacked and destroyed either with or without prior warning among others 'if armed'.[100] This short-cut formulation modifies the rule appearing in the 1955 *US Manual* which proceeded on the basis of a distinction between offensive and defensive armaments. The repeal was thought necessary since 'in light of modern weapons, it is impossible to determine, if it ever was possible, whether the armament on merchant ships is to be used offensively against an enemy or merely defensively. It is unrealistic to expect enemy forces to be able to make that determination.'[101] Without being expressly prohibited, therefore, for a belligerent merchant ship to carry armaments, such practice, whatever the nature or extent of the armaments involved, would result in the forfeiture of its civilian immunities. The *Handbook* does not contain an analogous principle concerning neutral merchant ships, which may lead to the view that these vessels may never be equipped with military hardware.

The US Naval Warfare Publication draws mainly upon the rules codified in the First Additional Protocol and so the observations made on those rules may equally apply to the *US Manual*. It is regrettable that the *US Manual* uncritically endorses the false flag naval 'tradition'. Opting for the continuation of such maritime practices, may lead to the erroneous assumption that perfidy, as a theoretical legal concept, is divisible and multifaceted. Moreover, it is more than questionable whether this usage would have any practical significance for the most technologically advanced navy of the world at the dawn of the twenty-first century. The provision on armed merchantmen has the advantage of refraining of entering into a sterile discussion or adopting unworkable criteria concerning the ceiling of firing power to be displayed lawfully by a merchant vessel. But unfortunately it differs from a clear ban in absolute terms which

---

is permissible though to feign disablement in order to induce the enemy to break off an attack. As the *Annotated Supplement* specifies, 'the practice of submarines in releasing oil and debris to feign success of a depth charge or torpedo attack has never been considered to be unlawful', at pp. 12–10. Finally, in much less rigorous terms, the *Handbook* lays down that 'the flag of the United Nations and the letters "UN" may not be used in armed conflict for any purpose without the authorization of the United Nations'; see para.12.4.

[100]See para.8.2.2.2.

[101]See *Annotated Supplement* at p. 8–11.

would have rendered great service to the compelling principle of distinction and protection of non-combatants.

The German Manual The 1992 German tri-service *Manual* essentially restates the relevant provisions of the First Additional Protocol. Perfidy is thus given a general definition as comprising 'acts misleading the adverse party to believe that there is a situation affording protection under international law (e.g. humanitarian agreement to suspend combat with the intention of attacking by surprise the adversary relying on it)'.[102] Explicitly prohibited are the 'improper use of a flag of truce, enemy or neutral national flags, military insignia and uniforms as well as of special internationally acknowledged protective emblems, e.g. the red cross or the red crescent'.[103] On the other hand, ruses of war and the employment of measures necessary for obtaining information about the enemy are declared permissible such as 'the use of enemy signals, passwords, signs, decoys, etc.; not, however, espionage'.[104]

More specifically, as far as the law of naval operations is concerned, the German *Manual* remains faithful to the idea of customary peculiarities of naval warfare, such as the legitimacy of approaching the enemy under false flags, closely following Article 39§3 of the 1977 Geneva Protocol; 'unlike land and aerial warfare, naval warfare permits the use of false flags or military emblems. Before opening fire, however, the true flag shall always be displayed.'[105] As regards the arming of merchantmen, the *Manual* does not contain any provision unreservedly forbidding that practice, but neither does it qualify it as generally acceptable. According to para.1025, for instance, enemy merchant ships may be treated as military objectives if *inter alia* they are attacking other merchant ships or actively resisting

[102]See *ZDv 15/2 Humanitäres Völkerrecht in bewaffneten Konflikten – Handbuch* [Humanitarian Law in Armed Conflicts – Manual], August 1992 at para.472.
[103]*Ibid.* at para.473.
[104]*Ibid.* at para.471.
[105]*Ibid.* at para.1018. See also para.1019 which reads as follows: 'perfidy is prohibited also in naval warfare. In particular, it is prohibited to misuse the emblem of the Red Cross or to give a ship, in some other way, the looks of a hospital ship for the purpose of camouflage. It is also prohibited to make improper use of other distinctive signs equal in status with that of the Red Cross and of the flag of truce, or to feign surrender or to feign distress by sending a distress signal or by the crew taking to life rafts.'

visit, search or capture, which would of course imply the presence of weapons systems on board.[106] Overall, one may reasonably conclude that the German *Manual* is clearly against the legitimization of adding firing power to merchant vessels.

5 Fresh academic initiatives

The San Remo Manual The document in its finalized form, adopted at Livorno in June 1994, devotes three paragraphs to the legal parameters of deception in sea warfare. Those provisions appear to be the product of an attempt to apply Articles 37–39 of the Geneva Protocol in the naval context eschewing critical evaluation or suggestions for reform. Thus, the false flag anomaly which has crept into Article 39§3 of the First Additional Protocol, has also found its way in para.110 of the *San Remo Manual* at the eleventh hour since it was omitted in the so-called Harmonized Text of March 1994; 'ruses of war are permitted. Warships and auxiliary vessels, however, are prohibited from launching an attack whilst flying a false flag.'[107]

Moreover, the *Manual* follows closely the distinction drawn in Article 38 and Article 37§1 of the Protocol between the mere improper use of recognized emblems and perfidious acts of simulation. Thus:

> warships and auxiliary vessels, are prohibited at all times from actively simulating the status of:
>
> (a) hospital ships, small coastal rescue craft or medical transports;
> (b) vessels on humanitarian missions;
> (c) passenger vessels carrying civilian passengers;
> (d) vessels protected by the United Nations flag;
> (e) vessels guaranteed safe conduct by prior agreement between the parties, including cartel vessels;

[106]With reference to neutral merchant ships, para.1139 simply stipulates that ships resisting inspection 'may be damaged or destroyed if it is not possible to prevent them from continuing their voyage by any other means'. As it is formulated, this proviso may well allude to an attempt of fleeing rather than to armed resistance.

[107]It is noteworthy that in order to underscore the uniqueness of naval usage in this respect, para.109 expressly provides that 'military and auxiliary aircraft are prohibited at all times from feigning exempt, civilian or neutral status'.

(f) vessels entitled to be identified by the emblem of the red cross or red crescent;
(g) vessels engaged in transporting cultural property under special protection.[108]

On the other hand, perfidy goes beyond the false pretence of protected status being associated with the fact of launching an attack whilst feigning innocence. By way of example, the Manual stipulates that:

> perfidious acts include the launching of an attack while feigning:
>
> (a) exempt civilian, neutral or protected United Nations status;
> (b) surrender or distress by, for example, sending a distress signal or by the crew taking to life rafts.[109]

On the issue of the permissibility of arming merchantmen, the *San Remo Manual* addresses enemy and neutral vessels separately. With regard to enemy ships, it appears that a limited belligerent right of arming merchantmen is recognized. This conclusion is derived from para.60(f) of the *Manual* which provides that one of the activities which may render enemy

[108]See *San Remo Manual on International Law Applicable to Armed Conflicts at Sea,* Prepared by a Group of International Lawyers and Naval Experts, June 1994 [hereinafter *Manual*] at para.110. The accompanying *Commentary* stresses that 'in order to commit a violation, the warship must actively endeavour to establish its identity as one of the vessels mentioned under this paragraph . . . This prohibited simulation could be achieved by using means of communications and terminology reserved for the shipping concerned'; see *Commentary on the Harmonized Document on International Humanitarian Law Applicable to Armed Conflicts at Sea,* Geneva, March 1994 [hereinafter *Commentary*] at para.110.2. The expression 'active simulation' is used here as the equivalent of the term 'deliberate misuse' employed in Article 38§1 of the 1977 Protocol. On that term, see the remarks of SANDOZ, SWINARSKI and ZIMMERMANN, *op. cit., supra* n.83, §§1549–50 at pp. 456–7. Concerning the use of UN colours, it should be noted that according to the *Harmonized Text* the use of the UN distinctive emblem should be prohibited 'except when the United Nations is a party to the conflict', an expression which was finally omitted in the *San Remo Manual. Cf.* the commentary on Article 38§2 of the First Protocol by SANDOZ, SWINARSKI and ZIMMERMANN, *op. cit., supra* n.83, §1509 at p. 439 and §1560 at p. 459.

[109]See *Manual* at para.111. While the Commentary adds a most important note: 'the examples provided in sub-paragraph (a) and (b) are self-explanatory. The crucial element in the examples listed is that while protected status is simulated by a warship or military aircraft, an act of hostility is prepared and executed. The Round Table therefore was of the view that the former British practice of Q-ships is no longer acceptable'; see *Commentary* at para.111.2.

merchant vessels military objectives and thus liable to attack on sight is that of 'being armed to an extent that they could inflict damage to a warship'.[110] This implies *a contrario,* therefore, that a level of armament which would represent no threat for a naval combatant would be acceptable and would not compromise the civilian character of the ship in question. In the same clause, it is further specified that 'light individual weapons for the defence of personnel, e.g., against pirates, and purely deflective systems such as "chaff" are excluded from the type of arms which would justify an attack'.[111]

As far as neutral merchantmen are concerned, para.69 in a somewhat cryptic fashion, stipulates that 'the mere fact that a neutral merchant vessel is armed provides no grounds for attacking it'. This clause would seem to once again implicitly support the legality of the much contested practice of installing heavy armaments on merchant bottoms. The astonishingly laconic *Commentary* confuses the matter further by stating that: 'piracy remains a genuine threat in some areas of the world. Further, under traditional law, merchant vessels may be armed, at times quite heavily, for self defence.'[112] The reference to modern peacetime threats to maritime navigation and piracy is believed to be largely irrelevant here since the real question involves fitting out merchant platforms with combat weapons systems in the context of naval armed conflict rather than the

[110]According to para.60(e), 'actively resisting visit, search or capture' might also endanger the destruction of the merchant ship.

[111]The *Commentary* at para.60.14 reads as follows: 'under the traditional law, enemy merchant vessels could be equipped with defensive weapons but were subject to attack on sight if they were equipped with offensive weapons. Paragraph 60 (f) changes the traditional law because in light of modern weapons, it is impossible to determine, if it ever was possible, whether the armament on merchant ships is to be used offensively or merely defensively. It is unrealistic to expect enemy forces to be able to make that determination. Enemy merchant vessels which are armed to the extent that they could damage any warship, including a submarine, may be attacked on sight. In this context, the ship's bow, which could be used to ram a submarine, is not considered to be a weapon. The ship's crew may be armed with personal weapons such as rifles or pistols, particularly in waters where piracy is prevalent, and the ship may be equipped with deflective systems such as "chaff" without the vessel being classified as armed'. See also *ibid.* at para.60.13.

[112]See *Commentary* at para.69.1. In another proviso, the *Manual* concedes a belligerent right to attack neutral merchant vessels if they *inter alia* 'intentionally and clearly refuse to stop, or intentionally and clearly resist visit, search and capture', which might include attack by opening fire and would thus presuppose preinstalled armaments; see para.67(a). See also *Commentary* at paras.67.1–67.27.

presence of small arms for personal use which was never a matter of controversy. As for the reference to a customary right of arming under the traditional law, despite the confident tone, it is a most disputed proposition which would need considerable elaboration.

In short, the Round Table of Experts steered away from openly codifying a right of arming belligerent or neutral merchant ships, but indirectly acknowledged the possibility of such a situation arising in practice and outlined the legal consequences which would thereby arise. The reviewed paragraphs, however, fragmented and poorly buttressed, are certainly not amongst the most convincing statements of the San Remo document. One can seriously doubt the propriety of replacing the problematic notion of defensive/offensive nature of arms with another equally unworkable concept of a 'firing power level sufficient to inflict damage'. This provision could prove even dangerous to the degree that it might justify the destruction on sight of any – however lightly – armed merchant ship on the (correct) assumption that modern warships can suffer considerably from even the lowest level of armed force.[113]

IV The legal theory at sea: the doctrinal discussion

The Lethal Disguise of Mystery Ships Although the literature on the adventurous voyages of Q-ships and secret raiders is plentiful, commentaries on their legal merits are rare. Jacques Bruneau, probably convinced that men-of-war are entitled to undertake whatever trickery they see fit, disposes easily of the question by concluding that 'toutes ces ruses ayant trait au camouflage des bateaux de guerre, sont parfaitement licites, car elles consistent uniquement à cacher à l'ennemi quelque chose qu'il aurait intérêt à savoir, et ce n'est évidemment pas à son ennemi de le prévenir de ces actes qui n'agissent pas directe-

[113]Moreover, the idea of 'damage' was left totally unqualified and could thus cover material harm of practically any nature (not to mention the fact that inflicting damage to an aircarft carrier would necessitate a level of firepower distinctly superior to that needed against a wooden-hull minesweeper). By way of illustration, it should be recalled that at the peak of the US intervention in the Gulf Tanker War, there was considerable concern about the vulnerability of the US Aegis-class cruisers' radar system – the ship's critical nerve centre – even when faced with the machine-gun fire of Iranian speedboats.

ment sur lui, mais qui ont pour but de l'induire en erreur dans ses appréciations des forces et des caractères de son ennemi'.[114] Even if one concedes, together with those who when speaking of the Q-ships crewmen praised 'the martyrdom of some forty or fifty brave fellows who had challenged death in order to deal out death by stratagem',[115] that such practice needed a great deal of nerve, the fact remains that it consisted of using the false cover of neutral and non-combatant status in order to engage the enemy.

With no intention to enter the *vexata quaestio*, or better the circular reasoning, as to whether the Q-ships device might be regarded as a legitimate measure of belligerent reprisals against the unlawful U-boat tactics, or instead, whether unrestrained submarine warfare was lawfully resorted to in retaliation for the generalized arming of merchantmen and the use of false flags, one has to admit that the British decoy ships contributed significantly to the escalation of war, making the rupture with the rule of law a foregone conclusion. As René Bourdoncle observed, 'la ruse des bateaux-pièges, le camouflage des croiseurs auxiliaries ont beaucoup contribué à cette dégradation du droit international'.[116]

Notwithstanding the pitfalls of the 1907 Hague Convention VII relating to the conversion of merchant ships into warships,

[114]See BRUNEAU, J., *op. cit., supra* n.14 at p. 73. In several war chronicles narrating the peculiar hunting operations of the disguised merchant vessels, an effort is made to present Q-ships tactics as little differing in substance from the allegedly well-established usage of false flags. Rear-Admiral Gordon Campbell, for example, who served as a mystery ship captain, begins his wartime memoirs in these words: 'il ne faut pas s'imaginer que les navires mystérieux sont une invention de cette guerre, car les tentatives pour tromper l'ennemi sont aussi vieilles que possible. L'emploi de faux pavillons nationaux est un très vieil usage, et il est tout à fait naturel que des officiers entreprenants aient essayé d'aller un peu plus loin pour déguiser leurs navires et aient inventé d'autres ruses'; see CAMPBELL, op. cit., supra n.15 at p. 20.

[115]See BYWATER, H.C. and FERRABY, H.C., *Strange Intelligence – Memoirs of Naval Secret Service*, 1931 at p. 207.

[116]See BOURDONCLE, *op. cit., supra* n.12 at p. 69. In the words of another writer, 'it would seem that the British were not entirely guiltless in bringing about a hardening of the U-boat war'; see HAMPSHIRE, *op. cit., supra* n.15 at p. 19. It is important to note at this point that the British Admiralty never advanced the thesis that the Q-ships strategy was contrived in return of the indiscriminate submarine attacks. The fact remains that by February 1917, when the unrestricted submarine campaign was officially announced, the German fleet had already lost seven of its U-boats due to surprise attacks by the so-called *bateaux pièges*. For all practical reasons, the cat-and-mouse game between the mystery ships and the submarines was over by the second year of the war already.

the British mystery ships, and to a lesser extent the German auxiliary cruisers, directly contravened certain provisions of the Convention, such as Article 2 which obliges converted ships to 'bear the external marks which distinguish the warships of their nationality', and Article 6 which requires belligerents to 'announce such conversion in the list of warships'.[117] As for the new definition of perfidy, announced in Article 37 of the 1977 First Additional Protocol, it is indeed difficult to see how the *bateaux-pièges* device could stay out of its scope and avoid the rebuke of perfidy. To borrow from the wording of the latter article, the 'feigning of an intent to surrender' (through the attitude of the 'panic party'), the 'feigning of civilian, non-combatant status', as well as the 'feigning of protected status by the use of neutral signs and emblems', were all central elements of the ploy.

The Case Against Armed Merchantmen The practices of arming merchantmen and flying false flags were not, as some would seem to suggest, uncontested. Both usages have excited vivid debate and unanimity was never reached among the authorities of international law. The experience of the World Wars only amplified the tenacity against the disorderly methods which, under the pretext of coping with the submarine threat, contributed to further lawlessness. Turning the entire merchant navy into a fleet of quasi-combatants, or ordering the systematic feigning of neutral colours, were, no doubt, partly to blame for the viciousness and confusion with which both the Great Wars were fought at sea.

[117]In one of the earliest critiques, a British naval officer, writing in 1923, expressed scepticism as to the licit and opportune character of resorting to Q-ship tactics; 'its legitimacy is somewhat obscure and liable to give offence to neutrals . . . it is very hard to reconcile our legal consciences should we tackle the problem from another standpoint – that of the conversion of a merchant ship into a man-of-war, which in fact is what we do to the decoy ship . . . from a pure moral standpoint we cannot disregard the fact that a certain onus is attached to deception. The Navy is a proud Service, and straightforwardness has always appealed to it'; see STEELE, G.C., 'Decoy as a Weapon in Naval Warfare', 68 *Journal of the Royal United Services Institution* (1923) at pp. 107–8. Moreover, on a number of occasions the disguised vessels acted in open violation of the 1907 Hague Convention XI relative to certain restrictions with regard to the exercise of the right of capture in naval war, Article 3§3 of which stipulates that belligerents must not 'take advantage of the harmless character of the said [fishing/local trade] vessels in order to use them for military purposes while preserving their peaceful appearance'.

However, collective as well as individual, academic and political efforts were made to retrace the line separating the status of civilian mariners from that of commissioned naval officers, and eventually the fates of coastal trawlers from that of ironclads.[118] According to Article 14 of the 1922 Washington Treaty on the Limitation of Armament, 'no preparations shall be made in merchant ships in time of peace for the installation of warlike armaments for the purpose of converting such ships into vessels of war, other than the necessary stiffening of decks for the mounting of guns not exceeding 6 inch (152 millimetres) calibre'.[119] The drafters of the Havana Convention on Maritime Neutrality of 1928 did not find it difficult in Article 12 to assimilate armed merchantmen to warships, auxiliary ships or formally converted vessels as far as 'the sojourn, supplying, and provisioning of belligerent ships in the ports of neutrals are concerned'.[120] While the Harvard Research on the Rights and Duties of Neutrals, drafted eleven years later, specified unreservedly that 'belligerent merchant vessels, whether surface or submarine, shall, if armed for defense or offense, be assimilated to warships'.[121]

For Charles Cheney Hyde, 'the merchantman when equipped with a gun of great destructive force and long range becomes itself a valuable weapon of offense . . . Thus the armed merchantman although its chief mission be the transportation of passengers and freight, becomes necessarily a participant in the conflict . . . Indeed, the development of armed merchantmen

[118]Already in 1917, a Committee of the Grotius Society, reflecting on the legal status of submarines, recommended that the practice of arming merchantmen should be considered unlawful. In the mind of the authors of that report, 'it is impossible to frame any satisfactory definition of the phrase armament for defensive purposes'; see 4 *GST* (1918) at p. xlii. According to the same proposals, 'a neutral merchantman should not under any circumstances be entitled to resist visit and search or capture [when duly exercised] by a belligerent submarine or other war vessel'; *ibid.* at p. xliii. *Cf.* the dissenting view of John MacDonell, ibid., p. xliv*ff*.

[119]See 16 *AJIL* (1922) *Suppl.* at p. 45. Although the clause makes explicit reference to the possibility of mounting guns of a prescribed calibre, it is evident that such eventuality was only envisaged for the purpose of *formally* converting merchant vessels into warships in accordance with the conditions set out in Hague Convention VII of 1907, and consequently is not at all related to the occasional arming of merchant bottoms.

[120]See 22 *AJIL* (1928) *Suppl.* at p. 154.

[121]See the commentary on Article 2, 33 *AJIL* (1939) *Suppl.*, p. 224*ff*.

as an institution may lead to sorry consequences.'[122] The 'only sound position' – wrote George Grafton Wilson – 'seems to be that a vessel entitled to be treated as a merchant vessel both by neutral and belligerent shall have an unequivocal status. This can be based only upon a prohibition of armament, and then aircraft, submarines or other vessels of war in dealing with merchant vessels can find no justification for failure to observe the laws of war'.[123] While for Robert Tucker:

> it is not easy to see why belligerent merchant vessels may be armed for the sole purpose of attacking enemy submarines on sight, but enemy submarines considered as without a similar right to take 'defensive' measures by attacking armed merchant vessels on sight . . . Yet the fact remains that the initial British decision to arm merchant vessels was taken prior to World War I. More important were the circumstances in which merchant vessels were armed and directed to use their arms, circumstances which hardly allowed the assumption that these vessels retained a peaceful and strictly non-combatant status.[124]

[122]See HYDE, C.C., *Maritime War*, 1918 at pp. 19–20. In another writing it has been pertinently remarked that 'the supposed distinction between offensive and defensive armament becomes not merely metaphysical but unintelligent'; see BORCHARD and LAGE, *op. cit., supra* n.28 at p. 86.

[123]See WILSON, G.G., 'Armed Merchant Vessels and Submarines', 24 *AJIL* (1930) at pp. 338–9. As Herbert Arthur Smith commented after the Second World War, 'in both of the world wars this reliance by the Allies on a technical right surviving from the past undoubtedly played straight into the hands of the enemy. Whether the Germans would in any case have obeyed any rules which did not suit them may perhaps be doubted, but it is undeniable that Allied practice gave them at least a plausible excuse for claiming that it was no longer practicable to distinguish at sea between one ship and another. Thus insistence upon a technical right was allowed to defeat the essential purpose of the law'; see SMITH, H.A., *The Law and Custom of the Sea*, 3rd edn (1959) at pp. 117–18.

[124]See TUCKER, R., *The Law of War and Neutrality at Sea*, USNWC, 50 *International Law Studies* (1955) at pp. 61–2. See also RONZITTI, N., 'Le droit humanitaire applicable aux conflits armés en mer', 242 *RCADI* (1993) at p. 106. *Cf.* the view of Karl Zemanek who holds that 'by simply being armed, a merchant ship is not transformed into an auxiliary cruiser', and that 'the arming of merchant ships is a lawful but "risky" act (like espionage) which because of its extremely dangerous potential effect on enemy submarines and aircraft, entitles the latter to take appropriate pre-emptive strikes against such enemy armed merchant ships'; see ZEMANEK, K., 'Merchant Ships, Armed' in BERNHARDT, R. (ed.), *Encyclopedia of Public International Law*, instalment 3 (1982) at pp. 258–9.

its merchantmen'.[127] Likewise, Article 20§1 of the 1939 Harvard Research on the Rights and Duties of Neutrals in Naval War also provided that belligerents were under an obligation to forbid their merchant vessels to simulate the appearance of neutral ships.[128]

Several scholars have also pleaded the suppression of the abusive display of neutral or enemy flags. In one of the most influential writings of the past century, it was asserted that 'le combat sous pavillon étranger est un acte de félonie; il est réputé acte de *piraterie*: ce serait vainement qu'on voudrait faire envisager *comme une ruse permise* pour surprendre l'ennemi, de s'être avancé vers lui, couvert d'un pavillon ami. Si, dans certaines circonstances, *la ruse est licite,* c'est uniquement, quand elle ne blesse ni l'honneur ni la morale.'[129] William Edward Hall was the first to point out the unreasonable nature of a rule which would prohibit a method of deception but only as long as there is no more use of employing it; 'it is not easy to see why it is more disloyal to wear a disguise when it is absolutely useless, than when it serves its purpose'.[130]

[127]See 4 *GST* (1918) at p.l. While in another draft, undertaken by the International Law Association in 1920, it was stipulated unconditionally: 'a merchant vessel, whether belligerent or neutral, *shall not, under any circumstances, fly a false flag or wear false colours'* (emphasis added); see Article 17B in 29 *Rep.ILA* (1920), Portsmouth Conf. at p. 172. The prohibition, however, referred to merchant vessels only and thus, left the question open as to the legitimacy of warships cruising under false flags. It is to be noted also that according to Article 19 of the 1923 Hague Rules of Aerial Warfare 'the use of false external marks is forbidden', while several states and prominently the United States had proposed that the misuse of foreign flags in air warfare should warrant the death punishment.

[128]See 33 *AJIL* (1939) *Suppl.*, p. 353*ff.* The draft convention remained silent, however, as to the use of neutral flags as a *ruse de guerre* by warships because neutrals are 'only indirectly concerned' in this latter case; see the commentary, *ibid.* at p. 359.

[129]See DE CUSSY, F., *Phases et causes célèbres du droit maritime des nations,* tome I (1856) at p. 257. *Antoine Pillet,* for his part, held that 'cette surprise n'est pas de celles que l'usage de la guerre peut autoriser. Sur un champ également ouvert aux belligérants et aux neutres, comme l'est la pleine mer, il ne faut pas qu'une équivoque habilement entretenue puisse aboutir à la perte d'un vaisseau qui n'a eu d'autre tort que de respecter la valeur conventionnelle du signe sous lequel son adversaire s'est abrité'; see PILLET, A., 'Le libre usage du pavillon en temps de guerre maritime – Nécessité de réforme', 5 *RGDIP* (1898) at p. 446.

[130]See HALL, W.E., *A Treatise on International Law,* 8th edn (1924) at p. 649. His argument was taken up four decades later by Myres McDougal: 'there is some practice to this effect, that to fly a neutral or enemy flag, so long as a warship strikes her true colors before commencing attack, is "perfectly legitimate". The logic of these assertions is not self-evident. They are open to the interpretation

To quote once more Herbert Arthur Smith, such usage should be deemed as outdated as the days of pirates and privateers:

> in earlier times there were good reasons for the old rule . . . but today the rule would seem to be an anachronism, one of those survivals which in law so often outlive their proper function. If the anomalous practices of the two world wars are not to become permanent, it is clear that we should aim at restoring, so far as possible, the traditional distinction between combatant and non-combatant ships, between ships which may lawfully be sunk at sight and those which, unless they resist, may only be halted for visit and search.[131]

Robert Tucker, although convinced that 'the use of false colors by belligerent warships is clearly permitted by custom', admits that 'the criticisms raised against the ruse is not without substantial merit'.[132] Among the academics involved in the current discussion on the laws of war at sea, Frits Kalshoven, referring to the 'ancient practice of approaching the adversary under

---

that the ruse becomes impermissible only from the moment its further use is rendered unnecessary, the deceitful force or warship having been enabled to assume a posture favorable for attack'; see McDOUGAL, M.S. and FELICIANO, F.P., *Law and Minimum World Public Order*, 1961 at p. 670.

[131]See SMITH, *op. cit., supra* n.123 at pp. 116–17.

[132]See TUCKER, *op. cit., supra* n.124 at pp. 140, 142. See also CASTRÉN, E., *The Present Law of War and Neutrality*, 1954 at p. 265; 'for reasons of principle – and evidently quite rightly – most authors condemn the use of a false flag both at sea and on land as being a deceitful mode of warfare, but practice is different'. Writing in 1974, Dieter Fleck affirms that 'the use of such [false] flags for the purpose of deception has been a controversial issue at all times', without arriving at any conclusive answers. In his study he draws a distinction between warships and merchant ships. As for the former, he seems favourable to a principle according to which 'flying false flags would be permissible only in self-defence and not with a view to fulfilling a specific military mission', recognizing all the same that the 'flying of false flags is much closer to perfidy than other ruses of war', while in the case of merchant ships 'it would be desirable for international law to adopt the principle that merchant vessels are not entitled to use the flags of foreign countries if this would pose an additional danger to the ships of the countries concerned'; see FLECK, *op. cit., supra* n.12 at pp. 294, 295. Jean de Preux who signed the commentary of Article 39§3 of the First Additional Protocol, published by the ICRC in 1987, appears equally undecided. For one thing, he asserts that 'it is true that when a *warship during pursuit* displays the *enemy* or a *neutral* flag, such conduct at sea is accepted, or at least tolerated, whether the ship in question is pursuing an enemy ship or is trying to escape from it'. Yet, his reference to 'complex rules which cannot be changed without a thorough study' is suggestive of his uncertainty; see SANDOZ, SWINARSKI and ZIMMERMAN, *op. cit., supra* n.83, §1582 at p. 470. Similarly, see RONZITTI, *op.cit., supra* n.124 at p. 105.

cover of a false flag', notes that 'it is doubted even in naval circles whether this practice should be maintained as a legitimate method of waging naval warfare'.[133]

From 1988 to 1994, the legal rules applicable to modern naval operations received fresh attention from scholars in the context of the so-called Madrid Plan of Action which saw a number of academics, experts from the Red Cross movement, and naval officers gather annually. At the Bochum Round Table of November 1989 the issue of ruses of war in naval warfare was raised on a number of occasions but was made the object of a rather cursory discussion. William Fenrick acting as Rapporteur went a certain way in attacking the relevant provisos of the First Additional Protocol, especially doubting the utility of the false flag rule in those words: 'one might question whether certain aspects of it [the law concerning ruses of war and perfidy in a naval setting], in particular the false flag rule, are not anachronistic and harmful to the underlying principles of the law of armed conflict when one considers the current state of weapons technology . . . It is unlikely that targeting decisions in a high technology naval conflict would be made at ranges where the colour of a flag flown by a ship would be a relevant consideration.'[134] In what concerns the defensive armament of merchant

[133]See KALSHOVEN, F., *Constraints on the Waging of War*, 1987 at p. 84. According to the suggestion of yet another scholar, 'sailing under false colours should be *strictly* prohibited and doing so should amount to perfidy. This rule is essential for the protection of immune vessels and for neutral states'; see DOSWALD-BECK, L., 'The International Law of Naval Armed Conflicts: The Need for Reform', 7 *It.YIL* (1986–7) at p. 281. As for recent practice, to the best of writer's knowledge, there is no verified information suggesting that any merchant vessels or warships, whether belligerent or neutral, venturing in the Gulf in the years 1981–8 made use of false flags. According to a recent source, however, 'most tankers in the Gulf during the war were at pains to wear no flag, and some wore counterfeit flags – the old offense of masquerade'; see WISWALL, F.L., 'Neutrality, the Rights of Shipping and the Use of Force in the Persian Gulf', 31 *VJIL* (1991), ftn.4 at p. 620. What is known with certitude, on the contrary, is that Iran made extensive use of decoys (dummy tankers and oil rigs) to decrease the efficacy of Iraqi air raids on Kharg Island; see *Middle East Military Balance* (1987–8) at p. 236. According to other reports, the shuttle service between Kharg and Larak islands was aslo protected by the deployment of barges as lure targets anchored along the route used by the chartered tankers; see OUDOT de DAINVILLE, A., 'Analyse de la guerre du Golfe', 44 *Défense Nationale* (Oct.1988) at p. 55, and SCHILLER, T.S., 'The Gulf War and Shipping: Recent Developments' in Parritt, B.A.H. (ed.), *Violence at Sea*, 1986 at p. 113.

[134]See FENRICK, W.J., 'Introductory Report – Military Objectives in the Law of Naval Warfare' in VON HEINEGG, H.W. (ed.), *The Military Objective and the Principle of Distinction in the Law of Naval Warfare – Report, Commentaries and*

ships, Fenrick concluded as follows: 'enemy merchant vessels may be attacked and destroyed when they are armed; the old concept of defensively armed merchant vessels is an anachronism'.[135]

The discussions of the Round Table resulted in a draft document which read in part: 'the following activities are liable to render enemy merchant vessels military objectives: (f) they are armed to an extent that they could inflict damage to a warship

---

Proceedings of the Round Table of Experts on International Humanitarian Law Applicable to Armed Conflicts at Sea, Bochum, Nov.10–14, 1989, 1991 at pp. 38–9. He sounded, however, sceptical as for the prospects of codification: 'it is clear that the identification issue is ripe for reconsideration. One should not, however, presume that such a reconsideration would be a simple task. It is relatively easy for states to agree not to abuse protective signs for a small number of immune objects such as hospital ships and medical transports. It may be much more difficult to reach agreement to consider warships disguised as neutral ships or as merchant vessels and belligerent merchant vessels disguised as neutral vessels as engaging in perfidious acts because states at war may gain substantial military benefits from such practices', *ibid.* at p. 40. Note also the commentary of O. Bring, *ibid.* at p. 47: 'it is also meaningful to change the traditional false flag rule, not because it would be of substantial importance in modern naval combat, but because the present legal permissibility of feigning civilian or neutral status blurs the principle of distinction upon which the law of warfare is built and confuses the clear-cut message the law should convey'. I.A. Shearer suggested that an 'effort should be made to abandon the old rules and to replace them with rules consonant with present realities and humanitarian concerns'. As he pointed out, 'the supposed generally recognized rules of international law applicable to the use of flags in the conduct of armed conflict at sea, specifically exempted from the prohibition of perfidy by Geneva Protocol I (1977) Article 39(3), have not commanded universal acceptance in the past . . . It is significant that no codification of the law of armed conflict at sea has positively endorsed the use of false colours or feigned status . . . Second, it is highly artificial to distinguish between perfidious and allowable ruses de guerre simply on the temporal criterion of opening fire'; *ibid.* at p. 73. For similar remarks, see D. Fleck, *ibid.* at p. 52, L. Doswald-Beck, *ibid.* at p. 76, and B. Godet, *ibid.* at p. 137. *Cf.* G.J.F. van Hegelsom, *ibid.* at p. 105. However atypical, the view was also defended that the practice of flying false flags instead of fading out has inspired comparable rules in the law of land warfare. G. Venturini, for instance, recognized in the provisions of Geneva Protocol I which allow a lawful combatant to hide his arms, provided that he carries them openly while he is engaged in a military deployment preceding an attack, a legal condition reminiscent of the rule that a warship must show her true colours before firing. Consequently, he argued, 'it may be questioned if the use of false colours is rather an early indicator of later trends than a legal anachronism in the law of armed conflicts'; *ibid.* at p. 131. In the event, the debate confirmed William Fenrick's fears. The participants were only unanimous insofar as feigning of protected status was concerned such as hospital ships or cartel vessels. On the contrary, the question of the deceptive use of enemy and neutral flags could not be resolved during the Bochum session and discussion was deferred for later meetings; *ibid.* at p. 177.

[135]*Ibid.* at p. 42. *Cf.* W.H. v. Heinegg, *ibid.* at p. 93, H. Fischer, *ibid.* at p. 97, F. Kalshoven, *ibid.* at p. 128, D.B. Rurikov, *ibid.* at p. 139.

(this excludes light individual weapons for the defense of personnel, e.g. against pirates, and purely deflective systems such as "chaff")'.[136] The next session of the Round Table of Experts, held in 1990 at Toulon, was devoted to the discussion of methods and means of combat in naval warfare. The introductory report by G.J.F. van Hegelsom, however, made only fugacious reference to the issues of ruses and perfidy. Regrettably enough, the debate seemed again consumed in reflecting upon the pertinence of the old false flag usage. The Rapporteur's main suggestion was that the rule should be modified and perhaps retailored along the model of Article 44 of the First Additional Protocol. His proposition implied that the already debatable practice would be recognized lawful as long as a vessel does not take part in a naval engagement, or in a 'visible deployment preceding the launching of an attack'.[137]

[136]*Ibid.* at p. 176. See also *supra* notes 110–113 and accompanying text. It is noteworthy also that the prevailing current trend as evidenced in most of the national manuals on the law of naval warfare is that armed enemy merchantmen are to be presumed as incorporated into the enemy war effort and thus liable to attack and destruction; see, for example, para.717 of the Canadian draft manual (1984) and para.822 of the Australian manual (1983) as quoted by Fenrick, *ibid.* at pp. 32–3. *Cf.* Article 2 of the 1965 French manual, *ibid.* at p. 34. According to some sources, the oil tankers employed by Iran in the shuttle service from Kharg to Sirri and later to Larak islands were fitted out with chaff launchers; see OUDOT de DAINVILLE, *op. cit., supra* n.133 at p. 55.

[137]See VAN HEGELSOM, G.J.F., 'Introductory Report – Methods and Means of Combat in Naval Warfare', in VON HEINEGG, H.W. (ed.), *Methods and Means of Combat in Naval Warfare – Report and Commentaries of the Round Table of Experts on International Humanitarian Law Applicable to Armed Conflicts at Sea, Toulon 19–23 October 1990*, 1992 at p. 16. *Cf.* L.C. Green, *ibid.* at p. 95. It is suggested, however, that to borrow the formulation of Article 44§3 would be unfortunate since it would be notoriously difficult to cope with the very notions of visibility and aggressive deployment in a meaningful way in the modern environment of armed conflict at sea. Besides, the suitability of referring to a clause specifically devised to deal with the problem of guerrilla warfare in land warfare in order to resolve the puzzle of false colours in naval warfare may appear highly questionable. Yet, even if an analogy with Article 44§3 was to prove of some pertinence, it would only concern the conduct of warships during or prior to a naval engagement, so that the question of merchantmen flying false flags would still remain unanswered. Few would disagree, of course, with Christopher Greenwood's observation that 'the existing law on this subject is a mess' [*ibid.* at p. 100], yet one would expect more fruitful discussion in view of such a finding. One of the few well-pointed remarks came from S. Lyons who pointed out that 'this is a complex subject that goes beyond flags and false funnels and would entail consideration of a wide range of electronic deception'; *ibid.* at p. 121. Since the Toulon session, these issues have not been taken up again, the last three meetings of the Round Table of Experts being focused on subjects such as visit, search and capture, the effects of the UN Charter on the law of naval warfare, or the theatre of naval operations.

V Chivalry in the electronic age: how far immaterial?

The ethics of chivalrous conduct has, throughout the ages, shaped two complementary principles, the prohibition of perfidious killing and the idea of giving the enemy a fair chance of defending himself. These tenets, stemming from an imperative sense of military honour, later found expression in concrete rules of law. Article 42§2 of the First Additional Protocol, for instance, referring to persons parachuting from an aircraft in distress, requires that these persons 'shall be given an opportunity to surrender before being made the object of attack', while Article 41§2(c) proscribes attacking an enemy *hors de combat*, that is to say, 'incapable of defending himself'. In a more general sense, the quest for increased protection of the civilian population which was the driving element of the Diplomatic Conference adheres to the same logic that the party who lacks the means of offering an armed resistance deserves protection and respect.

Nowadays, however, the increasing use of space-based technology and avant-garde electronic gadgetry to engage the enemy tends to turn the notion of chivalry obsolete, not to say meaningless. Devising an electronic checkmate may in certain cases significantly dilute the idea of fair play. In the case of a clearly inferior adversary unable to call upon similar electronic warfare capabilities, the contest could easily turn into a graceless chase of a 'sitting duck', for knocking out the enemy defences through sheer control of the electromagnetic field may lead to fighting an *a priori hors de combat* enemy in a general sense. Recent practice, although not of a naval character, spares us the task of resorting to fiction. In 1991, the troops of the international coalition, equipped with the best the western world had to offer in military sophistication, ruined the Iraqi army over a terrain where no courage or determination could match software. Experts unanimously stated that 'the credit for emasculating the Iraqi air defence assets must lie with the electronic developments that have now effectively blinded this type of weapon system. Electronic warfare was arguably the decisive element of the air campaign.'[138] The phenomenal unevenness of the Gulf

[138]See ESHEL, T., 'The Most Successful Air Campaign Ever?', 15 *Military Technology* (1991), no.4 at p. 38. It has now been established that in the first 48 hours or so of the campaign all Iraqi threat acquisition and early warning radars had been blinded, destroyed or forced to switch off. As it has been recently written,

duellists in advanced matériel, electronic warfare assets, and space-based support technology, soon led analysts to speak of a massacre.[139]

Prospects and Problems of Electronic Warfare Deception in modern warfare lies essentially with the amazing and ever-expanding sector of electronic warfare. Contact with the enemy comes, if at all, through computer screens and digital readouts, bloodshed is turned impersonal. In this age of contactless killing, the chances of survival depend less on skilful manoeuvring and more on ungovernable computing of some built-in homing device in a weapon warhead. Deception boils down to a contest of the artificial intelligence of electronically controlled weapons (the frequent allusion to weapons' 'smartness' is telling). In most cases, victory is to be claimed only by the weapon system which can offer the largest reserve of counter-measures. The margins for makeshift instruments and improvisation, therefore, seem extremely narrowed; 'the history of camouflage' – wrote Guy Hartcup – 'has now passed from the stage of inspired improvis-

---

'victory was virtually assured already during the night of Jan. 17, when the massive air assault neutralised the entire Iraqi command and control infrastructure . . . With the command and control structure totally deaf and blind, Saddam's military commanders were completely unaware of the coalition's intentions or their movements on the ground'; see ESHEL, D., 'Desert Storm: A Textbook Victory', 15 *Military Technology* (1991) at p. 29. As a result of what was aptly called 'Nintendo war', the Iraqis were compelled, as some analysts have pictured it, 'to look at the skies through a straw'. Having been deprived of any capability of either detecting or targeting, their only option was to resort to desperate mass flak fire. The televised pictures of the early Baghdad bombing were in fact a futile barrage of confused, random gunfire against invisible bombers delivering their payloads thousands of feet above the effective range of anti-aircraft shelling. Note, for instance, the following commentary: 'there is an age old fighter pilot adage that "you can't fight what you can't see" and it was true enough for the Iraqis in this war as well. When one combines stealth, surprise, large numbers, good coordination and healthy doses of effective electronic warfare, open wonderment at the feeble Iraqi resistance and low allied losses seems a bit naive'; see SHEARER, O.V. and DASKAL, S.E., 'The DESERT "electronic warfare" STORM', 15 *Military Technology* (1991) at pp. 22–3.

[139]In the words of Anthony Preston, 'the qualitative and quantitative imbalance of forces was so great as to make the "January Massacre" a foregone conclusion'; see PRESTON, A., 'Naval Aspects of the Gulf Conflict', 15 *Military Technology* (1991), no.4 at p. 60. See also LOPEZ, G.A., 'The Gulf War: Not So Clean', 47 *Bulletin of the Atomic Scientists* (Sept.1991), no.7, p. 30*ff*., and 'Highway to Hell – Whose Victory Are We Meant to Be Celebrating?', *New Statesman*, 21 June 1991, p. 21*ff*.

ation to the province of the scientist and technologist'.[140] Modern technology has forced military thinking to accept the premise that everything is both visible and vulnerable which, of course, renders deception particularly difficult.[141]

Electronic warfare, or EW for the inevitable acronym, is generally held to be a major force multiplier in the combat environment of today and an asset which is unceasingly required. It stands for the judicious exploitation of the electromagnetic spectrum for either launching or frustrating an attack. Modern EW systems provide for integrated passive and active capabilities. Passive techniques are those used for gathering valuable intelligence information, like monitoring enemy communications, or detecting enemy radar signals. Active techniques involve disrupting the enemy's command, control and communication (C^3) networks, blinding his radar systems, and deflecting an incoming guided missile, all implying the use of electronic counter-measures (ECM).[142]

[140]See HARTCUP, *op. cit., supra* n.54 at p. 147. At the time of sophisticated night vision equipment, camouflage may well be inadequate, dazzle-painting has been outshone by stealth technology, and satellite communications have eclipsed the wireless. Fake funnels and false flags in the days of sophisticated electronic signatures, 'Friend-or-Foe' identification techniques and military satellites sound somewhat of a romance. It is not without significance that in its 1985 Report to the Congress, the US Navy affirmed that it 'is by far the largest tactical user of spaced-based systems'; see BUNN, G., 'Satellites for the Navy: Shielded by Arms Control?', 38 *US Naval War College Review* (1985), no.5 at p. 55. See also 'Military Satellite Communications', 18 *International Defense Review* (1985), no.5, p. 701*ff.* Camouflage, however, may still claim pertinence in modern strategy since the eye has not ceased to be the most frequently used sensor. On current principles of application, see ERBE, J., 'Thoughts on Camouflage and Deception', 11 *Military Technology* (1987), no.9, p. 85*ff.*, KNORPP, F., 'Camouflage and Deception – A Challenge to Army Armament', *ibid.*, p. 88*ff.*, and CORDLE, J.P., 'Welcome to Our World', 120 *USNIP* (March 1994), p. 63*ff.* On IFF, see COOMBS, L., 'Electronic Warfare: The Role of IFF', 12 *Military Technology* (1988), no.5, p. 55*ff.*

[141]Deception today, as one study concludes, 'must fool a multiplicity of sensors and systems ... Both the criticality and the difficulty of deception efforts are qualitatively magnified ... In this age of fatal visibility, we may not know that our hiding place has been detected until enemy fires descend upon us. Since we cannot securely hide, we must blind our enemies in order to guarantee that the new visibility is fatal to opposing formations and not to our own'; see PETERS, R., 'The Age of Fatal Visibility', 68 *Military Review* (1988), no.8 at p. 54.

[142]Command, control and communication counter-measures (C^3CM) systems can intercept and exploit communications, introduce false information, distort true information and, through jamming or saturation, degrade communications. Decoy launching systems (DLS), known as chaffs or expendables dispensers, on the other hand, can effectively distract the missile homing device before it

Identifying the challenges of the electronic age which international humanitarian law will have to face up to is probably as far as one can get. Ever-progressing military technology is a bare reality and, to breed no illusions, it will probably continue to evolve at its hectic pace. No serious argument could be made, therefore, for parity in firepower, much less in technological potential. This is simply to point out that electronic warfare supremacy may well convert an unequal battle, which is always conceivable, to a doomed game of one-sided cruelty, which can be legally problematic. Under such circumstances, it is submitted, electronic warfare may lie anywhere between tactical ingenuity and faceless carnage. Yet, electronic warfare as a means of reducing the adversary to a hopelessly defenceless prey should bear little relationship with a bright ruse. The changing face of war, therefore, necessitates seminal ideas to the

acquires the ship target or break lock after the missile seeker has acquired the ship as a target by producing clouds of radar reflecting articles. On electronic warfare in general, see DE ARCANGELIS, M., *Electronic Warfare: From the Battle of Tsushima to the Falklands and Lebanon Conflicts*, 1987, and DEWAR, *op. cit., supra* n.5, pp. 131–63. On the state of development of shipborne electronic warfare, see KAMHI, M., 'Shipboard EW – Growing Awareness', 18 *International Defense Review* (1985) *Suppl.*, p. 33*ff.*, and COTTON, M., 'Naval Electronic Warfare', *ibid.*, p. 43*ff.* See also SUNDARAM, G.S., 'Shipborne Electronic Warfare', 22 *International Defense Review* (1989), no.3, p. 325*ff.*, and no.5, p. 645*ff.* For more on decoy launching systems, see DUBOSE, R.L., 'Radar Decoys', 18 *International Defense Review* (Dec.1985) *Suppl.*, p. 49*ff.*, and DICKER, B., 'Rubber Duck', *ibid.*, p. 55*ff.* See also HEWISH, M., 'The Shield Naval Decoy', 16 *International Defense Review* (1983), no.4, p. 475*ff.*, DICKER, R.J.L., 'Decoying the Homing Torpedo', 18 *International Defense Review* (1985), no.2, p. 245*ff.*, and STREETLY, M., 'Expendable Decoys', 23 *International Defense Review* (1990), no.8, p. 878*ff.* During the Falkland conflict, the Royal Navy resorted to a massive use of chaff off-board decoys in an effort to divert incoming missiles. In the event, as reports suggest, no British vessel that fired decoy expendables was hit by an air-launched missile. In an unfortunate incident, however, chaffs successfully launched from the carrier *Hermes* deflected a homing Exocet and diverted its seeker to a nearby converted vessel, the *Atlantic Conveyor.* Fitting out the tankers operating in the Persian Gulf during the Iran-Iraq War with decoy launching systems was given serious consideration for quite some time in naval circles of the west. Several industries came up with prototypes especially designed for the needs and capabilities of merchant vessels. The TOAD (Towed Offboard Active Decoy), for instance, comprised a small boat carrying a sophisticated jamming device, required no inputs from the parent ship, and was completely automatic in operation; see HEWISH, M., 'Shipborne Electronic Warfare', 21 *International Defense Review* (1988), no.2 at p. 176. There have been no verified reports, however, that this or similar equipment was ever put to use throughout the tanker war. Yet, according to one writer, Iran and Kuwait deployed radar-deflecting decoy barges around their offshore oil-loading complexes with unknown results; see O'ROURKE, R., 'The Tanker War', 114 *USNIP* (May 1988) at p. 34.

crucible of humanitarian law, decidedly more future-oriented than say those underlying the false flag rule. The limitations that the principle of restraint exacts upon belligerents need urgent reassessment in the light of modern conditions.

Blinding Weapons: Does Unnecessary Suffering Need Reassessment? A last remark may further illustrate the relativity with which the prohibition of perfidy, no less than the principle of humanity, should be approached in contemporary humanitarian law. One of the new horrors in military research is the contemplated use of the laser beam for incapacitating the enemy.[143] As experts assert, 'no war instruments, including chemical and/or biological attacks, could conceivably be regarded as nastier and meaner'.[144] In a number of incidents in the last six years, the

[143]Weapons based on laser technology feature certain characteristics likely to revolutionize current patterns of conventional warfare. The laser beam is not affected by gravity and reaches the target instantaneously (the energy moving at the speed of light, roughly 300 million metres per second). If, therefore, a laser pulse is fired at an aircraft travelling at the speed of sound from a distance of 1 kilometre the aircraft will move little more than 1 millimetre during the time it takes for the laser beam to reach the target. This makes a laser device a basically zero time-of-flight weapon rendering impossible any evasive action by the target. What is more, energy is delivered along a straight line making the problems of calculating ballistic trajectories a thing of the past. Other advantages of laser radiation are that it is normally silent and invisible, and that it does not need the huge ammunition logistic support all conventional weapons systems require at present. Apart from anti-personnel use, directed-energy weapons may also find anti-matériel applications such as, for instance, shooting down cruise missiles and aircraft or destroying sensitive combat sensors and optical equipment. For more, see JOHANNSEN, M.K., 'Future Weapon: Directed Energy', 115 *USNIP* (Aug.1989), p. 99*ff.*, and ROBERTSON, H.B., 'Modern Technology and the Law of Armed Conflict at Sea' in ROBERTSON, H.B. (ed.), *The Law of Naval Operations*, USNWC, 64 *International Law Studies* (1991), at pp. 374–7. See also KOKOSKI, R., 'Non-lethal Weapons: A Case Study of New Technology Developments', *Ybk.SIPRI* (1994), p. 367*ff.*

[144]See ANDERBERG, B. and WOLBARSHT, M.L., 'Blinding Lasers: The Nastiest Weapon?', 14 *Military Technology* (1990), no.3 at p. 58. See also ICRC, *Weapons That May Cause Unnecessary Suffering or Have Indiscriminate Effects: Report on the Work of Experts*, 1973, §§235–42 at pp. 67–9, and DOSWALD-BECK, L. and CAUDERAY, G.C., 'Le développement des nouvelles armes antipersonnel', 72 *RICR* (nov.–dec.1990), no.786, p. 627*ff.* Several projects, in fact, took off as from the early 1980s on the so-called directed-energy weapons in the field of laser and high-power microwaves. The *Stingray*, for instance, a high energy laser beam weapon is known to have reached the stage of full-scale development despite ethical considerations concerning a new category of weapon which would cause permanent blindness; see SUNDARAM, G.S. and PENGELLEY, R., 'Electronic Warfare and the US Army: A Time for Reflection', 22 *International Defense Review* (1989), no.9 at p. 1244.

crews of US naval aircraft were temporarily blinded by lasers aimed directly at their cockpits, while lower-power devices, believed unable to blind pilots, were deployed with British warships during the Falkland Islands conflict.[145]

The question of the legality of the offensive use of lasers was raised for the first time at the 1974–7 Diplomatic Conference on Humanitarian Law, and again at the UN Conference on Certain Conventional Weapons in 1978 but without any concrete results. In 1986, at the XXV International Conference of the Red Cross, Switzerland and Sweden proposed the prohibition of blinding laser weapons. Their joint resolution read in part:

> the development of laser technology for military use includes a risk that laser equipment of armed forces can be specifically used for anti-personnel purposes on the battlefield, such as causing permanent blindness of human beings and that such use may be considered already prohibited under existing international law.[146]

[145]By illuminating the cockpit area of low-flying Argentine aircraft, the cockpit material could be made to fluoresce, thus distracting the pilot; see TURBÉ, G., 'Laser Weapons at Sea', 23 *International Defense Review* (1990) at p. 854. The regular use of the blinding laser beam in the Falklands War is confirmed by the Commander of the British Task Force who speaks in his memoirs of 'equipment known as "flasher" which could stop the attack because it forces any incoming pilot to pull up sharply during the 40 second period in which he cannot see'; see WOODWARD, S., *One Hundred Days*, 1992 at p. 320. The 1972 US-Soviet *Agreement on the Prevention of Incidents on and over the High Seas* contained a clause against the 'use [of] searchlights or other powerful *illumination devices* to illuminate the navigation bridges of passing ships of the other Party', but 'lasing' was considered substantially different to warrant separate treatment; see Article III§6 of the *Agreement on Prevention of Incidents at Sea* in 11 *ILM* (1972) at p. 780. According to the terms of a second bilateral agreement, therefore, signed at Moscow in June 1989, the two powers agreed to take the necessary measures for preventing dangerous military activities, such as 'using a laser in such a manner that its radiation could cause harm to personnel or damage to equipment of the armed forces of the other Party'; see Article II§1(b) of the *Agreement on the Prevention of Dangerous Military Activities* in 28 *ILM* (1989) at p. 881. Article IV further required an attempt to be made to notify the other party of any intention to use lasers. For more, see NAGLE, T.J., 'The Dangerous Military Activities Agreement: Minimum Order and Superpower Relations on the World's Oceans', 31 *VJIL* (1990), p. 125*ff*.

[146]Quoted in DOSWALD-BECK, L., 'Obstacles to Regulating New Weaponry: Battlefield Laser Weapons' in FOX, H. and MEYER, M.A. (eds), *Effecting Compliance*, 1993 at p. 111. The draft resolution, however, met with no success. Two years later, in 1988, Sweden submitted at the UN Disarmament Committee and subsequently to the UN Third Special Session on Disarmament a modified proposal aiming at the probition of lasers as anti-personnel weapons *per se*, while admitting the legality of the use of laser technology for other military

It is doubtful, however, whether the legality of the use of blinding laser weapons can be addressed solely in terms of excessive inhumanity and unnecesary suffering. For, being overpowered by a laser beam is not any more inhumane as compared to being blown away by a lethal missile, or trapped inside a burning tank hit by an armour-piercing round. It is not that laser weapons cause unnecessary suffering on a greater scale, for they certainly do not, but that by their very nature they tend to deny the opponent the opportunity to put up a decent defence at the very least. Addressing the issue through the lens of the customary prohibition of declaring that no quarter will be given, Eric David has expressed essentially the same idea in the following manner:

> le droit de la Haye repose sur une idée d'effet aléatoire des armes utilisées: les nécessités de la guerre justifient qu'on détruise le potentiel militaire de l'adversaire, mais les combattants doivent toujours conserver une chance d'échapper à un anéantissement certain . . . Or, lorsqu'une arme ne laisse aucune chance de survie à sa victime, son effet n'est plus aléatoire; il devient certain et viole alors les règles précitées. Le combat mené dans ces conditions par un belligérant s'apparente à l'exécution d'une personne en son pouvoir. Pour que l'emploi d'une telle arme soit licite, il faudrait donc qu'elle soit moins précise (!) ou qu'elle occasionne le moins de mal possible lorsqu'elle touche des individus.[147]

---

purposes such as range finding or target acquisition. On the most recent Swedish attempt to raise the issue, see 13 *UNDY* (1988) at p. 337, and ROBERTSON, *op. cit., supra* n.143 at p. 375. Alerted by rapid technological developments and persistent reports which predict a proliferation of small and light laser weapons in the near future, the ICRC undertook efforts to assess the medical and legal implications of the use of blinding weapons in combat. From June 1989 to April 1991, four expert meetings were organized with a view to obtaining technical information before a legal evaluation of new weapons technologies be undertaken. The proceedings of these meetings are published in DOSWALD-BECK, L. (ed.), *Blinding Weapons – Reports of the Meetings of Experts Convened by the International Committee of the Red Cross on Battlefield Laser Weapons 1989–1991*, 1993.

[147]See DAVID, E., 'Les armes nouvelles à la lumière du *jus in bello*', 26 *RBDI* (1993/1) at pp. 172–3. While for other authors 'the use of laser technology, when specifically designed and employed for certain anti-personnel purposes, is in contravention of that part of international humanitarian law which prohibits superfluous injury or unnecessary suffering'; see ANDERBERG, B., BRING, O.E.

What is this that makes death more acceptable than blindness (if not the ingrained visualization since time immemorial of battlefield victims as lifeless corpses)?[148] Why is the irreversibility of the loss of eyesight any more harrowing (or should it be deemed legally objectionable) than the severe mutilation or total body paralysis due to other combat-inflicted injuries? A satisfactory answer to those questions cannot be a strictly medical one. It transcends scientific empiricism and goes straight into an abstract (essentially moral) judgment on human dignity. The traditional humanitarian principle of superfluous injury or unnecessary suffering is less than a half-answer to the ethical queries that new weapons technology introduces.[149] The repulsion that laser guns spontaneously provoke has not so much to do with excessive cruelty as with the psychological effect on a soldier who knows that he is under fire without hearing or seeing a shot.

Hence, in the light of the above, the use of laser weapons might be brought within the bounds of a perfidious – in a broad

---

and WOLBARSHT, M.L., 'Blinding Laser Weapons and International Humanitarian Law', 29 *Journal of Peace Research* (Aug.1992) at p. 289. And elsewhere: 'using any kind of technology for anti-personnel purposes that brings about permanent blindness is not in proportion to the legitimate object of warfare. In the balance between military interests and humanitarian considerations, an *irreversible* disablement such as blindness caused by a laser beam must be described as "unnecessary suffering" according to the formulas from St. Petersburg, The Hague and Geneva'; see ANDERBERG, B. and BRING, O., 'Battlefield Laser Weapons and International Law', 57 *Nordic Journal of International Law* (1988) at p. 467. See also PROKOSCH, E., *The Technology of Killing*, 1995, pp. 148–201. *Contra*, see CAMPBELL, C.P. and BORCH, F.L., 'Directed Energy Weapons and the Laws of Warfare', *Army* (Aug.1985) at p. 37.

[148]The often used argument that people can more easily resign themselves to the possibility of death than that of blindness because death forms part of the natural life cycle is, to say the least, a debatable since unverifiable metaphysical hypothesis. For a blinded soldier can always be questioned whether he would have prefered to have died but a killed soldier cannot confide whether he would have wished to suffer blindness instead of his life being taken.

[149]For some interesting reflections on that principle, see MEYROWITZ, H., 'Le principe des maux superflus', 76 *RICR* (mars–avril 1994), no.806, p. 107*ff.*, and DAVID, E., *Principes de droit des conflits armés*, 1994, pp. 265–80. One might even argue that *temporary* incapacitation by a laser device (known as flash-blinding) is perhaps one of the most humane means of engaging the enemy. Flash-blinding may be used, for example, against pilots, missile operators, tank crews or artillery controllers. It is estimated that if a pilot is flash-blinded for 15 to 30 seconds during the final phase of attack he will most certainly have to leave the aircraft or crash. It would in fact be a most desirable development if the traditional perception of corporal wounds could be replaced by a temporary disablement absolutely painless and not requiring any sort of medical treatment.

sense – method of warfare. For this view to hold true, however, perfidy should take off from the narrow construction of Article 37 and be redefined as to encompass the resort to distinctly perverse applications of military technology. The prohibition of treacherous conduct could thus cease to be an under-exploited principle and play a more substantive role in assessing the lawfulness of awe-inspiring new weapons technologies.[150] And yet, although the concept of blinding weapons is currently receiving much criticism, who would deny that lasers may well figure as the finest weapon of tomorrow? As effective counter-measures might have been devised by the time laser techniques achieve perfection,[151] and as the new fighting tool may, by then, be enjoying 'popularity', all voices against its inhumane or perfidious nature will, to no amazement, die out.[152]

[150]As Hans Blix had suggested in 1978, 'we should try to expand the laws of war to bring the marginal humanitarian gains that are possible. In the field of conventional weaponry we should use the general rules against unnecessary suffering and injury and against indiscriminate and *treacherous conduct* as compasses for our advice' (emphasis added); see BLIX, H., 'Should Weapons of Dubious Legality Be Developed?', 72 *Proc.ASIL* (1978) at p. 36.

[151]According to most recent information, however, 'there is no cheap, effective, and acceptable eye protection available, and it seems unlikely that such protective means will become available in the near or even not so near future, as the necessary technology does not seem to exist at present'; see ANDERBERG, B., 'Protection and Countermeasures Against Laser Weapons', 17 *Military Technology* (May 1993) at p. 30.

[152]As things now stand, all chances for a general ban on laser rifles and other blinding weapons appear to rely more on the fear that such weapons (given advancing miniaturization) might end in the hands of maverick governments and terrorist organizations, rather than on a widespread awareness of the morally repugnant nature of those devices. In a most welcome development, the Review Conference of the 1981 Inhumane Weapons Convention, held at Vienna from 25 September to 13 October 1995, adopted a fourth additional Protocol prohibiting the use of only those laser weapons exclusively designed to inflict *permanent* blindness. In the terms of Article 1, 'it is prohibited to employ laser weapons specifically designed, as their sole combat function or as one of their combat functions, to cause permanent blindness to unenhanced vision, that is to the naked eye or to the eye with corrective eyesight devices. The High Contracting Parties shall not transfer such weapons to any State or non-State entity.' Article 3 further clarifies that 'blinding as an incidental or collateral effect of the legitimate military employment of laser systems, including laser systems used against optical equipment, is not covered by the prohibition of this Protocol'. Apart from a few points which lend themselves to conflicting interpretations, it also remains to be seen whether the Protocol will be widely accepted. For more, see DOSWALD-BECK, L., 'New Protocol on Blinding Laser Weapons', 78 *RICR* (mai-juin 1996) no.312, p. 272*ff.*, and CARNAHAN, B.M. and ROBERTSON, M., 'The Protocol on Blinding Laser Weapons: A New Direction for International Humanitarian Law', 90 *AJIL* (1996), p. 484*ff.*

VI Concluding remarks

The Conference on the Reaffirmation and Development of International Humanitarian Law has elaborated a partly satisfactory definition of the concept of perfidy which offers some interesting clues for a retrospective assessment of past practices. It would now seem clearly established that to hoist a neutral flag practically until the first cannon-balls are shot, should bear no relation whatsoever with stratagem, or to prose as a harmless and often a shipwrecked mariner, only to conceal an attack, is anything but memorable bravery. It is reproachable, however, that the notion of perfidy was divested of its primary moral connotation and thus, greatly narrowed in scope.

Moreover, the 1977 Conference took no exception to the longstanding tradition which wants to keep the laws of naval warfare a somehow inviolable domain, thus preserving the lamentable illusion that conducting war at sea should follow distinct humanitarian principles from those applicable to land warfare. The clause of Article 39§3, seasoned with the usual mandarin ambiguity, which seeks to immunize some unspecified *'existing generally recognized rules of international law applicable to the use of flags in the conduct of armed conflict at sea'* against the unequivocal language of Article 37, is believed to aimlessly perpetuate the uncertainties of the past. Far from attesting to the existence of an international custom, the degenerated practices of the two World Wars demonstrated that there are no commonly admitted principles on the subject. Flying false flags should be strictly prohibited so that the laws of sea warfare be at long last harmonized with those of land warfare, for it does not make sense that the same usage be considered a grave breach of humanitarian law when it is resorted to on land, and permissible when it is practised at sea. Although visual deception through the use of false marks becomes more and more impracticable in the age of over-the-horizon targeting, international law would still have interest in rectifying what is a useless anomaly in the laws of armed conflict at sea.

As for the practice of arming merchantmen, it should equally be proscribed for it disturbs the cardinal distinction between combatants and defenceless traders, and tends to create a vicious circle where any vessel can be asserted to represent a legitimate target on the assumption that it may carry threatening armament. Such confusion of roles, means and practices, has always worked to the detriment of the innocent. The usages of maritime warfare related to deception and surprise tactics should be reappraised bearing in mind the stern realities that modern electronic warfare imposes. It is high time that the *jus belli al mare* be liberated from considerations which may have appeared opportune, or even lawful, at the time of piracy and prize looting, but which are irrelevant in the present-day context.

A caveat, however, against ready-made assumptions on the subject would appear most fitting to conclude this chapter. The issue of perfidy in war mirrors to a certain extent the paradox of war laws in general. The goal is to preserve morality, honour and good faith as if it were not true that taking lives is to deny all of these. Some would rejoin, and rightly so, that far from exalting virtue, an armed contest calls nonetheless for a modicum of orderly conduct. Yet, one has to remain conscious of the fact that what is addressed here is a legal prescription of variable cogency and normative content at best. Perfidy is rather a label, a charge of ignominy laying in wait for almost every major military innovation. It is the impulsive reproach of stupefied laymen to the well-bred lethal creativity of military laboratories. It should be remembered that when vessels designed for underwater navigation and capable of firing while submerged were first put out to sea, these were condemned as being detestably treacherous. It is only when fresh developments in weapons technology announce new scales of magnitude in destructive power that open wonderment recedes and debate refocuses on the latest novelty.

The stigma of perfidy, no less than this of inhumanity, related to certain weaponry would seem to coexist with its modernity. Yielding to new instrumentalities occurs only because proliferation and further evolution makes continued discussion pointless, and not because the means or methods in question somehow cease to be objectionable in nature. For instance no one today would think to solicit the abolition of the submarine, or denounce the use of sea mines, given their unchivalrous character, however valid those charges may still sound. To recall a magnificent phrase of Major G.V. Fosbery pronounced before the Royal United Services Institution in 1868,

> what is this humanity of which so much is made? Is it

indeed a branch of that quality which leads us to clothe the naked and feed the hungry, only developed in another direction? or is it not rather a term of variable quantity, applied to homicidal cruelty, and *so adjusted as to be always just one step behind the last military discovery of the day?* (emphasis added)[153]

[153]Quoted in KALSHOVEN, F., 'Arms, Armaments and International Law', 191 *RCADI* (1985) at p. 210.

PART TWO

Belligerent Interference with Neutral Property at Sea

γλυκύ δ' απείρω πόλεμος· πεπειραμένων δε τις
ταρβεί προσιόντα νιν καρδία περισσώς

To the inexperienced war is pleasant, but he that hath had experience of it, in his heart sorely feareth its approach

Pindar, *Dance Songs, Fragments,* §110
(transl. by J. Sandys, The Loeb Classical Library, 1968 at p. 577)

Chapter Four

THE NOTION OF MARITIME NEUTRALITY

I Introduction

War without neutrals has not been recorded in the history of mankind. Wars accompanied by violations of neutrality, on the part of either belligerents or neutrals, are the only wars fought to date. Neutrality to end war is an honourable, but not so realistic, policy, whereas collective action instead of neutrality is a realistic, but rarely politically accepted, option. These are only a few of the remarks one could make in an epigrammatic form in order to show the ubiquity of the concept of neutrality in the ever-troubled reality of international relations.

It is in attempting to grasp the ambit of the legal notion of neutrality that confusion begins. What Grotius called *medii in bello* and Bynkershoek described as *non hostes qui neutrarum partium sunt* has puzzled academics for centuries. From an etymological point of view, neutrality derives from the Latin *neuter*, which means with neither side. It envisages a situation whereby a state preserves friendly relations with all states, parties in an armed conflict, by refraining from giving active support to any of them. Oppenheim defines the concept 'as the attitude of impartiality adopted by third States towards belligerents and recognized by belligerents, such attitude creating rights and duties between impartial States and the belligerents'.[1]

[1]See LAUTERPACHT, H. (ed.), *Oppenheim's International Law*, 7th edn (1952), vol.II at p. 653. For Richard Kleen: 'la neutralité est la situation juridique dans laquelle un État pacifique est, autant que possible, laissé en dehors des hostilités qui ont lieu entre des États belligérants, et s'abstient lui-même de toute participation ou ingérence dans leur différend, en observant vis-à-vis d'eux une stricte impartialité'; KLEEN, R., *Lois et usages de la neutralité*, tome 1er, 1898 at p. 73. While Paul Fauchille observes more simply: 'la neutralité est la situation de tout Etat qui reste étranger à la guerre survenue entre deux ou plusieurs autres Etats.

The notion appeared vaguely for the first time in the maritime context around the eleventh century. With its origins trailing back to the age of European feudalism, neutrality found clear expression in the *Consolato del mare* of the fifteenth century, but it is generally considered to be, in its modern form, a fruit of the nineteenth century. The American proclamation of 22 April 1793, the permanent neutrality of Switzerland and Belgium, and the Paris Declaration of 1856 are acclaimed as the milestones in the course of the maturation of neutrality in international usage. By the end of the nineteenth century, the principles governing neutrality had taken the form of widely accepted conventional rules.[2]

Throughout this century, neutrality has generated more doubt than certainty, more inquisition than affirmation. After almost every major test of the laws of neutrality, scholars have striven to discover the new physiognomy of neutrality but invariably ended their probe in mystery; 'je sais bien' – stated Arnold McNair in the early 1930s – 'ce qu'était la neutralité avant la dernière guerre. Je ne puis en conscience vous dire ce qu'elle

C'est l'existence de l'état pacifique impartial d'une puissance envers chacun des belligérants'; FAUCHILLE, P., *Traité de droit international public*, tome II, 8ème édn (1921), §1441 at pp. 635–6.

[2]Neutrality as a temporary relationship during war *(neutralité occasionnelle)* should be distinguished from other related concepts such as *permanent neutrality* and *neutralism*. The former relates to a commitment not to become involved in any future armed conflict *(neutralité perpetuelle)* and to a policy which aims at the credible realization of that undertaking. This concept found its most earnest adherents among small European nations such as Switzerland which was granted the status of permanent neutrality at the Vienna Congress of 1815. Austria chose the route of permanent neutrality in 1955, and was followed by Sweden, Finland and Malta. On permanent neutrality, see DOLLOT, R., 'Essai sur la neutralité permanente', 67 *RCADI* (1939), p. 7*ff*. Neutralism (also known as non-alignment), on the other hand, is traditionally understood as a policy of keeping out of alliances and rival power blocs. Contrary to classical neutrality which presupposes a war relationship between at least two other states, neutralism is conceived as a strategy available in times of both peace and war. On neutralism, see MORGENTHAU, H.J., 'Neutrality and Neutralism', 11 *Yearbook of World Affairs* (1957), p. 47*ff*.; FENWICK, C.G., 'The Legal Aspects of Neutralism', 51 *AJIL* (1957), p. 71*ff*.; JANKOVIC, B., 'De la neutralité classique à la conception moderne des pays non-alignés', 21 *REDI* (1965), p. 89*ff*.; SCHWARZENBERGER, G., 'The Scope for Neutralism', 15 *Yearbook of World Affairs* (1961), p. 233*ff*.; LYON, P., 'Neutrality and the Emergence of the Concept of Neutralism', 22 *Review of Politics* (1960), p. 255*ff*. Still different is the notion of *neutralization* of states or territories by treaty, as for instance the neutralization of the Aaland Islands; see VEROSTA, S., 'Neutralization' in BERNHARDT, R. (ed.), *Encyclopedia of Public International Law*, instalment 4 (1982), p. 31*ff*.

est aujourd'hui.'[3] Others spoke of the birth, death and reincarnation of neutrality, while Charles Fenwick has expressed doubt whether neutrality is still a term of present law.[4] Karl Zemanek referred in 1989 to the chaotic status of the laws of neutrality, and Michael Bothe has been wondering what is left of the traditional law of neutrality.[5]

How is one to interpret such collective uneasiness if not as a clear warning that the subject is notoriously nebulous and messy? Common is the feeling among specialists that we have been navigating in uncharted waters for so long that it would need enormous effort to dispel misconceptions nurtured for decades and have major naval powers agree on clear and comprehensive rules for the future. Despite the rhetorical overtones, however, the situation should not be dramatized. Disorder is somewhat endemic in the law of neutrality which has been through the centuries more of a desideratum or an ephemeral expectation than a tangible set of rules. The threshold of abstention – the quintessence of neutral duties – has always been enveloped in mystery, and even after having been codified in the Hague instruments it remained an approximation at best.

Perhaps the most recurrent feature concerning the concept of maritime neutrality is that it strikes a balance between two sets of conflicting interests: those of the belligerent to cut off enemy supply routes, and those of the neutral to be affected as little as possible in its normal seaborne trade relations. Yet, it would be more correct to describe neutrality as a peculiar situation of mutual suspicion: on the one hand the distrust of the belligerent as to whether the neutral is genuinely indifferent with regard to the outcome of the conflict, and on the other hand the wariness of the neutral that the belligerent might not honour neutral immunities for long. Neutrality is certainly not a static point of equilibrium; it is a dynamic power relation. Neutrality is ultimately transient, ever-fluctuating and at best conditional.

[3]See 37 *Rep.ILA* (1933) Oxford Conf., 1932 at p. 185.
[4]See JESSUP, P.C., 'The Birth, Death and Reincarnation of Neutrality', 26 *AJIL* (1932), p. 789*ff*., and FENWICK, C.G., 'Is Neutrality Still a Term of Present Law?', 63 *AJIL* (1969), p. 100*ff*.
[5]See ZEMANEK, K., 'The Chaotic Status of the Laws of Neutrality' in *Im Dienst an der Gemeinschaft Festschrift für Dietrich Schindler*, 1989, p. 443*ff*., and BOTHE, M., 'Neutrality in Naval Warfare: What Is Left of Traditional International Law?', in DELISSEN, A.J.M. and TANJA, G.J. (eds), *Humanitarian Law of Armed Conflict – Challenges Ahead, Essays in Honour of Frits Kalshoven*, 1991, p. 387*ff*.

It is worth bearing in mind that neutrality, in its eventful history, has hardly come close to acquiring a standard definition of its substantive elements. With the exception of the 1907 Hague Conventions and the abortive London Declaration of 1909 (both of which soon proved no match for the test of a World War), the rights and duties of neutrals have remained the object of constant remodelling. The Vattelian conception of the duty of abstention, for instance, which is believed to portray the bedrock of traditional neutrality, saw nothing inconsistent with strict neutrality in neutral nations supplying levies of soldiers to all comers or in allowing free passage of belligerent troops across neutral territory. Since that time, the threshold of neutral duties has been greatly raised – the point at issue today being to what degree the law of the Charter has affected this fine tuning of the notion of neutrality. It so happens that the long diagnosed malfunction of the UN coercive mechanism saved neutrality from decline, for in a world where aggression has often prevailed with impunity while the Charter's chapter 7 has been kept in mothballs, there could still be room for abstention and impartiality, at least technically.

II Uncertain origins and tardy evolution of the concept of neutrality

1 From classical antiquity to the medieval world

The Meaning and Function of Neutrality in Ancient Greece Most studies devoted to the origins and evolution of the concept of neutrality espouse the view that neutrality as a legal notion, being unknown in classical antiquity, emerged for the first time in the Middle Ages. Paul Fauchille in his work on war and neutrality refers to 'une notion essentiellement moderne, inconnue à l'antiquité', while Richard Kleen affirms that 'la neutralité, comme principe de droit, était à peu près inconnue aux peuples anciens'.[6] As those scholars reason, neutrality as a legal institution presupposes a certain level of development of inter-state relations as well as adequately elaborate laws of war, which one could hardly observe in classical times when human communities were in a state of constant violence with barely

[6]See FAUCHILLE, *op. cit., supra* n.1 at p. 637, and KLEEN, *op. cit., supra* n.1 at p. 2.

any legal niceties to obey. Upon the outbreak of a war, bordering nations were expected either to join forces as allies, or to fight on the side of the enemy, while those refusing to take the part of either were to be treated as if they had opted for the enemy camp. As the Roman Senate had declared, *Romanos aut amicos aut hostes habere oportet; media via non est.*[7]

By contrast, other scholars have demonstrated that, for much of the debate surrounding the legal dimension of neutrality in modern times, parallels of astonishing similitude could be drawn from the history of ancient Greek city-states. Relying on copious evidence by great historiographers such as Thucydides, Herodotus, Polybius, Diodorus or Strabon, they were able to confirm not only that aloofness was an accepted feature in Hellenic inter-communal relations, but also that definite rights and duties stemmed from that condition.[8] The specific expression used to describe the attitude of neutrality was ουδετερων οντες, or its variants μηδετερων οντες, ουδε μεθ' ετερων, and μηδε μεθ' ετερων οντες, all connoting the quality of being with neither side, or denying assistance to either side (the conjunctives ουδε and μηδε were employed in that sense). The term is to be found practically unchanged in modern Greek (ουδετεροτης).

Examples of ancient cities claiming the benefits of neutrality abound in Greek history and it goes beyond the purview of this survey to recount them all. When the Peloponnesian War broke out, as Thucydides narrates, Argives and Achaeans were the only people south of the Corinthian isthmus not to ally with Spartans,[9] while the islands of Melos and Thera were among those who refused to coalesce with Athenians.[10] Even though

[7]Quoted in SULTAN, H., *L'évolution du concept de la neutralité*, 1938 at p. 6.
[8]See, for instance, SÉFÉRIADÈS, S., 'La conception de la neutralité dans l'ancienne Grèce', 16 *RDILC* (1935), p. 641*ff.*, BOTTIÉ, F., *Essai sur la genèse et l'évolution de la notion de neutralité*, 1937, pp. 19–34, and TÉNÉKIDÈS, G., 'Droit international et communautés fédérales dans la Grèce des cités', 90 *RCADI* (1956), pp. 557–61.
[9]Thucydides, *History of the Peloponnesian War* [translated by SMITH, C.F., *The Loeb Classical Library*, 1919], bk.II, §9: 'all the Peloponnesians south of the Isthmus with the exception of the Argives and Achaeans (these latter had *friendly relations with both sides*)'.
[10]*Ibid.*, bk.II, §9: 'those [allies] of the Athenians were . . . the islands which lie between the Peloponnesus and Creta toward the east, with the exception of Melos and Thera'. At the very origin of that war lay the effort by Corcyra to avoid entanglement in the internal affairs of Epidamnus. When the Corinthians interferred, however, Corcyra responded in arms and shortly after proposed to Athens to join its League. Corinth strove to secure the neutrality of Athens arguing that 'you will not merely become allies to them [Corcyraeans], but also

the usages respecting neutrals were not always uniform in character or precise in content, it is safe to assume that neutrals might lawfully claim the inviolability of their territory, the protection of the population and the inalienability of their property. Violations of such neutral rights, however, were not uncommon. At the beginning of the Peloponnesian War, for instance, Lacedaemonians treated as foes all those captured at sea, regardless of their being allies of Athenians or neutrals.[11]

By far the most eloquent episode to be found in ancient Greek history is the confrontation of neutral Melians with the powerful Athenian navy in the sixteenth year of the Peloponnesian War. Melos, although a colony of Sparta, had remained neutral from the very outset of the war and wished to preserve its neutrality despite Athens' threats to impose an alliance by force. In 416 B.C., when Athenian envoys came to convince the Melians about the futility of any resistance, the Melians appealed to the sanctity of their island secured by neutrality. The passage containing the Melian plea is an ageless tribute to morality and law and merits quotation *in extenso*:

> you would not consent to our remaining at peace and being friends instead of enemies, but allies of neither combatant? . . . Just as you force us to abandon all pleas of justice and seek to persuade us to give ear to what is to your own interests, that we, too, tell you what is to our

---

enemies to us instead of being at truce with us. For it will be necessary for us, if you go with them, to include you when we proceed to take vengeance upon them. And yet, the right course for you would be, preferably, to stand aloof from us both – or else to go with us against them'; *ibid.*, bk.I, §40. During the expedition against Sicily, although most of the Sicilian cities united for the defence of Syracuse, Agrigentans remained neutral; *ibid.*, bk.VII, §33: 'almost the whole of Sicily – except the Agrigentines, who were *neutral*, but the rest without exception had united with the Syracusans'. See also RUBIN, A.P., 'The Concept of Neutrality in International Law', 16 *Denver Journal of International Law and Policy* (1988) at p. 355.

[11]*Ibid.*, bk.II, §67: 'for at the beginning of the war all persons whom the Lacedaemonians captured at sea they destroyed as enemies, whether they were fighting on the side of the Athenians or not even *taking part on either side*'. Among the obligations falling upon neutrals, one should cite the prohibition of financial support towards belligerents, of recruiting volunteers for a belligerent army, or of allowing belligerent vessels into neutral ports. Yet, authorization for anchoring within a neutral port, or for obtaining water supply, might be exceptionally given; *ibid.*, bk.VII, §44: 'they sailed along the coast of Italy – some of the cities not receiving them with a market nor into the town, though furnishing them with water and anchorage, and Tarentum and Locri not even with these – until they came to Rhegium, a promontory of Italy'.

> advantage and try to persuade you to adopt it, if that happens to be your advantage also. How, we say, shall you not make enemies of all who are now neutral, as soon as they look at our case and conclude that some day you will come against them also? And in this what else are you doing but strengthening the enemies you already have, and bringing upon you, against their inclination, others who would never have thought of becoming your enemies? . . . But we propose to you that we be your friends, but enemies to neither combatant, and that you withdraw from our territory, after making such a truce as may seem suitable for both of us.[12]

In conclusion, although neutrality in a legal sense remained unrefined in classical antiquity, it is beyond doubt that the ancient Greek communities were familiar with the posture of neutrality, that is not taking sides. A policy of abstention was in fact a surprisingly frequent feature in ancient Greek warfare, although it failed to assume a specific legal connotation of its own. What is more, neutrality in the classical period was linked more to concerns about the city's security and independence rather than to commercial interests.[13] The concept practically

[12]*Ibid.*, bk.V §§94,98,112. See also RUBIN, *op. cit.*, *supra* n.10 at p. 356. Finally, the Athenians, for fear of disintegration of their League should small client states have been allowed to decide for themselves whether to fight or not, invaded the island killing all adult men and enslaving all women and children. They later colonized Melos with 500 of their own settlers. As regards the concept of permanent neutrality, it was not foreign to the ancient Greeks, the most notable case being the neutrality of the city of Plateae for a duration of one half of a century (from 479 to 429 B.C.). At the time of the Persian wars, the allied Greek states had sworn perpetual respect of the city and its citizens. Fifty years later, amidst the Peloponnesian War, the Lacedaemonians invoking those oaths asked the Plateans to remain peaceful and taking neither side to receive both parties as friends; *ibid.*, bk.II. §72: 'therein you should take part, if possible, and yourselves abide by the oath's; otherwise keep quiet, as we have already proposed, continuing to enjoy your own possessions; *take part with neither side, receive both sides as friends but for hostile purposes neither*'. Related to the idea of permanent neutrality was also the status of sacrosanct cities and territories such as the island of Delos.

[13]As a recent study on the subject concludes, 'the first thing that one notices about states that stay out of wars in the classical period, especially when one compares them with modern neutral states, is the lack of connection between their policy and commercial interests. In this respect neutrality in the classical period differs distinctly from neutrality as it has evolved since the seventeenth century . . . Neutrality of the classical period is more often directly involved with self-defense and the safety of the state than with protection of trade and profit. The various restrictions that neutrals imposed or attempted to impose on

disappeared in the Roman world for neutrality was simply incompatible with Roman imperialism. Not only rarely did Rome adopt a neutral status, but it refused to recognize any neutral immunities for other peoples.[14]

The Genesis of the Modern Concept of Maritime Neutrality It is generally accepted that the formative period of the law of maritime neutrality extends from roughly the end of the fifteenth century to the mid-eighteenth century. Although historical evidence exists to demonstrate that the word neutrality was used in the modern sense of non-participation in a war as early as the fourteenth century, and while it is also true that the *Consolato del Mare*, published in 1494, embodied existing practices and rules of Mediterranean nations regarding neutral rights at sea, it is commonly assumed that the emergence of the concept of maritime neutrality as a legal status presupposed the confluence of certain conditions which did not arise earlier than the end of the fifteenth century. Even by the time the concept had reached a high stage of development, i.e., the sixteenth and seventeenth centuries, specific rules remained often changeable and ill-defined.[15]

Among the factors which led to the progressive concretization of the notion of neutrality, mention may be made of the radical change in seaborne trade following the period of great discoveries, and the unprecedented commercial rivalry at sea that the newly explored riches in America, the East Indies or Africa inaugurated among the leading maritime nations. Equally instrumental was the disappearance of feudal entities and the advent of modern state structures with the parallel substitute of public wars for the unregulated private wars. The long process of transition from privateers to standing navies was chiefly

the activities of belligerents, such as prohibiting passage across neutral territory, limiting to a single ship the access of belligerents to a neutral harbor, refusing to allow belligerents within the city walls, and even denying water and withholding the sale of food, all represent distinctly self-defensive measures'; see BAUSLAUGH, R.A., *The Concept of Neutrality in Classical Greece*, 1991 at pp. 70, 73.

[14]See BOTTIÉ, *op. cit., supra* n.8, pp. 35–47.

[15]It is for this reason that Francis Deák and Philip Jessup in their leading work on neutrality correctly suggest that 'it is unimportant to dispute the size and shape of the embryo at different moments in the intervening centuries'; see JESSUP, P.C. and DEÁK, F., *Neutrality – Its History, Economics and Law,* vol.I (1935) at p. 17.

marked by the diminishing interest in issuing private letters of reprisal,[16] the set-up of admiralty jurisdictions and the organization of prize courts which announced new standards for orderly treatment of enemy property at sea. By and large, the historic development of the law of maritime neutrality offers an important lesson in the fragility of the law of nations.

2 The formative period of the law of maritime neutrality

Early Rules, Early Discord: Seizing Neutral Property at Sea and Maritime Custom One of the most elementary propositions of the rules of economic warfare at sea is the belligerent right to capture enemy property. As the *Consolato del Mare* indicated, there was never much doubt about the soundness of the principle that enemy goods aboard enemy ships made good prize: 'there is no need to discuss a situation when an armed vessel sets out on a journey, is cruising around, or is returning to its home port and intercepts a merchantman, and the latter vessel and its cargo belong to enemy nationals, because all informed persons know what will happen under such circumstances, and what is to be done, and therefore it would be misleading to try to set some sort of a rule about this'.[17]

The situation was not at all clear, however, as to enemy goods in neutral ships, and neutral goods in enemy ships. According to the *Consolato*, enemy property loaded on a neutral vessel was subject to confiscation, while the vessel was not. Conversely, neutral goods on enemy ships were immune whereas the ship was not. In both cases, therefore, no interference was permitted with neutral property. The neutral could send his goods on a belligerent carrier, or he could use his own merchantmen to transport enemy goods without worrying about loss of either his cargo or his ship. Moreover, when enemy freight was seized on a neutral ship, or an enemy ship carrying neutral goods was captured, the captor was liable to pay full compensation to the

[16]The theory that private persons might be licensed to seize enemy property so as to obtain redress for previously sustained damages first appeared in the last quarter of the thirteenth century and was made the object of numerous bilateral treaties as from the early fourteenth century. For an interesting study of the evolution of English practice in these matters, see CLARK, G., 'The English Practice with Regard to Reprisals by Private Persons', 27 *AJIL* (1933), p. 694*ff.*
[17]See JADOS, S.S., *Consulate of the Sea and Related Documents*, 1975, §276.

neutral owner. The provisions of the *Consolato* were in fact as favourable as they could possibly be towards neutral property.[18]

As from the fifteenth century, however, a noticeable change took shape. For England under Henry VI, for instance, enemy goods were liable to capture under a neutral flag while neutral goods were liable to capture under an enemy flag. Still more stringent were the French marine ordinances of 1543 and 1584 according to which neutral vessels engaged in carriage of enemy goods as much as neutral cargoes entrusted to belligerent merchantmen made good prize. Under this latter provision, which was the exact opposite of the liberal clauses of the *Consolato*, only neutral goods shipped in neutral vessels were exempt from belligerent seizure. Apart from this minimal exception, therefore, the new policy could be condensed to the principles *enemy ships – enemy goods,* but also *enemy goods – enemy ships* (which is the rejection, to put it differently, of the rule *free ships – free goods*).[19]

The Eighteenth Century: Rising Principles Amidst Anarchy and Con-

[18]As a number of treaties in the fourteenth century show, these rules were generally observed in Medieval Europe. The treaties concluded between England and the cities of Biscaye in 1351, with Portugal in 1353, with the Duke of Bourgogne in 1406, 1417 and 1426, or with the Republic of Genoa in 1462, are indicative in this respect.

[19]State practice, however, remained largely inconsistent, France, for instance, in 1559 and 1564 entered into agreements with England to the effect that neither state would interfere with the ships of the other which, of course, implied the restoration of the rule *free ships – free goods.* Similarly, in 1646 France signed a treaty with the Netherlands conceding a four-year suspension of the ordinance of 1584 as regards Dutch vessels. Even more strikingly, in 1655 the French granted to the Hansa Towns not only the same favour accorded to the Netherlands, but also immunity of neutral goods found aboard enemy ships (thus abandoning even the rule *enemy ships – enemy goods*). Thus, far from reflecting solidly established usages, the bilateral treaties of the sixteenth and seventeenth centuries gave only expression to occasional arrangements in order to satisfy transient interests. Consequently, while it is correct to assert that by 1680 the strongest maritime powers of Europe adhered to the rules *enemy ships – enemy goods* and *free ships – free goods* (as confirmed by the 1659 treaty of the Pyrenees between France and Spain, the 1662 French-Danish and French-Dutch treaties, the 1667 treaty between Sweden and the Netherlands, as well as the English-Dutch and English-Spanish treaties of the same year), by the turn of the century the context was once more modified, with most countries denying that free ships made free goods, e.g., the French *règlement* of 1704, the Spanish ordinances of 1702 and 1718, or the 1706 English treaty with Danzig; see JESSUP and DEÁK, *op. cit., supra* n.15, pp. 137–47. The theory and practice of neutrality as evolved in the seventeenth and eighteenth centuries is analysed in BAUDENET D'ANNOUX, H., *Le développement de la neutralité de Grotius à Vattel*, 1910.

flict The controversy over whether *la robe ami couvre la marchandise ennemie* continued to provide the setting for the further evolution of maritime neutrality throughout the eighteenth century. Whereas the treaty of Utrecht of 1713, as much as the treaties concluded by France with the Kingdom of Denmark-Norway in 1742, with the Dutch in 1739 or with the Kingdom of the Two Sicilies in 1745, endorsed the principle *free ships – free goods*, England as the leading naval power stood firmly by the rule of the *Consolato del Mare* affirming its right to capture enemy property aboard neutral vessels. It was against this backdrop of recurrent Anglo-French rivalry and war that the most remarkable legal developments occurred in this century, namely the promulgation of the so-called Rule of 1756 and the elaboration of the principles of *Armed Neutrality* mainly among the Scandinavian kingdoms.

The Rule of 1756 is a striking example of the continual process of redefining belligerent rights in response to creative neutral practices. It stemmed from the resolve of the English admiralty to curb the French practice to license neutral merchants to enter the colonial trade – a peacetime monopoly for French seafarers. The capture of several Dutch vessels engaged in the transport to France of supplies from her overseas colonies was vested in the legal construction that a neutral vessel when put in the service of a belligerent and operating under its control is, in effect, incorporated into the hostile fleet and thus liable to capture and condemnation. The principle was further refined to deal with fraudulent landing and reloading of enemy colonial goods in neutral ports, giving birth to the doctrine of continuous voyage.

As for the system of Armed Neutrality, it exemplified the potency of neutral defences against belligerent abuses, especially when expressed in a concerted action. The first of these alliances for joint protection of the security of navigation and commerce was concluded in 1691, and reaffirmed in 1713, between Sweden and Denmark-Norway. The two kingdoms agreed to assure the protection of neutral merchants against privateers by providing armed escorts, thus laying the basis for the doctrine of neutral convoys as elaborated a century later. Moreover, they undertook to claim reparation in case any of their subjects suffered damages from belligerent action, and to resort to necessary reprisals if reparation was not promptly awarded. The dress-rehearsal in armed neutrality was a success since England and the Netherlands discontinued interfering with Scandinavian shippers trading with France and released some captured vessels.

In 1756, Sweden and Denmark–Norway reiterated their commitment in yet another treaty, while in 1780, at the time of the American War of Independence, the posture of armed neutrality appealed to a much larger number of countries. At the origin of the League of 1780 was a declaration of Empress Catherine II of Russia which announced five guiding principles concerning the neutral right to trade in time of war. Apart from reaffirming the *free ships – free goods* principle, with the exception of contraband, the declaration laid down a narrow definition of contraband items, and stressed the need for effectiveness in maintaining a naval blockade. These propositions were endorsed in the treaties that Russia signed with Denmark–Norway, Sweden and Prussia, while by 1783 four more countries, the Netherlands, Portugal, Austria, and the Two Sicilies, had adopted the Russian scheme. One more treaty was concluded in 1794 between Sweden and Denmark–Norway calling for armed accompaniment of neutral merchantmen. As a result, England had to give way and repeal her instructions for capture of neutral vessels carrying wheat to France.

The final chapter in the story of Armed Neutralities of the northern European states was written in 1800 on the occasion of a Danish convoy intercepted by an English squadron while resisting visit and search. Shortly after the incident, Sweden, Denmark-Norway and Prussia signed treaties with Russia reviving the principles of the 1780 League. The most significant innovation related to neutral convoys, to the effect that neutral merchantmen when escorted by warships would not be subject to visit and search since the convoy commander could certify the absence of contraband. The controversy over neutral immunities turned swiftly to confrontation as Nelson was instructed to convince, by arms if necessary, the Scandinavian states to withdraw from the League. In 1801, the Danish-Norwegian fleet was attacked at Copenhagen. According to the terms of the treaties restoring good relations between Russia, Sweden and Denmark-Norway on the one hand, and England on the other hand, the rule *free ships – free goods* was renounced in favour of the old principle of the *Consolato* to the effect that enemy property aboard neutral vessels made good prize. As for the belligerent right of halting and boarding merchant vessels, it was stipulated that neutral convoys would only be exempt from visit by privateers but not by commissioned warships.[20]

Another assumption lying at the foundation of modern maritime neutrality is the inviolability of neutral territory by which it is understood, first, the belligerent obligation to refrain from conducting operations within the realm of a neutral power, and second the corresponding neutral obligation to prevent as much as possible the commission of such hostile acts. A number of early instances and treaty provisions seem to corroborate the view that the sanctity of neutral territory came to be recognized by and large in the course of the seventeenth century.[21] During the endless little wars that kept Europe in flames for most of that century, there were frequent abuses against neutral jurisdiction. Neutrals, however, such as Portugal, Genoa, or the Netherlands, which appeared to have particularly suffered in this regard, never missed the opportunity to press strongly for indemnity or restitution of seized vessels by invoking a prevalent principle of law.[22]

[20]For a concise survey of armed neutralities, see BOYE, T., 'Quelques aspects du développement des règles de la neutralité', 64 *RCADI* (1938), pp. 166–90, and PHILLIPS, W.A. and REEDE, A.H., *Neutrality – Its History, Economics and Law*, vol.II (1936), pp. 91–111. See also KULSRUD, C.J., *Maritime Neutrality to 1780*, 1936.

[21]See JESSUP and DEÁK, *op. cit., supra* n.15, pp. 249–56. Most authors do not fail to notice, however, that in all probability the rule stemmed from pure economic interest, i.e. the desire to safeguard the uninterrupted continuation of neutral trade, rather than from a legal conviction connected to neutral detachment. For, if this was not so, then neutrals should have also objected to other practices, notably the transit of belligerent troops through neutral territory, which continued unopposed through the seventeenth century. As early as 1562, Queen Elisabeth protested to Queen Mary of Scotland against ships taken within Danish territorial waters arguing that 'the territory of an indifferent and meane prince is sauf conducte in lawe', while two years later the Privy Council restyled the principle as follows: 'whate so ever the enemye dothe take from thenemye in the harborowe of a frende, that is no prise; for the proprietie thereof is not altered, but remayneth still in lawe with the first owners'. In 1605, as Spain waged war against the United Provinces, James I of England, seeking to protect the non-involvement of his kingdom, issued a proclamation forbidding hostilities in any of the ports or other maritime areas lying within his dominion.

[22]In 1634, the English Admiralty court adjudicated damages and costs to be paid by the captor to the original owner of a ship seized within neutral waters. In 1668, Charles II of England issued a proclamation of neutrality very similar to that of 1605 concerning the interdiction of all belligerent action within English waters. In 1689, upon Danish protests over French captures in ports of Norway,

By the mid-eighteenth century, the principle of the inviolability of neutral waters had taken solid root in the law of nations. According to the English royal instructions of 1739, naval commanders were prohibited from engaging in hostilities or capturing prizes within neutral waters. Famous prize decisions, such as the *Two Sisters* of 1740, or the *Maria* of 1764, further recognized that the rule was firmly established by that time, while in 1759 the English offered solemn apologies to Portugal for having infringed upon the sanctity of its territory by capturing two French vessels and setting ablaze another two near Portuguese forts.

As for another requirement of the traditional laws of neutrality, namely that prizes might not be disposed of in neutral ports, it had been far less certain in its early origins. Whereas as early as 1613 reference is made in a doctrinal work to the neutral obligation to restore a captured ship to its owners and to release its crew if the belligerent had intended to sell its prize within the bounds of a neutral nation, and whereas a French royal decree of 1649 specified that foreign prizes would not be permitted to anchor in French ports for more than 24 hours unless constrained by sea conditions, it was regular practice for neutrals to allow foreign prizes to be condemned in their ports. Despite occasional protests and diplomatic debate, most European nations had at one time or another tolerated their ports being used by a belligerent as a prize haven.[23]

The old practice of issuing *letters of marque* and *letters of reprisal* enabling private individuals to take active part in hostilities had

the King of France released the prizes and ordered French privateers to refrain thereafter from operating along the coasts of Norway. Occasionally, the aggrieved belligerent might hold the neutral responsible for having failed to prevent the violation of its neutrality. When in 1665, for example, the Dutch fleet attacked English merchantmen in the port of Hamburg, the latter was asked to pay reparation for damages.

[23]When, for instance, in 1656 England protested to the Netherlands over allowing Spaniards to bring prizes into Dutch ports, the Dutch responded that such practice had long been approved by the English Court of Admiralty. Similarly, Sweden in 1659 objected to the English move to release Swedish prizes brought into then-neutral English ports recalling consistent English practice in the past. The controversy continued through most of the eighteenth century. As late as 1779, for instance, France enacted legislation endorsing the right to take prizes into neutral ports.

also ended up being a source of embarrassment and conflict.[24] Privateers in most cases waged an unruly war of plunder little different from piracy. The establishment of prize jurisdictions was in part designed to check the abusive usages of marauders, the understanding being that a valid title to booty could only be obtained after the ship and cargo were brought into port and condemnation as a lawful prize was awarded. Towards the end of the eighteenth century, opposition against privateering was on the rise. Certain powers solicited stricter regulation, while others opted for definitive abandonment. Great Britain, for instance, in the Jay Treaty of 1794 inserted an article to the effect that, before putting out to sea, privateers had to deposit securities against which eventual claims for damages could be made.[25] Prussia and the United States in their treaty of friendship and commerce of 1785 agreed not to issue any commission to private armed vessels.[26]

3 Crystallization in international usage: maritime neutrality in its modern cast

The Nineteenth Century: The Time for Codification At the dawn of the nineteenth century, the principles which had inspired the Armed Neutrality of 1800 seemed defeated. The quest of Scandinavian powers for orderly conduct of economic warfare at sea had been set back. England had managed to reimpose the *Consolato* rule allowing for the capture of enemy property aboard neutral vessels, while the principle of effectiveness in

[24]The term *marque* is most often associated with frontiers such that *lettres de marque* were official documents authorizing trespassing of frontiers and incursion into enemy territory. In the fourteenth century, *marquer* was used to signify *piller,* that is to plunder, to pillage, or to levy contributions. A distinction is often attempted between private reprisals and acts of privateering on the ground that the former were authorized as a means of securing compensation and had no direct relation to war or peace, whereas the latter were authorized during war only and sought to inflict injury upon the enemy; see CLARK, *op. cit., supra* n.16 at p. 702.

[25]On the Jay Treaty, see PHILLIPS and REEDE, *op. cit., supra* n.20, pp. 56–90, and SCHLOCHAUER, H.G., 'Jay Treaty' in BERNHARDT, R. (ed.), *Encyclopedia of Public International Law,* instalment 1 (1981), p. 108*ff.*

[26]*Letters of marque* were extensively issued for the last time during the French Revolutionary Wars when French privateers operating from American ports ravaged British shipping. On privateering, see SCHEUNER, U., 'Privateering' in BERNHARDT, R. (ed.), *Encyclopedia of Public International Law,* instalment 4 (1982), p. 152*ff.*, and RABUS, W, 'Booty in Sea Warfare', *ibid.*, instalment 3 (1982), p. 68*ff.*

maintaining a naval blockade was generally paid no attention. The conclusion of the Napoleonic Wars occasioned no major development regarding neutral rights and duties and the Congress of Vienna avoided any discussion of this subject.

At the time of the French-Spanish War of 1823, France declared its intention not to arm privateers and not to interfere with private shipping, whether enemy or neutral, except for blockade runners. On the same occasion, US President Monroe called upon European nations to conclude an international convention laying down the principles of neutral commerce during wartime. His proposal, drawing principally upon the rules of Armed Neutralities, entailed the abolition of privateering and the inviolability of private property at sea. Despite a rather favourable reception, nothing concrete came out of the Monroe initiative. In the wars that opposed Austria to Sardinia and Denmark to Prussia (1848–9), no use was made of privateers, while France inserted an explicit provision on the abolition of privateering in certain treaties such as those concluded with Tunisia (1830) and Sardinia (1832).

As regards the rule *free ships – free goods*, it surfaced again owing primarily to the influence of the United States such that in the period from 1815 to 1854 it was adopted in several treaties concluded between European states and the US as well as in the treaties that the US concluded with some of the newly independent Latin American states, such as Colombia, Chili, Venezuela, Peru, Bolivia and Equador. By the second quarter of the nineteenth century, renewed interest was also manifested for the requirement of effectiveness of naval blockades. A few attempts by Spain, Brazil, and Portugal to establish paper blockades were met with strong protests and failed. In the Danish-Prussian treaty of 1818, it was stipulated that a locality in order to be deemed validly besieged or blockaded should be surrounded by warships at sea and gun batteries on land. Similar clauses were included in the military instructions of Prussia and those of Denmark of 1848.

A Few Milestones: The Paris Declaration, the Alabama Case and the Hague Conferences In view of the above developments, when the Crimean War broke out in 1854, it was felt that the moment had arrived for agreeing upon common regulations with regard to the treatment of neutral property at sea. The need for uniformity was all the more pressing as the English were to join forces with the French against the Russians; England traditionally opted for the capture of enemy property on board neutral vessels, yet respected neutral property on board enemy vessels, whereas France was not against enemy goods being transported by neutral ships, but resolved to seize neutral goods aboard enemy ships.

In the event, it was agreed that each power would give up that part of its policy which was most annoying to neutral interests while maintaining the rules which were most beneficial to the merchant. In concrete terms, England accepted not to interfere with enemy goods found on neutral vessels, and France recognized the immunity of neutral property on board enemy ships. Shortly after those principles were announced, Russia made an analogous declaration pledging compliance with the *free ships – free goods* rule.

Two years later, at the Paris Congress which marked the end of hostilities, the representatives of England, France, Austria, Prussia, Sardinia and Turkey signed a declaration with a view to codifying some fundamental principles of the law of naval war and maritime neutrality including those which had for so long divided maritime nations. The Declaration of Paris read:

> (1) Privateering is, and remains, abolished; (2) The neutral flag covers enemy's goods, with the exception of contraband of war; (3) Neutral goods, with the exception of contraband of war, are not liable to capture under the enemy's flag; (4) Blockades, in order to be binding, must be effective, that is to say, maintained by a force sufficient really to prevent access to the coast of the enemy.[27]

[27]See SCHINDLER, D. and TOMAN, J. (eds), *The Laws of Armed Conflicts – A Collection of Conventions, Resolutions and Other Documents*, 3rd edn (1988) at p. 788. The 1856 Paris Declaration is given an exhaustive treatment in PIGGOTT, F., *The Declaration of Paris 1856*, 1919, especially pp. 173–218. See also FUJITA, H., 'Commentary on the Paris Declaration' in RONZITTI, N. (ed.), *The Law of Naval Warfare – A Collection of Agreements and Documents with Commentaries*, 1988, p. 66*ff*., and JOHNSON, D.H.N., 'Prize Law' in BERNHARDT, R. (ed.), *Encyclopedia of Public International Law*, instalment 4 (1982), p. 155*ff*. The drafting of the four principles was not free of criticism. The first principle, although expressed in absolute terms, would not be opposable to non-adherent nations. What is more, it is by no means clear whether the signatories were ready to forfeit the right to issue commissions to privateers in the event of a war against a non-adherent state. With regard to the second and third principles, the Declar-

Half a century after the ideas of the Secondly Armed Neutrality had to surrender to the might of the Nelsonian fleet, they were consecrated, for the most part, in the first truly international conventional instrument concerning neutral maritime commerce.[28] Only Spain, Mexico and the United States did not adhere to the Paris Declaration, having wished that the abolition of privateering had been coupled with an unconditional recognition of the inviolability of private property at sea.

The legal implications of neutrality underwent further refinement on the occasion of the American Civil War (1861–5). The main source of controversy related to the propriety of English shipyards constructing and delivering steamships on order of the Southern Confederacy for the purpose of being subsequently transformed into privateers. The most infamous cruiser put out to sea from English ports, the *Alabama*, was built at Liverpool but converted into a commerce raider on the high seas. It was basically by reason of her exploits against the merchant fleet of the Union that after the war the government of the United States sought from England compensation for damages on the grounds that Britain had not prevented the

ation excluded explicitly the contraband of war from their scope of application, but remained silent as to the case of blockade running – which would seem to make up a further exception. This is not to mention, of course, the absence of any indication as to what should be understood by contraband. Regarding the prohibition of paper blockades contained in the fourth principle, much could be said about the obscurity of terms such as 'effective' or 'sufficient' force, so that the drafters of the Paris Declaration were reproached for having left the question as unsettled as it always had been.

[28]As was shown later, the British consent to let enemy goods pass unmolested on board neutral vessels was dictated more than anything else by outstanding commercial interest. Suffice here to recall that the trade volume between Russia and Great Britain before the Crimean War was ten times greater than the trade between Russia and any other country. In particular, English industry was heavily dependent upon Russian produce of flax and tallow. A unique arrangement was thus promoted according to which Russian commodities were routed to Prussian ports whence they were shipped on board neutral vessels to England. In the words of one scholar, 'in this manner the blockade of the Baltic ports of Russia was neutralized . . . The doctrines of continuous voyages and ultimate consumption, so drastic in their results in modern times, were set aside and it was, in fact, a practical exmple of that anomaly – a military war and a commercial peace'; see STOCKTON, C.H., 'The Declaration of Paris', 14 *AJIL* (1920) at p. 360. For historical notes on the political calculations that induced the British government to surrender the right to seize enemy goods on neutral ships in return for the abolition of privateering, see MALKIN, H.W., 'The Inner History of the Declaration of Paris', 8 *BYIL* (1927), p. 1*ff*., and ANDERSON, O., 'Some Further Light on the Inner History of the Declaration of Paris', 76 *Law Quarterly Review* (1960), p. 379*ff*.

fitting out of Confederate warships within its jurisdiction and had done nothing to seize them while they were in British ports.[29]

By virtue of the treaty of Washington, signed in 1871, the dispute was submitted to an arbitral tribunal which was asked to apply the following principles of international law:

> A neutral government is bound: first, to use due diligence to prevent the fitting out, arming, or equipping, within its jurisdiction, of any vessel which it has reasonable ground to believe is intended to cruise or to carry on war against a Power with which it is at peace; and also to use like diligence to prevent the departure from its jurisdiction of any vessel intended to cruise or carry on war as above, such vessel having been specially adapted, in whole or in part, within such jurisdiction to warlike use. Secondly, not to permit or suffer either belligerent to make use of its ports or waters as the base of naval operations against the other, or for the purpose of the renewal or augmentation of military supplies or arms, or the recruitment of men. Thirdly, to exercise due diligence in its own ports and waters, and, as to all persons within its jurisdiction, to prevent any violation of the foregoing obligations and duties.[30]

Yet, ten years before the arbitral award in the *Alabama* case, the English rules of 1862 had been equally influential on another

[29]In less than two years, that is from 1862 until June 1864 when it was sunk by the Union's warship *Kearsarge* off Cherbourg, the *Alabama* sank, burned or ransomed nearly 70 ships of the Union on the Atlantic, the Indian Ocean, and even the China Sea; see SEIDEL, P., 'The Alabama' in BERNHARDT, R. (ed.), *Encyclopedia of Public International Law,* instalment 2 (1981), pp. 11–13. Another case making up the 'Alabama Claims' dispute was that of the *Florida.* First known as the *Oreto,* the *Florida* was the first Southern cruiser to be built in English shipyards. Upon being fitted out with arms and ammunition at the port of Nassau, it set out upon its hunting operations against Northern merchantmen making regular use of the British port facilities in the Bahama and Bermuda islands. It was finally captured in October 1864 by the Union warship *Wachusett* while within neutral Brazilian waters; see SEIDEL, P., 'The Florida', *ibid.,* pp. 100–1.

[30]At the time the Washington treaty was concluded, both governments involved agreed that third powers would be invited to adhere to the principles enunciated in the treaty. Notwithstanding the fact that such prospect was ultimately frustrated by the opposition of the English House of Commons, it is widely held that the so-called Washington Rules laid down the foundation of modern standards concerning the neutral duty of prevention.

score. Enacted at the time of the American Civil War in order to meet the protests of the Unionists, these rules provided that belligerent warships would not be admitted in English harbours for more than 24 hours except for repairs, that coal replenishment should be limited to the quantity necessary to arrive at the nearest home port, and that new calls for supplies would be denied before three months time. As for reparation works, only those related to the seaworthiness of the ship would be authorized, and not those intended to improve its war fighting capacity. The English rules of 1862 were clearly followed in the Italian legislation of 1864, the Dutch legislation of 1866 and the American legislation of 1870, and they were also later adopted by the Scandinavian countries.

At the turn of the century, two major events were destined to mark the process of codification of maritime neutrality. On the one hand, the first Hague Peace Conference in 1899 succeeded in codifying the customary principles of the *jus in bello* insofar as land warfare was concerned. On the other hand, the Russo-Japanese War of 1904–5 drove to the foreground the problems of war and neutrality at sea and provided the central theme for the upcoming Second Peace Conference. In the event, the 1907 Conference embarked upon an extremely ambitious undertaking which went from international arbitration to international prize court and from the prohibition of the use of force for recovery of contract debts to naval bombardment and submarine mines.[31]

Three of the four Commissions of the Conference were in fact assigned to study questions regarding the laws of war. The work of the Conference resulted in the adoption of thirteen conventions and one declaration. The drafting of a comprehensive instrument on the laws and customs of war at sea was deferred to a later conference although specific aspects of naval warfare were regulated, e.g. the conversion of merchant vessels into warships in Convention VII, the laying of contact mines in Convention VIII, the bombardment by naval forces in Convention IX, as well as certain restrictions on the right of capture in Convention XI. In matters of neutral rights and duties, the Conference gave birth to Conventions V and XIII concerning neutral powers in land and sea warfare, respectively, and also

[31]On the achievements of the Hague Conferences, see MÖSSNER, J.M., 'Hague Peace Conferences of 1899 and 1907' in BERNHARDT, R. (ed.), *Encyclopedia of Public International Law,* instalment 3 (1982), pp. 204–11.

to Convention XII on the establishment of an international prize court.

The Thirteenth Hague Convention of 1907 set out to regulate the relations between belligerents and neutrals within neutral territory. Its scope was therefore limited to neutral ports and coastal waters, while the broader issues of treatment of neutral property on the high seas (carriage of contraband, visit and search, seizure or destruction, blockade running) were not dealt with. The inviolability of neutral territory (Article 1) was reaffirmed in relation to the belligerent prohibition against the use of neutral ports and waters as a base of naval operations (Article 5), against resort therein to any act of hostility including the exercise of the right to capture or search (Article 2), or against the establishment of a prize court (Article 4).

Belligerents, on the other hand, were entitled to sail through the territorial waters of a neutral together with their prizes (Article 10), employing neutral licensed pilots if necessary (Article 11). The 24-hour rule for the stay of belligerent warships in neutral harbours was codified in Article 12, while Articles 17–18 proscribed belligerent warships when calling at a neutral port to carry out repairs of their armaments or to seek to increase their complement and supplies of ammunition. Moreover, these vessels could only be provided with sufficient fuel to reach the nearest port in their own country (Article 19), and that only every three months (Article 20).

Emanating directly from the principle of sanctity of neutral waters, the neutral power was burdened with the duty of preventing any belligerent violation therein, although that obligation was given a rather narrow reading being confined to the surveillance that the means at the disposal of the neutral state would allow (Article 25) – an elegant formulation to evade the 'due diligence' criterion of the Washington Rules. Subject to this limitation, a neutral was obliged to prevent the fitting out or arming of vessels intended to engage in hostile operations (Article 8), was further obliged to release any prize which might have been unlawfully captured within neutral jurisdiction (Article 3), and was equally expected to intern a belligerent ship and its crew each time the rules concerning the sojourn, replenishment, or bringing in of prizes were violated (Articles 21 and 24).

Faithfully reflecting the *laissez-faire* logic of the time, Hague

Convention XIII stipulated in Article 7 that a neutral power was not bound to prevent its private citizens from exporting war sinews for the use of either belligerent. The neutrality status would only be affected when the state itself supplied war matériel to the fighting armies (Article 6). Finally, it was incumbent upon the neutral to apply without distinction to all belligerents the same conditions, restrictions or prohibitions it might wish to adopt concerning the admission into its ports, roadsteads or territorial waters, of belligerent men-of-war or their prizes (Article 9).[32]

III The theory and practice of neutral conduct at sea in the twentieth century

1 Traditional rules to the test of World Wars

Following Robert Tucker's fine schematization, maritime neutrality imposes four duties upon states wishing to preserve friendly relations with belligerent powers: *abstention, impartiality, prevention* and *toleration*. Abstention and impartiality are so intimately connected to the common meaning of non-involvement or detachment that it would be fair to suggest that if abstention is the *alter ego* of neutrality, impartiality is the overriding obligation among the conditions defining that abstention.[33]

The Duty of Abstention and Impartiality Defining neutrality in terms of abstention nears a tautology, for staying out of an armed conflict means before anything else abstaining from furnishing belligerents with certain goods or services indispensable to their war effort. In the maritime context, abstention is concretized in the obligation incumbent upon the neutral state not to supply in any manner, directly or indirectly, a belligerent power with warships, ammunition, or war materials of any kind. Although Article 6 of the 1907 Thirteenth Hague Convention, which codified the above rule, is not free of controversy,

[32]For succinct remarks on that Convention, see SCHINDLER, D., 'Commentary on Hague Convention XIII' in RONZITTI, *op. cit., supra* n.27, pp. 211–22.

[33]The theory and practice of maritime neutrality after the Hague codification is reviewed in WILLIAMS, W.L., 'Neutrality in Modern Armed Conflicts: A Survey of the Developing Law', 90 *MLR* (1980), pp. 9–48; DINSTEIN, Y., 'The Laws of Neutrality', 14 *IYHR* (1984), pp. 80–110; TUCKER, R.W., *The Law of War and Neutrality at Sea*, USNWC, 50 *International Law Studies* (1955), pp. 202–62.

especially in relation to what may amount to an 'indirect' supply, the veritable paradox – in fact a predominant principle of the traditional edifice of neutrality – is that the duty of abstention does not extend to private transactions. This principle, enshrined in common Article 7 of the Thirteenth and the Fifth Hague Conventions, provided the canvass for unfathomable polemic and continues to divide legal theory even today.

By impartiality, again a notion which should normally be free of any doubt, the traditional law expects neutrals to fulfil their duties and perform their rights in a non-discriminatory manner towards all belligerents. Yet, legal doctrine has attempted here also a fine distinction – often more of a sophism – between impartiality in law and impartiality in operation, maintaining that neutrality is not compromised for the simple reason that neutral measures, although impartially applied, affect unequally the two contestants. It is clear that behind such pretensions is most often hidden the desire to side decisively with one of the belligerents without liquidating neutral status. To retain similar propositions, however, would have no more sense than saying that to allow *both* belligerents to make free use of neutral waters for launching naval operations, or to deliver to *both* belligerents any amount of military hardware requested, is consonant with neutrality law since it is perfectly impartial.

The Duty of Prevention Under the duty of prevention, a neutral power is required to avoid by all reasonable means certain belligerent conduct which if permitted might give a definite military advantage to one of the contestants. Apart from this negative aspect of prevention, the neutral carries also the duty, in a positive sense, to act swiftly and terminate any belligerent act which would infringe upon the inviolability of its territory. Thus, to react in protection of such inviolability pertains more to a duty than to a mere right. Concretely, under the relevant provisions of the Thirteenth Hague Convention, belligerents are prohibited from using neutral ports and waters as a base of naval operations, which corresponds to the duty of a neutral power to exercise such surveillance as the means at its disposal allow to prevent any violation occurring within its territory, ports, roadsteads or in its waters.

Neutral status is not affected by the mere passage of belligerent warships and prizes, provided: that warships do not remain in neutral territorial waters for more than 24 hours; that no more than three warships of the same belligerent power are anchored simultaneously in one of the ports of a neutral state; or that warships do not leave harbour until 24 hours have elapsed from the departure of an enemy merchant ship.[34] Belligerent warships are authorized to carry out in neutral ports only those repairs which are linked to their seaworthiness and not any work which may add to the fighting capacity. In the case where a belligerent warship fails to comply with neutral restrictions or prohibitions in regard to the entry of foreign men-of-war into ports or roadsteads, the neutral state must detain the ship and crew.[35]

As for replenishment, Article 19 of the Convention permits belligerent warships to obtain stores in neutral ports up to the normal supply limit and to be refuelled only for the purpose of reaching the nearest port in their own country.[36] Prizes may also be brought into neutral ports but only on account of unseaworthiness, stress of weather or want of fuel, and must leave as soon as conditions permit; should it fail to obey neutral

[34]The famous *Altmark* incident of the Second World War concerned precisely the application of the 24-hour rule in conjunction with Article 10 of the Hague Convention. On the *Altmark* incident of February 1940, see WALDOCK, C.H.M., 'The Release of the *Altmark*'s Prisoners', 24 *BYIL* (1947), p. 216*ff.*; BISSCHOP, W.R., 'The *Altmark*', 26 *GST* (1940), p. 67*ff.*; BORCHARD, E., 'Was Norway Delinquent in the Case of the Altmark?', 34 *AJIL* (1940), p. 289*ff*,; TELDERS, B.M., 'L'incident de l'Altmark', 48 *RGDIP* (1941–5), p. 90*ff.*; McCHESNEY, B., 'The Altmark Incident and Modern Warfare – Innocent Passage in Wartime and the Right of Belligerents to Use Force to Redress Neutrality Violations', 52 *Northwestern University Law Review* (1957–8), p. 320*ff.*; SCHÜTZ, H.-J., 'The Altmark' in BERNHARDT, R. (ed.), *Encyclopedia of Public International Law*, instalment 3 (1982) at p. 14.

[35]The conditions surrounding the scuttling of the German pocket battleship *Graf Spee* off the harbour of Montevideo in December 1939 illustrated the delicate problem of interpretation related to Article 17 of the Hague Convention. On the *Graf Spee* incident, see MIRWART, J., 'Guerre maritime – Séjour d'un navire de guerre belligérant dans un port neutre – Incident du Graf von Spee', 20 *RDILC* (1939), p. 823*ff.*; O'CONNELL, D.P., *The Influence of Law on Sea Power*, 1975, pp. 27–39; BERG, A., 'The Graf Spee', in BERNHARDT, R. (ed.), *Encyclopedia of Public International Law*, instalment 3 (1982), p. 200*ff.*

[36]The *Attilio Regolo* incident of September 1943 involved Italian warships which, after having been supplied with fuel in Spanish ports, refused to leave in accordance with the 24-hour rule and were subsequently interned by Spanish authorities. For more on the incident, see LEROY, P., 'L'affaire de l'*Attilio Regolo* et autres navires', 11 *AFDI* (1965), p. 278*ff.*

orders, the neutral power must employ all available means to release its original officers and intern the prize crew.[37]

The Duty of Acquiescence By toleration is understood the neutral duty to acquiesce in the legitimate exercise of certain belligerent measures such as those aimed at controlling contraband traffic. A belligerent navy has the right to intercept, board and search neutral merchantmen everywhere outside neutral territorial waters and, if carriage of contraband is established, eventually escort them into port for prize adjudication. Faced with such interference, neutrals have the obligation to submit, the only exception being the right to convoying. The underlying rationale, as explained in detail in the next two chapters, is that the trade in contraband was traditionally tolerated but only as a purely private venture which could never give rise to any claim of diplomatic protection; private neutrals were given the possibility of significant gain in return for the risk of capture and confiscation. Likewise, neutrals had no right to protest even against more severe treatment that the belligerent might exceptionally reserve for neutral shipping such as the outright destruction of a seized vessel under certain conditions.[38]

[37]The controversy over the *City of Flint* incident, concerning the release of a German prize in Norwegian waters in October 1939, typified the problems relating to treatment of prizes within neutral jurisdiction and the exact conditions of application of Article 21 of the Hague instrument. On the *City of Flint* incident, see EAGLETON, C, 'The City of Flint', 34 *AJIL* (1940), p. 89*ff.*; MIRWART, J., 'Guerre maritime – Admission de prises dans un port neutre: The City of Flint', 20 *RDILC* (1939), p. 830*ff.*; MÜNCH, I., 'The City of Flint' in BERNHARDT, R. (ed.), *Encyclopedia of Public International Law,* instalment 3 (1982), p. 85*ff.* See also MADDERS, K.J., 'Internment' in BERNHARDT, R. (ed.), *Encyclopedia of Public International Law,* instalment 3 (1982), p. 224*ff.*, and TRAUTTMANSDORFF, F., 'Disarming of Belligerents by Neutrals', *ibid.*, p. 155*ff.*

[38]Mention should also be made at this juncture to the right of angary since it concerned neutral vessels found in belligerent ports. The right of angary consists in the requisition of neutral merchant ships in the case of imperative need and upon the conditions that full compensation is paid and that they would be restored to their owners as soon as they would be no more needed. Among the abundant writings on angary, see HARLEY, J.E., 'The Law of Angary', 13 *AJIL* (1919), p. 267*ff.*; BULLOCK, C.L., 'Angary', 3 *BYIL* (1922–3), p. 99*ff.*; WILSON, G.G., 'Taking Over and Return of Dutch Vessels, 1918–1919', 24 *AJIL* (1930), p. 694*ff.*; WOOLSEY, L.H., 'The Taking of Foreign Ships in American Ports', 35 *AJIL* (1941), p. 497*ff.*; LAUTERPACHT, H., 'Angary and Requisition of Neutral Property', 27 *BYIL* (1950), p. 455*ff.*; GRAWITZ, M., 'L'angarie', 58 *RGDIP* (1954), p. 538*ff.*; DOWNEY, W.G., 'Captured Enemy Property: Booty of War and Seized Enemy Property', 44 *AJIL* (1950), p. 488*ff.*; VAN BOGAERT, E., 'L'angarie', 21 *NILR* (1974), p. 251*ff.*; LAGONI, R., 'Right of Angary' in BERNHARDT, R. (ed.), *Encyclopedia of Public International Law,* instalment 3 (1982), p. 18*ff.*

2 Recent practice: continuity, transformation or outright abandonment?

In the post-Second World War era, the traditional institutions of maritime neutrality have only rarely operated. Apart from the protracted Egyptian interdiction campaign against Israel interests in the Suez Canal, the short-lived Indo-Pakistani confrontation of 1971, and, to a much lesser extent, the Korean and Vietnam conflicts, the rights and duties of neutrals at sea did not occasion much polemic either in theory or in practice. Symptomatic of the lack of interest in the laws of war in general after 1945, the customary principles of sea warfare were relegated to a shadowy subsistence while it was even suspected that they might have been totally eclipsed by Charter law. It was the amplitude of state practice during the so-called Gulf Tanker War that stimulated the reappraisal of long-forgotten issues and revived interest in the subject.

Some twenty years after isolated French visit and search operations during the Algerian War and similar US measures in the context of the Cuban missile crisis, the world needed urgent answers to matters ranging from neutral and belligerent rights within international straits to neutral convoys or capture, and from unneutral service to minesweeping. Even though the validity of traditional concepts was not seriously called into question, the real issue concerned their possible transformation in the light of current conditions. Most of the Persian Gulf experience relating to the particulars of prize law is analysed in chapter 6 below, yet two aspects which stirred discussion on the general theory of neutral duties would be pertinent to address here. In fact, it was the policies and actual conduct of two states, namely the United States and Kuwait, which were made most often the object of considerable controversy and thus merit a cautious review.

Forcible Protection of Neutral Rights: The US Stance On one level, US interventionism in the Persian Gulf claimed the immunities proper to a neutral power. On another level, they affirmed rights well within the scope of application of the Charter's prescriptions on self-defence. For the purposes of this analysis, however, the question to be examined is whether the US naval presence and the incidents it occasioned were truly suggestive of a neutral commitment and to what extent they remained respectful of the obligations resulting therefrom. The crux of the matter is how to identify the exact moment of transition when neutrality cedes to partisanship and abstention converts into entanglement and even provocation.

Could a state which led a sweeping diplomatic campaign in order to cut the arms supply lines of one of the two belligerents (an initiative sponsoring an arms embargo against *both* belligerents would certainly be different), as the United States did with Operation Staunch,[39] pretend in good faith to be a neutral? Could a state which was chiefly responsible for the Security Council's idleness before the Iraqi aggression and which slowly drove that body into partiality (since the only attacks explicitly ever condemned by the Security Council throughout the eight-year war were those of Iran in 1984 against Kuwaiti and Saudi vessels) still be labelled a neutral?[40] If one adds to this the fact that the United States, like so many other nations, tilted in favour of the original aggressor, its policy should be criticizable not only under the customary principles of neutrality but also under the Charter values.[41]

[39]The policy was advocated in these words: 'we are actively working to persuade Iran's leaders of the futility of their pursuit of the war by limiting their ability to buy weapons. This effort – "Operation Staunch" – is aimed specifically at Iran because that country, unlike Iraq, has rejected all calls for negotiations'; see statement by Under Secretary for Political Affairs M.H. Armacost, 16 June 1987, reprinted in 26 *ILM* 1431 (1987).

[40]As one author remarked, 'continued and demonstrable United States partiality for Iraq only prolonged this tragic conflict by discouraging Iran from working with the United Nations Security Council to end the war because one of the latter's permanent and most important members was eviscerally and implacably prejudiced against it. For this very reason, those inexcusably few United Nations Security Council resolutions that have so far been adopted on the Gulf War were all clearly and admittedly biased in favor of Iraq'; see BOYLE, F.A., 'International Crisis and Neutrality: United States Foreign Policy Toward the Iran-Iraq War', 43 *Mercer Law Review* (1992) at p. 545. It may be recalled at this point that it took the Security Council seven long years of 'culpable mildness' [the expression belongs to Judge BEDJAOUI, M., 'The Gulf War of 1980–1988 and the Islamic Conception of International Law' in DEKKER, I.F. and POST, H.H.G. (eds), *The Gulf War of 1980–1988: The Iran-Iraq War in International Legal Perspective* (1992) at p. 281] before determining that there exists a breach of peace as regards the conflict between Iran and Iraq (see Security Council Resolution 598 of 1987) according to its Charter mandate. What is more, one had to wait eleven years to see a UN organ surrendering to the evident reality of the Iraqi responsibility for having commenced the war of aggression against Iran.

[41]As Louis Henkin pertinently remarked in this respect, 'no one would accuse us of being a friend of Iran, but there is a strong case that Iraq is probably the

It could be argued, of course, that a state not party to an armed conflict does not forfeit its neutral status by challenging the unlawful acts of belligerents that affect its interests. As Article 14 of the 1939 Harvard Research on the Rights and Duties of Neutral States provided, for instance, 'a neutral State shall not be deemed to have violated Article 4 of this Convention by resorting to acts of reprisal or retaliation against a belligerent because of illegal acts of the latter'.[42] Impartiality remains, however, an absolute neutral duty. This is all the more so when unlawful acts, equally detrimental to neutral interests, are com-

---

aggressor. No one has mentioned that for some years now . . . Neutral means impartial. Is Kuwait neutral, or is it perhaps a co-belligerent? Is the United States supporting Kuwait, and, if so, are we also co-belligerents? If so, we may not be only supporting the aggressor but if the old laws of war apply – we also may be violating the laws of war. I suggest we may not only have slipped into the war, but, from the international lawyer's point of view, we seem to have slipped into a particular position on international law without much thought about it and without any thought to the long-term consequences'; see 'Conference Report – The Persian/Arabian Gulf Tanker War: International Law or International Chaos?', 19 *ODIL* (1988) at p. 310. As has been written with regard to the reflagging operation, 'the United States was protecting the Kuwaiti-owned vessels with "cellophane flags" that Iran sees through . . . While the war rages between Iraq and Iran, the United States continues to claim that it is neutral and has the right of innocent passage in the Persian Gulf. But neutrality is generally indicated by not taking sides or demonstrating forms of partisan protection. Would it not have been better initially for the United States to have abstained from *any* involvement in the Persian Gulf? Rather than trying to police the Kuwaiti convoys while hiding behind the mask of neutrality, the United States could have backed the United Nations in protecting the convoys under the U.N. flag'; see PHILLIPS, T.A., 'Exchanging Excuses for Uses of Force – The Tug of War in the Persian Gulf', 10 *Houston Journal of International Law* (1988) at p. 292. In the same vein another scholar concluded that 'in the case of the U.S. reflagging operation, the 11 tankers continued to be owned and controlled by Kuwait. Under either formulation of the laws of war, if Kuwait is characterized as a belligerent, the character of the tanker was not altered by the U.S. reflagging, and Iran would not have been required by international law to respect the neutral character of the U.S. flag'; see CARON, D.D., 'Choice and Duty in Foreign Affairs – The Reflagging of the Kuwaiti Tankers' in JOYNER, C.C. (ed.), *The Persian Gulf War – Lessons for Strategy, Law, and Diplomacy*, 1990 at p. 165.

[42]See 33 *AJIL* (1939) *Suppl.* at p. 329 . Article 4 stipulated that 'a neutral State, in the exercise of its neutral rights and in performance of its neutral duties, shall be impartial and shall refrain from discrimination between belligerents'. This would be the concrete application in the *jus in bello* of a far more general principle of the law of nations which recognizes that a state is not bound to abstain from exercising a right which another state has unlawfully denied; see Corfu Channel Case, Merits, *ICJ Rep. 1949*, at p. 30. For an attempt at systematization of what he names 'armed self-protection short of self-defense', or a right which would fall conceptually between self-defence and law-enforcement, see GILL, T.D., 'The Forcible Protection, Affirmation and Exercise of Rights by States under Contemporary International Law', 23 *NYIL* (1992), p. 105*ff.*

mitted by both belligerents. Whenever a neutral is confronted, therefore, with the same token of illegality on the part of belligerents, to commit itself to resisting, nay using force against, the unlawful deeds of one (while leaving unchallenged the offences perpetrated by the other) could hardly be in conformity with the predominant onus of impartiality.

If American forces felt that they should do something about the Iranian unwarranted attacks on neutral shipping, would it not be reasonable to wonder why they did not demonstrate the same commitment to challenging the equally unlawful, and much more destructive, Iraqi air strikes against neutral shipping?[43] If Iran should not be allowed to sow mines and strafe tankers unchallenged, would it not be consistent to expect that Iraq should also be prevented from launching indiscriminate lethal missile attacks on merchant vessels? American airborne early warning assets could, in fact, keep track of any Iraqi air force sortie much easier and earlier than US surface units could follow the movement of Iranian Boghammers on their radar screens. And yet, no US aircraft was ever ordered to intercept an Iraqi bomber in order to frustrate an imminent attack. Instead, naval commanders proved eager to give chase to Iranian speedboats.

Washington's reaction to the *USS Stark* and the *USS Samuel Roberts* incidents is especially significant in this respect. If the former surprises with its passivity and cool-headedness, the latter is clearly suggestive of a vengeance-prone stance. Despite

[43]One should be very critical of all facile assumptions like the one that holds lawful the Iraqi air campaign against 'legitimate naval targets' but unlawful the Iranian hit-and-run tactics against vessels trading with 'neutral' Kuwait and Saudi Arabia. Consider, for instance, the following statement: 'while Iraqi attacks have been on shipping serving a belligerent, Iranian retaliatory attacks have been against a wide range of third country neutral shipping serving non-belligerent Arab Gulf ports in international waters'; Weinberger Report to the Congress on Security Arrangements in the Persian Gulf, 15 June 1987, reprinted in 26 *ILM* (1987) at p. 1445. Domestically, Washington's ill-defined Gulf policy often met with strong opposition. Senator Nunn, reflecting upon the Weinberger Report in June 1987, had this to say: 'the challenges to freedom of navigation originate with Kuwait's ally Iraq. It is difficult to justify U.S. actions on this principle when America is indirectly protecting the interests of Iraq who started the "tanker war" and who has conducted about 70 percent of the ship attacks'; see 26 *ILM* 1467 (1987). Senator Nunn continued further in the same document: 'with a highly visible effort to assist the close ally of a belligerent, U.S. claims of neutrality will lose credibility. Moreover, if the U.S. aim is to prevent an Iranian victory, there are better means than encouraging a direct confrontation with Iran', *ibid.*

the heavy casualty toll to deplore in the *Stark* attack, and the persistent rumour that Iraq might have intentionally delivered that blow in order to provoke the internationalization of the Iran-Iraq conflict, the US promptly accepted the Iraqi apologies and abstained from any 'proportionate response'. In striking contrast, when the *Samuel Roberts* struck a floating mine, suffering minor damage and only ten seamen reportedly injured, the US naval presence was immediately and significantly stepped up and plans for more than a tit-for-tat strike got under way.[44]

Some could argue that an official policy of 'benevolent' or 'qualified' neutrality had been announced, as the following statement lays bare: 'we do not wish to see an Iranian victory in that terrible conflict. Nevertheless, the United States remains formally neutral in the war.'[45] However, 'non-belligerency' has never acquired a firm grip on international law, being, in the apt metaphor of a scholar, 'un concept essentiellement politique, par definition indefinissable'.[46] Yet, even those who believe it has become firmly established in law define it as the state of overt support for one belligerent, sort of taking part in active hostilities on its side, whereas the American intervention in the Gulf apparently overstepped the limits of such a problematic notion.

As from mid-1987, the conduct of American forces, it is submitted, came more and more closer to active participation in hostilities against Iran.[47] On 10 August 1987, a US Navy F-14

[44]For more on the *Stark* incident, see VLAHOS, M., 'The *Stark* Report', 114 *USNIP* (May 1988), pp. 64–7. A final settlement to the compensation issue occurred in March 1989; see 28 *ILM* (1989), pp. 644–8.

[45]See statement by Under Secretary for Political Affairs M.H. Armacost, 16 June 1987, reprinted in 26 *ILM* (1987) at p. 1430.

[46]See MEYROWITZ, H., *Le principe de l'égalité des belligérants devant le droit de la guerre*, 1970 at p. 327.

[47]It should be noted that at the time of the *Sea Isle City* incident in October 1987, former US President Jimmy Carter said that the United States was acting 'in effect as a belligerent' in the war because of the increased American naval presence; quoted in RAMAZANI, R.K., 'The Iran-Iraq War and the Persian Gulf Crisis', 87 *Current History* (Feb.1988) at pp. 61, 86. It is common knowledge today that American AWACS had literally played the role of air controllers for Iraqi air force missions in the Gulf; see BARRY, J. and CHARLES, R., 'Sea of Lies – Special Report', *Newsweek*, 13 July 1992, at p. 15. It is also believed that the United States passed targeting and intelligence information to Iraq to enable successful air strikes against the Iranian storage sites on Farsi Island at the end of 1987; see BOYLE, *op. cit., supra* n.40 at p. 538. In addition, according to recent revelations, the United States had been conducting since 1987 extensive covert

Tomcat fired two Sparrow air-to-air missiles at an Iranian aircraft over the Hormuz Strait but both missed their target. On 8 October 1987, US frigate-based helicopters attacked and sank four Iranian speedboats about 15 miles south west of Farsi Island. During the already reviewed action of 18 April 1988, an impressive number of American warships entered into large-scale clashes with Iranian forces.[48]

By the end of April 1988, the US State Department had announced that all foreign merchant vessels could enjoy the protection of the US Navy.[49] This meant that American forces would attempt, to every possible extent, to interpose themselves, engage or chase away any Iranian platform which would interfere with transiting merchant ships. During Gulf missions, as the Iranian Airbus incident depicted in a most tragic fashion, US warships were clearly instructed to operate as if under a constant Iranian threat. Speaking, therefore, of simple support to Iraq in the circumstances prevailing in the course of the final year of the Iran-Iraq War would be an understatement. Unlike the practice of its European partners in the Gulf armada,[50] the

---

operations in Gulf waters against Iran. It all began in July 1987 with Operation Eager Glacier, the CIA's reconnaissance programme that sent spy planes and helicopters over Iranian bases. Next, special forces manning patrol boats and helicopters were stationed on two giant floating barges to carry out secret night missions; see BARRY and CHARLES, *supra* at p. 14. The capture of the *Iran-Ajr* red-handed was arguably the fruit of such a mission.

[48]It is worth remembering that, at the same time, a decisive Iraqi offensive was unfolding in the north of the Gulf for the recapture of the Faw peninsula. Iran was convinced that the two-pronged attack was a coordinated US-Iraqi action and further accused the United States of providing air cover to the Iraqi Faw offensive; see ENTESSAR, N., 'Superpowers and Persian Gulf Security: The Iranian Perspective', 10 *Third World Quarterly* (July 1988) at pp. 1446–7. Faced with the increasingly assertive American presence, Iran had to deplore, in a single day, several gunboats sunk and two oil platforms wrecked, for one helicopter downed. It would be, no doubt, difficult to conceive of these actions in terms other than those of active hostilities.

[49]In the words of Secretary of Defence Frank Carlucci, the United States could not 'stand by and watch innocent people be killed or maimed by malicious, lawless actions when [it has] the means to assist, and perhaps prevent them . . . This policy should not be construed as a tilt in either direction in the war. Our policy has been and will continue to be one of strict neutrality'; see 88 *US Department of State Bulletin* (July 1988), No.2136 at p. 61.

[50]It is worth comparing in this respect the *modus operandi* of the European naval contingents. In fact, the naval forces of several European countries deployed in the Gulf were extremely cautious not to get entangled in a type of action which could lead them astray of their narrowly defined duties, that is to say, according protection to merchant ships of their flag and minesweeping the Gulf shipping routes. It was the same foreseeable risk that had for a long time kept the

United States was the only power to undertake combat action against one of the Gulf belligerents, and this was not the first time that the US interpreted neutrality as affording measures that few would identify with abstention or impartiality.

Kuwait's Hazardous Advances to Non-belligerency A brief review of Kuwait's pretence of neutrality illustrates the perennial dilemmas of an aggrieved belligerent *vis-à-vis* a *mala fide* neutral. At an early stage, Iran confined itself to traditional contraband control measures against merchant vessels *en route* to Kuwaiti ports and made repeated requests to its Arab neighbours to abide by the 1907 Hague Conventions.[51] There is sufficient evidence, however, that Tehran as from the fourth year of the war utterly disbelieved Kuwait's pledges of neutrality, and that in 1987 Iran formally decided to act towards Kuwait as Iraq's closest ally. Statements, and later deeds, confirm the view that Iran resolved that it should no longer suffer illusions but that it had better put an ultimate end to Kuwait's duplicity by directly attacking its territory.

Iran insisted that Kuwait was not playing by the rules and that, in truth, was making a mockery of its declared neutrality by regularly allowing Iraqi forces to make use of its territory in order to launch air strikes against Iranian oil production centres. Denounced also was the generous financial and logistical assistance to Iraq.[52] Tehran published every so often information to substantiate its accusations and constantly demanded a reappraisal of the 'impartial stance purported by the Kuwaiti

---

Europeans indecisive as to the prudence of committing naval forces to the Persian Gulf. European governments were certainly hostile to a Gulf mission as a western crusade against Iranian fundamentalism for fear of unpredictable consequences. In a statement of 17 June 1987, for instance, the French government expressed its reservations in these words: 'il serait, en particulier, dangereux de donner le sentiment que se constitue une force navale multinationale pour la protection des navires marchands, laquelle ne manquerait pas de susciter un engrenage de réactions qui feraient du Golfe un lien d'affrontement entre puissances extérieures'; see 33 *AFDI* (1987) at p. 948.

[51]See, for instance, UN Doc. *S/17482*, 20 September 1985, and UN Doc. *S/17496*, 25 September 1985.

[52]It will be recalled that under the 'War Relief Crude Oil' Agreement of February 1983 between Saudi Arabia/Kuwait and Iraq, the Saudis/Kuwaitis committed themselves to the payment of the sale-proceeds to Iraq of the oil produced in the oil fields of Khafji to make up for the oil revenue it had lost due to the destruction of its port facilities on Shatt-al-Arab; see MEHR, F., 'Neutrality in the Gulf War', 20 *ODIL* (1989) at p. 105.

government'. Kuwait, for its part, insisted on the sincerity of its policy of abstention, and refused Iran's allegations – although its replies remained largely rhetorical.

According to information obtained by a captured Iraqi pilot in September 1986, all Iraqi air strikes on merchant ships and coastal installations in the Persian Gulf were facilitated by transit-flight through Kuwaiti airspace.[53] In a series of intrusions into Iran's airspace in October and November 1987, Iraqi planes fled back to their bases through Kuwait, while in an earlier incident an Iraqi fighter made an emergency landing on Kuwait's Boubian Island wherefrom it departed two days later.[54] Iran protested anew on 22 December 1987, maintaining that a formation of 16 Iraqi planes, 4 fighter bombers and 12 tankers, overflew Kuwait on its way to Larak oil terminal in the southern Gulf.[55] Another Note was addressed in March 1988 claiming continued availability of Kuwaiti territory for Iraqi flights by reference to a further incident on 20 January 1988 when an Iraqi aircraft, after having attacked the Resalat oil platform, made a safe return flying through Kuwaiti airspace.[56]

In light of the above, in July 1987, Iranian President Ali Kham-

[53]It was further claimed that 'the Iraqi use of Kuwaiti airspace was co-ordinated in advance, so that no radio transmission would be required while the war planes were in the air'; see UN Doc. *S/18557*, 5 January 1987. Kuwait's reply is in UN Doc. *S/18582*, 12 January 1987.

[54]See UN Doc. *S/19409*, 7 January 1988. Kuwait rejected the Iranian accusations as inaccurate, indicating, for instance, that there is no airfield on Boubian Island; see UN Doc. *S/19417*, 11 January 1988.

[55]For Tehran it was clear that Kuwait by consenting to such practices was adopting an allied posture with Baghdad: 'the Government of Kuwait, by granting air corridor and flight permission to the Iraqi planes, has clearly cooperated with the Iraqi regime'; see UN Doc. *S/20003*, 11 July 1988. Kuwait once more negated the truthfulness of the information; see UN Doc. *S/20015*, 14 July 1988.

[56]See UN Doc. *S/19841*, 26 April 1988. See also UN Doc. *S/19849*, 24 April 1988, and UN Doc. *S/19872*, 9 May 1988 for the reaction of Kuwait. It is of interest to recall at this juncture that, to the extent the Iranian allegations were accurate, Kuwait would bear responsibility for failing 'to prevent the entry within its jurisdiction of belligerent military aircraft, and to compel them to alight [every time] they have entered such jurisdiction', that is to say for violating Articles 40 and 42 of the 1923 Hague Rules of Aerial Warfare; see Commission of Jurists to Consider and Report upon the Revision of the Rules of Warfare – General Report, 32 *AJIL* (1938) *Suppl.* at pp. 34–6. Some of the Hague Rules, although never adopted in a legally binding form, would still be regarded as corresponding to international customary principles. Similar neutral duties were specified in Article 14 of the 1928 Havana Convention on Maritime Neutrality, and Article 95 of the 1939 Draft Convention on Rights and Duties of Neutral States in Naval and Aerial War, 33 *AJIL* (1939) *Suppl.* at pp. 766–8.

anei was reported as saying: 'we do not know of any party that so openly supports Iraq and makes facilities available to it; therefore, Kuwait will be the target of our assault'. A spokesman of the Iranian Parliament went on to explain this new policy in these words: 'we have abandoned our former policy of overlooking the damage done to our installations and not attacking those of Iraq's partners, and have decided to apply henceforth a policy of tit-for-tat in proportion to the evils Iraq is perpetrating. So if an oil tanker is attacked, we shall likewise attack tankers, while if terminals and wells are attacked, we shall attack terminals and wells.'[57] In August 1987, the UN Secretary-General was informed of the Iranian intentions in a letter that read in part: 'until the official announcement by Kuwait of its guaranteed withdrawal of financial, political and logistical support for Iraq and hence a position of complete neutrality, Kuwait will be regarded as a partner of Iraq in the war. The Islamic Republic of Iran will adjust its policies *vis-à-vis* Kuwait accordingly.'[58]

Following the substance and the tone of this diplomatic correspondence, it becomes manifest that Iran for at least the last two years of the Gulf War considered Kuwait's pretended neutrality ended since the latter had for all practical purposes joined Iraq's camp. From August 1987, therefore, Iran mounted systematic attacks against Kuwaiti freighters,[59] vessels of third states

[57]See UN Doc. *S/19005*, 29 July 1987.

[58]See UN Doc. *S/19041*, 14 August 1987. In later statements Kuwait was charged with 'official complicity on the part of the aggressor regime of Iraq in the latter's imposed war against the Islamic Republic of Iran' and of 'total disregard for the rules of neutrality'; see UN Doc. *S/19797*, 18 April 1988, and UN Doc. *S/19865*, 5 May 1988. A similar Note was once addressed to the government of Saudi Arabia. It concerned two instances in January and April 1988 in which Iraqi planes, on their return trip from Gulf missions, made use of Dahran and Abu Jobil airports. Based on these facts, Iran spoke of 'all-around Saudi co-operation with and support for the aggressive Iraqi regime' and 'unequivocal violation of the principles of neutrality'; see UN Doc. *S/19971*, 29 June 1988. Riyadh denied the allegations as completely unfounded; see UN Doc. *S/20007*, 11 July 1988.

[59]It should be recalled that ships of Kuwaiti ownership or in Kuwaiti service had been singled out well before. Of 52 Iranian attacks on shipping from September 1986 through July 1987, 34 were directed against Kuwaiti vessels or vessels bound to or from Kuwaiti ports; see 'The Iran-Iraq War and the American Naval Intervention', *Middle East Military Balance* (1987–8) at p. 65. On 31 August 1987, the *Jabal Ali* came under fire from an Iranian warship in the southern Gulf; see UN Doc. *S/19093*, 1 September 1987. On 16 October 1987, the Kuwaiti-owned *Sea Isle City* anchored in Kuwaiti territorial waters was hit by a missile; see UN Doc. *S/19215*, 16 October 1987.

trading with Kuwait,[60] and later on refinery plants and military posts.[61] Although the language of the Iranian declarations has often led commentators to speak of a policy of reprisals against an insincere and foul neutral, a different construction is also possible. Convinced that Kuwait was deeply and irrevocably involved in Iraq's war effort, Iran might have found it opportune to impose against the former the retaliation in kind that it was not possible to apply against the latter. Under this interpretation, Kuwait would have thus forfeited its non-belligerent status by having assumed a co-belligerent posture instead.

The essential question to be asked, therefore, is the following: are the Iranian attacks against Kuwait and Kuwait-related interests to be deemed as peacetime forcible reprisal measures, or should they rather be considered as belligerent reprisals? Following the first mentioned assumption, the unprovoked raids against Kuwaiti or Kuwait-destined shipping would be difficult to plead as having any legitimacy.[62] In the second hypothesis, however, a more defensible case might be made for the Iranian practices. In other words, in order to convince Iraq to discontinue its unlawful preying on merchant vessels carrying Iranian oil, Iran could meet like with like and attack merchant ships trading with *belligerent* Kuwait.[63]

[60]On 15 October 1987, a missile attack was launched against a Liberian tanker while in the territorial waters of Kuwait; see UN Doc. *S/19210*, 15 October 1987.

[61]On 22 October 1987, Iran fired a Silkworm missile hitting an oil-loading platform; see UN Doc. *S/19227*, 22 October 1987. On 7 December 1987, another Silkworm was launched against Kuwaiti oil installations; see UN Doc. *S/19328*, 8 December 1987. On 30 March 1988, three Iranian gunboats entered Kuwaiti territorial waters and opened fire against military positions on Boubian Island; see UN Doc. *S/19709*, 30 March 1988. Iran denied any implication in the incident; see UN Doc. *S/19729*, 4 April 1988. On 20 April 1988, a Scud missile was fired into Kuwaiti territory and exploded near installations of the Getty Oil Company in the Wafra area; see UN Doc. *S/19811*, 20 April 1988.

[62]It is under this assumption that most of the legal commentaries have addressed the issue; see, for instance, JENKINS, M., 'Air Attacks on Neutral Shipping in the Persian Gulf: The Legality of the Iraqi Exclusion Zone and Iranian Reprisals', 8 *Boston College International and Comparative Law Review* (1985) at p. 547; LECKOW, R., 'The Iran-Iraq Conflict in the Gulf: The Law of War Zones', 37 *ICLQ* (1988) at p. 640; ROACH, A.J., 'Missiles on Target: Targeting and Defense Zones in the Tanker War', 31 *VJIL* (1991) at p. 603.

[63]A few publicists approached the issue from that angle, but left the question basically unanswered; see RUSSO, F.V., 'Neutrality at Sea in Transition: State Practice in the Gulf War as Emerging International Customary Law' 19 *ODIL* (1988) at p. 394, and BOCZEK, B.A., 'Law of Warfare at Sea and Neutrality: Lessons from the Gulf War', 20 *ODIL* (1989) at pp. 259–60. For T.S. Schiller, however, the fact appears indisputable that Iran considered itself to be at war

Where We Are Today and Where We Are Going How is then one to interpret that anthology of violations of the old law of neutrality? What else can be made out of that messy experience if not the outright abandonment of traditional neutral standards? Before racing to such fatalistic conclusions, however, it may be worth remembering that the very legal evaluation of those practices is only possible by constant reference to that 'obsolete' body of legal norms. Admitting that those rules have now *in toto* disappeared would create a legal vacuum for which the law of self-defence would only be a poor subsitute.

This radical approach could thus lead to the absurd conclusion that practices such as the boarding or diversion of foreign vessels, the confiscation of contraband, the capture or destruction of foreign ships chartered by the enemy, armed reprisals against a non-participant state that wilfully offers military assistance to the enemy, and so many other practices which there is no need to mention here, are simply not regulated by modern international law in the sense that there are no explicit principles neither prohibiting nor allowing such acts. Instead of assessing classical neutrality as merely non-existent, therefore, care should be taken to reformulate it in order to become compatible with what one might call the self-defence working environment and in order to be able to run new applications thereby. Or, as Eric David wrote in 1990, 's'il est donc trop tard pour la neutralité, la guerre Iran-Irak montre aussi qu'il est encore trop tôt pour la sécurité collective'.[64]

---

with Kuwait; see SCHILLER, T.S., 'The Gulf War and Shipping: Recent Developments' in PARRITT, B.A.H. (ed.), *Violence at Sea*, 1986 at p. 121. *Cf.* Dietrich Schindler's view: 'on ne saurait non plus invoquer l'*inobservation de ses devoirs* par un Etat neutre pour justifier le recours à la force contre celui-ci. Même la déchéance des droits d'un Etat neutre ne confère aucun droit au belligérant lésé de recourir à la force contre lui. Seules les mesures non armées sont encore permises'; see SCHINDLER, D., 'L'emploi de la force par un Etat belligérant sur le territoire d'un Etat non belligérant' in *Estudios de derecho internacional Homenaje al Profesor Miaja de la Muela*, 1979, vol.II at p. 858. A similarly restrictive approach is adopted by another scholar who notes with relation to Iranian attacks against Kuwait: 'même si les attaques menées contre le territoire de certains Etats tiers pouvaient se fonder, au regard du droit de la neutralité, sur le non-respect par ces Etats de leur devoir de neutres – ce qui doit être démontré *in concreto* – elles restaient inadmissibles au regard des règles contemporaines de l'interdiction du recours à la force'; see DAVID, E., 'Le droit de la neutralité à l'épreuve de la guerre du Golfe (1980–1988)', 11 *Cahier du Cedsi* (1990) at p. 51.

[64]See DAVID, *op. cit., supra* at p. 51.

IV New challenges, old values: collective security versus neutrality

1 Neutrality and the UN Charter: an awkward coexistence

The League's Legacy All the classical definitions of neutrality given at the very beginning of this chapter remain no doubt descriptive of an international legal order that found nothing irregular in having states vacillate between peace and war. The well-settled triple schematization of nations, as nations at peace, nations at war and neutral nations, stood firm and intact through the First World War and the creation of the League of Nations. However, as soon as the Wilsonian idealism inspired the vision of an ecumenical peace-guarding organization, war, and consequently neutrality, were impetuously declared outmoded.

Heralding the transition from *balance of power* to *collective security*, or, 'safety for all by all', to use Alfred Zimmern's phrase,[65] the League of Nations Council affirmed in 1920 that 'the conception of neutrality of the Members of the League is incompatible with the principle that all Members will be obliged to cooperate in enforcing respect for their engagements'.[66] The Covenant's breakthrough was some years later coupled with the Paris Pact which, in essence, discarded the resort to war as a dispute settlement mechanism among civilized nations. Article 16 of the Covenant, combined with the 1928 renunciation of war, therefore, led the great majority of writers to toll the death-bell of neutrality.

Commenting on the meaning of the Paris Pact, Quincy Wright concluded that, 'war cannot occur without violation of the Pact, and armed violence cannot be justified except within the legal concept of self-defence. Neutrality posited upon isolation and impartiality has lost its legal foundation',[67] while Malbone

[65]See ZIMMERN, A., 'The Problem of Collective Security' in Wright, Q. (ed.), *Neutrality and Collective Security*, 1935 at p. 4. See also McNAIR, A.D., 'Collective Security', 17 *BYIL* (1936), p. 150*ff.*

[66]See League of Nations, *Official Journal*, no.2 (March 1920) at p. 57. A detailed treatment of the question is found in MICHAILIDÈS, P., *La neutralité et la Société des Nations*, 1933.

[67]WRIGHT, Q., 'The Meaning of the Pact of Paris', 27 *AJIL* (1933) at p. 61. And elsewhere, 'a little reflection will make it clear that this impartiality in the presence of violence, required by the nineteenth century law of neutrality, is a principle which can logically exist only under conditions of complete or partial

Graham maintained that, 'the specific instances of war – i.e., of the result of negative jurisdiction over states – and of its concomitant function, neutrality, are due progressively to lessen and eventually to disappear'.[68] John Whitton, for his part, argued: 'on a voulu consacrer, dans l'organisation du monde sous l'égide d'une grande constitution universelle, la véritable fin de la neutralité. On a soutenu qu'au point de vue de la logique et de la pure raison, la neutralité et la Société s'excluaient l'une l'autre; car tandis que neutralité voulait dire non-participation aux différends d'autrui, la Société au contraire visait à assurer la paix par l'action solidaire de tous les Etats.'[69]

Expressing himself in more moderate terms, Hersch Lauterpacht maintained that 'to say that the Covenant has abolished neutrality among the members of the League is as misleading as to maintain that it has not affected it at all . . . It is true to say that collective security and neutrality are mutually exclusive. The more there is the one, the less there is of the other . . . collective security and neutrality are inherently antagonistic and

anarchy'; see Id., 'Neutrality and Neutral Rights Following the Pact of Paris for the Renunciation of War', 24 *Proc.ASIL* (1930) at p. 85.

[68]GRAHAM, M.W., 'The Effect of the League of Nations Covenant on the Theory and Practice of Neutrality', 15 *California Law Review* (1927) at p. 377. Hans Morgenthau shared the same view and reasoned: 'for the principle of collective security, which is the very foundation of the League, means confederacy, partiality, intervention; whereas neutrality implies aloofness, impartiality, abstention. Therefore, these two principles can neither in theory nor in practice exist together'; see MORGENTHAU, H.J., 'The End of Switzerland's Differential Neutrality', 32 *AJIL* (1938) at p. 559. As for Clyde Eagleton, he suggested that, 'it is not only true that the abolition of neutrality follows from the abolition of war; it is true also that the abolition of neutrality is a positive and potent weapon for the control of war'; see EAGLETON, C., 'Neutrality and Neutral Rights Following the Pact of Paris for the Renunciation of War', 24 *Proc.ASIL* (1930) at p. 92.

[69]WHITTON, J.B., 'La neutralité et la Société des Nations', 17 *RCADI* (1927) at pp. 551–2. While James Leslie Brierly noted that 'neutrality in the traditional sense, except perhaps in the unlikely event of both belligerents having violated the treaty [Pact of Paris], would only be conceivable on the assumption that the state violating the treaty could not be identified, and the immense importance of article 2 is that for practical purposes it rules out this contigency'; see BRIERLY, J.L., 'Some Implications of the Pact of Paris', 10 *BYIL* (1929) at p. 210. Similarly, the resolution submitted by W.A. Bewes at the Oxford Conference of the International Law Association in 1932, postulated the inadmissibility of neutrality in the case of a violation of the Paris Pact and suggested that 'in the event of any violation of the Briand-Kellogg Pact being committed by any Power party thereto, it would be a breach of the law of nations that any other High Contracting Party, its citizens or subjects should trade with such violating Power so long as such violation continues'; see 37 *Rep.ILA* (1933), Oxford Conf., 1932 at pp. 169–70.

antinomous.'[70] Few scholars, in fact, espoused at the time the views of Edwin Borchard who, as one of the most devout supporters of traditional neutrality, had this to reply: 'the very suggestion that neutrality ought to be abolished is an indication of the now common divorce between reason and experience . . . the notion that by abandoning neutrality peace could be promoted, while passions were inflamed, is one of the delusions of an unbalanced and slogan worshipping age'.[71]

After all was said, it appeared that national egoism and apathy had come full circle, and were now surrendering to internationalism, so that many saw a return to Grotian precepts of just wars. The attitude of impartiality was charged with all the vicious 'neutral' practices experienced during the World War, as world peace was discovering with exaltation its new elixir in the name of discrimination. One reads among the Articles of Interpretation of the Kellogg-Briand Pact adopted by the International Law Association at the Budapest Conference of 1934:

> (6) in the event of a violation of the Pact by a resort to armed force or war by one signatory State against another, any signatory State, not being a party to the original dispute, may, without thereby committing a breach of the Pact or of any rule of international law, do all or any of the following things:
>
> (b) supply the State attacked with financial or material assistance, including munitions of war . . .
>
> (d) decline to observe towards the State violating the Pact the duties prescribed by international law, apart from the Pact, for a neutral in relation to a belligerent.[72]

[70]LAUTERPACHT, H., 'Neutrality and Collective Security', 2 *Politica* (1936–7) at pp. 135, 149. In parallel reasoning, Paul de La Pradelle thought that 'on doit constater qu'à l'heure actuelle la neutralité subsiste, mais que le régime de 1907 est dépassé'; see LA PRADELLE, P.de, 'L'évolution de la neutralité', 14 *Revue de Droit International* (1934) at p. 221.

[71]BORCHARD, E., 'Sanctions Versus Neutrality', 1 *Hungarian Quarterly* (1936) at pp. 263, 265.

[72]See 38 *Rep.ILA* (1935), Budapest Conf., 1934 at pp. 5–6. The Draft Convention on Rights and Duties of States in Case of Aggression, prepared by the Harvard Research in International Law in 1939, coined the term of a *supporting* state, to wit, a state discriminating against the aggressor, save using force, and enjoying the rights which, if it were neutral, it would have against a belligerent; see Article 10, 33 *AJIL* (1939) *Suppl.* at p. 902. Moreover, a third state which wishes to become neither co-defending nor supporting, would not have in its relations

The degree of intellectual confusion concerning neutrality on the eve of another World War is best indicated in the cryptic resolution, adopted by the International Law Association at the Amsterdam Conference of 1938, according to which 'neutrality still exists and is not abrogated even as between members of the League although the rights and duties of a neutral cannot now be defined without consideration of the provisions of the Pact of Paris'.[73] With the League approaching the precipitous end of its existence, there were those who categorically insisted that 'considérée comme une institution la neutralité est le produit de l'anarchie internationale',[74] and others who responded that neutrality had shown an undeniable longevity and had well resisted the League's onslaught.[75]

The UN Blueprint for a Warless World The neutrality debate was to be revived in the early days of the UN Charter. The inoperativeness of neutrality within a functioning arrangement of collective security – so amply demonstrated by the experience of Switzerland during the Italo-Abyssinian war – was addressed, but, on the whole, left undecided at the San Francisco Conference. Paul Boncour, the French delegate to the conference, pleaded unavailingly for the insertion in the Charter of the United Nations of an explicit provision, according to which no state would be allowed to invoke its neutrality as a means to evade its obligations under the Charter. Along the same lines,

with the aggressor the duties which, if it were neutral, it would have to a belligerent but it would have the rights which, if it were neutral, it would have against a belligerent; see Article 12, *ibid.* at p. 903. Many saw, in the Harvard Research and the Budapest Articles, a formal endorsement of the controversial concept of non-belligerency. In reality, they continued to translate the rights and duties emanating from the Covenant or the Paris Pact in terms suggestive of the pre-League order, rather than in terms of a fresh, autonomous obligation of discrimination. In any case, however, non-belligerency is nowhere referred to *expressis verbis* in these documents.

[73]See 40 *Rep.ILA* (1939), Amsterdam Conf., 1938 at pp. 88–9. It is not by coincidence that the work of the Neutrality Committee of that Society had been suspended in 1932, the subject of neutrality being reintroduced only in 1937.

[74]POLITIS, N., *La neutralité et la paix*, 1935 at p. 11.

[75]See, for instance, D'ASTORG, B., *La neutralité et son réveil dans la crise de la S.D.N.*, 1938, and MORGENTHAU, H.J., 'The Resurrection of Neutrality in Europe', 33 *APSR* (1939), p. 473*ff.* See also ROYEN, W.P.J.A.van, *Analyse du problème de la neutralité au cours de l'évolution du droit des gens*, 1938, and TÉNÉKIDÈS, C.G., 'La neutralité en son état d'évolution actuelle', 20 *RDILC* (1939), p. 256*ff.*

a distinguished non-governmental committee drafted in January 1944, a document entitled, The International Law of the Future: Postulates, Principles and Proposals, which *inter alia* laid down the following principle: 'the duty would rest upon all States, and no State would be free to frustrate the efforts of the Community of States by relying upon the nineteenth-century law of neutrality'.[76]

A few years after the foundation of the United Nations, it was asserted that, 'there is perfect unanimity in the doctrine that if the machinery of the United Nations works normally – that is the Security Council is able to exercise its functions – there is no room for neutrality so far as member-states are concerned, as neutrality would be contrary to the letter and spirit of the Charter'.[77] As Louis Henkin observed in 1963, 'the difficult issue is whether, in the event of an aggression which becomes a war of the kind we have known, Members of the United Nations may sit it out, may deal equally with victim and aggressor, may even supply the aggressor with the means of war. I know of no basis for a certain answer. Any guess is academic and, hopefully, will remain so. But it is fair to say that any claim to traditional neutrality will have and deserve little sympathy.'[78]

[76]See 38 *AJIL* (1944) *Suppl.* at p. 87.

[77]KOMARNICKI, T., 'The Place of Neutrality in the Modern System of International Law', 80 *RCADI* (1952) at p. 472. Dehn, speaking before the Grotius Society in 1945, concluded: 'the renunciation of neutrality is the minimum contribution which assuredly every State – great and small – is expected to make'; DEHN, C.G., 'The Problem of Neutrality', 31 *GST* (1945) at p. 149.

[78]HENKIN, L., 'Force, Intervention, and Neutrality in Contemporary International Law', 57 *Proc.ASIL* (1963) at p. 161. In the words of another scholar, 'il est vrai que dans certains cas le recours à la guerre peut avoir lieu et par la suite le problème de la neutralité peut se poser. Mais la guerre reste illicite et la neutralité par conséquent, sans fondement . . . la neutralité avec son double caractère d'abstention et d'impartialité ne trouve plus de crédit dans l'opinion publique et de fondement dans la conscience des peuples'; see CALOGEROPOULOS-STRATIS, S., 'La neutralité et la paix' in *Eranion en l'honneur de G.S. Maridakis*, vol.III (1964) at pp. 402–3. Writing at about the same time, Dietrich Schindler commented: 'Ce système a réintroduit la distinction entre les guerres justes et les guerres injustes, de sorte qu'a disparu l'une des conditions qui avait permis l'établissement du droit de la neutralité au XIX siècle . . . En un certain sens, le nouveau régime de maintien de la paix est l'exact opposé de celui qui s'était institué au XIX siècle. Tandis qu'au XIX siècle on s'efforcait de localiser les guerres et que l'on favorisait à cette fin la neutralité, le régime de la sécurité collective conduit, en un certain sens, à une universalisation des guerres. Ce système exige des Etats, non pas une abstention et une impartialité, mais au contraire une intervention active en faveur des Etats attaqués contrairement

Despite the plethora of academic affirmations, however, neutrality has not passed away. In 1975, 'the right to neutrality' found formal reaffirmation in the Helsinki Final Act.[79] The UN Security Council, after a long period of reluctance in the context of the Iran-Iraq War, finally recognized the facts and spoke of 'attacks on *neutral* shipping'.[80] During the UN-authorized military action against Iraq, Iran and, to a lesser extent, Jordan claimed the status of traditional neutrality, pledging impartiality and interning numerous Iraqi aviators who fled their country to Iran.[81] Lately, certain academic societies and learned scholars have proved particularly active in undertaking a restatement (the term in itself denotes the continued validity of the traditional law) of the old rules.[82] The same old rules have preserved their place in recent naval manuals where notions such as contraband, prize condemnation, unneutral service or continuous voyage are treated exhaustively.[83]

Most importantly, the International Court of Justice in its recent Advisory Opinion on the Legality of the Threat or Use

au droit. La neutralité se présente ainsi comme une atteinte à la solidarité internationale'; see SCHINDLER, D., 'Aspects contemporains de la neutralité', 121 *RCADI* (1967) at p. 237. See also TAUBENFELD, H.J., 'International Actions and Neutrality', 47 *AJIL* (1953), p. 377*ff*.; GUGGENHEIM, P., 'La sécurité collective et le problème de la neutralité', 2 *ASDI* (1945), p. 9*ff*.; LALIVE, J.-F., 'International Organization and Neutrality', 24 *BYIL* (1947), p. 72*ff*.; ACCIOLY, H., 'Guerre et neutralité, en face du droit des gens contemporain' in *Hommage d'une génération de juristes au Président Basdevant*, 1960, p. 1*ff*.

[79]See 'Declaration on Principles Guiding Relations between Participating States', 14 *ILM* (1975) at p. 1294. As has been written in this connection, 'l'intérêt de la formule de l'Acte final de la CSCE est de poser un droit général à la neutralité'; see GHEBALI, V.-Y., 'L'Acte final de la Conférence sur la Sécurité et la Coopération en Europe et les Nations Unies', 21 *AFDI* (1975) at p. 92. See also SUBEDI, S.P., 'Neutrality in a Changing World: European Neutral States and the European Community', 42 *ICLQ* (April 1993), p. 238*ff*.; KARSH, E., 'International Cooperation and Neutrality', 25 *Journal of Peace Research* (1988), p. 57*ff*.; ANDRÉN, N., 'On the Meaning and Uses of Neutrality', 26 *Nordic Journal of International Studies* (1991), p. 67*ff*.

[80]See Security Council Resolution 582 (1986) at para.2, and Security Council Resolution 598 (1987) at the fourth preambular paragraph.

[81]See ROBERT, E., 'Le statut des Etats neutres dans le Golfe' in Université libre de Bruxelles, *La guerre du Golfe et le droit international*, 1991, p. 91*ff*.

[82]The allusion refers to the ongoing codification work of the ILA's Maritime Neutrality Committee's on Neutrality and Naval Warfare, as well as to the *San Remo Manual on International Law Applicable to Armed Conflicts at Sea* adopted by a group of international lawyers and naval experts in June 1994.

[83]See, for instance, chapter 7 of the US *Commander's Handbook on the Law of Naval Operations* (NWP9-Rev.A) of 1989, paras.7.1–7.10, and chapter 11 of the German *ZDv 15/2 Humanitäres Völkerrecht in bewaffneten Konflikten – Handbuch* [Humanitarian Law in Armed Conflicts – Manual] of August 1992, §§1101–55.

of Nuclear Weapons, referred to the principle of neutrality as 'an established part of the customary international law' and added:

> the Court finds that as in the case of the principles of humanitarian law applicable in armed conflict, international law leaves no doubt that the principle of neutrality, whatever its content, which is of a fundamental character similar to that of the humanitarian principles and rules, is applicable (subject to the relevant provisions of the United Nations Charter), to all international armed conflict, whatever type of weapons might be use.[84]

On yet another level, it is not without significance that peace-keeping contingents from so-called permanent neutral countries such as Sweden continue to be most welcome in any theatre of crisis – the last deployment of peace-keepers from Nordic countries being that in the Former Yugoslav Republic of Macedonia (FYROM) in 1993 – while neutrality still features as a *sine qua non* principle on which the action of humanitarian agencies such as the Red Cross is based.[85]

Neutrality persists and defies the eloquent rhetoric of new world orders as much as war defies those who have dreamt that peaceful negotiation could claim any sort of exclusivity in the settlement of international disputes.[86] Neutrality has been at times presented as the talisman for national prosperity, or criticized as an unmistakable road to war and hardship. It has frequently been the companion of national policy as far as pre-

[84]See Legality of the Threat or Use of Nuclear Weapons, Advisory Opinion of 8 July 1996, *ICJ Reports 1996*, §§88–9. See also *ibid.*, §§51, 93.

[85]For remarks on neutrality as a key element of Red Cross action, see HAUG, H., *Humanity for All – The International Red Cross and Red Crescent Movement*, 1993, p. 461*ff.*; DOMINICÉ, C., 'La neutralité et l'assistance humanitaire', 35 *Annales de droit international médical* (1991), p. 118*ff.*; KALSHOVEN, F., 'Impartialité et neutralité dans le droit et la pratique humanitaires', 71 *RICR* (nov.–déc.1989), no.780, p. 541*ff.*; HARROFF-TAVEL, M., 'Neutralité et impartialité – De l'importance et de la difficulté pour le Mouvement international de la Croix-Rouge et du Croissant-Rouge, d'être guidé par ces principes', 71 *RICR* (nov.–déc.1989), no.780, p. 563*ff.*; VAN BOVEN, T.C., 'Some Reflections on the Principle of Neutrality' in SWINARSKI, C. (ed.), *Studies and Essays on International Humanitarian Law and Red Cross Principles in Honour of Jean Pictet*, 1984, p. 643*ff.*

[86]War, in the somewhat cynical allusion of one writer, remains 'the traditional, if unfortunate, method of readjusting the tenure of the earth's crust, and until we find a better method, the old one will be hard completely to outlaw'; see BORCHARD, E., 'Neutrality', 48 *YLJ* (1938–9) at p. 40.

texts can hold, extending over a terrain where commitments become juridically blurred. Legal paradoxes, such as benevolent or qualified neutrality and non-belligerency, would suffice to demonstrate just how openly the notion of neutrality has been abused. Charles Chaumont was thus led to reflect:

> la neutralité n'est plus (en admettant qu'elle l'ait jamais été) un concept cristallin. L'expérience montre que les Etats belligérants et neutres se satisfont d'à-peu-près, de neutralités approximatives dont le contenu est déterminé par la marge, la frontière mouvante qui sépare l'Etat non-belligérant de la pleine participation aux hostilités . . . On pourrait en conclure qu'il s'agit là de fausses situations de neutralité et . . . qu'il vaut mieux franchement reconnaître l'existence de situations intermédiaires ne relevant pas plus du concept de neutralité que du concept de belligérance.[87]

Collective Inaction and Abstention: Causes for Failure Who would have imagined that half a century after the adoption of the UN Charter, jurists would have still to grapple with the relationship between the principle of collective security and that of neutrality? The query is all the more puzzling as the two concepts seem to draw upon divergent, if not mutually exclusive, rationales, so that there should be practically no room to argue that the old logic of neutrality has not been carried away by the tide of the Charter principles. And yet, everyday experience comes to refute theoretical confidence.

Echoes of neutrality still fill the air at a time when state aggression should normally impose but one course of action. Idyllic representations of an international community wholeheartedly mobilized against wrongdoers have dramatically failed to convince us of their sincerity. The influence of the UN Charter on the corpus of neutrality laws might therefore be better addressed under the following two headings: first, has the notion of neutrality survived the arrival of the Charter, and if so, what purposes might it still fulfil today? Second, has a right of non-belligerency emerged as a manifestation of the duty to 'act' against the Charter violator, giving also tangible

[87]CHAUMONT, C., 'Nations Unies et neutralité', 89 *RCADI* (1956) at p. 11.

expression to that sentiment of collective responsibility for the maintenance of international peace?

Traditional neutrality relies upon non-entanglement, pleads indifference and promises inaction. Collective security, on the other hand, is intended to spark off international concern, inspired by communal solidarity and translated into decisive action. Despite the evident contradiction between the logic underlying the perception of neutrality and that permeating the Charter values, the everlasting debate about neutral rights and duties does not appear to have lost any of its steam. Hardly any post-1945 international conflict has been fought without relevant issues of neutrality being raised at some point. In 1982, the British victory over the disputed sovereignty of the Falkland Islands was not achieved without some discussion on the implications a US resolute neutrality stance might have on the final outcome of the military confrontation. At the climax of the 1980–8 Gulf War, Iran made repeated calls for genuine neutrality on the part of its Arab neighbours and reminded Kuwait and Saudi Arabia of their obligations under the relevant 1907 Hague Conventions. The UN Security Council, for its part, asked belligerents to respect the legitimate interests of states non-parties to the conflict, while the western armada was eventually gathered for the protection of neutral shipping and the enforcement of neutral rights.[88]

Hence, if neutrality preserves its place within contemporary international law, it can only be so either because it still serves some purpose or because the regime which was meant to succeed it failed to work. The truth lies, in fact, in both explanations. The UN machinery for centralized action remained for decades a significantly underused asset, and in that context the law of neutrality seemed to offer a modicum of orderliness. Faced every so often with the inability of the UN Security

[88]Even more striking, at the time of the UN-mandated collective action against Iraq in 1991, which is widely held as an almost exemplary performance of the Charter collective security blueprint, there was still question of some states wishing to remain neutral. Iran, for instance, claimed an attitude of traditional neutrality and accordingly interned Iraqi pilots who had taken refuge in great numbers in its territory, but also protested the use of Iranian coastal waters by coalition warships; see UN Doc. *S/22163*, 28 January 1991; UN Doc. *S/22379*, 23 March 1991; UN Doc. *S/22141*, 23 January 1991 for the internment of Iraqi pilots, and UN Doc. *S/21902*, 24 October 1990; UN Doc. *S/21903*, 24 October 1990; UN Doc. *S/21904*, 24 October 1990; UN Doc. *S/21905*, 24 October 1990 for the protection of the territorial waters.

Council to discharge its functions, states were forced to rediscover the old familiar terrain of neutrality. Not only has it proved next to impossible to identify the culprit every time an act of aggression has called for collective response, but also the Charter is lacking in any operational guidance beyond the idolized right of self-defence.

It quickly became clear, however, that inter-state violence, often drawn out for years, as well as delicate questions related to third non-involved states, could never be satisfactorily regulated by a sterile invocation of the right of self-defence. Neutrality, therefore, subsists owing to its proven utility as a back-up or substitute source of legal reference in the case, of the regrettably frequent failure of the Charter scheme for concerted action to materialize. In the words of Judge Ammoun,

> if the provisions of the Charter concerning collective security could have been implemented according to the letter and in the spirit of the San Francisco Conference, there would have been no place for neutrality, at least among States Members of the United Nations . . . The Security Council's action has been paralysed by the veto, or by the fear of a veto as in the Namibia question. Consequently, neutrality persists so long as wars are tolerated, whether deliberately or through weakness.[89]

If anything is clear about the Charter's collective security machinery, it is that Security Council decisions in matters of breach of peace, threat against peace or act of aggression rob any discretionary power member states might originally have had to remain inactive faced with situations endangering international peace and security. Not only are they deprived of the faculty to pretend abstention and neutrality, but they are duty-bound to implement in full the enforcement measures the organization may command. What is more, there is no escape from the obligation to discharge one's own part in the community effort since obligations assumed under the Charter prevail over all other international commitments. These

[89]See Legal Consequences for States of the Continued Presence of South Africa in Namibia (South West Africa) notwithstanding Security Council Resolution 276 (1970), Separate Opinion of Judge Ammoun, *ICJ Rep. 1971*, §13 at p. 92.

obligations found clear expression in Articles 25 and 103 of the Charter.[90]

There still remain two questions, however, to be addressed at this point: first, would it be possible for a state to obtain an exemption from UN-mandated sanctions? And second, are there any corresponding obligations incumbent upon non-member states? The answers to both questions may appear crystal-clear in theory, yet grey in practice. As regards the application of sanctions, a member state may consult the Security Council with a view to resolving 'special economic problems arising from the carrying out of those measures' (Article 50), which implies that in principle all member states must implement the sanctions whatever the negative consequences to their national economies may be. The understanding in this respect is that a state particularly affected by the break-off of economic relations and lines of communication with the targeted state may ask for measures of alleviation rather than outright exemption and still less a licence for traditional neutrality.

Insofar as military coercion is concerned, member states may well abstain from committing armed forces on condition that the Security Council determines that action should be taken by only some of the members (Article 48). Here again, nothing seems to permit the conclusion that member states may assert neutrality status of the classical sort even if they are exonerated from contributing military assets to the UN-led campaign. Yet, this is as far as legal theory can go. In practice, those principles appear somewhat diluted, if not seriously compromised. If one turns to the question of obligations possibly arising for non-member states, the problem lacks no theoretical interest, but tends to become a peripheral one since the number of states that prefer not to join the world organization is not only constantly shrinking, but also the most notable of these, Switzerland, is

[90]These provisions are commented upon in GOODRICH, L.M. and HAMBRO, E., *Charter of the United Nations – Commentary and Documents*, 3rd edn (1969), pp. 207–11, 614–17, and COT, J.-P. and PELLET, A. (eds), *La Charte des Nations Unies*, 2e edn (1991), pp. 471–8, 1381–9. Authors unanimously agree that under such ideal conditions, a claim of traditional neutrality would simply be inadmissible since it would be incompatible with the hierarchy of values struck by the UN blueprint. As Lester Woolsey clearly noted in the mid-1930s, the ideas of neutrality and collective sanctions 'are as immiscible as oil and water'; see WOOLSEY, L.H., 'The Fallacies of Neutrality', 30 *AJIL* (1936) at p. 259.

showing increasing readiness to align itself fully with UN-mandated coercive action.

International Sanctions: The Swiss Case Over the last six years, Switzerland has on several occasions adopted economic sanctions resembling those decreed by the UN Security Council. However, Bern has not missed the opportunity to point out that this was only the fruit of a free political choice of the federal government in order to assist the UN effort and that it could be in no way construed as an explicit recognition of the universally binding character of the decisions of the UN Security Council in matters of international peace and security. Switzerland has long adhered to a principle of strict non-participation in economic sanctions as a key premise of its policy of permanent neutrality.

The so-called integral conception of neutrality was temporarily abandoned in the 1930s on the occasion of the Italo-Ethiopian crisis. Shortly after that embarrassing experience, Switzerland returned to its traditional aloofness staying clear of any suggestion for participation in collective economic warfare. It was only in 1965, at the time of the Rhodesian crisis and the UN economic sanctions against the Smith régime, that Switzerland inaugurated a new policy of the 'autonomous' application of UN measures.[91] To date, the official position remains unaltered to the effect that the occasional participation of the Swiss Confederation in UN-imposed sanctions remains a matter of free sovereign decision of the federal government.

In August 1990, the Swiss government responded promptly to the Security Council call for a comprehensive trade embargo against Iraq. In a parliamentary report, the federal authorities reasoned as follows:

[91]On Swiss policy in the Italian and Rhodesian operations, see ROSS, J.F.L., *Neutrality and International Sanctions – Sweden, Switzerland and Collective Security*, 1989, pp. 87*ff*., 157*ff*. As has been rightly observed, 'the Swiss measures were "autonomous" only in a narrow legal sense. In a political sense they came about under the pressure of international public opinion. The Swiss could not afford to ignore this spirit of solidarity and since they no longer adhered to the conception of differential neutrality that had applied to the League of Nations they had no conceptual basis from which to operate. Hence the tortuous argumentation which does very little to convince the informed public of the usefulness of the official conception of neutrality'; see GABRIEL, J.M., 'Switzerland and Economic Sanctions: The Dilemma of a Neutral' in MILIVOJEVIC, M. and MAURER, P. (eds), *Swiss Neutrality and Security*, 1990 at p. 241.

> l'adoption de sanctions économiques n'est pas contraire au droit de la neutralité. Ce droit n'impose pas à l'Etat neutre le devoir de maintenir des relations économiques avec une partie impliquée dans un conflit . . . La Suisse se doit donc de soutenir la communauté des Etats lorsque celle-ci réagit contre l'entité qui a violé le droit d'une manière flagrante . . . Les mesures décidées par le Conseil de sécurité de l'ONU lient tous les Etats membres de cette organisation, y compris les Etats neutres d'Europe . . . La participation de la Suisse à ces sanctions s'imposait également du point de vue de la solidarité internationale. La Suisse, n'étant pas membre de l'ONU, a été amenée à prendre une décision autonome . . . Dans un conflit opposant deux parties aussi inégales, à savoir, d'un côté, l'entité qui a violé le droit et, d'autre, l'ensemble de la communauté internationale, le principe du traitement paritaire n'est guère applicable.[92]

Meanwhile, on 12 April 1992, the Swiss *Conseil fédéral* explained in these terms its decision to apply Security Council Resolution 748 (1992) concerning the air embargo against Libya:

> Le Conseil fédéral a décidé de mettre en oeuvre *de façon autonome* les sanctions demandées par le Conseil de sécurité des Nations Unies à l'encontre de la Libye. En effet, le Conseil fédéral estime que la Suisse doit se montrer *solidaire* des efforts de la communauté internationale dans la *lutte contre le terrorisme.* Comme la grande majorité des nations s'est ralliée aux sanctions décidées par l'ONU, le Conseil fédéral a jugé que la nécessité de participer activement à la lutte contre le terrorisme passait avant des considerations relevant de la politique de neutralité. (italics in the original)[93]

Likewise, in June 1992, the Swiss government strained its economic relations with the Federal Republic of Yugoslavia (Serbia and Montenegro) by following closely the terms of the Security Council Resolution 757 (1992). The press statement read as follows:

> le Conseil fédéral condamne de la façon la plus rigoureuse les agressions qui frappent durement les populations de

[92]See 1 *RSDIE* (1991) at pp. 561–2.
[93]See 3 *RSDIE* (1993) at pp. 745–6.

> Bosnie-Herzégovine. Il considère qu'il est du devoir d'un Etat de droit de tout entreprendre en vue de faire respecter les principes du droit international, gravement bafoués par des éléments serbes. C'est la raison pour laquelle, se fondant sur la Résolution 757 du Conseil de sécurité de l'ONU, le Conseil fédéral a décidé de prendre des mesures à l'encontre de la Yougoslavie (Serbie et Monténégro) dans les domaines suivants: relations commerciales, transferts financiers, navigation aérienne.[94]

As those statements amply demonstrate, Switzerland has gradually surrendered to the truth that the closer the United Nations approaches universality in its membership, the more the Security Council may validly claim a binding effect of its decisions upon the entire international community of states.

The foregoing discussion focused on the relationship between neutrality and collective security if and when the Charter is to apply to the letter. It has been shown that in such a case the two concepts are proved mutually exclusive in principle, yet occasionally coexistent in practice. It so happens, however, that a properly performing UN Security Council has been for decades more of an academic hypothesis than an everyday reality, for, as Inis Claude has observed, the Charter represents no more than 'an agreement to agree' on collective security provisions.[95] It remains to be examined, therefore, the function of neutrality in the all too frequent case whereby the UN machinery stays idle and so member states receive no centralized instructions for a community response against the international wrongdoer.

[94] *Ibid.* at pp. 746–7. See also 4 *RSDIE* (1994) at pp. 627–8. On another level of action, Switzerland has on numerous occasions indirectly supported UN peacekeeping operations by allowing overflight and landing to troop carriers, but also by undertaking the transport of UN contingents. For more on this kind of contribution to UN action, see DEYRA, M., *Aspects contemporains de la neutralité*, 1979, p. 262*ff.* The latest example of such a participation came in September 1994 when Switzerland provided the means for the deployment of UN observers along the frontier between the Serb-controlled territory of Bosnia-Herzegovina and the Federal Republic of Yugoslavia (Serbia and Montenegro).

[95] See CLAUDE, I.L., *Power and International Relations*, 1962 at p. 175.

2 Institutionalizing non-belligerency: the threshold of abstention or the absence of a threshold?

Towards a Protean Neutrality It has occasionally been argued that in the absence of authoritative designation of the law-breaker by the UN Security Council states may decide the issue for themselves and discriminate in favour of the belligerent who appears to their eyes as the victim of aggression. In the latter case, it is further submitted, the aggrieved belligerent would be under a legal obligation to tolerate the neutral differential treatment while he would be deprived of any right to retaliate against the self-styled non-belligerent. The proposition should be dismissed as both imprudent and unbalanced.

On the one hand, it is rash, perhaps even dangerous, to over-simplify such an infinitely complicated issue as the pinpointing of the aggressor. Not only, is it a fact of life today that even the clearest instance of naked aggression may put up a case for self-defence, but also political interests are so diversified that it is most common to have several states ready to support such a case.[96] On the other hand, it is a weak assertion since it would be naive to believe that the aggrieved belligerent (who may happen to be the real victim of aggression) would passively accept unneutral measures being taken against him.

A few examples might help to highlight the complex situations one should expect in practice. In September 1980, Iraq invaded and occupied Iranian territory, a fact that at least today seems undisputed.[97] Yet, for reasons which are unnecessary to recount here, the majority of western states not only refused to extend a helping hand to Iran but, to the contrary, generously

[96]The point is made by Robert Tucker although in somewhat vague terms: 'general international law may be interpreted as presently permitting states to discriminate against an aggressor, but it cannot prevent third states from reaching mutually contradictory decisions as to the identity of the aggressor'; see TUCKER, *op. cit., supra* n.33 at p. 170.

[97]Despite Iran's persistent requests that the United Nations determine the aggressor, it was not until December 1991 that the UN Secretary-General for the first time alluded to the Iraqi responsibility for the 1980–8 Gulf War. In particular, the Secretary-General, reporting to the UN Security Council on the implementation of para.6 of Resolution 598 (1987) which refers to the prospect of inquiring into responsibility for the Iran–Iraq conflict, concluded: 'the outstanding event . . . is the attack of 22 September 1980 against Iran, which cannot be justified under the Charter of the United Nations, any recognized rules and principles of international law or any principles of international morality and entails the reponsibility for the conflict'; see UN Doc.S/23273, 9 December 1991, para.6 at p. 2.

offered their partiality to the regime of Baghdad. Following the above-described views, should Tehran accept to suffer discriminatory treatment without having the possibility to take reprisals against the *mala fide* neutrals or, better, non-belligerents. Could it be argued, on the basis of law or good reason, that those short-sighted neutrals tilting in favour of the aggressor-Iraq should enjoy all benefits of neutrality and no duties *vis-à-vis* the attacked-Iran? It might be also relevant to recall in this respect that several states furnished assistance to *both* belligerents, thus elevating the idea of non-belligerency to the heights of sheer absurdity.

Even in the context of the second Gulf War, where the case for Iraq-initiated aggression is as uncontroversial as can ever be, there should be no doubt that under slightly different circumstances (e.g. occupation or annexation of only a disputed pocket of territory) there might well have been powers which would have tolerated or supported the Iraqi action as justifiable, and even defensive in nature. As for the recent Bosnian war, it is far more typical with respect to the often insoluble question of attributing responsibilities for the commencement of hostilities. Setting aside the fact that the UN Security Council has imposed economic sanctions against a power 'involved' in the conflict and so the freedom of action for member states is drastically curtailed, would it be conceivable to apply the theory of non-belligerency in relation to the warring nations of former Yugoslavia without risking utter confusion? Recent practice, far from containing the least indication that the concept of non-belligerency is becoming rooted in contemporary international law, serves as a reminder of the endless complexity that pseudo-legal constructions can only beget.[98]

[98]Among the writers who have pointed out the dangerous consequences of such a concept, the most convincing remarks have come from the gifted pen of Philip Jessup: 'if the legal position of nonparticipants in the conflict is to be regulated by some international agreement short of a return to the old status of war and neutrality, it would be disastrous to agree that every state may decide for itself which of the two contestants is in the right and may govern its conduct according to its own decision . . . The ensuing conflict among Members of the United Nations would be destructive of the ordered world community which the Charter must seek to preserve. State C would be shipping or permitting its nationals to ship war supplies to A, while State D would be assisting State B. The history of neutrality teaches that out of such situations conflict between nonparticipants and contestants readily results, and it would not be long before C and D would be enmeshed in the struggle out of self-defense'; see JESSUP, P.C., *A Modern Law of Nations – An Introduction*, 1948 at p. 205.

A further note may be in order here; according to the proponents of non-belligerency, every state may decide for itself the victim of aggression and discriminate in its favour accordingly, that course of action being sufficient to create a new intermediate legal situation between neutrality and belligerency (partial but still neutral). If one transposed *ex arguendo gratia* the same logic to the thorny question of self-defence, it would have meant that an intermediate status between self-defence and aggression could also be envisaged which would eventually release states from the prohibition of use of aggressive force (to initiate aggression but still within the law). Hopefully, a similar construction has not as yet been suggested (the controversial notion of 'defensive reprisals' may be an exception), but it demonstrates the risk of arbitrariness latent in any recognition of intermediacy in law.

Perhaps the most compelling consideration speaking against the alleged validity of non-belligerency is the fact that never has a 'benevolent' neutral state attempted to justify its conduct on the grounds of a firmly established right. Not a single policy statement has ever been recorded making reference to a special, intermediate status of non-belligerency as an accepted institution flowing from a dynamic interpretation of the Charter. In the absence of such theoretical apology, therefore, it is extremely difficult to see how one could demonstrate a conviction in law, the indispensable *opinio juris,* to substantiate the emergence of the new concept.

Dietrich Schindler in some recent remarks upholds the right of third states to render assistance short of military involvement to the victim of aggression by virtue of Article 51 whenever the Security Council is unable or unwilling to identify the aggressor. In his view,

> benevolent neutrality or non-belligerency have become legally admitted attitudes. Neutrality has become purely optional. State practice since 1945 shows that States have in fact assumed a great variety of intermediate positions regarding armed conflicts between other States.[99]

[99]See SCHINDLER, D., 'Transformations in the Law of Neutrality since 1945' in DELISSEN, A.J.M. and TANJA, G.J. (eds), *Humanitarian Law of Armed Conflict – Challenges Ahead, Essays in Honour of Frits Kalshoven,* 1991 at p. 373. A central issue in his construction is whether the non-belligerent offers assistance to the

In view of the inexorable difficulty of defining the aggressor, he is led to conclude somewhat contradictorily that 'only if it is *objectively impossible* to identify one belligerent as the aggressor, e.g. because the armed conflict has slowly escalated by mutual provocations, third states cannot be held entitled to make use of the right of collective self-defence' (emphasis added).[100] But is it logical to expect that states might ever adopt common criteria as to when it is 'objectively impossible' to designate the aggressor? To put it differently, however 'impossible' the identification of the aggressor may seem, how and why should a state be stopped from taking sides in what it at least regards as a crystal-clear case of aggression? The point made here is that one should think twice before opening a door to abuse. As Georges Scelle observed, 'non seulement la neutralité s'est raréfiée, mais, en fait, l'égale abstention, qui en est l'âme, s'est camouflée sous des formes plus ou moins hypocrites de concours indirect à l'un des partis, ou "l'attente sournoise" de l'occasion d'intervenir directement'.[101]

The vagaries of the notion of non-belligerency are clearly portrayed in a recent commentary by Wolff Heintschel von Heinegg. The point he essentially makes is that in attempting to provide legal justification for states' action in favour of victims of aggression, one should be careful not to create instead a legal vacuum of unregulated violence: 'if certain neutral duties

victim of aggression or the aggressor, assuming that the question can always be objectively and conclusively answered. His submission is that 'in all future considerations on the law of neutrality a distinction should be drawn between the rules applicable to all States not parties to an armed conflict and the rules applicable to genuine neutrals only . . . It would no longer be feasible to include both of them in one regulation as was done in 1907', *ibid.* at p. 385. In fact, he favours the institutionalization of non-belligerency although he promptly admits that 'an aggressor state will never concede to have committed an armed attack and therefore never recognize the right of third states to make use of the right of self-defence in favor of its adversary', and also that 'the legal situation will always be controversial, even if the facts are clear'; see SCHINDLER, D., 'Neutrality and Non-Belligerency in Armed Conflicts at Sea', Report submitted at the 1993 Geneva session of the Round Table of Experts on International Humanitarian Law Applicable to Armed Conflicts at Sea (copy on file with author) at p. 6.

[100]*Ibid.* at pp. 6–7.

[101]See SCELLE, G., 'Quelques réflexions sur l'abolition de la compétence de guerre', 58 *RGDIP* (1954) at p. 16. For further arguments in favour of non-belligerency as a legal institution, see GIOIA, A., 'Neutrality and Non-Belligerency' in POST, H.H.G. (ed.), *International Economic Law and Armed Conflict*, 1994, p. 76*ff.*

are said not to apply to the "non-belligerent" then the same must be true with regard to the alleged aggressor. The situation would not be governed by any legal rule at all. The (alleged) aggressor would not be obliged to accept being discriminated against... Because there is no duty of acquiescence on behalf of the aggrieved belligerent the differentiation between "benevolent" and "strict" neutrals is counter-productive.'[102] His overall conclusion is that 'as a matter of legal principle and in view of state practice a legal status on "non-belligerency" has to be rejected'.[103]

Non-belligerency: Where Is the Evidence? It would be misguided to legitimize any departure from the law of neutrality by simply pigeon-holing it as a manifestation of an autonomous legal institution lying in between neutrality and belligerency. The main flaw of such a theory lies with the fact that an elastic concept of neutrality, or neutrality of variable normativity as one might call it, cannot truly be expected to provide legal guidance but only subterfuge for any sort of abusive conduct. Recent experience confirms that states still prefer to fall back on outdated instruments as the only apparent modicum of orderly conduct.

During the 1980–8 Iran-Iraq War there were many instances where states turned to the old Hague Conventions or the London Declaration as the only legal yardstick available. On the contrary, no state has ever suggested that the legality of

[102]See VON HEINEGG, H.W., 'Neutrality and Non-Belligerency', paper presented at the 1993 Geneva session of the Round Table of Experts on International Humanitarian Law Applicable to Armed Conflicts at Sea (copy on file with author) at pp. 10, 14.

[103]*Ibid.* at p. 13. It is also noteworthy that for the purposes of drafting the 1994 *San Remo Manual*, 'the participants carefully debated whether a distinction should be made between rules applicable to "non-belligerents" and those applicable to "neutrals", and decided that such a distinction should not be recognized; the designation of a state as "neutral" or "non-belligerent" would inevitably be arbitrary and would therefore produce extreme uncertainty about the rules applicable to the shipping of states not party to the conflict and to the protection of their waters'; see DOSWALD-BECK, L., 'The San Remo Manual on International Law Applicable to Armed Conflicts at Sea', 89 *AJIL* (1995) at pp. 197–8. Maurice Torrelli, speaking of 'neutralité à la carte', or 'variations sur la gamme de la neutralité', tends to admit the validity of the status of non-belligerency in contemporary international law. He does not fail to notice, however, that 'ces notions n'ont aucun contenu juridique précis' and that 'c'est alors, pour l'essentiel, en dehors du droit de la neutralité qu'il faut peut-être aller chercher les droits et les devoirs du non-belligérant'; see TORRELLI, M., 'La neutralité en question', 96 *RGDIP* (1992) at p. 14.

neutral activities should be measured by reference to a new customary right of benevolent neutrality. At the climax of Iranian interference with neutral merchant shipping most western powers referred back to the time-honoured belligerent right of visit, search and capture only urging Iran to respect the customary conditions of its exercise. Kuwait or Saudi Arabia throughout the conflict claimed nothing less than traditional 'strict neutrality', while they never attempted to justify their support to Iraq as a matter of legal right by reference to the concept of non-belligerency.

Not only is juridical evidence lacking to the effect that states decide to discriminate following only their own findings as to the responsibility for conflict, but, in fact, those states (whether one wishes to call them non-belligerents or foul neutrals), have consistently sought to conceal their active participation on the side of one belligerent. How should one interpret the fact that whenever such non-belligerent services have been brought to public attention, the states concerned first deny categorically the allegations and second offer reassurances about their strict neutrality, if not as an affirmation of the flimsy legal moorings of the concept of non-belligerency in contemporary international law? Had the subtleties of non-belligerency been refined and clearly established by now, would it not be logical to expect that a state opting for such a position would firmly stand by and defend its decision in legal terms instead of simply negating the essence of its policy?

In the absence of conclusive evidence in favour of the acceptance of the concept in modern international law, the proponents of non-belligerency infer such endorsement from a number of precedents in state conduct as well as from a terminological peculiarity slipped into the 1949 Geneva Conventions and the 1977 Additional Protocol.[104] As regards the alleged affirmation in state practice, one may notice the lack of consistency in legal policies as revealed in the oft-quoted precedents. In any event, those precedents can be perfectly considered as mere violations of the international law in force. As Michael Bothe has rightly observed, 'this kind of involvement in the armed conflict,

[104]Article 122 of Geneva Convention III of 1949 draws a distinction between 'neutral and non-belligerent powers', while Articles 2(c), 9§2a, 19, 22§2a, 31, 39§1 and 64 of the 1977 First Additional Protocol refer to 'neutral and other States not parties to the conflict'.

however, does not lead, as a matter of law, to a kind of intermediate status between neutrality and belligerency. The rendering of unneutral services is indeed a violation of the law of neutrality and may give rise to an appropriate reaction by the belligerent party which is the victim of that violation.'[105]

It is true that the draft Additional Protocol prepared for the purposes of the 1974–7 Diplomatic Conference on the Reaffirmation of International Humanitarian Law in Article 19 and Article 32 referred solely to states not parties to the conflict and that Jean Pictet had explained the position of the ICRC by saying that 'it had been considered appropriate to replace the former term "neutral" by "states not parties to a conflict", since there were now varying degrees of neutrality, such as non-belligerency'.[106] It was only following an amendment originally proposed by Austria, Finland, Sweden, Switzerland and the United Kingdom that the classical term 'neutral' reappeared alongside the expression 'states not parties to the conflict' in a way that inevitably lends itself to confusion.

By way of comparison, however, it is interesting to note that the draft Protocol in its provision concerning the prohibition of the use of false flags, military insignia and uniforms had opted for the single term neutral avoiding any reference to states not parties to the conflict.[107] Similarly, Article 2 of the draft Protocol defining the term 'Protecting Power' referred simply to a 'State not engaged in the conflict', as did draft Article 9.[108] Besides, the drafting history of Article 22§2(a) referring to hospital and coastal rescue crafts that a neutral or other state not

[105]See BOTHE, *op. cit., supra* n.5 at p. 391. Similarly, see RONZITTI, N., 'Le droit humanitaire applicable aux conflits armés en mer', 242 *RCADI* (1993) at p. 135. See also BINDSCHEDLER, R.L., 'Neutrality, Concept and General Rules' in BERNHARDT, R. (ed.), *Encyclopedia of Public International Law,* instalment 4 (1982) at pp. 13–14.

[106]See LEVIE, H.S. (ed.), *Protection of War Victims: Protocol 1 to the 1949 Geneva Conventions*, vol.1 (1979) at p. 528, and vol.2 (1980) at p. 166.

[107]In its final form, however, Article 39§1 resumes the familiar formulation 'neutral or other States not Parties to the conflict' following the proposal of European neutrals. The representatives of the US, the UK and Venezuela also expressed the view that it would be preferable to refer to states not parties than to neutral states; see LEVIE, *op. cit., supra,* vol.2 at pp. 320–1.

[108]Here again it was the editorial intervention of Austria, Finland, Sweden, Switzerland and the United Kingdom in order 'to avoid the difficulty which may result from this diversity of terms' which led to the adoption of the clause 'neutral or other State not a Party to the conflict'; see LEVIE, *op. cit., supra* n.106, vol.1 at pp. 87, 316.

party to the conflict might lend to a belligerent,[109] or of Article 64 concerning the civil defence organizations of neutral or other states not parties to the conflict operating in belligerent territory[110] sheds no light on the matter.

The negotiating history does not allow for any conclusive assessment as to the reasons that finally led to the codification of such a mysterious distinction between genuine neutrals and non-belligerents. For the Austrian delegation, at least, the change in terminology although 'a matter of form rather than of substance' was undesirable on several accounts:

> it would be confusing to have regulations directed to neutral States in the [1949] Conventions and additional regulations for States not parties to the conflict in the Protocols, and there would inevitably be difficulties of interpretation. Furthermore, the term "States not parties to the conflict" might endanger the very concept of neutrality. Neutral status, where States did not, and did not intend to, enter into armed conflict carried certain well-defined rights and duties. It implied a policy in wartime which was foreseeable and could be relied upon. The use of an ill-defined and vague term, with no legal protection, would weaken the concept of neutrality and upset international legal safety.[111]

In short, there is hardly anything in the voluminous proceedings of the Diplomatic Conference which would reveal a clear intention on the part of the participating states to institutionalize non-belligerency or to attach to it legal consequences distinct from those of traditional neutrality. The notable CDDH/45 amendment of March 1974 sponsored by Austria, Finland, Sweden, Switzerland and the United Kingdom had been recognized time and again as a result of a compromise,[112] aiming at

[109] *Ibid.*, vol.2 at pp. 13–41.
[110] *Ibid.*, vol.3 at p. 504.
[111] *Ibid.*, vol.1 at p. 528 and vol.2 at p. 167. Most commentators attach little significance to the distinction between 'neutrals' and 'other states not parties to the conflict'; see, for instance, BOTHE, M., PARTSCH, K.J. and SOLF, W.A., *New Rules for Victims of Armed Conflicts – Commentary on the Two 1977 Protocols Additional to the Geneva Conventions of 1949*, 1982 at p. 106, and SANDOZ, Y., SWINARSKI, C. and ZIMMERMANN, B. (eds), *Commentary on the Additional Protocols of 8 June 1977 to the Geneva Conventions of 12 August 1949*, 1987 at p. 61.
[112] See the statement to that effect of Haas, LEVIE, *op. cit., supra* n.106, vol.1 at p. 318.

making the negotiated text uniform rather than tracing new paths in neutrality law.[113]

It would appear safer to interpret the views in support of the expression 'states not parties to the conflict' as an attempt to avoid as much as possible terms alluding to an old legal order built upon notions of war and neutrality. Much in the same way as the four Geneva Conventions had concluded with terms such as 'belligerents' or 'belligerency', for instance, the drafters of the Protocol may have wished to eschew delicate questions of interpretation for the future by adopting a more colourless term than the much-laden 'neutrality'. Be that as it may, one has still to remark the irony of such a witch-hunt exercise (as if new terms would suffice to exorcise outlawed practices) by pointing out that although the term 'armed conflict' has chased away the 'evil' term of war from modern international documents, the Additional Protocol still refers to prisoners of *war* and *war* crimes.

To conclude this brief note on the troubled relationship between collective security and neutrality, one should remain sceptical about the suggestion that the advent of collective security has wiped out the entire body of the law of neutrality in unqualified terms. The UN Charter has laid down a number of objectives and outlined a scheme for their attainment. It worked out a pattern for concerted effort, not a guarantee of automated solutions and unfailing success. If one should conclude that the collective security arrangement enunciated in the Charter has caused the outright extinction of classical neutrality rules, then what should be the analogous impact of Article 2§4 upon the international humanitarian law?

Applying the same logic one should be forced to assume that the interdiction of the use or threat of force in international relations has disposed of the laws of war as a whole, except for those rules which would remain pertinent in cases of action in self-defence. For what could possibly be, for instance, the continued need for rules related to offensive bombardment, to reprisals against civilian population, to attacks against military objectives, or of so many other codified provisions which continue to envisage fighting armies and protracted hostilities in an era when only an extremely limited right of self-defence

[113]See the statement of Kussbach, *ibid.*, vol.1 at p. 324.

is exceptionally open to national states? Yet, inter-state armed conflicts continue to take their toll on human communities, forcing nations to rediscover and further develop humanitarian law. Similarly, collective security has not materialized, save on rare and selective occasions, and thus neutrality has preserved most of its aptness.

V Concluding remarks

Neutrality – A Lasting Story War still exists, peace remains precarious, neutrality proves chimerical. Extending over the moving ground between peace and war, the legal concept of neutrality is bound to alter every time the legal understanding or attitude towards the problems related to war and peace itself changes. The obscurity surrounding the original concept of neutrality is to be attributed to three main sources: first, to the experience of two World Wars which afforded little room for neutrals pushing traditional law close to irrelevance; second, to the rise of various notions of differential, qualified, benevolent neutrality, or non-belligerency, all conveying the assumption that neutral duties can be discharged at will or by degrees; and third, to the adoption of the Kellogg-Briand Pact and later of the UN Charter that have presumably outlawed war (and even elevated its prohibition to the heights of *jus cogens*), thus depriving neutrality of its material field of application.

The legal literature of the last three-quarters of a century is replete with obituaries offered to the law of war and neutrality. True, neutrality has been for the most of that time shrinking to a mere ante-room of belligerency, often dissimulating duplicity and contempt for law. It is also true that the advancing awareness of problems of transnational solidarity and interdependence tend to stigmatize neutrality as a somewhat anti-social, egocentric policy. Yet, *volens nolens* neutrality has proved to be an attitude that states are not ready to relinquish. It occasionally stands for measure, reason or a balanced *modus vivendi* and therefore may still be serviceable.

Hence, instead of delivering obituaries, it would be preferable to calibrate classical neutrality to present-day conditions. For there is nothing surprising about neutrality being in the melting-pot; in fact, because of its dynamic character it is condemned to constant transformation and evolution. As one scholar remarked, paraphrasing an older expression of Hersch Lauterpacht's, 'the international affairs of both the pre- and post-World War II eras have undoubtedly proved that there is more of neutrality and less of collective security. Not only has collective security failed to banish the political and legal phenomenon of neutrality from the international scene, but the formidable obstacles entailed in the application of the concept have most concretely highlighted the viability and merits of neutrality as a foreign policy instrument.'[114]

Although the sovereign discretion to opt for abstention has largely been eroded in these days of modern collective security arrangements, the institutional gear by which classical neutrality functioned has given far less rise to dispute. For several decades now jurists have been trying to discredit the concept of neutrality by revealing its systemic weaknesses, its all too common insincerity, its final vulnerability, its evident disharmony with collective security doctrine. Whatever the merits of such an exercise, however, it should be acknowledged that neutrality has shown an amazing endurance. It cannot be denied that it continues to float on the rough seas of inter-state relations and that it will apparently commence yet another century of juridical life coupled with what always made its company: eternal mystery and vivid debate.

Neutrality and the Crisis of Legitimacy of the UN Security Council Neutrality may further assume the connotation of a policy of dissidence within a UN system in which important decisions remain the prerogative of a limited number of powers and thus appear occasionally arbitrary. As long as the Security Council continues to act as the least representative directorate, unsusceptible to democratic control,[115] neutral postures might

[114]See KARSH, E., 'International Co-operation and Neutrality', 25 *Journal of Peace Research* (1988) at p. 67.

[115]A growing number of publicists appear to cast doubt on the very legitimacy of the Security Council decision-making since it involves an aberrantly small number of states. As argued in a recent article, 'the ambivalence of many states toward a stronger UN is now coupled with apprehension about a pax Americana, even a UN-centered one, without a Soviet counterweight . . . The more active and assertive the council becomes, the more the 150-plus member states not on the council will mutter about decisions it makes in their name but without their input'; see LUCK, E.C. and GATI, T.T., 'Whose Collective Security?', 15 *Washington Quarterly* (spring 1992) at pp. 43,45. For another commentator, 'la légitimité du "Directoire" des Cinq grandes puissances peut être discutée à juste

come to illustrate a 'protest mood' against UN dictates whenever regarded unjust or biased.[116] The Iranian and Jordanian stance of neutrality during the international campaign against Iraq in 1990–1 was to a certain degree motivated by considerations of this nature. The UN-led action was opposed on several grounds, e.g. cultivation of fratricidal trends within the Muslim world,

titre ... Quelles que soient les solutions adoptées, on ne peut imaginer que les 165 membres des Nations Unies reconnaîtront indéfiniment le privilège que se sont octroyé, en 1945, les vainqueurs de la seconde guerre mondiale'; see MERLE, M., 'Maintien de la paix et l'idée d'un nouvel ordre mondial – Rapport général' in DAUDET, Y. (ed.), *Aspects du système des Nations Unies dans le cadre de l'idée d'un nouvel ordre mondial*, 1992 at p. 58. Recent remarks by Michael Reisman point in the same direction: 'with the end of the Cold War, the Council not only has revived atrophied functions, but also has undertaken activities that, arguably, may not have been contemplated at its inception. Magnifying the disquiet is the fact that, as the Council has become more effective and powerful, it has become more secretive. Like a parliamentary matryoshka (doll), it now contains ever-smaller "mini-Councils", each meeting behind closed doors without keeping records, and each taking decisions secretly ... Decisions that appear to go further than at any time in the history of the United Nations are now ultimately being taken, it seems, by a small group of states separately meeting in secret'; see REISMAN, W.M., 'The Constitutional Crisis in the United Nations', 87 *AJIL* (1993) at pp. 85–6. Consider also the following commentary: 'pour certains, le directoire international institué par la Charte sous la forme d'un Conseil de sécurité, fait planer, lorsqu'il fonctionne, l'ombre de Metternich sur les relations internationales. Aujourd'hui, le Conseil ne serait-il pas le masque à l'abri duquel les Etats-Unis légitiment leur hégémonie sans partage?'; see TORRELLI, M., 'Le Conseil de sécurité: un directoire mondial?', *Trimestre du monde* (1992/4) at p. 28. See also CARON, D.D., 'The Legitimacy of the Collective Authority of the Security Council', 87 *AJIL* (1993), pp. 552–88; CHUBIN, S., 'The South and the New World Order', 16 *Washington Quarterly* (autumn 1993) at p. 103; GAJA, G., 'Réflexions sur le rôle du Conseil de sécurité dans le nouvel ordre mondial', 97 *RGDIP* (1993), pp. 297–320; DUPUY, R.-J. (ed.), *The Development of the Role of the Security Council*, 1993.

[116]In a recent essay, Clark Arend identified three possible models for maintaining international order in the post-Cold War era, namely US hegemony, Great Power concert, and new multilateralism, and advanced the proposition that if the Security Council member states 'continue to take this special leadership position in the international system, the "new world order" could be a system of Great Power management'; see AREND, C.A., 'The United Nations and the New World Order', 81 *Georgetown Law Journal* (March 1993) at p. 494. For yet another scholar, 'in at least one sense, the Cold War schism provided a measure of sovereign security to smaller nations which has not as yet been recovered under the new world order ... The exercise of expanded authority by the Security Council will, as a practical matter, directly affect only those nations seeking a course that is truly independent from the views of the permanent members of the Council ... Only by restoring legitimacy to the Security Council system can faith be restored in the international legal system at large'; see ROBERTS, L.D., 'United Nations Security Council Resolution 687 and Its Aftermath: The Implications for Domestic Authority and the Need for Legitimacy', 25 *New York University Journal of International Law and Politics* (1993) at p. 626.

double standards and unfair treatment of the Palestinian question, criminal apathy during the Iraqi war of aggression against Iran, all of which reflected a sentiment of resentment and disapprobation of UN handling finally expressed in the declaration of neutrality.

Thus, hidden behind the seemingly exemptory clause of Article 48§1 of the Charter and vows to neutrality, there will often be in reality a mute condemnation of UN practices in matters concerning the maintenance of international peace and security. There are two facets of recent Security Council action which would seem relevant here. The first would be connected with the mode of enforcement of certain sanctions which is genuinely reminiscent of the nineteenth-century practice of pacific blockades as the instrument of global policing in the hands of the Concert of Europe, and which in a sense illustrates the attitude of neo-colonialism currently criticized in the Security Council. The second equally controversial aspect would concern the vexed question of how exactly the priorities for UN action are set.[117] One should simply try the exercise of ranking the Haitian case, by measure of its gravity on a global scale, among the rising tide of international crises seeking to attract world attention, to realize the logical opacity of the Security Council approach.

[117]As one commentator has put it, the prime consideration seems to be 'to steer clear of those cases where the wounds are too severe to be attended to because that would tie up too many of the organization's resources for little or no gain whereas the lightly wounded would not be helped because they could live with their wounds'; see FREUDENSCHUSS, H., 'Article 39 of the UN Charter Revisited: Threats to the Peace and the Recent Practice of the UN Security Council', 46 *Austrian Journal of Public and International Law* (1993) at p. 39. See also GOULDING, M., 'The Evolution of United Nations Peacekeeping', 69 *International Affairs* (July 1993) at p. 461.

ΛΟΦΟΠΟΙΟΣ οίμ' ως προθέλυμνόν μ', ω Τρυγαί; απώλεσας.
ΤΡΥΓΑΙΟΣ. τί δ' έστιν, ώ κακόδαιμον; ού τί που λοφάς;
ΛΟ. απώλεσάς μου την τέχνην και τον βίον,
και τουτουί και τού δορυξού 'κεινουί.
ΤΡ τί δήτα τουτοινοί καταθώ σοι τοίν λόφοιν;

ΘΩΡΑΚΟΠΩΛΗΣ. τί δαί δεκάμνω τώδε θώρηκος κύτει
ενημμένω κάλλιστα χρήσομαι τάλας;
ΤΡΥΓΑΙΟΣ. ούτος μέν ου μή σοι ποιήσει ζημίαν.
αλλ' αίρε μοι τούτόν γε τής ισωνίας·
εναποπατείν γαρ εστ' επιτήδειος πάνυ,

CREST-MAKER. O you've destroyed me root and branch, Trygaeus.
TRYGAEUS. How now, poor wretch! what ails you? got a crestache?
C.-M. You have destroyed my living and my trade,
And this man's too, and yon spear-burnisher's.
TR. What shall I give you then, for these two crests? [. . .]
BREASTPLATE-SELLER. O what's the use of this habergeon now?
So splendidly got up: cost forty pounds.
TR. Well, well, you shan't lose anything by that:
I'll buy it of you at its full cost price.
'Twill do superbly for my chamber-pan [. . .]

Aristophanes, *The Peace*, l.1210–14, 1224–9, 1245–54, (transl. by B.B. Rogers, The Loeb Classical Library, 1961 at pp. 111–15)

Chapter Five

THE THEORY OF ABSOLUTE CONTRABAND

I Introduction

Neutrality presupposes war. War presupposes arms. And arms presuppose humans, sometimes alleged neutrals, disposed to furnish them in abundance. This vicious circle has, at the same time, disturbed the notion of neutrality, altered the scope and nature of war, and, most certain of all, cost millions of human lives. This chapter focuses on what seems a logical absurdity, for professing neutrality and yet supplying arms to belligerents seem mutually exclusive. History, however, shows that for a long time the law of nations tolerated this paradox since the theory of neutrality was founded on an all too fragile compromise according to which neutral governments were under an obligation not to supply arms while they were under no obligation to prevent their nationals from doing so.[1]

Rough estimations claim that since the end of the Second World War, there have erupted some 150 armed conflicts around the globe, causing the death of over 20 million.[2] Despite the development of indigenous arms industries in several Third World countries, all recorded conflicts have only been made

[1]See Articles 6 and 7 of the 1907 Hague Convention XIII Concerning the Rights and Duties of Neutral Powers in Naval War. See also Article 7 of the Hague Convention V Respecting the Rights and Duties of Neutral Powers and Persons in Case of War on Land.

[2]More than half of the member states of the United Nations have participated in one or more of these conflicts which were fought in the territories of over 71 countries; see *Study on Conventional Disarmament*, published in 1985, UN Doc.A/39/348, §§55–6 at p. 15. The great majority of these wars have occurred or continue to tear apart developing countries and have been fought with conventional weapons, with some exceptions such as the use of chemical weapons in the Iran-Iraq War.

possible as a result of a, more often than not, freewheeling flow of conventional arms traded by the major industrialized countries. The patterns of the arms trade in the post-war period, followed between donor and recipient states, have obeyed practically nothing but the dictates of commercial greed and political imperialism. The militarization of the Third World, for the most part, proceeded unchecked and as a result it may now backfire.

The legal problems of neutrality and the traffic in arms have been gathering dust ever since the Hague Conferences. Neutrality has supposedly been eclipsed by the Charter vision which renders inactivity incompatible with active membership *vis-à-vis* a threat or breach of international peace, while the issues of arms trade and conventional disarmament have been largely ignored by legal science. The question to be addressed here, therefore, is what the contemporary international law prescriptions governing the arms sales of a country which has declared or implied itself neutral in a conflict unpronounced upon by the United Nations? Have any general principles of law crystallized over the past decades, or, is it still the Hague law of 1907 that sets the limits of legitimacy in the field? Are, in the end, Thomas Jefferson's words to enjoy perpetuity or should they be in all urgency revisited? Let us remember his legacy: rejecting British complaints in 1793 concerning reports that French agents had been purchasing arms in the United States with a view to exporting them to France, he declared:

> our citizens have always been free to vend and export arms; that it is the constant occupation and livelihood of some of them; to suppress their callings, the only means perhaps of their subsistence, because a war exists in foreign and distant countries in which we have no concern would scarcely be expected; it would be hard in principle and impossible in practice.[3]

[3]Quoted in ATWATER, E., *American Regulation of Arms Exports*, 1941, pp. 7–15. See also HYNEMAN, C.S., *The First American Neutrality*, 1934, pp. 145–50. While at the time of the Russo-Turkish War of 1822, Jefferson was even more explicit: 'that the life of the feeder is better than that of the fighter . . . let us milk the cow while the Russian holds her by the horns and the Turk by the tail'; quoted in JESSUP, P.C. and DEÁK, F., *Neutrality – Its History, Economics and Law*, vol.I (1935) at p. 260.

The query today persists whether in the two hundred years that have since elapsed humanity cannot claim to have advanced further than contending that armaments, exported by private (to name but a few) French, Dutch or Italian industries, to keep the Gulf War flames burning for eight years were but a legitimate commercial enterprise, and did not contravene the French, Dutch or Italian appearance of neutrality. Does it hold true any more, in the light of mandatory arms exports licensing and frequent embargo practices, that private persons have *always* been free to vend and export? And, bearing in mind the extensive state interventionism prevailing in defence matters, is it credible that there do exist major arms industries that rest *exclusively,* literally and metaphorically, in private hands? Can one still share the view that, in the age of collective security arrangements, conflicts may exist *in foreign and distant countries* which leave unconcerned the international community? Is there still room today to argue persuasively that enforcing restraint and national controls, *is hard in principle and impossible in practice*?

War hurts everybody, benefits nobody except the profiteers, and settles nothing, wrote Field Marshal Sir William Robertson, his words echoing an epoch in which people discovered with horror that cannons and warships were being built not only for national defence but also for profit. Deplorable though it may be, profit has yet to be taken out of war, though rationalism has cried out for it ever since the achievements of the legendary personality of Zaharoff were brought to light.[4] Numerous initiatives floated on the unilateral or multilateral level since the early days of the League were all calculated to fail. Pacifism has been, more often than not, criticized as incurably romantic and utopian. The grave objections to unchecked arms trafficking remained for decades muted. The prospects for the foreseeable future appear no more comforting. Who could have imagined

[4]Zaharoff's eventful life thrilled the imagination of several biographers; see LEWINSOHN, R., *The Man Behind the Scenes – The Career of Sir Basil Zaharoff,* 1929; NEUMANN, R., *Sir Basil Zaharoff – Le roi des armes,* 1934. See also COLLIER, B., *Arms and the Men,* 1980, p. 80*ff.*; BROCKWAY, F., *The Bloody Traffic,* 1933, p. 38*ff.*; ENGELBRECHT, H.C. and HANIGHEN, F.C., *Merchants of Death – A Study of the International Armament Industry,* 1934, p. 95*ff.*; SELDES, G., *Iron, Blood and Profits,* 1934, p. 179*ff.*

that these very 'grave objections',[5] spelled out by the League of Nations in 1921, would remain today more valid than ever?[6]

Already in the late 1930s eloquent arguments had been made on whether a meaningful distinction between *state* and *private* was still sustainable in the realm of arms manufacture and arms export. The works of Wolfgang Friedmann and Lawrence Preuss have led the way to suggest that the old Hague rule was to enjoy only theoretical validity, since the basis on which it was devised had disappeared and therefore the concept of neutrality was moving towards complete abstention. Following their reasoning, Articles 6 and 7 of the 1907 Thirteenth and Fifth Hague Conventions should be deemed to have been superseded by a comprehensive prohibition of sending arms to belligerents on the part of neutrals, whether government agents or private citizens. At a time, when the prohibition of 'oiling' the war machines of belligerents seems to stem not only from some obsolete laws of neutrality, but from positive dictates of the United Nations Charter, it is at least ironic that need would arise to reaffirm the most essential of neutral duties.

What follows is a description of the current anomalies and legal niceties of an international trade in arms which seems more than ever before constrained by national and international commitments, and yet thrives in practice. Unorthodox though it may seem to start out with findings, here are the two principal observations which shape the legal controversy. First, the largest arms-producing countries have long brought arms exports to the centre of the public interest and committed themselves, as

[5]See *infra* n.29 and accompanying text.

[6]One should avoid the easy assumption that present day Zaharoffs, Krupps, or Vickers are the only ones to blame. Frantic global militarism certainly took more than a handful of powerful arms dealers to reach today's heights. For it is simplistic to believe that $65 billion worth of armaments consumed in the Iran-Iraq War were transacted by such dark personalities like Adnan Khashoggi or Manucher Ghorbanifar alone. For thousands of tanks, aircraft and heavy artillery exported to the Persian Gulf during the 1980s cannot be classified singularly as the fruits of black marketing, which means that they were simply stolen from state inventories; see KLARE, M.T., 'Secret Operatives, Clandestine Trades: The Thriving Black Market for Weapons', 44 *Bulletin of the Atomic Scientists* (April 1988), p. 16*ff.* See also KARP, A., 'The Trade in Conventional Weapons' in *Ybk.SIPRI* (1988), p. 190*ff.*, and 'The Covert Arms Trade: The Second-Oldest Profession', *The Economist*, 12 February 1994, p. 19*ff.* 'The real culprit today [wrote Thayer in 1969] has become diffuse, an abstraction, a zephyr that often defies precise identification. In a way the villain is an attitude that has run unchecked for decades, and with particular intensity since the end of the Second World War'; see THAYER, G., *The War Business*, 1969 at p. 307.

a matter of official policy or enacted law, not to supply arms to warring nations. Several among them have gone even further, declining in principle to sell arms to areas of tension, countries experiencing internal disturbances, or governments with a poor human rights record. Second, the very same states have, nonetheless, frequently proved unable or unwilling to act in a manner fully compatible with their pledges in the context of a real situation.

The eight-year-long Iran–Iraq War provides a perfect illustration of such inconsistency between words and deeds. At the peak of the Gulf War's frantic demand for arms, most western states were prepared to pervert their alleged neutrality through the argument that abstention could be equated with strict impartiality in supplying *both* sides. To pursue restraint unilaterally, as the pedestrian view has it, is pointless in a world full of alternative suppliers. This *cosi fan tutti* type of argument, however, risks a regression to the *si omnes* logic long discarded both in legal theory and practice. While the 1990–1 Gulf campaign and the pursued dismantlement of the Iraqi military potential brought to the forefront the industrialized world's proper responsibility for fomenting instability through unscrupulous arms transfer policies.[7]

II The legal and factual parameters of the issue

1 The theory of risk and absolute contraband now and then

Unviolability of private property in wartime does not hold true in the maritime context. Traditional rules have codified the neutral *state obligation* not to furnish munitions of war to bel-

[7]It may be worth remembering that 80 per cent of the weapons delivered to belligerent Iraq throughout the 1980s came from three of the five permanent members of the United Nations Security Council (the Soviet Union, France and China) which are purported to hold 'primary responsibility for the maintenance of international peace and security' (Article 24), which also means that they are bound to 'promote the establishment and maintenance of international peace and security with least diversion for armaments of the world's human and economic resources' (Article 26); see *Fact Sheet on Military Expenditure and Iraqi Arms Imports*, SIPRI, 8 August 1990 at p. 4. In the words of the UN Secretary-General, 'paradoxically, those expressing great concern over the rising stocks of arms worldwide are also the source of that phenomenon. The five permanent members of the Security Council account for 86 per cent of the arms supplies now flowing to the countries of the world'; see *An Agenda for Development and International Economic Cooperation*, UN Doc.A/48/935, 6 May 1994, §32 at p. 8.

ligerents, but have also expressly provided for a neutral *private right* of trade in arms. The underlying logic was that private acts can by no means affect or compromise national policies, and therefore a neutral state was under no obligation to prevent such private acts, however unneutral or detrimental to one of the belligerents, these might be. Private seaborne commerce could thus legitimately carry on, the only risk arising from the corresponding belligerent right to intercept and confiscate all cargoes destined to enemy territory and susceptible of belligerent use. In this latter case, the private merchant might not count on his government for any sort of protection and should suffer the consequences of his venture.

In other words, international law in its classical and long respected form found nothing illogical or improper about private neutral trade with warring nations for as long as the belligerent right to seize contraband prevailed in case of conflict. The so-called 'theory of risk' (*théorie de l'aventure*), based on a net dichotomy between public interest and private profit, was expounded in great many prize decisions. As the British privy council reasoned in 1920, 'the ownership of contraband goods, though often spoken of as if it were a guilty departure from the neutral duty of impartiality, is now well recognized as being in itself no transgression of the limits of a neutral's duty, but merely the exercise of a hazardous right, in the course of which he may come into conflict with the rights of the belligerent and be worsted'.[8]

Contraband, the term originally designating goods banned from commerce by a prince or by the Church, has assumed a particular significance in the context of the laws of sea warfare. It consists of goods susceptible to confiscation provided that

[8]See *The Kronprinsessan Margareta* (1920), 1 *Appeal Cases* at p. 505. And elsewhere: 'neutrals who carry contraband do not break the law of nations; they run a risk for adequate gain, and, if they are caught, take the consequences. If they know what they are doing, those consequences may be very serious; if they do not, they may get off merely with some inconvenience or delay; this must suffice them'; see *The Prins der Nederlanden* (1921), *ibid.* at p. 760. Writing shortly before the outbreak of the Second World War, Philip Jessup summarized the state of development of the modern law of contraband in these propositions: 'twentieth-century ideas of the law of contraband of war imply three things: on the part of a belligerent, the right to seize and to confiscate certain goods going to his enemy; on the part of a neutral government, no obligation to prevent the shipment of such goods; on the the part of a neutral individual, risk of loss if his shipment is intercepted by the belligerent'; see JESSUP and DEÁK, *op. cit., supra* n.3 at p. 51.

two determinant requisites are met, that is to say they are susceptible to use in armed conflict and they are consigned to a hostile destination.[9] Traditionally, contraband has been divided in two categories: absolute and conditional. The distinction dates back to Grotius' treatise on war and peace and his reference to 'things, such as weapons, which are useful only in war; other things which are of no use in war, as those which minister to pleasure; and others still which are of use both in time of war and at other times, as money, provisions, ships, and naval equipment'.[10]

Absolute contraband, which is the object of the present analysis, comprised all those goods to be used for warlike purposes, such as arms, ammunition, uniforms, etc. Lists of items to be treated as absolute contraband could be freely issued by every belligerent state upon the outbreak of hostilities. A shipment of absolute contraband might then be seized on board a neutral vessel if a destination in enemy or enemy-occupied territory could be established. Conditional contraband, on the other hand, referred to goods equally susceptible to peaceful and warlike purposes, e.g. foodstuffs, fuel, gold, etc. These articles might be seized only if specifically destined to enemy's armed forces or public services.

Viewed in historical perspective, the practice of proclaiming a list of prohibited contraband goods emerged only as a progressive refinement of the idea of total bans on trade common

[9]On the historical development of the law of contraband, see PYKE, H.R., *The Law of Contraband of War,* 1915; COLOMBOS, C.J., *A Treatise on the Law of Prize,* 3rd edn (1949), pp. 186–230; ORTOLAN, T., *Règles internationales et diplomatie de la mer,* tome 2 (1864), pp. 175–247; KLEEN, R., *Règles et usages de la neutralité,* tome 1er (1898), pp. 348–452; DUPUIS, C., *Le droit de la guerre maritime d'après les doctrines anglaises contemporaines,* 1899, pp. 237–80; WHITEMAN, M.M., *Digest of International Law,* vol.10 (1968), pp. 791–852; HACKWORTH, G.H., *Digest of International Law,* vol.VII (1943), pp. 14–99. See also TUCKER, R.W., *The Law of War and Neutrality at Sea,* USNWC, 50 *International Law Studies* (1955), pp. 263–82; MENG, W., 'Contraband' in BERNHARDT, R. (ed.), *Encyclopedia of Public International Law,* instalment 3 (1982), p. 122*ff.*

[10]See SCOTT, J.B. (ed.), *The Classics of International Law – De Jure Belli ac Pacis by Hugo Grotius,* 1925, vol.II at p. 602 [bk.III, ch.I, section V]. In an early reference to the notion of conditional contraband, Lord Stowell had stated: 'these instances shew that articles of human food have been so considered [contraband], at least where it was probable that they were intended for naval or military use . . . And I take the modern established rule to be this, that generally they are not contraband, but may become so under circumstances arising out of the particular situation of the war, or the condition of the parties engaged in it'; see *The Jonge Margaretha* (1799), 1 C. *Robinson's Admiralty Reports* at p. 193.

as of the early thirteenth century through to the sixteenth century. By the end of the sixteenth century, a belligerent was still held free in principle to prohibit all trade with the enemy. It was only when powerful neutrals vigorously protested that by way of concession the prohibition was confined to those trade items which the enemy needed most, in particular munitions. The first treaty to announce a selective range of products as prohibited goods for neutral transactions with the enemy was the Anglo-Dutch treaty of 1625, while by the time the Anglo-Dutch war broke out in 1652, the concept of contraband had assumed the clear and definite meaning of a legal doctrine.

Prize courts made frequent reference to the rules of contraband and free lists although serious discrepancies persisted as to the exact content of those rules. Owing to her naval supremacy England wished the extension of contraband lists to include, beyond the incontrovertible category of arms and munitions of war, ship-building materials and foodstuffs. On the other hand, France, as a major exporter of wines, victuals and cloth, and the Netherlands, as the preferred transporter of French commodities, argued for wide-ranging free lists. The controversy over whether provisions and naval stores would qualify as contraband goods remained unresolved through the eighteenth century. Doctrine and practice were only developed through the conclusion of numerous bilateral treaties often including detailed descriptions of contraband articles and free goods.

Articles 22 and 24 of the unratified London Declaration of 1909 are believed to have codified the customary law as it then stood concerning the typology of contraband goods. According to its terms, absolute contraband would include, to name but a few, arms of all kinds, projectiles, charges, powder and explosives, armour plates, warships, gun-mountings, military wagons, saddle, draught and pack animals, or articles of camp equipment. Conversely, foodstuffs, forage and grain, clothing, gold and silver or paper money, vehicles of all kinds, vessels, craft and boats of all kinds, railway material, balloons and flying machines, fuel, lubricants, field glasses, telescopes or all kinds of nautical instruments would be only be treated as conditional contraband. The Declaration of London gave also expression to a third category of goods known as 'free goods', or goods immune from capture and condemnation. By virtue of Articles

27–9, non-contraband articles would include, for instance, raw cotton, wool, silk, oil seeds and nuts, rubber, resins, gums, raw hides, horns and ivory, metallic ores, earth clays, lime, chalk, stone, chinaware and glass, paper, soap, bleaching powder, precious stones, clocks, feathers and articles of household furniture.

World War experience, however, changed drastically, and in all likelihood irrevocably, the law of contraband. The idea of 'nations at war' which meant that the entire population without exception contributed to the war effort made increasingly irrelevant whether seized goods were destined for an enemy government and its armed forces or for consumption by the civilian population. Contraband lists were expanded to every imaginable category so that the distinction between absolute and conditional contraband vanished in practice. The burden of proof shifted to the claimant who had to rebut all kinds of presumptive evidence. As Herbert Arthur Smith has written, 'no topic of the law of nations has had a longer or more contentious history'.[11]

2 World military expenditure and arms trade: a briefing

World military expenditure is the appellation for the aggregate global resources devoted to human self-destruction and is indicative of the feverish pace of the world arms race. In the twentieth century, the assets the world commits annually to armaments has increased 85-fold.[12] The pace at which poor nations fritter away their national assets in arming themselves becomes all the more impressive when one looks at military expenditures as a percentage of gross national product. By way of indication, while the figures for NATO countries have varied between 3.5 per cent and 6.5 per cent in recent years, Iraq's spending climbed from 6.3 per cent in 1980, to 24.4 per cent in

[11]See SMITH, H.A., *The Law and Custom of the Sea*, 3rd edn (1959) at p. 145.

[12]In 1982, the global figure for military spending was believed to move in the neighbourhood of US $600 billion. For 1985, it was estimated at US $870 billion, while the US $1,000 billion per year barrier could be breached before the end of the century. These numbers are to be compared with US $65 billion in 1948, and less than US $10 billion in the year 1900; see BARNABY, F. and HUISKEN, R., *Arms Uncontrolled*, SIPRI, 1975 at p. 5.

1983, and 29.1 per cent in 1984.[13] Current figures on the total conventional weapons inventory on earth speaks of some 140,000 battle tanks, 35,000 combat aircraft, 21,000 helicopters, 1,100 major surface warships and 700 attack submarines.

The international arms trade represents only a fraction of the mammoth world military expenditures. It covers essentially the spending for the acquisition of weapon systems from foreign countries. With the exception of recent signs of contraction,[14] the world arms trade has never deviated from its two constant parameters, namely, the ever-soaring amount of money involved, and the fixed direction of arms flow from the industrialized north to the underdeveloped south.[15] The number of arms exporters has grown from 32 in 1963, to 48 in 1984, whereas the number of states importing weapons has risen from 91 in 1963, to 118 in 1986. The increase of flow of major weapons has been substantial. In volume, it was three times greater in the second half of the 1960s than in the first half of the 1950s.

Marketing arms abroad has been supported by various political, industrial and economic reasons. Enhancing the consolidation of hegemonistic relationships and galvanizing

[13]Other Middle Eastern countries, like Saudi Arabia or Oman, kept their expenditures at an average of 21 per cent throughout the decade, while Syria around 15 per cent. In Central America, Nicaragua accorded 34.2 per cent of its domestic product to arms in 1987, the corresponding figure for 1988 being 28.3 per cent. And in Africa, the recorded statistics for Angolan military spending gave 28.4 per cent in 1985–6 and 21.5 per cent in 1988; see *Ybk.SIPRI* (1991) at pp. 175–6, 178.

[14]In 1990, conventional arms worth US $21.7 billion were exported to 132 countries around the world, a 35 per cent decrease from the 1989 level and a 45 per cent decrease from the peak year of 1987 when US $39.8 billion in arms were traded; see ANTHONY, I., 'The Global Arms Trade', 21 *Arms Control Today* (June 1991) at p. 3.

[15]Among the various monographs on the dynamics of the international trade in arms, see BLACKABY, F. et al., *The Arms Trade with the Third World*, SIPRI, 1971; BRZOSKA, M. and OHLSON, T. (eds), *Arms Production in the Third World*, SIPRI, 1986; BRZOSKA, M. and OHLSON, T., *Arms Transfers to the Third World, 1971–85*, SIPRI, 1987; WULF, H. (ed.), *Arms Industry Limited*, SIPRI, 1993; HARKAVY, R.E., *The Arms Trade and International Systems*, 1975; KLARE, M.T., *American Arms Supermarket*, 1984; FARLEY, P.J., KAPLAN, S.S. and LEWIS, W.H., *Arms Across the Sea*, 1978; PIERRE, A.J., *The Global Politics of Arms Sales*, 1982; SJÖQUIST, B. and WILLIAMSON, R. (eds), *Selling Weapons: A Deadly Business*, 1993; SAMPSON, A., *The Arms Bazaar*, 1977; STANLEY, J. and PEARTON, M., *The International Trade in Arms*, 1972; FRANK, L.A., *The Arms Trade in International Relations*, 1969; COLLINSON, H., *Death on Delivery: The Impact of the Arms Trade on the Third World*, 1989; KEMP, G., 'Arms Traffic and Third World Conflicts', 577 *Int.Con.* (1970).

alliances, by increasing the military and hence the political dependence of the recipient country, is thought to be the prime political determinant in arms transfers.[16] Among the industrial incentives, it has somewhat axiomatically asserted that domestic demand alone would be insufficient to allow the production of advanced weapons systems without exorbitant cost. As far as economic considerations are concerned, arms deals are often counted on to beautify foreign trade balance sheets, cure budget deficits and ensure full employment in troubled or sensitive sectors.[17] For better or for worse, arms exports are now globally seen as an imperative precondition for the viability of any defence industry.[18]

If anything is clear, it is the fact that arms manufacture, and the arms exports resulting therefrom, have largely been lying, over the last decades, in the hands of governments rather than private industrialists, and that, in any case, the important decisions necessitate direct involvement and supervision of the public power. As it was attested some twenty years ago, 'not only do governments generally control the defence industry, either through ownership or by virtue of their monopolistic position, but they also bear a large share of the responsibility

[16]See OBERG, J., 'Arms Trade with the Third World as an Aspect of Imperialism', 12 *Journal of Peace Research* (1975), p. 213*ff.*

[17]See STANLEY and PEARTON, *op. cit., supra* n.15, p. 122*ff.*; BLACKABY, *op. cit., supra* n.15, p. 377*ff.*; BAJUSZ, W.D. and LOUSCHER, D.J., *Arms Sales and the U.S. Economy – The Impact of Restricting Military Exports*, 1988, p. 97*ff.* Yet, for some analysts, 'although economic considerations undoubtedly play a role in arms sales decisions, they are seldom, if ever, paramount. The international trade in arms has become such a prevalent implement of foreign policy for many countries, that economic criteria are subordinated to political considerations'; see HESSING CAHN, A., 'The Economics of Arms Transfers' in NEUMAN, S.G. and HARKAVY, R.E. (eds), *Arms Transfers in the Modern World*, 1979 at p. 182. See also SMITH, R., HUMM, A. and FONTANEL, J., 'The Economics of Exporting Arms', 22 *Journal of Peace Research* (1985), p. 239*ff.*

[18]In the words of a United Nations study, 'the high technology content of major weapons systems means two different but related things: only a few countries can produce and supply such weapons and even they must be able to export arms because they must recover at least a part of their development costs. The technological and economic imperative to export is accompanied by domestic political pressures, associated with employment in arms production facilities or with foreign policy objectives. In such circumstances, the limitation of conventional arms transfers is not regarded, by many Governments, as a desirable goal'; see *Study on the Economic and Social Consequences of the Arms Race and Military Expenditures*, published in 1989, UN Doc.A/43/368, §55 at p. 25. See also *Study on Ways and Means of Promoting Transparency in International Transfers of Conventional Arms*, published in 1991, UN Doc.A/46/301, §§42–52, p. 21–4.

for organizing and promoting the export of weapons. Less than 5% of the arms trade is in the hands of private dealers, and only a minute proportion of these dealers operate without government approval.'[19]

Several facets of the international arms trade seem to be undergoing considerable change in the 1990s, such as the number of suppliers and the types of commodities sold.[20] From 1975 to 1982, six countries (the United States, the former Soviet Union, the United Kingdom, France, West Germany and Italy) together supplied 84 per cent of all munitions ordered by developing states, the figure falling by the mid-1980s to 75 per cent. Second-tier suppliers like the Netherlands, Spain, Sweden, Switzerland, Belgium, East Germany and Poland accounted for most of the remainder. Yet, more important than the growing competitiveness of mid-size European suppliers was the emergence of powerful world-class suppliers among the Third World, notably China and Brazil. Analysts have been advancing worrying predictions for the prospects of the world arms trade. Most of them foretell a thriving future in a world of deep-rooted

[19]BLACKABY, *op.cit., supra* n.15 at p. 4.

[20]Among the most recent evaluations, see ADAM, B., 'Evolution du contexte politique et économique du commerce des armes', 26 *RBDI* (1993/1), p. 3*ff.*; KARP, A., 'Controlling Weapons Proliferation: The Role of Export Controls', 16 *Journal of Strategic Studies* (March 1993), p. 19*ff.*; CORDESMAN, A.H., 'After the Gulf War: The World Arms Trade and its Arms Races in the 1990s', 102 *RUSI and Brassey's Defence Yearbook* (1992), p. 205*ff.*; O'HANLON, M., FARRELL, V. and GLAZERMAN, S., 'Controlling Arms Transfers to the Middle East: The Case for Supplier Limits', 22 *Arms Control Today* (Nov.1992), p. 18*ff.*; KLARE, M.T., 'Wars in the 1990s – Growing Firepower in the Third World', 46 *Bulletin of the Atomic Scientists* (May 1990), p. 9*ff.*; Id., 'The Arms Trade: Changing Patterns in the 1980s', 9 *Third World Quarterly* (1987), p. 1257*ff.*; Id., 'The Unnoticed Arms Trade – Exports of Conventional Arms-making Technology', 8 *Int.Sec.* (1983), p. 68*ff.*; NEUMAN, S.G., 'The Arms Market: Who's on Top?', 33 *Orbis* (1989), p. 509*ff.*; Id., 'The Arms Trade in Recent Wars: The Role of the Superpowers', 40 *Journal of International Affairs* (1986), p. 77*ff.*; HARTUNG, W., 'Nations Vie for Arms Markets', 43 *Bulletin of the Atomic Scientists* (Dec.1987), p. 27*ff.*; BRZOSKA, M., 'The Arms Trade – Can It Be Controlled?', 24 *Journal of Peace Research* (1987), p. 327*ff.*; WILES, P., 'Whatever Happened to the Merchants of Death? Normal Supply Versus Catastrophic Demand', 15 *Millennium* (1986), p. 295*ff.*; YAKEMTCHOUK, R., 'Le commerce des armes', 45 *Studia Diplomatica* (1992); PEARSON, F.S., *The Global Spread of Arms*, 1994; COLLET, A., *Armements et conflits contemporains de 1945 à nos jours*, 1993. By way of general reference, the most reliable and comprehensive sources on world military expenditures and arms trade, are the annual publications of SIPRI, *Yearbook of World Armaments and Disarmament*, and ACDA, *World Military Expenditures and Arms Transfers*.

instability, increasing intolerance and unfolding redistribution of roles in global power.[21]

III Arms sales and the delusion of international control

1 Early efforts and the Hague codification

The questions of manufacture and trade in arms have presented major challenges to the international public order through the whole of our century. The two issues have always gone hand in hand since controlling arms transfers without controlling arms production would have given a definite advantage to arms-producing countries over arms-dependent ones. Almost no initiative was staged to tackle these problems prior to the creation of the League of Nations. Nineteenth-century worship of *laissez-faire* attitudes as reflected in the customary law of neutrality left nations virtually free to supply munitions as they pleased; private profit was not subordinated to any perception of public interest.[22]

The first multilateral effort calling for concerted action against the unsound diffusion of arms came out of the scramble for continued colonial domination over the African continent. The conference against the slave trade, held at Brussels in 1899–90, led to the conclusion of an international document stipulating the prohibition of arms trade within a defined geographical zone. The Brussels General Act, signed by seventeen States on 2 July 1890 and entered into force as from 2 April 1892, envisaged in fact the interruption of flow of arms directed to African colonies situated between the latitudes 20° North and 22°

[21]As one expert has noted, 'in an ironic twist of fate, the forthcoming Soviet and American arms reductions in Europe will produce massive supplies of surplus weapons which are likely to be funneled into the arms inventories of emerging Third World powers'; see KLARE, M.T., 'The Arms Trade with the Third World – Changing Patterns in the 1990s', paper presented in an Amnesty International colloquium, entitled *Arms Trade and Human Rights,* Lausanne, 10 November 1990. See aslo KLARE, M.T., 'L'accroissement des ventes d'armes au tiers-monde annonce d'autres tensions', *Le Monde Diplomatique*, septembre 1990, p. 10*ff.*, and NEUMAN, S.G., 'Controlling the Arms Trade: Idealistic Dream or Realpolitik', 16 *Washington Quarterly* (summer 1993), p. 53*ff.*

[22]For a detailed account on the diplomatic efforts for arms transfers control, up to the Second World War, see YAKEMTCHOUK, R., *Les transferts internationaux d'armes de guerre,* 1980, pp. 24–123. See also BLACKABY, *op. cit., supra* n.15, p. 86*ff.*; HUDSON, M.O., *Munitions Industry – International Regulation of the Trade in and Manufacture of Arms and Ammunition – A Report,* 1935.

South.[23] The Parties agreed also to keep each other informed of measures taken, and in this connection some functions were conferred to an International Office at Brussels. The Act was later supplemented by the Protocol of 22 July 1908, and by special treaties relating to Abyssinia.

The Hague Peace Conferences of 1899 and 1907, contrary to the *raison d'être* commonly assumed to underlie their inception, never dealt with disarmament. Instead, they codified usages of wa and neutrality such as the prevalent *théorie de l'aventure*. Although a neutral state should abstain, in principle, from furnishing material assistance to any of the warring nations, private industries should not be obliged to interrupt arms deliveries to belligerents. Common Article 7 of Hague Conventions V and XIII put down in black and white the popular belief that neutrality, if anything, was all about freedom of trade and that private commercial adventurism in no way jeopardized state policies. This legal prescription, which still pretends to be valid today, merits quotation in full:

> *a neutral power is not bound to prevent the export or transit, for the use of either belligerent, of arms, ammunition, or, in general, of anything which could be of use to an army or fleet.*

[23]The geographical coordinates of the zone could be roughly conceived as a line traversing Mauritania, Mali, Nigeria and Chad in the north, and another one crossing through Namibia, South Africa, Rhodesia and Madagascar in the south. Article 8 of the Act read as follows: 'l'expérience de toutes les nations qui ont des rapports avec l'Afrique ayant démontré le rôle pernicieux et prépondérant des armes à feu dans les opérations de traite et dans les guerres intestines entre tribus indigènes, et cette même expérience ayant prouvé manifestement que la consecration des populations africaines dont les Puissances ont la volonté expresse de sauvegarder l'existence, est une impossibilité radicale si des mesures restrictives du commerce des armes à feu et des munitions ne sont établies les Puissances décident, pour autant que le permet l'état actuel de leurs frontières, que l'importation des armes à feu et spécialement des armes rayées et perfectionnées, ainsi que de la poudre, des balles et des cartouches, est, sauf dans le cas et sous les conditions prevues à l'Article suivant, interdites dans les territoires compris entre le 20° parallèle nord et le 22° parallèle sud et aboutissant vers l'ouest à l'océan Atlantique, vers l'est à l'océan Indien et ses dépendances, y compris les îles adjacentes au littoral jusqu'à 100 milles marins de la côte'. The Act was adopted under the necessity for orderly colonial expansionism. It was furthering the spirit of the Berlin Act of 1885, which had established, among others, the neutrality of the Congo River basin, and it was generalizing practices already agreed upon in earlier bilateral treaties. For more, see YAKEMTCHOUK, R., 'Les antécédents de la réglementation internationale du commerce d'armes en Afrique', 13 *RBDI* (1977), p. 144*ff*.

2 The League of Nations and disarmament

The years following the First World War saw the heyday of anti-war passion. Boosted by the 1914–18 ordeal, the disarmament cause seemed for once to be making noble headway. Woodrow Wilson's fourth point had prayed for 'adequate guarantees that national armaments will be reduced to the lowest point consistent with domestic safety'.[24] The League of Nations took up the Wilsonian theme and incorporated it into Article 8 of the Covenant. That Article made reference to the 'evil effects' and 'grave objections' raised in respect of private manufacture of arms, and urged a frank and complete exchange of information related to the level of armaments. Its fifth paragraph ran as follows:

> The members of the League agree that the manufacture by private enterprise of munitions and implements of war is open to grave objections. The Council shall advise how the evil effects attendant upon such manufacture can be prevented, due regard being had to the necessities of those Members of the League which are not able to manufacture the munitions and implements of war necessary for their safety.[25]

[24]It is worth recalling, that in Wilson's original draft for the League, dated 16 July 1918, Article 21 called for the suppression of the private manufacture of munitions and implements of war as follows: 'the contracting Powers agree that munitions and implements of war shall not be manufactured by private enterprise and that publicity as to all national armaments and programmes is essential'. In support of Wilson's thought, General Smuts recommended on 16 December 1918, 'that all factories for the manufacture of direct weapons of war shall be nationalized' and that 'their production shall be subject to the inspection of the officers of the Council'.

[25]Moreover, in the terms of Article 23(d), the member states would 'entrust the League with the general supervision of the trade in arms and ammunition with the countries in which the control of this traffic is necessary in the common interest'. The League's record in matters of disarmament is reviewed in SLOUTZKY, N., *Le contrôle du commerce international des armes de guerre*, 1969; DE BROUCKÈRE, L., 'Les travaux de la Société des Nations en matière de désarmement', 25 *RCADI* (1928), p. 365*ff.*; JOUHAUX, L., *Le désarmement* 1927; WEHBERG, H., 'La limitation des armements', 28 *RGDIP* (1921), p. 504*ff.*; LAVALLAZ, M. de, *Essai sur le désarmement et le Pacte de la Société des Nations*, 1926, p. 3*ff.*; SMITH, H.A., 'The Problem of Disarmament in the Light of History', 10 *International Affairs* (1931), p. 600*ff.*; NOEL-BAKER, P.J., *Disarmament*, 2nd edn, 1927. See also GHEBALI, V.Y., *A Répertoire of League of Nations Serial Documents, 1919–1947*, 1973, vol.I, p. 203*ff.*, and OTTLIK, G., *La Société des Nations et le désarmement*, 1932, p. 102*ff.*

Within the larger Paris peace settlement which marked the conclusion of the First World War, twenty-three powers signed on 10 September 1919 the Saint-Germain Convention, with the principal intention of further regulating arms export in regions outside Europe.[26] All exports should be consigned to governments that were signatories of the convention, and should be accompanied by an official licence by the authorities of the exporting country (Article 1). The much desired publicity, long thought to be the handmaid of disarmament, was to be safeguarded through the Central International Office, a special organ to be monitoring and publishing the annual reports on export licences communicated to the League by the member states (Article 5). The United States felt that the Saint-Germain system was so inextricably interlocked with obligations emanating from the League membership as to make it unsuitable to adhere to it. In the event, the fact that the Convention was not ratified by many of the powers principally involved in the international trade of arms robbed it of any real significance.

From 1920 to 1923, the League attempted to bring about a more general acceptance of the St. Germain Convention. The First Assembly, in December 1920, noted the value of the St. Germain Convention 'as an instrument of civilization'. Again in 1921, the Second Assembly stressed the 'urgent importance of ratifying the Convention at the earliest possible moment'. Hardly three years had passed from the euphoric launch of the League's disarmament crusade, however, when the Third Assembly felt obliged to conclude, after the latest US refusal to

[26]The text of the Convention is in League of Nations Doc.C.758 M.258.1924.IX, p. 29*ff*. In what amounted to a major update of the Brussels General Act, the Convention of Saint-Germain enunciated the prohibition of exports of arms and munitions to a zone comprising the entire African continent (with the exception of Algeria, Libya and South Africa), the Arabian peninsula (including the maritime areas of the Red Sea, the Gulf of Aden, the Persian Gulf and the Gulf of Oman), the Transcaucasus, Persia and the ex-Ottoman dependencies in Asia. In essence, Britain and France sought eagerly to prevent their colonial holdings in Africa and the Middle East from being flooded with large supplies of munitions left over from the World War. The British and French delegations had placed before the Peace Conference three draft conventions: one for control of the trade in arms, another relating to liquor traffic in Africa and a third revising the Berlin General Act of 1885 and the Brussels General Act of 1890. It was only in late June 1919 that a Commission on the revision of the Acts of Berlin and Brussels was created and whose work subsequently led to the signing of the St. Germain Convention.

adhere to the Convention, that 'this reply puts an end to the hopes that the Convention of St. Germain in its present form would receive general acceptance'.[27]

On 19 May 1920, the Council of the League adopted a resolution establishing a Permanent Advisory Commission for Military, Naval and Air Questions, and instructed this Commission 'to begin immediately the study of such technical questions as are required for the execution of Articles 1 and 8 of the Covenant'.[28] In 1921, a Temporary Mixed Commission, composed not of government representatives but of independent personalities, was assigned the inquiry into the evils of private manufacture.[29] By 1924, the League's Temporary Mixed Commission had also elaborated in three sessions a Draft Convention, partly revising the St. Germain Convention of 1919, and partly regulating the international traffic in arms and

[27]On the first steps of disarmament through to 1924, see WHEELER-BENNETT, J.W., *Information on the Reduction of Armaments*, 1925.

[28]For the text of this resolution, see 14 *AJIL* (1920) *Suppl.* at p. 365.

[29]In attempting to list the *grave objections*, alluded to by the Covenant, the Commission reported, in what is probably the most appealing and often quoted document on the subject:

> the objections that are raised to untrammeled private manufacture may be grouped under the following headings;
> (1) that armament firms have been active in fomenting war scares and in persuading their own countries to adopt warlike policies and to increase their armaments,
> (2) that armament firms have attempted to bribe government officials, both at home and abroad,
> (3) that armament firms have disseminated false reports concerning the military and naval programmes of various countries in order to stimulate armament expenditure,
> (4) that armament firms have sought to influence public opinion through the control of newspapers in their own and foreign countries,
> (5) that armament firms have organized international armament rings through which the armament race has been accentuated by playing off one country against another,
> (6) that armament firms have organized international armament trusts which have increased the price of armaments sold to governments (see League of Nations Doc.A.81.1921.C.321 at p. 11)

Although the Commission had no difficulty in pronouncing that 'it is a common belief that wars are promoted by the competitive zeal of private armament firms, and would be rendered less frequent were the profit-making impulse brought under control or eliminated altogether', it confessed it could not 'at the present stage of deliberations either recommend the abolition of private manufacture or advise upon the particular steps to be taken to control it should it be decided that on the balance of advantage private manufacture must be allowed to continue', *ibid.*

munitions of war.[30] The Committee's draft convention was submitted to the Council of the League and then forwarded to both member and non-member states, with a further invitation to participate in an international conference to be intended to deal with the same issues.

The Conference was finally held at Geneva, from 4 May to 17 June 1925, with the participation of forty-five states. One of the documents adopted by the conference was the Convention for the Supervision of the International Trade in Arms and Ammunition and in Implements of War, or simply the Arms Traffic Convention, which was eventually signed by over thirty-five states.[31] The Geneva Convention of 1925, although clearly geared to make the US acceptance more likely, never managed to attract sufficient number of ratification instruments. When the US Senate acceded belatedly to the Convention in 1935, the prospects for it being revitalized had already vanished.[32] Powerless

[30]For the Draft Convention see League of Nations Doc.A.13.1925.IX, pp. 17–26. The prepared text betrayed a surface resoluteness at best. Article 2 reassured that the High Contracting Parties would be duty-bound to prohibit the export or import of arms and munitions, with the stupefying exception of arms deliveries directed to a recognized government, which could continue unobstructed (Article 3). Most important of all, according to Article 25, in the event of war, the application of Articles 2–5 would be suspended; thus the parties to the convention would be authorized to furnish freely arms to belligerents.

[31]For the Official Records of the Geneva Conference, see League of Nations Doc.A.13.1925.IX. Extracts from the work of the Temporary Mixed Commisssion, submitted drafts and related documents, as well as a historical survey on disarmament up to 1924, are to be found in League of Nations Doc.C.758. M.258.1924.IX. The text of the Arms Traffic Convention is in League of Nations Doc.A.16.1925.IX. The Convention classified the arms, munitions, and implements of war into five categories. As for arms making up the first category, i.e. arms constructed and destined exclusively for war, all deliveries to private individuals were to be strictly prohibited. On the other hand, arms exports to recognized governments should be given due publicity; exporting countries were asked to subject all arms exports to a compulsory government authorization to be issued in response to a formal demand addressed by the governemnt of the prospective importing country (Article 2). The publicity of the negotiated contract was intended to engage the double responsibility of both the exporting and the importing states. The Convention, following closely the Temporary Mixed Commission's draft, provided for the suspension of the regulatory regime at time of war *vis-à-vis* all belligerent states (Article 33). Unlike the Saint-Germain agreement, arms exports were not to be limited only among signatory states, nor was there any provision for an international authority like the Central International Office to collect documents and statistics.

[32]Until 1932, the United States invoked constitutional limitations inhibiting participation in the conclusion of an international agreement and insisted on a declaration of principle, first floated in 1927, to the effect that its government was 'powerless to prescribe or enforce a prohibition or a system of licenses

resolutions exorcizing private arms trafficking and praying for more publicity followed the unfortunate undertaking of 1925.[33]

The future of disarmament was finally entrusted to a Preparatory Commission which was to lay the groundwork for an

upon private manufacture which takes place under the jurisdiction of the States which form the Union of the Government of the United States'; see HUDSON, M.O., 'The Treaty-Making Power of the United States in Connection with the Manufacture of Arms and Ammunition', 28 *AJIL* (1934), p. 736*ff.*; POTTER, P.B., 'Inhibitions Upon the Treaty-Making Power of the United States', 28 *AJIL* (1934), p. 456*ff.* The American alibi was questioned accurately by a Danish delegate: 'you have done it for opium; why not for arms?'; cited in DREXEL, C., 'A Brief Outline of Efforts to Control the Manufacture and Sale of Munitions and Implements of War' in JOHNSEN, J.E., *International Traffic in Arms and Munitions*, 1934 at p. 54. The constitutional argument was finally dropped in November 1932, when the US announced to the Bureau of the Disarmament Conference that all previously made reservations for constitutional reasons had now been withdrawn. The Convention appeared relatively more successful in getting under way a series of official publications aimed at bringing the world arms trade under public notice; the *Military Yearbook* and the *Statistical Yearbook on the Trade of Arms, Munitions and Implements of War* were issued regularly from 1924 until 1938. The former included updates on the ground naval and air forces of the member states, as well as studies of several national defence budgets. The latter contained detailed information on the arms exports of the six largest producers, i.e. Great Britain, France, the United States, Germany, Italy and Czechoslovakia. For more on the ill-fated Geneva Convention of 1925, see DUPRIEZ, L., 'Le contrôle des armes et munitions et des matériels de guerre', 7 *RDILC* (1926), p. 57*ff.* The Temporary Mixed Commission had also finalized its proposals in respect of private manufacture of arms. The adopted scheme, based on draft submitted by the British representative, provided *inter alia*, that no company should engage in the production or sale of armaments without a government licence; that no such licence should be granted if the applying company had any controlling interest in the public press; that a licensed company should be obliged to inform the government of all the foreign orders it accepts, and finally that its directorship should refrain from carrying on propaganda of any kind relating to the war matériel, or from running for legislative elections; see League of Nations Doc.A.31.1922 C.631 at p. 22; Doc.A.35.1923.IX; Doc.A.16.1924.IX at p. 22.

[33]For instance, the Assembly resolution of 21 September 1926, 'once again draws attention to the close connection which exists between the question of the supervision of the private manufacture of arms and ammunition and of implements of war and the international trade in these articles [and] hopes that the efforts which are being made to obtain the ratification [of the 1925 Arms Traffic Convention] of the principal producing countries will soon be successful'; see League of Nations Doc.A.92.1.1926.IX. In another resolution of 24 September 1927, the Assembly declared itself 'convinced that the establishment of a Convention] of the supervision of private manufacture and the publicity regarding manufacture is of the highest importance for the putting into force of the Convention on the International Trade'; see League of Nations Doc.A.118.1927.IX. A Draft Convention, elaborated in 1928–9, seemed for a moment to afford the basis for the work of an international conference, but after progress was stalemated in the Assembly; see League of Nations Doc.A.43.1928.IX, pp. 2–7, and Doc.A.30.1929.IX, pp. 6–9.

International Disarmament Conference.[34] The International Disarmament Conference met for the first time in 1932, gathering delegations from sixty-two states in an atmosphere of mixed feelings ranging from melancholy to euphoria.[35] The unresolved issues of international arms trafficking were touched upon by the Conference only marginally.[36] The final impasse concerned

[34]See CECIL, V., *Lord Cecil Describes the Work of the Preparatory Commission for the Disarmament Conference*, League of Nations Union pamphlet no.290, 1931. Twenty-six states participated in the work of the Commission which lasted from May 1926 to January 1931. The *travaux préparatoires* resulted in the adoption of a Draft Convention on Disarmament on 9 December 1930. The provisions of the Draft Convention are commented upon in LYON, J., *Les problèmes du désarmement*, 1931.

[35]Wrote Viscount Cecil a few months before the opening of the conference: 'twelve years after the League of Nations was founded, three years after the signature of the Pact for the Renunciation of War, the nations are spending over $4.5 billion a year on preparations to fight one another, and this vast expenditure is still growing. That is a colossal and sinister fact, a proof in the eyes of ordinary men and women of governmental insincerity and inconsistency which saps their faith in all covenants and pacts and obliges the organization of international society to proceed painfully and fitfully in an atmosphere of cynicism and unreality'; see CECIL, V., 'Facing the World Disarmament Conference', 10 *Foreign Affairs* (Oct.1931) at p. 15. While the Spanish delegate Salvador de Madariaga expressed the expectations in terms of a telling practical calculation: 'si les nations du monde avaient bien voulu envoyer au Trésorier du Secrétariat général de la Société, en 1930, 5%, rien que 5% de ce qu'elles ont dépensé en 1930 pour leur défense nationale et si le Trésorier de la Société des Nations avait placé cette somme à 5% dans une banque, ces 5% de 5% auraient suffi et suffiraient à soutenir la Société des Nations, le Bureau international du Travail et la Cour permanente de Justice internationale de la Haye pendant tout le reste de l'histoire du monde, sans avoir jamais à demander un centime aux membres de la Société'; see MADARIAGA, S.de, 'La Société des Nations et le travail préparatoire pour la conférence pour la réduction des armements', 9 *Revue de Droit International de Sciences Diplomatiques et Politiques* (1931) at p. 395. On the outlook of such an ambitious undertaking as it appeared in 1932, see POLITIS, N., 'La base des travaux de la conférence du désarmement', 2 *Nordisk Tidsskrift for International Ret* (1931), p. 123*ff.*; DULLES, A.W., 'The Disarmament Puzzle', 9 *Foreign Affairs* (July 1931), p. 605*ff.*; MONTLUC, L.de, 'La question du desarmement', 9 *Revue de Droit International de Sciences Diplomatiques et Politiques* (1931), p. 268*ff.*; JAEQUEMYNS, R., 'La question dite du désarmement devant la Société des Nations', 10 *RDILC* (1929), p. 1*ff.*; MOLLER, A., 'La Société des Nations et la réduction des armements', 1 *Nordisk Tidsskrift for International Ret* (1930), p. 19*ff.*; SCIALOJA, V., 'Obstacles to Disarmament', 10 *Foreign Affairs* (Jan.1932), p. 212*ff.*

[36]A special committee, known as the Committee for the Regulation of Trade in the Private and State Manufacture of Arms, was assigned the inquiry into the suitability of amending the 1925 Geneva Convention and the 1929 Draft Convention, but soon decided to abandon the idea of revising either of the two instruments. For more, see SLOUTZKY, *op. cit.*, *supra* n.25, p. 83*ff.* It should be recalled, however, that on 27 February 1933, four governments officially proposed the nationalization of arms manufacture; see the joint memorandum of Denmark, France, Poland and Spain, in League of Nations Disarmament Confer-

the German claim for parity in armaments. The German delegation left the Conference in September 1932, returning temporarily thereafter only to leave the League itself in October 1933.[37] The deadlocked Conference, as one commentator observed, was 'maintaining its precarious existence only by the process of repeated postponements'.[38] It was finally dissolved in 1937, after five years of most stagnant and otiose negotiations.

The League's swan-song in soliciting international disarmament came on 30 September 1937, in the form of an Assembly resolution urging 'the Members of the League each in so far as

---

ence, Conf.D.31. For more see WHITE, F., *Traffic in Arms,* League of Nations Union pamphlet no.269, 1934, p. 46*ff.* Other radical proposals were submitted on 15 June 1934, by the American delegation, following President Roosevelt's expressed willingness to negotiate 'a convention containing provisions for the supervision and control of the traffic in arms much more far-reaching than those which were embodied in the convention of 1925', and his public denunciation of 'the uncontrolled activities of the manufacturers and merchants of engines of destruction'; see League of Nations Disarmament Conference, Conf.D.171. For more see CRICHTON, R.M., *Steps Toward Control of the Munitions Industry,* YWCA National Board, 1935, p. 13*ff.*

[37]On the first two turbulent years of the Conference and the German struggle for equality, see WHEELER-BENNETT, J.W., *The Pipe Dream of Peace – The Story of the Collapse of Disarmament,* 1935. See also STONE, W.T., 'The World Disarmament Conference – First Stage', 8 *Foreign Policy Reports* (11 May 1932), p. 60*ff.*; STONE, W.T., 'The World Disarmament Conference – Second Stage', 8 *Foreign Policy Reports* (18 January 1933), p. 268*ff.*; DULLES, A.W., 'Progress Toward Disarmament', 11 *Foreign Affairs* (Oct.1932), p. 54*ff.*; STONE, W.T., 'The Disarmament Crisis – 1933', 9 *Foreign Policy Reports* (25 October 1933), p. 186*ff.*

[38]See STONE, W.T., 'The Disarmament Impasse', 175 *Ann.AAPSS* (Sept.1934) at p. 82. The Vice-President of the Conference, Nicolas Politis, had already avowed in 1934: 'si, par l'idéale beauté de son programme, cette Conférence est l'Assemblée internationale la plus grandiose de l'histoire, le spectacle qu'elle offre aujourd'hui a quelque chose de dramatique. Car, destinée à contribuer à consolider la paix, elle risque d'en compromettre le maintien . . . Juridiquement, la promesse contenue dans le préambule de la partie V du traité de Versailles ne tient plus; l'engagement assumé en vertu de l'article 8 du Pacte a cessé de valoir. Si, déjà en 1932, on eût été en droit de s'opposer à la réunion de la Conférence de Genève, on serait à plus forte raison aujourd'hui autorisé à en réclamer la dissolution'; see POLITIS, N., 'Le problème du désarmement', 8 *L'Esprit International* (1934) at pp. 3, 25. While Hanighen and Engelbrecht wrote: 'these conferences resulted in nothing except interminable speeches and the usual thick and unreadable book containing the minutes of the proceedings. But one thing was revealed by all these turgid, polyglot debates – the attitude of the various governments toward this Frankenstein which they professed to be willing to destroy. From all the polite speeches of the delegates one thing stood out. The non-producing countries were panic-stricken when they considered the possibility that any restrictions might be placed on their "right to buy" and they insisted that no such action be taken'; see HANIGHEN, F.C. and ENGELBRECHT, H.C., 'Don't Blame the Munitions Makers', *American Mercury* (Sept.1934), reprinted in JOHNSEN, *op. cit., supra* n.32 at p. 141.

it is concerned and to the extent that this has not already been done, to examine the possibility of adopting internal measures with a view to the effective supervision of the manufacture of and trade in arms, ammunition and implements of war, on the basis of the work done by the Special Committee of the Disarmament Conference'.[39] The League's crusading zeal fell tragically short of producing anything more durable than *pia vota* with a view to curbing world militarism.[40]

3 The follow-up of the Hague rule in the inter-war period

The Fifth and the Thirteenth Hague Conventions of 1907 on the Rights and Duties of Neutral Powers in case land and sea warfare respectively are widely deemed to have codified patterns of state behaviour prevalent in the eighteenth and nineteenth centuries. Common Article 7 of the two Conventions was inspired by the logic, popular at that time, that acts by private citizens can by no means affect national policies and hence leave the neutrality of their state intact and irreproachable. The whole contraband theory was anchored for a long time to this very reasoning. Impartiality and duty of abstention – long held as the cardinal elements of neutrality – referred exclusively to state conduct and not at all to private ventures.

It would, in fact, contradict reality to argue that Article 7 was not reflecting at the dawn of the present century a fair consensus of doctrine and practice as to the meaning and function of neutrality, despite the fact that, as the preamble of the Fifth Hague Convention made clear, the arrangement concerning neutral subjects was only transitory 'pending the possibility of settling, in its entirety, the position of neutral individuals in their relations with the belligerents'. Notwithstanding this last remark, the import of the Hague prescriptions of 1907 was

[39]For the replies of various countries, see League of Nations Disarmament Conference, Conf.D.183. One year later, another Assembly resolution asked those governments that had not yet acted upon the 1937 recommendation to promptly do so.

[40]Outside the League framework, the only regional initiative of some significance was the Convention for the Limitation of Armaments, which was signed in February 1923 at Washington by Guatemala, El Salvador, Honduras, Nicaragua and Costa Rica and which laid down a prohibition on arms exports between the signatories; see Article 3 of the treaty, in 17 *AJIL* (1923) *Suppl.* at p. 116.

reaffirmed on several occasions during the first half of our century.

After the First World War, the principle endorsing the private trade in contraband was restated in 1923 in the Commission of Jurists' Report on the Control of Radio in time of War and Rules of Aerial Warfare, the latter commonly known as the Hague Rules of Aerial Warfare, Article 45 of which read as follows:

> subject to the provisions of Article 46, a neutral Power is not bound to prevent the export or transit on behalf of a belligerent of aircraft, parts of aircraft, or material, supplies or munitions for aircraft.[41]

In like regard, the 1923 judgment of the Permanent Court of International Justice on the *Wimbledon* case adhered to the same theory of risk related to contraband trade.[42] The Court, in perfect harmony with the customary contraband theory, refuted the argument that 'Germany's neutrality would have necessarily been imperilled if her authorities had allowed the passage of the *Wimbledon* through the Kiel Canal, because that vessel was carrying contraband of war consigned to a state then engaged in an armed conflict'.[43] On yet another occasion, three years

[41] *Ibid.* at p. 256.

[42] *PCIJ, Series A,* No.1. It will be recalled that the case arose in the context of the Russo-Polish War, and involved a British steamship carrying a munitions load consigned to the Polish forces at Danzig. As the vessel proceeded to enter the Kiel Canal, the German authorities denied passage on the grounds of some neutrality regulations issued by Germany with respect to the war. The first of these Orders, enacted in 1920, had laid down an export and transit prohibition of arms, munitions, powder, explosives and other war matériel to Poland and the Soviet republics.

[43] *Ibid.* at p. 28. Judges Anzilotti and Huber, however, in their dissenting opinion, registered their serious doubts as to whether the long-established usages in respect of contraband trade were in conformity with principles of justice and morality, especially in the light of the League's Covenant. Although well aware of the written law and usages of neutrality, 'the undersigned feel called upon to make a reservation with regard to the recognition of a right to international protection for the transport of contraband. It is not disputed that present international law allows neutrals the option of suppressing or tolerating in their territory commerce in and transport of contraband, and more especially of arms and munitions. Again the transport of such commodities, even under a neutral flag, is not protected against a belligerent, and the latter is entitled, in certain conditions, to confiscate as a penalty even the neutral vessel and that part of its cargo which is not contraband. This is explained by the fact that commerce in and transport of contraband, although not necessarily affecting the neutrality of States, *is regarded under the law of nations as unlawful because it assumes the guise of peaceful commerce for warlike purposes.* This idea seems to acquire still greater force when considered in the light of the Covenant of the League of

after the *Wimbledon* judgment, the International Law Association in its Draft Convention on Maritime Neutrality found it pertinent to repeat verbatim the Hague provision.[44] And again, Article 6 of the Draft Convention on the Rights and Duties of Belligerents with regard to Neutral Property at Sea, debated by the same Society at the Oxford Conference of 1932, echoed to the letter Article 7 of the 1907 Conventions.[45]

Moreover, the Havana Convention on Maritime Neutrality,[46] adopted in February 1928 at the Sixth International Conference of American States, remained faithful to the idea of perfect separability of state and private transactions with belligerent nations, and laid down accordingly in Article 15: 'of the acts of assistance coming from the neutral states, and the acts of commerce on the part of individuals, only the first are contrary to neutrality'.[47] Whereas Article 22 was phrased in more recurrent terms: 'neutral states are not obligated to prevent the export or transit at the expense of any one of the belligerents of arms, munitions and in general of anything which may be useful to their military forces'.[48]

It was only in the late 1930s, that the professorial board con-

---

Nations, and more especially of its Articles 8 and 23 paragraph (d)' (emphasis added); *ibid.* at p. 42. See also the reasoning of Judge Schücking in his dissenting opinion, *ibid.* at pp. 46–7.

[44]See 34 *Rep.ILA* (1927), Vienna Conf., 1926 at p. 47. The Draft Convention was eventually referred back to the Neutrality Committee for further consideration. As J.C. Witenberg of Poland said, 'il est parfaitement inutile que la Conférence de Vienne adopte un projet qui, non seulement a été un projet, mais qui a eu forme dans cette Convention de la Haye dont l'expérience a prouvé l'insuffisance'; *ibid.* at p. 99.

[45]See 37 *Rep.ILA* (1933), Oxford Conf., 1932 at p. 161. See also Article 5 of the Draft Convention on Neutrality in Land Warfare, ibid. at p. 170. Objections like the one raised by L.M. Isaacs appeared isolated; commenting on the draft, he suggested that a neutral Power should be bound to prevent the export of war material, for 'if the neutral is not so bound he is simply prolonging the war and, for a little profit, increasing the danger to the world', *ibid.* at p. 186. Others doubted the continuing validity of the concept of neutrality in general. Arnold D. McNair, for instance, asked rhetorically: 'is it right at this stage of the world's history that this body should do anything to crystallise a conception of neutrality which most of us regard as completely out of order?', *ibid.* at p. 185. And James Leslie Brierly, speaking of drafts closely following the Hague Conventions, noted: 'they are based on a notion of the relations between neutrals and belligerents which was all right in 1899 and 1907 at the Hague Conferences, which was all right, possibly, as late as 1913, but which in 1932 belongs to an utterly outlawed order of ideas', *ibid.* at p. 175.

[46]See 22 *AJIL* (1928), p. 151*ff.*

[47]*Ibid.* at p. 155.

[48]*Ibid.* at p. 156.

ducting the Harvard Research on the Rights and Duties of Neutral States, ventured to suggest a rule slightly departing from the lines of the Hague tradition. Article 11 of the 1939 Draft Convention provided that:

> a neutral state *may*, for the purpose of conserving its own supplies or *of safeguarding its neutrality*, place prohibitions upon the shipment or departure from or transit through its territory of arms, ammunition and implements of war ... of articles or materials other than arms, ammunition or implements of war ... or upon the granting of loans or credits by persons subject to its jurisdiction. (emphasis added)[49]

Although not directly opposing the basic premise of the Hague rule of private *laissez-faire*, the Harvard Research hinted at a practice, which if institutionalized would certainly discredit that rule to a large extent. Article 11 spelt out a right rather than an obligation but, even in its optional form, established for the first time a causal link between the conduct of private citizens and the preservation of state neutrality.[50] It is clear that Article 11 echoed the intellectual ferment of the inter-war period, especially the ebb and flow of American isolationism, but above all it reflected the growing understanding that the rationale behind the Hague rule was turning stale.

4 The United Nations era

The Second World War put an end to the parody of the disarmament talks crushing ruthlessly all hopes rested upon the League. For at least two decades after 1945, the world seemed disinterested in rejuvenating the League's romance with disarmament. It was not until 30 November 1965, that the first proposal directly related to arms trade was taken down in the

[49]See Draft Convention on Rights and Duties of Neutral States in Naval and Aerial War, reprinted in 33 *AJIL* (1939) *Suppl.* at p. 177.

[50]The accompanying commentary is even more explicit: 'there appears to be a growing opinion in favor of *imposing upon neutral States a duty to do* that which this article states they are permitted to do' (emphasis added), *ibid.* at p. 283. And elsewhere, in somewhat more ambiguous language: 'it should be repeated that trade in contraband has never been "lawful" although it has been true that a neutral government was not under a duty to suppress it', *ibid.* at p. 301.

United Nations records. A Maltese resolution was submitted to the First Committee of the General Assembly:

> *believing* [in the words of its preamble] that a general and effective system of publicity to transfers between States, whether by way of trade or otherwise, of arms, ammunition and implements of war, would be a constructive contribution towards the relaxation of international tension and the development of relations of mutual trust between States [and] *recognizing* that such publicity would improve the possibility of making progress towards the goal of general and complete disarmament under effective international control.[51]

On another level of action, the UN General Assembly decided to convene in 1978, 1982 and 1988 Special Sessions devoted to disarmament but with only relative success.[52] At the conclusion of the First Session a Final Document was adopted, which in two paragraphs touched upon the issue of arms transfers. Para.22 of this Final Document read as follows:

[51]See UN Doc.A/C.1/L.347 of 30 November 1965. The reception of the Maltese move was anything but encouraging. Eighteen countries voted in favour of the draft resolution, 19 others opposed it and as many as 39 abstained. It should be underscored that the Maltese proposal pleaded anything but a novelty, and that after all the need for publicity had already been recognized since the League days. The issue was stirred up again in 1968 and 1976 on the occasion of another two resolutions, submitted by Denmark and Japan respectively, both pleading transparency in arms transactions. These draft resolutions were strenuously opposed and finally defeated before being put to a vote; see UN Doc.A/C.1/L.446 of 21 November 1968, and UN Doc.A/C.1/31/L.20 of 22 November 1976. For brief comments on the UN role in advancing the cause of disarmament, see GASPARINI, P., 'Beyond Disarmament: Catching-Up with the Arms Trade?', 26 *RBDI* (1993/1), p. 58*ff.* See also GOLDBLAT, J., 'The Role of the United Nations in Arms Control: An Assessment', 7 *Arms Control* (1986), p. 115*ff.*, and RÖLING, B.V.A., 'The Law of Arms Control and Disarmament' in MAKARCZYK, J. (ed.), *Essays in International Law in honour of Judge Manfred Lachs*, 1984, p. 731*ff.*

[52]For an overview of the discussions during the First Special Session, see 3 *UNDY* (1978), p. 404*ff.* The proposal for holding such a session dates back to the first conference of heads of state of the non-aligned countries at Belgrade in 1961. The proposal was reiterated on numerous subsequent occasions, and led to the GA Resolution 31/189 B of Dec.21, 1976, which provided for the Special Session to be held in May/June 1978. Working papers and other documents submitted to the Preparatory Committee were addressing chiefly issues of nuclear disarmament, with the only exception of proposals put forward by Japan, 'concerning the conventional arms race including, in particular, the international transfer of conventional arms and mutual limitation of conventional armaments and armed forces on the regional level'; see UN Doc.A/AC.187/86 of 13 December 1977.

> there should also be negotiations on the limitation of international transfer of conventional weapons, based in particular on the same principle, and taking into account the inalienable right to self-determination and independence of peoples under colonial or foreign domination and the obligations of States to respect that right, in accordance with the Charter of the United Nations and the Declaration on Principles of International Law concerning Friendly Relations and Cooperation among States, as well as the need of recipient States to protect their security.[53]

While para.85 set out the following:

> consultations should be carried out among major arms supplier and recipient countries on the limitation of all types of international transfer of conventional weapons, based in particular on the principle of undiminished security of the parties with a view to promoting or enhancing stability at a lower military level, taking into account the need of all States to protect their security as the inalienable right to self-determination and independence of peoples under colonial or foreign domination. . . .[54]

By Resolution 33/71 H, the General Assembly decided that a Second Special Session should be convened in 1982.[55] In his opening address the UN Secretary-General sounded anything but sanguine on the prospects of the new undertaking; 'the fact must now be faced that the Programme of Action has largely remained a dead letter. Indeed, the goals set forth in the Programme are further from our reach now than they were four years ago. The hope and euphoria of 1978 have been replaced

[53]See 3 *UNDY* (1978) at pp. 476–7.

[54]*Ibid.* at p. 483. In what amounts to just another disheartening reality about the United Nations record, the 1970s, declared by the General Assembly as a Disarmament Decade, proved to be hosting instead the most phenomenal explosion of world militarization of all times. In view of such undisguised contempt of its effort, the General Assembly confined itself to express 'deep concern at the meagre achievements of the Disarmament Decade in terms of truly effective disarmament and arms limitation agreements and the detrimental effects on world peace and economy of the continuing unproductive and wasteful arms race'; see UNGA Resolution 3470(XXX) of 11 December 1975, and UNGA Resolution 31/68 of 10 December 1976.

[55]This forum was held from 7 June to 10 July 1982. A summary of the views expressed in that Session is to be found in 7 *UNDY* (1982), p. 393*ff*.

by stalemate.'[56] Being finally unable to reach consensus on any course of action, the Assembly only approved the Concluding Document, which contained a record of the proceedings and a list of its conclusions.[57]

By Resolution 41/60 G, adopted in 1986, the General Assembly decided to convene its Third Special Session on disarmament in 1988, and a preparatory Committee was assigned the task of preparing a draft agenda.[58] Javier Pérez de Cuéllar, in his address, emphasized what he thought should be guiding the deliberations: 'the time had also come for it [international community] to recognize the need to deal squarely with the mounting toll of death, destruction and human suffering inflicted by the use of conventional weapons in conflicts around the world. The term "conventional" should not hide or minimize the vast destructive powers of some of those weapons, nor should the innocuous sounding phrase "arms transfers" make people forget the devastating effect of the supply of weapons in local conflicts'.[59] In the end, the General Assembly was still

[56]See 5 *Disarmament* (Nov.1982) at p. 9. Among the diverse schemes advanced during the session, there was an Italian proposal suggesting the creation of an *ad hoc* organ, an international disarmament centre, which would be responsible for the control and limitation of the volume of the international transfer of conventional weapons. In the words of the Italian document, the centre would 'be entrusted with the task of keeping a register of all international transactions in conventional weapons on the understanding that member countries would provide the center regularly with all the information relevant and necessary to the performance of that task'; see UN Doc.A/S-12/AC.1/20 of 18 June 1982. Bangladesh suggested that special fees should be levied on arms transactions and that the funds be used by the United Nations for international development assistance. Others, like Singapore, Uganda or Japan, advocated restraints and proposed international monitoring of state inventories and analysis of transfers of conventional weapons. The Soviet Union expressed its readiness to resume bilateral talks with the United States on the question of conventional arms transfers, while some countries, like Australia, Honduras or Turkey, invited the session to examine thoroughly the problem of clandestine arms trade.

[57]See UN Doc.A/S-12/32 in 7 *UNDY* (1982), p. 497*ff.* On the miscarried work of the 1982 Special Session on disarmament, see DAHLITZ, J., 'The Second Special Session of the General Assembly Devoted to Disarmament – An Account and Evaluation', 5 *Disarmament* (Nov.1982), p. 49*ff.*; CORRADINI, A., 'National Arms Policies and the Message of the 1978 and 1982 Special Sessions on Disarmament', 5 *Disarmament* (Nov.1982), p. 61*ff.*

[58]By resolution 42/40 of 30 November 1987, the Session was scheduled for the period from 31 May to 25 June 1988; see 13 *UNDY* (1988), p. 37*ff.*

[59]The debate reflected a heightened international awareness of disarmament issues, although the traditional priority accorded to nuclear weapons remained unchanged. In fact, despite the large number of states that called attention to the question of the ever-expanding arms trade, no documents or concrete proposals were ever submitted dealing specifically with it. Delegations from

unable to adopt by consensus a final document. Despite the definitely improved political atmosphere and the converging outlook in several issues, the third General Assembly's Special Session managed to produce even less fruit than the second one.

In a UN *Study on Conventional Disarmament*, published in 1985, the question of arms trade was treated with extreme delicacy and received only superficial attention. In the Secretary-General's words, 'arms transfers are important in the context of the conventional arms race but are not at the centre of conventional disarmament problems'.[60] In the five paragraphs dealing with agreements on the reduction of international arms transfers between suppliers and recipients, the Secretary-General noted the 'sensitivities' which surround the problem and which have caused the failure of all past attempts.[61].

In November 1988, Colombia submitted a resolution on the regulation of international arms transfers. The draft resolution, eventually cosponsored by some fifteen states, among them the UK, the Federal Republic of Germany, the Netherlands and Sweden, was finally adopted by 110 to 1 votes with 38 absten-

---

Albania, Argentina, Australia, Belgium, Colombia, Ghana, Indonesia, Italy, Luxembourg, the Philippines, Spain, the Soviet Union and the United States, that intervened on the question went very little further than restating the challenges, underscoring the perplexities and deploring the realities of the problem. The United States noted that in the five years 1977–81, some US $128 billion-worth of arms had been delivered to developing countries. In the following five years, ending in 1986, the figure had risen to US $180 billion, or an increase of some 40 per cent. Australia denounced arms exports as a cure for domestic financial problems; as the Australian delegate put it, arms transfers should not be allowed to become 'a new cash crop'. Belgium insisted on the idea of creating an international register of arms transfers. Developing countries, in general, stressed that they would have preferred to allocate their resources to social-economic development, but were obliged to confront the increasing militarization of neighbouring countries or rebel groups.

[60]See UN Doc.A/39/348 [publication sales No.E.85.IX.1] §67 at p. 20.

[61]He concluded, first that 'all countries must be satisfied that the proposals are not discriminatory: this entails even-handedness for arms suppliers and arms recipients alike'. Second, the consultations should never contradict 'the principle of undiminished security of the parties . . . the inalienable right to self-determination and independence of peoples under colonial or foreign domination'. Third, in the case of possible agreement between some recipient and supplier states, sufficient guarantees should be explored so 'that supplier countries which may not join in such arrangements would not simply expand their transfers to fill any vacuum arising from agreed restraint in arms transfers'. Finally, he thought that the reopening of US-Soviet bilateral talks on conventional arms transfers would be a desirable first step in order to set arms trade control mechanisms in motion; *ibid.*, §§165–9 at pp. 45–6. See also §198 at pp. 53–4.

tions.[62] According to the terms of Resolution 43/75 I, the General Assembly noted 'increasing illicit and covert arms trafficking', and requested the member states to consider *inter alia* measures such as 'reinforcement of their national systems of control and vigilance concerning production and transport of arms' and 'examination of the ways and means of providing for more openness and transparency with regard to world-wide arms transfers'.[63] On 15 December 1989, the General Assembly finally adopted Resolution 44/116N on international arms transfers which *inter alia* invited all member states to make available to the Secretary-General their views and proposals on the matter.[64]

Following on from Resolution 43/75 of December 1988 and the recent study by the UN Secretariat, and because of the definitely improved political atmosphere, the General Assembly voted overwhelmingly in December 1991 for the creation of a Register of Conventional Arms.[65] States were invited to provide the Secretary-General with an annual report on their imports-exports and national production of seven categories of conventional weapons. According to the provisions of the resolution, the Register was established on 1 January 1992, its first edition to be completed in April 1993. The first report was finally released on 11 October 1993 containing the replies of eighty-three states.[66]

[62]See UNGA Resolution 43/75 I of 7 December 1988. See also 13 *UNDY* (1988), p. 371*ff.*

[63]The resolution also mandated a study by the UN Secretariat on international arms transfers, which was eventually produced in July 1991; see *Study on Ways and Means of Promoting Transparency in International Transfers of Conventional Arms*, UN Doc.A/46/301 of 9 September 1991 [publication sales no.E.93.IX.6].

[64]To date, no more than 17 governments had responded; see UN Doc.A/44/444 of 14 August 1989 and UN Doc.A/44/444, Add.1–3. See also UN Doc.A/45/363 of 20 August 1990, and UN Doc.A/45/363/Add.1 of 25 October 1990.

[65]See UNGA Resolution 46/36 L of 9 December 1991. No country voted against the resolution while only China and Cuba abstained. See also UNGA Resolution 46/36 H of 6 December 1991 on illicit arms trade, and UNGA Resolution 47/52 L of 1992 by which the General Assembly declared its determination to ensure the effective operation of the Conventional Arms Register, and the Report of the Secretary-General on the Register of Conventional Arms, UN Doc.A/47/342 of 14 August 1992.

[66]See UN Doc.A/48/344 and Add.1–2. More specifically, 24 countries reported exports and 38 governments reported imports. The number of countries who submitted reports represented less than 50 per cent of the UN membership. For background information on this voluntary system of standardized reporting, see 'Transparency and the Arms Register', 18 *UNDY* (1993), p. 63*ff.* See also

Outside the United Nations forum, there is no major progress to report on the problems of disarmament and arms transfers.[67] The European Parliament in its resolution on the European arms exports, adopted on 14 March 1989, pleaded for publicity in the arms deals and stressed the need for stricter controls.[68] Being convinced, 'qu'il est important de limiter et de contrôler le commerce des armes pour diminuer l'ampleur des conflits armés dans le monde et atténuer la souffrance humaine', the Parliament requested the competent organs of the European Union, to refine a common arms transfers policy within the larger context of European political cooperation. To this end, it

---

FEINSTEIN, L., '52 Countries Volunteer Reports to New UN Arms Register', 23 *Arms Control Today* (June 1993) at p. 30, SMITH, R.J., 'U.S. and Germany Lead in Export of Weapons', *International Herald Tribune*, 22 October 1993 at p. 2, and ASTOR, R.J., 'A Register of Arms Sales is a Silly Idea', *International Herald Tribune*, 8 August 1991 at p. 4. For some of the first reflections on the problems and prospects of the UN Arms Register, see CHALMERS, M. and GREENE, O., *Taking Stock: The UN Register after Two Years*, 1995; ANTHONY, I., 'Assessing the UN Register of Conventional Arms', 35 *Survival* (winter 1993–4), p. 113*ff.*; WAGENMAKERS, H., 'The UN Register of Conventional Arms: A New Instrument for Cooperative Security', 23 *Arms Control Today* (April 1993), p. 16*ff.*; LAURANCE, E.J., 'The UN Register of Conventional Arms: Rationales and Prospects for Compliance and Effectiveness', 16 *Washington Quarterly* (spring 1993), p. 163*ff.*; WULF, H., 'The United Nations Register of Conventional Arms', *Ybk.SIPRI* (1993), p. 533*ff.*; GOLDBLAT, J., *Arms Control – A Guide to Negotiations and Agreements*, 1994, pp. 182–7; Special Issue, 'The United Nations Register of Conventional Arms: Whence? Whither? . . . and Why?', 17 *Disarmament* (1994/1).

[67]As regards academic consideration, note, for instance, the principle of disarmament which figured in the list of Principles of Peaceful Coexistence, drafted by the International Law Association in 1964: '(6) le principe du désarmement, en vertu duquel les Etats sont tenus d'assurer par voie d'accords le désarmement général et complet sous contrôle effectif'; see 51 *Rep.ILA* (1965), Tokyo Conf., 1964 at p. 806, and 812*ff.* Note also what M. Radojkovic had to say, reporting on the problem of disarmament before the Committee on international security and cooperation of the same Society: 'le problème du commerce des armes mérite à plus d'un titre d'être examiné et reglé par une nouvelle convention, le trafic des armes prenant une extension toujours plus grande dans les échanges internationaux sans égard pour les prohibitions contenues dans les arrangements conclus dans un passé relativement récent. A plus forte raison le commerce du trafic des armes devra-t-il faire l'objet d'une étude objective au sein de l'International Law Association'; see 55 *Rep.ILA* (1974), New York Conf., 1972 at p. 290.

[68]See EP Resolution No.C96 of 14 March 1989. The resolution was adopted by 85 to 19 votes with 67 abstentions. See also the Report of the Political Affairs Committee on European Arms Exports, Doc.A2-398/88 of 22 February 1989. See further Council of Europe, Parliamentary Assembly Resolution 928 of 27 September 1989. On the ongoing debate concerning the elaboration of a common European policy on arms exports, see MUELLER, H., 'The Export Controls Debate in the "New" European Community', 23 *Arms Control Today* (March 1993), p. 10*ff.*, and REINICKE, H., 'Arms Sales Abroad: European Community Export Controls Beyond 1992', 10 *Brookings Review* (summer 1992), p. 22*ff.*

invited the Council of the Foreign Ministers of the member states to adopt a declaration of principles on arms sales along certain lines, such as, for example, the security interests of the European Union as a whole, and the human rights record, real needs and degree of democracy in recipient states.

Amongst diplomatic initiatives on the bilateral level, reference should be made to the US-Soviet Talks on Conventional Arms Transfers, better known with the acronym CAT talks.[69] These negotiations were launched by the Carter administration in 1977, as a concrete manifestation of an attempted reorientation in United States arms sales policy. The first formal CAT meeting was held in Washington in December 1977. Three more rounds of talks took place in Helsinki and Mexico City, before collapsing over the American refusal to envisage arms exports cuts to China, South Korea and Iran. The 1979 Soviet invasion of Afghanistan and the debut of Reagan's hardline foreign policy deprived the negotiations of any serious prospect of success.[70]

In the aftermath of the 1991 war against Iraq, the five permanent members of the UN Security Council, and largest arms suppliers, committed themselves to the elaboration of a 'code of conduct' in regard to arms sales. Three rounds of discussions were held at Paris, London and Washington in July and October 1991 and May 1992. According to the proposed set of guidelines, the leading arms exporters would pledge to avoid arms transfers which would deplete recipient countries' economic resources, which would prolong or aggravate ongoing conflicts, increase tension or create a destabilizing military capacity, and which

[69]For a brief review of those negotiations and of the causes of their collapse, see HUSBANDS, J.L. and CAHN, A.H., 'The Conventional Arms Transfers Talks: An Experiment in Mutual Arms Trade Restraint' in OHLSON, T. (ed.), *Arms Transfer Limitations and Third World Security*, 1988, p. 110*ff*. See also BLECHMAN, B.M., NOLAN, J.E. and PLATT, A., 'Pushing Arms', 46 *Foreign Policy* (1982), p. 138*ff*. On the European dimension of the CAT talks, see FRANKO, L.G., 'Restraining Arms Exports to the Third World: Will Europe Agree?', 21 *Survival* (1979), p. 14*ff*.

[70]Yet the CAT talks at one point came near adopting a framework of principles of restraint. In fact, by the end of the third round of negotiations, both sides had agreed on a threefold framework for arms transfers restraint. The framework included political-legal criteria by which to judge potential recipients, military-technical criteria limiting the exports of certain weapon systems, and plans for implementing these guidelines in specific regions. Restraints in arms sales were preferably envisaged against racist, or human rights violating regimes, countries proned to aggression or militarism, and countries defying disarmament efforts or staging unfound territorial claims.

would violate an international embargo or support international terrorism. The five powers also agreed to meet regularly, at least once a year, and seek harmonization of their respective national export control mechanisms with particular reference to arms of mass destruction.[71]

In retrospect, the efforts to control international arms trafficking throughout the present century presents no occasion for recounting glorious successes. The jurist has still to cope with the discomfiting truth that the Brussels Act of 1890 remains the only international agreement regulating arms trade to have entered into force. The few proposals have been drafted with modesty and destined to oblivion – calculated stagnancy, or a sense of *déjà vu* at best, the pessimist would say.[72] Today, is there any reason why one should sound less frustrated in assessing the impact of more than 800 General Assembly resolutions, passed since the United Nations was founded, in matters of arms control?

Not many would deny the disquieting truth that the discussion over the control of the international arms trade has not genuinely advanced since the days of the Geneva Convention of 1925. The context has changed dramatically, but the core issues and obstacles display unrelenting intertemporality. Disarmament is as much a burden to be discharged by UN member states, bound by Article 26 of the Charter, as it was an urgent goal to be attained by League's members, which had committed themselves to Article 8 of the Covenant, but still the idolization of national security needs works to cancel the hopes of 'general and complete' disarmament. Far from inhibiting rifles trade to

[71]See MUSSINGTON, D., 'The International Control of the Arms Trade', 26 *RBDI* (1993/1), p. 43*ff*. The future of those talks remains in considerable doubt since the US offer to sell 150 F-16 fighters to Taiwan in September 1992 and the subsequent withdrawal of China from the annual meetings.

[72]To borrow from Klein's colourful language,'les négociations débutent toujours par une vaine bataille de plans, se poursuivent par des discussions byzantines d'une haute technicité et s'achèvent par l'adoption d'un procès-verbal de carence comme si le désir d'entretenir une négociation n'avait d'égal que la volonté de ne pas la conclure'; see KLEIN, J., *L'entreprise du désarmement depuis 1945*, 1964 at p. 299. Lehmann-Russbüldt writing in 1930 noted with frustration: 'since 1921, 121 sessions of Council commissions and sub-commissions have taken place, and ink and words have flowed freely in streams on the subject of disarmament. In all, 111 resolutions on the subject have been passed the League having sponsored 53 of these, and the Council 58. And yet armaments, and the roaring traffic in armaments, do not diminish, but are constantly on the increase'; see LEHMANN-RUSSBÜLDT, O., *War for Profits*, 1930 at p. 159.

Sub-Saharan Africa, the world today addresses missile proliferation and market saturation with sophisticated weaponry, but the non-discrimination complex still vexes the relations between arms-dependent and arms-producing countries. Publicity and transparency over the international arms transactions are still overpowered by considerations of state secrecy.

What Alfred Zimmern was thinking in 1932 apropos of the chances of the Disarmament Conference, is a fitting epilogue to all miscarried disarmament plans within the span of our century:

> suffice it to say that any man's judgment on whether this new system will prove practicable depends ultimately on whether he believes that we have reached a point in human history in which the play of power, which must always exist in human affairs, will henceforward be carried on along less barbaric and destructive lines than through mutual slaughter.[73]

IV From neutrality to non-belligerency: the American paradigm

Americans did not invent neutrality. They did, however, elevate neutrality to the heights of a commanding and constant parameter of their foreign policy for at least one and a half centuries. What is more, occasionally they did much also to retailor neutrality's fundamentals showing little respect for the institution. For better or worse, the policies followed by successive US administrations in the course of the first half of our century have chiefly influenced the fate of the concept of neutrality and hence merit a cautious review.

1 The First World War

The twentieth century *roman-fleuve* of American neutrality commences with the Wilsonian proclamation of 1914, which committed the United States to detachment with regard to the First World War. The pretended neutral policies of Washington in the period 1914–17 soon came under attack, both domestically

[73]See ZIMMERN, A., 'Disarmament: The Decisive Phase', 131 *Fortnightly Review* (Dec.1932) at p. 691.

and abroad. The internal front dwelt on pacifism and Christian morality and accused the administration of allowing the making of unethical profit out of other people's ruination. The external front, that is Germany and its allies, based their charges on the international codes of neutral conduct maintaining that the latter should be given more than simply a technical reading.

During the opening stages of the First World War, as the great American Power opted for impartiality, a massive public campaign was set off with the aim of halting the shipment of munitions to the European belligerents. Embargo resolutions were introduced in December 1914 in the House by R. Bartholdt and H. Vollmer, and in the Senate by G. Hitchcock.[74] Congressional initiative for an arms embargo surfaced again in February 1915. As one of the most fervent proponents of the move, Senator La Follette, argued, the munitions trade had 'but one purpose and that is to sacrifice human life for private gain', and insisted on the need of nationalizing the arms manufacture – a counsel sounding premature at the time but fated to impose itself some fifteen years later.

In the aftermath of the *Lusitania* disaster, the isolationist camp was linked principally with the idea of prohibiting travel on belligerent ships, but the question of arms trade came also to the fore. Congressman Works doubted American innocence in the *Lusitania* affair. By supplying munitions to one side, he claimed, 'we are hypocritical in claiming that we are neutral'.[75] As the U-boat campaign attained unrestrained proportions in early 1917, attention again focused on the question of arms

[74]On the Hitchcock resolution of December 1914 and the activities of the so-called American Embargo Conference, see GRATTAN, C.H., *Why We Fought*, 1929 at pp. 142–4, 150–1. The advocates of these bills denounced the immoral basis of arms trade and preached sincere neutrality. Congressman Vollmer, for example, supported his resolution in the name of 'genuine and not merely sham neutrality', and asserted that it would keep the United States from standing 'as the arch hypocrite among the nations of the earth, praying for peace . . . and furnishing the instruments of murder to one side only of a contest in which we pretend that all the contestants are our friends'; quoted in COOPER, J.M., *The Vanity of Power – American Isolationism and the First World War 1914–1917*, 1969 at p. 29. An arms embargo, of course, would clearly serve the cause of the Central Powers. It is not by coincidence, therefore, that the staunchest support for arms exports prohibition came from pro-German pressure groups such as the National German-American Alliance.

[75]While W. Kenyon lashed out at big business; 'the jingle of the bloody dollar can not drown the sound of the groans and cries of misery arising from the battle fields of Europe. International law may permit it; moral law condemns it'; cited in COOPER, *op. cit., supra* at p. 108.

deliveries. The proposed Cooper amendment of spring 1917 would have prevented armed American merchantmen from transporting munitions to the belligerent countries.

The Spirit of True Neutrality: The Diplomatic Quarrel In proclaiming the American neutrality on 4 August 1914, President Wilson made clear that the right of private citizens to trade in contraband with warring nations was not to be impaired by the official neutral stance of the government of the United States. Such commerce, however, might be undertaken at the exclusive risk of American citizens. As the proclamation read in the preamble:

> and whereas the laws and treaties of the United States, without interfering with the free expression of opinion and sympathy, or with the commercial manufacture or sale of arms or munitions of war, nevertheless impose upon all persons . . . the duty of an impartial neutrality . . . and I do hereby warn all citizens of the United States . . . that while all persons may lawfully and without restriction by reason of the aforesaid state of war manufacture and sell within the United States arms and munitions of war, and other articles ordinarily known as 'contraband of war', yet they cannot carry such articles upon the high seas for the use or service of a belligerent . . . without incurring the risk of hostile capture and the penalties denounced by the law of nations in that behalf.[76]

[76]See 9 *AJIL* (1915) *Suppl.* at p. 110, 114. While on 15 October 1914, the Department of State circulated an explanatory statement as to whether American merchants could sell to governments at war contraband articles without violating the neutrality of the United States. The statement recited the long-standing principle codified in the Hague Conventions of 1907, namely, that a neutral state bears no obligation to prevent private sales to a belligerent, in these words: 'In the first place it should be understood that, generally speaking, a citizen of the United States can sell to a belligerent government or its agent an article of commerce which he pleases. He is not prohibited from doing this by any rule of international law, by any treaty provisions, or by any statute of the United States. It makes no difference whether the articles sold are exclusively for war purposes, such as firearms, explosives, etc., or are foodstuffs, clothing, horses, etc., for the use of the army or navy of the belligerent. Furthermore, a neutral government is not compelled by international law, by treaty, or by statute to prevent these sales to a belligerent. Such sales, therefore, by American citizens do not in the least affect the neutrality of the United States'; *ibid.* at p. 125.

The US policy of permitting private citizens to export freely arms and munitions to belligerents markedly disadvantaged the Central Powers which lacked the sea command in order to benefit themselves from such a market. As the arms industry experienced a dramatic expansion in the United States, and the orders from the Allies outpaced production, Germany and Austria-Hungary started questioning whether neutrality was still a precise description of American policies.[77] The issue of unrestrained private arms sales to the Allies was in fact the object of several memoranda filed by Germany and Austria-Hungary beginning in the second year of the war. On 16 February 1915, for instance, the German Foreign Minister communicated these lines to his counterpart in Washington:

> The German Government believe that they are obliged to point out very particularly and with the greatest emphasis, that a trade in arms exists between American manufacturers and Germany's enemies which is estimated at many hundred million marks. The German Government have given due recognition to the fact that as a matter of form the exercise of rights and the toleration of wrong on the part of neutrals is limited by their pleasure alone and involves *no formal breach of neutrality*. The German Government have not in consequence made any charge of formal breach of neutrality . . . Conceded that it is the formal right of neutrals not to protect their legitimate trade with Germany and even to allow themselves knowingly and willingly to be induced by England to restrict such trade, it is on the other hand not less their good right, although unfortunately not exercised, to stop trade in contraband, especially the trade in arms, with Germany's enemies . . . the German Government ventures to hope that the American Government upon reconsideration will see their way clear to a measure of

[77]Suffice it to recall that as from mid-1915, the Allies had established a Central Purchasing Bureau in the United States, which soon spent, on the average, US $10 million a day. It is believed that between August 1914 and February 1917, more than US $10.5 billion worth of goods were shipped out of America. The legal aspects of the export of arms and munitions to the Entente Powers are fully analysed in GARNER, J.W., *International Law and the World War*, 1920, vol.II, p. 375*ff*.

race during peacetime, or *Essenizing*,[82] as they called it euphemistically. A comprehensive arms embargo, it was argued, would leave the victim of an international aggression defenceless; '*why aid the wolf and hamstring the lamb?* Why by a change of law and policy aid and encourage the predatory policy and debilitate defence? Such change must stimulate war and discourage peace' (italics in the original).[83] Ethical objections were also regarded with scepticism. As James Garner rhetorically asked, 'is selling arms in time of peace any less immoral than furnishing them in time of war and then why arms exportation should be considered as more reprehensible morally than delivering raw materials such as coal for warships?'[84]

Confronted with such a remarkably solid case, the advocates of the prohibition of private arms exports attacked the very nature of such a concept of neutrality and turned to portray the vagaries of a system which permits to neutral citizens what it forbids to neutral states. In the words of one scholar:

> the highly artificial distinction now drawn between the duty of the state, as such, not to furnish a belligerent with munitions of war or other contraband, and the absence of any such duty on the part of all its citizens, is a hybrid of very recent origin. It is one of the very few unhealthy products of the modern interdependence of states. That this distinction between the duty of the people and the duty of the state has become more firmly established since the rise of democracies and the increasing identification of the people with the state is one of the anomalies of history.[85]

[82]The metaphor alluded to the impressive Krupps arms industry at Essen; for more, see MENNE, B., *Blood and Steel – The Rise of the House of Krupp*, 1938.
[83]See GREGORY, C.N., 'Neutrality and the Sale of Arms', 10 *AJIL* (1916) at p. 554.
[84]See GARNER, J.W., 'Some True and False Conceptions Regarding the Duty of Neutrals in Respect to the Sale and Exportation of Arms and Munitions to Belligerents', 10 *Proc.ASIL* (1916) at pp. 26–7.
[85]See BUTTE, G.C., 'The Reform of the Law of Contraband', 9 *Proc.ASIL* (1915) at p. 120. While Philip Marshall Brown argued that 'a fictitious impartiality which, under the guise of affording equal opportunities to all, really affords special facilities for the only side able to avail itself of the chance . . . is plainly a euphemism for unneutral neutrality'; see BROWN, P.M., 'Munitions and Neutrality', 10 *Proc.ASIL* (1916) at p. 37. See also MACH, E.von, 'An Argument Against the Exportation of Arms', 60 *Ann.AAPSS* (1915), p. 192*ff*. Furthermore, the viciousness of the private trade in arms and the dominant lobbying power of arms manufacturers, or *kruppism*, had not gone unnoticed. Already in 1914, George Perris was prefacing his book on the war traders in these words: 'war does not pay the nations. But war panics and preparations do, all the time and

In earlier correspondence, Vienna had attempted to demonstrate that American practices went far beyond what the drafters of Article 7 of the Thirteenth Hague Convention of 1907 had intended. According to the Austro-Hungarian argumentation, the treaty rule allowing the private trade in war materials originated in the need to protect private industries in neutral countries from suffering substantial losses as a result of a war erupted between third states, but it could not under any construction be read as envisaging the unprecedented expansion of these industries due to such a war. The view of Foreign Minister Burian deserves to be quoted in length:

> It can not certainly have escaped the attention of the American Government, which has so eminently cooperated in the work of The Hague, that the meaning and essence of neutrality are in no way exhaustively dealt with in the fragmentary provisions of the pertinent treaties. If one takes into consideration particularly the genesis of Article 7 of the Fifth and Thirteenth Conventions, respectively, upon which the Federal Government clearly relies in the present case, and the wording of which, as is in no way to be denied, affords it a formal pretext for the toleration of traffic in munitions of war now being carried on by the United States, it is only necessary, in order to measure the true spirit and import of this provision . . . to point out the fact that the detailed privileges conceded to neutral states are limited by the requirements of neutrality which conform to the universally recognized principles of international law . . . The question now before us is surely not whether American industries which are engaged in the manufacture of war material should be protected from loss in the export trade that was theirs in time of peace. Rather has that industry soared to unimagined heights. In order to turn out the huge quantities of arms, ammunition and other war material of every description ordered in the past months by Great Britain and her allies from the United States, not only the full capacity of the existing plants but also their transformation and enlargement and the creation of new large plants, as well as a flocking of workmen of all trades into that branch of industry, in brief far-reaching changes

> of economic life encompassing the whole country, became necessary.[79]

The central issue of such diplomatic correspondence is worth holding on to. Germany and Austria-Hungary never set out to challenge the continued validity of the Hague rule sanctioning the private trade in contraband. They simply asserted that to allow extensive reconfiguration of the country's industrial planning and wholehearted investment in arms production was far distant from what the ordinary meaning and intention of the Hague principle would justify. Their claim alluded to a progressive transformation of the concept of neutrality which would suggest that the trade in arms between warring nations and neutral private industries should cease to obey exclusively to mercantilistic considerations of demand and supply.

To Sell or Not to Sell: The Doctrinal Debate The defenders of free private arms trade with belligerents had no doubt a solid case to support. State practice, jurisprudence and conventional texts never questioned the right of citizens of neutral countries to supply the belligerents with arms and munitions of war without impairing the neutral status of their home state. Most of the American publicists saw in that nothing but a consistently reaffirmed legal principle ever since the 1793 proclamation of neutrality.[80] The *loci classici* of the American jurisprudence bear

[79]See 9 *AJIL* (1915) *Suppl.* at pp. 147–8. The American replies to these observations enjoyed all the protection that the written law could afford. The State Department confined itself to recounting the ample practice of states, the prominent authorities, and above all the unmistakable letter of the Hague Conventions upholding the right of private persons to pursue trade in contraband with belligerents; see Bryan's answer to a German Note, dated 21 April 1915, *ibid.*, p. 127*ff*, and Lansing's Note of 12 August 1915, *ibid.*, p. 166*ff*. See also the reply to the Chairman of the Senate Committee on Foreign Affairs, dated 8 January 1915 on the question of arms sales to Great Britain and her allies, *ibid.* at pp. 259–60.

[80]For an excellent treatment of the question of private arms sales, and a review of the American policy standpoint on the issue, see MOREY, W.C., 'The Sale of Munitions of War', 10 *AJIL* (1916), p. 467*ff*. See also DENNIS, W.C., 'The Right of Citizens of Neutral Countries to Sell and Export Arms and Munitions of War to Belligerents', 60 *Ann.AAPSS* (1915), p. 168*ff*.; MOORE, J.B., *A Digest of International Law*, vol.7, p. 955*ff*. Their views reflected basically a strict adherence to the Jeffersonian conception of American neutrality standing for indifference and unobstructed pursuit of commercial gain. Moreover, they seem to subscribe to an understanding of international affairs according to which the isolation or self-containment of a world power were still perfectly feasible.

the names of the *Santissima Trinidad*, and the *Bermuda*. As Justice Story pronounced in February 1822:

> there is nothing in our laws or in the law of nations that forbids our citizens from sending armed vessels, as well as munitions of war, to foreign ports for sale. It is a commercial adventure which no nation is bound to prohibit, and which only exposes the persons engaged in it to the penalty of confiscation.[81]

According to the apologists of the established usage, to bar the private export of arms and munitions of war would feed international militarism and force small states to an armaments

[81]See *The Santissima Trinidad*, 7 *Wheat.* (20 U.S.) at p. 339. To be reaffirmed in December 1865; 'neutrals in their own country, may sell to belligerents whatever belligerents choose to buy . . . So, too, except goods contraband of war, or conveyed with intent to violate a blockade, neutrals may transport to belligerents whatever belligerents may agree to take . . . a neutral may convey contraband to a belligerent, subject to no liability except seizure in order to confiscation of the offending goods'; see *The Bermuda*, 3 *Wall.* (70 U.S.) at pp. 551, 555. On two more occasions, United States tribunals were found confronted with private suits demanding the prohibition of private trade in arms or implements of war with a belligerent state. The first case, *Pearson et al. vs. Parson et al.* of 1901, arose in the context of the Boer War, and involved the shipment of horses and mules which were contraband of war to the British forces. The Circuit Court of Louisiana in interpreting the treaty of Washington of 1871, pronounced that 'it would become necessary to determine whether the United States intended by the above declaration of the treaty to subvert the well-established principle of international law that the private citizens of a neutral nation can lawfully sell supplies to belligerents. It is almost impossible to suppose, a priori, that the United States would have done so, and would have thus provided for the most serious and extensive derangement of and injury to the commerce of our citizens whenever two or more foreign nations should go to war; and it would seem that there is nothing in the treaty, especially when its history and purposes are considered, which would warrant the belief that the United States insisted upon inserting therein a new principle of international law, from which the greatest damage might result to the commerce of this country, and which was absolutely different from and antagonistic to the rule and policy which the government of this country had theretofore strenuously and invariably followed'; see 11 *AJIL* (1917) at p. 880. The second case, *Samuel Pearson vs. Allis-Chalmers Co.*, concerned large consignments of ammunition by the Bethlehem Steel company to the Entente powers during the First World War. The Circuit Court of Wisconsin had no difficulty in lining-up with earlier decisions, and stressed that 'the right of the defendant as a subject of the United States to manufacture and sell contraband articles, with the risk of having the goods condemned if captured, has been recognized by all the nations of the earth since the administration of President Washington, as a practice violative of neither the laws of nations nor the standards of neutrality'; *ibid.* at p. 895. In the Court's view, 'the allegation that the war would cease if the shipment of shrapnel shell is stopped is only an expression of opinion, hope, or expectation, and is not susceptible of proof, and cannot be made the basis of judicial action'; *ibid.* at p. 898.

race during peacetime, or *Essenizing*,[82] as they called it euphemistically. A comprehensive arms embargo, it was argued, would leave the victim of an international aggression defenceless; '*why aid the wolf and hamstring the lamb?* Why by a change of law and policy aid and encourage the predatory policy and debilitate defence? Such change must stimulate war and discourage peace' (italics in the original).[83] Ethical objections were also regarded with scepticism. As James Garner rhetorically asked, 'is selling arms in time of peace any less immoral than furnishing them in time of war and then why arms exportation should be considered as more reprehensible morally than delivering raw materials such as coal for warships?'[84]

Confronted with such a remarkably solid case, the advocates of the prohibition of private arms exports attacked the very nature of such a concept of neutrality and turned to portray the vagaries of a system which permits to neutral citizens what it forbids to neutral states. In the words of one scholar:

> the highly artificial distinction now drawn between the duty of the state, as such, not to furnish a belligerent with munitions of war or other contraband, and the absence of any such duty on the part of all its citizens, is a hybrid of very recent origin. It is one of the very few unhealthy products of the modern interdependence of states. That this distinction between the duty of the people and the duty of the state has become more firmly established since the rise of democracies and the increasing identification of the people with the state is one of the anomalies of history.[85]

[82]The metaphor alluded to the impressive Krupps arms industry at Essen; for more, see MENNE, B., *Blood and Steel – The Rise of the House of Krupp*, 1938.
[83]See GREGORY, C.N., 'Neutrality and the Sale of Arms', 10 *AJIL* (1916) at p. 554.
[84]See GARNER, J.W., 'Some True and False Conceptions Regarding the Duty of Neutrals in Respect to the Sale and Exportation of Arms and Munitions to Belligerents', 10 *Proc.ASIL* (1916) at pp. 26–7.
[85]See BUTTE, G.C., 'The Reform of the Law of Contraband', 9 *Proc.ASIL* (1915) at p. 120. While Philip Marshall Brown argued that 'a fictitious impartiality which, under the guise of affording equal opportunities to all, really affords special facilities for the only side able to avail itself of the chance . . . is plainly a euphemism for unneutral neutrality'; see BROWN, P.M., 'Munitions and Neutrality', 10 *Proc.ASIL* (1916) at p. 37. See also MACH, E.von, 'An Argument Against the Exportation of Arms', 60 *Ann.AAPSS* (1915), p. 192*ff*. Furthermore, the viciousness of the private trade in arms and the dominant lobbying power of arms manufacturers, or *kruppism*, had not gone unnoticed. Already in 1914, George Perris was prefacing his book on the war traders in these words: 'war does not pay the nations. But war panics and preparations do, all the time and

2 The inter-war period

From Ephemeral Isolation to Diaphanous Neutrality The two decades separating Versailles from Pearl Harbor represented a period of transition for the American theory of neutrality. Political foresight, public sentiment and academic debate gave shape to three rival streams of thought, all arguing they could resolve the troubles of the American foreign policy. The intellectual discussion was stirring and the literature prolific as never before.[86] For the proponents of *traditional neutrality*, or *classicists*, to promote business with belligerents in time of war and to engage in lucrative trade were unobjectionable goals for private individuals and in no sense ran counter to neutrality status assumed by their own governments. The founding fathers of American neutrality had acted upon such an understanding, and a dozen neutrality acts passed between 1794 and 1919 read in the same vein. Neutrality was translated as indifference and holding back from all but economic enterprise.[87]

For others, in a world of ever-growing interdependence, to turn a 'foreign' war into a blessed source of national wealth, while remaining immune from war turmoil, was an illusion at best. Neutrality was to be too easily defeated if it meant exclusively government abstention. *Isolationism*,[88] responding to that

---

on an enormous scale, pay powerful groups of men in each nation; and it may be doubted whether any real peace will be achieved till this association of political power and the private trade in arms is broken'; see PERRIS, G.H., *The War Traders*, 1914.

[86]This ebullient period of the American legislative history is recapitulated in DEÁK, F., 'The United States Neutrality Acts – Theory and Practice', 358 *Int.Con.* (1940), p. 73*ff.*; KUNZ, J., 'Le problème de la neutralitè aux Etats-Unis 1920–1939', 47 *RGDIP* (1940), p. 66*ff.* For a penetrating historical account, see DIVINE, R.A., *The Illusion of Neutrality*, 1962.

[87]As has been remarked in one analysis of American neutral policies, 'in American history, the notion of neutral economic rights preceded that of neutral military duties'; see GABRIEL, J.M., *The American Conception of Neutrality After 1941*, 1988 at p. 204. The traditional view lacked no support from such distinguished jurists as John Bassett Moore, and Edwin Borchard, while Senators Borah and Johnson remained the chief spokesmen for the traditionalists in the US legislature.

[88]For an excellent historical reflection on the parentage of concepts, such as isolation, non-entanglement or insulation, see WEINBERG, A.K., 'The Historical Meaning of the American Doctrine of Isolation', 34 *APSR* (1940), p. 539*ff.* See also THOMPSON, K.W., 'Isolationism and Collective Security: The Uses and Limits of Two Theories of International Relations' in DECONDE, A. (ed.), *Isolation and Security*, 1957, p. 159*ff.* Among the several research works on American isolationism, see JONAS, M., *Isolationism in America 1935–1941*, 1966; ADLER,

challenge, favoured a reconsideration of the traditional definition of neutral rights in the light of the World War experience. Private financial stakes invested in foreign trade were seen as decisive in precipitating the United States' entanglement in the European war.[89] Addressed to a people torn by the Great Depression, shocked by the Nye committee's revelations, and alarmed by the Chaco or the Manchurian conflicts and the once again darkening horizon over Europe, the counsel of isolationists carried much persuasion.[90]

The third school of thought, the so-called *sanctionists* or *interventionists,* attempted to accommodate neutrality within the philosophy of the Kellogg-Briand Pact and of the League's Covenant. Unlike the neo-isolationist advocacy of a mandatory or automatic embargo directed against *both* belligerents, the interventionists pushed for selective, discretionary and partial embargo, imposed only on the aggressor and not the victim state.[91] According to them, following the Italo-Ethiopian war

S., *The Uncertain Giant 1921–1941: American Foreign Policy Between the Wars,* 1965; GUINSBURG, T.N., *The Pursuit of Isolationism in the United States Senate from Versailles to Pearl Harbor,* 1982.

[89]Under the label of revisionism, a current among historians and political scientists poised to rethink the real motives that induced America into the frenzy of the World War, it was argued that the German U-boat campaign was no more than a seeming reason and that American entanglement was unmistakably brought about by the machinations of bankers and business men who tied American prosperity to the Entente cause. Most popular among the first revisionist studies, the works of BARNES, H.E., *The Genesis of the World War,* 1926; FAY, S.B., *The Origins of the World War,* 1928; GRATTAN, *op. cit., supra* n.74; MILLIS, W., *Road to War,* 1935. See also COHEN, W.I., *The American Revisionists – The Lessons of Intervention in World War I,* 1967.

[90]For most students of American politics, isolationism is a whole cluster of ideas and emotions related to isolation, ranging from zeal for economic and social reform to ethnic bias and from pacifist militancy to fervour over American tradition. On the influence of American isolationism and its gradual metastasis from 'touchstone of patriotism' to 'virtually disloyalty', see DECONDE, A., 'On Twentieth Century Isolationism' in DECONDE, *op. cit., supra* n.88, p. 3*ff.* See also RIESELBACH, L.N., *The Roots of Isolationism,* 1966.

[91]The case of neutrality in the service of collective security was indefatigably pleaded by the pen of such prominent scholars as Quincy Wright, Charles Fenwick, and Clyde Eagleton. The writer, wrote Wright, 'knows of [no instance where] peace has been secured or a war shortened by neutrality . . . It seems probable that neutrality has never been a constructive force for peace at all but merely a consequence of the recurrence of war in an anarchic but trading world'; see WRIGHT, Q., 'The Future of Neutrality', 242 *Int.Con.* (1928) at p. 367. While Fenwick referred to neutrality as 'an inherently illogical and inconsistent attitude, that it puts you in the position where you have to choose between abandoning your rights or fighting to maintain them . . . it would be the supreme folly to go to war to maintain your right to stay out of war'; see FENWICK,

and the Spanish Civil War,[92] the mandatory embargo, however sincerely inspired by neutrality convictions, proved too inflexible as an instrument of foreign policy. Yet the most compelling reason for relinquishing the impartial arms and credit embargo remained the earnest commitment to aid Great Britain and France against the perilous German expansionism.

The Heyday of Isolationism As from the late 1920s, the isolationists, or embargoists, called for a drastic curtailment of private rights and principally for a self-activating embargo on the sales of arms and ammunition. The Burton resolution, introduced in December 1927, declared it 'to be the policy of the United States of America to prohibit the exportation of arms, munitions or implements of war to any nation which is engaged in war with another'. Following a presidential proclamation of neutrality, specified the bill, 'it shall be unlawful, except by the consent of Congress, to export or attempt to export any arms, munitions, or implements of war from any place in the United States or any possession thereof to the territory of *either* belligerent or to any place if the ultimate destination . . . is within the territory of *either* belligerent or any military or naval force of *either* belligerent' (emphasis added).[93]

Neutrality was reappraised as entailing much more sacrifice than gain. Neutral trading rights were dismissed and replaced by burdensome duties; a duty not to tolerate the private arms sales or the private loans to belligerents, and a duty to refrain from sending ships and goods to zones known to be the theatre of naval operations. Yet, it was not until 1933 that the drift

---

C.G., *American Neutrality – Trial and Failure,* 1940 at p. 3. For a comment from a European scholar endorsing the sanctionist approach, see PELLOUX, R., 'L'embargo sur les exportations d'armes et l'évolution de l'idée de neutralité', 41 *RGDIP* (1934), p. 58*ff.*

[92]See BUELL, R.L., 'U.S. Neutrality in the Spanish Conflict', 13 *Foreign Policy Reports* (1937), p. 206*ff.* See also FAIRMAN, C., 'La loi américaine de neutralité du 31 août 1935 appliquée au conflit italo-ethiopien', 42 *RGDIP* (1935), p. 678*ff.*

[93]See WOOLSEY, L.H., 'The Burton Resolution on Trade in Munitions of War', 22 *AJIL* (1928), p. 610*ff.* See also the editorial comment, 'The Arms Embargo Resolution and American Neutrality', 42 *YLJ* (1933), p. 1109*ff.* The specific properties of such embargo were destined to make up the core issue of all the neutrality legal battles to be fought in the U.S. Congress from 1935 to 1939. For an overview of the rival theories based on representative clipping, see PHILLIPS, C.F., *The American Neutrality Problem,* 1939, pp. 276–307.

toward isolation became noticeable.[94] At about that time, Charles Warren intervened in the academic debate to speak first of a *de facto* revision of the historic notion of neutrality. For the former Assistant Attorney General, the best policy 'would be, to admit frankly that, in a war between great powers, there are no such things as neutral rights of trade, to admit that to wrest admissions of such rights from a belligerent nation is impracticable, to admit that a belligerent nation will only concede such privileges to trade as it believes will be compatible with its own victory, in the war'.[95]

[94]Paladins of American neo-isolationism in the 1930s rallied around eminent statesmen such as Senators Clark, Maverick, Vandenberg, or Senator Gerald Nye who presided over the congressional investigation into American arms industries. For an evaluation of the work of the Munitions Industry Investigation Committee, see WILTZ, J.E., 'The Nye Committee Revisited', 23 *The Historian* (1960–1), p. 211*ff*. See also BEARD, C.A., *The Devil Theory of War,* 1936; Anonymous, 'Arms Manufacturers and the Public', 12 *Foreign Affairs* (July 1934), p. 639*ff*. Numerous publications set out to unveil the 'blood brotherhood' and the 'sinister conspirators' – all substitutes for the more stereotyped 'merchants of death'. Among the most influential works, see ENGELBRECHT, H.C., *One Hell of a Business,* 1934; BACCUS, J.H. (ed.), *Arms and Munitions,* 1935; ALLARD, P., *La vérité sur les marchands de canons,* 1935; GALTIER-BOISSIÈRE, J. and LEFEBURE, R., *Les marchands de canons,* 1933; Anonymous, *Marchands de canons,* 1933; BROCKWAY, F. and MULLALLY, F., *Death Pays a Dividend,* 1944. The moral indignation concerned two practices: first, the prospect of selling arms to one's own enemy, even during the war, and second, the idea of furnishing means of destruction to both belligerents while being technically neutral. No modern observer would hesitate to brand it a period of reigning naivety, that people revolted at the thought that national arms industries might have furnished arms to enemies. Some conspicuous examples had been recurring in all publications against war profiteering. The British fleet, for example, in the battle of Skagerrak, was equipped with optical instruments for its guns delivered only six months before by Zeiss of Iena and Goetz of Anschütz to Holland. Vickers guns were used to kill British soldiers during the Gallipoli campaign, while German soldiers attacking Fort Donaumont at Verdun found themselves entangled in barbed wire furnished to France through Switzerland by Magdeburger Draht und Kabelwerke two months earlier. What is more, France shipped poison chemicals to Germany during the war, while the Krupps gave their fuses to Vickers for a royalty.

[95]WARREN, C., 'What Are the Rights of Neutrals Now, in Practice?', 27 *Proc.ASIL* (1933) at p. 133. Being convinced that 'there is no magic in the word neutrality as protection against war', he urged that 'in order to avoid friction and complications with the belligerents, it [United States] must be prepared to impose upon the actions of its citizens greater restrictions than international law requires'; see WARREN, C., 'Troubles of a Neutral', 12 *Foreign Affairs* (April 1934) at p. 378. See also WARREN, C., 'Safeguards to Neutrality', 14 *Foreign Affairs* (Jan.1936), p. 199*ff*. Later, Warren submitted a 210-page memorandum elaborating on the measures to be taken if the essence of neutrality was to be preserved: mandatory arms embargo against all belligerents, limitation of trade with belligerents to pre-war levels, and a travel prohibition on belligerent vessels were among his

The stern verdict then of the Nye committee, growing revisionism among international lawyers, militant pacifism cultivated in publications and above all a profoundly vehement *vox populi*, led to the triumph of isolationist neutrality as mirrored in the first Neutrality Act of August 1935. This Act echoed the unyielding conviction that staying out of war was only attainable by means of drastic legislation. In the apt metaphor of a publicist, 'it is hardly too much to say that neutrality legislation became the American Maginot line',[96] or 'the isolationists had strait-jacketed American diplomacy'.[97] In the words of President Roosevelt, the 1935 legislation stamped the abandonment of 'dollar diplomacy' in favour of the policy of the 'good neighbor'.[98]

The Neutrality Act of 31 August 1935, provided for a mandatory embargo on arms, ammunition and implements of war, as defined in the Arms Traffic Convention of 1925 to include little else besides lethal weapons.[99] The Neutrality Act that followed on 29 February 1936, to the great disappointment of traditionalists, extended the embargo provisions to comprise credits and loans granted by private bankers to belligerents.[100] A new section introduced in the 1936 legislation declared the embargo clauses

principal recommendations. In fact, the 1935 neutrality legislation followed very closely Warren's suggestions. While Charles Cheney Hyde suggested: 'the law that serves to free the neutral from an obligation to prevent the exportation of war material from its shores is in sharp contrast to, and difficult to reconcile with obligations which are imposed upon the neutral to endeavor to prevent the use of its territory as a base of supply for a belligerent fleet or the fitting out, arming and departure ... There exists therefore today what may be called a law of neutrality that operates in a grotesque fashion'; see HYDE, C.C., 'The Arms Traffic from the Standpoint of International Law', 16 *Proc.APS* (Jan.1935) at pp. 6–7.

96See DONOVAN, J.C., 'Congressional Isolationists and the Roosevelt Foreign Policy', 3 *World Politics* (April 1951) at p. 304.

97The description belongs to GUINSBURG, *op. cit., supra* n.88 at p. 205.

98See message to the Congress, 3 January 1936; cited in BELIN, J., 'La portée de la neutralité américaine', 43 *RGDIP* (1936) at p. 425. In reality, the good neigbour policy, or, the policy of 'tilling our own garden' as Charles Beard preferred to put it, had been set forth as early as 1933, in Roosevelt's inaugural address: 'in the field of world policy, I would dedicate this nation to the policy of the good neighbor – the neighbor who resolutely respects himself and, because he does so, respects the rights of others'.

99For a short commentary on the 1935 neutrality legislation, see JESSUP, P.C., 'The New Neutrality Legislation', 29 *AJIL* (1935), p. 665*ff*; FENWICK, C.G., 'Neutrality and Responsibility', 29 *AJIL* (1935), p. 663*ff*.

100For a brief assessment of the 1936 Act, see GARNER, J.W., 'Recent Neutrality Legislation of the United States', 17 *BYIL* (1936), p. 45*ff*.

inapplicable in case an American republic would be engaged in war with a non-American state. Although manifestly a gesture offered to American solidarity, such a proviso seriously discredited the American pretensions of impartiality.

Cash-and-Carry and the Road to Interventionism Isolationism suffered its first setback with the adoption of the Cash-and-Carry scheme, or 'policy of transferred risk' to use Francis Deák's description,[101] in the 1937 Neutrality Act. Although the neutrality laws remained strongly isolationist in inspiration and mandatory restrictions were not yet lifted, the Cash-and-Carry compromise pointed at the unwillingness of the American people to bear the full consequences of a genuine neutrality, or, as Divine has put it, 'faced with the apparent choice between peace and prosperity, they searched for a magic formula that would preserve both'.[102] The ambitious idea had been originally advanced by Bernard Baruch under the assumption that 'we will sell to any belligerent anything except lethal weapons, but the terms are cash on the barrel-head and come and get it'.[103]

The Cash-and-Carry plan of 1937 produced the first crack in the isolationist front, long wrestling for ironclad rules and unflinching neutrality. The temper appeared to change rapidly as from early 1938. The outright repeal of the 1937 Act, or some radical amendment which would have permitted discriminatory embargoes against aggressors, were argued for in as many as

[101]For sharp critical remarks on the 1937 neutrality act, see DEÁK, F., 'The Pitfalls of the New American Neutrality', 340 *Int.Con.* (May 1938), p. 179*ff.*; GARNER, J.W., 'The United States Neutrality Act of 1937', 31 *AJIL* (1937), p. 385*ff.*; GARNER, J.W., 'The United States Neutrality Law of 1937', 19 *BYIL* (1938), p. 44*ff.*

[102]DIVINE, *op. cit., supra* n.86 at p. 162.

[103]BARUCH, B.M., 'Neutrality', 44 *Current History* (June 1936) at p. 43. The aim was to minimize the risk of entanglement without negating the economic profits of neutral trade. The US President was conferred the power to confine to foreign vessels the carrying of exports other than munitions, and to require cash payment for them and that title be transferred to a foreign owner before such exports could set sail. Moreover, the time limitation contained in the arms embargo provisions of the earlier acts disappeared, so that the indiscriminate prohibition of arms export to warring nations was to become a ritual in enforcing American neutrality. On the economic dimensions of neutrality, see DULLES, A.W., 'Economic Implications of American Neutrality Policy', 186 *Ann.AAPSS* (1936), p. 41*ff.*; PATTERSON, E.M., 'Economics of Neutrality', 186 *Ann.AAPSS* (1936), p. 155*ff.*; SOULE, G., 'Economic Preparation for Neutrality', 192 *Ann.AAPSS* (1937), p. 93*ff.*; CASE, W.W., 'Economic Problems of U.S. Neutrality in War-time', 15 *Foreign Policy Reports* (1939–40), p. 22*ff.*

twenty bills by spring 1938.[104] Given the precarious military balance in Europe, the Executive felt it should be given the widest margin of discretion to cope with potential aggressors without damaging America's neutral status.

Under the circumstances, the mandatory arms embargo, although assuring a genuine impartiality and abstention, had to be baptized immoral and unneutral. Secretary of State Hull, who three years before had urged for a mandatory arms embargo at the Buenos Aires Conference, now considered that an arms embargo was a 'hazardous departure from the principle of international law which recognizes the right of neutrals to trade with belligerents and of belligerents to trade with neutrals' and 'directly opposed to the idea of neutrality'.[105] President Roosevelt was now calling for 'greater consistency through the repeal of the embargo provisions and a return to international law'. His address to Congress of 21 September 1939, ended in these words: 'I seek reenactment of the historic and traditional American policy which, except for the *disastrous* interlude of the

[104]Some of the major bills before the Congressional Committees are briefly analysed in JESSUP, P.C., 'The Reconsideration of Neutrality Legislation in 1939', 33 *AJIL* (1939), p. 549*ff*. See also WILCOX, F.O., 'The Neutrality Fight in Congress: 1939', 33 *APSR* (1939), p. 811*ff*. Midway between those supporting the abolition of the arms embargo clause, and those pushing for it to be retained, there were some who maintained that an arms export prohibition should be imposed automatically to all belligerents upon the outbreak of hostilities, to be converted to a discriminatory embargo as soon as the aggressor is denominated; the Thomas amendment of 1939 argued along these lines. See also EAGLETON, C., 'Revision of the Neutrality Act', 33 *AJIL* (1939), p. 119*ff*. It should be remembered that bills calling for a discriminatory embargo against countries violating the 1928 Pact of Paris had already appeared in the late 1920s. In the terms of the Capper resolution of February 1929, for instance, 'whenever the President determines and by proclamation declares that any country has violated the multilateral treaty for the renunciation of war, it shall be unlawful . . . to export to such country arms, munitions, implements of war, or other articles for use in war'; see WOOLSEY, L.H., 'The Porter and Capper Resolutions Against Traffic in Arms', 23 *AJIL* (1929), p. 379*ff*. Moreover, the Stimson doctrine, promulgated in 1932, and refusing recognition for any territorial conquest made by force moved very much along the same lines.

[105]Quoted in BORCHARD, E. and LAGE, W.P., *Neutrality for the United States*, 2nd edn, 1940 at p. 401. Even to the ears of firm adherents of traditional neutrality, such as Edwin Borchard, these remarks sounded barely consistent: 'it was noticed that Executive faith in embargoes was still strong when applied to Japan, thus putting the Government in the paradoxical position of maintaining that an arms embargo on the Atlantic made for unneutrality and war, whereas an arms embargo on the Pacific against Japan made for neutrality and peace'; *ibid.* at p. 404.

Embargo and Non-Intercourse Acts, has served us well for nearly a century and a half' (emphasis added).

After long legislative procrastination and fierce debate, the 1937 Neutrality Act was repealed, and on 4 November 1939, Roosevelt's signature sealed the new legislation. The 1939 Act contained no time limit making some to speak of permanent neutrality for the United States.[106] The Cash-and-Carry principle was generalized so as to apply to all exports. Severe travel restrictions and prohibited combat zones were decreed. Moreover, to signal the much acclaimed 'return to international law', American exporters could resume shipments of arms, ammunition and implements of war to belligerents on condition that all trade would be carried away by foreign ships and that title over cargoes would be tranferred before the goods left the United States. For the Neutrality Act of 1939, the trade in 'guns or butter' needed no separate treatment. Only an extra-legal 'moral embargo' was specified concerning aircraft deliveries to countries accused of bombing civilian sites.

3 The Second World War

The Destroyers Deal During the summer of 1940, the prospect of an early Allied defeat appeared all too serious, with the battle of Britain approaching its climax, most of the European countries already overpowered by the Nazi blitzkrieg tactics, and increasing demoralization among the Allied forces.[107]. Almost half of Britain's destroyer fleet had been put out of action while the sunk tonnage in July towered to 400,000 tons. Given the dreadful memories of the unrestricted U-boat campaign of 1917 which nearly brought Great Britain to its knees, it was realized that aiding Britain should take the form of strengthening its naval power,

[106]For short commentaries on the 1939 Act, see EVERETT, G., 'The Neutrality Act of 1939', 211 *Ann.AAPSS* (Sept.1940), p. 95*ff.*; DULLES, A.W., 'Cash and Carry Neutrality', 18 *Foreign Affairs* (1940), p. 179*ff.*; JESSUP, P.C., 'The Neutrality Act of 1939', 34 *AJIL* (1940), p. 95*ff.*

[107]On the estimated needs of Britain in late 1940, see GREEN, J.F., POPPER, D.H. and DeWILDE, J.C., 'U.S. Aid to Britain', 16 *Foreign Policy Reports* (Jan.1941), p. 242*ff.*

and more particularly, facing effectively the German submarine challenge.[108]

Winston Churchill's pleas for urgent and massive aid (such as the cable to the US President on 31 July 1940 which read: 'I must tell you that in the long history of the world this is a thing to do NOW') were for some time being given a cool reply. The British Cabinet, under the circumstances, was forced to reverse its previous decision not to grant base sites in the West Indies to the United States in return for warships and aircraft. According to the British proposals, as finally submitted to the State Department on 8 August 1940, the following facilities were included:

> (i) continuation of the facilities already granted to the United States government in June 1939, allowing US aircraft and ships to use the waters of Trinidad, St. Lucia and Bermuda and permitting the US authorities to lease premises there, (ii) right to lease small areas on British Guiana, Trinidad and Jamaica where aerodromes could be constructed, and (iii) authorization for US military aircraft to make occasional training flights to Newfoundland and to make use of the airport there.

The list of the British requirements for the facilities offered comprised 96 destroyers complete with torpedoes and anti-aircraft ammunition, 20 motor torpedo boats at the time under construction for the US Navy, over 50 aeroplanes and 250,000 rifles.[109] Americans would favour instead an agreement which

[108]It should be recalled that the US Navy held in reserve about 170 destroyers of First World War vintage since the Washington naval limitation treaty of 1922. In September 1939, 68 of these vessels had been returned to service in the American Navy for use on the so-called Neutrality Patrol, which was set up at the beginning of the war to deter German warships from operating too close to the coasts of the western hemisphere. The full historical account on the destroyers transfer is given in GOODHART, P., *Fifty Ships that Saved the World – The Foundation of the Anglo-American Alliance,* 1965. On the political aspects, see LANGER, W.L. and GLEASON, S.E., *The Challenge to Isolation 1937–1940,* 1952, p. 742*ff.* See also BAILEY, T.A. and RYAN, P.B., *Hitler vs. Roosevelt – The Undeclared Naval War,* 1979, pp. 82–98; REYNOLDS, D., *The Creation of the Anglo-American Alliance 1937–41,* 1981, pp. 121–44; Id., 'Roosevelt, Churchill, and the Wartime Anglo-American Alliance, 1939–1945: Towards a New Synthesis' in LOUIS, W.R. and BULL, H. (eds), *The Special Relationship: Anglo-American Relations since 1945,* 1986, pp. 17–41; PONTING, C., *Myth and Reality,* 1990, pp. 196–215.

[109]See GOODHART, *op. cit., supra* at pp. 157–8.

would authorize the use of Newfoundland, Bermuda, Bahamas, Jamaica, St. Lucia, Trinidad and British Guiana as naval and air bases, the understanding being that the necessary land would be acquired through purchase, or through ninety-nine-year lease.[110] Throughout August, Roosevelt was concerned with how to bypass Congress and overcome neutrality legislation, while Churchill's vexation was how to convince the public that the Empire was not handing over any of its overseas sovereign territories. Churchill, points out Goodhart, 'was prepared to give the sites but not to sell them and Roosevelt was prepared to buy them and not to accept them as a gift'.

Eventually, in less than four months of pressing negotiations, the controversial transaction widely known as the *Destroyers Deal* was concluded.[111] When everything was arranged, President Roosevelt announced to the Congress that his country was about to receive from Great Britain ninety-nine-year leases on certain naval bases in the Caribbean in exchange for fifty destroyers, the United States neutrality status not being impaired or otherwise modified:

> the rights to bases in Newfoundland and Bermuda are gifts – generously given and gladly received. The other bases mentioned have been acquired in exchange for fifty of our over-age destroyers. This is not inconsistent in any sense with our status of peace. Still less is it a threat against any nation. It is an epochal and far reaching act of preparation for continental defence in the face of grave danger.[112]

[110]*Ibid.* at p. 165. On how the negotiated base sites were expected to enhance America's Atlantic defences, see ELLIOTT, A.R., 'U.S. Strategic Bases in the Atlantic', 16 *Foreign Policy Reports* (Jan.1941), p. 258*ff.*

[111]The negotiations which led to the destroyers for bases agreement are reviewed also in LANGENBERG, W.H., 'Destroyers for Naval Bases: Highlights of an Unprecedented Trade', USNWC, 62 *International Law Studies* (1980), p. 519*ff.* Cordell Hull and Lord Lothian, the British ambassador in Washington, sealed the final document on 2 September 1940, while the Secretary for the Navy Admiral Stark, certified the next day that the destroyers were not essential to national security. D-day for delivery was to be 6 September 1940 at Halifax, Nova Scotia. The vessels were to be handed over in groups of eight at fortnightly intervals, and were to be carried across the Atlantic by British crews.

[112]See 34 *AJIL* (1940) *Suppl.* at p. 184. The presidential message was accompanied by an opinion on the constitutional and international law aspects of the concluded agreement by the US Attorney General; see 34 *AJIL* (1940), p. 728*ff.* The text of the agreement is in 35 *AJIL* (1941) *Suppl.*, pp. 134–44.

Reactions to the unprecedented deal were unexpectedly muted. The legal irregularities were promptly identified and criticized by a large number of distinguished American lawyers, but the storm of disapproval that many feared failed to materialize. The main sophistry invoked in order to overcome the Neutrality Act of 1917, Section 3 of which prohibited the sending outside of US jurisdiction of vessels built, armed or equipped with intent to be delivered to a belligerent nation, was that the over-age ships 'were clearly not built, armed or equipped with any such intent or with reasonable cause to believe that they would ever enter the service of a belligerent'.[113]

The destroyers deal received its first official legal defence only two weeks after the signature of the US President made it effective, in an address of the US Attorney General to the Inter-American Bar Association on 27 March 1941.[114] The speech is at best an hymn to the philosophy of collective security as promoted by the League of Nations and the Kellogg-Briand Pact which toppled long outdated perceptions of war and neutrality and revitalized international law. Drawing a parallel with just war theories, R.H. Jackson suggested that discrimination against the aggressor should fall as a duty upon the shoulders of those affected. Quincy Wright aligned with the Attorney General's opinion, holding that 'the United States has a complete answer

[113]See 34 *AJIL* (1940) at p. 736. It was on the same grounds that Attorney General Jackson did oppose the transfer of the so-called 'mosquito boats' which were still under construction for the US Navy. Cunning legal quibbling pretended to have glossed over all juridical obstacles, or, as Selig Adler's gifted pen has put it, 'H. Jackson's opinion, which found warrant for the transaction under a forgotten domestic statute, split hairs to the point where a misplaced comma was pressed into service! The violation of international law was beyond question'; see ADLER, *op. cit., supra* n.88 at p. 237. Several scholars criticized the stretched interpretation of the provisions of the 1917 Act. As Herbert Briggs wrote, 'it is not the *building* with such intent or for such use which is prohibited by Section 3, but the *sending out* with such intent or for such use . . . the destroyers have by now been transferred; but let no one say that it was accomplished legally. The supplying of these vessels by the U.S. government to a belligerent is a violation of our neutral status, a violation of our national law, and a violation of international law' (italics in the original); see BRIGGS, H.W., 'Neglected Aspects of the Destroyer Deal', 34 *AJIL* (1940) at p. 578. Edwin Borchard shared the same view: 'the history of this statute clearly shows that the words with any intent relate back to the words it shall be unlawful to *send* any vessel out of the jurisdiction of the U.S. with intent that it shall be used in belligerent service' (italics in the original); see BORCHARD, E., 'The Attorney General's Opinion on the Exchange of Destroyers for Naval Bases', 34 *AJIL* (1940) at p. 694.
[114]See 35 *AJIL* (1941), p. 348*ff*.

to any challenge to the propriety of the destroyer transaction under international law'.[115]

However, the Attorney General's views met also with caustic remarks. Leslie Buell noticed: 'the difficulty with present American policy is that is belated, unconscious, and ineffectual. We try to satisfy our consciences without taking any risks. We want to be good in the world, provided it does not cost anything, or at least not very much.'[116] To cite once more Edwin Borchard, 'by the marshalling of no much evidence, not a scintilla of which has any claim to being international law, the Attorney General has demonstrated the lack of any actual basis for his proposals for departure from the law, proposals now advanced as the foundations for the maintenance of peace'.[117]

From a military perspective, the destroyers deal appeared little advantageous. The skippers of these decrepit vessels experienced tremendous difficulties in keeping them running. Their monumental steering and maintenance deficiencies stopped them from making any measurable contribution to the desperate struggle against the submarine threat. Although the anecdotes about extremely poor manoeuvrability and malfunc-

[115]WRIGHT, Q., 'The Transfer of Destroyers to Great Britain', 34 *AJIL* (1940) at p. 689. Clyde Eagleton commenting at about the same time would see no violation of international law in having the US Congress repealing neutrality legislation in wartime with the manifest intention to help one of the two belligerents; see EAGLETON, C., 'The Duty of Impartiality on the Part of a Neutral', 34 *AJIL* (1940), p. 99*ff*. Georg Schwarzenberger, for his part, pointed out the ultimate moral challenge neutral powers would face in a blatant war of aggression to undertake discriminatory action 'because they are morally and legally entitled to disregard their duties as neutral powers in defence of the world's *Magna Carta*', although he admitted that such attitude would technically contravene neutral obligations; see SCHWARZENBERGER, G., 'The Aid Britain Bill and the Law of Neutrality', 27 *GST* (1941) at p. 28.

[116]BUELL, R.L., *Isolated America*, 1940 at p. 331.

[117]BORCHARD, E., 'War, Neutrality and Non-Belligerency', 35 *AJIL* (1941) at p. 624. And elsewhere; 'there is no possibility of reconciling the destroyer deal with neutrality, with United States statutes, or with international law. It can only be explained by the legal fact that the United States is now, and it is submitted, has been for some time, in a state of limited war'; see BORCHARD, *op. cit., supra* n.113 at p. 697. While the press in general commented sarcastically on the transaction speaking of 'a raw piece of chicanery', 'a highly diaphanous neutrality', or of the United States having 'one foot in the war and the other on a banana peel'; quoted in LANGER, W.L. and GLEASON, S.E., *The Undeclared War*, 1940–1, 1953, pp. 772–3.

tion may be true,[118] during 1941 the Town-class ships made up between a fifth and a quarter of the escorts available in the Battle of the Atlantic. Military historians have handed down their verdict as to the ultimate importance of the deal noticing that it did not live up to neither Churchill's nor Roosevelt's hopes and estimates. The true significance of the deal rests in the fact that it marked the moment of the United States' irrevocable commitment in support of the Allied cause, or a telling prelude to the Lend-Lease and a decided epitaph to neutrality.

The Lend-Lease Act Three months before the fifty over-age destroyers were to fly the British colours, Washington committed itself to the urgent rearmament of the British forces. The enormous losses of material at Dunkirk had left the British Isles critically exposed. With industrial output not yet accelerated, the colossal orders filed by the Anglo-French purchasing commission could only be satisfied through the US Army and Navy's own stocks. Since international law provided for a stringent prohibition on sales from a neutral government to a belligerent, and since the US administration was still at that time placing great importance on the guardianship of its neutrality, it was decided that the Army and the Navy could turn weaponry back to the manufacturers and the latter could then resell the equipment to the British. Under this arrangement – the first tactful symptom of non-belligerency – no less than thirty freighters with gun loads sailed between the end of June and the beginning of August.[119]

Upon his re-election, on 5 November 1940, President Roosevelt announced that thereafter 50 per cent of the American arms production would be automatically turned over to British and Canadian forces. Naturally enough, British bank reserves were

[118]As Goodhart notes, 'no less than 12 of the 50 Town class ships were involved in collisions with friendly ships. At times the Town class destroyers seemed to show signs of homesickness – for on five separate occasions they rammed American ships'; see GOODHART, *op. cit., supra* n.108 at pp. 208–9.

[119]The first vessel to reach the English coast, the *Eastern Prince*, arrived on 23 June. As many as 140 bomber planes were also traded in to the air industries and resold to the British and French. America's first steps in joining the Allied camp are best traced in DIVINE, R.A., *The Reluctant Belligerent – American Entry into World War II*, 2nd ed.(1979), DIMBLEBY, D. and REYNOLDS, D., *An Ocean Apart – The Relationship Between Britain and America in the Twentieth Century*, 1988, pp. 126–49, and STETTINIUS, *op. cit., infra*, p. 24*ff*.

soon depleted from the massive dollar and gold-drain. New British contracting in the United States practically stopped by the end of 1940. It was the lawyers of the Treasury Department who then came up with the idea of lend-leasing.[120] According to a 1892 statute, they had found out that the Secretary of War, 'when in his discretion it will be for the public good', could lease Army property 'not required for public use', for a period of no more than five years. The bill was drafted, discussed and revised in the haste that the war developments imposed.

House Resolution 1776, or *Lend-Lease Bill* sparked off a vociferous national debate over the propriety and the ramifications of the all-out Aid Britain policy.[121] The much controverted bill contained a principle concerning eligibility for Lend-Lease aid to 'any country whose defense the President deems vital to the defense of the United States', and authorizing the President to 'sell, transfer title to, exchange, lease, lend, or otherwise dispose of . . . any defense article' to them. The United States would receive in return 'payment or repayment in kind or property, or any other direct or indirect benefit which the President deems satisfactory'.[122]

The Lend-Lease programme was inaugurated on 11 March 1941, with the first two Presidential directives. The first declared the defence of Great Britain vital to the defence of the United States, and authorized the Secretary of the Navy to turn over to the British twenty-eight fast torpedo boats, originally included in the destroyers package. The second directive declared the defence of Greece, at the time engaged in repelling

[120]The story of the Lend-Lease supply plan has been thoroughly narrated by one of its chief administrators, STETTINIUS, E.R., *Lend-Lease: Weapon for Victory*, 1944. See also the judicious essay by KIMBALL, W.F., *The Most Unsordid Act: Lend-Lease, 1939–1941*, 1969. The history of American *soi-disant* neutrality from the telling repeal of 1939 to the Lend-Lease aberration is minutely rehearsed also in LANGER and GLEASON, *op.cit., supra* n.108, pp. 213–89, 419–63; BAILEY and RYAN, *op. cit., supra* n.108, pp. 99–117; DRUMMOND, D.F., *The Passing of American Neutrality 1937–1941*, 1955.

[121]On the passionate hearings before the US Congress, see STETTINIUS, *op. cit., supra*, p. 71*ff*. For highlights of the debates, see also BEARD, C.A., *President Roosevelt and the Coming of the War 1941*, 1948, pp. 33–68, and COLE, W.S., *Roosevelt and the Isolationists, 1932–45*, 1983, p. 35*ff*.

[122]The dress-rehearsal of the Lend-Lease had already taken place in June 1940 with the signature of the Pittman Act by which the US Congress authorized the Secretary of War and Secretary of the Navy to manufacture in government owned arsenals munitions for direct sale to the government of any threatened American republic.

the Italian invasion, equally vital to the defence of the United States, and ordered the transfer of artillery guns to the Greek troops. The Lend-Lease scheme grew steadily into a vast and complex system of rationing critical war resources – anything from foodstuffs to planes and tanks – among the fighting Allies from Britain to Burma, and from North Africa to the Soviet front. Shiploads under the Lend-Lease programme represented one-fifth of the consignments of war supplies for which the Allies paid cash.[123]

Ironically enough, the Roosevelt administration which had been urging the arms embargo repeal of 1939 in the hope of rediscovering the dictates of international law, was now departing from the Hague rules in big steps. In April 1941, it concluded an arrangement with the anti-Nazi Danish minister in Washington providing for American occupation of Greenland.[124] Early in July 1941, the US forces were for the first time commissioned to assist the Allies militarily by taking over the defence of Iceland. In September, the US President, with his shoot-on-sight address, ordered the American Navy to attack without warning German and Italian warships wherever found within the patrol zone. Finally, on 17 November 1941, that is less than a month before the United States were forced to end its neutrality and join the war, the combat zones provisions of the 1939 Neutrality Act were repealed so that American

[123]STETTINIUS, *op. cit., supra* n.120 at p. 99. Beside the direct government arms deliveries, Lend-Lease funds were allocated to permit repairs of damaged Allied warships in American shipyards. The British aircraft carrier *Illustrious* underwent extensive repairs for five months at Norfolk before it was reconditioned and returned to fight. Hundreds of Allied merchant vessels have been laid up in American dry-docks for repairs and mounting of guns. At the time of the adoption of the Lend-Lease, the idea of US Navy escorting convoys of Lend-Lease cargoes had been temporarily ruled out. Washington came up instead with a makeshift manoeuvre; United States warships would patrol vigilantly on all sides of the Americas to secure the western hemisphere's approaches. But these, as Roosevelt reasoned, 'were patrolling operations not convoying. There is the same difference between the two operations as between a cow and a horse. If one looks at a cow and calls it a horse that is all right with the President, but that does not make a cow a horse'; cited in BEARD, *op. cit., supra* n.121 at p. 100.

[124]Under the Greenland agreement of 9 April 1941 the United States were accorded 'the right to construct, maintain, operate, and protect defense facilities' in Greenland. The US would also enjoy exclusive jurisdiction over such defence areas they would see pertinent to lease for as long as the agreement remained in force. For comments, see BRIGGS, H.W., 'The Validity of the Greenland Agreement', 35 *AJIL* (1941), p. 506*ff.*

merchantmen could be armed and sail to ports of warring nations, while American pilots could ferry aircraft from the assembly lines to Allied airfields.[125]

Qualified Neutrality or Non-belligerency It was with the circuitous transfer of surplus US Army matériel to Great Britain and France in June 1940 that American foreign policy initiated flattering overtures with the idea of *non-belligerency,* yet another product of sheer legalistic inventiveness, or 'un concept essentiellement politique, par definition indefinissable'.[126] No-one held illusions as to what the destroyers deal really meant. As Winston Churchill had written later, by 'all standards of history' this act would have 'justified the German government in declaring war' against the United States.[127] As the Lend-Lease was being devised in order to circumvent British pecuniary straits, 'nothing short of an immediate declaration of war could have rendered

[125]The idea of a neutrality law amendment to authorize US Navy convoys across the Atlantic was first put forward in spring 1941. On this debate, see COLE, *op. cit., supra* n.121, p. 155*ff.* The act of 17 November 1941, repealing the prohibition of arming US merchantmen, of trading with belligerent ports, and of travelling through combat zones, ended in all practical sense the renunciatory neutrality policy launched in 1935; see WRIGHT, Q., 'Repeal of the Neutrality Act', 36 *AJIL* (1942), p. 8*ff.* It cannot be reasonably argued that impartiality bore any relevance to American foreign policy at a time when the British and US staffs held conversations 'to determine the best methods by which the armed forces of the United States and British Commonwealth . . . could defeat Germany . . . should the United States be compelled to resort to war'. The British-American staff conversations were concluded in March 1941 reaching agreement on several issues of joint war planning. Does one need to refer further to the Argentia meeting and the Atlantic Charter declaration of August 1941 to illustrate this policy of declaring war by instalments? It should be noted that the United States had concluded in August 1941 a joint convoy agreement with England that exposed the US Navy even more to war risks and open confrontation. In a series of incidents from September to October 1941, American destroyers clashed with German submarines. Historical research has established that some of those incidents were deliberately misrepresented and largely exploited to support what was branded Roosevelt's 'unneutral neutrality'. The sinking of the *USS Greer* gave rise to the 'Rattlesnake Address' and the shoot-on-sight order of 11 September 1941. In October, the *USS Reuben James* and the *USS Kearny* were torpedoed while escorting convoys. On the 'shooting phase of the undeclared war', see MANSON, J.M., *Diplomatic Ramifications of Unrestricted Submarine Warfare, 1939–1941*, 1990, pp. 138–7, and BAILEY and RYAN, *op. cit., supra* n.108, pp. 168–213. See also DEAC, W.P., 'America's Undeclared Naval War', 87 *USNIP* (Oct.1961), p. 70*ff.*

[126]MEYROWITZ, H., *Le principe de l'égalité des belligérants devant le droit de la guerre,* 1970 at p. 327.

[127]Quoted in DRUMMOND, *op. cit., supra* n.120 at p. 169.

[US] alignments more clear'.[128] Lend-Lease, wrote Stettinius in 1943, 'has been a measure of war, a program through which the United Nations have pooled their economic resources for winning victory. *It has never been intended as a way of doing business in peace'* (emphasis added).[129]

The unprecedented clamour for effective barriers to prevent the recurrence of entrapment in a World War, the prospect of the announced New Deal to be built on social justice, and the crumbling illusion of a war-less world, have led to the twenty-year-long intellectual ferment, commonly known as the Neutrality Debate. From the legacy of George Washington's farewell address, through to the heyday of isolationism in the mid-1930s, or to the disguised belligerency behind the Lend-Lease programme, American neutral politics have sustained a long period of trial and error, a painful experimentation in a world that no longer appeared willing to afford neutrals the luxury of detachment.

The laborious process lacked no contradictions, miscalculations, or pitfalls. It is to be regretted that, under the compelling force of circumstances, the mandatory and indiscriminate arms embargo, coming closest to the idea of abstention and impartiality, was abrogated and largely regarded as ephemeral departure from 'the solid footing of real and traditional neutrality'. The isolationist blueprint for peace through neutrality and neutrality through stiff abstention became immaterial when the Japanese finally lashed out at Pearl Harbor; 'gone, probably for ever, was the unfounded notion that Providence had blessed the New World with a unique destiny unrelated to the fortunes and misfortunes of other nations and continents'.[130]

V Trading arms in the 1980s: between euphoria and reality

This section juxtaposes the characteristics of state practice in arms sales during the past decade to the internal institutional frameworks and political or legal directives which the arms exports of different countries are supposed to obey. As will be shown, overemphatic reassurances and seemingly stiff policies of restraint abound. It is no exaggeration to assert that if the

[128]*Ibid.* at p. 212.
[129]STETTINIUS, *op. cit., supra* n.120 at p. 331.
[130]ADLER, *op. cit., supra* n.88 at p. 285.

legal prohibitions were to be taken at face value there would be no need to probe into the international arms trade, since arms exports would steadily be shrinking before dying out. Yet, the gap between words and deeds has never been broader.[131]

1 National arms export regulations and declared policies, or the triumph of restraint

Arms Sales and US Foreign Policy During the period 1950–79 the United States transferred abroad over US $110 billion in arms and related military services, more than half of the world total.[132] US-made weapons systems are transferred to foreign countries, for the most part, through three different channels; foreign military sales (FMS), foreign military construction sales (FMCS) and the military assistance programme (MAP). All military export transactions are to be approved by the State Department pursuant to the Arms Export Control Act (AECA) of 1976, while dual-use items are to be licensed by the Commerce Department. The licensing authority to approve exports is exercised by the State Department's Office of Munitions Control (OMC),[133] or as it was renamed in January 1990, the Center for Defense Trade.

[131]In the decades that followed the Second World War, the drums of war never were silent. For a succinct review of the state practice in the post-1945 period and up to the mid-1970s as far as arms transfers to belligerents are concerned, see NORTON, P.M., 'Between the Ideology and the Reality: The Shadow of the Law of Neutrality', 17 *HILJ* (1976), p. 297*ff.*

[132]PIERRE, *op. cit.*, *supra* n.15 at p. 45.

[133]The Office of Munitions Control originates in the Interdepartmental National Munitions Control Board, which was constituted under the Neutrality Act of 1935, with a view to blocking arms exports that might compromise the American neutrality. On the key provisions of the Arms Export Control Act and the function of the Office of Munitions Control, see SUCHINSKY, A.E., 'The Lawful Trafficking in Arms' in UNSINGER, P.C. and MORE, H.W. (eds), *The International Legal and Illegal Trafficking of Arms*, 1989, p. 73*ff.* See also SMITS, W.H., 'The Illegal Sales of U.S. Arms Abroad', *ibid.*, p. 97*ff.*, and ANTHONY, I., 'The United States' in ANTHONY, I. (ed.), *Arms Export Regulations*, SIPRI, 1991, p. 183*ff.* An export licence is required if the items to be exported figure in the OMC's munition list. The munition list encompasses the whole gamut of weapons, military services and technical data, grouped in 21 regularly updated categories. The OMC receives an average 45,000 applications per year, 90 per cent of which are eventually approved. Contested arms deals may need the President's final consent, upon recommendation of the National Security Council. The US Congress also has the power to oppose within 30 days arms exports exceeding a certain value, without being able, however, to enact restrictions unilaterally. More on the role of Congress in MOOSE, R.M. and SPIEGEL, D.L., 'Congress and Arms Transfers' in PIERRE, A.J. (ed.), *Arms Transfers and American Foreign Policy*, 1979, p. 228*ff.*

Parallel to these long-standing regulations, every newly elected administration traditionally sets the political guidelines to be pursued in the sensitive domain of arms trade in the form of Presidential directives. A Defense Department directive, for instance, issued on 10 March 1970, under Nixon laid down that 'it is the policy of the Department of Defense consistent with over-all national policy and the protection of security interests of the United States to permit the export to friendly nations of munitions articles and services and related technical data including manufacturing licence and technical assistance agreements'. Compared to an earlier version of the directive, dating from 1954, which specified that it was the policy to promote and encourage such exports and not just to permit, the directive of 1970 introduced a change in perspective concerning the arms exports.[134]

Although a new arms sales policy does not necessarily mean changes in the export control procedures, it may affect significantly the nature, degree and ambit of government involvement in foreign military sales. The dissimilar Carter and Reagan policies in arms transfers offer a clear illustration of the political parameters of the issue.[135] Under the Carter directive of 19 May 1977, arms transfers were to be regarded as an 'exceptional foreign implement', and not as a normal instrument of United States foreign policy, 'to be used only in instances where it can

[134]By the mid-1970s, the campaign pushing for a drastic reappraisal of the American arms transfers policy was gaining momentum so that the Arms Export Control Act of 1976 was couched in the following terms: 'it shall be the policy of the United States to exert leadership in the world community to bring about arrangements for reducing the international trade in implements of war and to lessen the danger of outbreak of regional conflict and the burdens of armaments. United States programs for or procedures governing the export, sale, and grant of defense articles and defense services to foreign countries and international organizations shall be administered in a manner which will carry out this policy'. Overall, the Nixon and the Ford administrations did little to prevent the substantial growth in American arms sales, despite occasional embargo practices. Their policies definitely lacked coherence and willingness for effective control. For more, see SORLEY, L., *Arms Transfers Under Nixon – A Policy Analysis*, 1983. See also WOOD, R.J., 'Military Assistance and the Nixon Doctrine', 15 *Orbis* (1971), p. 247*ff.*; TAYLOR, T., 'President Nixon's Arms Supply Policies', 26 *Yearbook of World Affairs* (1972), p. 65*ff.*

[135]On the swings of US policy under the Carter and the Reagan administrations, see KLARE, *op. cit., supra* n.15, p. 39*ff.*; LABRIE, R.P., HUTCHINS, J.G., REURA, E.W.A. and RICHMAN, D.H., *U.S. Arms Sales Policy – Background and Issues*, 1982, p. 10*ff.*; KLARE, M.T., 'U.S. Policy on Arms Transfers to the Third World' in OHLSON, *op. cit., supra* n.69, p. 84*ff.*

be clearly demonstrated that the transfer contributes to our national security interests'.[136] On the other hand, the permissive policy promulgated by the Reagan administration in 1981 looked on military exports as a vital adjunct to the United States' own military preparedness. According to the directive issued on 9 July 1981, the United States must 'not only strengthen its own military capabilities, but be prepared to help its friends and allies to strengthen theirs through the transfer of conventional arms and other forms of security assistance'.[137]

With the exception, therefore, of the explicit criteria for recipient eligibility, announced but not consistently enforced by the Carter administration, Washington's preferred pattern for arms sales has avoided hard and fast commitments in the interest of political manoeuvring. The genuine security needs of

[136]His programme provided that the United States would not be the first to introduce advanced systems into a region, that development of weapons systems designed solely for export would no longer be permitted, that coproduction agreements involving significant weapons would cease to be entered into, that government personnel would not be tolerated to be involved in arms sales promotion, and that approvals of weapons sales would be tied up to the human rights record of recipient governments. The much-hailed Carter's effort drastically to curb the arms trade ended in no miracles. In the words of one commentator, 'philosophically wrong, practically infeasible and never seriously implemented, the policy needed only the *coup de grâce* administered by the Soviets in December 1979'; see BETTS, R.K., 'The Tragicomedy of Arms Trade Control', 5 *Int.Sec.* (1980) at p. 80. See also BALL, N. and LEITENBERG, M., 'The Foreign Arms Sales Policy of the Carter Administration', 4 *Alternatives* (1979), p. 527*ff.*; HUSBANDS, J.L., 'The Arms Connection: Jimmy Carter and the Politics of Military Exports' in CANNIZZO, C. (ed.), *The Gun Merchants: Politics and Policies of the Major Arms Suppliers,* 1980, p. 18*ff.*; SALOMON, M.D., LOUSCHER, D.J. and HAMMOND, P.Y., 'Lessons of the Carter Approach to Restraining Arms Transfers', IISS, 23 *Survival* (1981), p. 200*ff.*; SIMMONS, H.T., 'U.S. Arms Sales and the Carter White House', 12 *International Defense Review* (1979), p. 339*ff.* A Report by the Congressional Research Service, published in September 1977, on the 'Implications of President Carter's conventional arms transfer policy', equally cast doubt on the viability of Carter's policies and confirmed that sales continued on a routine basis. For approving remarks on Carter's policy, see BENSON, L.W., 'Turning the Supertanker: Arms Transfer Restraint', 3 *Int.Sec.* (1979), p. 3*ff.*

[137]Arms transfers were to be viewed thereafter as an 'essential element of its [administration's] global defence posture and an indispensable component of its foreign policy'. The new outlook was expressed in Reagan's apologia to realism when he said that 'we will deal with the world as it is rather than as we would like it to be'. And the Under Secretary of State for Security Assistance of his administration, in his first address, claimed that the Carter administration had adopted policies on the sale of arms that 'substituted theology for a healthy sense of self-preservation'; cited in PIERRE, *op. cit., supra* n.15 at p. 62.

the recipient country, freely appraised by the US State Department, seem to afford the only limits in the process, or as the Deputy Assistant Director of the Arms Control and Disarmament Agency has written, 'we do make the critical distinction between *stabilizing* and *destabilizing* arms transfers. Arms transfers which meet the legitimate national security requirements of the recipient in ways which do not contribute to the build-up of tension or the eruption of conflict between neighbouring states contribute to stability. Arms transfers which we consider to be destabilizing exceed reasonable self-defense needs, permit offensive power projection, stimulate arms race and tend to heighten regional tension and conflict' (emphasis in the original).[138]

Pleading Secrecy: Soviet and Chinese Arms Exports The Soviet Union before its disintegration had been for years the largest single arms supplier to the Third World. In recent decades, the value of arms deliveries to developing countries amounted to between six and eight times the value of economic or relief aid, a figure to be compared to the 1:1 ratio for the United States, or the 1:3.5 for West Germany.[139]

By virtue of the Constitution of the Union of Soviet Socialist Republics of 1923, replaced later by the Constitution of 1936, a People's Commissariat for External Trade was established to direct all external trade activities of the Union on the basis of

[138]See DECAIN, V.F., 'Promoting Restraint in International Arms Transfers: An American Perspective', 13 *Disarmament* (1990) at p. 146. See also JOHNSON, J.L., 'In Search of a Sensible US Arms Transfer Policy', 15 *Military Technology* (Oct.1991), p. 12*ff.*

[139]See KRAUSE, J., 'Soviet Arms Transfer Restraint' in OHLSON, *op. cit., supra* n.69 at p. 97. During the period 1930–45, the Soviet Union accounted for less than 6 per cent of the market in aircraft and tanks, while by 1970 it was selling 30 per cent of the world's exports of aircraft, helicopters, tanks and submarines; see MENON, R., 'The Soviet Union, the Arms Trade and the Third World', 34 *Soviet Studies* (1982) at p. 379. See also Id., 'Soviet Arms Transfers to the Third World: Characteristics and Consequences', 40 *Journal of International Affairs* (1986), p. 59*ff.* Soviet military equipment became attractive because of the comparatively low prices and beneficial repayment terms. In the early 1980s, it was estimated that roughly 10 per cent of Moscow's total hard currency earnings came from arms sales to less developed nations; see PIERRE, *op. cit., supra* n.15 at p. 79. See also HOLLOWAY, D., 'The Soviet Union' in BALL, N. and LEITENBERG, M. (eds), *The Structure of the Defense Industry – An International Survey*, 1983 at p. 67.

state monopoly.[140] The chief restriction in Soviet military exports, at least in principle, flowed from the dominant doctrine of peaceful coexistence. Although Soviet military aid to countries resisting western imperialism should continue, the prevention of direct confrontation between the superpowers remained imperative. Other relevant considerations were apprehension concerning uncontrollable diffusion of Soviet military technology, furtherance of Soviet global strategic interests, and pursuit of bilateral relationships in traditional spheres of influence.[141]

Russia, the most powerful among the successor states of the Soviet Union is currently pursuing an aggressive and insufficiently controlled arms transfer policy in order to avoid the imminent collapse of its military industry. Most analysts have expressed concern about the risks involved in such a desperate arms-for-cash process. Yet, it is too early to evaluate the regulations, motives and organization of arms sales under the new Russian leadership.[142]

China ranks fifth in the list of the largest exporters of arma-

[140]For more on the early Soviet legislation, see League of Nations Conference for the Reduction and Limitation of Armaments, *National Control of the Manufacture of and Trade in Arms, Geneva, April 14, 1938, Conf.D.184*, pp. 189–90.

[141]In all, there were nine different ministries in charge of military production and exports. Overall responsibility, however, for implementing the arms transfer policy was assigned to the Chief Engineering Directorate (GIU) – a branch of the Soviet State Committee for Foreign Economic Relations. The GIU conducted the negotiations with recipient countries, consulted with the Ministry of Defence on the types and quantities of equipment to be exported, and acted as the supplier in military contracts. Finally, it coordinated the shipment of ordered weaponry with the Ministry of Foreign Trade; see PAJAK, R.F., 'Soviet Arms Transfers as an Instrument of Influence', 23 *Survival* (1981), p. 165*ff.* See also WULF, H., 'The Union of Soviet Socialist Republics' in ANTHONY, *op. cit., supra* n.133, p. 165*ff.*

[142]On the new Russian arms export policy, see BLANK, S., 'Challenging the New World Order: The Arms Transfer Policies of the Russian Republic', 6 *Journal of Slavic Military Studies* (June 1993), p. 234*ff.*; KARAOGLANOV, S.A., 'Russian Arms Export Policy Detailed', 16 *Military Technology* (Oct.1992), p. 53*ff.*; 'Russian Defence Sales: The Insider's View', 17 *Military Technology* (Dec.1993), p. 40*ff.*; ALMQUIST, P. and BACON, E., 'Arms Exports in a Post-Soviet Market', 22 *Arms Control Today* (July/Aug.1992), p. 12*ff.*; KHRIPUNOV, I., 'Russia's Arms Trade in the Post-Cold War Period', 17 *Washington Quarterly* (autumn 1994), p. 79*ff.*; WILLETT, S., 'Economic Incentives to Export Arms: Russia and the Ukraine', 103 *RUSI and Brassey's Defence Yearbook* (1993), p. 257*ff.* The Russian Federation Law on Conversion of the Defence Industry of March 1992, and some subsequent decrees such as that on arms sales licensing of January 1993 are analysed in SERGOUNIN, A. and SUBBOTIN, S., 'In Search of a New Russian Arms Export Policy', 29 *International Spectator* (1994/1), p. 33*ff.*

ments, while it is the only Third World nation among the major arms exporters. Over the past thirty years, the Chinese had generally refused to sell military goods and preferred instead to offer arms selectively to Third World nations. The need for foreign exchange, however, has forced Beijing to a reversal of policy. China's prominence in the field is owed principally to her ability to sell cheaply and deliver immediately. Official information about Chinese weapon production and the amount of exported matériel is rare.[143] Domestic restraints on sales are believed to be ill-defined, if at all existent.

Selling Arms: The French Approach The legal prescriptions and policies of the leading European industrial powers merit also a close survey. Aggressive salesmanship has recently led the European exporters to overtake the superpowers in Third World arms sales with 31 per cent of the market in 1985. For second-tier suppliers such as France, Germany, the United Kingdom or Italy, arms sales resemble more a commercial than a strategic venture. In the post-war period, France has consistently been among the ten leading arms exporting countries, and recently has occupied the third place, with an average turnover of US $4 billion, or 12 per cent of world exports.[144]

[143]For one of the latest studies, see GILKS, A. and SEGAL, G., *China and the Arms Trade*, 1985. See also JAMMES, S., 'China' in BALL and LEITENBERG, *op. cit., supra* n.139, p. 257*ff.*; GILL, R.B., 'Curbing Beijing's Arms Sales', 36 *Orbis* (1992), p. 379*ff.*; BITZINGER, R.A., 'Arms to Go: Chinese Arms Sales to the Third World', 17 *Int.Sec.* (1992), p. 84*ff.*; BLACKABY, *op. cit., supra* n.15, p. 359*ff.* As from 1980, all Chinese defence industries have been reorganized into companies along western lines in order to promote efficiency; see FURLONG, B., 'China's New Arms Export Policy', 17 *International Defense Review* (1984) at p. 1795. See also YENG, B.S., 'Understanding the Chinese Defence Industry', 11 *Military Technology* (1987), p. 36*ff.*

[144]France has been frequently reproached for being willing to sell anything, 'from tents to tanks', to just about anybody. Arms deliveries rose from 2,673 million francs in 1970 to 20,500 million in 1980, or an approximately fivefold increase in constant francs. French arms manufacture consists of three main industrial groupings. A government agency, called Délégation Générale pour l'Armement (DGA), owns 25 arsenals and employs 60,000 persons. Three nationalized companies, the Société Nationale des Industries Aérospatiales, the Société Nationale d'Études et de Construction de Moteurs d'Avions and the Société Nationale de Poudres et Explosives, employ another 70,000 people. The third component of the French defence industry are the private companies, altogether employing 150,000 persons. The French defence industry is often cited as one of the world's most export-oriented. It has been estimated that 50 per cent of French aerospace workers, 38 per cent of all electronics workers and 67 per cent of naval construction workers derive their jobs from arms exports. Today, one half of its output

The export of all instruments of war is, as a matter of law, strictly prohibited in France by virtue of 1939 legislation.[145] Ever since, arms contracts have been concluded on the basis of exceptional authorization derogating from the law in force. The decree of 1939 was supplemented and amended in 1971 and 1973, but the export prohibition principle has never been lifted.[146] The Commission Interministérielle pour l'Étude des Exportations de Matériels de Guerre (CIEEMG), composed of twenty-five government members, meets periodically in closed session, and examines the various export projects.[147] Every application for a prospective export operation is subject to two inspections: the first examines the substance of the project, while the second verifies that all formalities have been respected. Before an export authorization is even applied for, the arms industry must obtain three preliminary licences: first, to prospect the market, then to negotiate the contract and finally to conclude the sale by signing the contract.

Beyond the appearances, however, of watertight export control mechanisms the Quai d'Orsay has maintained a *tous azimuts* policy relating to arms transfers. Not surprisingly, pub-

---

(others say 55 per cent to 60 per cent) is directed to foreign countries. The French policies on arms exports have been scrutinized in several writings; KOLODZIEJ, E.A., *Making and Marketing Arms – The French Experience and its Implications for the International System*, 1987; PIERRE, *op. cit., supra* n.15, p. 83*ff.*; KLEIN, J., 'France and the Arms Trade' in CANNIZZO, *op. cit., supra* n.136, p. 127*ff.*; HEBERT, J-P., *Les ventes d'armes*, 1988; ANASTASSOPOULOS, J-P. and DUSSAUGE, P., 'French Savoir-faire in Selling Arms: A New Way of Doing Business?', 18 *Long Range Planning* (1985), p. 13*ff.*; DELHOMBRE, J., 'Exportations françaises d'armements et commerce exterieur', 46 *Défense Nationale* (1990), p. 57*ff.*; ABEN, J., 'Commerce de guerre ou commerce de paix: Un dilemme pour les relations entre la France et le Tiers Monde', 41 *Défense Nationale* (1985), p. 61*ff.*

[145]See COLLET, A., *Armements – Mutation, réglementation, production, commerce*, 1989, p. 31*ff.*

[146]Close government supervision and control over the defence industry was first established, under various decrees of October/December 1935 and of May/June 1936. Export permits were needed since the decree of 3 September 1935. On the main provisions of the early enactments, see League of Nations Doc., *op. cit., supra* n.140, p. 77*ff.* For commentaries on this legislation, see JÈZE, G., 'Le régime juridique des entreprises de fabrication ou de vente de matériels d'armement', 54 *Revue du Droit Public et de la Science Politique en France et à l'étranger* (1937), p. 456*ff.*

[147]The CIEEMG was created in 1955, and was assigned the responsibility of authorizing exceptional deviations from the law prohibiting arms exports. Each year the CIEEMG receives almost 5,000 applications for exemption, 85 per cent of which are finally approved; see COURADES ALLEBECK, 'Arms Trade Regulations', *Ybk.SIPRI* (1989) at p. 325. See also WARUSFEL, B., 'Strategic Exports Control and Disarmament in France', 15 *Disarmament* (1992), p. 43*ff.*

licity on concluded sales or arms deliveries has been kept to a minimum.[148] Only occasionally have government spokesmen referred to broad principles of restraint giving sporadic assurances that France as a matter of principle refuses to export arms to a war zone, or to belligerent states, while caution is exercised in selling weapons systems to areas of tension.[149] François Mitterand's platform, prior to the 1978 elections, included some detailed proposals for 'lifting the secrecy' and introducing 'democratic control', over the various sectors engaged in arms manufacture and exports.[150]

Controlling British Arms Sales In the first decade after the Second World War, Britain was the second largest exporter of weapons in the world. Ever since, its importance as a major supplier has decreased, yet still today, arms exports account for 25 per cent to 30 per cent of Britain's total military production and constitute an estimated 3.5 per cent of its external trade.[151] Permanent peacetime control of the export of war material in Great Britain may be said to have begun with the Order-in-Council of 24 March 1921, which prohibited the export of fifteen categories of arms, ammunition, explosives, and military and naval stores, without licence from the Board of Trade.[152]

[148]The *secret d'État* fetish enjoys a prodigious reverence in France. In the words of one analyst, 'the impressive size, pervasive organizational structure and formidable political influence of the arms industry within the government and within the French economy and society create a subgovernmental system that sustains and reinforces the commitment of the Fifth Republic to an open-door arms sales policy . . . at this juncture of history, the fate of the arms complex and the French republic appear inextricably entangled'; see KOLODZIEJ, *op. cit.*, *supra* n.144 at p. 298.

[149]See PIERRE, *op. cit.*, *supra* n.15 at p. 90.

[150]Parliamentary control would be provided for, public reports on French arms sales would be issued annually, and a Secretariat of State for the arms industry would be created, as well as a special Council for Disarmament and Security to elaborate proposals for the limitation and the reorientation of arms sales; see 27 *AFDI* (1981) at pp. 860–1. In the years that followed, Defence Minister Charles Hernu at times announced arms sales policy directives, specifying that France would refuse to sell arms to 'racist and fascist regimes'. While his fellow Cabinet Minister Claude Cheysson, further excluded from France's future clientele dictatorial, or repressive regimes and governments of countries at war.

[151]PIERRE, *op. cit.*, *supra* n.15 at p. 101.

[152]This Order was supplemented by the Arms Export Prohibition Order of 13 December 1921, and further amended in 1931, 1937 and 1970. A full account of the early British legislation is given in ATWATER, E., 'British Control Over the Export of War Material', 33 *AJIL* (1939), p. 292*ff.* See also League of Nations Doc., *op.cit.*, *supra* n.140, p. 34*ff.*

In essence, the Import Export and Customs Powers (Defence) Act of 1939, as much as the Export of Goods (Control) Order of 1987, as amended in 1988, entrusts to the government the overall management of foreign military sales. However, apart from the arms exports licensing and the registry procedures, no explicit criteria for export authorization are enunciated in the British legislation. Nor have relevant government guidelines been issued to clarify the orientations of the British government in the field.[153] Applications for weapon export licenses are first submitted to the Ministry of Trade and then channelled to the Ministry of Defence. Within the MoD, the Defence Sales Organization, created in 1966 and recently renamed Defence Export Services Organization (DESO), is responsible for the processing of applications while the Foreign Office is also consulted.[154]

Legal Constraints of German Arms Sales Policy The Federal Republic of Germany entered the international arms market as late as the mid-1960s. In fact, following the decision to rearm West Germany in 1955, military production, which had been banned since the war, was permitted under the control of the Western European Union. The defence industry was gradually redesigned, its production capacity augmented, and the value of exports became ten times higher in a period of ten years (1974–84).[155]

The Constitution *(Grundgesetz)* of the Federal Republic of

[153]In the words of one expert, 'the ultimate criteria, arguably, are expediency and pragmatism: the expediency of not embarrassing the British government and the practicality of being as flexible as possible in order to be able to respond to new challenges'; see EDMONDS, M., 'The Domestic and International Dimensions of British Arms Sales, 1966–1978' in CANNIZZO, *op. cit., supra* n.136 at p. 96. See also PEARSON, F.S., 'The Question of Control in British Defense Sales Policy', 59 *International Affairs* (1983), p. 211*ff.*; Id., 'Problems and Prospects of Arms Transfer Limitations Among Second-Tier Suppliers: The Cases of France, the United Kingdom and the Federal Republic of Germany' in OHLSON, *op. cit., supra* n.69, p. 126*ff.*; PIERRE, *op. cit., supra* n.15, p. 100*ff.*; JONES, I. and WYNREES, G., 'Britain and Post-Cold War Arms Transfers', 15 *Contemporary Security Policy* (April 1994), p. 109*ff.*

[154]The most delicate deals, however, are referred to the Defence and Overseas Policy Committee, which is chaired by the Prime Minister. Nearly 97 per cent of an average 70,000 applications examined every year are granted; see COURADES ALLEBECK, *op. cit., supra* n.147 at p. 327.

[155]See HUEBNER, B., 'The Importance of Arms Exports and Armament Cooperation for the West German Defence Industrial Base' in HAGLUND, D.G. (ed.), *The Defence Industrial Base and the West*, 1989 at p. 137.

Germany, in Article 26§2, provides that the manufacture or transport of arms is only permissible with the authorization of the federal government.[156] According to the War Weapons Control Act (KWKG) of 20 April 1961, as subsequently amended in 1978 and 1990, sales of military equipment are to be supervised by the Ministries of Economics, Defence and Foreign Affairs. The three Ministries, upon consultation, approve or reject applications for export licence, while politically sensitive transactions are referred to the larger Federal Security Council. Among other grounds, authorization may be refused, if 'there is a risk that the weapons will be used in an action disturbing the peace, in particular in an offensive war', and if 'there is reason to believe that the transaction could damage the Federal Republic's commitments under international law or threaten their fulfilment'.

Further criteria for arms export licensing were announced by the Federal Security Council in June 1971 and again in April 1982 bearing, however, the character of internal cabinet regulations rather than of binding legal enactments. According to the 1971 directives, all exports to 'areas of tensions' *(Spannungsgebiete)* should be prohibited, while under the 1982 guidelines, arms shipments would be allowed even to areas of tension, if 'vital foreign policy and security interests' so dictate. These guidelines have been given liberal interpretation by both the Schmidt and the Kohl governments.[157]

The Czechoslovakian Defence Industry: A Thriving Past What was known up to its dissolution as the Czech and Slovak Federal

[156]Before the Second World War, private manufacture in Germany was equally subjected to state authorization, in accordance with the law of 18 March 1938, while exports were only permitted upon licence, under the law of 6 November, 1935. For more, see League of Nations Doc., *op. cit.*, *supra* n.140, p. 119*ff.*

[157]See PEARSON, F.S., 'Of Leopards and Cheetahs: West Germany's Role as a Mid-Sized Arms Supplier', 29 *Orbis* (1985), p. 165*ff.* See also ALBRECHT, U., 'The Federal Republic of Germany and Italy: New Strategies of Mid-Sized Weapons Exporters', 40 *Journal of International Affairs* (1986), p. 129*ff.* For more on the German arms export policy debate, see PEARSON, F.S., 'Necessary Evil: Perspectives on West German Arms Transfer Policies', 12 *Armed Forces and Society* (1986), p. 525*ff.* See also BRZOSKA, M., 'The Erosion of Restraint in West German Arms Transfer Policy', 26 *Journal of Peace Research* (1989), p. 165*ff.*; KRAUSE, J. and MATTOX, G.A., 'From Kiel to Port Stanley: The Arms Sales Debate', 110 *USNIP* (March 1984) at p. 179; WEITBRECHT, A., 'The Control of Arms Exports in the Federal Republic of Germany', 15 *Disarmament* (1992), p. 57*ff.*

Republic bears a long tradition of armament production dating as far back as the 1880s while the most recently published statistics bring it to seventh place among the leading exporters of major conventional weapons for the period 1986–90. Over the years, the Czechoslovakian defence industry became the second most important in Eastern Europe after the Soviet one, consisting principally in licensed production of Soviet weapons systems such as tanks and aircraft but also in the production of indigenously developed jet trainers, radar equipment and light arms.[158]

Under the law of 13 May 1936, the export of war materials was permitted only upon authorization by the Military Administration.[159] Since 1948 all foreign arms trade contracts were handled by Omnipol Foreign Trade Corporation (HTS), a government agency. Weapons have been routed to other Warsaw Pact members according to Moscow's central planning but also exported to Arab countries, Afghanistan, Cuba, Ethiopia and Vietnam. In the peak years of the mid-1970s, the military industry represented 8.1 per cent of all Czechoslovak commercial exports.[160]

Law and Policy of Italian Arms Exports According to a White Book on Defence, published in 1977, there are in Italy 150 defence-related industries employing some 150,000 workers. Most firms are to be found in the electronics subsector or the engineering industry. As many as 58 per cent of these companies are state-owned or state-controlled with state ownership especially predominant in the aircraft and naval subsectors. Military production in Italy relies heavily on exports at a rate of 60

[158]See TIEDTKE, S., 'Czechoslovakia' in BALL and LEITENBERGER, *op. cit., supra* n.139, p. 181*ff.*; CHECINSKI, M., 'The Warsaw Pact/Comecon and the Polish and Czechoslovak Military-Industrial Complex', 33 *Osteuropa Wirtschaft* (1988), p. 37*ff.*

[159]For more, see League of Nations Doc., *op. cit., supra* n.140, p. 49*ff.*

[160]By way of illustration of the apparently unrestrained policy of arms transfer, it was recently revealed that under the previous regime 1,000 tonnes of Semtex explosive were sold to Libya, or in President Vaclav Havel's own words, 'enough quantity for international terrorism to last the next 150 years'; see 36 *KRWE* (1990) at p. 37327. For the orientations of the new leadership, see ZUKROWSKA, K., 'Organisation of Arms Exports in Eastern Europe and Prospects for Limitation of Arms Transfers', Polish Institute of International Affairs, Occasional papers no.15, 1990, p. 10*ff.* For some of the most recently enacted export laws, see MATOUSEK, J., 'Czechoslovakia' in ANTHONY, *op. cit., supra* n.133, p. 50*ff.*

per cent for the aircraft and about 70 per cent for the electronics industry.[161]

Following the League of Nations recommendations, Italy envisaged state control over private manufacture of arms and foreign trade in munitions by the decrees of 18 November 1929 and 18 June 1931 respectively. A General Commissariat of War Material Manufacture, instituted by the decree of 14 July 1935, enjoyed wide powers with regard to arms production planning and supervision.[162] These early enactments have been complemented by ministerial decisions, such as the recent ones of 4 December 1986, 19 October 1987, and 14 July 1990, on military exports.[163]

The regulations currently in force require ministerial authorization before commercial negotiations involving the possible export of weapons and strategic materials could be entered into. Requests for such authorizations are then processed by the competent authorities, chiefly by the Ministries of Defence, Foreign Affairs and Trade. Each body can refuse authorization, whereas major or sensitive sales may also involve also the National Security Authority of the Prime Minister's Office.[164] The new law, passed in 1988, purports to make the licensing procedure more sensitive to considerations of foreign policy and international law. Arms exports inconsistent with Italian international engagements, national security, anti-terrorism efforts and the maintenance of friendly relations with third countries, are to be prohibited, as are deliveries to countries in war, or countries with a poor human rights record.

Arms Contracting: Dutch Incentives and Limitations The basic law

[161]For more see ROSSI, S.A., 'Italy' in BALL and LEITENBERG, *op. cit., supra* n.139, p. 214*ff.*

[162]See League of Nations Doc., *op. cit., supra* n.140, p. 129*ff.*

[163]On the decision-making process and the legal conditions concerning Italian arms exports, see CORSI, C., 'Arms Exports Controls: Developments in Domestic Legislation – Italian Legislation on the Export of Armaments', 15 *Disarmament* (1992), p. 29*ff.* See also BLACKABY, *op. cit., supra* n.15, p. 276*ff.*, and COURADES ALLEBECK, *op. cit., supra* n.147, p. 332*ff.*

[164]Under recently enacted legislation the Italian Parliament has to be presented with a detailed report on all arms deals once a year. The Ministerial decree of 4 December 1986, on regulations regarding the issuance of authorizations for the export and transit of armament material is to be found in 7 *It.YIL* (1986–7), pp. 609–12. See also MIGGIANO. P., 'Italy' in ANTHONY, *op. cit., supra* n.133, p. 92*ff.*

in the Netherlands prescribing administrative regulation of the imports, exports, transit and manufacture of fire-arms and ammunition, dates back to 7 June 1919,[165] while licensing of arms exports was first introduced by the Import-Export Law of 1962. The Dutch kingdom has since developed into a mid-sized arms producer of great ambition, recently ascending to eighth place among the world's largest arms suppliers. From the available material on the Dutch practice, it seems safe to conclude that a state of active hostilities constitutes the prime policy consideration and the most cogent reason for blocking arms deliveries to foreign nations.[166]

The regular licensing procedure involves an application to the General Imports and Exports Service *(Centrale Dienst voor In-en Uitvoer)* which forwards it to the Ministry of Economic Affairs. Next, the Ministry of Economic Affairs requests the Defence and the Foreign Affairs Ministries to consider all relevant aspects of the prospected contract. The political criteria by reference to which the application is judged include, *inter alia,* the nature of the material, the situation in the recipient country, relevant international engagements, the character of the recipient country's defence needs, the economic situation of the country concerned, previous experience and the employment pay-off in the defence sector involved. After the inter-ministerial consultations, and if no objection is raised, a licence is issued by the Minister of Economic Affairs. Withdrawal of licences is, in principle, not possible except 'for very weighty reasons'.[167]

Nordic Policies: The Swedish Experience Sweden, although a com-

[165]On the Dutch early enactments, see League of Nations Doc., *op. cit., supra* n.140, p. 141*ff.*

[166]See 2 *NYIL* (1971) at p. 201; 9 *NYIL* (1978) at p. 247; 12 *NYIL* (1981) at p. 261, and 14 *NYIL* (1983) at p. 338. See also COLIJN, K. and RUSMAN, P., 'The Netherlands' in ANTHONY, *op. cit., supra* n.133, p. 110*ff.*, and Id., 'Dutch Arms Export Policies' in BOZZO, L. (ed.), *Exporting Conflict – International Transfers of Conventional Arms*, 1991, p. 80*ff.*

[167]The mechanism of arms export licensing and the policy considerations involved in the decision-making process is given in 13 *NYIL* (1982), pp. 270–2. On the occasion of a parliamentary debate, related to controversial arms exports to Kuwait, the Dutch Foreign Minister explained the position of his government, not without a touch of purposeful vagueness. The Netherlands, in principle, he said, abstains from sending arms to countries in war, or to areas of tension, although an 'inevitable subjective assessment' may dictate otherwise in not 'clearly definable cases'; see 17 *NYIL* (1986) at pp. 213–14.

mitted devotee of non-alignment and neutrality in international affairs, is still included among the ten largest exporters of major weapon systems.[168] In response to the League of Nations initiatives to curb world militarization, Sweden by the Royal decree of 19 December 1930, laid down a general prohibition on export of specified war materials. Authorizations for such exports could, nevertheless, be granted exceptionally by the government.[169] The early legislation was supplemented by laws in 1935 reinforcing state control, while in 1946 the Swedish War Matériel Inspectorate (KMI) was accorded the authority to oversee also foreign military sales.

Export guidelines were issued in 1950, 1967, 1972, 1983 and 1988.[170] According to the guidelines formulated in 1971, as amended in 1988, a distinction is to be made between *unconditional* and *conditional* obstacles in authorizing arms sales. In case of the former, arms exports shall not be pemitted, under any circumstances, in the following instances: (a) when it is prohibited by an international agreement binding upon Sweden such as the non-proliferation treaty, (b) when a UN Security Council resolution explicitly orders so, or (c) when it would involve a violation of the rules of international law. The conditional obstacles, on the other hand, concern cases like: (a) states engaged in armed conflicts with other states, regardless of whether war has been officially declared, (b) states involved in international conflicts that may lead to armed conflicts, (c) states in which internal armed disturbances are taking place,

[168]On Sweden's domestic regulations and declared policies, see HOLMSTRÖM, P. and OLSSON, U., 'Sweden' in BALL and LEITENBERG, *op. cit., supra* n.139, p. 140*ff.*; HIRDMAN, S., 'Sweden's Policy on Arms Exports', 14 *Military Technology* (1990), p. 47*ff.*; HAGELIN, B., 'Arms Transfer Limitations: The Case of Sweden' in OHLSON, *op. cit., supra* n.69, p. 157*ff*; BLACKABY, *op. cit., supra* n.15, p. 333*ff*. For the history and the capabilities of the Swedish defence industry, see OLSSON, U., *The Creation of a Modern Arms Industry, Sweden 1939–1974*, 1977. For a comparative analysis of the formal and actual defence-related policies in four neutral European countries, see HAGELIN, B., *Neutrality and Foreign Military Sales – Military Production and Sales Restrictions in Austria, Finland, Sweden, and Switzerland*, 1990, p. 49*ff*.

[169]See League of Nations Doc., *op. cit., supra* n.140, p. 165*ff*.

[170]The governing principles were described by the Swedish Prime Minister Tage Erlander before the Parliament, in April 1956: 'in accordance with long accepted general guidelines concerning exports of military equipment, permits are not granted for exports to countries that are involved in war, whether a war between nations or a civil war. Nor are export permits granted in cases where the situation seems disturbing or critical, even if a state of war does not exist'; cited in HIRDMAN, *op. cit., supra* n.168 at p. 51.

and (d) states that as a result of declared intentions or of current political conditions can be expected to employ Swedish weapons to suppress human rights.[171]

The Swiss Model The viability of the Swiss defence industry depends heavily on exports, for it has been reckoned that almost 30 per cent of its total military output ends up in a foreign country.[172] According to a Constitutional provision approved in February 1938, the manufacture, import and export of arms, ammunition, explosives and other war matériel is subject to a system of authorization issued by the federal authorities.[173] By virtue of 1949 law, all export or transit of war matériel is formally prohibited. Derogation from the law was to be allowed only in exceptional cases. Licensing is further specified in the Federal Law on War Material (KMG) of 1972. The Military Department is primarily responsible for granting such export licences often cooperating with the Political Department. The overarching principle in according export permits is 'not to allow arms exports to areas of armed conflict, where such conflict might break out or other dangerous tensions exist'.[174]

[171]See COURADES ALLEBECK, *op. cit., supra* n.147 at p. 332. As a government official has ironically commented, 'the Swedish defence industry can only export to those customers who can clearly demonstrate that they do not need the weapons and that they will not use them'; cited in HAWES, M.K., 'The Swedish Defence Industrial Base: Implications for the Economy' in HAGLUND, *op. cit., supra* n.155 at p. 179. Nevertheless, in an attempt to advertise its credibility as a military supplier, the Swedish government has given assurances that all defence contracts would, in principle, be fulfilled even if the recipient country was to be engaged in an armed conflict after these contracts were signed. In the words of the Swedish Inspector General of military equipment, 'once an export permit has been granted, it is not withdrawn unless the unconditional obstacles to exportation or other special circumstances intervene'; see HIRDMAN, *op. cit., supra* n.168 at pp. 52–3.
[172]Swiss arms transfers policies are reviewed in BLACKABY, *op. cit., supra* n.15, p. 350*ff*. See also SAUERWEIN, B., 'The Swiss Defense Industry', 21 *International Defense Review* (Sept.1988), p. 1143*ff*.
[173]For more, see League of Nations Doc., *op. cit., supra* n.140, p. 183*ff*.
[174]In a study on the theme of 'Exportation d'armes et neutralité', the Direction du Droit International of the Département Fédéral des Affaires Étrangères has reported as follows: 'La loi [fédérale] sur le matériel de guerre prohibe l'exportation d'armes vers des régions où règne la tension, vers des régions donc où se déroule une guerre aussi bien que vers celles où un conflit armé risque d'éclater. Cette réglementation permet à la Suisse de remplir les obligations qui incombent en tant qu'Etat perpétuellement neutre, du point de vue du droit autant que de la politique de neutralité'; see 46 *ASDI* (1989) at p. 254. See also 40 *ASDI* (1984) at p. 195. In September 1972, an *initiative populaire* was rejected which would

Curbing Belgian Arms Sales: Political Concerns and Legislative Efforts In Belgium, state control over the armaments industry was first introduced under the Royal decrees of 3 January 1933 and 14 June 1933, as modified by the decrees of 9 January 1934, 29 July 1934 and 4 May 1936.[175] Arms transfers are regulated in a general fashion by the 1962 law on the import, export and transit of goods, as amended in 1968. In the wake of a heated public debate in recent years, and a two-year parliamentary inquiry into Belgian involvement in illegal arms transfers, these enactments have now been superseded by the Decree of 5 August 1991 and the Royal decree of 6 April 1993 on imports and exports of war material.[176]

In a report issued by the Foreign Ministry, for example, entitled 'Note sur l'exportation d'armes et de munitions de guerre' and dated 1 January 1981, the following principle is announced: 'toute licence *peut être suspendue* ou retirée lorsque le pays destinataire est engagé dans un conflit interne ou international. C'est expressément stipulé sur la licence elle-même. Cette règle est appliquée pour des exportations à destination de pays où sont déclenchées des hostilités armées' (emphasis added).[177]

The Sleeping Giant: Japan's Potential Because of severe consti-

have provided for a constitutional amendment with a view to prohibiting all arms exports except those destined to European neutral countries. The Federal Council's debate on the motion offered the occasion the Swiss concept of armed neutrality to be forcefully reaffirmed; see 28 *ASDI* (1972), pp. 278–9, and 29 *ASDI* (1973), pp. 384–7.

[175]See League of Nations Doc., *op. cit.*, *supra* n.140, p. 21*ff*. For commentaries on the Belgian laws of 1933, see CONSTANT, J., *Le régime des armes et des munitions – Commentaire de la loi du 3 janvier 1933 et des arrêtés subséquents*, 1936. On the Belgian defence industry, see TURBÉ, G., 'The Belgian Defense Industry – An Overview', 19 *International Defense Review* (1986), p. 481*ff*.

[176]For some preliminary remarks on the new legislation, see VINCINEAU, M., 'Introduction à la législation sur le commerce des produits de guerre', 26 *RBDI* (1993/1), p. 101*ff*., and VINCKE, C., 'L'Office National du Ducroire (O.N.D.) et l'exportation d'armes, de munitions et de matériel à usage militaire', *ibid.*, p. 257*ff*.

[177]See 18 *RBDI* (1984–5) at p. 367. A second document, published only two months later, on 19 March 1981, appears more categorical. Among the arms transfers principles enumerated in that text one reads: '(7) *suspension immédiate* des livraisons d'armes à tous les pays déclenchant un conflit avec leur voisins' (emphasis added), *ibid.* at p. 359. Although the text seems to imply an arms embargo as against the aggressor, it has been clarified that what is truly envisaged is an arms embargo which would apply equally to all participants of an international conflict. See also 19 *RBDI* (1986) at p. 428, and 16 *RBDI* (1981–2) at p. 591.

tutional limitations, Japan has long refrained from exporting arms on the scale that its industrial capacity and expertise would have permitted.[178]. In fact, Article 9 of the 1946 constitution stipulates that Japan renounce war as a 'sovereign right of the nation and the threat or use of force as a means of settling international disputes', and adds that 'land, sea and air forces, as well as other war potential, will never be maintained'. Having created its own self-defence forces only in 1954, and having enacted an Arms Manufacturing Law in December 1952, Japanese exports to developing countries have been extremely small. Licensing is compulsory and export permission requests have to be filed with the Export Section of the Ministry of International Trade and Industry.[179]

Despite pressures from the industrial community to ease restrictions on exports, Japan's political leadership remains extremely cautious of the risks attached to becoming a major arms exporter.[180] Japan has kept its defence expenditures admirably low, or less than 1 per cent of GNP, and has achieved autonomy in national security by constructing domestically 95 per cent of the equipment of its armed forces. For the rest, few would disagree with the view that given Japan's leading technological expertise, it 'could become a medium-sized arms exporter almost overnight if Tokyo reached a political decision to follow this path'.[181]

[178]See the study on the Japanese defence industry by DRIFTE, R., *Arms Production in Japan*, 1986.

[179]Prime Minister Sato, in a statement of April 1967, had declared the three principles on arms exports to be followed by his government; 'export of arms is limited by the Export Trade Control Law and in the following cases, no approval is to be given. The first case is when they are intended for a communist country; second, to the countries to which United Nations resolutions forbid the export of arms; third, to the parties of international disputes or to countries which might become involved in such disputes.' These principles were reconfirmed in 1976 by the government of Takeo Miki.

[180]For Japan's arms trade policy of restraint, see BLACKABY, *op. cit., supra* n.15, p. 320*ff*. On some loopholes of the arms export ban, see DRIFTE, *op. cit., supra* n.178, p. 74*ff*.

[181]According to a 1982 study on the theoretical possibilities of the Japanese defence industry, if Japan was to have a free hand as far as weapons production and export are concerned, today it would be the world's third aeronaval power with a level of forces equivalent to that of the French and British forces combined. As for export sales, the study foresaw that Japan would control 60 per cent of the naval shipbuilding market, 40 per cent of the military electronics market and 30 per cent of the aerospace market; see GIORGERINI, G., 'Economy and Defence: The Japanese Dilemma', 7 *Military Technology* (1983), p. 34*ff*. See also AOKI, T., 'Japan's Defence Industry', 9 *Military Technology* (1986), p. 47*ff*.

2 When interest defies commitment: recent practice, or fanning the flames as a global ritual

A The 1982 Falkland Islands conflict

When the ostensibly limited war in the South Atlantic broke out, France and the Federal Republic of Germany had to decide whether their military alliance and economic partnership with the United Kingdom should prevail over their contractual commitments with Argentina, long showing a marked preference for European arms. France was eagerly trying at the time to prove its expertise in aeronautical construction and advanced guided missiles technology, while the Federal Republic of Germany was seeking to consolidate its position in regional markets such as the South East Asia, the Eastern Mediterranean or Latin America.[182] France had already delivered to Argentina five Super Etendard fighter-bombers, armed with Exocet AM-39 missiles, with another nine remaining on order. The arms sale relationship with the Germany, on the other hand, concerned an extensive naval programme including the purchase of several Blohm and Voss MECO-360 destroyers, MECO-140 frigates, escort vessels and submarines, as well as the construction of other vessels under licence in Argentine shipyards.[183]

Eventually, in April 1982, both France and the Federal Republic of Germany imposed a comprehensive arms embargo against Argentina, which included arms deliveries and contracts signed before the trade sanctions were decided. France discontinued the Super Etendard deliveries, and refused to provide the technical assistance for the final phase of installing the Exocet missiles on the five aircraft already in Argentine possession.[184] The unilaterally imposed arms embargo was later superseded by larger economic sanctions against Buenos Aires decided by the European Community.[185] France moved to end

[182]For some interesting observations, see ANTHONY, I., *The Naval Arms Trade*, 1990, pp. 20–32.

[183]See DICKER, R.J.L., 'The German Submarine Industry – Will the Success Continue?', 16 *International Defense Review* (1983), p. 1289*ff.* See also KRAUSE and MATTOX, *op. cit., supra* n.157 at p. 181.

[184]Reports that a nine-man team of French technicians may have actually helped the Argentines install Exocet missiles launchers were never verified. On the French arms embargo against Argentina, see also 28 *AFDI* (1982), pp. 1025–6, 1093.

[185]On the EEC policy during the conflict, see EDWARDS, G., 'Europe and the Falkland Islands Crisis 1982', 22 *Journal of Common Market Studies* (1984), p. 295*ff.*

its arms embargo in August 1982, while Germany did not lift its own until February 1983. Shipbuilding was resumed under the submarine and MECO projects, the first destroyer having been delivered in March 1983 and the first submarine in 1984.

The attitude adopted by the United States during the Falklands conflict appeared to be, at least at an initial stage, far less resolute and neatly designed. Having to perform the delicate task of sticking by principles and condemning aggression, without bruising relations with Latin America, Washington opted for a neutral policy and proposed even-handedness between the two contenders. Besides the declared impartiality, United States throughout the conflict favoured a diplomatic solution which would have avoided a potential US military participation and hence would have least impaired its regional interests. The United States ended its policy of non-involvement on 30 April, or 1 May, with the decision of the National Security Council to tilt Britain's way.

There have been persistent allegations, however, that the United States long before the official endorsement of the British cause had been furnishing invaluable military assistance to the British Task Force. Some analysts have even suggested that without the decisive American support Operation Corporate might well had ended in a dreadful military defeat. And that all this help simply could not have started as late as 1 May. Although the allegations about the *sub rosa* US role in the then still-deepening Falklands crisis contrary to its proclaimed neutrality cannot but remain unconfirmed they seem to be based on plausible and hardly exaggerated evaluations.

The handicaps and perils of the South Atlantic venture for the British forces were never denied. Those in charge of the campaign to recapture the islands have been even more emphatic in underlining these hazards; a desperately fragile logistics tail, an all too vulnerable surface fleet against the submarine threat, definite lack of air superiority, limited airborne early warning capability, inadequate satellite communication and advanced intelligence systems, and shortage of reliable guided missiles or anti-missile countermeasures. A fatal blow on an aircraft carrier or on a troop-carrying liner would have, in all probability, caused the suspension of the entire enterprise and yet such eventuality could not be excluded. In view of such critical setting, the United States are believed to have contributed enormously in order to avoid the British undertaking end up in a military disaster. All decisive weaponry was asked for and rapidly furnished by American inventories.[186]

On another level of active collaboration, less susceptible to money evaluation, the United States are believed to have provided advanced satellite communication channels and crucial intelligence services. According to certain sources, the detection of the position of the *General Belgrano*, the breaking of the Argentine military codes, and the communication between the fleet headquarters and the deployed nuclear submarines are all to be credited to the US Pentagon. Almost 98 per cent of British intelligence was gathered by American sources. It has even been suggested that Britain persuaded the American government to move a military satellite from its ordinary orbit over the southern hemisphere to cover the South Atlantic war zone. The British had, nevertheless, to buy US $4 million-worth of satellite communication equipment from the United States.

Far more indispensable for the recapture of the islands proved to be the USAF Wideawake air base on Britain's Ascension Island. The air base was soon capable of coping with an air traffic exceeding that of Chicago's airport. Kerosene stockpiles on the island were turned over to British planes while another 12.5 million gallons of aviation fuel had to be diverted from American defence supplies. As an indication of the close military planning between US and British officials, it has been contended that US Defence Secretary Caspar Weinberger had worked out contigency plans according to which, should anything happen to either of the British carriers, the United States would immediately replace it by the amphibious assault ship *USS Guam* which in the event would be transferred to the Royal Navy.[187]

[186]As many as 200 Sidewinder, AIM-9L air-to-air missiles which accounted for most of the Argentine 'kills', Harpoon anti-ship missiles, Stinger anti-aircraft systems, a complete Vulcan Phalanx anti-missile gun system mounted on *HMS Illustrious*, Shrike air-to-ground radar-seeking missiles, and thousands of tons of ammunition were transferred to Ascension Island and forwarded to British units. The arms and matériel so provided are estimated at well over US $60 million-worth.

[187]Most of the preceding information on the US role draws on 'America's Falklands War', *The Economist*, 3 March 1984, pp. 23–5. The British ambassador in Washington at that time, Sir Nicholas Henderson, evaluating the overall American stance in the crisis had this to say: 'some measure of the significance

Chile is also known to have gained profits by offering military concessions to Britain during the Falklands conflict in defiance of its declared neutrality. Under the terms of a secret package deal, arranged with the Pinochet government by John Heath, the British ambassador at Santiago, RAF could use the southern Chile base of Punta Arenas to fly reconnaissance missions with Canberra PR9 spy planes which would be finally turned over to the Chilean air force. It is estimated, that at least six Canberras were flown secretly to Belize, repainted in Chilean markings and forwarded in mid-April of 1982 to Punta Arenas. It was also agreed, that SAS special units should be allowed to infiltrate from southern Chile into Argentina for sabotage missions, probably destruction of Argentine aircraft on the ground, and that the Chilean Naval Intelligence staff should pass any information such as codebreaking of Argentine signals to British forces.[188]

Argentina, for its part, sought and received assistance in the form of either direct arms sales or grants of military equipment from a very limited number of countries. Israel stood as its major source of arms and the deliveries included as many as 20 Dagger fighters, 24 American-built A-4 Skyhawk fighters, a large number of Gabriel air-to-ship and Shafrir air-to-air missiles and spare parts for US-made weapons systems. While Israel was officially assuring London of its attitude of non-interference, press accounts confirmed confidently that arms sales to Argentina were going on 'par le biais de multiples stratagèmes'.[189]

Moreover, Argentina's critical need for intelligence was served by the Soviet Union. Soviet Bear reconnaissance aircraft and

---

of American support for Britain over the Falklands can be gathered by imagining what it would have been like for Britain to have been detached from its most powerful ally as we were at Suez. From my discussions with service leaders since the events, I conclude that it is difficult to exaggerate the difference that America's support made to the military outcome'; see *The Economist*, 12 November 1983 at p. 60.

[188]The *quid pro quo* arrangement provided for the transfer of six Canberras and eight Hawker Hunter aircraft to Chile, relaxation of British restrictions on arms sales to Chile, collaboration in nuclear research programmes, and diplomatic support within the United Nations over the issue of the Chilean human rights record. Yet other allegations alluded to an Antarctic base, Adelaide Island, offered by the British in exchange for permanent rights to use the remote Chilean air base of Diego Ramirez; see the revealing journalistic account on 'The Chilean Connection', *The New Statesman*, 25 January 1985, pp. 8–10.

[189]See KLICH, I., 'Israel et l'Amérique Latine', *Le Monde Diplomatique*, février 1983 at p. 17. See also BEITHALLAHMI, B., *The Israeli Connection – Who Israel Arms and Why*, 1987 at p. 102.

military imaging reconnaissance (MIR) satellites were reported to have supplied signals intelligence, communications intelligence, electronic intelligence and satellite intelligence to Argentina. Finally, three Latin American countries, Peru, Venezuela and Brazil, responded to Argentine requests by possibly transferring a small number of French Mirages and Exocet missiles as well as spare parts and aviation fuel. Four other countries, Libya, Saudi Arabia, South Africa and Ecuador, were involved in supplying missiles to Argentina in conditions which resembled more those of black market.[190]

B The 1980–8 Persian Gulf War

The Persian Gulf Market: A Global Pattern All experts agree that the Iran-Iraq War broke out at a moment of general decline in the global arms trade.[191] Throughout the 1980s, however, statistics showed clear signs of 'recovery' owing principally to the phenomenal volume of arms trade in the Gulf which did not leave disinterested any industrialized nation of the world. Analysts are unanimous that the intensity and the universality of the arms flow were simply unprecedented.

Arms exporters acted upon a global pattern, seeking to sell the most sophisticated of their products but still not willing to give any of the belligerents the potential of inflicting a decisive defeat.[192] All foreign policy or legal constraints were quickly drowned in the arms export wave. Forgery and bribery were extensively practised, cracks in the legislation exploited, and customs controls relaxed; above all, deep secrecy was solicited in order to achieve gains at no political cost. Before long, however, practically all western nations found themselves, one way or

[190]The part on the suppliers of Argentina relies heavily on SLAUGHTER, R.L., 'The Politics and Nature of the Conventional Arms Transfer Process During a Military Engagement: The Falklands-Malvinas Case', 4 *Arms Control* (1983), p. 16*ff*.

[191]The persistent world economic recession, the sharp debt crisis in the Third World and the market saturation during the 1970s contributed to arms transfers agreements with Third World countries plunging from US $46.8 billion in 1982 to US $24.7 billion in 1983, or a drop of 47 per cent; see KLARE, M.T., 'New Merchants in the Arms Bazaar', 41 *Bulletin of the Atomic Scientists* (Jan.1985) at p. 15.

[192]To offer but one example, it was reported in 1987 that the US Central Intelligence Agency had supplied deliberately distorted intelligence information and falsified satellite photographs to both belligerents in an effort to ensure that neither of them built up a commanding position; see 33 *KRWE* (1987) at p. 35160.

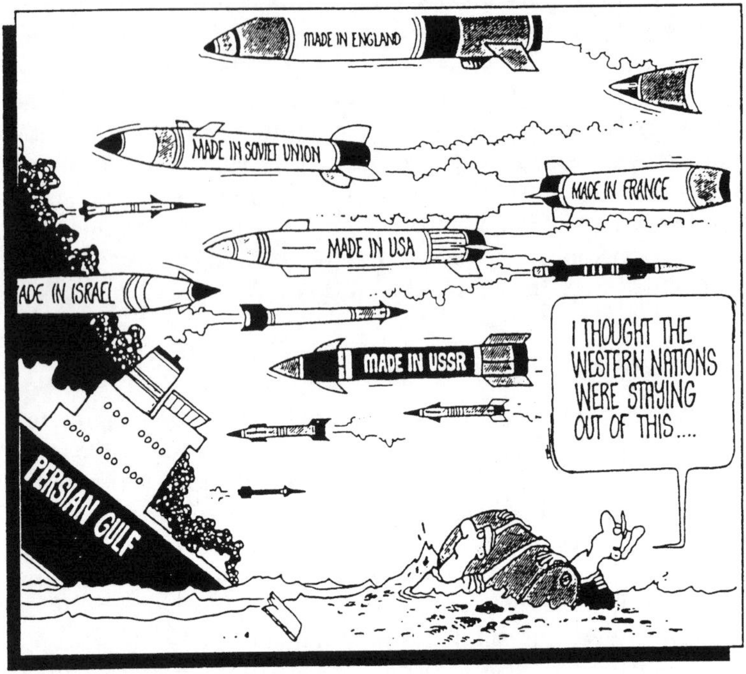

Figure 14 *The Gulf Tanker War and the Neutrals*
Source: 41 *Bulletin of the Atomic Scientists* (Jan.1985) at p. 16. © Reaside/ Rothco

the other, embroiled in controversies over what was invariably termed illegal arms shipments to the Persian Gulf.[193] In 1986 a survey by the Stockholm International Peace Research Institute raised the total number of countries fuelling the Iran-Iraq War to fifty-three, or, to put it allegorically, one-third of the 'peace-loving' United Nations member states. Even more startling, twenty-eight of these countries saw no reason why they should not let their weaponry land on both banks of the Shatt-al-Arab.

According to one estimate, Iran and Iraq have jointly spent

[193]Among the most recent studies, see DE BOCK, W. and DENIAU, J.-C., *Des armes pour l'Iran – L'Irangate européen,* 1988; MATTHEWS, R., 'The Neutrals as Gunrunners', 35 *Orbis* (1991), p. 41*ff*.; VINCINEAU, M., 'Les ventes d'armes à l'Irak avant la deuxième guerre du Golfe' in Centre de Droit International, Université Libre de Bruxelles, *La guerre du Golfe et le droit international,* 1991, p. 137*ff*.; KRAUSE, K., 'Transferts d'armement et gestion des conflits: Le cas de la guerre Iran-Irak', 4 *Cultures et Conflits* (1992), p. 13*ff*.

US $64 billion in the period 1980–7 to acquire implements of war for their mutual annihilation.[194] Iran and Iraq's tremendous appetite for instruments of war in the period 1980–8 was satisfied only by consuming 25 per cent of all Third World military imports.[195] Only one-third of this mammoth trafficking was effected by private dealers, the other two-thirds slipping through state controlled channels.[196] To assert that the arms commerce of such gigantic proportions was carried through without government knowledge, or that it is to be credited exclusively to blackmarketeers, cannot stand up any serious scrutiny.[197]

Arms Exports Imbroglios: A Challenge to Public Conscience With the quest for arms nearing its apogee in the Persian Gulf, one of the most stupefying revelations was made: the United States

[194]See KLARE, M.T., 'Deadly Convergence: The Perils of the Arms Trade', 6 *World Policy Journal* (1988–9) at p. 141.
[195]See *Ybk.SIPRI* (1990) at p. 246. Iraq is listed in the first place among the Middle Eastern countries in overall arms imports between 1983–7 with US $15.7 billion worth of matériel; see COUVRAT, J.-F. and PLESS, N., *La face cachée de l'économie mondiale*, p. 117*ff*.
[196]BRZOSKA, M., 'Profiteering on the Iran-Iraq War', 43 *Bulletin of the Atomic Scientists* (June 1987) at p. 42.
[197]In the words of Judge Mohammed Bedjaoui what the Iran-Iraq War most remarkably evidenced was 'pour la première fois, semble-t-il, dans l'histoire de la polémologie, l'existence d'Etats nombreux qui, toute sympathie exclue pour la cause de l'un et de l'autre belligérants ont massivement fourni des armes simultanément à l'un et à l'autre camps et je pèse mes mots. Il ne s'agissait pas là sans doute simplement de l'application impitoyable de la loi du commerce international des armes, il semblait bien aussi que l'on pouvait relever dans cette manière de servir indistinctement les deux belligérants à la fois en armes et en autres moyens de destruction réciproque une stratégie d'affaiblissement des belligérants jusqu'à leur commune extinction ... le droit international ne serait porteur ni de la paix ni de justice, s'il devait rester indifférent à des situations de cette nature'; see Centre de Droit International, Université Paris X-Nanterre, *Les aspects juridiques de la crise et de la guerre du Golfe – Actes du colloque des 7 et 8 juin 1991*, 1991 at p. 88. While in November 1990, commenting on the poor showing of the Security Council in the context of the Iran-Iraq War, he noticed: 'there is absolutely no getting away from the comparison between the 1980–8 Gulf War and the present crisis in the Gulf. Now the Security Council has taken in ten weeks more decisions than it took in eight years previously, when an actual war was raging ... The most that emanated from the Security Council was an occasional request that third states "refrain from any action likely to intensify or widen the conflict". One could hardly be more culpably mild'; see BEDJAOUI, M., 'The Gulf War of 1980–1988 and the Islamic Conception of International Law' in DEKKER, I.F. and POST, H.H.G. (eds), *The Gulf War of 1980–1988: The Iran-Iraq War in International Legal Perspective*, 1992 at p. 281.

while counselling abstention and neutrality,[198] had surreptitiously been shipping arms to Iran. The very same senior advisers of the National Security Council who had recommended Operation Staunch[199] against the Ayatollah's regime had all the same covertly channelled arms to Teheran.[200] If it was not for the clandestine arms shipments to Iran in 1986, the United States could perhaps safely claim the title of the most self-restrained arms exporter in the context of the Iran-Iraq War.

On 12 November 1986, President Reagan admitted to having initiated the arms transfers and announced that without his knowledge profits from the sale had been transferred to the contras, the Nicaraguan rebels. The revelations led to the dismissal of Colonel Oliver North, and the resignation of the National Security Adviser Vice Admiral John Poindexter. Five Congressional committees probed into what came to be known as the Irangate affair.[201] Far beyond the military advantage that

[198]It should be remembered that President Carter had stated on 22 September 1980 that the US attitude would be one of 'strict impartiality'; see 27 *KCA* (1981) at p. 31011.

[199]Operation Staunch, launched in spring 1983, was designed to dissuade those nations aligned with the United States from supplying weapons to Iran. Up to when the first accounts on the Irangate affair leaked, the campaign was moderately successful with the US having persuaded Argentina, Italy, Portugal, South Korea and Spain to cancel planned exports to Iran.

[200]On 3 November 1986, the *Al Shiraa*, a pro-Syrian Lebanese newspaper, disclosed that the United States had clandestinely sold arms to Iran and that Robert McFarlane, former US National Security Adviser, had visited Teheran to meet Iranian officials.

[201]In August 1985, McFarlane had briefed President Reagan on Israel's proposal to sell US-made TOW anti-tank missiles to Iran and obtained the White House's approval. The sale was intended to facilitate the liberation of the American hostages held by pro-Iranian groups in Lebanon. By mid-September, a load of 500 TOWs had reached Iran while an American hostage had been freed. In November the sale of Hawk anti-aircraft missiles was similarly arranged. On 17 January 1986, Reagan signed an order authorizing the Central Intelligence Agency to purchase 4,000 TOWs from the Defence Department and to sell them to Iran via Israel. One shipment of these missiles was accompanied by McFarlane on a secret visit to Teheran. In July 1986, seven more tons of US-made weapons systems were delivered to Iran via Spain and Yugoslavia. For a short account of Irangate, see HIRO, D., *The Longest War: The Iran-Iraq Military Conflict*, 1989, p. 215ff. For a critical review of the Report of the Congressional Committees Investigating the Iran-Contra Affair, see BANKS, W.C., 'While Congress Slept: The Iran-Contra Affair and Institutional Responsibility for Covert Operations', 14 *Syracuse Journal of International Law and Commerce* (1988), p. 291*ff*. For other commentaries, see JENKINS, E. and BRINK, R.H., 'The National Security Council and the Iran-Contra Affair', 18 *Georgia Journal of International and Comparative Law* (1988), p. 19*ff*.; KOH, H.H., 'Why the President (Almost) Always Wins in Foreign Affairs: Lessons of the Iran-Contra Affair', 97 *YLJ* (1988), p. 1255*ff*.;

the few thousand missiles may have given to Iran, the US covert sales carried a hurtful symbolism; the country which had shown the staunchest opposition to the Ayatollah's regime still found it acceptable to disregard domestic laws and do business with it. In the words of the official United States Congressional Report 'the common ingredients of the Iran and Contra policies were secrecy, deception, and disdain for the law'.[202]

The French arms transfer policy *vis-à-vis* the Gulf belligerents is often cited as the most eloquent example of a country's effort to intensify its arms sales in the pursuit of definite economic gains, despite pledges of non-involvement. France had been receiving every year, since 1976, regular Iraqi orders for military equipment and regularly furnished armaments in quantities that only the Soviet Union surpassed.[203] The frequent answer to criticisms was that should France fail to exploit the Iraqi need for war matériel, Iraq 'peut se tourner vers d'autres',[204] which made the then Iranian President A.H. Banisadr accuse France of 'pretended neutrality'.[205]

SHARPE, K.E., 'The Real Cause of Irangate', 68 *Foreign Policy* (1987), p. 19*ff.*; Symposium, 'Legal and Policy Issues in the Iran-Contra Affair: Intelligence Oversight in a Democracy', 11 *Houston Journal of International Law* (1988), pp. 7–270. For a brief analysis of the various statutory rules applicable in the affair, see SCHEFFER, D.J., 'U.S. Law and the Iran-Contra Affair', 81 *AJIL* (1987), p. 696*ff.*

[202]During the Kuwait crisis in autumn 1990, it was further revealed that the US Commerce Department had approved as many as 14 export shipments to Iraq between 1985 and 1990 that directly helped Baghdad's development of nuclear, chemical and ballistic missile capabilities.

[203]In the period 1974–80, Iraq filed orders with French industries for 200 helicopters, 60 Mirage aircraft, 320 armoured vehicles and large stocks of guided missiles. When hostilities broke out over the Shatt-al-Arab boundary, none of these items had been delivered. In the ensuing eight years of war, despite temporary freezes and hesitations, France delivered considerable amounts of weaponry to Iraq. By 1982, Iraq was already absorbing 40 per cent of all arms exported by France. The value of the exports was estimated at US $40 million a week, or US $2,100 million a year; see HIRO, *op. cit., supra* n.201 at p. 165. For a detailed analysis of the orientations and incentives of the French Gulf policies, see METGE, P., 'La France dans le conflit irano-irakien: Commerce d'armes ou guerre par procurations?', 7 *Paix et Conflits* (1984), p. 3*ff.*

[204]Statement of the French Foreign Minister J. Francois-Poncet in late September 1980, as quoted in METGE, *op. cit., supra* at p. 7.

[205]On the other hand, *l'affaire Luchaire*, to the extent it became publicly known, concerned regular illegal shipments of artillery consumables to Iran between 1983 and 1986 by the French firm Luchaire, with the consent and political coverage of Defence Minister Charles Hernu and other top government officials; see ZAKS, A. and GIRONDEAU, G., 'Les affaires Luchaire: Le gouvernement français éclaboussé' in *L'Europe des armes*, Collection GRIP-informations, no.16–17, p. 21*ff.* For the full text of the Rapport Barba, the official investigation report on the Luchaire scandal, see DE BOCK and DENIAU, *op. cit., supra* n.193, p. 247*ff.*

The French approach to the Gulf War can be best described as a typical slide from professed neutrality to unreserved non-belligerency. For the first two years at least, the official statements concerning the Iran-Iraq War alluded to a French policy of non-involvement, cautiously avoiding, however, any explicit reference to classical neutrality. On 3 May 1982, the Foreign Minister had this to say:

> La position française sur le conflit irako-iranien est connue: la France déplore ce conflit bilatéral qui, tout en provoquant des pertes humaines et des destructions matérielles considérables, constitue un facteur de déstabilisation dans la région. Elle estime que la seule solution juste et durable réside dans un règlement politique négocié reconnaissant les droits légitimes des deux parties et garantissant notamment leur intégrité et leur souveraineté contre toute forme d'ingérence extérieure, dans un cadre internationalement reconnu.[206]

It was only in June 1983 that France came to designate Iran as aggressor, when Iran refused to heed a ceasefire after having recaptured all the territories originally invaded by Iraq and turned on the offensive. At that time the following declaration was made: 'nous apporterons notre soutien à l'Irak... parce que ce pays est agressé sur son sol et que le monde arabe a au sommet de Fès, reconnu que cette agression l'affectait dans son

[206]See 28 *AFDI* (1982) at p. 1095. The delivery of Mirage aircraft to Iraq in 1981 was justified solely on grounds of faithful execution of contracts concluded prior to the outbreak of hostilities. Note the following statement of the French Foreign Minister of 18 May 1981: 'Le Gouvernement a autorisé la livraison de Mirage à l'Irak en se fondant sur les deux considèrations suivantes: la nécessité d'honorer les contrats signés, dont dépend la crédibilité de notre pays auprès de ses partenaires actuels et potentiels; la date de conclusion du contrat relatif à cette fourniture (juillet 1977) qui est antérieure au conflit irako-iranien. L'application de ce contrat ne saurait donc être considérée comme une intervention dans un conflit sur lequel le Gouvernement a pris immédiatement une position très claire. Comme le ministre des affaires étrangères a eu l'occasion de le déclarer à plusieurs reprises, la France n'est nullement impliquée dans le différend de nature bilatérale qui oppose Bagdad et Téhéran. Elle souhaite que ce différend trouve le plus rapidement possible une solution par la négociation. Son action diplomatique s'exerce dans ce sens. En outre, le principe de l'exécution des contrats conclus vaut aussi bien pour l'Iran que pour l'Irak. Aussi, dès que la décision prise dans le cadre des Neuf de ne plus livrer de matériels militaires à l'Iran a été levée, le Gouvernement a-t-il fait savoir aux autorités iraniennes qu'il était disposé à autoriser la livraison des vedettes commandées par l'Iran'; see 27 *AFDI* (1981) at p. 859.

ensemble'.[207] Moreover, the French Foreign Minister identified the objectives of the new policy of qualified neutrality in these words: 'notre rôle vis-à-vis de cette guerre . . . n'est pas de participer à la guerre avec l'Iran ni de donner a l'Irak des facilités d'agression . . . les avions dont on parle actuellement seraient, le cas échéant, un élément parmi d'autres de rééquilibrage des forces à un moment où le gouvernement irakien renouvelle ses offres de négociations'.[208]

The Soviet Union, despite its formal stance of neutrality,[209] is known to have satisfied 85 per cent of Iraq's military needs in the years 1976–80 and 53 per cent of the same market in 1980–9, while its exports to Iran were significantly lower. The aggregate Soviet arms sales to Iraq for the period 1980–9 were of an estimated value of US $13,396 million, the Soviet Union thus figuring as by far the leading arms supplier to the Gulf belliger-

[207]See 29 *AFDI* (1983) at p. 909. By the time the Iran-Iraq War had entered its twenty-ninth month, France decided to deliver another 29 Mirage F1 aircraft to Iraq. Five Super-Etendard attack-bombers were also to be supplied 'on loan'. The latter were formally decommissioned from the French airforce, repainted and flew to Iraq. On 28 October 1983, the French President set clearly the genuine priorities of the French policy by announcing that 'les Super-Etendards sont là où ils doivent être si la France respecte ses contracts'; *ibid.* at p. 854. The transfer of the five Super-Etendard was later qualified as a 'vente classique'; see 30 *AFDI* (1984) at p. 952. The aircraft, however, were returned to France, apparently upon the expiration of a two-year lease term, in September 1985 with the further agreement that another 24 Mirage F1 would be soon bearing the Iraqi colours on their wings; see 31 *AFDI* (1985) at pp. 962–3.

[208]*Ibid.* The contradictions of the French arms supply policies were later acknowledged by President Mitterand himself: 'donc, nous vendons en effet des armes. Le problème pour nous est d'éviter d'alimenter les lieux où se déroulent des combats. Je pourrais dire que *je me trouve en contradiction dans un seul cas, c'est celui de la guerre entre l'Irak et l'Iran*' (emphasis added); see 30 *AFDI* (1984) at p. 951. Jean Charpentier, who signs the anthology of the French international practice in the *Annuaire Français de Droit International*, prefaces his commentary on the rubric *ventes d'armes* as follows: 'décidément, la question des ventes d'armes est le domaine de prédilection de l'hypocrisie, pour ne pas dire de la duplicité gouvernementale'; see 31 *AFDI* (1985) at p. 962. France continued her indecipherable course, professing at one time strict impartiality and at another whole-hearted support for peace-loving Iraq. While the Elysée was affirming that 'la France n'a pas choisi son camp; il se trouve qu'elle a une amitié, elle ne veut pas avoir un ennemi', [the Quai d'Orsay was informing the Senate that] 'nous avons continué à apporter un soutien à celui des deux belligérants qui acceptait toutes les propositions faites pour la paix, qui acceptait toutes les résolutions des Nations Unies et qui cherchait ardemment la paix'; *ibid.* at pp. 1012–13.

[209]It should be remembered that on 25 September 1980, it was announced that Soviet Foreign Minister Andrei Gromyko and his US counterpart Edmund Muskie had agreed to preserve neutrality in the conflict; see 27 *KCA* (1981) at p. 31011.

ents.[210] But even during periods of Soviet reluctance both belligerents had assured access to Soviet-made weaponry. Iraq received armoured vehicles, arms and ammunition from countries such as Czechoslovakia, Hungary, Romania, Poland, Egypt, North Korea, Yugoslavia and China. Iran, on the other hand, had to turn to Libya, Syria, North Korea and China. Other reports have suggested that Iran received tanks, missiles, fighter aircraft and artillery equipment from several Warsaw Pact states.[211]

As regards China, its most serious contribution to the intensification of the Gulf War proved to be the delivery of Silkworm cruise missiles to both belligerents. Although an accurate assessment of the Chinese arms exports remains difficult, it is believed that in the period 1985–9 China sold US $1,488 million-worth of arms to Iran and US $988 million to Iraq.[212] During the war, China accounted for 50 per cent of Iranian and 80 per cent of Iraqi imports of military hardware.[213] Some estimates suggest that overall China exported US $8 billion in arms to both belligerents during their war.

The Federal Republic of Germany proved mainly involved in Iraq's plans for strategic weapons production. Plentiful revelations came to light in the aftermath of the Iraqi invasion of Kuwait in August 1990.[214] Several West German chemical companies have since been accused of having master-minded the construction of the Iraqi chemical plant at Samarra (capable of producing mustard and nerve gases) while others have been linked to biological weapons production and the transfer of nuclear technology.[215] The West German Finance Minister announced consequently that as many as fifty-nine firms were under investigation in an apparent move to ease criticisms over

[210]See *Fact Sheet*, *op.cit.*, *supra* n.7 at p. 5.
[211]See *Ybk.SIPRI* (1990) at pp. 246–7.
[212]See *Ybk.SIPRI* (1991) at p. 209.
[213]See *Ybk.SIPRI* (1989) at p. 197.
[214]See 'Who Armed Baghdad?', *Time*, 11 February 1991, p. 26*ff*.; 'The German Connection', *Newsweek*, 4 February 1991 at p. 37; 'A New Regime for Arms Sales', *International Herald Tribune*, 14 February 1991 at p. 6; 'Make Arms, Not War?', *Economist*, 16 February 1991, p. 23*ff*.
[215]See CHARLES, D., 'Exporting Trouble – West Germany's Freewheeling Nuclear Business', 45 *Bulletin of the Atomic Scientists* (1989), p. 21*ff*.; BRZOSKA, M., 'Behind the German Export Scandals', 45 *Bulletin of the Atomic Scientists* (1989), p. 32*ff*.; ALBRIGHT, D. and HIBBS, M., 'Iraq's Shop-till-you-drop Nuclear Program', 48 *Bulletin of the Atomic Scientists* (1992), p. 27*ff*.

governmental liability in the transactions with Baghdad. The War Weapon Control Act and the Foreign Trade Act went through several amendments in 1990–1 and now provides for new export limitations on dual-use technology, increased penalties for violators and more scrupulous licensing procedures.[216]

The British policy during the Iran-Iraq War revealed two facets worth analysing. First, the British government seemed to link its official stance of neutrality directly to a general prohibition to export arms to belligerents. Repeatedly in the first three years of the conflict, the British government offered assurances that it had not supplied either belligerent with any war materials, as its neutrality was deemed to imply. The Minister of State in the Foreign and Commonwealth Office, responding to questions posed in the House of Commons, wrote in March 1982:

> sales of arms and military equipment are subject to customary licensing procedures. Applications are considered in the light of all relevant circumstances, including our relations with the countries involved and, in the case of Iran and Iraq, *our neutrality during the present state of hostilities.* (emphasis added)[217]

The second interesting aspect of the British attitude is the shift as from 1983 in the arms transfer policy which appeared to suggest that not the export of *any* but that of *lethal* defence equipment should be prohibited on account of Britain's neutrality. As Douglas Hurd declared at the time: 'we are neutral in this war and we have not supplied *lethal equipment* to either side' (emphasis added).[218]

[216]See WULF, H., 'German Defence Exports: Laws and Rules', 15 *Military Technology* (Nov.1991), p. 56*ff.*, and Id., 'The Federal Republic of Germany' in ANTHONY, *op. cit., supra* n.133, p. 72*ff.* See also 37 *KRWE* (1991) at p. 38020.

[217]See 53 *BYIL* (1982) at p. 559. And again in November of the same year: 'we are neutral in the war and *we have not supplied arms or ammunition to either side'* (emphasis added), ibid.

[218]See 54 *BYIL* (1983) at p. 549. And in June 1984, in the course of a parliamentary debate, this position was restated: 'I repeat that our policy is one of neutrality and a refusal to sell *lethal arms* to either side. We believe that it would be both constructive and helpful if all nations followed that policy' (emphasis added); see 55 *BYIL* (1984) at p. 597. See also 57 *BYIL* (1986) at p. 644, and 58 *BYIL* (1987) at p. 638. The set of guidelines that London decided to apply to all deliveries of defence equipment to Iran and Iraq as of December 1984 read as follows: '(i) we should maintain our consistent refusal to supply any lethal equipment to either side; (ii) subject to that overriding consideration, we should

Leaving aside the vague 'lethality' criterion,[219] it is important to note that in the mind of the British government the faithful execution of contracts criterion is subject to the 'overriding consideration' of not letting the belligerents replenish their war machines by importing weapons – contrary to what has been noticed, for instance, with respect to the French policies. The drafting of these guidelines, however, does not permit confident conclusions as to whether the British government halted arms deliveries, or whether it would be generally willing to halt arms deliveries under similar circumstances, as a matter of expediency, or as a matter of legal obligation flowing from its much emphasized neutrality.

Italy, lacking until very recently a comprehensive legal framework, followed throughout the Iran-Iraq War a virtually unrestrained policy of arms exporting. In the years 1982–8, for instance, Rome is believed to have exported US $132 million worth of arms to Iraq (mainly helicopters and missiles). Italy's biggest bank financed to a great extent the Iraqi arms procurement programme around the world. In another concrete instance of such trade, the Valsella Meccanotecnica Co. had produced, between 1981 and 1984, 250,000 anti-personnel mines for Iran in cooperation with Bofors of Sweden. It has been reported that until the belated ban on arms sales in mid-1987, Rome had renewed or issued thirty-nine authorizations for arms sales to Iran and Iraq.[220]

---

attempt to fulfil existing contracts and obligations; (iii) we should not, in future, approve orders for any defence equipment which, in our view, would significantly enhance the capability of either side to prolong or exacerbate the conflict; (iv) in line with this policy, we should continue to scrutinise rigorously all applications for export licences for the supply of defence equipment to Iran and Iraq'; see 56 *BYIL* (1985) at p. 534.

[219]In Pearson's view, 'the criteria of conflict exacerbation and prolongation can be even more subjective than weapon lethality'; see PEARSON, F.S., 'Problems and Prospects of Arms Transfer Limitations Among Second-Tier Suppliers: The Cases of France, the United Kingdom and the Federal Republic of Germany' in OHLSON, *op. cit., supra* n.69 at p. 138. The transfer of Plessey radars to the Khomeini regime in 1986, or the sale of 58 armoured personnel carriers to Iraq in 1982–3, may be said to illustrate what Whitehall meant by non-lethal weapons; see SCHMITZ, M., 'L'Europe des marchands d'armes: Un tableau très hétéroclite' in *L'Europe des armes*, Collection GRIP-informations, no.16–17 at p. 144. On another occasion, in April 1984 the Foreign and Commonwealth Office confirmed reports that Iranian personnel were receiving training in England in the operation of Swiss-made anti-aircraft fire control systems; see 30 *KCA* (1984) at p. 33058.

[220]See HIRO, *op. cit., supra* n.201 at pp. 231–2.

Yet, in June 1984, the Italian Minister for Relations with the Parliament had expressed the view of the Italian government concerning the arms trade with the Gulf belligerents in the following terms:

> on the level of military supplies, the two countries had been, before the conflict, important purchasers in our arms industries. For this reason, since the start of hostilities and even more at the present stage, the Government has decided to maintain a policy of scrupulous vigilance, believing that it is its *duty* to refrain from any act that might increase the level of the armed conflict. We have been following this restrictive policy not only as far as new military supplies are concerned . . . but also with regard to *previous commitments*. In fact, while taking into account the necessity to respect contracts that have already been signed, for obvious reasons of credibility and good faith at the international level, we have avoided supporting, with Italian supplies, any attempt to staunchly pursue the conflict to the bitter end, or, worse still, to raise its threshold. (emphasis added)[221]

The chain of industrialized nations that kept propelling the war effort in the Gulf is long and stretches around the globe. Brazil's striking performance in marketing domestically developed weaponry was closely linked to spinning out of the Iran-Iraq War. It has been reckoned that the Persian Gulf market represented 40 per cent of Brazil's total military exports between 1985 and 1989.[222] Brazil typifies the emerging arms-exporting country which sought to consolidate its defence industrial base by feeding the gargantuan needs of Iran and Iraq without the slightest restraint.[223] Figures show that Brazilian weapons satis-

[221]See 7 *It.YIL* (1986–7) at pp. 470–1. This is, no doubt, one of the rare statements which refers implicitly to abstention from shipping arms to belligerents as an international obligation incumbent upon states. What is more, the Italian policy statement would seem to envisage the suspension even of those contracts concluded before the Gulf War broke out.

[222]See *Ybk.SIPRI* (1990) at p. 247.

[223]By 1986, arms had replaced coffee beans as Brazil's principal foreign exchange earner; see MATTHEWS, *op. cit., supra* n.193 at p. 44. In many respects Brazil's expanding industrialization, or the Brazilian economic miracle as some prefer to call it, has been spurred by military production and thriving arms exports. For a critical insight into Brazil's defence industry, see BRIGAGAO, C., 'The Brazilian Arms Industry', 40 *Journal of International Affairs* (1986), p. 101*ff.*

fied 4 per cent of the aggregate Iraqi demand for arms throughout the 1980s.

The attitudes of the so-called European neutrals merit a particularly thoughtful examination. Sweden's illegal transactions so far disentangled by the media, political parties and several commissions of inquiry pertain to shipments of missile systems to Iran by Sweden's leading arms company, Bofors, to large ammunition deliveries to Iran by another Swedish firm Nitro Nobel AB, as well as to other shadowy arms sales by the state-owned company FFV.[224] As regards the missiles supplied to Iran, the illicit trade was channelled through several South East Asian countries, notably Singapore and Thailand, both faithful clients of AB Bofors. The arms were then forwarded to Middle Eastern end-users particularly Bahrain, Oman and Iran.[225]

In arming the Gulf belligerents, Switzerland's participation was peripheral, yet not negligible.[226] Bern is believed to have delivered to Iraq and Iran more than 120 aircraft, Pilatus and others, officially classified as trainers. In 1983, for example, the weapons sales to Iraq peaked at US $38 million, while as late as 1987 the Swiss Confederation kept furnishing arms in the amount of US $21 million, by far exceeding the respective arms sales of countries like the UK and Germany.[227] Despite growing concern over the probable military use of Pilatus planes by the Gulf belligerents, deliveries were not frozen even after it was widely rumoured that the Swiss-made aircraft were used in Iraqi gas attacks against Kurdish villages. More indirectly, the Swiss firm EMS-Patrag, specializing in weapon ignition systems, was implicated in the Bofors scandal, while huge quantities of aluminium products were ordered by Iran's war ministry from Alusuisse. In Austria, illegal transactions with Tehran and Baghdad created a major political scandal. The Noricum ord-

[224]See AGRELL, W., 'La Suède et les affaires Bofors: La fin d'un mythe?' in *L'Europe des armes*, Collection GRIP-informations, no.16–17, p. 47*ff*. See also DE BOCK and DENIAU, *op. cit., supra* n.193, p. 64*ff*.

[225]The five-member Citizen's Commission on Arms Exports, set up to investigate the country's controversial practices, recommended that arms exports be continued 'when it is deemed necessary to ensure a requisite supply of equipment to the Swedish defence forces and when it is compatible with the principles and aims of Sweden's foreign policy'; cited in HAWES, *op. cit., supra* n.171 at p. 185.

[226]See SCHMITZ, M., 'La loi suisse sur les ventes d'armes: Un véritable gruyère' in *L'Europe des armes*, Collection GRIP-informations, no.16–17, p. 15*ff*.

[227]See *Fact Sheet, op.cit., supra* n.7 at p. 6.

nance and the Hirtenberger munition factories, subsidiaries of the state-owned Voest-Alpine AG, were revealed to have delivered over 200 howitzers to Iraq and 140 of the same type to Iran in 1985–6. Several high officials and statesmen were implicated, among them the former Austrian Chancellor Fred Sinowatz.[228]

During the 1980s, Belgium became a major transit-state of illegal arms shipments to countries like Iran or Iraq.[229] Reports speak, for instance, of forty vessels having completed at least sixty voyages in 1985–6, plying between the Belgian ports of Anvers and Zeebrugge and the Iranian port of Bandar Abbas. The cargo almost invariably included military equipment seemingly destined for Honduras, Paraguay, Argentina, Kenya or Nigeria. It has been established that the Belgian firm Transammo and Poudreries Réunies de Belgique S.A. regularly supplied Iran with ammunition while another Belgian firm, ASCO, was accused of having imported US military equipment and having re-exported it to Iran. The illegal deliveries were piped through Italian (Tivena), Greek (Elviemek) or Spanish (Empressa Nacional Santa Barbara) companies engaged in falsifying documents in order to conceal the real destination.

The official attitude of Brussels has been to deny all allegations of government complicity. As Members of the Belgian government often pointed out, although they could not exclude the possibility of Belgian weapons being found in the hands of belligerents, they could nonetheless assure that such weapons would have been exported illegally. As was stated in December 1984 before the Belgian parliament:

> je puis néanmoins assurer à l'honorable membre qu'en vertu de *la politique constante du gouvernement belge d'interdire toute fourniture de ce genre de matériel à des pays impliqués dans un conflit armé*, aucune licence de transit n'a été délivrée

[228]In February 1991, fourteen industrialists were convicted of violating Austrian neutrality and legislation on war matériel; see 37 *KRWE* (1991) at p. 38020. According to a 1982 enactment, exports of weapons should not be allowed *inter alia* to areas of armed conflict or where other dangerous tensions exist. For more on Austrian regulations and policies, see WULF, H., 'Austria' in ANTHONY, *op. cit., supra* n.133, p. 24*ff.*; LOIBL, G. and BRANDSTETTER, W., 'The Amendments of the Austrian Legal Provisions Concerning the Export and Transit of War Materials and the Gulf Crisis 1990/91', 43 *Austrian Journal of Public and International Law* (1992), p. 73*ff.*

[229]See ADAM, B., 'La Belgique, plaque tournante du trafic d'armes' in *L'Europe des armes*, Collection GRIP-informations, no.16–17, p. 35*ff.*

> pour l'Iran depuis que ce pays est en guerre. Il est exclu, dès lors que des armes qui lui sont expédiées par des pays tiers soient transbordées de façon légale dans nos ports ou aéroports. (emphasis added)[230]

During the Gulf War, several Dutch industries were often reported to have supplied defence equipment to belligerents. On the Iranian side, the Damen Scheepswerven shipyards constructed ten tankers, the Holwerde and the Muiden Chemie companies exported large quantities of explosives and ammunition. On the other hand, companies such as the KBS Holland BV, Melchemie Holland BV or Oldelft furnished, among other things, strategic chemical substances and night vision equipment to Iraq.[231] Other transactions, such as the delivery of Fokker F-27 jet aircraft to Iran, fell in the grey area of so-called dual-purpose equipment. Yet, the Dutch government took pains on every possible occasion to declare its official neutrality. In reply, for instance, to allegations that the Royal Dutch airlines agreed to carry out maintenance work on Iranian civil aircraft with a military character the following statement was issued: 'the Government wishes to maintain its attitude of *absolute impartiality* in the war between Iran and Iraq'. (emphasis added)[232]

According to estimates, during the Gulf War Czechoslovakia exported to Iraq weapons worth US $614 million, or 2 per cent of all Iraqi imports for the period 1980–9.[233] In the 1991 edition of the Stockholm International Peace Research Institute's yearbook, Czechoslovakia is listed to have forwarded in 1986–90 US $251 million-worth of matériel to Iran and US $132 million to Iraq.[234] For their part, Greece and Portugal responded promptly to Iraq and Iran's endless quest for light ammunition. The Danish Elsinore shipyards are believed to have delivered to Iraq three landing vessels in 1983, while the Finnish firms Forcit and

[230]See 20 *RBDI* (1987) at p. 340. And Foreign Minister Tindemans declared in April 1985 that 'si dans le conflit du Golfe des armes belges sont utilisées, les pays belligérants doivent les avoir importées de façon illégale', *ibid.* at p. 341.
[231]See SCHMITZ, *op. cit., supra* n.219 at pp. 140–1.
[232]See 16 *NYIL* (1985) at pp. 416–17. And when a squadron of Dutch and Belgian minesweepers was deployed in the Persian Gulf, the Dutch government repeated with caution: 'the Government wishes to emphasize that its decision to send mine-hunters in no way alters its *strictly neutral stance* in the conflict between Iran and Iraq' (emphasis added); see 19 *NYIL* (1988) at p. 360.
[233]See *Fact Sheet, op.cit., supra* n.7 at p. 5.
[234]See *Ybk.SIPRI* (1991) at p. 209.

Kemira sent large quantities of chemicals to Iran through Yugoslavia. The Iraqi inventory included also helicopters from Spain and Canada, fighter aircraft from Egypt, cluster bombs from Chile and small arms from Pakistan. Iran, on the other hand, had to turn to Israel, South Korea and Taiwan for loads of spare parts of US-made weapons.[235]

Beyond Confusing Deeds and Words: An End Note By way of recapitulation, it is crucial to appreciate the thrust of the various national structures reviewed here. First, it needs to be stressed that most of the leading industrial powers, when they decided to enact national legal prescriptions for their arms exports in late 1920s and early 1930s, found it pertinent to lay down a prohibition of arms exports as a matter of general principle. Most of these laws remain still today in force. Selling and exporting arms to foreign countries was envisaged, and is still perceived following the letter of these decrees, as only exceptionally permissible.

The second aspect of the numerous national control mechanisms examined above, is the true meaning and legal implications of arms export licensing, now a standard feature in the legislation of almost every arms-producing country. It may be said that the institutionalization of a compulsory licensing procedure involving governmental decision-making has ended all discussion or doubt as to who is ultimately responsible for arms exports. Although the 'private' arms industries may still be responsible for the substantive part of the construction, commercialization and even the negotiation of foreign contracts, as soon

[235]The recently ended war in Bosnia-Herzegovina presents a clearly different case and will not be addressed here. In fact, since September 1991 a UN embargo on all arms shipments to warring factions in former Yugoslavia was enforced so that the question of neutral rights and duties did not arise in that context; see Security Council Resolution 713 (1991) at para.6, Security Council Resolution 724 (1991) at para.5(a), Security Council Resolution 727 (1992) at para.6, Security Council Resolution 740 (1992) at para.8. Despite the mandatory embargo, however, a flow of arms of considerable proportions is believed to have fuelled the fighting. Slovenia and Croatia have reportedly spent US $150 million on arms imports from Lebanon, the former Soviet Union, several countries of Eastern Europe (particularly Hungary and Romania), South Africa, Singapore, but also from German and Austrian sources. For more, see PEARSON, F.S., BRZOSKA, M. and CRANTZ, C., 'The Effects of Arms Transfers on Wars and Peace Negotiations', *Ybk.SIPRI* (1992), p. 407*ff.*, and 'Yugoslav Crisis Renews Debate on Ending Bosnian Arms Embargo', 23 *Arms Control Today* (May 1993) at p. 21.

as they apply for an export licence to be accorded by the state they cannot be deemed responsible for the export itself. The decision to bestow the export permit divests the transaction of any private character it might originally have had and transforms it into a governmental one.

The universality of the licensing system leads, therefore, to the conclusion that as much in theory as in practice, and with the exception of clandestine arms trafficking, private arms exports proper are virtually non-existent.[236] To be noted also, in this respect, the finding of the Royal Commission on the Private Manufacture of and Trading in Arms in its Report of October 1936:

> important as we feel the moral and humanitarian considerations that have been advanced to be, they do not, in our opinion, afford sufficient ground for abolishing the private industry in this country, but we think it is the duty of the government, on general grounds, to subject the industry to such measures of public regulation and control as would *establish clearly that its conduct is a matter of government responsibility.* (emphasis added)[237]

This is precisely the reason why all the murky arms deals that often made headlines during the Iran-Iraq War were invariably treated as punishable frauds which had one way or the other escaped government scrutiny; to admit that all administrative procedures had been well respected would have given rise to grave charges of government duplicity. What is more, in most cases governments promptly investigated the illegal transactions, parliaments enacted stricter controls and courts pronounced on criminal charges. To put it another way, in none of these cases did the government in question find it justified to come to the defence of the right of private citizens to sell arms to belligerents in a situation of professed neutrality. Nor has a government ever pretended impartiality by affirming that

[236]For some, however, 'the fact that the Government permits export which it could prevent by means of withholding the licence does not make it a party to the transaction. Its responsibility is engaged only when in thus acting it discriminates between the opposing belligerents'; see LAUTERPACHT, H. (ed.), *Oppenheim's International Law,* 7th edn (1952), vol.II at p. 658.

[237]See *Cmd.5292,* §56 at p. 24. And further in the same document: '*the government's ultimate responsibility for whatever consequences may result from the export of arms abroad is incontestable*' (emphasis added); *ibid.,* §145 at p. 48.

both belligerents could contract for arms without fear of discrimination. And yet, these are the very prescriptions of the Hague law of 1907.

Certainly there is nothing new in what has just been said. The view that significant changes in global socio-economic structures since the days of the Hague Conventions had an impact on matters of arms transactions has no claim to novelty in legal science. Writing in 1938, on the 'gradual intrusion of the state into spheres which constituted formerly a reserve of the individual', Wolfgang Friedmann pointed out that 'the control of the arms trade is perhaps the one field in which the change from private to state control can be said to be sufficiently definite and general not only to have destroyed the old law but also to make possible an outline of the new law', and concluded that '*a general consensus of state practice* has already destroyed the customary rule of law that a neutral state need not prevent the export of war materials to belligerents' (emphasis added).[238]

[238]FRIEDMANN, W., 'The Growth of State Control Over the Individual, and Its Effect Upon the Rules of International State Responsibility', 19 *BYIL* (1938) at pp. 135–6. Lawrence Preuss, in a somewhat more moderate commentary, suggested that 'even though mere control has no positive legal effect upon neutral duties at the present time, it seems probable that it will in the future have the effect of accelerating the extension of governmental duties of neutral prevention into the sphere within which it may now permit individual freedom of action. Throughout the history of neutrality, there has been a constant progression and cumulation of neutral duties of impartiality, abstention and prevention'; see PREUSS, L., 'Some Effects of Governmental Controls on Neutral Duties', 31 *Proc.ASIL* (1937) at pp. 118–19. As for Jean-Florien Lalive, drawing upon the previous works, he noted that although 'le développement de l'étatisme a eu pour conséquence d'affaiblir la portée de la distinction entre les *actes publics* et les *actes privés* qui est à la base du droit de neutralité traditionnel [il serait] prématuré de soutenir que l'augmentation des devoirs d'abstention et de prévention (conséquence d'un étatisme toujours grandissant) appartient aujourd'hui au droit positif. C'est de nouveau attribuer au droit de neutralité un caractère rigide qu'il n'a pas du tout'; see LALIVE, J-F., *Le droit de la neutralité et le problème des crédits consentis par les neutres aux belligérants*, 1941 at pp. 176, 186. While Robert Tucker speaks of the 'gradual invalidation of an assumption fundamental to almost the whole of the traditional law of neutrality – that a clear distinction could be drawn between the public and private spheres and that the neutral state would not enter into economic activities long considered outside its proper functions'; see TUCKER, *op. cit., supra* n.9 at p. 194. And Judge Ammoun in his Separate Opinion in the Namibia case of 1971 pointed out: 'governments must show due diligence in preventing any individual or collective act contrary to neutrality. This obligation relates to nationals and subjects, and to foreign residents. Showing due diligence means that adequate measures must be taken, including legislative measures providing for penalties. For a State which undertakes an obligation commits its own subjects and those who live under its law, and must employ every kind of means, legislative, administrative and judicial,

VI The threshold of abstention: the law in the books

Unlike the growing interest, accrued over the last twenty years, in the political issues of world military expenditures and arms trade, the academic community seems to have gone through a period of intellectual aphasia concerning the legal questions of war and neutrality. And yet, war shows no signs of retraction from being the 'ultimate *arbiter rerum*', while neutrality continues to be 'suspended between an ideology which denies its premises and a reality which finds it useful, if not necessary'.[239] The array of authorities who have debated the subject in the post-war period is neither long nor impressive. For the most part, carefully made, one might say balanced, assessments that lead no further than the point to which Wolfgang Friedmann had taken us when he wrote still before the war:

> it is far more difficult to say what law, at the present stage has replaced the old one. The new practice, which is developing through international treaties ... has probably not yet hardened into a legal rule. All one can say is that a new customary rule is in the process of formation.[240]

Doctrinal Opinions: Divided as Ever For some jurists, contemporary neutrality is only conceivable as imposing a blanket prohibition to supply arms to countries at war, regardless whether the trade involves state or private companies. Note, for instance, the view of Francis Deák: 'obviously, the relief of a neutral state from the duty of preventing trade in war materials by private individuals – whether nationals or alien residents in that country – no longer has justification'.[241] In the same vein,

---

by which it governs. It is not therefore sufficient to refuse diplomatic protection to those who transgress'; see Legal Consequences for States of the Continued Presence of South Africa in Namibia (South West Africa) notwithstanding Security Council Resolution 276 (1970), *ICJ Rep. 1971*, §14 at p. 95.

[239]See NORTON, *op. cit., supra* n.131 at p. 249.

[240]See FRIEDMANN, *op. cit., supra* n.238 at p. 137.

[241]See DEÁK, F., 'Neutrality Revisited', in FRIEDMANN, W., HENKIN, L. and LISSITZYN, O. (eds), *Transnational Law in a Changing Society: Essays in Honour of Phillip C. Jessup*, 1972 at p. 153. In a much earlier publication, it was argued that 'la notion de contrebande absolue doit être énergiquement maintenue, et qu'alors, modifiant comme il convient l'art.7 de la 5e Convention de La Haye, on doit considérer comme dérogatoire à la neutralité leur envoi à un belligérant'; see DUMAS, J., *Les aspects économiques du droit de prise avant la guerre mondiale*, tome I (1926) at p. 162. And elsewhere: 'peut-être objectera-t-on que c'est là un

Walter Williams argues that 'the developing trend of customary law is that a neutral state is under a duty to take all reasonable measures to prevent provision of materials and other assistance to a belligerent by individuals and associations under its control'.[242] One of the clearest statements espousing that view is to be found in the 1992 German military manual which reads:

> state practice has modified the former conventional rule that a neutral state is not bound to prohibit export and transit of war matériel by private persons for the benefit of one of the parties to the conflict (Art.7 HC V). To the extent to which arms export is subject to control by the state, the

point de vue d'ordre moral et non pas d'ordre économique, parce que l'esprit de lucre est la condition même de l'activité économique, et que l'appréciation des produits fabriqués doit se faire, non pas d'après l'usage licite ou illicite auquel ils peuvent servir, mais d'après leur plus ou moins grand degré de rareté et de désirabilité . . . Raisonner ainsi, ce n'est pas seulement méconnaître la part qu'il convient de réserver aux intérêts généraux de l'Humanité dans l'évaluation du profit qui résulte d'une production déterminée, mais c'est encore formuler un sophisme économique puisque l'on compte à l'actif de la production des objets qui ne servent qu'à la destruction et qui n'ont aucun emploi possible en dehors de leur rôle destructif. La richesse d'une nation se compose de l'ensemble de ses forces productives, et classer au rang de celles-ci des forces qui ne sont susceptibles d'être utilisées que pour la destruction, c'est exactement comme si, dans une statistique démographique, on ajoutait le nombre des morts au nombre des vivants, ou si, dans un bilan, on additionnait l'actif et le passif pour calculer leur différence qu'une soustraction seule peut faire apparaître', *ibid.* at pp. 163–4.

[242]See WILLIAMS, W.L., 'Neutrality in Modern Armed Conflicts: A Survey of the Developing Law', 90 *MLR* (1980) at p. 33. As for Natalino Ronzitti, he subscribes to the view that 'en ce qui concerne le transfert d'armes, la distinction entre le commerce d'Etat, qui est interdit, et le commerce des particuliers, qui est admis, n'a probablement aucune raison d'être retenue, car aujourd'hui le commerce d'armes est totalement entre les mains de l'Etat ou, du moins, sous le contrôle étatique'; see RONZITTI, N., 'Le droit humanitaire applicable aux conflits armés en mer', 242 *RCADI* (1993) at p. 123. For his part, Maurice Torrelli, in one of the latest essays on modern neutrality, refers to 'l'évolution consistant à limiter voire à interdire les prêts à des belligérants et la fourniture de matériel de guerre car dans la mesure où les exportations d'armes sont pratiquement soumises à des licences d'exportation, la vieille distinction du droit de la Haye peut difficilement trouver à s'appliquer aujourd'hui'; see TORRELLI, M., 'La neutralité en question', 96 *RGDIP* (1992) at p. 25. Likewise, another study concludes that 'the concept of a strict separation between the spheres of national policy conducted by state organs on the one hand and an autonomous sphere of private commercial activity on the other hand is nothing but a fiction today'; see OETER, S., *Neutralität und Waffenhandel*, 1992 at p. 256. Note also the following commentary: 'l'Etat qui autorise une firme privée à vendre des armes à un belligérant se distingue mal de l'Etat qui procède directement à cette vente, et par conséquent, l'interdiction qui s'applique au second devrait également s'appliquer au premier'; see DAVID, E., 'Le droit de la neutralité à l'épreuve de la guerre du Golfe (1980–1988)', *Cahier du Cedsi*, no.11, Grenoble, 1990 at p. 44.

> permission of such export is to be considered as unneutral service.[243]

Other scholars defend the thesis that to abstain from shipping arms to a theatre of war has become an imperative of the modern law of peace, quite irrespective of neutrality considerations, without, however, making it clear whether they write *de lege ferenda* or *de lege lata*. Says Romain Yakemtchouk:

> le coeur de la problématique des transferts internationaux d'armes et le critère de base qui doit servir à leur éventuelle réglementation, c'est l'interdiction des envois d'armes aux pays du champ de bataille: par qui que ce soit, par quelle voie que ce soit, avec ou sans l'embargo décidé au niveau de l'Organisation internationale.[244]

In the view of Andrea Gioia,

> modern practice shows a tendency to impose on all States not party to an armed conflict certain duties, flowing from

[243]See *ZDv 15/2 Humanitäres Völkerrecht in bewaffneten Konflikten – Handbüch* [Humanitarian Law in Armed Conflicts – Handbook], August 1992, para.1112 at p. 114. While Michael Bothe in his latest report for the ILA's Maritime Neutrality Committee expressed serious doubt whether Article 7 can be still regarded as part of international customary law: 'the following text is taken from Articles 6 and 8 of Hague Convention no.XIII which, it is submitted, constitute the expression of customary rules of international law. It has to be noted that according to the rules relating to naval warfare, duty of abstention implies a duty to control private activities which may be helpful for a belligerent. Whether the same applies nowadays also in relation to activities on land and to export of war materials is a question which remains to be discussed if and when this or another Committee will deal with more general issues of neutrality'; see *Report on Neutrality and Naval Warfare* for ILA's Buenos Aires Conference (1994), commentary on para.1.5. Note also the explicit terms of an earlier report: '*de lege ferenda*, it is highly desirable to introduce a duty of neutral states to control and restrict private activities like arms exports or engaging in foreign military service . . . *Thus, a strict control – or still better: a simple prohibition of arms exports to belligerent countries – appears to be the desirable rule*' (emphasis added); see 65 *Rep.ILA* (1992), Cairo Conference, para.1.6 at p. 168.

[244]See YAKEMTCHOUK, R., 'Le respect de la destination des armes acquises à l'étranger: La clause de finalité d'emploi et de non-reexportation', 24 *AFDI* (1978) at p. 149. And elsewhere: 'nous disons: il faut les interdire tous les deux [government and private arms sales], car quelle que soit la provenance de ces transferts, leur finalité est la même. Aujourd'hui, il n'y a pas d'acquéreurs privés d'armements: c'est l'Etat qui les achète et qui en est responsable politiquement et juridiquement. Par conséquent, les transactions et les livraisons privées n'ont lieu que sous le contrôle de l'Etat, qui doit en être responsable, lui aussi, politiquement et juridiquement'; see YAKEMTCHOUK, R.,'Le transit international des armes de guerre', 83 *RGDIP* (1979) at p. 413.

> principles other than the principle of impartiality, that neutral States did not have under the traditional law of neutrality: for example, as far as the trade in arms and war materials is concerned, it is possible to detect a tendency to impose upon all States a duty to abstain – as well as a duty to prevent private persons – from supplying belligerents with arms the employment of which is prohibited under the *jus in bello*, such as chemical and biological weapons, and from helping belligerents to produce such arms.[245]

Arto Kosonen supports the idea of an automatic arms embargo *vis-à-vis* the belligerents, but only as a *de lege ferenda* proposition: 'it would be better, if the neutral states would have a certain kind of legal duty to undertake at least some measures in regard to all (severe) armed conflicts. At this point of the study this would include first of all stopping of military export to all (state) parties to these conflicts – totally irrespective of their geographical position which could possibly be far from the actual source of the crisis'.[246]

For another segment of the regrettably poor literature, the idea of an arms embargo against warring nations, despite perhaps its logic and moral force, has always fallen short of proving its legally binding character. Louis Dubouis, for instance, writing in 1967, expressed the view that 'vis-à-vis d'un Etat en guerre l'embargo est licite mais non obligatoire, tout en tendant, au moins en droit à échapper à la compétence des Etats'.[247] In the same vein, Jean-Claude Martinez considers that the principle proscribing arms exports to countries at war 'semble découler

[245]See GIOIA, A., 'Neutrality and Non-Belligerency' in POST, H.H.G. (ed.), *International Economic Law and Armed Conflict*, 1994 at p. 109.

[246]See KOSONEN, A., 'New Legal Horizons of Neutrality and Military Export', *Finnish Branch of International Law Association 1946–1986, Essays on International Law*, 1987 at p. 106. Elsewhere in his study, Kosonen supports the view that distinguishing between state and private exports would be meaningless: 'one can somewhat safely argue that already the world-wide existence of peacetime licence systems . . . supports the view that nowadays private arms export must be subscribed to the state . . . with the exception of illegal transfers over the border of the state – it is the state alone that has the responsibility for all military export, not only in wartime, but in all circumstances. This approach is also in quite a good harmony with the view according to which military export is a matter connected to foreign politics in such a total way that the control of the whole arms business must be in the hands of the state from manufacture to possible export and even after this event'; *ibid.* at pp. 103–4.

[247]See DUBOUIS, L., 'L'embargo dans la pratique contemporaine', 13 *AFDI* (1967) at p. 116.

logiquement des règles de la neutralité ... semble a priori aller de soi ... [mais] sa force obligatoire reste incertaine'.[248]

By far the oddest thesis advanced by legal scholars is the one pleading the outright repeal of the duty of abstention for the neutral states. Although it seems to be fading today, that thesis, some thirty years ago, received support from such eminent authorities as Julius Stone and Wolfgang Friedmann. Writes Stone:

> trading activity of neutral Governments with belligerents should be assimilated to private trading in both respects. First, that the duty of the neutral Government not to supply arms, munitions or to grant loans should be abolished. Second, that the ships, and cargoes, and other instrumentalities of the neutral Government engaged in such trade should be subject to the ordinary penalties for contraband carriage, blockade breach, and the like, and should not enjoy the immunities ordinarily enjoyed by State owned ships and property.[249]

His view found renewed advocacy in Friedmann's writings; 'the equilibrium should be restored by assimilating the trading activities of neutral governments to private trading by relieving, on the one hand, neutral governments of their duties of abstention from supplies, loans, etc., to belligerents, and subjecting them, on the other hand, to the liabilities of search and seizure for contraband goods, to which private traders are exposed under the rules of international law'.[250]

It calls, no doubt, for reflection that there would be in our days thinkers inclined to uphold not the stiffening but, to the contrary, the relaxation of the legal framework elaborated at The

[248]See MARTINEZ, J.-C., 'Le droit international et le commerce des armes', *Société Française pour le Droit International – Le droit international et les armes*, Proceedings of the sixteenth SFDI colloquium at Montpellier 1982, 1983 at p. 160.

[249]See STONE, J., *Legal Controls of International Conflict*, 1959 at p. 413. Julius Stone admits that he was forced to such conclusion, for states 'are certainly still far from the point at which they commit economic self-immolation for the sake of the law of neutrality'; *ibid.*

[250]See FRIEDMANN, W., *The Changing Structure of International Law*, 1964 at p. 348. See also Id., 'Some Impacts of Social Organization on International Law', 50 *AJIL* (1956) at pp. 487–91. In much the same spirit Morris Greenspan concludes: 'only if a state-owned enterprise conducted its transactions on other than a purely commercial basis and discriminated in favor of a particular belligerent could there be real cause for complaint of breach of neutrality'; see GREENSPAN, M., *The Modern Law of Land Warfare*, 1959 at pp. 551–2.

Hague. For one thing, it is difficult to see what would remain of the concept of neutrality if the duty of abstention was to be extracted from its core.[251] And secondly, from a Charter perspective, to argue for the sheer liberalization of the international commerce of arms on the eve of the twenty-first century, and in terms that even the Hague Conferences had not dared to suggest, appears an inopportune retrogression in aims and means.

Finally, a number of scholars take satisfaction in simply stating the issue or find it inopportune to advance any proposal. Dietrich Schindler, for instance, commenting upon the Hague Convention XIII, contents himself with saying: 'only the suply of war materials by a neutral Power itself is prohibited (Article 6). This still seems to be the law in force today'.[252] Similarly, Dieter Fleck notes: 'but neutral states are still not bound to prevent their nationals from supplying one of the parties to the conflict with war material, as explicitly stated in Article 7 of Hague Convention No XIII. Rather, they have to avoid the application of different standards in their arms export control policies'.[253]

[251]Note apropos the pertinent remark by Oppenheim: 'at a time when warfare is becoming increasingly mechanised, to permit a neutral State as such to supply the belligerents with vast masses of arms, munitions, and implements of war might amount to rendering its neutrality purely nominal'; see LAUTERPACHT, *op. cit.*, *supra* n.236 at p. 658.

[252]See SCHINDLER, D., 'Commentary on the 1907 Hague Convention XIII' in RONZITTI, N. (ed.), *The Law of Naval Warfare*, 1988 at p. 216. Note also the Report of the Swiss Federal Council on the Swiss foreign policy of the 1990s, dated 29 November 1993: 'ce droit de l'Etat neutre à commercer librement par la voie terrestre ou maritime a d'ailleurs été codifié dans les Conventions de La Haye de 1907. De fait, il est même stipulé à l'article 7 de la Ve Convention (. . .) qu'une puissance neutre n'est pas tenue d'empêcher l'exportation ou le transit, pour le compte de l'un ou de l'autre des belligérants, d'armes, de munitions et, en général, de tout ce qui peut être utile à une armée ou à une flotte'; see 4 *RSDIE* (1994/5) at p. 637.

[253]See FLECK, D., 'Comments on F.V. Russo's paper' in DEKKER, I.F. and POST, H.H.G. (eds), *The Gulf War of 1980–1988: The Iran-Iraq War in International Legal Perspective*, 1992 at p. 196. See also DELBRÜCK, J., 'International Traffic in Arms – Legal and Political Aspects of a Long Neglected Problem of Arms Control and Disarmament', 24 *GYIL* (1981), pp. 114–43; Id., 'Arms Traffic' in BERNHARDT, R. (ed.), *Encyclopedia of Public International Law*, instalment 3 (1982), pp. 38–40; ROUSSEAU, C., *Le droit des conflits armés*, 1983, §248, pp. 394–7.

VII In search of positive law: the moral dimension

There is no doubt that the principles of international law governing the issues of neutrality and arms trade announce a crucial moral dimension. The problematic reconciliation of the practice of selling arms with the status of declared neutrality, by moral standards, has not escaped attention. In a speech before the United States Senate, Senator Works had said in January 1916:

> I believe the trade to be immoral and demoralizing to the people of the United States. I believe that most of the complications that have grown up between this and foreign nations now at war have been the result of the trade in munitions of war. I believe that if it had not been for the fact that we are dealing in that nefarious trade, the people upon the *Lusitania* would not have lost their lives . . . We cannot justify ourselves in that position or in that trade by saying that it is allowed by the laws of neutrality. *There is something higher that should control the people of the United States than the mere strict law of neutrality.* (emphasis added)[254]

Morality vs. Legality As one might argue, the practice of selling arms to belligerents, while immoral, is not necessarily illegal. True, no one has ever asserted that enacted law is scheduled to function in a morally irreproachable fashion:

> a concept of law [says Hart] which allows the invalidity of law to be distinguished from its immorality, enables us to see the complexity and variety of these separate issues; whereas a narrow concept of law which denies legal validity to iniquitous rules may blind us to them.[255]

[254]Cited in GARNER, *op. cit., supra* n.77 at p. 399.
[255]See HART, H.L.A., *The Concept of Law,* 1961, at p. 207. Note also Nardin's view: 'no doubt the temptation is very great to regard the laws of war as a moral institution that ought to mirror our moral judgments about war or else suffer our rejection . . . The impulse to subject the law to moral scrutiny cannot be faulted . . . What is wrong with this propensity to *criticize* the laws of war for failing to provide defensible moral standards for making such judgments, is simply that the laws of war are not a moral code, but a legal one'; see NARDIN, T., 'The Laws of War and Moral Judgment', 3 *British Journal of International Studies* (1977), at pp. 134–5. For yet another thinker, 'it is a philosophical commonplace that legality and morality are not the same. What is legal may be

The immanent cry for justice and reform is precisely due to the imperfection of the law. The codes of rights and duties are not drafted solely at the behest of canons of morality. *Summum jus, summa injuria,* was the adage by which the Romans used to denote that applying law with rigour is not always administering justice in the sense of fairness and equity.

Morality is about right conduct and thus points to an ideal. Discrepancies, therefore, between the exigencies of a higher moral code and the letter of a negotiated *pactum* are inevitable. The problem discussed here from a moral analysis perspective should be phrased as follows: had it been possible to ascertain that the routine of shipping arms by whatever means to belligerents while professing neutrality, is universally recognized as morally objectionable, would then the moral evaluation suffice to mould a new principle of law consonant with its claim?

As Ralph Newman has depicted the dilemma in more general terms, 'the problem narrows to how we can most effectively apply moral values to the solution of problems of social control through law; how the moral convictions of the place and time can be formulated in terms appropriate for translation into legal norms'.[256] To explore then the borderline between the *legal being* and the *moral should,* or, as Fuller has put it, finding the proper resting place of the 'imaginary pointer that marks the line dividing *duty* from *aspiration*',[257] is to work with fine distinctions at best and tends to be rather conjectural; 'the line is difficult to draw at times, since it is constantly shifting, not that moral rules ever cease to be moral rules, but rather because many moral rules are adopted also as legal rules'.[258]

Morality and the Law of Nations To ponder on Vattel's thought that the state is a *moral person,* or Jellinek's definition of law as

immoral, and that what is moral may be illegal . . . the law does not try to be a perfect reflection of the moral universe or to make us perfectly moral . . . [although] laws that seem no longer tied to morality lose their grip on our conscience; laws that seem to flout morality inspire rebellion'; see COHEN, S.M., *Arms and Judgment: Law, Morality, and the Conduct of War in the Twentieth Century,* 1989, at pp. 7–8. In the same vein, see also HONORÉ, T., 'The Dependence of Morality on Law', 13 *Oxford Journal of Legal Studies* (1993), p. 1*ff.*

[256]See NEWMAN, R. (ed.), *Equity in the World's Legal Systems,* 1973 at p. 26.

[257]See FULLER, R.R., *The Morality of Law,* 1964 at p. 10.

[258]See WRIGHT, H., 'The Moral Bases of International Law', 35 *Proc.ASIL* (1941) at p. 55.

a *minimum éthique,* or again to look back at the age-old conflict between *nomos* and *physis* so magnificently impersonated in Antigone's hesitancy between obeying the laws of the *polis* or the voice of her moral conscience, would deflect this analysis to interminable philosophical inquiries. To enter the perennial debate between positivists and naturalists over the ontology of international law would likewise exceed our compass. It appears apposite, however, even at the risk of inconclusiveness to refer momentarily to the nexus linking international morality to international law. Moral discourse is an integral part of any legal essay: 'the content of law [wrote Alessandro d'Entrèves] is a moral one. Law is not only a measure of action. It is a pronouncement on its value.'[259] And Terry Nardin adds: 'international morality and international law are contingently as well as conceptually related. Few would deny that international law has from its origins been parasitic on moral ideas and that it continues to be so.'[260]

The moral foundations of the law of nations were never questioned, with the exception perhaps of the Machiavellian perception of state conduct.[261] The desire to secularize the law, however, lies in the origin of the intellectual stream which eventually led to the separation of moral discourse from modern jurisprudence. Liberating law from theology proceeded essentially through abating the tenor of moral oration. The rupture did not occur without consequences, or, as James Brown Scott colourfully pictured it, 'unfortunately it does seem to imply that the moral law is the law of the church and not of the state, and that the law with which we are concerned in the relations of individuals is the law of the state and not of the church. The trouble seems to have been that by the union of church and state, the church became political, without the state becoming

[259]D'ENTREVES, A.P., *Natural Law – An Introduction to Legal Philosophy,* 1951, at p. 80.

[260]See NARDIN, T., *Law, Morality and the Relations of States,* 1983, at p. 306.

[261]For a historical retrospective on theories of moral philosophy that carried weight in the development of international law, see ROEMER, W.F., *The Ethical Basis of International Law,* 1929. Natural law theories are also reviewed in VERDROSS, A. and KOECK, H.F., 'Natural Law: The Tradition of Universal Reason and Authority' in McDONALD, R.S.J. and JOHNSTON, D.M. (eds), *The Structure and Process of International Law: Essays in Legal Philosophy Doctrine and Theory,* 1983, p. 17*ff.*

moral. The law of the layman, is what we may call a six day law; the moral law is too often of the seventh day alone.'[262]

Yet even today, several thinkers would maintain that international law is not genuinely law but rather a loose code of universal morality.[263] Some would identify morality with international custom. Nardin, for example, concludes, although with some reservations, that 'the moral element in international law is to be found in those general principles of international association that constitute customary international law'.[264] Still others would search for morality in that large reservoir of principles *quo omnes gentes utuntur,* which we commonly call general principles of law.[265]

Despite the link between law and morality, however, little attention was paid in the past to moral claims in shaping and structuring international law principles. One can think of many reasons for the unenthusiastic analysis of the moral elements in the philosophy of international relations. There is a tendency, for example, to dismiss moral claims as sheer moralism, as nothing but the rationalization of simple desires. There is the problem of establishing standards by which to judge the content and the applicability of a system of moral values for the international community. Moreover, moral expectations, as a matter of everyday experience, are continually disappointed in the confused realm of international politics. In sum, the reign of legal positivism was precisely to this effect: to sterilize international law against any naturalistic influence, to fortify consent in the face of moral duty.

The challenge to the positivist doctrine came along with the

[262]See also SCOTT, J.B., 'A Single Standard of Morality for the Individual and the State', 26 *Proc.ASIL* (1932) at p. 10.

[263]For a painstaking attempt to refute such a theory, see HART, *op. cit., supra* n.255, p. 221*ff.*

[264]See NARDIN, *op. cit., supra* n.260 at p. 233.

[265]This is how Lord Asquith was led to speak of a 'modern law of nature'; see *Abu Dhabi Arbitration,* 18 *ILR* (1951) at p. 149. As Judge Tanaka declared some years later: 'it is undeniable that in Article 38, paragraph 1(c), some natural law elements are inherent. It extends the concept of the source of international law beyond the limit of legal positivism according to which, the States being bound only by their own will, international law is nothing but the law of the consent and auto-limitation of the State'; see South West Africa, Second Phase, Dissenting Opinion, *ICJ Rep. 1966* at p. 298. An attempt to formulate a list of principles of international morality is undertaken in POLITIS, N., *La morale internationale,* 1943, at pp. 51–153, and JENKS, C.W., *A New World of Law?,* 1969, at pp. 291–300.

dawn of the Charter era. In the decades that followed, the world community traced directions and endorsed ideas, bearing clearly the mark of the hitherto exorcised naturalism. Today, everyone agrees that the growth of human rights law, the ascendancy of notions of equity and distributive justice,[266] or the maturation of ideas such as the commonality of resources signal a return to some sort of natural law discourse. In the words of one scholar, 'this "moralization" of international law, the outstanding instances of which are the recognition of the dignity of the human person, the introduction of a ban on the use of force in international relations, as well as the strengthening of the international duty of cooperation, may be acclaimed as a decisive step forward on the way to the establishment of a genuine international community'.[267]

[266]Equity – wrote Herbert Kraus in his Hague course in 1927 – 'n'est pas autre chose qu'une manifestation spéciale de la justice sous un aspect ouvertement moral'; see KRAUS, H., 'La morale internationale', 16 *RCADI* (1927) at p. 506.

[267]See TOMUSCHAT, C., 'Ethos, Ethics and Morality in International Relations' in BERNHARDT, R. (ed.), *Encyclopedia of Public International Law,* instalment 9 (1986) at p. 134. Note also the following remark by Christian Dominicé: 'telle est bien la question qu'évoque aujourd'hui la notion de droit naturel. Non pas l'idée qu'il existerait un système de normes juridiques d'origine transcendante, mais plutôt l'idée que certaines règles du droit international sont identifiées comme telles en raison de la nature de leur contenu – particulièrement important du point de vue éthique – ou encore font l'objet d'un processus de création lui aussi quelque peu différent du mode usuel en raison du poids moral particulier attaché à leur teneur'; see DOMINICÉ, C., 'Le grand retour du droit naturel en droit des gens' in *Mélanges en l'honneur de Jacques-Michel Grossen*, 1992 at p. 401. See also DIMITRIJEVIC, V., 'A Natural or Moral Basis for International Law' in GRAHL-MADSEN, A. and TOMAN, J. (eds), *The Spirit of Uppsala*, 1984, p. 383*ff*., and GABOU, A., 'Le fondement naturel ou moral du droit international', *ibid.*, p. 397*ff*. In 1949, Judge Alvarez, referring to those profound changes which by far transcended old conceptions of law and morality, noted: 'in consequence of profound changes that had taken place in international relations, a new international law had arisen; it is founded on social interdependence . . . Briefly, it is the realization of social justice. It is entirely different from the old law, which was strictly juridical; it approaches nearer to the notion of equity, without however being merged in it. This new international law is not a *lex ferenda*, as is often believed; it has a real existence and it has essential and actual foundations'; see Corfu Channel case, Judgment of April 9, 1949, *ICJ Rep. 1949* at p. 40. It is true, of course, that the plain moralization of laws, that is, the subordination of laws to loosely defined ethics, is equally undesirable. In 1966, the World Court stated: 'humanitarian considerations may constitute the inspirational basis for rules of law, just as, for instance, the preambular parts of the United Nations Charter constitute the moral and political basis for the specific legal provisions thereafter set out. Such considerations do not, however, in themselves amount to rules of law. All States are interested – have an interest – in such matters. But the existence of an "interest" does not of itself entail that this interest is specifically juridical in character'; see South West Africa, Second

Morality and Legal Reform Much of the question relates essentially to the mystical process by which the transition from *lex ferenda* to *lex lata* could be fixed with certainty in time. Should we look stoically for the formal adoption of an international instrument, as the positivist cult of state-will seems to ordain, or is it legitimate to infer from accumulating state practice the emergence of a novel customary principle? In fact, manifestations of juridical conviction abound, and as O'Connell has observed, 'to await their final and conscious adoption by governmental authorities before deciding that *lex ferenda* has become *lex lata* is to impose on international law an unnecessary and frustrating halter'.[268] The dilemma highlights the broader issue of the system of sources of international law. In the words of Michel Virally:

> il en résulte une tension croissante entre la *lex lata* et la *lex ferenda* qui s'écartent sans cesse davantage dans une société en pleine mutation, et une tentation difficile à réprimer de passage de l'une à l'autre, c'est-à-dire de confusion, tant au niveau de l'affirmation (ou création) du droit, qu'à celui de son application. Comme à ses origines, on demande de plus en plus au droit international de transformer les rapports internationaux en y insufflant plus de justice, plutôt que de consacrer juridiquement (au risque de l'immobiliser) l'état actuel de leur évolution.[269]

Law and morality both function at the service of justice; 'there is one idea [writes Hart] that of justice which seems to unite both fields: it is both a virtue specially appropriate to law and the most legal of the virtues. We think and talk of "justice

Phase, Judgment, *ICJ Rep. 1966*, §50 at p. 34. While the International Law Association, in its Report on the *Theory and Methodology of International Law* of 1978, reflected the ambivalence prevailing among its members by noting that 'the existence of a moral duty or obligation may encourage the need for a legal rule but is not in itself legally enforceable', only to add, immediately after this, that 'the international community has not shown itself to be entirely irresponsible or insensitive' to principles of equity and distributive justice and that 'issues with a strong moral element have acquired great prominence in recent years ... It may be that a legal obligation carries more weight than a merely moral obligation, but where is no effective protection or enforcement machinery, it is certainly not unreasonable to question the value of calling a rule "legal" as opposed to anything else'; see 58 *Rep.ILA* (1978), Manila Conf. at pp. 191–2.

[268]See O'CONNELL, D.P., *International Law*, 2nd edn, 1970, vol.1 at p. 20.

[269]See VIRALLY, M., 'A propos de la *lex ferenda*' in *Mélanges offerts à Paul Reuter – Le droit international: Unité et diversité*, 1981 at p. 521.

according to law" and yet also of the justice or injustice *of* the laws' (italics in the original).[270] The demand for justice *lato sensu*, motivating force of all social change, relates to the call for harmonization of legal command with moral conviction.[271] This process is fated to incompletion *in perpetuum*, or for as long as the real lags behind the ideal. That there may exist, however, an incrongruity between established law and cherished morality should not make one believe that there is an element of vanity in aspiring to law reform.

Morality exerts a magnetizing effect on law, while law aims eternally at the embodiment of higher moral norms without always reaching them.[272] But as the gap between morality and law persists, and will *volens nolens* continue to exist, we should not lose sight of these fine words of caution offered by James Leslie Brierly, who passionately sought in ethics the ultimate foundations of international law:

> mais nous sommes tentés trop souvent d'oublier que la connexion qui lie le droit à la morale est réellement beaucoup plus fondamentale que la distinction qui existe entre elles, et que la base ultime de l'obligation à l'obéissance à la loi ne peut être que morale.[273]

Summing Up This analysis contends that legal orienteering, in a milieu of antiquated legal prescriptions, cannot operate in a

[270]See HART, *op. cit., supra* n.255 at p. 7.

[271]As Ginsberg correctly points out, 'what we aim at in dealing with changing law is an adjustment by means of the ethical considerations such that it can thenceforth be neutrally applied . . . Thus, while legal reasoning in its "normal" exercise has a practical logic of its own not explicitly ethical, yet the consideration of ethical principle is inevitable in the crucial reasoning of the law'; see GINSBERG, R., 'Legal Reasoning and Ethical Principles', in HUBIEN, H. (ed.), *Le raisonnement juridique – Actes du Congrès mondial de philosophie du droit et de philosophie sociale*, 1971, at pp. 496, 500.

[272]For Nicolas Politis, there is a linear path linking *comitas gentium*, morality and law. Arguing that, 'la courtoisie évolue vers la morale [et] la morale évolue vers le droit', he suggested that, 'on peut dire, dans une certaine mesure, que la morale est une courtoisie consolidée, codifiée . . . [et] que le droit est une morale rendue obligatoire et munie de plus grandes sanctions'; see POLITIS, *op. cit., supra* n.265 at p. 43.

[273]See BRIERLY, J.L., 'Le fondement du caractère obligatoire du droit international', 23 *RCADI* (1928) at p. 547. Or, as Richard Falk said succinctly, 'there is no necessary coincidence of moral and legal norms, although adherence to law rests ultimately upon the *moral confirmation* of its rules' (emphasis added); see FALK, R.A., *Law, Morality and War in the Contemporary World*, 1963, at p. 9.

moral vacuum.[274] Juridical anachronisms, such as the one examined here, to be remedied, need to respond sensitively to the environment of moral precepts at the time of reappraisal. To argue that the Hague Conventions of 1907 have preserved their validity up to our days would be essentially to paralyse all moral sensibilities which may have grown ripe throughout the present century.[275] In short, the content of law must be in accord with the evolving standards of morality that mark the progress of a maturing society. Contending that the remote Hague rules have frozen the law on the subject, all the rest being an elevating but immaterial excursion in the domain of higher ethics, is to deny that the law should be freed of the constraints of narrow legalism in the instances where the departure from elementary international moral standards is manifest.

VIII Concluding remarks

If law is to maintain a minimum contact with logic, it is unthinkable to argue that in the dawn of the twenty-first century, neutrals' obligations *vis-à-vis* ongoing conflicts are exhausted in the letter of Article 6 of the Thirteenth Hague Convention of 1907. To allow citizens to furnish armaments to countries in war is not only a violation of true neutrality but a defiance of fundamental principles of the United Nations Charter. The law of the Charter has superseded the law of neutrality in a most fundamental way; where one used to read *rights* and duties of neutral states with regard to a foreign war, at the time of the United Nations one should refer solely to *duties* of member states. It is indeed least credible to consider that the Charter, in

[274]In fact, conditions of a moral vacuum, or of lacunae in moral ideas, comparable to these in law, are hardly perceivable. As Herbert Kraus has put it convincingly, 'la morale, à l'inverse des autres branches prédesignées, remplit absolument tout le domain des relations internationales. Assurément on peut se représenter, au moins théoriquement, un espace vide de droit, une friche juridique, située en dehors de toute réglementation de droit international, où ne s'applique non plus aucune considération politique et où ne s'exerce aucun principe international. Mais il n'y a rien qui ne soit soumis à la loi morale, rien qui ne soit susceptible d'un jugement moral'; see KRAUS, *op. cit., supra* n.266 at p. 500.

[275]It is to be noted in this respect that validity should not be exclusively interpreted in a mechanistic or technical sense. For Aarnio, to name but one thinker, it should also mean efficacy *(factual validity)* and acceptability *(axiological validity)*, the latter implying the required conformity of a legal prescription to ethics and natural law; see AARNIO, A., *The Rational as Reasonable – A Treatise on Legal Justification*, 1987, p. 33*ff*.

the matter of an armed conflict, confers to its parties anything other than concern and shared responsibility in contributing to the fair and expeditious settlement of the conflict.

The once legitimate expectations of unimpeded economic gain, inborn in the traditional concept of neutrality, are today displaced by broader communal interests, in preserving the general well-being and peaceful coexistence through collective effort[276] Although states have not yet realized the full meaning of interdependence, or attained a *conscience planétaire,* to recall René-Jean Dupuy's dearest abstraction,[277] international law ethics can now claim to have veered away from state-centrism to universal human values, the defence of which cannot leave indifferent the entire international community.

In the preamble of the Charter, 'the *peoples* of the United Nations' commit themselves 'to practise tolerance and live together in peace with one another as good neighbours, and to unite [their] strength to maintain international peace and security', while in the terms of the General Assembly's Declaration on Friendly Relations, 'States parties to an international dispute, *as well as other States,* shall refrain from any action which may aggravate the situation so as to endanger the maintenance of international peace and security' (emphasis added). Would it not be consonant then with the philosophy of the Charter to infer from the principle that all states have a share in the responsibility not to allow international frictions to degenerate into disputes of threatening proportions, an equally heavy legal burden for the states witnessing an ongoing armed conflict not to provide the means which may allow the belligerents to go on with their conflict? One can hardly avoid the conclusion that the second-best option after UN conflict resolution is abstention from anything that could permit the continuation of killing.

Admittedly, states have refrained from codifying the prohibition into an international treaty rule. It is also true that the practice of *ad hoc* national arms embargoes can be generally seen

[276]As a recent UN study has put it, 'the international transfer of conventional arms is a unique part of international trade and relations; in the final analysis it involves tools designed to kill and destroy. It should not be therefore primarily driven by economic or commercial considerations'; see UN Doc. A/46/301, 9 September 1991, §148 at p. 49.

[277]See, for instance, DUPUY, R.-J., 'A la recherche d'un nouvel ordre mondial?', *Le Trimestre du Monde* (1992) at p. 13.

more as a vehicle of foreign policy interests than as a legal imperative connected with neutrality.[278] The thesis here submitted though is that, even in the absence of an appeal on the part of UN organs, third countries professing neutrality should remain under an obligation to prohibit and effectively prevent *all* military exports to states committed in an armed contest. There have been significant developments in the last seventy years which could sustain the conclusion that today. As a matter of ordinary policy, most of the arms-exporting states subscribe to the principle that no war material should be consigned to countries participating in an armed conflict, except when the United Nations Security Council has identified the aggressor, or when the provisions on collective self-defence are deemed applicable.[279]

Tracing the steps that paved the way in this long evolutionary

[278]An international arms embargo, of course, imposed by the United Nations presents a different situation. As Richard Baxter argued in 1968, 'an order or even a recommendation of this character must take precedence over any freedom a state would otherwise have to permit the provision of military supplies by private persons'; see BAXTER, R.R., 'The Legal Consequences of the Unlawful Use of Force Under the Charter', 62 *Proc.ASIL* (1968) at p. 73. On the few occasions that an arms embargo has been decided by the UN Security Council, it has been devised in the context of international sanctions under chapter VII of the Charter against a specific government, be it the South Rhodesian, Security Council Resolution 232(1966); the South African, Security Council Resolution 418(1977); the Iraqi, Security Council Resolution 661(1990); or, lately, the Libyan government, Security Council Resolution 748(1992) and the Haitian régime, Security Council Resolution 841(1993). In four recent cases, however, the Security Council imposed 'a general and complete embargo on all deliveries of weapons and military equipment' (of a preventive and not punitive character) to all parties of an armed conflict 'for the purposes of establishing peace and stability'; see Security Council Resolution 713 of 25 September 1991 on former Yugoslavia at para.6, Security Council Resolution 733 of 23 January 1992 on Somalia at para.5, Security Council Resolution 918 of 17 May 1994 on Rwanda at para.13, and Security Council Resolution 924 of 1 June 1994 on Yemen at para.2. See also S/PRST/1994/43 of 11 August 1994 concerning Afghanistan. For a general overview, see SCHRIJVER, N., 'The Use of Economic Sanctions by the UN Security Council: An International Perspective', in POST, H.H.G. (ed.), *International Economic Law and Armed Conflict*, 1994, p. 123*ff.*, and 'United Nations Arms Embargoes', *Ybk.SIPRI* (1994), pp. 493–502.

[279]As a recent essay concluded, 'support is found for the policy not to supply to combatants or states close to war, a policy formally adopted by several countries, unless one wants one side to win'; see PEARSON, BRZOSKA and CRANTZ, *op. cit.*, *supra* n.235 at p. 415. *Cf.* BOTHE, M. and MARAUHN, T., 'The Arms Trade: Comparative Aspects of Law', 26 *RBDI* (1993/1) at p. 42, who maintain that 'state practice is too diverse in order to derive a common standard from the confused material even less to be considered as a basis for an emerging rule of customary international law'.

process, one should first refer to *the decisive shift towards nationalization of arms production.* As the memories of the early days of the Industrial Revolution, which had seen the bulk of technological potential concentrated in private hands, were fading away, upon recovery from the shock of a World War, and under the strong instigation of the League, states thought it opportune to take such a sensitive concern away from private entrepreneurs. Parallel to the de-privatization of the arms industry, there was a move towards *concerted enactment of sweeping state controls on arms exports.* Where the state did not proceed to outright expropriation on the production level, it assumed responsibility on the foreign trade level through a compulsory licensing system. On the whole, the combined result of these two parameters was to erase the distinction between the state and private citizens as regards arms manufacture and their transfer to third states.

Next in the evolution of the idea of sheer incompatibility between formally declared neutrality and continued private arms trade came *the practice of instituting arms embargoes against states at war.* Although America's pioneering legislative experiment of the years 1935–9, stipulating an automatic arms embargo against both belligerents, did not show signs of durability, the use of *ad hoc* arms embargoes (perhaps less resolute, but politically more flexible) envisaging specific countries, preparing for, or, already engaged in armed conflict, becomes more and more an international practice. The ritual of introducing arms embargoes seems, nowadays, well respected, without it being, however, always clear whether they are decreed more out of a sense of legal obligation, moral constraint or mere political expediency.[280]

Along the same path of development, one should mention lastly *the Charter prescriptions which assign to every member state considerable responsibility for the preservation of world peace.* The proscription against facilitating the prolongation of a conflict by shipping war requisites to belligerents seems no longer to

[280]Remarks Robert Harkavy apropos of such practice and it is indeed difficult to disagree with his thought: 'the rationale for this type of embargo seems almost incomprehensible. It appears to be merely a demonstration of disapproval and now seems to have become a traditional ritual of self-righteousness on the part of arms suppliers who feel compelled, for the benefit of world opinion, to act outraged when their arms are finally put to use'; see HARKAVY, *op. cit., supra* n.15 at pp. 220–1.

emanate from an abstract and often fugitive appreciation of neutrality, but rather from stern and irrevocable commitments attached to United Nations membership.[281]

As a matter of empirical observation, it is to be noticed that states have long ceased to defend their nationals' 'right' to sell weapons to belligerents. States seem increasingly sensitive to revelations that they fan war flames by shipping arms to belligerent nations. Instances of clandestine arms trade with nations at war, whenever disclosed, are invariably exposed as scandals rather than as defensible ordinary commercial transactions. Many reasons may account for this; professing leadership in the guardianship of world ethics, cultivating a political profile compatible with United Nations principles, or fear of reprimand from public opinion – *mobilization of shame* is the expression used in the neigbouring domain of human rights. State practice, therefore, demonstrates increasingly the signs of consistency and uniformity that would point to an emerging international custom. As for the sentiment of legal obligation, it may be said to be spreading out, although at times it seems diluted in considerations of moral dictate or political suitability.[282]

The question discussed in this chapter, one should not fail to acknowledge, in the larger context of the preservation of world peace, is helplessly narrow. Even if neutrals came to recognize unreservedly their legal obligation not to furnish arms to belligerent nations, the problems of unrelenting world militarization and soaring trade in weaponry would still remain far from solved. If the arms race in peacetime is to keep up at the same hectic pace, to urge neutrals not to trade munitions of war with countries engaged in an armed conflict, and only for as long as the military engagements persist, would not make a potential aggressor any less pugnacious. It is believed, however, that to suspend the arms flow to the fighting armies once an

[281]In fact, should the world organization had been effective in discharging its responsibilities in full, neutrality would have lost even its academic interest, but this is a long way from being the case, or, in Patrick Norton's renowned words, 'caught between this reality and the failed ideal, the law of neutrality will continue its shadowy existence'. Neutrality, therefore, or its modern variants of 'strict impartiality' and 'non-interference', remain juridically valid and are frequently advanced as the prime motivation whenever states decide to suspend arms transfers to warring nations.

[282]On this point, see the remarks of HARKAVY, R.E., 'Arms Resupply During Conflict: A Framework for Analysis', 7 *Jerusalem Journal of International Relations* (1985) at p. 16.

armed conflict erupts is for the world community an absolute least.

No apology would be needed if we closed by reiterating that if neutrality is to fit into the larger Charter picture, if national governments are to discharge in full the responsibilities emanating from their sovereign power, and if, at last, morality is to claim any kinship with law, then the practices evidenced during the world's bloodiest conflict of the 1980s should never be reproduced under any pretext and certainly not in the name of a much deformed neutrality. To interpret the present state of affairs otherwise would be to confess the supremacy of a derailed pragmatism over law, or, to paraphrase Jefferson's credo: our defence industries have adamantly been seeking arms perfection and ruthlessly competing for foreign markets; to suppress these callings because a war exists in foreign and distant countries should not naively be expected; it would be highly Christian in principle but outrageous in practice.

'αλλ' ο πρώτος τα χρήματα νείρα των πραγμάτων προσειτών εις τα
τού πολέμου πράγματα μάλιστα βλέψας τούτ' ειπείν έοικε."

He who first declared that money is the sinews of the state seems to have said this with special reference to war

Plutarch, *Life of Cleomenes*, sect.27,
(transl. by B. Perrin, The Loeb Classical Library, 1959 at p. 111)

Chapter Six

PRIZE LAW REVISITED

I Introduction

Among the fundamental axioms of the laws of naval warfare as it has evolved over the last eight centuries, and one of the most striking dissimilarities with the law of land warfare, is that private property (enemy and to a lesser extent also neutral) encountered at sea is liable to confiscation. As Hugo Grotius argued in 1604 in his *De Jure Praedae,* as killing in war is not murder, so the capture of enemy property is not robbery.[1] It was only natural, therefore, that around such a central proposition a whole body of legal rules be erected regulating *who* can do *what* to *whom* and *how* in matters of seizure of ships and cargoes. In the interminable tug-of-war between belligerent and neutral interests through the centuries, the evolution of prize law has consisted in developing new antidotes to counteract fraudulent or casuistic practices.

Whenever neutral resourcefulness resorted to new techniques in order to evade belligerent constraints, admiralty courts had to elaborate fresh legal doctrines. Hence, when visit and search at sea became impracticable because of the cargo's volume, or simply ineffective by reason of false papers, prize courts were ready to uphold the legality of diverting merchantmen into port; when contraband shipments were smuggled into enemy territory through neighbouring neutral ports, judges came up with the doctrine of continuous voyage; and when continuous voyage became arduous to prove, 'irrefutable' evidence was sought and found in the form of presumptions and statistics.

[1]Quoted in DUMBAULD, E., 'Grotius on the Law of Prize', 1 *Journal of Public Law* (1952) at p. 381.

The picture is admirably depicted by Philip Jessup who asks: 'how can it ever fail to be true that the belligerent will wish to cut off *all* his enemy's commerce and that the neutral will wish to continue *all* his trade even with the parties at war?'[2] One answer, so finely given by Robert Tucker several years later, reminds us of the end at which any scholarly writing in the field should ultimately aim: 'it need hardly be stated that "in logic" there is no satisfactory way out of the situation, save by an examination of state practice and the possible efficacy of novel belligerent measures in altering traditional procedures'.[3]

Economic warfare at sea was a practical reality from the Late Middle Ages (1300–1500). The first regulations of neutral rights were enunciated in the famous *Consolato del mare*. Administering seizures of property at sea, however, was not to assume the clear lines of an established branch of the law of nations until the late eighteenth century. Lord Stowell, as a Judge in the British court of Admiralty in the years 1798–1828, is generally acknowledged as the founder of the modern law of prize. His pronouncements on prize cases arising from the Napoleonic Wars are considered for all their authority and clarity to be the starting point for all subsequent judicial development. Other landmarks followed, such as the Second Armed Neutrality of 1800, the Declaration of Paris of 1856, the American Civil War, and the Russo-Japanese War.

Rich jurisprudence was soon to be complemented by academic reflection, renowned bodies such as the Institut de Droit International seeking to systematize contraband law, while later came the time for legal codification with the Hague Peace Conferences. Despite significant efforts, however, prize law was never codified in a single conventional instrument and the prospective creation of an International Prize Court in 1907, as well as the 1909 London Declaration, ultimately failed. The experience of the two World Wars, which completes this fascinating trail in the evolution of the law of maritime neutrality, added only a few but important elements in matters of capture and destruction at sea. By and large, however, one cannot say that the law of prize has departed in any appreciable sense from the

[2]See JESSUP, P.C. and DEÁK, F., *Neutrality – Its History, Economics and Law,* vol.I (1935) at p. 78.
[3]See TUCKER, R.W., *The Law of War and Neutrality at Sea,* USNWC, 50 *International Law Studies* (1955) at p. 333.

tradition endowed by Lord Stowell at the end of the Napoleonic Wars.

A real cornerstone in prize legal tradition is the principle that any capture effected at sea has to be adjudicated (*toute prise doit être jugée*). The principle was consecrated in national instructions as early as 1373 and was consistently reaffirmed through the centuries. At the origins of prize proceedings lay the desire to accord judicial guarantees to the often arbitrary practices of privateers. Yet, even after the abolition of privateering, transfer of title over seized goods and ships remained dependent upon proper legal procedure. As an essay on the evolution of that principle concluded, 'tel est le dernier terme de l'évolution de la règle que toute prise doit être jugée: les motifs qui ont inspiré la naissance de cette règle onte été fort divers, mais au cours de l'évolution historique, ils se sont épurés par une suite "d'ascensions spirituelles" remarquables pour aboutir à cette idée de légalité pure: la capture n'est point une opération arbitraire et la meilleure garantie en est donnée avec une juridiction qu'aucun intérêt individuel ne vient mettre en mouvement, mais seulement l'intérêt supérieur de la loi'.[4]

The principle was reiterated in innumerable prize decisions such as this of the Mixed Arbitral Tribunal hearing claims against Bulgaria pronounced in 1926:

> en matière de prises, le principe fondamental, universel et plusieurs fois séculaire, est que toute prise doit être jugée . . . Il est nécessaire qu'une procédure judiciaire soit suivie, au cours de laquelle les deux parties sont entendues et il faut que les sentences, veritables jugements, soient basées, non seulement sur les lois et les intérêts nationaux, mais aussi sur la loi internationale.[5]

When the world looked back again into Stowellian sharpness and eloquence some forty years after the Second World War,

[4]See REUTER, P., *Étude de la règle: Toute prise doit être jugée*, 1933 at p. 32.

[5]See *Vlasios D. Katrantsios v. Bulgaria* (No 533), in *Recueil des décisions des Tribunaux Arbitraux Mixtes*, vol.VII (1927) at pp. 43–4. A prominent characteristic of prize jurisdiction is precisely the fact that municipal courts are supposed to apply international law. As Justice Gray said, 'this rule of international law is one which prize courts, administering the law of nations, are bound to take judicial notice of, and to give effect to, in the absence of any treaty or other public act of their own government in relation to the matter'; see *The Paquete Habana* (1900), 175 *US Supreme Court Reports* at p. 708.

the impetus was found in that particularly law-defying armed conflict which opposed Iraq and Iran for much longer than anyone could have ever foreseen. As from the mid-1980s, Iran claimed the right to intercept third ships heading to neutral destinations suspecting that contraband cargoes might then reach its enemy by land – an unmistakable allusion to the doctrine of *continuous voyage*. The United States warned the Gulf belligerents that no interference with their tanker escort missions would be tolerated since established legal principles exempt *convoyed* neutral merchantmen from belligerent visitation. From various quarters it was suggested that foreign ships chartered by the Iranian government to ferry oil from Kharg Island to safer terminals in the south might well have forfeited their neutral immunity since they were clearly engaged in acts of *unneutral service*.

These are some of the occasions which marked the forceful come-back of prize law and called into question the self-sufficiency of the Charter system. The Persian Gulf events compelled the jurist to rediscover long-abandoned concepts and jargon, and hence to rehabilitate ideas which apparently have not lost any of their functionality. The purpose here is, first, to review the content and evolution of some of the most fundamental notions of what is generically termed prize law and, second, to examine their continued currency, if any, in contemporary practice.

II The belligerent right of visit and search

1 Origins, scope and content of the concept

The right of visit and search finds its legal justification in the basic premise of sea warfare according to which private property, enemy but also neutral under certain conditions, can be confiscated.[6] Capture is only conceivable through the modalities of visit and search. In the words of Emmerich de Vattel, 'on ne

[6]Among the leading studies on the subject, see HIGGINS, A.P., 'Le droit de visite et de capture dans la guerre maritime', 11 *RCADI* (1926), pp. 65–170; Id., 'Visit, Search, and Detention', 7 *BYIL* (1926), p. 43*ff.*; WISE, J.C., 'The Rights of Visit and Search, Capture, Angary and Requisition', 16 *AJIL* (1922), p. 391*ff.*; FRASCONA, J.L., *Visit, Search, and Seizure on the High Seas*, 1938. See also ROJAHN, O., 'Ships, Visit and Search' in BERNHARDT, R. (ed.), *Encyclopedia of Public International Law*, instalment 4 (1982), p. 224*ff.*

peut empêcher le transport des effets de contrebande, si l'on ne visite pas les vaisseaux neutres, que l'on rencontre en mer. On est donc en droit de les visiter.'[7] As Lord Stowell reasoned in 1799, 'the right of visiting and searching merchant ships upon the high seas, whatever be the ships, whatever be the cargoes, whatever be the destinations, is an incontestable right of the lawfully commissioned cruisers of a belligerent nation . . . This right is so clear in principle, that no man can deny it who admits the legality of maritime capture; because if you are not at liberty to ascertain by sufficient inquiry whether there is property that can legally be captured, it is impossible to capture.'[8]

Early Development The historic origins of such practice can be traced back to the collection of maritime usages known as the *Consolato del mare*, first published at Barcelona in 1494, and to a number of later treaty provisions explicitly recognizing the right of visit for the purposes of verifying the neutral character of encountered merchantmen.[9] Also prescribed in certain treaties and national enactments was the right to capture all ships which would resist visit and search.[10] Most important among those early sources is the Treaty of the Pyrenees, concluded in 1659

[7]See VATTEL, E.de, *Le droit des gens ou principes de la loi naturelle*, 1758, tome II, liv.III, chap.VII, §114, reproduced in SCOTT, J.B. (ed.), *The Classics of International Law – Le Droit des Gens by E. de Vattel*, 1916, vol.II at p. 91.
[8]See *The Maria* (1799), 1 *C. Robinson's Admiralty Reports* at p. 360. While in 1815, Chief Justice Marshall pronounced: 'belligerents have a full and perfect right to capture enemy goods, and articles going to their enemy which are contraband of war. To the exercise of that right, the right of search is essential. It is a means justified by the end. It has been truly denominated a right growing out of, and ancillary to the greater right of capture'; see *The Nereide* (1815), 9 *W. Cranch's US Supreme Court Reports* at p. 426.
[9]In an early instance, France and Holland by the Tournai treaty of 1407 decided that, although their commerce should carry on unaffected by the war against England, French ships would have the right to visit Dutch merchant vessels to verify their cargoes' origin; see HIGGINS, *op. cit., supra* n.6 at p. 74. To cite another example, in 1625 England reached an agreement with Holland according to which they should request their allies or any other country interested in defeating Spain to prohibit all trade relations with the Spaniards and that if they did not consent they would stop and search merchant vessels from those countries for contraband; see NYS, E., *Les origines du droit international*, 1894 at p. 230.
[10]To that effect, for instance, the British Order-in-Council of 1664, the French Ordinance of 1681, and the Spanish Ordinance of 1718; see *The Maria* (1799), 1 *C. Robinson's Admiralty Reports* at pp. 364–5.

between France and Spain, Article 17 of which describes in detail the normal procedure to be followed and the formalities to be respected in approaching and boarding a suspect vessel.[11] The 1797 Convention between England and Russia further stipulated that visit and search should be performed with utmost constraint.[12]

A common feature in those early treaties was that the captor should send a boat and men to the summoned vessel rather than require the master of the latter to come over, and that violence against the crew or damage to the cargo of the inspected ship should be strictly avoided. As a general rule also, visitation was confined to examining the arrested ship's papers while actual search of the cargo was prohibited. The gradual elaboration of procedural rules of an almost customary character relating to visit and search reflected a careful design to protect neutral merchantmen against unruly seizure through intimidation or even pillage, but equally the captor against possible deception.[13]

Forms and Procedure As a belligerent right, visit and search operations may be conducted only in those sea areas where a belligerent can lawfully engage his enemy, that is to say, everywhere beyond neutral territorial waters. As Article 2 of 1907 Hague Convention XIII Concerning the Rights and Duties of Neutral Powers in Naval War provides, 'any act of hostility,

[11]Subsequently, a great many agreements of the seventeenth century followed the model of the Treaty of the Pyrenees. The 1713 Anglo-French Treaty of Commerce and Navigation, for instance, signed at Utrecht, adopted to the letter the terms of the Pyrenees treaty; see NYS, E., *La guerre maritime – Etude de droit international*, 1881 at p. 74.

[12]See also *The Maria* (1799), 1 *C. Robinson's Admiralty Reports* at p. 361: 'the right must unquestionably be exercised with as little of personal harshness and of vexation in the mode as possible'. Occasionally neutrals were not prepared to acquiesce in the enforcement of such belligerent right. In 1652, for instance, in a quarrel that eventually led to the first Anglo-Dutch War, the admiralty of Holland, Zeeland and Friesland charged their fleet 'to free the ships of this country from all search by anyone whatever'; see JESSUP and DEÁK, *op. cit., supra* n.2 at p. 161.

[13]On the early history of visit and search, see ORTOLAN, T., *Règles internationales et diplomatie de la mer*, tome 2nd (1864), pp. 248–82; DUPUIS, C., *Le droit de la guerre maritime d'après les doctrines anglaises contemporaines*, 1899, pp. 296–321; KLEEN, R., *Règles et usages de la neutralité*, tome 2 (1900), pp. 246–320; JESSUP and DEÁK, *op. cit., supra* n.2, pp. 157–200; KULSRUD, C.J., *Maritime Neutrality to 1780*, 1936, pp. 156–202.

including capture and the exercise of the right of search, committed by belligerent warships in the territorial waters of a neutral Power, constitutes a violation of neutrality and is strictly forbidden'.

Traditionally, only duly commissioned warships could exercise the right of visit and search. The performance of submarines and aircraft in both World Wars added fresh controversy to the lawful exercise of the traditional right of visit and search. The new formidable challenge to established law stemmed from the fact that both those platforms were best suited and most optimally used to carry out surprise attacks, whereas they were least appropriate to conduct visit and search in the normal mode.[14] The Commission of Jurists to Draft Rules of Aerial Warfare refrained from drafting an article on this issue in view of the irreconcilable submissions of some states,[15] while the 1939 Draft Convention on the Rights and Duties of Neutral Powers in Naval and Aerial War prepared by Harvard Law School reaffirmed in Article 54 the obligation of aircraft to conform to the rules of international law to which surface vessels are subject.[16]

The purpose of ordering a ship to heave to and accept being boarded and searched is to establish its nationality, the conditions of its voyage, as well as the ownership, nature and destination of its cargo. While approaching, the belligerent warship may order the suspect vessel to stop, either by raising the international flag-signal, by siren or by radio communi-

[14]See ROTOCKI, Z., 'Aircraft and Prize Law in Sea Warfare', 4 *PYIL* (1971), p. 187*ff.*, and SMITH, H.A., *The Law and Custom of the Sea,* 3rd edn (1959), pp. 196–204. During the First World War, air action in relation to visit and search was limited and rather incidental. On some occasions German hydroplanes or Zeppelins visited vessels at sea and escorted them into port for prize proceedings. More frequently, aircraft ordered merchant ships to change course without prior visitation (either towards a friendly port or to a near sailing warship) or simply attacked them on sight.

[15]Great Britain, for instance, supported the idea that, although belligerent aircraft should in all circumstances abide by the rules applicable to warships, they should be recognized the right of diversion. The United States, on the other hand, opposed the view that an aircraft could divert without board first.

[16]As regards diversion, Article 109§3 attempted an innovation stipulating that 'if the belligerent aircraft is unable to alight, it may require the vessel to proceed on its course under instructions as to speed until the sea moderates or until a naval vessel of the belligerent appears; if visit and search are not affected by either means within six hours, or if the aircraft does not remain within sight or hearing of the merchant vessel, the vessel may resume its course at normal speed'.

cation. Frequent also is the practice of hoisting the flag and firing a blank charge, or affirming gun (*coup de semonce* or *coup d'assurance*). If the merchant vessel refuses to take heed, the warship may fire across the bows, and, if necessary, disable the ship's steering gear.

A boarding party is sent next to examine the ship's papers in order to verify its flag of registry, its provenance and next port of call, the consigner, the consignee and the character of its cargo.[17] Fraudulent or missing documents and even papers filled out in incomplete manner are held to offer 'probable cause' for capture, although the neutral must be subsequently allowed to refute the charges before a prize court. Should suspicion remain as regards the nationality of the ship or the nature of the cargo, the visiting officers may also interrogate the crew and search the ship's holds. If the inquiry shows nothing irregular which may validate the ship's seizure, the boarding party should cause no more delay and release the vessel after having signed an entry to the vessel's log-book.[18]

The Contested Practice of Diversion and Detention Although visit and search were traditionally performed on the high seas, novel

[17]Commonly, the boarding party looked at the ship's *Register* (certifying ship's nationality, technical characteristics and owner), *Master Role* (giving information about number, names and contracts of crewmen), *Log* (daily details of journey), *Charter-party* (contract if on a chartered voyage), *Manifest* and the *Bills of Lading* (description of type and volume of cargo), and *Clearance* (document delivered by customs authorities at last port of call); see HIGGINS, *op. cit., supra* n.6 at p. 116. Philip Jessup notes that these documents related chiefly to the cargo and not to the ship itself, and that therefore from the fifteenth century ships were provided with a document specifically indicating the nationality of the ship (often named congé, pass, passport, cocket, sea-letter, sea-brief or certificate); see JESSUP and DEÁK, *op. cit., supra* n.2 at p. 176.

[18]The belligerent right of visit and search should not be confounded with similar powers conferred to warships of all nations under the peacetime law of the sea. In accordance with a long-established customary principle, warships may stop, board, and search private vessels on the high seas if there is reasonable ground to suspect that the ship in question is engaged in activities such as piracy, slave trade or unauthorized broadcasting. This exception to the exclusiveness of the flag jurisdiction over ships on the high seas is now codified in Article 110 of the 1982 LOS Convention which also extends the right of visit to military aircraft or 'any other duly authorized ships or aircraft clearly marked and identifiable as being on government service'. Analogous rights of inspection, boarding and searching may be granted by specific treaty provisions such as Article 17 of the 1989 Geneva Convention against Illicit Traffic in Narcotic Drugs and Psychotropic Substances. For more, see JENNINGS, R. and WATTS, A. (eds), *Oppenheim's International Law*, 9th edn (1992), vol.I, pp. 736–9.

conditions at the time of the First World War linked to the development of the steam engine, the increased tonnage of ships and the introduction of unrestricted submarine campaign, contributed to the emergence of an alternative technique. Under the rapidly generalized practice, neutral suspect vessels were diverted to a friendly port for the purpose of search. If the master of the vessel refused to change course, an armed guard was placed on board to ensure compliance. The method became known under the terms of 'diversion' or 'detention', both denoting the idea that a ship safely berthed in port would render easier the thorough search of its cargo, but also would allow a better evaluation of circumstantial evidence based on commercial intelligence which might substantiate the presumption of ultimate enemy destination and thus enable a decision as to the initiation of prize proceedings.

Shortly after the outbreak of the First World War, the governments of the United States and Great Britain exchanged views on the propriety of the new arrangement. In a note dated 7 November 1914, the State Department maintained that 'the belligerent right of visit and search requires that the search should be made on the high seas at the time of the visit, and that the conclusion of the search should rest upon the evidence found on the ship under investigation, and not upon circumstances ascertained from external sources'.[19] The British Foreign Office replied on 7 January 1915 as follows: 'it is, however, essential under modern conditions that where there is real ground for suspecting the presence of contraband, the vessels should be brought into port for examination: in no other way can the right of search be exercised, and but for this practice it would have to be completely abandoned'.[20]

[19]See 9 *AJIL* (1915) *Sp.Suppl.* at p. 74. On 26 December 1914, the US government reiterated its objection in these terms: 'The Government of the United States readily admits the full right of a belligerent to visit and search on the high seas the vessels of American citizens or other neutral vessels carrying American goods and to detain them when there is sufficient evidence to justify a belief that contraband articles are in their cargoes; but His Majesty's Government, judging by their own experience in the past, must realize that this Government can not without protest permit American ships or American cargoes to be taken into British ports and there detained for the purpose of searching generally for evidence of contraband, or upon presumptions created by special municipal enactments which are clearly at variance with international law and practice', *ibid.* at pp. 58–9.

[20]*Ibid* at p. 63. And elsewhere: 'the growth in the size of steamships necessitates in many cases that the vessel should go into calm water, in order that even the

In March 1915, after Germany had declared the waters around the British Isles to be a war area and ordered its U-boat fleet to sink on sight all ships found therein, the British and the French governments adopted retaliatory measures in order to prevent commodities of any kind from reaching Germany. As they framed it, 'the British and French Governments will therefore hold themselves free to detain and take into port ships carrying goods of presumed enemy destination, ownership, or origin. It is not intended to confiscate such vessels or cargoes unless they would otherwise be liable to condemnation'.[21] Washington expressed its surprise in these words: 'the first sentence claims a right pertaining only to a state of blockade. The last sentence proposes a treatment of ships and cargoes as if no blockade existed. The two together present a proposed course of action previously unknown to international law'.[22]

Also regrettable in the eyes of the US was the new rule adopted by the British prize court which departed from traditional practice to consider at the first hearing only the ship's papers and documents and the goods found on board, and

right of visit, as apart from the right of search, should be exercised. In modern times a steamer is capable of pursuing her voyage irrespective of the conditions of the weather. Many of the neutral merchantmen which our naval officers are called upon to visit at sea are encountered by our cruisers in places and under conditions which render the launching of a boat impossible ... If a belligerent is to be denied the right of taking a neutral merchantman, met with under such conditions, into calm water in order that the visiting officer may go aboard, the right of visit and of search would become a nullity ... No Power in these days can afford during a great war to forego the exercise of the right of visit and search. Vessels which are apparently harmless merchantmen can be used for carrying and laying mines and even fitted to discharge torpedoes. Supplies for submarines can without difficulty be concealed under other cargo. The only protection against these risks is to visit and search thoroughly every vessel appearing in the zone of operations and if the circumstances are such as to render it impossible to carry it out at the spot where the vessel was met with the only practicable course is to take the ship to some more convenient locality for the purpose. To do so is not to be looked upon as a new belligerent right, but as an adaptation of the existing right to the modern conditions of commerce', *ibid.* at pp. 75–6.

[21]*Ibid.* at p. 102.

[22]*Ibid.* at p. 103. On 21 October 1915, the US State Department refuted once more the British contentions, arguing that 'an examination of the instructions issued to naval commanders of the United States, Great Britain, Russia, Japan, Spain, Germany, and France from 1888 to the beginning of the present war shows that search in port was not contemplated by the Government of any of these countries ... [and] an examination of the opinions of the most eminent text writers on the laws of nations shows that they give practically no consideration to the question of search in port'; see 10 *AJIL* (1916) *Sp.Suppl.* at p. 75.

which allowed for additional evidence – or 'seizures upon conjectural suspicion' as it was termed:

> under these new rules there is no longer a 'first hearing' on the evidence derived from the ship, and the prize court is no longer precluded from receiving extrinsic evidence for which a suggestion has not been laid in the preparatory evidence. The result is, as pointed out above, that innocent vessels or cargoes are now seized and detained on mere suspicion while efforts are made to obtain evidence from extraneous sources to justify the detention and the commencement of prize proceedings.[23]

The British reply to those complaints came on 24 April 1916, in the form of a memorandum where it was stressed that 'new devices for despatching goods to the enemy must be met by new methods of applying the fundamental and acknowledged principle of the right to intercept such trade'.[24] With regard to the alterations in the prize court procedure allowing for extraneous evidence, the British Foreign Office observed:

> in the days when the old rules were developed the ship's papers were a safe and satisfactory guide as to the nature and destination of the cargo . . . Nowadays the conditions have changed; the papers may outwardly be perfectly genuine and complete, yet they may have been prepared with the express purpose of concealing the real nature of the transaction . . . Consequently the old rule that the papers on board the ship must alone be taken into consideration, and evidence from other sources excluded, is no longer practicable; indeed, the system of attributing to the ship's papers the character of final and conclusive proof upheld in the United States would encourage shippers of contraband to falsify the papers, as they would thereby ensure absolute immunity from capture.[25]

The British practice apart, it would seem that diversion to port and detention for search was also provided for in the German Prize Regulations and the Italian Naval Instructions of 1915 and 1917 respectively, while French prize courts on numerous

[23] *Ibid.* at p. 77.
[24] *Ibid.* at p. 121.
[25] *Ibid.* at pp. 126–7.

occasions upheld the validity of *déroutement*.[26] As a leading authority in the field has concluded, 'in view of the experience of the two World Wars it does not appear very realistic to continue to question the legitimacy – in principle – of diverting neutral vessels into port for search'.[27]

2 Resisting visit and search

By Enemy Merchantmen All enemy merchantmen are a priori liable to capture and condemnation, and since interception by an enemy warship would in most cases lead to such capture, it has been argued that enemy merchant vessels should be conferred the right to resist forcibly visit and search. That view was strongly solicited by a considerable number of authorities,[28] and equally upheld in the jurisprudence of prize courts and the national manuals of naval warfare. What is open to question, however, is whether one could translate the right to resist visit and search as an unlimited right of carrying armaments in order to engage and defeat a potential captor.

The question of the legality of so-called *defensively armed merchantmen* provoked ardent debate and remains unsettled. It is noteworthy that the Institut de Droit International, in undertaking a codification of the rules of sea warfare based on the right of capture, firmly endorsed the right of merchant vessels to respond by force when *unlawfully attacked*, which is of course profoundly different from the proposition that they should be empowered to attack an approaching warship while lawfully exercising the belligerent right of visit and search. Article 12 of the 1913 *Oxford Manual* provided that, 'neither public nor private vessels, nor their personnel, may commit acts of hostility against

[26]See, for instance, the prize decisions of *The Federico, The Barcelo, The Rioja, The Alfonso*, in VERZIJL, J.H.W., *Le droit des prises de la Grande Guerre*, 1924 at p. 1169. *Cf. The Carthage* (France v. Italy), Award of 6 May 1913, in SCOTT, J.B., *The Hague Court Reports*, 1916 at p. 559. See also JESSUP, P.C., 'The Diversion of Merchantmen', 34 *AJIL* (1940), p. 312*ff.*, and HILL, D.J., 'Visit, Search and Capture', 16 *Proc.ASIL* (1922), p. 49*ff.*

[27]See TUCKER, *op. cit., supra* n.3 at p. 340. See also WOLF, J., 'Ships, Diverting and Ordering into Port' in BERNHARDT, R. (ed.), *Encyclopedia of Public International Law*, instalment 4 (1982), p. 223*ff.*

[28]See, for instance, HIGGINS, A.P., 'Armed Merchant Ships', 8 *AJIL* (1914), p. 705*ff.*, and GARNER, J.W., *International Law and the World War*, vol.I (1920), p. 384*ff.* See also ZEMANEK, K., 'Merchant Ships, Armed' in BERNHARDT, R. (ed.), *Encyclopedia of Public International Law*, instalment 3 (1982), p. 258*ff.*

the enemy. Both may, however, use force to *defend themselves against the attack* of an enemy vessel' (emphasis added).[29]

By Neutral Merchantmen The traditional law of capture makes a distinction between neutral merchantmen attempting to escape upon being summoned and neutral vessels resisting by force visit and search. In the former case the vessel is not necessarily deemed liable to capture and confiscation for the sole fact of fleeing. A belligerent warship is of course entitled to pursue and use force as appropriate in order to bring the vessel to halt. Its owner would eventually have no right to claim compensation for damages or destruction caused during the pursuit. Yet, even if the neutral vessel was finally condemned, e.g. for transport of contraband, it should still bear no legal consequences for having taken flight.[30] At the time of the First World War, Germany and France followed the established trend. On the contrary, Article 64(a) of the 1917 US Instructions for the Navy included flight as a valid reason for capture.[31]

In contrast, in the case where the neutral vessel opposes visitation by forcible means, it is openly engaged in hostile acts and by that reason it is to be treated as an enemy merchantman, which is to say it would be liable to capture and condemnation.[32]

[29]See 26 *Ann.IDI* (1913), Oxford Session, pp. 610–40. The text can also be found in SCHINDLER, D. and TOMAN, J. (eds), *The Laws of Armed Conflicts – A Collection of Conventions, Resolutions and Other Documents*, 3rd edn (1988), pp. 857–75, and RONZITTI, N., *The Law of Naval Warfare – A Collection of Agreements and Documents with Commentaries*, 1988, pp. 277–328.

[30]As Lord Stowell put it, 'I am not aware that a mere attempt to escape, before any possession is assumed, has ever been held to draw with it the consequences of condemnation'; see *The St. Juan Baptista* (1803), 5 *C. Robinson's Admiralty Reports* at p. 35. Chief Justice Marshall argued in the same vein: 'if the property be neutral, what mischief is done, by its escaping a search? In so doing, there is no sin, even as against the belligerent, if it can be effected by lawful means. The neutral cannot justify the use of force or fraud, but if, by means, lawful in themselves, he can escape this vexatious procedure, he may certainly employ them'; see *The Nereide* (1815), 9 *W. Cranch's US Supreme Court Reports* at p. 428.

[31]See VERZIJL, *op. cit., supra* n.26 at p. 1183.

[32]Already included in the French Prize Instructions of 1584 and 1681, the rule appears founded on a long-established practice; see ORTOLAN, *op. cit., supra* n.13, tome 2 at p. 260. To cite once more Lord Stowell, 'by the law of nations, as now understood, a deliberate and continued resistance to search, on the part of a neutral vessel to a lawful cruiser, is followed by the legal consequence of confiscation'; see *The Maria* (1799), 1 *C. Robinson's Admiralty Reports* at p. 369. Lord Stowell continued elsewhere: 'if a neutral master attempts a rescue, he violates a duty, which is imposed upon him by the law of nations, to submit to come in for enquiry, as to the property of the ship or cargo; and if he violates

This rule was codified in Article 63 of the 1909 London Declaration which stipulated:

> forcible resistance to the legitimate exercise of the right of stoppage, search, and capture, involves in all cases the condemnation of the vessel. The cargo is liable to the same treatment as the cargo of an enemy vessel. Goods belonging to the master or owner of the vessel are treated as enemy goods.[33]

This formulation was later reproduced in several national manuals. The United States, Germany, Austria-Hungary, France, Italy and Japan all included prescriptions reflecting that rule.[34]

3 Visit and search in recent practice

A The Persian Gulf Tanker War

The Iranian Campaign Given Iran's most favourable controlling position in the Hormuz narrows, but also the fact that the Iranian navy operated throughout the war virtually unchallenged by Iraqi forces, it brings no surprise that neutral vessels were systematically stopped and boarded at the entrance of the Persian Gulf, and eventually diverted and detained in Iranian ports. In the first instance of a neutral merchantman being visited and searched in the vicinity of the Strait of Hormuz, the Danish vessel *Elsa Cat* was seized in August 1981 with a cargo of military hardware bound for Iraq. The Iraqi government promptly filed a protest claiming that 'the vessel's cargo was destined to owners in Kuwait and the United Arab Emirates'.[35]

---

that obligation by a recurrence to force, the consequence will undoubtedly reach the property of his owner; and it would, I think, extend also to the confiscation of the whole cargo entrusted to his care, and thus fraudulently attempted to be withdrawn from the rights of war'; see *The Catharina Elizabeth* (1804), 5 C. *Robinson's Admiralty Reports* at p. 232.

[33]At the London Conference there was some support for the claim that a neutral ship should be liable to capture and condemnation for an attempt to take flight no less than for forcible resistance, but this view did not prevail; see General Report of the Drafting Committee, USNWC, 9 *International Law Topics* (1909) at p. 145.

[34]See VERZIJL, *op. cit.*, *supra* n.26 at p. 1177.

[35]See letter dated 19 August 1981 from the Minister of Foreign Affairs of Iraq addressed to the President of the Security Coucil, UN Doc. *S/14637*, 21 August 1981. Presumably acting in defence of neutral interests, Iraq maintained that 'the act of seizure committed by Iran constitutes a flagrant violation of the established rules of international law of freedom of navigation through straits used for international navigation', *ibid.*

But it was not until 1985 that Iran stepped up its contraband control measures. Since no neutral vessel could reasonably be expected to slip through the Iranian blockade and reach an Iraqi port, Iran became increasingly concerned about the volume of neutral trade with Iraq's neighbouring Gulf states, especially Kuwait. In what is probably the most publicized incident, on 20 June 1985, the Iranian navy intercepted the Kuwaiti vessel *Al-Muharraq* some 22 nautical miles south of the Strait of Hormuz while *en route* to several ports in the Gulf and diverted it to the port of Bandar Abbas for thorough inspection of her cargo. As the Iranian authorities asserted, 'out of 10,500 tons of cargo aboard the vessel, 4,500 tons of logistical support were destined for Iraq', which could therefore be confiscated as contraband of war.[36]

It is not without significance that, as described in a communiqué issued by the shipping company on the incident, the manner in which the *Al-Muharraq* was ordered to halt and subsequently boarded and diverted does not seem to raise any legal objection.[37] What also flows from the same document is that a consignment of 2,856 tons bound for Kuwait port was listed as transit cargo. To justify its action, Iran made explicit reference to the 1907 Hague Convention XIII Respecting the Rights and Duties of Neutral Powers in Naval War,[38] probably alluding to Article 6 of the said convention which forbids 'the supply, in any manner, directly or indirectly, by a neutral Power to a belligerent Power, of warships, ammunition, or war material of any kind whatever'.

In the months that followed, several Kuwaiti ships were likewise detained and inspected for contraband such as the *Al-Wattyah* on 4 September 1985, the *Al-Massilah* on 9 September,

[36]See letter dated 19 July 1985, from the Permanent Representative of Iran to the UN addressed to the Secretary-General, UN Doc. *S/17348*, 22 July 1985. The ship was finally released on 12 July 1985, with the remaining cargo to proceed with her scheduled voyage. The government of Kuwait protested, although it remains unclear whether it opposed the act of boarding and diverting as such, or solely the prolonged detention. The Gulf Cooperation Council which was convened in the meantime adopted a resolution condemning the Iranian action as a 'flagrant violation of international law concerning navigation on the high seas as well as freedom of navigation in international waterways'; see letter dated 10 July 1985, from the Permanent Representative of Kuwait to the UN addressed to the President of the Security Council, UN Doc. *S/17335*, 11 July 1985.

[37]See Communiqué issued by the Board of Directors of the United Arab Shipping Company, UN Doc. *S/17335*, 11 July 1985, Annex at pp. 2–3.

[38]See UN Doc. *S/17348*, 22 July 1985.

or the Chinese ship *Jing Jiang*, chartered by Kuwait, on 12 September.[39] An Italian ship, the *Merzario Britania*, was searched by a helicopter-borne boarding party on 6 September while on a northbound voyage.[40] Kuwait's formal protests relating to these incidents failed to specify any precise grounds on which the Iranian contraband control measures should be considered contrary to international law. In a letter dated 19 September 1985, and addressed to the UN Secretary-General, the Minister of Foreign Affairs of Kuwait simply claimed that 'those commercial ships were sailing in international waters, and the Iranian authorities therefore had no right to intercept them'.[41]

By way of reply, Tehran made clear reference to the doctrine of continuous voyage and accused Kuwait of violating its neutral obligation of abstention. The Iranian note of 25 September 1985, to the UN Secretary-General read in part:

> the Government of the Islamic Republic of Iran has repeatedly announced that it would not allow the transport of arms from the Persian Gulf waters to the Iraqi aggressors. It has unfortunately been established in different cases that, contrary to the principles of good neighbourly relations, cargo ships destined for Kuwait have had on board logistical goods and arms headed for Iraq via Kuwait . . . The Government of the Islamic Republic of Iran, while fully respectful of the freedom of navigation for all vessels destined for Kuwait, has every right to prevent the transportation of military hardware to Iraq through the Persian Gulf. Therefore, *in accordance with the established rules*

[39]The allegedly Iraq-bound cargo removed from the *Al Wattyah* comprised automobile spare parts, electric appliances, oil-drilling equipment, water cooling parts and toys, while a corn cargo was seized on board the *Jing-Jiang*; see SCHILLER, T.S., 'The Gulf War and Shipping: Recent Developments' in PARRITT, B.A.H. (ed.), *Violence at Sea*, 1986 at p. 115.

[40]A number of similar incidents involved: the Cypriot *Mathildalia* and the Japanese *Tohgo Maru* both intercepted on 20 September 1985. In the case of the Danish *Arnold Maersk* seized on 22 September, some 650 tons of her cargo were confiscated because of ultimate enemy destination. On 26 September 1985, three vessels, the German *Arkona*, the Yugoslavian *Briber* and the Panamanian *Express Lato*, were detained for four days. Iran announced that in September alone more than forty foreign merchant vessels had been searched; see 32 *KCA* (1986) at p. 34514. Six more incidents involving German, Dutch, Panamanian, Kuwaiti and Japanese vessels were reported in November, while in late December 1985, 78 tons of explosives were discovered and confiscated aboard the Danish ship *Horneland*; see SCHILLER, *op. cit., supra* at p. 117.

[41]See UN Doc. *S/17482*, 20 September 1985.

> *of international law regarding the rights and duties of neutral Powers in naval war,* the Islamic Republic of Iran will continue its inspection of ships in the Persian Gulf suspected of carrying arms to Iraq. (emphasis added)[42]

On 8 November 1985, in a somewhat differing incident, a Greek tanker, the *Canaria*, and a Dutch salvage vessel, the *Amsterdam*, were reportedly fired upon by Iranian gunboats and taken under escort to Sirri Island.[43] At the time of the incident, the Greek vessel damaged by an Iraqi missile attack was being towed to Dubai for repairs. The *Amsterdam* was subsequently diverted to Bandar Abbas where it was detained until 25 November. The Iranian authorities suspected the Dutch vessel of having used its sophisticated radio equipment in order to collect information on ship movements in the Gulf. It remains unclear, however, whether the vessels came under fire for sailing inside the Iranian defensive sea area without permission, or if the action was related to the charge of unneutral service.

The Iranian campaign of close surveillance of Gulf shipping was to intensify at certain periods over the next two years. On 9 January 1986, the *Ville du Sahara* registered in West Germany was intercepted by the Iranian navy and released three days later. On 12 January 1986, five cargo ships, the American *President Taylor*, the Panamanian *Barber Perseus*, the Greek *Artemis*, the German *Jork* and the Sri Lankan *Seedevi*, were stopped in the Gulf of Oman, searched and released the same day. In mid-May 1986, the English *Columbia* and the German *Frankfurt Oder* underwent cargo inspection before being released. On 2 September 1986, a cargo vessel flying the Soviet flag, the *Yemtsov*, was seized while sailing ten miles south of Sirri island.[44] On 13 September 1986, four Panamanian tankers, the *Golden Bear*, the *Gulf Pioneer*, the *Acacia* and the *Pal Pal*, were boarded by Iranian search parties off the southern coast of Iran. According to the fleet Commander of the Iranian navy, more than 1,000 merchant ships had been inspected by the end of 1986.[45]

[42]See UN Doc. *S/17496*, 25 September 1985.
[43]See SCHILLER, *op. cit., supra* n.39 at pp. 116–17.
[44]According to other information there were no less than ten interceptions on 2 September, two involving Soviet vessels; see 33 *KRWE* (1987) at p. 35160.
[45]See MOMTAZ, D., 'Commentary on the Iranian Practice' in DE GUTTRY, A. and RONZITTI, N. (eds), *The Iran-Iraq War (1980–1988) and the Law of Naval Warfare*, 1993 at p. 24.

In January 1987, the *Hual Ingrita* registered in the Philippines was seized, while in April 1987 the Kuwaiti *Jebel Ali* was temporarily detained. In July of the same year, the Panamanian *Cosmobile Ace* was taken under escort to Bandar Abbas and delayed for four days. On two occasions, with regard to the seizure of the Yugoslavian *Bribir* and the Danish *Chastine Maersk* in August and October 1987 respectively, warning shots across the bows were reported. In late December 1987, a Swiss container ship, the *Norasia Pearl*, was subjected to a several day-inspection in the port of Bandar Abbas.[46]

On the whole, the Iranian navy discontinued the boarding and diversion practices as from early September 1988, although the last recorded incident involving a British tanker occurred on 12 December 1988.[47] The right of visit and search of vessels proceeding to and from the Shatt-al-Arab waterway figured high on the agenda of peace talks initiated shortly after the ceasefire of 20 August 1988. In fact, the face-to-face negotiations, opened

[46]These boarding/diversion incidents have been cited in the annual reports of the UN Secretary-General in pursuance of Security Council Resolution 552 (1984); see UN Doc. *S/16877*, 31 December 1984 at p. 6; UN Doc. *S/16877/Add.2*, 31 December 1985 at pp. 7–11; UN Doc. *S/16877/Add.3*, 31 December 1986 at pp. 3,6,9; UN Doc. *S/16877/Add.5*, 31 December 1987 at pp. 4,6,8–9,13,19. This listing of incidents, however, calls for a commentary. In fact, the UN Secretary-General was requested under para.7 of Security Council Resolution 552 (1984) to report regularly on the progress of the implementation of that resolution. In carrying out this mandate the Secretary-General requested from all states and the International Maritime Organization information on any relevant incident which subsequently appeared in his reports. As one might expect, such inventory contains primarily the reported attacks of both belligerents against neutral shipping by aircraft-launched missiles, surface gunfire, or mines – as was most often the case. The question then arises whether the visit and search incidents mentioned therein represent for the UN acts of comparable illegitimacy. True, the UN Secretary-General refrained from any judgment on the lawful or unlawful character of the indexed incidents in his reports. Yet, the empowering resolution was couched in fairly general terms. It will be recalled that the said resolution condemned the *attacks* on commercial ships *en route* to and from the ports of Kuwait and Saudi Arabia but also demanded that such attacks should cease and 'that there should be *no interference* with ships en route to and from states that are not parties to the hostilities' (emphasis added). Since stopping, boarding and even more so diverting of neutral vessels can hardly be deemed anything else than interference, there would be enough room to argue that the exercise of traditional rights of visit and search appeared to the Security Council to be as abusive as the unwarranted destruction of neutral merchantmen by surprise attacks. In view of the obscurity of such a conclusion, it appears clearly ill-advised for the Secretary-General to have classified a priori unobjectionable incidents of visit and search together with conspicuously unlawful attacks which in most cases signified numerous casualties and material damage.

[47]See 35 *KRWE* (1989) at p. 36570.

on 25 August 1988, were soon deadlocked over this very issue. Iraq asked for unimpeded movement of its vessels through the Persian Gulf, while Iran insisted that as long as the state of belligerency had not formally ended it conserved the right to inspect shipping.

Neutral Acquiescence Several foreign governments, through various statements, admitted the legitimacy of the Iranian maritime inspection campaign. As US Assistant Secretary Richard Murphy stated, for instance, in respect of the boarding of US-flagged ship *President Taylor* on 12 January 1986, 'there is a basis in international law for ship searched by belligerents. At the same time . . . we have stated our deep concern about this incident because of the danger of misunderstandings, overstepping of rights and norms, and even violence which is inherent in all ship search incidents'.[48] On 29 April 1988, Secretary of Defense Frank Carlucci announced the extension of US assistance to all neutral ships by pointing out that 'such aid will be provided to friendly, innocent neutral vessels flying a non-belligerent flag, outside declared war/exclusion zones, that are not carrying contraband or resisting *legitimate visit and search* by a Persian Gulf belligerent' (emphasis added).[49]

The British government, for its part, acquiesced to the Iranian contraband control measures, but only to the extent they might be covered by the right of self-defence. As a memorandum dated 12 April 1988, on the UK policy towards the Iran-Iraq conflict read,

> under Article 51 of the UN Charter, a state actively engaged in armed conflict (as in the case of Iran and Iraq) is entitled in exercise of its inherent right of self-defence to stop and search a foreign merchant ship on the high seas if there is reasonable ground for suspecting that the ship is taking arms to the other side for use in the conflict. This is an exceptional right: if the suspicion proves to be unfounded and if the ship has not committed acts calculated to give rise to suspicion, then the ship's owners have

[48]See 86 *US Dept. of State Bulletin* (March 1986), no.2108 at p. 41.
[49]See 88 *US Dept. of State Bulletin* (July 1988), no.2136 at p. 61. On the US acquiescence in the Iranian measures of visit and search, see also DE GUTTRY and RONZITTI, *op. cit., supra* n.45, doc.3.3 at p. 188.

> a good claim for compensation for loss caused by the delay. This right would not however extend to the imposition of a maritime blockade or other forms of economic warfare.[50]

In contrast, the French government was the only one among the western naval powers present in the Gulf to challenge the Iranian policy and threaten to react militarily. When on 8 October 1985, the French merchant ship *Ville d'Anvers* received the order to stop and submit to search, a French warship on patrol in the vicinity warned that it would prevent by force the boarding of the merchantman. The Iranian gunboat desisted from further action and the French vessel was allowed to continue its voyage to Bahrain.

Most legal commentators have expressed the view that the Iranian practice of boarding or diverting neutral vessels for inspection kept in line with customary law prescriptions and reaffirmed the continued validity of established principles on the subject.[51] It appears that at least on the diplomatic level Tehran proved more mindful than its neighbours of furnishing a sound legal basis for its naval strategy in the Gulf. Unfortunately, the prize court provided for in the Iranian enactment of 31 January 1988, was never instituted since it would have given better opportunity to test the validity of legal arguments.

[50]See 59 *BYIL* (1988) at p. 581. See also 57 *BYIL* (1986) at p. 635, and GRAY, C., 'The British Position in Regard to the Gulf Conflict', 37 *ICLQ* (1988) at pp. 422–3. Note also the following commentary: 'in the Gulf war, limited to Iran and Iraq, it would ill become this country to make clamour about the exercise of a belligerent right in relation to our merchant ships when, as a belligerent over the centuries, we have been among the foremost in asserting and exercising the full amplitude of the right of visitation against neutral merchant shipping'; see DRAPER, G.I.A.D., 'Rights of Search at Sea', letter to *The Times*, 23 January 1986 at p. 17.

[51]See GIOIA, A. and RONZITTI, N., 'The Law of Neutrality: Third States' Commercial Rights and Duties' in DEKKER, I.F. and POST, H.H.G. (eds), *The Gulf War of 1980–1988*, 1992 at p. 232; BOTHE, M., 'Neutrality at Sea', *ibid.* at p. 210; BOCZEK, B.A., 'Law of Warfare at Sea and Neutrality: Lessons from the Gulf War', 20 *ODIL* (1989) at p. 261; RUSSO, F.V., 'Neutrality at Sea in Transition: State Practice in the Gulf War as Emerging International Customary Law', 19 *ODIL* (1988) at p. 385; LECKOW, R., 'The Iran-Iraq Conflict in the Gulf: The Law of War Zones', 37 *ICLQ* (1988) at p. 638; VON HEINEGG, H.W., 'Visit, Search, Diversion, and Capture in Naval Warfare: Part II, Developments since 1945', 30 *CYIL* (1992) at pp. 102–4.

B Visit and search in current UN-mandated naval operations

Over the last four years, the international community has experienced extensive visit and search operations arising in the context of UN sanctions against Iraq, the Federal Republic of Yugoslavia (Serbia and Montenegro) and Haiti. Owing principally to the end of the Cold War which allowed for smoother functioning of the UN Security Council and the re-activation of the Charter's chapter 7, the world organization was able to adopt on three occasions (August 1990, May 1992 and October 1993) compulsory coercive measures calling *inter alia* for international maritime interception campaigns as a sanction enforcement measure.

There is no doubt that the legal basis for the UN-mandated naval operations lies with the relevant Security Council resolutions under Article 41 and/or Article 42 of the Charter, and in that sense it may seem inappropriate to include an analysis of UN-decreed maritime embargoes in the present review of state practice related to the exercise of belligerent contraband control rights. Notwithstanding this crucial dimension, a survey of recent interdiction campaigns set up in the Persian Gulf, the Gulf of Oman, the Red Sea, the Adriatic or the Caribbean remains useful especially with regard to the *modus operandi* of the naval forces involved.

The War for Kuwait: Operation Desert Shield On 25 August 1990, the UN Security Council passed Resolution 665 which called upon

> those Member States co-operating with the Government of Kuwait which are deploying maritime forces to the area to use such measures commensurate to the specific circumstances as may be necessary under the authority of the Security Council to *halt all inward and outward maritime shipping, in order to inspect and verify their cargoes and destinations* and to ensure strict implementation of the provisions related to such shipping laid down in resolution 661 (1990). (emphasis added)[52]

[52]The United States and the United Kigdom, naval forces of which had already been deployed in the Gulf, had announced even before the adoption of Resolution 665 (1990) that they would use their warships to prevent any violation of

The Maritime Interception Forces (MIF) eventually comprised 45 US warships, including 4 aircraft carriers, as well as 50 more naval vessels provided by 18 allies.[53] In some cases, boardings were effected by parties of US Marines landed by helicopter, while low-level passes by allied aircraft were also used to induce compliance of vessels defying orders.[54] In total, more than 9,000 ships were challenged by all participating forces, 1,100 were boarded and more than 60 diverted.[55]

---

the trade sanctions decreed under Resolution 661 (1990). Accordingly, interceptions began on 17 August with the *USS John J. Hall* in the Red Sea (the Iraqi tanker *Al Fao*) and with the *USS England* in the Persian Gulf (the northbound *Al Abid* and *Al Byaa*). On 18 August, US warships fired their first warning shots at two outbound Iraqi oil tankers; see 50 *Facts on File* (24 August 1990) at p. 615. For other reported incidents, see UN Doc. *S/21564*, 20 August 1990; UN Doc. *S/21568*, 20 August 1990; UN Doc. *S/21707*, 5 September 1990; UN Doc. *S/21861*, 10 October 1990; UN Doc. *S/21874*, 15 October 1990; UN Doc. *S/21910*, 29 October 1990.

[53]See 14 *Military Technology* (Oct.1990) at p. 19. Other sources suggest that units from as many as 23 navies became involved in the maritime campaign; see FREEDMAN, L. and KARSH, E., *The Gulf Conflict 1990–1991, Diplomacy and War in the New World Order*, 1993 at p. 153. See also CYR, B.L. et al., 'Naval Operations' in WATSON, B.W. (ed.), *Military Lessons of the Gulf War*, 1991, pp. 121–34, and VALAISON, G., 'Les forces navales dans le Golfe', 47 *Défense nationale* (juin 1991), pp. 188–91. A US commander was reported on 30 August 1990, as saying that the US Navy was challenging 75 ships daily (mostly interrogated by bridge-to-bridge radio), while three to four of those vessels were being boarded; see 50 *Facts on File* (21 September 1990) at p. 687. For a description of some particular incidents, see DELERY, T., 'Away, the Boarding Party!', 117 *USNIP* (May 1991), pp. 65–71. The US ships carried specially trained and experienced Coast Guard Law Enforcement Detachments for checking shipboard documents; see BRIGHAM, L.W., 'The U.S. Coast Guard in 1990', 117 *USNIP* (May 1991) at p. 146.

[54]See FRIEDMAN, N., *Desert Victory – The War for Kuwait*, 1991 at pp. 71–3. Maritime patrol aircraft offered invaluable surveillance support to interdiction efforts querying more than 6,500 vessels during Operation Desert Shield. The Outlaw Hunter-configured P-3 patrol aircraft, featuring unique capabilities of global positioning and satellite communication, was indeed a key platform in the embargo enforcement. For more, see BROOKS, R., HISER, S. and HOHL, T.K., 'If It Was There, P-3s Found It', 117 *USNIP* (Aug.1991), pp. 41–3.

[55]See BAYLISS, J.F.T., 'The Law and Practice of the Maintenance of Maritime Embargoes and Blockades in the Context of UN Security Council Enforcement Measures', paper presented at the ASIL/NVIR Second Joint Conference, The Hague, 22–4 July 1993 at p. 9. According to other accounts, by October 1991, some 35,000 ships had been controlled; see DUVAL, M., 'Les crises du Golfe vues de la mer', 47 *Défense nationale* (déc.1991) at p. 63. Eleven warning shots were fired, but none to disable. Most of the challenges were in the Gulf, while 90 per cent of the diversions and boardings were in the Red Sea; see FREEDMAN and KARSH, *op. cit., supra* n.53 at p. 153. For more on the multinational force operated in the Persian Gulf and the Red Sea, see STALEY, R.S., *The Wave of the Future – The United Nations and Naval Peacekeeping*, International Peace Academy, Occasional Paper Series, 1992, pp. 36–42.

War in Europe: Operation Sharp Guard Turning to UN involvement in the ongoing war in the former Yugoslavia, shortly after the adoption of Security Council Resolution 752 (1992), NATO as well as the Western European Union (WEU) examined the possibility of undertaking naval operations with a view to monitoring compliance with Security Council Resolution 713 (1991) and Security Council Resolution 757 (1992). By 15 July, the North Atlantic Council had worked out the operational arrangements and announced that NATO monitoring operations in the Adriatic (code-named Operation Maritime Monitor) would commence on 16 July 1992. The maritime surveillance effort would be complemented by a WEU force operating in an adjacent area of responsibility. The WEU force, engaged in Operation Sharp Vigilance, was initially composed of two Italian and one French warships, but it was soon reinforced with naval units from Belgium, Spain, Portugal and Great Britain totalling six vessels, while maritime patrol missions were flown by aircraft from Germany, the Netherlands and France. By November 1992, NATO and WEU forces deployed in the Adriatic had followed the movements of some 3,649 ships of which 71 were suspected of violating the UN embargo.[56]

On 16 November 1992, the UN Security Council passed Resolution 787 further tightening its economic sanctions against Serbia and aiming at preventing the reportedly ongoing infringements of the trade embargo.[57] By virtue of para.12, the Security Council called upon States:

[56]See UN Doc. *S/24847*, 25 November 1992. See also PERROS, Y., 'Présence en Adriatique: Un an déjà!', 41 *Défense nationale* (oct.1993) at p. 179, VAN EEKELEN, W., 'Western European Union – The European Security Nucleus', 38 *NATO's Sixteen Nations* (1993/3) at p. 15, and REMACLE, E., 'L'UEO et l'OTAN dans le conflit de l'(ex)-Yougoslavie', *Trimestre du Monde* (1993/4), pp. 153–65. It is important to note that, in the absence of an explicit authorization by the UN Security Council, the deployed naval forces had the limited role of tracking merchant shipping and shadowing suspect vessels without, however, being able to undertake visit and search, diversion or boarding procedures – let alone to use force – against those vessels. Another crucial limitation in the tightness of the UN trade embargo against Serbia concerned the fact that it was not at all clear whether warships could freely enter for the purposes of their mission the territorial waters of Albania as well as those of the former Yugoslav federal states.

[57]The US Permanent Representative to the Security Council stated that 'the Adriatic will not be allowed to become a Serbian supply line' and announced that Maltese-flagged vessels of Greek and Italian ownership as well as vessels belonging to an Egyptian shipping company were believed to have delivered on numerous occasions oil shipments to the Yugoslav port of Bar; see UN Doc. *S/PV.3135*, 13 November 1992 at pp. 11–12. See also the statement of Cyrus Vance, UN Doc. *S/PV.3134*, 13 November 1992 at p. 16.

> acting nationally or through regional agencies or arrangements, to use such measures commensurate with the specific circumstances as may be necessary under the authority of the Security Council to *halt all inward and outward maritime shipping in order to inspect and verify their cargoes and destinations* and to ensure strict implementation of the provisions of resolutions 713 (1991) and 757 (1992). (emphasis added)[58]

Pursuant to Resolution 787 (1992), the naval forces present in the Adriatic could intercept merchant vessels, board them in order to verify their cargo, and divert or take them into custody for inspection to a neighbouring port. Operation Sharp Fence succeeded Operation Sharp Vigilance, and Operation Maritime Guard succeeded Operation Maritime Monitor, as of 22 November 1992.[59] By early 1993, a total of some forty warships was operating in the 350-mile long Adriatic sea.[60]

In the aftermath of the adoption of Security Council Resolution 820 (1993) which further tightened the economic isolation of Serbia, providing *inter alia* for the seizure, detention and eventual confiscation of sanctions-busting vessels, it was decided that a combined NATO/WEU Task Force should be created under a unified command. The principal aim of Operation Sharp Guard, as the new arrangement was called, and which began in June 1993, was to prevent all unauthorized shipping from entering the territorial waters of the Federal Republic of Yugoslavia (Serbia and Montenegro). The task was demanding because of the density of maritime traffic; sometimes there were close to 300 contacts in a 50-mile radius. Furthermore,

[58]For Croatia, naval operations should be confined to the Yugoslav coast and ports; see UN Doc. *S/24856*, 26 November 1992. The Federal Republic of Yugoslavia replied that, since an arms embargo had been imposed on all republics of the former Yugoslavia, merchant shipping heading to or leaving Croatian territorial waters should be equally inspected; see UN Doc. *S/24877*, 1 December 1992.

[59]The WEU and NATO decided to step up the close cooperation of their naval assets although they were still under separate command; see BOORDA, J.M., 'The Southern Region – NATO Forces in Action', 38 *NATO's Sixteen Nations* (1993/2) at p. 8, and DESJAMETS, A., 'Mission Balbuzard: Le déploiement d'une force aéronavale en Adriatique', 49 *Défense Nationale* (avril 1993), pp. 190–3.

[60]Apart from the NATO and WEU forces, three carrier-led naval Task Groups (British, French, and American) were also present in the Adriatic, all operating under national command; see FURSDON, E., 'Poised in the Adriatic', 98 *Navy International* (May/June 1993), pp. 170–4.

apart from sealing off Serbia and Montenegro, naval forces had also to ensure the strict implementation of the general arms embargo against all former Yugoslav states which implied checking the merchant traffic moving across the Adriatic which amounts to a daily average of fifty ships or more.

Twelve NATO member states contributed some 20-odd surface ships of which 8 to 9 were continuously at sea in the Otranto Channel and off Montenegro immediately in front of the ports of Kotor and Bar. The combined T.F. 440 was also supported by maritime patrol aircraft from nine NATO countries, as well as by airborne early warning assets assigned to Operation Deny Flight (enforcing the no-fly zone over Bosnia-Herzegovina). From 22 November 1992, to 15 June 1993, over 12,000 ships had been challenged, of which 803 were stopped and 176 were diverted for cargo inspection; among these, 9 violations were detected.[61] Since Operation Sharp Guard started, over 18,000 merchantmen have been challenged, of which 1,775 have been halted, inspected or diverted.[62]

Restoring Democratic Rule: Operation Support Democracy The next occasion for a maritime interception campaign as a UN sanctions enforcement mechanism arose during the Haitian constitutional crisis. By Resolution 841 (1993), Resolution 861 (1993) and Resolution 873 (1993), the Security Council acting under chapter 7 imposed, lifted and reimposed a selective oil and arms embargo against the Caribbean island, while by Resolution 875, adopted on 16 October 1993, it called upon:

> Member States acting nationally or through regional agencies or arrangements, cooperating with the legitimate Government of Haiti, to use such measures commensurate with the specific circumstances as may be necessary under

[61]See KRIENDLER, J., 'NATO's Changing Role – Opportunities and Constraints for Peacekeeping', 41 *NATO Review* (June 1993) at p. 19.

[62]See NATO's Fact Sheet on Operation Sharp Guard, 14 April 1994. The Italian coastguard designated specific diversion areas and the ports of Bari and Brindisi in case thorough cargo inspection could not be performed at sea. In the event, about 15 ships were impounded in Italian ports for violation of the UN resolutions; see VENTURONI, G, 'The Italian Navy in Allied Adriatic Operations', 39 *NATO's Sixteen Nations* (1994/1) at p. 40. See also BOORDA, J.M., 'Loyal Partner – NATO's Forces in Support of the United Nations', *ibid.*, pp. 8–12; CAIRNS, P.W., 'Maritime Training for Peacekeeping Operations', *ibid.*, pp. 17–20; ANNATI, M.A., 'Stand By, We Are Boarding', 120 *USNIP* (March 1994), pp. 53–7.

> the authority of the Secretary-General to ensure strict implementation of the provisions of resolutions 841 (1993) and 873 (1993) relating to the supply of petroleum products or arms and related matériel of all types, and in particular to *halt inward maritime shipping as necessary in order to inspect and verify their cargoes and destinations*. (emphasis added)[63]

The first freighter *en route* to Haiti to be intercepted by a US ship was the *Don José* registered in the Turks and Caicos Islands. The ship was detected while sailing some 13 miles north of Haiti and stopped only after two warning shots were fired across its bows.[64] On 19 October 1993, a ship carrying food and medical supplies from a Miami-based relief organization to Haiti was reportedly turned back by warships enforcing the oil and arms embargo.[65] Although the US-Canadian flotilla was scheduled to patrol just outside the 3-mile territorial sea limit of Haiti, on 21 October 1993, US President Bill Clinton was reported to have ordered the US warships to operate within the Haitian territorial waters.[66] Consequently, General Raoul Cédras asked his Prime Minister to file a protest against the presence of US warships in Port-au-Prince bay as a violation of Haiti's territorial sovereignty.[67]

Finally, on 6 May 1994, the Security Council passed unanimously Resolution 917 setting up the long-threatened total trade embargo. In the terms of para.9, all maritime traffic should be prohibited from entering or leaving the territory or territorial sea of Haiti with the exception of regularly scheduled shipping lines calling in Haiti carrying non-prohibited commodities or commodities in transit to other destinations, while para.10 reframed the authorization to those member states wishing to

[63]Six US destroyers and three Canadian naval vessels were already stationed off Haitian coasts at the time the UN embargo went into effect; see 'In and Out with the Tide', *Time*, 25 October 1993 at p. 24; 'No Way to Cut and Run', *Newsweek*, 25 October 1993 at p. 15; 'Waiting for Something Horrid', *Economist*, 23 October 1993 at p. 53. Shortly after, France, the United Kingdom, the Netherlands, Argentina and Chile announced that they were ready to commit naval vessels in support of Operation Support Democracy; see 'Britain and the Netherlands to Join UN Blockade of Haiti', *International Herald Tribune*, 20 October 1993 at p. 7.

[64]See FRENCH, H.W., 'Aristide Team, with Help, Blocks the Sale of Gasoline', *New York Times*, 22 October 1993 at p.A10.

[65]See 'U.S. Warns Army in Haiti not to Seize Gasoline Supplies', *International Herald Tribune*, 23–4 October 1993 at p. 5.

[66]See FRENCH, H.W., 'Haiti's Premier and General Meet as Drive to Settle Crisis Intensifies', *New York Times*, 26 October 1993 at p.A13.

[67]See FRENCH, H.W., 'New Haiti Road Could Become Lifeline', *New York Times*, 28 October 1993 at p.A16.

participate in naval enforcement 'to halt *outward as well as inward* maritime shipping as necessary in order to inspect and verify their cargoes and destinations' (emphasis added).[68]

The Next Step: Stocktaking If one is to compare the above experiences, it is clear that they match hardly at all. Despite an apparent resemblance reflected in the wording of the relevant Security Council resolutions, the maritime operations under discussion are part of distinct 'sanction-packages'. No doubt, the Security Council in the post-Cold War era appears prepared to add a naval dimension to its coercive action, yet at varying times, pursuing often dissimilar objectives, and calling upon diverse agents for its accomplishment.

However, on the operational level which interests us here, several important conclusions are to be drawn. Stopping and searching a merchant ship in the traditional mode has lost nothing of its *raison d'être*. Warning shots across the bows remain the last resort for bringing a ship to halt, while boarding parties are still confronted with the same age-old frauds with regard to ship's papers. Maritime patrol aircraft and helicopters are now fully integrated and greatly appreciated in interception operations. Cargo inspection at sea is occasionally impossible (modern container-ships carrying 2,000–3,000 densely packed containers offer the best example), so that diversion to port appears a logical necessity where doubt persists.[69]

[68]Given the often denounced lack of coordination among the actors, as experienced in the Persian Gulf and the Adriatic campaigns, Security Council Resolution 917 for the first time called for regular reporting of the naval contingents to the UN Sanctions Committee.

[69]The recent UN-authorized naval operations pose a certain number of other queries. From the point of view of legal theory, there is the problem of the exact constitutional basis of such operations. Are they evocative of economic sanctions under Article 41, military coercion under Article 42, or something in between? As regards legal practice, it would be interesting to explore whether any pattern is being moulded to serve as the post-Cold War model in securing compliance, or if this is all simply due to the overheating of the UN's engine. And last, in relation to legal history, are current UN exercises in economic warfare truly different from collective naval enterprises of the last century recorded in history under the euphemism of 'pacific blockades'? On these points, see POLITAKIS, G.P., 'UN-Mandated Naval Operations and the Notion of Pacific Blockade: Comments on Some Recent Developments', 6 *RADIC* (1994), p. 173*ff.* See also SCHRIJVER, N., 'The Use of Economic Sanctions by the UN Security Council: An International Perspective' in POST, H.H.G. (ed.), *International Economic Law and Armed Conflict*, 1994 at pp. 152–4.

4 Evading visit and search: the convoy device

A Neutral Vessels Under National Convoy

Neutrals' persistent attempts to circumvent the obstacles that belligerents so often imposed to the seaborne trade eventually gave rise to the practice of neutral convoys. This arrangement envisaged a group of neutral merchantmen sailing under the orders and protection of a warship of their home state with the expectation that, upon being summoned, the convoy commander would give ample and sufficient assurances that the escorted vessels were not engaged in carriage of contraband and, therefore, they should be spared the visit and search procedure. The innovation proved, however, to be an irritant to belligerent interests promising lasting friction. For Philip Jessup, the use of convoys sought to achieve the same purpose as the classical demonstration of ship's papers, yet on an entirely different assumption:

> in the case of ship's papers, ownership, destination, innocent character of cargo, etc., were to be ascertained or proved on the basis of what may be called legal evidence. This evidence was submitted to and passed upon by the belligerent, first at sea, and, on occasion, subsequently in his prize courts. On the other hand, in the case of convoy, the neutral made an assertion of fact or law and the belligerent could accept the *ipse dixit* or fight.[70]

As a substitute device for the traditional right of visit, neutral convoys were first introduced in the seventeenth century. In 1653, during the war between Great Britain and Holland, Queen Christina ordered her merchantmen to sail in convoy and instructed the escort captains to resist any belligerent inter-

[70]See JESSUP and DEÁK, *op. cit., supra* n.2 at p. 200. The legal controversy over neutral convoys is treated in KLEEN, *op. cit., supra* n.13, pp. 346–89; GORDON, E., 'La visite des convois neutres', 41 *RGDIP* (1934), p. 566*ff.*; AKZIN, B., 'Neutral Convoys in Law and Practice', 40 *Michigan Law Review* (1941–2), p. 1*ff.* See also STÖDTER, R., 'Convoy' in BERNHARDT, R. (ed.), *Encyclopedia of Public International Law,* instalment 3 (1982), p. 128*ff.* It must be stressed that by 'right to convoy' in a legal sense is only meant a *neutral* claim to offer protection against visit and search and it should not be confounded with *belligerent* convoy techniques as a means of protecting merchant shipping.

ference.[71] In the eighteenth century, during the Seven Year War (1756–63), the Dutch reinstated their claim to exempt all escorted vessels from the right of visit and search but Britain obstinately refused to acquiesce to that pretension. The War of Independence of the United States (1776–83) marked the first time that a belligerent power, to wit the United Provinces of the Netherlands, in conformity with its previous commitment abstained from boarding neutral merchant vessels sailing in convoy.[72] From 1782 to 1800 the convoy principle was reaffirmed in several treaties entered into by some Scandinavian powers and also the United States. Great Britain, for her part, sought by all means to retain the right of visit and search unfettered.[73]

The emerging right of neutral convoy caused renewed dispute between Denmark and Britain in 1799 leading to the formation of the Second Armed Neutrality between Russia, Prussia, Sweden and Denmark under Tsar Paul's leadership in 1800. The Second Armed Neutrality raised specifically the issue of freedom from visitation and search of neutral merchantmen sailing in neutral convoy maintaining that a declaration of the commanding officer concerning the absence of contraband was all that could lawfully be required.[74] The controversy continued

[71]See NYS, *op. cit., supra* n.11 at pp. 77–8. On the early history of neutral convoys, see also ORTOLAN, *op. cit., supra* n.13, pp. 262–79.
[72]See DUPUIS, *op. cit., supra* n.13 at pp. 305–6.
[73]As Lord Stowell eloquently asserted with relation to a 1798 incident involving a Swedish convoy of 33 vessels seized in the English Channel, 'two sovereigns may unquestionably agree, if they think fit, by special covenant, that the presence of one of their armed ships along with their merchant-ships shall be mutually understood to imply that nothing is to be found in that convoy of merchant-ships inconsistent with amity or neutrality . . . But surely no sovereign can legally compel the acceptance of such a security by mere force. The only security known to the law of nations upon this subject, independent of all special covenant, is the right of personal visitation and search, to be exercised by those who have the interest in making it. I am not ignorant, that amongst the loose doctrines which modern fancy, under the various denominations of philosophy and philanthropy, and I know not what, have thrown upon the world, it has been within these few years advanced, or rather insinuated, that it might possibly be well if such a security were accepted. Upon such unauthorized speculations it is not necessary for me to descant: the law and practice of nations give them no sort of countenance; and until that law and practice are new-modelled in such a way as may surrender the known and ancient rights of some nations to the present convenience of other nations, no reverence is due to them'; see *The Maria* (1799), 1 *C. Robinson's Admiralty Reports* at pp. 362–3.
[74]See Article 3§5 of the Russo-Swedish Convention for the Re-establishment of an Armed Neutrality of 16 December 1800: 'that the declaration of the commanding officer of the vessel or vessels of the royal or imperial navy, which

unabated throughout the nineteenth century. Continental writers invoked the principle of good faith and maintained that the affirmation of the convoy's commanding officer should be sufficient warranty of the convoy's regularity.[75]

The 1909 London Declaration gave further evidence of the validity of the long-contested convoy principle. Article 61 of this instrument recognized that neutral merchantmen under escort should enjoy immunity from visit and search in these terms:

> neutral vessels under national convoy are exempt from search. The commander of a convoy gives, in writing, at the request of the commander of a belligerent warship, all information as to the character of the vessels and their cargoes, which could be obtained by search.[76]

While Article 62 further affirmed that the convoying officer was alone authorized to inquire into any allegations that a vessel under his protection carried contraband:

---

accompanies the convoy of one or more merchant ships, that his convoy carries no contraband merchandise, must be considered sufficient, and that thereupon there shall be no occasion to visit either his vessel or those of his convoy'; see SCOTT, J.B. (ed.), *The Armed Neutralities of 1780 and 1800,* 1918 at p. 533. Identical provisions had been included in the Convention between Russia, Denmark and Norway of 16 December 1800, and the Convention between Russia and Prussia of 18 December 1800; see *ibid.* at pp. 539, 546. Documents related to the First and Second Armed Neutralities are also collected in PIGGOTT, F. and OMOND, G.W.T., *Documentary History of the Armed Neutralities 1780 and 1800,* 1919.

[75]The right of convoy was explicitly admitted in the 1870 French naval instructions, while England, for its part, favoured an integral right of visit and search which would afford no exceptions. The latter view was vigorously supported by a number of learned scholars such as Robert Phillimore, William E. Hall, and Thomas J. Lawrence. Their main objection to the proposed immunity was related to the fact that the convoying officer would be in most cases in a material impossibility to verify personally and in advance the regularity of his convoy. It appeared, therefore, understandable to them why Britain felt reticent to substitute a neutral paper control for a genuine contraband control performed by the most interested state, that is the belligerent. In Article 16 of the Draft International Rules on Maritime Capture, adopted by the Institut de Droit International in 1882, it was provided that 'lorsque des navires de commerce neutres sont convoyés, ils ne seront pas visités, si le commandant du convoi remet au navire du belligérant qui l'arrête une liste des navires convoyés et une déclaration signée par lui et portant qu'il ne se trouve à leur bord aucune contrebande de guerre et quelles sont la nationalité et la destination des navires envoyés'; see 6 *Ann.IDI* (1882–3) Torino Session at p. 215.

[76]Drawing upon the idea of good faith and international comity, the General Report of the Drafting Committee of the London Declaration considered that the commander of the belligerent cruiser 'cannot question the assurances given by the official representative of a neutral Government, without failing in international courtesy'; see USNWC, 9 *International Law Topics* (1909) at p. 139.

> if the commander of the belligerent warship has reason to suspect that the confidence of the commander of the convoy has been abused, he communicates his suspicions to him. In such a case it is for the commander of the convoy alone to investigate the matter. He must record the result of such investigation in a report of which a copy is handed to the officer of the warship. If, in the opinion of the commander of the convoy, the facts shown in the report justify the capture of one or more vessels, the protection of the convoy must be withdrawn from such vessels.[77]

By the time the First World War broke out, most countries, with the notable exception of Great Britain, had adopted rules following the provisions of the unratified London Declaration.[78] In 1922, a subcommittee of the American Society of International Law, which set out to study and report on the commonly accepted rules regarding visit, search and capture, arrived at the conclusion that the exemption of neutral convoys from visit and search made part of the 'common law' on the subject having been long recognized as binding law by all maritime nations.[79] In 1939, the Harvard Research on Neutral Rights and Duties in Naval War in Articles 56–7 followed closely the provisions of the London Declaration.

B Neutral vessels under belligerent convoy

The practice of neutral merchantmen sailing under enemy convoy for reasons of protection should not be confounded with the right of neutral warships to convoy merchant vessels of their home flag in order to eschew belligerent search and possibly diversion. The latter is a recognized mechanism permitting evasion of *contraband control,* and perhaps the most formal way to certify the innocent character of the shipment, whereas the former pertains clearly to the rules governing the conditions

[77]Interestingly enough, the Drafting Committee in its report left open the possibility for the convoy commander to invite the officer of the belligerent warship to join the inspection should the suspicion persist, but only 'as an act of courtesy or good policy'; *ibid.* at p. 143.

[78]See, for instance, Articles 51–3 of the 1917 US Instructions, or Article 87 and Articles 103–4 of the 1912 French Instructions in VERZIJL, *op. cit., supra* n.26 at pp. 1173–4. See also Article 10 of the 1915 Italian Naval Prize Regulations, 10 *AJIL* (1916) *Suppl.* at p. 120.

[79]See 16 *Proc.ASIL* (1922) at p. 53.

under which a belligerent can engage his enemy and results in an unequivocal waiver of neutral rights. One could also say that sailing under national convoy is to escape seizure by honouring neutrality, whereas sailing under belligerent convoy is to escape seizure by defying neutrality.[80]

The most common approach is to address the issue under the heading of unneutral service which, of course, is not totally satisfactory. It is clear that in the case under consideration the escorted neutral vessels offer no service whatsoever to the belligerent (beyond the carrying of contraband). To the extent that the voyage placed under belligerent protection has an enemy destination, it might be argued that it evokes as much carriage of contraband as unneutral service. It would be certainly justified to assume that a neutral vessel under these circumstances would be most likely chartered by the enemy government or in any event subject to the full control of the latter which alludes to the rules of unneutral service. The fact remains, however, that merely sailing under belligerent convoy does not amount in itself to a case of unneutral service.

Belligerent convoys lay at the origin of heated controversy between Denmark and the United States in the period 1810–30. At the time of the Anglo-Danish War, American vessels often sought protection in British convoys when sailing in the North Sea and the Baltic Sea. As a result, Denmark modified its naval instructions and announced that any neutral ship voyaging under enemy protection would be condemned as lawful prize. In the event, some eighteen American ships were seized. In the protracted diplomatic quarrel that ensued, the American government argued that a belligerent convoy was an established practice which did not imply resistance to seizure at least on the part of neutral vessels and which accordingly did not authorize enemy action other than the exercise of the right of visit and search. The dispute ended in 1830 with an agreement which provided for monetary compensation to be paid to the United States, while Denmark obtained an explicit treaty provision by

[80]On belligerent escort of neutral shipping, see GORDON, E., 'Le navire de commerce neutre sous convoi de la marine militaire d'un belligérant', 17 *RDILC* (1936), p. 165*ff*. See also 33 *AJIL* (1939), pp. 674–80, and ROSKILL, S.W., '*Capros* Not *Convoy*: Counter-Attack and Destroy!', 82 *USNIP* (Oct.1956), p. 1047*ff*.

which the negotiated settlement was to bear no precedential value as to the issue of belligerent convoys.[81]

At the time of the First World War, only the Japanese *Regulations* of 1914 and the US *Instructions for the Navy* of 1917 contained explicit provisions concerning the capture of neutral vessels under convoy of enemy warships. The French *Instructions,* for their part, simply mentioned that a ship should bear full responsibility for the damage or destruction it might suffer in the event of a naval engagement. The question did not arise, however, in any prize decision.[82] When the American steamship *Gulflight* was torpedoed and sunk in May 1915 in the vicinity of the Scilly Islands, it was apparently escorted by two small

[81]According to one commentator, 'il est impossible de tirer de l'affaire dano-américaine aucune conclusion, soit en faveur de l'une, soit en faveur de l'autre des deux thèses'; see GORDON, *op. cit., supra* at p. 171. It may be noted, however, that American jurisprudence and doctrinal opinion had already ceded to the widely held view according to which sailing under belligerent convoy forfeits neutral immunity. In 1815, Justice Story, referring to the Danish claim that 'none of the powers in Europe have called in question the justice of this principle', admitted that 'it cannot be denied, that our government acquiesced in the truth and correctness of this statement', and reasoned as follows: 'The resistance of the convoy is the resistance of all the ships associated under the common protection, without any distinction whether the convoy belong to the same or to a foreign, neutral sovereign; for upon the principles of natural justice, a neutral is justly chargeable with the acts of the party, which he voluntarily adopts, or of which he seeks the shelter and protection . . . It is because there is a constructive resistance, in law, from the common association and voluntary protection against search, under a full knowledge of the intentions of the convoy. Then, the principle applies as well to a belligerent as to a neutral convoy; for it is manifest, that the belligerent will, at all events, resist search; and it is quite as manifest, that the neutral seeks belligerent protection, with an intent to evade it . . . There can be but little doubt, that it is upon the latter principle, that the penalty of confiscation is applied to neutrals. The law proceeds yet further, and deems the sailing under convoy as an act *per se* inconsistent with neutrality, as a premeditated attempt to oppose, if practicable, the right of search, and therefore, attributes to such preliminary act, the full effect of actual resistance'; see *The Nereide* (1815), in 9 *W. Cranch's US Supreme Court Reports* at pp. 438–42. Three years later, Justice Johnson declared: 'a convoy is an association for a hostile object; in undertaking it, a nation spreads over the merchant vessel an immunity from search, which belongs only to a national ship; and by joining a convoy, every individual ship puts off her pacific character, and undertakes for the discharge of duties which belong only to the military marine, and adds to the numerical, if not to the real, strength of the convoy. If then, the association be voluntary, the neutral in suffering the fate of the whole, has only to regret his own folly, in wedding his fortune to theirs'; see *The Atalanta* (1818), in 3 *H. Wheaton's US Supreme Court Reports* at p. 423. For an account of the Danish-American dispute and a detailed critique of the American position, see KLEEN, *op. cit., supra* n.13, vol.II (1900) at pp. 382–9.
[82]See VERZIJL, *op. cit., supra* n.26 at p. 1176.

British naval vessels. In responding to the American protests, the German government did not attempt to justify its action by reference to belligerent convoys as one might expect, but expressed its regret for the 'unfortunate accident' and offered 'full recompense for the damage'.[83]

Beginning in 1916, the British Admiralty decided to escort allied and neutral ships on a regular basis, the most notable case being that of Norwegian ships supplying Britain with nitrate of ammonia and plying between different Norwegian ports and Lerwick. The elaborate convoy techniques developed in 1917 proved highly effective against the threat of submarine attack.[84] A noteworthy aspect of these Norwegian convoys is that in the early voyages the British warships entered the neutral ports but weighed anchor before the 24-hour visit time expired. In 1918, however, due to the increased activity of German U-boats in coastal areas, it was decided that British men-of-war should accompany the convoys no further than the Norwegian territorial sea limits, the remainder of the voyage to be effected under Norwegian convoy.

Under Article 64(a) of the 1939 Harvard Draft Convention, a neutral vessel sailing under the escort of enemy warships was to be treated as an enemy merchant vessel. The Commentary admits that the question is not firmly settled and notes: 'the present tendency in this mater, as in many other questions of the law of neutrality, is undoubtedly toward increasing belligerent rights. A large majority of writers seem to favour the right of belligerents to condemn neutral vessels under enemy convoy.'[85] The view has also been put forward that a neutral vessel under belligerent convoy should be liable to attack on sight and to destruction no less than the accompanying enemy warships. For Robert Tucker, 'there is now a substantial consensus that the mere fact of enemy convoy is sufficient to assimilate a neutral vessel to the status of the belligerent warships providing protection'.[86]

[83]See 9 *AJIL* (1915) *Sp.Suppl* at p. 137.
[84]In October 1917, 99 convoys comprising as many as 1,502 vessels safely arrived in England while the losses did not exceed 1.57 per cent. In November of that year, 70 new convoys made the North Sea crossing, the losses being 0.57 per cent; see GORDON, *op. cit., supra* n.80 at p. 176.
[85]See 33 *AJIL* (1939) *Suppl.* at p. 680.
[86]See TUCKER, *op. cit., supra* n.3 at p. 321.

C Neutral convoys in the 1980–8 Persian Gulf War

The Reflagging Scheme In a move that was destined to bring foreign naval intervention to its climax, Kuwait requested in December 1986 that both superpowers take upon themselves the protection of its oil tankers while navigating inside the Persian Gulf.[87] By February 1987, it appeared that the idea was favourably received and that Kuwait would place five of its tankers under the Soviet flag and another six under the American one. Concerned about the prospect of increased Soviet influence in the Gulf region, US diplomacy sought to exclude Soviet naval presence by proposing the reflagging of all eleven tankers under consideration. In early April, Kuwait formally approved the US offer, thus limiting the Soviet participation to a simple charter arrangement. The three Soviet-flagged chartered vessels entered into service in May while, later in 1987, the UK agreed also to reflag three more Kuwaiti tankers.

In a statement of 19 May 1987, before the House Foreign Affairs Committee, US Assistant Secretary Richard Murphy defended the scheduled reflagging operation in these words: 'in providing this protection, our actions will be fully consistent with the *applicable rules of international law, which clearly recognize the right of a neutral state to escort and protect ships flying its flag which are not carrying contraband*. In this case, this includes the fact that US ships will not be carrying oil from Iraq. Neither party to the conflict will have any basis for taking hostile action against U.S. naval ships or the vessels they will protect' (emphasis added).[88]

On 15 June 1987, Secretary of Defense Caspar Weinberger presented a report to the US Congress on Security Arrangements in the Persian Gulf in which he described more accurately the escort mission:

> international law clearly recognizes the right of a neutral state to escort and protect its flag vessels in transit to neutral ports. The tankers will carry Kuwaiti oil to neutral

[87]A chronology of the negotiated reflagging arrangement with the United States is in 26 *ILM* (1987), pp. 1461–3.

[88]*Ibid.* at p. 1425. Hardly could a solicitation of the traditional right to convoy be made in more unmistakable terms. To be noted, however, the erroneous perception of Iraqi oil exports as contraband.

> ports and will return in ballast; they will not carry contraband for either of the belligerents. If a belligerent seeks to exercise the right of visit and search for contraband, the U.S. escorts will certify its absence . . . Therefore, the United States will be in full compliance with international law concerning neutrality and the use of force. Neither the tankers nor their U.S. escorts will be legitimate objects of attack, and the United States will exercise the right to use reasonable force only to protect them from attack.[89]

Under the traditional law of naval warfare, neutral convoys aim at certifying the absence of contraband aboard neutral merchantmen. It could be argued that in the case of the Gulf experience only the northbound branch of the transit passage consisted in the exercise of the neutral right to convoy *stricto sensu*. During the Kuwait-bound voyage, in fact, the captains of US warships were instructed to give all necessary guarantees that escorted tankers transported no contraband since unloaded, and consequently to resist any attempt on the part of the Iranian navy to interfere with the convoy. On the contrary, during their southbound passage the reflagged tankers transported neutral (Kuwaiti) oil to non-hostile destinations, thus the question of carriage of contraband could not arise and therefore one should not speak of a neutral convoy in the traditional sense.[90]

Although not directly related to the convoy operations that interest us here, a few words should be said about the legal aspects of reflagging as such. Under US domestic law, the Kuwaiti tankers before being permitted to fly the US flag should have met US ownership and manning requirements and to have submitted to inspection regarding their conformity with US

[89] *Ibid.* at p. 1458.

[90] The legal aspects of the US convoy undertaking as a traditional neutral right are examined in DAVIDSON, S., 'United States Protection of Reflagged Kuwaiti Vessels in the Gulf War: The Legal Implications', 4 *International Journal of Estuarine and Coastal Law* (1989), p. 173*ff*.; McDONALD, W.L., 'The Convoy Mission', 114 *USNIP* (May 1988), p. 36*ff*.; GAMLEN, E. and ROGERS, P., 'U.S. Reflagging of Kuwaiti Tankers', in RAJAEE, F. (ed.), *The Iran-Iraq War: The Politics of Aggression*, 1993, p. 123*ff*.; CARON, D.D., 'Choice and Duty in Foreign Affairs: The Reflagging of the Kuwaiti Tankers' in JOYNER, C.C. (ed.), *The Persian Gulf War – Lessons for Strategy, Law, and Diplomacy*, 1990, p. 153*ff*.

U. S. Navy Convoys, July 1987-December 1988

Month	*Number of Convoys Begun*	*Number of Merchant Ships Escorted*
1987		
July	1	2
August	5	13
September	4	9
October	4	8
November	5	16
December	3	11
1988		
January	7	16
February	7	18
March	6	10
April	7	18
May	6	14
June	10	16
July	8	13
August*	10	17
September	7	17
October	10	19
November	12	22
December**	15	20
Total	127	259

Source: Department of Defense, 17 January 1989.
*Cease-fire went into effect 20 August 1988.
**Data for December include some "accompanying" operations.

Table 3 *The Reflagged Tanker Convoy Mission*
Source: O'ROURKE, R., 'Gulf Ops', 115 *USNIP* (May 1989) at p. 49

Coast Guard safety standards.[91] This procedure raised the recurrent question of the *genuine link* in respect of ship registration. Given the vagueness of the concept, as crystallized in the 1958 High Seas Convention, or the 1982 Law of the Sea Convention, and equally preserved in the 1986 Registration of Ships Convention, it cannot be easily denied that the United States in carrying out the reflagging scheme complied with international law standards.[92]

On 21 July 1987, the first two Kuwaiti tankers to be re-registered under US law, the *Bridgeton* and the *Gas Prince*, were transferred to the Chesapeake Shipping Company established under US law, and the next day they entered the Gulf escorted by US warships.[93] By the end of 1988, the US Navy had conducted 136 convoy operations, escorting a total of 270 merchant ships at an average rate of seven convoys per month and two merchant ships per convoy.[94] Following the ceasefire of 20 August 1988, the US Navy announced the formal suspension of convoy operations in December 1988. More precisely, American naval forces' role was downgraded first to *accompanying* US-flagged ships, and then to simply *monitoring* US merchant traffic in the Persian Gulf.[95]

It has been commonly acknowledged that Iran did not challenge the US convoys mainly because of political realism, but this does not reduce the precedential value of Tehran's acquiesc-

[91]With regard to ownership, all that was needed was to transfer the Kuwaiti vessels to a US company in which the chief executive, the chairman of the board and the majority of the directors were American citizens. As to the nationality of the crew, since the tankers would not depart from or call at US ports, it could have been non-American except for the master. Finally, on account of national security interests, the Department of Defence conceded waivers from certain safety specifications (e.g. required life-saving equipment or drydocking); see 26 *ILM* (1987) at pp. 1450–1.

[92]The reflagging operation from the point of view of peacetime law of the sea has been analysed in NORDQUIST, M.H. and WACHENFELD, M.G., 'Legal Aspects of Reflagging Kuwaiti Tankers and Laying of Mines in the Persian Gulf', 31 *GYIL* (1988), p. 138*ff.*, and WOLFRUM, R., 'Reflagging and Escort Operation in the Persian Gulf: An International Law Perspective', 29 *VJIL* (1989), p. 387*ff.* On the evolution of the concept of genuine link, see McCONNELL, M.L., '. . . Darkening Confusion Mounted Upon Darkening Confusion: The Search for the Elusive Genuine Link', 16 *Journal of Maritime Law and Commerce* (1985), p. 365*ff.*

[93]It was during this maiden voyage under the American flag that the *Bridgeton* struck a mine while 120 n.m. south east of Kuwait; on this incident, see SEITZ, F.C., '*SS Bridgeton*: The First Convoy', 114 *USNIP* (May 1988), p. 52*ff.*

[94]See O'ROURKE, R., 'Gulf Ops', 115 *USNIP* (May 1989) at p. 49.

[95]See DE GUTTRY and RONZITTI, *op. cit., supra* n.45, doc.3.20 at pp. 209–10.

ence to the campaign. It can also be said that Iran refrained from asserting its belligerent right of visit and search since the escorted vessels, at least the reflagged Kuwaiti tankers, in the northbound voyage were sailing in ballast, and by construction they were unsuitable for transport of contraband (except of course for oil and gas of which Iraq was definitely not in need). In any event, it appears that not only Iran desisted from interfering with neutral convoys in practice but also never claimed in the abstract the right to do so. The Iranian conduct can thus be interpreted as a confirmation of the continued validity of the customary principle of exemption of neutral convoys from belligerent contraband control measures.

The US Escort Mission For the purposes of tanker protection the United States gathered an impressive naval force of some thirty-five warships including an aircraft carrier, a battleship, missile destroyers and missile frigates, landing ships and auxiliary craft, minesweeping vessels and minesweeping helicopters. Given such massive deployment, besides being commonly acknowledged to have a clear offensive profile, the US Navy could afford to escort merchant ships in even these excessive numbers. As was noted in a British report, the US Navy did not hesitate to use 'as many as eight warships to protect three merchant vessels'.[96] As part of the 'reflag and convoy deal', Kuwait agreed to grant landing rights to US aircraft engaged in escort operations and supply free fuel to the US warships. In contrast, US vessels were not allowed to enter or station in Kuwaiti territorial waters.[97]

The end points of US escort missions were Kuwaiti territorial sea limits and Fujairah-Khor-Fakan in the Gulf of Oman, where the oil was trans-shipped to other tankers for transport to its final destination. In early 1988, the operation proceeded at the rate of one convoy per week, and two or three tankers per convoy. In November 1987, the largest until then convoy, com-

[96]*Ibid*, doc.2.a.37 at p. 303. The US Navy escort operations put in the larger context of the American naval intervention in the Gulf region are also examined in MENEFEE, S.P., 'Commentary on the United States' Practice', *ibid.*, pp. 92–132.
[97]It is possible, however, that this position was later modified since in December 1987 Kuwait reportedly approved a US request to anchor a barge fortress near Kuwait's offshore oil terminal, in Kuwaiti territorial waters; see BROWN, J., 'The Superpowers in the Middle East: Lessons from the Persian Gulf', *Brassey's Defence Yearbook* (1989), ftn.18 at p. 145.

prising five vessels of which one non-Kuwaiti, non-reflagged freighter carried US arms, was coupled with the appearance for the first time of the battleship *USS Missouri* in the Gulf.[98]

The Soviet Convoy Operations The first Soviet warship was intitially deployed in September 1986 after an incident in which Iranian gunboats had fired upon, stopped and searched the Soviet merchant vessel *Pyotr Emtsov* while heading to Kuwait with an arms shipment ultimately destined for Iraq.[99] The one-year lease agreement with Kuwait for three Soviet tankers was signed on 1 April 1987, and was renewed in 1988. On 17 May 1987, during its first trip under Kuwaiti charter, the Soviet tanker *Marshal Chuykov* struck a mine near the Kuwaiti port of Al-Ahmadi and had to proceed to Dubai for repairs. In the second half of 1987 the Soviet naval forces present in the Gulf region were to increase markedly. By the end of September 1987 no less than 1,500 men on board several warships were deployed in the area.[100]

In contrast to the US Task Force, the Soviets avoided the deployment of large combatants such as aircraft carriers and battleships, opting instead for destoyers, frigates and minesweepers, some 20 vessels in total, of which between 4 and 7 plied the Persian Gulf itself.[101] The number of escort missions undertaken by the former Soviet Union's navy was roughly similar to that of the French or the Italian navy. In February 1988, for instance, there was recorded six Soviet convoys as compared to seven French and five Italian.[102] Assessing the surface threat to be predominant within and around the Strait of Hormuz while that of mines throughout the rest of the voyage to Kuwait, a Soviet destroyer or frigate at anchorage in the Gulf of Oman was usually assigned the escort task through the strait up to the vicinity of the port of Dubai, while for the second leg

[98]See *Middle East Military Balance* (1987–8) at p. 84.
[99]On the Soviet naval presence in general, see CIGAR, N., 'The Soviet Navy in the Gulf: Naval Diplomacy in a Combat Zone', 42 *US Naval War College Review* (spring 1989), pp. 56–88.
[100]See OUDOT DE DAINVILLE, A., 'Analyse de la guerre du Golfe', 44 *Défense Nationale* (oct.1988) at p. 59.
[101]See *Middle East Military Balance* (1987–8) at p. 83.
[102]See DE GUTTRY and RONZITTI, *op. cit., supra* n.45, doc.2.a.37 at p. 299.

of the journey ship protection was entrusted to small minesweepers.[103]

Although in a number of cases Iranian frigates or speedboats approached and challenged escorted Soviet ships, there have been no reports of armed incidents.[104] Particularly displeased with Iranian halt and search tactics, the Soviet navy had placed special 'counterboarding groups' on its warships while on escort mission. In fact, the low-profile of the Soviet involvement changed distinctly in the wake of the *Ivan Koroteev* incident of 6 May 1987, in which two Iranian speedboats closed to the unescorted Soviet freighter while *en route* to Damman, Saudi Arabia, and strafed it with machine-gun fire inflicting material damage. Moscow filed a protest with Tehran over the incident reaffirming its commitment to defend freedom of navigation while reportedly sending fifty aircraft into Iranian airspace as a clear sign of its determination.

The British Naval Action In September 1980, the British government launched Operation Armilla which originally consisted in dispatching two Royal Navy warships with a view to offering 'assistance' if needed to British shipping in the Gulf.[105] As was later reported to the House of Commons, 'the role of the Armilla Patrol was to remain in the Gulf of Oman and to provide a visible naval presence to British merchant shipping entering the Gulf, while being prepared to enter the Gulf if necessary. The object was to encourage merchant shipping to continue to transit the Strait of Hormuz, without giving any suggestion that military intervention was planned'.[106] Formal arrangements for

[103]One minesweeper had completed 14,000 miles in escort duty in the Gulf in just two months; see CIGAR, *op. cit., supra* n.99 at p. 69. Up to four ships were taken in convoy at a time. It is of particular interest to note that the Soviet warships were in all probability the only among all foreign navies in the Gulf to have escorted merchantmen not only to Arab ports but to Iranian ones as well, such as the *Khudozhnik Gabashvili* to Bandar Abbas in 1987; *ibid.* at p. 66.

[104]Most of the time the Soviet warships went to action stations by locking on the Iranian ships following which the latter broke off and sailed away. For an account of such incidents, see *ibid.* at pp. 64–5.

[105]See statement of the Secretary of State for Foreign and Commonwealth Affairs on 7 December 1983, in DE GUTTRY and RONZITTI, *op. cit., supra* n.45, doc.2.a.5 at p. 260. On the nature, extent and the policy objectives of the British naval intervention in the Gulf in general, see also LOWE, A.V., 'Commentary on the British Practice', *ibid.*, pp. 241–53.

[106]*Ibid.*, doc.2.a.19 at pp. 271–2.

convoy missions were not envisaged given the limited assets available, but also by reason of the risk of escalation that convoys were believed to involve.[107]

Towards the end of 1986 the British naval presence was reinforced by a third warship while in September 1987 four minehunters also joined the Armilla Patrol. Despite the increased potential, however, the British government refrained from ordering systematic convoy operations. The mission of British naval forces was officially described as providing reassurance to British ships. On 21 July 1987, for instance, Geoffrey Howe declared that 'the Armilla Patrol provides cover for British shipping when it is in the relevant area', maintaining a 'self-defensive', 'non-provocative and de-escalatory' posture.[108] Whenever possible, these vessels were accompanied, although no further than 40 miles north of Dubai where the area of operations of the Armilla Patrol ended.[109]

As regards reflagging, the first Kuwaiti tanker, the *Tonbridge* (ex-*Al-Fariha*) sailed under the British flag in September 1987.[110] As it was affirmed in July 1987, 'the reflagging of merchant shipping is a commercial and administrative matter. It does not require our approval but does require applicants to satisfy certain requirements imposed by the Department of Trans-

[107]In July 1984, for instance, the British Parliament was informed that 'all effort is going into seeking restraint in the area by diplomatic means, and therefore there is at present no policy to escort merchant ships or tankers . . . For us to go a stage further and provide convoy protection would involve serious and wide political implications which we should seek to avoid'; *ibid.*, doc.2.a.8 at p. 264.

[108]*Ibid.*, doc.2.a.22 at pp. 277, 279. According to yet another statement, 'the job of the Patrol will be to help and to stay in the vicinity of British merchantmen'; see *ibid.*, doc.2.a.20 at p. 274.

[109]The normal procedure was that merchant vessels eligible for protection should wait at the entrance of the Hormuz Strait (at times for as long as 36 hours) until an Armilla warship became available. It would then be for the latter to specify the day and time the escorted passage should begin. While transiting the strait, merchant ships were navigating in a line, staying roughly half a mile apart; *ibid.*, doc.2.a.37 at p. 295.

[110]It is interesting to note that although the British government initially regarded reflagging as a purely administrative affair, it later expressed its 'concern that the foreign element in the British register is increasing steadily, with possible consequences for the workload of the Armilla Patrol' and discouraged a move to reflag 50 to 60 Norwegian ships; *ibid.* at p. 298. Apart from the three reflagged Kuwaiti tankers, it appears that three more ships that were already on the Gibraltar register were leased by Kuwait; *ibid.*, doc.2.a.37 at p. 319.

port'.[111] As for accompaniment operations, they commenced on 12 January 1987, and by the end of that year some 405 ships had been so protected.[112] As the Secretary of State for Foreign and Commonwealth Affairs stated in November 1987, 'the Armilla Patrol exists to provide reassurance to British ships, and to accompany their passage to the best of its limited resources. It provides no guarantee of protection and does not convoy or escort. Nor does it operate beyond the Strait of Hormuz and the southern Gulf'.[113] In total, 1,026 ships were accompanied through to November 1988 when the Armilla Patrol switched to a simple patrol role.[114]

The overall record shows that the Royal Navy had been more active than all the other western navies put together. In February 1988, for example, the Armilla Patrol undertook 60 accompanied transits while the US Navy was involved in 15, the French navy in 7, and the Italian navy in only 5 convoy missions.[115] Entitled to Armilla Patrol accompaniment were in the first place vessels on the British register (including ships registered in the Channel Islands and the Isle of Man) and on those of British dependent territories (i.e. Hong Kong, Cayman Islands, Bermuda, Gibraltar). In early 1988, however, protection was extended over foreign-flagged vessels having a clear majority UK or dependent territory interest in the ownership.[116]

Unlike the US or the French attitude at the final stage of the conflict, the British government denied any suggestion that it was providing protection to foreign merchant vessels save on strict humanitarian grounds.[117] Among the few reported inci-

[111]See 58 *BYIL* (1987) at p. 614. See also DE GUTTRY and RONZITTI, *op. cit., supra* n.45, doc.2.a.33 at p. 281.
[112]See DE GUTTRY and RONZITTI, *op. cit., supra* n.45 at p. 354. It will be recalled that in May 1988 the Armilla Patrol consisted of one frigate, two destroyers, three minesweepers and three auxiliary vessels; see BROWN, *op. cit., supra* n.97 at p. 145.
[113]See DE GUTTRY and RONZITTI, *op. cit., supra* n.45, doc.2.a.24 at p. 281.
[114]*Ibid.*, doc.2.b.12 at p. 379, and doc.2.a.47 at p. 362.
[115]*Ibid.*, doc.2.a.37 at p. 299.
[116]*Ibid.*, doc.2.a.28 at p. 283. As it was reported in June 1988, of the 133 ships which operated in the Gulf and were qualified for protection, 33 were British-owned although not flying the British flag. Thus foreign-owned and foreign-registered vessels with British crew or carrying British-owned cargo remained excluded from the expanded protection scheme; *ibid.*, doc.2.a.37 at p. 296.
[117]The British understanding was that the American forces had been authorized to adopt a 'retaliatory approach' whenever they encountered neutral vessels being attacked, i.e. an important enlargement of the scope of protection which London was not ready to follow; see *ibid.* at pp. 305–6.

dents: in November 1987, the *HMS Battleaxe* deployed a helicopter to search for and rescue survivors of the Romanian vessel *Fundulea* after it had been attacked and set on fire; in December 1987, the *HMS Scylla* assisted with her helicopter in the rescue of twenty survivors from the assailed Korean-flagged *Hyundai*; while in March 1988 medical assistance was provided to injured crewmen of the Singapore-flagged *Havglimt* and the Danish *Karama Maersk*.[118] Yet, humanitarian assistance was once described in terms of an eventual interposition of a Royal Navy warship between the attacking platform and the merchant ship in distress,[119] which would of course confer the right to British forces to open fire in self-defence should they be attacked.

French and Italian Practice Until July 1987 the French naval presence in the Gulf was kept at a rather limited level. Following the break-off of diplomatic relations with Tehran, however, the naval potential was considerably upgraded with the deployment of the *Clemenceau* aircraft carrier group.[120] Presumably these assets were never assigned the role of formally planning and carrying out convoys of French-flagged merchant vessels along the model of US Navy missions. Instead, they were authorized to keep a close watch on maritime traffic and eventually to escort one or more French merchant ships at their own request, a course of action which was given the name of *assistance* or *accompagnement*.

As was announced on 17 June 1987, during a parliamentary debate, 'nous avons toujours agi avec fermeté et clarté, notamment au conseil de sécurité, en faveur de la liberté et de la sécurité de la navigation. Nos bâtiments sont présents dans le Golfe: ils n'*escortent* pas les navires marchands, mais peuvent leur prêter *assistance* en fonction des circonstances. Mais cet

[118] *Ibid.* at pp. 327–8.
[119] *Ibid.* at pp. 304, 336.
[120] From summer 1987 to September 1988, the French navy operations in the North Indian Ocean involved a total of 33 warships, which represented 70 per cent of the total French logistical potential, 25 per cent of the total force of combat vessels and 20 per cent of the total mine warfare potential; see VILLADRET, F., 'Le groupe aéronavale regagne la Méditerranée', 44 *Défense Nationale* (nov.1988) at p. 181.

effort demeure volontairement contrôlé.'[121] In the context of Operation Prométhée, therefore, the French warships were expected to be at such a distance from French vessels which could permit them to intervene, without giving the impression, however, that they were engaged in a regular convoy mission – a delicate way to express the French concern for a naval intervention at the lowest level compatible with the defence of national interests. In the opinion of one analyst, the French practice of accompaniment may set a precedent as a reasonable adaptation of maritime convoy rules to times of crisis.[122]

The Italian government announced its intention to offer escort protection to its merchant vessels transiting the Persian Gulf on 4 September 1987, following the flare-up of the Tanker War since the end of August and the attack against the Italian-flagged vessel *Jolly Rubino*. The Italian naval squadron, known as Naval Group 18, consisted of three frigates, three minehunters, one support and one supply vessel and was assigned the dual mission of ensuring the safety of Italian shipping and assisting the clearing of mines in the busiest sea lanes in the Gulf. Beginning in October 1987, the Italian naval forces completed forty convoy missions in the first seven months,[123] with their presence continuing up to November 1988.

Concerning the question of the belligerent right to visit and search, Rome appeared from the outset to adhere to the traditional rules of neutral convoy, making explicit reference to the relevant provisions of the London Declaration. Thus on 24 September 1987, the Minister of Defence stated: 'it is emphasized

[121]See 33 *AFDI* (1987) at p. 948. As late as March 21, 1988, it was maintained that 'le déploiement de la Marine nationale dans le golfe Persique est insuffisant pour organiser la protection des navires marchands français en convoi à l'exemple de ce que fait la marine des Etats Unis au profit des navires du Koweït passés sous pavillon américain'; see 34 *AFDI* (1988) at p. 964. It will be recalled that in May 1988 the French naval forces comprised one aircraft carrier, four frigates, two destroyers, three minesweepers and three auxiliary ships; see BROWN, *op. cit., supra* n.97 at p. 145.

[122]See MALLEIN, J., 'Commentary on French Practice' in DE GUTTRY and RONZITTI, *op. cit., supra* n.45 at p. 403. It was further argued, in a somewhat exaggerated fashion, that accompaniment should be considered as juridically distinct from escort: 'the French practice of accompaniment did not have the authoritarian character which is recognized for military escort. It had a "passive" character, whereas that of escort is active'; *ibid.* at p. 401. However, despite the operational details in which the French and US missions might well differ, there is nothing to suggest that something less of a traditional neutral convoy was envisaged, especially as far as the legal implications were concerned.

[123]*Ibid.*, doc.2.a.10 at p. 465.

that unescorted Italian merchant ships will be subject to the right of visit on the part of the belligerents, whereas, following a convention of 1909, this right will not apply to escorted vessels. As an alternative the commander of the escort will issue all the information asked for and may himself conduct any check.'[124] Shortly after, however, it was announced that the captains of belligerent warships wishing to exercise the right of visit and search should be invited to accompany the captain of the convoy in carrying out any inspection.[125] As such an occasion never arose in practice, it remains unclear whether the Italian government inverted in reality its previous stance on the exemption of neutral convoys from belligerent interference, or whether it only wished to offer further concrete proof of its *bona fide* neutral policy.[126]

To conclude, it would appear that the multiple escort missions as conducted by American, British, French or Italian warships in the last two years of the Iran-Iraq War matched squarely with the time-honoured practice of neutral convoys under customary law and reaffirmed its lasting validity.

5 Visit, search and convoying in current theory

Recent developments in state practice, as reviewed above, have certainly had their impact on the rules governing the rights of visit, search and convoying as they now appear in some revised national naval manuals and academic drafts. The belligerent right to intercept and board or divert merchant ships, as well as the neutral right to escort vessels flying the same flag so that they eschew visit and search, are reaffirmed in much the same terms and there seems to be general agreement on their customary character.

[124]*Ibid.*, doc.2.a.5 at p. 455.

[125]In the words of the President of the Council, Giovanni Goria, 'our ship's captains have been asked to allow the captain of the belligerent's ship (or his representatives) to accompany them on visits to merchant ships sailing under the escort of naval vessels. This, it is clear, is an attitude which, while respecting our material and non-material interests, underscores even more clearly the peaceful and neutral character of our naval presence'; *ibid.*, doc.2.a.6 at p. 460.

[126]On this point, see also the remarks of DE GUTTRY, A., 'Commentary on Italian Practice', *ibid.* at pp. 431–2. It will be recalled in this connection that, in a very analogous gesture, Italy had decided to communicate to all Gulf states, including Iran and Iraq, the essential terms of the Rules of Engagement under which its naval squadron was to operate.

For example, the 1989 *US Commander's Handbook on the Law of Naval Operations* defines visit and search as:

> the means by which a belligerent warship or belligerent military aircraft may determine the true character (enemy or neutral) of merchant ships encountered outside neutral territory, the nature (contraband or exempt free goods) of their cargo, the manner (innocent or hostile) of their employment, and other facts bearing on their relation to the armed conflict.[127]

As regards the right of ordering a ship into port, the *US Manual* provides as follows: 'if visit and search at sea is deemed hazardous or impracticable, the neutral vessel may be escorted by the summoning or another US Navy warship or by a US military aircraft to the nearest place (outside neutral territory) where the visit and search may be conveniently and safely conducted'.[128] Finally, neutral convoys 'are exempt from visit and search, although the convoy commander may be required to provide in writing to the commanding officer of an intercepting belligerent warship information as to the character of the vessels and of their cargoes which could otherwise be obtained by visit and search'.[129]

In similar terms the 1992 publication of the German Defence Ministry stipulates that 'warships of a party to the conflict are

[127]See *Commander's Handbook on the Law of Naval Operations* (NWP9-Rev.A) at para.7.6. On the peacetime right of approach, see *ibid.* at para.3.8. The manual goes on to describe the procedure to be followed by warships in exercising the right of visit and search: it should be carried out 'with all possible tact and consideration'; before summoning, the warship 'should hoist its national flag'; if the summoned vessel takes flight, 'she may be brought to by forcible means if necessary'; the boarding officer should examine the ship's papers although 'regularity of papers is not necessarily conclusive, and, should doubt exist, the ship's company may be questioned and the ship and cargo searched'; see *ibid.* at para.7.6.1 §§1–8. The *Handbook* recognizes that not only warships but also military aircraft may lawfully exercise visit and search rights, although this may present certain difficulties in practice. What is more, visit and search of an aircraft by another aircraft can also be envisaged, the intercepting aircraft in this case directing and escorting the intercepted aircraft to the nearest belligerent landing area; see *ibid.* at para.7.6.2.

[128]*Ibid.* at para.7.6.1§5.

[129]*Ibid.* at para.7.6. With reference to this proviso, the commentary notes: 'this has been the consistent position of the United States which, while previously not commonly accepted, appears to have recently achieved such acceptance. Certainly, the experience of the convoying by several nations in the Persian Gulf during the tanker war between Iran and Iraq (1984–8) supports the US position'; see *Annotated Supplement to Commander's Handbook* at p. 7–32.

entitled to stop, visit and search merchant ships wearing the flag of a neutral state on the high seas and to control the contents and destination of their cargo'.[130] The German *Manual* makes no explicit reference to the right of diversion, whereas with regard to convoys it lays down the following: 'the right of control shall not apply to merchant ships wearing neutral flags when they are escorted by a neutral warship (convoy). In this case, however, a warship of a party to the conflict may request the commander of the neutral warship to provide information on the type and destination of the cargo.'[131]

As far as the 1994 *San Remo Manual* is concerned, it lays down as a basic rule that 'belligerent warships and military aircraft have a right to visit and search merchant vessels outside neutral waters where there are reasonable grounds for suspecting that they are subject to capture'.[132] When the 'visit and search at sea is impossible or unsafe', the intercepting warship may order the merchant vessel to proceed to an appropriate area or port for the purpose of papers and/or cargo inspection.[133] An escorted merchant vessel is exempted from belligerent halting and boarding procedures if it meets the following conditions:

(a) it is bound for a neutral port; (b) it is under the convoy

[130]See *ZDv 15/2 Humanitäres Völkerrecht in bewaffneten Konflikten – Hanbuch* [Humanitarian Law in Armed Conflicts – Manual], August 1992, para.1138 at p. 118.

[131]*Ibid.*, para.1141 at p. 119. See also para.1147.

[132]See *San Remo Manual on International Law Applicable to Armed Conflicts at Sea*, Prepared by a Group of International Lawyers and Naval Experts [hereinafter *Manual*], June 1994, at para.118. The Round Table, with an apparent intention to innovate, added a provision which offers to the neutral merchant vessel the possibility to change course as an alternative to visit and search. As the commentary explains, 'the rationale behind paragraph 119 is to meet both the interests of belligerents as well as of neutral merchant shipping. Visit and search, and diversion for the purpose of visit and search, are relatively time consuming and hazardous to both the merchant vessel and the intercepting warship . . . it is not necessarily in the belligerent's interest to confiscate the merchant vessel in question. There are situations in which it will suffice to keep merchant vessels out of certain areas instead of diverting them to a belligerent port'; see *Commentary on the Harmonised Document on International Humanitarian Law Applicable to Armed Conflicts at Sea*, March 1994 [hereinafter *Commentary*], para.119.2 at pp. 209–10.

[133]See *Manual* at para.121. As the commentary observes, 'in view of modern state practice, as e.g. during the Iraq-Kuwait conflict, as well as according to modern military manuals, the right of diversion for this purpose is undisputed'; see *Commentary*, para.121.1 at p. 213.

> of an accompanying neutral warship of the same nationality *or a neutral warship of a state with which the flag state of the merchant vessel has concluded an agreement providing for such convoy;* (c) the flag state of the neutral warship warrants that the neutral merchant vessel is not carrying contraband or otherwise engaged in activities inconsistent with its neutral status; (d) the commander of the neutral warship provides, if requested by the commander of an intercepting belligerent warship or military aircraft, all information as to the character of the merchant vessel and its cargo as could otherwise be obtained by visit and search. (emphasis added)[134]

As regards the work of the International Law Association's Maritime Neutrality Committee, Michael Bothe in his latest report refers to various belligerent control measures over neutral shipping and specifies *inter alia* the following rule: 'belligerent warships have a right to visit and search *vis-à-vis* neutral commercial ships in order to ascertain whether those ships carry contraband. Measures of coercion necessary to exercise this right are permissible. This includes a right to divert a ship where visit and search at the place where the ship is encountered are

[134]See *Manual,* at para.120. Two remarks from the commentary should be retained here: first, that convoying 'does not imply a duty on the accompanying warship to travel in close vicinity of the merchant vessels', and second that neutral convoys may consist of vessels flying different (neutral) flags. The latter proposition is clarified as follows: 'the element of progressive development in paragraph 120 is to be seen in the right of neutral states to form multinational convoys. These are also exempt from visit and search if all the conditions in subparagraphs (a)-(d) are fulfilled. Accordingly, not every neutral merchant vessel encountered in the vicinity of a neutral warship flying a different flag is exempt from visit and search. Only if the flag state of the neutral warship has concluded an agreement with another neutral state whose flag the merchant vessel concerned is flying, will multinational convoys be regarded as exempt from visit and search'; see *Commentary,* paras.120.2, 120.4 at pp. 211–13. The idea is certainly interesting, but it would be most problematic in its application. Furthermore, it may be argued that it contravenes the rationale of the traditional convoy principle, which is to surrender a belligerent right out of comity and respect for the specific neutral government that substitutes its word for the word of its private citizen (symbolized precisely by the presence of a public ship and not by the presence of *any neutral* warship). The *San Remo Manual* further extends the right of convoy to neutral civil aircraft to which it applies by analogy the same conditions for merchant vessels; see *Manual* at para.127, and *Commentary,* para.127.1 at p. 219. Despite the absence of customary rule or long-standing practice on this question, the Round Table probably wished to apply whenever possible the same rules to air or sea operations.

not practical.'[135] The draft rule on the principle of convoying reads: 'the right of convoy is recognized. Consequently, neutral states have the right to accompany commercial ships flying their own *or another neutral state's flag* by their warships. The exercise of a right of transit or passage by such convoys does not constitute a forbidden use of force' (emphasis added).[136]

III The right to capture and the duty of initiating prize proceedings

The Seizability of Private Property in Sea Warfare By the term 'capture', in a technical sense, one understands all the possible means by which a belligerent warship assumes control over an enemy or neutral vessel with a view to bringing it before a prize court since a probable cause for confiscation arose after it was duly visited and searched. For that purpose, the captor may provide a prize crew unless the captured vessel accepts to steer by the instructions of the captor. With the exception of the clearly defined instances of lawful destruction of the seized vessel, the act of capture does not confer any right over the ship, its crew, or its cargo other than the mere faculty to control its course, speed and mode of navigation.

Beyond the technical sense of escorting a prize into port, capture also has a broader legal significance; *the right to capture*, by which one determines the liberties and constraints of belligerent interference with private property at sea. Despite isolated attempts to distinguish seizure from capture,[137] one has

[135]See *Report on Neutrality and Naval Warfare* for ILA's Buenos Aires Conference (1994) at para.5.2.1.
[136]*Ibid.* at para.6.1. The accompanying commentary relates to the Persian Gulf practice as a most reliable precedent: 'the formation of such convoys was indeed a practice during the Iran-Iraq War, although it was not always claimed that this constituted the exercise of a "right of convoy". The recognition of such rights nevertheless seems to be the best explanation of what actually happened'. See also 65 *Rep.ILA* (1992), Cairo Conference, paras.3.1, 4.1, 4.2, 4.4 at pp. 171, 173–5. It is doubtful, however, whether, under customary principles, neutral convoys could comprise vessels and warships of different nationalities. In this sense, therefore, Bothe's draft, as much as the *San Remo Manual*, can be seen as pertaining more to progressive development than to codification of existing law.
[137]See, for instance, SMITH, H.A., *The Law and Custom of the Sea*, 3rd edn (1959), pp. 126–8. On the delicate terminological issue concerning the use of the words 'capture', 'seizure', 'detention', 'prize' or 'sequestration' in different languages, see HIGGINS, *op. cit., supra* n.6 at pp. 145–7, and VERZIJL, *op. cit., supra* n.26 at

to admit the often interchangeable use of these terms. Jurisprudence of prize courts is, in fact, replete with statements like the following:

> every ship, indeed, may, in time of war, be brought to and examined; but she is not to be seized and captured, without the captors have just grounds to think she is the property of an enemy, and not the property of subjects of a nation in peace and friendship, or neutrality. If such seizure and capture are made without just grounds, the party injured is entitled to have an action for damages: and it is the policy of all nations at war, to oblige the captains of privateers to give bond and security, to enforce a proper conduct while at sea, and to prevent seizures and captures from being wantonly made.[138]

According to an early view, capture upon completion was even deemed to imply an immediate transfer of title over the captured property. By completed capture, one implied the moment when effective possession was secured, or when some clear evidence of submission was received, or when all hope of recapture *(spes recuperandi)* had vanished. Lord Stowell in the *Santa Cruz* case gave an account of the diversity of views in matters of title over prizes:

> respecting the time when property vests in the captor . . . It may be fit there should be some rule, and it might be either the rule of immediate possession, or the rule of pernoctation and twenty-four hours possession; or it might be the rule of bringing *infra praesidia*; or it might be a rule requiring an actual sentence of condemnation: either of these rules might be sufficient for general practical convenience, although in theory perhaps one might appear more just than another: but the fact is, there is no such rule of practice; nations concur in principle indeed, so far as require firm and secure possession; but their rules of evidence respecting the possession are so discordant, and lead to such opposite

pp. 1200–6. See also QUIGLEY, H.S., 'The Immunity of Private Property from Capture at Sea', 11 *AJIL* (1917), p. 22*ff.*; HUDSON, M.O., 'Seizures in Land and Naval Warfare Distinguished', 16 *AJIL* (1922), p. 375*ff.*; RICHMOND, H., 'The Value of the Right of Capture at Sea in Time of War', 9 *BYIL* (1928), p. 50*ff.*

[138]See *The Resolution* (1781), 2 *A.J. Dallas' US Supreme Court Reports*, at p. 21.

conclusions, that the mere unity of principle forms no uniform rule to regulate the general practice.[139]

Prize Law: Basic Principles It has been firmly established that all property captured at sea must be submitted to a prize court as the sole competent organ to pronounce upon the condemnation of the ship or her cargo, and that consequently ownership can only be transferred following a reasoned prize decision. This elementary principle was paid an eloquent tribute by Lord Stowell:

> in later times, an additional formality has been required, that of a sentence of condemnation, in a competent Court, decreeing the capture to have been rightly made, *jure belli*; it not being thought fit, in civilized society, that property of this sort should be converted without the sentence of a competent Court, pronouncing it to have been seized as the property of an enemy, and to be now become *jure belli* the property of the captor. The purposes of justice require, that such exercises of war, should be placed under public inspection; and therefore the *mere deductio infra praesidia* has not been deemed sufficient. No man buys under that title; he requires a sentence of condemnation, as the *foundation of the title* of the seller; and when the transfer is accepted, he is liable to have that document called for, as the foundation of his own. From the moment that a sentence of condemnation becomes necessary, it imposes an additional obligation, for bringing the property, on which it is to pass, into the country of the captor; for a legal sentence must be the result of legal proceedings, *in a legitimate Court*, armed with competent authority upon the subject matter, and upon the parties concerned – a Court which has the means of pursuing the proper enquiry, and enforcing its decisions. These are principles of universal jurisprudence applicable to all Courts.[140]

[139]See *The Santa Cruz* (1798), 1 *C. Robinson's Admiralty Reports* at p. 59.
[140]See *The Henrick and Maria* (1799), 4 *C. Robinson's Admiralty Reports* at p. 55. Consider also the following pronouncement: 'the legality of a capture is open for question and examination, until a competent jurisdiction has decided the question, and a decree passes for condemnation as prize; then, and not before,

It would appear that the rule knows a single exception in the rare eventuality of enemy warships being captured. In such case, it is generally admitted that title passes upon seizure and that no need arises for prize adjudication.[141] If the prize court determines that the capture, as a matter of both substance and procedure, was carried out in conformity with existing national prize regulations, it may order the confiscation of the captured property, that is, the definitive transfer of the hitherto foreign property to the captor state. Upon condemnation by a prize court the original owner of the confiscated ship or cargo is deemed to have surrendered his property rights retroactively at the time of the capture.[142]

Although prize cases were adjudicated by consular commercial courts established in principal maritime ports as early as the fourteenth century, it is generally admitted that the seventeenth and eighteenth centuries represent the truly formative

all further questions and examinations are precluded; then, all parties, and all foreign courts, are estopped to say, "the capture is not legal"; and if the decree be erroneous or iniquitous, the party injured must apply for redress to that nation, whose courts have committed the error or inquity'; see *The Resolution* (1781), 2 *A.J. Dallas' US Supreme Court Reports* at pp. 4–5. And elsewhere: 'for I know no other definition of prize-goods, than that they are goods taken on the high seas, *jure belli*, out of the hands of the enemy; and there is no axiom more clear, than that such goods, when they come on shore, may be followed by the process of this Court'; see *The Two Friends* (1799), 1 *C. Robinson's Admiralty Reports* at p. 283. For the different theories concerning the transfer of ownership, see HERZOG, S.A., 'When Does Title to Prize Pass?', 18 *AJIL* (1924), p. 483*ff.* See also JOHNSON, D.H.N., 'Prize Law' in BERNHARDT, R. (ed.), *Encyclopedia of Public International Law*, instalment 4 (1982), p. 154*ff.*

[141]Early practice as regards capture of warships is reviewed in HIGGINS, A.P., 'Ships of War as Prize', 6 *BYIL* (1925), p. 103*ff.*

[142]Apart from the judicial action concerning title over captured property, prize proceedings were also understood to cover institutionalized practices such as bounty money, prize money, or military salvage. *Bounty* has been a reward for courage *in specie* distributed *pro rata* to all men serving on ships after fighting a victorious battle. *Prize money* represented a part of the value of a captured vessel or cargo to be shared out among the captors. Bounty and prize money were abolished in the United States following a 1899 Act restructuring the Navy, while Britain continued to award such payments during both World Wars. Finally, *military salvage* was allotment of money for a successful recapture of ships and cargoes prior to their condemnation. For more, see KNAUTH, A.W., 'Prize Law Reconsidered', 46 *Columbia Law Review* (1946) at pp. 70–6. See also RABUS, W., 'Booty in Sea Warfare' in BERNHARDT, R. (ed.), *Encyclopedia of Public International Law*, instalment 3 (1982), p. 68*ff.*, and SMITH, H.A., 'Booty of War', 23 *BYIL* (1946), p. 227*ff.*

period of traditional prize law.[143] It was in fact under the combined influence of both the maturation of neutrality law and the expansion of maritime commerce that the major seafaring nations felt the necessity of setting up separate prize jurisdictions. In England and the Netherlands prize courts were organized as separate sittings in admiralty, whereas in France or Spain these were considered *ad hoc* tribunals.[144] Despite their character as national courts, the judiciary involved in prize proceedings were supposed to apply international law standards.

Prize procedure was regulated in a considerable number of treaties. Primary among the guiding principles enunciated in those treaties was the rule that a captured vessel, before being condemned, should enjoy all the guarantees of an orderly legal process. In more concrete terms, mention was often made of the required impartiality and integrity of the judges, of the need to pronounce according to the law of nations, that is justice and equity, or of the obligation to avoid undue delays. Another often prescribed safeguard was the prohibition to dispose in any way of the captured goods before the prize court rendered its decision as to condemnation of the vessel. Only perishable goods might be exceptionally unloaded and sold, the proceeds of the sale to be given in custody of the court. Failure to comply

[143]It may be noted that until the early seventeenth century it was widely held, especially in France, that title over the captured vessel passed 24 hours after seizure. England never accepted the 24-hour rule considering that condemnation and transfer of ownership lay within the exclusive jurisdiction of prize courts. As the US Federal Court of Appeals once put it, 'it is alleged, that . . . after a capture and occupation for twenty-four hours, the legality of the capture is not open for question and examination. This doctrine must never be suffered; there is no example or precedent for it to be found in any of our books; it breaks down and destroys the distinction between right and wrong; it gives a sanction to injustice, robbery and piracy, and it is reprobated by the laws, usage and practice of nations'; see *The Resolution* (1781), 2 *A.J. Dallas' US Supreme Court Reports* at p. 4. On the so-called 24-hour rule, see DUPUIS, *op. cit., supra* n.13, pp. 360–9, and NYS, *op. cit., supra* n.11, pp. 262–3.

[144]A thorough survey of early practice relating to prize proceedings is in JESSUP and DEÁK, *op. cit., supra* n.2, pp. 201–48; KLEEN, *op. cit., supra* n.13, tome 2, pp. 390–434, 587–745; NYS, *op. cit., supra* n.11, pp. 117–32; DUPUIS, *op. cit., supra* n.13, pp. 370–405; POTTER, H., 'The Foundations of Modern Prize Law', 10 *GST* (1924), p. 37*ff.*; BATY, T., 'Neglected Fundamentals of Prize Law', 30 *YLJ* (1920–1), p. 34*ff.* On the rules concerning jurisdiction, applicable law, evidence and procedure of prize courts in general, see COLOMBOS, C.J., *A Treatise on the Law of Prize*, 3rd edn (1949), pp. 15–66, 342–71. On the organization and evolution of the British prize courts, see ROSCOE, E.S., *A History of the English Prize Court*, 1924. The procedure before the French prize courts is reviewed in REUTER, *op. cit., supra* n.4, pp. 46–70.

with such procedural rules often provoked neutral protests and perhaps even refusal of third governments to recognize the regularity of title conferred by the prize decision. Concerned about the damage undisciplined proceedings could inflict on the sale of future prizes, belligerent captors had just as much interest as neutral owners in honouring the proper function of prize courts.

The prize court's jurisdiction extended to every case in which there had been a maritime seizure *jure belli*, and in exercising this jurisdiction the court could deal with all incidental matters. Owing to the contentious nature of prize proceedings, these were instituted by the captors who filed claims for the condemnation of the ship and its cargo. The owners of the captured vessel were entitled to file claims for its release, while the owners of the cargo might only be heard as intervening parties. The hearing of the parties included oral and written pleadings, the latter consisting of memorials, replies and rejoinders presented by the captor, the claimant, or the intervening parties. The right of appeal was explicitly recognized in several treaties. According to most of these treaty provisions, an appeal to a prize decision could only be initiated upon the complaint of the ambassador of the claimant's country, while the judgment should be rendered within a specified time which often did not exceed three months.

Prize law in its early development firmly adhered to the principle which held that all evidence relating to the prize proceedings should be secured from the ship itself, a doctrine widely known under the expression that the captured ship's fate must be determined *'out of her own mouth'*.[145] The doctrine in its material application implied that the ship's papers, correspondence or other documents found on board, and the collected testimonies of the crew were to be considered as affording the sole source of evidence as to nationality, ownership, or destination of ship and cargo. As provided in several national jurisdictions, upon arrival of a captured ship in port, admiralty officers or judges were charged with carrying out the usual preparatory procedure which comprised boarding the vessel for the purpose of ascertaining its condition, making up

[145]See, for instance, *The Haabet* (1805), 6 C. *Robinson's Admiralty Reports* at pp. 55–6.

an inventory, sealing its cargo, collecting all documents and interrogating the crew.

As it turned out, the principle of exclusive reliance on ship's papers for the purposes of prize decisions was honoured more by continental countries such as France or Spain, whereas in England a practice was soon developed which allowed judges to consider extrinsic evidence and even base themselves on presumptions. In view of the widespread use of false papers, the English High Court of Admiralty could invite extrinsic evidence to be introduced under an order for further proof. What was sought, in essence, was the creation of parallel procedural and substantive rules justifying condemnation whenever condemnation of the ship could not be pronounced 'out of her own mouth'.[146]

As from the beginning of the First World War, extraneous or sheer conjectural evidence were so extensively used, especially for the purpose of establishing real enemy destination, that the examination of the ship's papers or the interrogatories were relegated to a rather meaningless routine. The techniques employed to unmask these 'dummy consignees' in neutral countries often consisted in intercepting messages, investigating the true financial capacity of the consignee, examining general trade

[146]Among the most frequently invoked presumptions were the destruction or concealment of papers, attempted resistance or flight, testimonies contradicting seized papers, the suspicious change in ship's customary pattern of voyage (e.g. the regular call to a port suspected of clandestine trade trafficking with the enemy), or the appearance of the ship's name in a blacklist. As a result, the recourse to presumptions, already current in the seventeenth and eighteenth centuries, easily defeated the somewhat unrealistic idea of judging a prize solely 'out of her own mouth'. In a case decided by the US Federal Court of Appeals towards the end of the eighteenth century, the prevailing opinion as to the evidentiary weight of ship's papers was neatly presented: 'every commercial country has directed, by its laws, that its ships shall be furnished with a set of papers called ship papers: and this criterion the law of nations adopts, in time of war, to distinguish the property of different powers, when found at sea; not indeed as conclusive, but presumptive evidence only . . . Such then is the evidence which the law of nations admits on a question of prize or no prize; and it is on this evidence, that vessels with their cargoes are generally acquitted or condemned. And therefore, if, in this case, the papers on board affirm the ship and cargo to be such property as is not prize, there must be an acquittal, unless the captors are able, by a contrariety of evidence, to defeat the presumption which arises from the papers, and can show just grounds for condemnation. On the other hand, if the papers affirm the ship and cargo to be property of an enemy, there must be a condemnation, unless they who contest the capture can produce clear and unquestionable evidence to prove the contrary'; see *The Resolution* (1781), 2 *A.J. Dallas' US Supreme Court Reports* at p. 22.

statistics of the neutral country and thereby deducing a marked increase of imports, obliging the neutral merchant to produce all his commercial books for examination for the period starting prior to the outbreak of war and until the actual seizure, and many others.[147]

It is noteworthy that the British prize court had contrived other means to exclude at all events the possibility that seized goods might reach any suspect or undesirable destination. According to the 1921 Privy Council's decision in the case of the *Falk*, for instance, a prize order for the release of seized goods did not suffice *per se* to enable the owner to get his goods removed out of the realm. Upon being released, therefore, the goods could only be re-exported in conformity with the general licensing procedure and it was for the owner to arrange to carry them away as he could.[148]

Ordering the sale of seized goods pending the outcome of

[147]See RICHARDS, E., 'The British Prize Courts and the War', 1 *BYIL* (1920–1) at pp. 25–9. See also ROSCOE, E.S., 'Prize Court Procedure', 2 *BYIL* (1921–2), p. 90*ff.* As it was decided in 1916 in a case before the British prize court, 'experience also shows not only the ingenuity and multitudinous characters of the devices and shams resorted to in carrying on contraband trading, but how often it is only the interception of letters, or cables, or wireless messages, that the deceptions can be detected and disclosed. And even if there is not, in truth, any actual knowledge, is the trader to defeat belligerent rights by taking care not to know by a species of "voluntary ignorance"? I hazard the opinion that not many of the shipowners or masters of ships belonging to the Scandinavian or Dutch countries are suffering from any want of knowledge of how articles of a contraband character are sent to Germany, either by water or by land, from neutral ports, which could not reach Germany by direct voyages to her own ports. Knowledge of the destination of such articles in particular cases may be difficult to establish by actual and direct proof'; see *The Maracaibo* (1916), in GRANT, A.W., *British and Colonial Prize Cases*, vol.II (1916–17) at p. 299. See also LEWIS, M.M., 'Domicile as a Test of Enemy Character', 4 *BYIL* (1923–4), p. 60*ff.*, and DUKE, H., '*Mens Rea* in Prize Law', 6 *GST* (1920), p. 99*ff.*

[148]As the prize decision read, 'a decree for release does not warrant actual ability to remove the goods from the realm. This might be impossible for want of bunker coals, or of labour, or of repairs, and yet it could not be said that the redress given by the Prize Court was made inefficacious by reason of something of which that Court ought to take notice. As is assumed in *The Dusseldorf*, release means release out of the custody of the Marshal in this country, where the goods are, and it is for the owner of them to arrange to remove or dispose of them as he can. The Court of Prize cannot give itself a more extensive jurisdiction in cases where the neutral is unable to remove his property out of the realm, or award damages against the Procurator-General for consequences arising from matters to which he is a stranger . . . The jurisdiction of the Court of Prize is to condemn or to release, not to override the executive after release has taken place'; see *The Falk* (1921), in GRANT, A.W., *British and Colonial Prize Cases*, vol.III (1917–22) at pp. 966–7.

prize proceedings was another measure which for all practical purposes reduced significantly the importance of condemnation as such. Beyond the obvious case of perishable commodities, a prize court could justify its decision on various circumstances such as difficulties in warehousing, unaffordable expenses for the preservation of merchandise and others. In such a case, the goods were liquidated and their sale prize stood in the Prize Court in lieu of them. If they were finally released the owner would have to content himself with the proceeds of the sale and not the goods. If there was condemnation, on the contrary, the same sum of money would go to the Exchequer.[149] By resorting to these contrivances, and regardless the positive or negative result of the prize decision, it was safe that shipments to presumed (though not proved) hostile destinations might still be frustrated.[150]

[149]In the words of a memorable prize decision, 'persons who lay claim to property captured or seized, have no right by any rule of international law to demand that the property should be preserved *in specie* until the final decree determines whether it is to be released or to be condemned. Prize Courts have always acted upon the principle that the capture is lawful, until claimants establish the contrary. All that it is necessary for captors to allege in prize proceedings is that the capture was made, and that the property captured is claimed as prize; thereupon claimants must establish their claim to release. If their claim to release is sustained they may have the property delivered up, if it has been kept intact; or they will receive its value if it has been sold or otherwise disposed of, with or without costs and damages against the captors as the circumstances may require . . . If the claimants have no such legal right to have the property delivered up *in specie*, it matters not whether the property is sold for good reasons, and so converted into money, or is requisitioned by the Crown (instead of going through the form of sale) upon an undertaking to pay into Court the appraised value'; see *The Zamora* (1915), in TREHERN, E.C.M., *British and Colonial Prize Cases*, vol.I (1914–15) at pp. 320–1. The novel techniques in prize proceedings are also reviewed in FITZMAURICE, G.G., 'Some Aspects of Modern Contraband Control and the Law of Prize', 22 *BYIL* (1945), p. 73*ff*.

[150]Similar was the prize policy followed in the Second World War; see SERENI, A.P., 'Italian Prize Courts', 37 *AJIL* (1943), p. 248*ff*.; ROWSON, S.W.D., 'Italian Prize Law, 1940–1943', 23 *BYIL* (1946), p. 282*ff*.; Id., 'Prize Law During the Second World War', 24 *BYIL* (1947), p. 160*ff*.; GERVAIS, A., 'Le droit des prises maritimes dans la seconde guerre mondiale – La jurisprudence française', 52 *RGDIP* (1948), p. 82*ff*.; Id., 'La jurisprudence britannique des prises maritimes dans la seconde guerre mondiale', 53 *RGDIP* (1949), p. 201*ff*., 425*ff*.; GUTTINGER, P., 'Réflexions sur la jurisprudence des prises maritimes de la seconde guerre mondiale', 79 *RGDIP* (1975), p. 25*ff*.

1 Lawful prize – the doctrine of unneutral service

By unneutral service, one implies all acts of assistance committed by neutrals, other than blockade running and trade in contraband, which would contravene the duty of impartiality and which would justify sanctions on the part of the offended belligerent.[151] The term is thought to be unfortunate in that it fails to stress the distinct nature of the acts falling into the two categories. Upon being captured, a neutral merchantman laden with contraband runs the risk of confiscation although its neutral character remains. On the contrary, a merchant vessel flying neutral colours engaged in operations directly beneficial to a belligerent navy (e.g. intelligence gathering) is to be treated as having forfeited its neutral nature and having assumed the status of an enemy merchantman or warship, depending on the gravity of the act of cooperation with enemy forces. Yet, from another perspective, the carriage of contraband or an attempted breach of blockade can be regarded as equally unneutral.[152]

Despite its currency, the expression *unneutral service* should be replaced by another more evocative term which comprises the fact that the acts in question result in the forfeiture of the neutral character and the adoption of a co-belligerent stance with all the emanating consequences. It may be noticed, in this respect, that the French term *assistance hostile* is more expressive of the quasi-belligerent character of the act performed by the neutral. A possible explanation for the unsatisfactory terminology may be that, in its traditional variant, unneutral service was deemed to comprise the transport of certain persons of belligerent nationality (troops and diplomats in particular), as well as the transport of parcels and letters for a belligerent, both of which, of course, do not seem very dissimilar from contraband carrying.[153]

[151]For an exposition of the traditional law prescriptions on unneutral service, see DUPUIS, *op. cit., supra* n.13, pp. 281–95, and COLOMBOS, *op. cit., supra* n.144, pp. 231–45.

[152]In this sense, the Drafting Committee of the 1909 London Declaration addressed the trade in contraband and blockade running as clear instances of unneutral service, and added: 'but there are cases where such *unneutral service is particularly disctinctive* and, for which it has been thought necessary to make special provision'; see USNWC, 9 *International Law Topics* (1909) at p. 99.

[153]Throughout the seventeenth and eighteenth centuries the transportation of enemy troops aboard neutral vessels was deemed as a common act of trade in contraband, soldiers being regularly listed at that time as contraband articles.

In any event, to describe as unneutral service acts which may be lawfully treated by the offended belligerent as sheer acts of war on the part of his enemy is no doubt anomalous. This may well suggest an antiquated or unfortunate legal terminology but

---

This early confusion is reflected in expressions like 'contraband persons' or 'analogues of contraband', or 'quasi-contraband'. To draw once again upon the wealth of Stowellian jurisprudence, 'the carrying of military persons to the colony of an enemy, who are there to take on them the exercise of their military functions, will lead to condemnation, and that the court is not to scan with minute arithmetic the number of persons that are so carried. If it has appeared to be of sufficient importance to the government of the enemy to send them, it must be enough to put the adverse government on the exercise of their right of prevention; and the ignorance of the master can afford no ground of exculpation in favour of the owner'; see *The Orozembo* (1807), 6 *C. Robinson's Admiralty Reports* at p. 436. For the British Admiralty the vessel would be liable to condemnation irrespective of the fact that the transported military might not be directly destined to join fighting forces of the enemy: 'the substance of the thing is this, whether they are vessels hired by the agents of the Government, for the purpose of conveying soldiers or stores in the service of the state? That is the substance; and it signifies nothing whether the men so conveyed are to be put into action on an immediate expedition or not. The mere shifting of draughts in detachments, and the conveyance of stores from one place to another, is an ordinary employment of transport vessels, and it is a distinction totally unimportant, whether this or that case may be connected with the *immediate active service* of the enemy'; see *The Friendship* (1807), *ibid.* at p. 426. Equally irrelevant was held the voluntary or not character of the troops transport: 'if this vessel had been taken in *delicto*, I should have felt no hesitation in saying, that she must have been subject to condemnation. Whether the troops were received on board voluntarily, or involuntarily, could make no difference'; see *The Carolina* (1802), *ibid.*, vol.4 at p. 260. And elsewhere: 'that the simple carrying of dispatches between the colonies and the mother country of the enemy, is a service highly injurious to the other belligerent, is most obvious ... The consequence of such a service is indefinite, infinitely beyond the effect of any contraband that can be conveyed. The carrying of two or three cargoes of stores is necessarily an assistance of a limited nature; but in the transmission of dispatches may be conveyed the entire plan of a campaign, that may defeat all the projects of the other belligerent in that quarter of the world ... It is a service, therefore, which, in whatever degree it exists, can only be considered in one character, as an act of the most noxious and hostile nature'; see *The Atalanta* (1808), *ibid.*, vol.6 at pp. 454–5. See also HIGGINS, A.P., 'Carriage of Belligerent Troops by a Neutral Transport: The *Creta* Case', 3 *BYIL* (1922–3), p. 188*ff.* On the early stages of development of the rules of unneutral service, see HILL, N.L., 'The Origin of the Law of Unneutral Service', 23 *AJIL* (1929) at pp. 56–61. The term 'unneutral service' first appeared in the last decade of the nineteenth century, probably introduced by Lawrence in 1895. On this point, see *ibid.* at pp. 66–7. The term does not figure in any of the early documents, either judicial pronouncements or conventional texts, which moulded it into a settled legal principle. Lord Stowell refers to cases of 'active interposition in the service of the enemy, concerted and continued in fraud, and marked with enemy species of malignant conduct'; see *The Atalanta* (1808), *supra.* at p. 460. For a review of nineteenth-century practice relating to the law of unneutral service, see 33 *AJIL* (1939) *Suppl.*, pp. 660–5.

may also indicate that the law of unneutral service has simply grown unchecked.

Legal Codification The unratified London Declaration draws a distinction between two categories of unneutral acts according to the seriousness of the violation of the neutral duty of impartiality they involve, and attaches different penalties to each. According to the less consequential type of unneutral activity (Article 45), the vessel is to receive the same treatment as if it was engaged in carriage of contraband:

> a neutral vessel will be condemned and will, in a general way, receive the same treatment as a *neutral* vessel liable to condemnation for carriage of contraband:
> (1) if she is on a voyage specially undertaken with a view to the transport of individual passengers who are embodied in the armed forces of the enemy, or with a view to the transmission of intelligence in the interest of the enemy.
> (2) if, to the knowledge of either the owner, the charterer, or the master, she is transporting a military detachment of the enemy, or one or more persons who, in the course of the voyage, directly assist the operations of the enemy.
>
> In the cases specified under the above heads, goods belonging to the owner of the vessel are likewise liable to condemnation.[154]

Aside from the liability to capture, the vessel does not lose its neutral character and continues to be entitled to the protection otherwise accorded to neutral vessels. It has to be seized while the suspect voyage endures; once terminated, it may not be captured since it is considered to have infringed upon the law of neutrality in a single act and not continuously. If the vessel is condemned on account of unneutral service the goods belonging to the owner are also liable to condemnation. The Article specifies four instances of this somewhat low-intensity collaboration with the enemy; the first two, the transmission of information and the transport of passengers serving in the enemy's armed forces, are punishable only if connected with a

[154]See 3 *AJIL* (1909) *Suppl.*, pp. 179–220. The text can also be found in SCHINDLER and TOMAN, *op. cit., supra* n.29, pp. 843–56, and RONZITTI, *op. cit., supra* n.29, pp. 223–56.

voyage especially undertaken for that purpose. It should be proved, therefore, that the vessel deviated from its usual course, or that it has called at a port ordinarily not visited, in order to effect the acts charged against it. The other two cases, i.e. the transport of enemy troops and the direct assistance to enemy operations by a passenger (e.g. by signalling), require the knowledge of the owner or the master to give rise to capture liability.

On the other hand, more severe treatment would be expected by neutral merchantmen if they were assimilated to enemy forces. As Article 46 provides:

> a neutral vessel will be condemned and, in a general way, receive the same treatment as would be applicable to her if she were an *enemy* merchant vessel:
> (1) if she takes a direct part in the hostilities;
> (2) if she is under the orders or control of an agent placed on board by the enemy government;
> (3) if she is in the exclusive employment of the enemy government;
> (4) if she is exclusively engaged at the time either in the transport of enemy troops or in the transmission of intelligence in the interest of the enemy.
>
> In the case covered by the present article, goods belonging to the owner of the vessel are likewise liable to condemnation.[155]

In those cases, the vessel is likewise condemned but as an enemy merchant vessel and no longer as a neutral one carrying contraband. This would imply among other things that the rules of precaution regarding the destruction of neutral prizes are not applicable in this case. It would also entail a rebuttable presumption of enemy character for the goods found on board. Finally, a neutral merchant engaged in the acts enumerated in Article 46 would be deprived of his right to seize the jurisdiction of the contemplated International Prize Court. Much like the rule laid down in Article 45, goods belonging to the owner of the vessel are also liable to condemnation.

The four cases specified in Article 46 demonstrate clearly that the aid afforded by the neutral, in this case, takes a qualitatively different form bearing direct consequences on the conduct of

[155] *Ibid.*

military operations as such. As regards the fourth proposition, it should be noted that this relates to an exclusive, that is to say permanent, employment of the neutral vessel for transporting troops or intelligence acquisition. Consequently, contrary to what was said with relation to Article 45(1), the vessel is liable to capture even though at the moment of its seizure it might neither carry troops, nor pass on information.[156] The rules as contained in the London Declaration were reiterated almost *expressis verbis* in Articles 45, 46 of the Laws of Naval War,[157] drafted by the International Law Association in 1920, while Article 46 of the London Declaration was also taken up in Article 12 of the 1928 Havana Convention on Maritime Neutrality.[158]

Case Law A number of prize cases which have arisen in the context of the First World War concerned unneutral service.[159] In the case of the *Pontoporos* the point in question was whether being forced to refuel an enemy raider, the *Emden* should still qualify as an act of unneutral service implying the condemnation of the neutral vessel. The British prize court rejected this notion arguing that 'Articles 45, 46, and 47 [of the London Declaration] are all grouped under the heading "unneutral service" or "assistance hostile", and, in my opinion, the use of that term implies some act or acts in violation of neutrality on the part of a neutral having authority over the neutral vessel, and the existence of some contractual relation, such as that of employer and employee, between the belligerent and such neutral. No such relation existed in this case.'[160]

[156]See the commentary on Article 45–6, USNWC, 9 *International Law Topics* (1909), pp. 99–109.

[157]See 29 *Rep.ILA* (1920) Portsmouth Conference, pp. 165–206.

[158]See 22 *AJIL* (1928) *Suppl.*, pp. 151–7. The text can also be found in SCHINDLER and TOMAN, *op. cit., supra* n.29, pp. 961–8, and RONZITTI, *op. cit., supra* n.29, pp. 769–78.

[159]First World War prize decisions in matters of unneutral service are reviewed in VERZIJL, *op. cit., supra* n.26, pp. 962–95.

[160]See *The Pontoporos* (1915), in TREHERN, E.L.M., *British and Colonial Prize Cases*, vol.I (1914–15) at p. 384. On another occasion the condemnation of a neutral vessel was upheld on grounds of Article 46 although at the moment of capture it was not supplying an enemy vessel ship: 'so the intention of [Article 46] paragraph (3) becomes obvious when you read the official commentary. This document expressly brings transports within the scope of the paragraph, and adds the words: "such is the position of colliers which accompany a hostile fleet". Counsel for the claimants, in a supreme effort, argued that you cannot accompany a hostile fleet if there is no hostile fleet to accompany; but I think

In another context, a neutral vessel was declared a lawful prize on account of supplying coal to an enemy warship even if the capture was proven to have taken place within neutral territorial waters:

> on the assumption that the *Bangor* was in fact captured within the territorial waters of a neutral – the question is whether the vessel was immune from legal capture and its consequences according to the law of nations. In other words, can the owners of the vessel, who are, *ex hypothesi*, to be treated as enemies, rely on the territorial rights of a neutral state and object to the capture? Or must the objection to the validity of the capture come from the neutral state alone? No proposition in international law is clearer, or more surely established, than that a capture within the territorial waters of a neutral is, as between enemy belligerents, for all purposes rightful; and that it is only by the neutral state concerned that the legal validity of the capture can be questioned. It can only be declared void as to the neutral state, and not as to the enemy.[161]

In a 1920 judgment it was found that the mere transport of a third officer of an enemy merchant vessel did not amount to a sufficient reason for confiscation in terms of Article 45 of the London Declaration. In the words of the British Privy council:

> his case, therefore, cannot be placed in the same category at all as the cases where the officers of a belligerent state have engaged a vessel to perform a particular service, or have paid for the carriage of particular passengers, or where

the offence lies rather in the intention of the employment than in its literal fulfilment'; see *The Thor* (1914), *ibid.* at p. 232.

[161]See *The Bangor* (1916), in GRANT, A.W., *British and Colonial Prize Cases*, vol.II (1916–17) at pp. 208–9. For a similar case, see *The Heina* (1915), in SCOTT, J.B. and JAEGER, W.H.E., *Cases on International Law*, 2nd edn (1937) at pp. 936–8. In the case of *The Hanametal*, the Supreme Court of Hong Kong declared that Articles 45 and 46 of the London Declaration call for hard evidence and that therefore unneutral service could not be established on mere suspicion; 'there is no such direct evidence against her as would be required to stamp as illegal an apparently innocent voyage within the ordinary rights of a neutral ship. There is, I think, room for suspicion, but that is not sufficient. Some positive breach of neutrality must be proved before the vessel of a friendly State can be condemned, and here none has been established'; see *The Hanametal* (1914), in TREHERN, E.L.M., *British and Colonial Prize Cases*, vol.I (1914–15) at p. 358.

> persons, already embodied in the service of the belligerent country, are being transported upon some purpose of state . . . At any rate, if there is no sufficient evidence of an act which would constitute an unneutral service, or a cause of condemnation under that or any analogous title, the mere deceptions of the captain of the *Svithiod* in themselves would not, either in justice or according to authority, be a ground for confiscating the vessel.[162]

As far as the Italian and French prize jurisdictions are concerned, in the case of *La Bella Scutarina* (1916), the Italian Prize Commission ordered the confiscation of an Albanian ship in conformity with Article 45§2 of the London Declaration. The captured vessel, which carried a large load of high-quality fuel as well as navigational instruments of great precision and detailed maps, was believed to act as a collier for enemy submarines and hydroplanes in the Adriatic.[163] In the case of the *Evangelistria* (1916), the French Conseil des Prises invoked Article 46 of the London Declaration in support of the condemnation of a merchantman of doubtful nationality engaged in refuelling operations of enemy submarines.[164]

On yet another occasion, a neutral ship, the *Adelphotis* (1917), was declared lawful prize for transporting an oil cargo destined to enemy submarines.[165] The *Iro-Maru* (1916), a Japanese vessel was captured while transporting the German consul in China on a special journey to Bangkok. The prize decision interpreted Article 45 of the London Declaration in a sense encompassing the travel of diplomats and not only of militaries: 'un navire,

[162]See *The Svithiod* (1920), in GRANT, A.W., *British and Colonial Prize Cases*, vol.III (1917–22) at pp. 576–7. In two other cases, the question arose as to the validity of capturing a vessel on grounds of being under the control of an enemy government (Article 46) while on a voyage following the suspect one; 'could she be captured on the voyage on which she was, that being either the second or the third voyage after the one upon which she had taken the coal to the German fleet? If it was merely a question of contraband, she could not. If it was a question of her being an auxiliary, in the sense of being in some way part of the fleet, possibly she might'; see *The Edna* (1919), *ibid.* at p. 417. See also *The Alwina* (1918), *ibid.* at pp. 58–9.

[163]See FAUCHILLE, P. and BASDEVANT, J., *Jurisprudence italienne en matière de prises maritimes*, 1918 at pp. 49–50. In the case of *The Chrysopolis* (1917), it was upheld that a suspected act of replenishment of enemy submarines, if effected under constraint, did not amount to unneutral service; *ibid.* at p. 165.

[164]See FAUCHILLE, P., *Jurisprudence française en matière de prises maritimes*, 1916 at p. 283.

[165]*Ibid.* at p. 385.

quel que soit son pavillon, neutre ou allié, est de bonne prise lorsqu'il voyage spécialement en vue du transport d'un agent de l'Etat ennemi chargé de porter des plis ou nouvelles dans l'intérêt de cet Etat'.[166] The *Olympia* (1915) was confiscated upon evidence, especially the transport of several enemy militaries, that warranted the combined application of Article 45 and Article 46§§1,2,3 of the London Declaration.[167]

Finally, with regard to the German jurisprudence, the Berlin Supreme Prize Court had scarcely ever the opportunity to deal with cases touching upon the concept of unneutral service.[168] In a number of cases pleaded before the Mixed Arbitral Tribunals in the aftermath of the First World War, the question arose as to the legal consequences of a neutral vessel if at the time of capture fully chartered by a belligerent government. As those arbitral awards invariably admitted, neutral vessels should in that case receive no better treatment than enemy merchant ships, Article 46 of the London Declaration reflecting in that respect existing customary law. In the case of *Marouli v. Germany* (4 October 1928), for instance, the Greek-German Mixed Arbitral Tribunal affirmed: 'que d'après les principes généralement admis et consacrés par l'art.46 de la déclaration de Londres, le

[166]*Ibid.* at p. 326.

[167]*Ibid.* at p. 125. In the case of *The Federico,* the French prize court applied Article 45 to a Spanish vessel carrying passengers of enemy nationality although they were not as yet embodied in the armed forces of the enemy but they intended in all probability to do so; 'whereas it is proved from the inquiry that the steamer Federico is not a packet employed in the regular transportation of passengers; whereas, at the time of its capture at sea the special object of its voyage was the transportation from Barcelona to Genoa of numerous German and Austro-Hungarian passengers, the great majority of these belonging by their age to the classes mobilized by their respective governments and travelling in response to this call; whereas, under these circumstances, these passengers should be regarded as incorporated in the armed force of the enemy in the sense of article 45 cited above, and whereas the ship was thus, according to the terms of the said article, subject to confiscation'; see *The Federico* (1915), in SCOTT, J.B. and JAEGER, W.H.E., *Cases on International Law,* 2nd edn (1937) at pp. 940–1.

[168]In the case of *The Dahlia,* the Court declared that the presence of a neutral fishing boat in the immediate zone of naval operations coupled with the absence of ship papers justified seizure on grounds of unneutral service (intelligence gathering) in favour of the enemy; see FAUCHILLE, P. and DE VISSCHER, C., *Jurisprudence allemande en matière de prises maritimes,* 1924 at p. 118. In the case of *The Liesbeth Betty,* the Court accepted that a neutral ship emitting a thick smoke screen upon being approached by German warships might be lawfully seized upon reasonable suspicion of signalling their position to the enemy; *ibid.* at p. 119.

navire de commerce neutre affrété en totalité à un gouvernement ennemi est passible du traitement qu'il subirait s'il était un navire de commerce ennemi'.[169]

Similar to what happened with relation to so many other aspects of the laws of war at sea, all belligerents entered the war with an express commitment to abide by Article 45 and 46 of the London Declaration but soon distorted the codified principles on unneutral service beyond recognition.[170] The French decree, for instance, of 27 August 1918, or the Italian decree of 10 October 1918, declared guilty of unneutral service any neutral vessel which would agree to sail under an enemy safe-conduct. The French enactment was arguably in retaliation for a German amendment of a Prize Ordinance which asserted that the entire merchant fleet of a neutral country, the greater part of whose tonnage was sailing in enemy interest, would be presumed as engaged in unneutral service and should suffer the consequences.

A major change that First World War practices are believed to have provoked regarding unneutral service concerns the assimilation of the neutral vessel with an enemy warship in the case of active participation in the hostilities, a legal fiction totally unknown at the time of the London Naval Conference. Article 46 of the London Declaration which deals with the most objectionable forms of unneutral service did not go further than affording to the neutral offender the same treatment as that reserved to enemy merchantmen. Already before the outbreak of the Second World War, however, French, German or Italian naval instructions and prize regulations provided for the outright attack and destruction of a neutral ship which was in any way taking part in the naval operations of the enemy.[171]

[169]See *Recueil des décisions des Tribunaux Arbitraux Mixtes*, vol.8 (1928–9) at p. 348. The case concerned *The Kyma*, a Greek ship chartered by the French government and torpedoed off the West African coast. Identical was the reasoning in the cases of *Costomenis and Valmadis v. Germany* (21 February, 1929), *ibid.* at p. 850, and *Embiricos v. Germany* (24 July, 1930), *ibid.*, vol.10 at p. 106. Both cases concerned Greek ships sunk by German submarines while chartered by the British government.

[170]National navy regulations and their progressive departure from the letter of the London Declaration are traced in VERZIJL, *op. cit., supra* n.26, pp. 952–62.

[171]According to Article 2 of the French instructions of 1934 a neutral vessel would be subject to attack 's'il se livre à des actes de guerre tels que mouillage de mines, rupture de cables sous-marin, visite de navires neutres, attaque de

While the 1939 Harvard Research laid down in Article 65 that:

> a belligerent may treat as an enemy warship:
> (a) a neutral vessel taking a direct part in hostilities on the side of the enemy;
> (b) a neutral vessel exclusively engaged at the time in the transportation of enemy troops.[172]

2 Lawful prize – the doctrine of continuous voyage

The Genesis of the Concept The doctrine of continuous voyage was formatted along the perpetual process of clash and readjustment between the neutral claim to pursue lucrative trade and

navires de commerce battant pavillon français ou allié . . . s'il participe aux opérations de guerre de l'ennemi en lui donnant par radiocommunication ou par tout autre procédé, des renseignements destinés à son usage immédiat (par exemple en lui signalant votre présence, en l'aidant à régler son tir, etc.)', while Article 141 of the Italian law of 1938 speaks of 'warlike acts in favour of the enemy or transmit military information for his immediate use or take part in his military operations in any other manner'; see 33 *AJIL* (1939) *Suppl.* at pp. 672–4. For Second World War practice concerning removal of enemy persons from neutral vessels, see BRIGGS, H.W., 'Removal of Enemy Persons from Neutral Vessels on the High Seas', 34 *AJIL* (1940), p. 249*ff.*; MUNSTER, J.H., 'Removal of Persons from Neutral Shipping', *US Judge Advocate General's Journal* (Oct.1952), p. 3*ff.*; MÜNCH, I., 'Asama Maru Incident' in BERNHARDT, R. (ed.), *Encyclopedia of Public International Law,* instalment 3 (1982), p. 40*ff.*

[172]See 33 *AJIL* (1939) *Suppl.*, pp. 654–80. Although the Commentary refrains from specifying what acts might suggest a 'direct part in hostilities', it is generally agreed that the act of assistance must intervene at the time of actual hostilities and have a direct bearing upon the progress of those naval operations. It will be recalled, at this juncture, that the so-called Hague Radio Rules adopted in 1923 contained some closely parallel provisions. According to Article 6§1, 'the transmission by radio by a vessel or an aircraft, whether enemy or neutral, when on or over the high seas of military intelligence for the immediate use of a belligerent is to be deemed a hostile act and will render the vessel or aircraft liable to be fired upon'; see 17 *AJIL* (1923) *Suppl.*, pp. 242–5, and 32 *AJIL* (1938) *Suppl.*, pp. 1–11. The text can also be found in RONZITTI, *op. cit.*, *supra* n.29, pp. 367–70. This clause bears a close resemblance with Article 65 in that it exacts immediacy between the passing of intelligence report and enemy action so that the neutral vessel can be regarded as directly involved in hostilities. Under Article 6§2, 'a neutral vessel or neutral aircraft which transmits when on or over the high seas information destined for a belligerent concerning military operations or military forces shall be liable to capture. The prize court may condemn the vessel or aircraft if it considers that the circumstances justify condemnation'; *ibid.* This in turn is comparable with Article 64(c) in that it concedes that the claim to assimilate the neutral vessel to enemy warship evaporates if the act of hostile assistance is clearly unconnected with any enemy operation undertaken immediately thereafter.

the belligerent preoccupation to cut off all enemy supply routes. It was developed by the English prize courts to counter the ingenious device by which American traders sought to evade the rule according to which a trade in which neutrals were forbidden to engage in time of peace might not be opened to them in time of war. This latter principle, known as the Rule of War of 1756, was promulgated and enforced by the British government in order to destroy the colonial trade of its enemies.[173]

American shippers, in turn, although denying international validity to the Rule of War of 1756 resorted to a circuitous technique which consisted in transporting goods from the French, Dutch or Spanish colonies to a US port before forwarding them in the same vessels to the mother countries. It was against this legal fiction of a two-leg voyage allegedly transforming enemy goods and enemy destination to pure neutral venture that the British prize courts countered the theory of continuous voyage holding that what was as a matter of fact a single, continuous voyage from a foreign colony to its mother country could not be altered by the deceptive insertion of an intermediate neutral port.[174]

[173]At the outbreak of the war between England and France in 1756 the latter power was forced to relax its colonial trade monopoly and allowed Dutch merchantmen to carry on the trade between metropolitan territory and the overseas dependencies. The English prize courts responded by declaring 'good prize' all Dutch vessels engaged in this traffic on the ground that such vessels would be deemed to be part of the merchant fleet of the enemy, or 'French by adoption'. As Lord Stowell reasoned: 'without reference to accidents of the one kind or other, the general rule is, that the neutral has a right to carry on, in time of war, his accustomed trade to the utmost extent of which that accustomed trade is capable. Very different is the case of a trade which the neutral has never possessed, which he holds by no title of use and habit in times of peace, and which, in fact, can obtain in war by no other title, than by the success of the one belligerent against the other, and at the expense of that very belligerent under whose success he sets up his title; and such I take to be the colonial trade, generally speaking'; see *The Immanuel* (1799), 2 *C. Robinson's Admiralty Reports* at p. 198. For the British view on the origin, nature and the consequences of the Rule of 1756 and of the concept of continuous voyage, see STEPHEN, J., *War in Disguise or the Frauds of the Neutral Flags*, 1805, 3rd edn by F.Piggott (1917), pp. 11–115.

[174]Among the numerous studies on the concept of continuous voyage, see BRIGGS, H.W., *The Doctrine of Continuous Voyage*, 1926; ELLIOTT, C.B., 'The Doctrine of Continuous Voyage', 1 *AJIL* (1907), p. 61*ff*.; WOOLSEY, L.H., 'Early Cases on the Doctrine of Continuous Voyage', 4 *AJIL* (1910), p. 823*ff*.; ARIAS, H., 'The Doctrine of Continuous Voyages in the Eighteenth Century', 9 *AJIL* (1915), p. 583*ff*.; BALDWIN, S.E., 'The "Continuous Voyage" Doctrine During

For Briggs, the doctrine finds its legal basis in 'the principle *dolus non purgatur circuitu* – that one is not permitted to do by indirection what one is forbidden to do directly'.[175] In the words of another scholar, 'the admitted principle is applied to facts as they are and not as they are made to appear to be. The doctrine does not rest upon a fiction; it looks beneath the fiction to the facts and if, as has been said, there is no place in international law for fictions, the doctrine should be accepted without further objection.'[176] On the contrary, for Paul Fauchille, 'la doctrine du voyage continu est en elle-même une véritable anomalie juridique. Infliger à un voyage entre deux ports neutres les conséquences pénales d'un voyage entre un port neutre et un port ennemi, sous prétexte que, parvenue au port neutre de destination, la cargaison sera réexpédiée dans un port ennemi, c'est de fait assimiler des voyages successifs à un voyage unique. La théorie repose ainsi sur une fiction de droit.'[177]

The Evolution of the Concept in Prize Law The difficult element to establish, if not presumptorily, was whether the call at a neutral port was made *bona fide* or simply to conceal a preconceived violation of neutrality laws:

> it is certainly true that a continued voyage from the colony of the enemy to the Mother Country, or to any other ports but those of the Country to which the vessel belongs, will subject the cargo to confiscation . . . It certainly is not a novel principle . . . On the contrary, it is an inherent and settled principle in all cases in which the same question can have come under discussion, that the mere *touching* at any port without importing the cargo into the common stock of

the Civil War and Now', 9 *AJIL* (1915), p. 793*ff.*; FAUCHILLE, P., 'La théorie du voyage continu en matière de contrebande de guerre', 4 *RGDIP* (1897), p. 297*ff.*; BATY, T., 'Continuous Voyage: The Present Position', 9 *GST* (1923), p. 101*ff.*; WILSON, G.G., 'Continuous Voyage', 15 *Proc.ASIL* (1921), P.45*ff.*

175 See BRIGGS, *op. cit., supra* at p. 28.

176 See ELLIOTT, *op. cit., supra* n.174 at p. 96.

177 See FAUCHILLE, *op. cit., supra* n.174 at p. 304. Likewise, Thomas Baty defended the view that 'it is essentially incompatible with any reasonable and coherent doctrine of neutrality in a maritime war' and traced its origins in some controversial practice: 'three highly-controverted cases in 1863; four cases where the attempt failed in 1898–1900; numerous cases at a time of chaos and wild reprisals, 1915–1918. This is not sufficient in itself to support a great new principle'; see BATY, *op. cit., supra* n.174 at pp. 102, 104.

> the country, will not alter the nature of the voyage, which continues the same in all respects, and must be considered as a voyage to the country, to which the vessel is actually going for the purpose of delivering her cargo at the ultimate port.[178]

Although the doctrine was brought into life in connection with some attempts to liberalize the colonial trade, it was later asserted to be equally valid as a contraband control mechanism. For instance, in one particular case which arose in the context of the Crimean War (a cargo of saltpetre bound from Lisbon to Hamburg and condemned on the ground that its real destination was an enemy port in Russia), the French prize court held that 'inasmuch as a shipment of contraband of war prepared in fraud of the political measures prescribed by an allied government in the interest of a common war, continued under a false name, with dissimulation on the ship's papers, and sent to parts nearer enemy country and serving habitually as a channel for provisions of the enemy, must be made on behalf and to the destination of the enemy, and therefore confiscation of the articles seized should be pronounced by application of articles 1 and 2 of the Regulations of July 1778'.[179]

As one of the earliest among the numerous prize decisions of the American Civil War reasoned:

[178]See *The Maria* (1805), 5 *C. Robinson's Admiralty Reports* at p. 368. A year later, Sir William Grant reaffirmed the principle: 'if the voyage from the place of lading be not really ended, it matters not by what acts the party may have evinced his desire of making it appear to have been ended. That those acts have been attended with trouble and expense cannot alter their quality or their effect. The trouble and expense may weigh as circumstances of evidence, to show the purpose for which the acts were done; but if the evasive purpose be admitted or proved, we can never be bound to accept as a substitute for the observance of the law, the means, however operose, which have been employed to cover a breach of it. Between the actual importation by which a voyage is really ended, and the colourable importation which is to give it the appearance of being ended, there must necessarily be a great resemblance. The acts to be done must be almost entirely the same; but there is this difference between them. The landing of the cargo, the entry at the custom-house, and the payment of such duties as the law of the place requires, *are necessary ingredients* in a genuine importation; the true purpose of the owner cannot be effected without them. But in a fictitious importation they are *mere voluntary ceremonies*, which have no natural connection whatever with the purpose of sending on the cargo to another market'; see *The William* (1806), *ibid.* at p. 396.

[179]See *The Frau Houwina* (1855), in SCOTT, J.B., *Cases on International Law*, 1922 at p. 997.

> the commerce is in the destination and intended use of the property laden on board of the vessel, and not in the incidental, ancillary, and temporary voyage of the vessel, which may be but one of many carriers through which the property is to reach its true and original destination. If this were not the rule of the prize law, a very wide door would be opened for fraud and evasion . . . This court holds that, in all such cases, the transportation or voyage of the contraband goods is to be considered as a unit, from the port of lading to the port of delivery in the enemy's country; that if any part of such voyage or transportation be unlawful, it is unlawful throughout.[180]

At the time of the American Civil War, a further attempt was made to apply the doctrine of continuous voyage with regard to blockade running. British merchantmen plying between England and Nassau, although ultimately destined to blockaded Confederate ports, gave rise to some well-known prize decisions such as the *Bermuda*,[181] or the *Springbok*.[182]

[180]See *The Stephen Hart* (1863), *ibid.* at pp. 992–3. The *Peterhoff* case stands as another *locus classicus* of the continuous voyage rule: 'contraband merchandise is subject to a different rule in respect to ulterior destination than that which applies to merchandise not contraband. The latter is liable to capture only when a violation of blockade is intended; the former when destined to the hostile country, or to the actual military or naval use of the enemy, whether blockaded or not . . . Hence, while articles, not contraband, might be sent to Matamoras [Mexico] and beyond to the rebel region [Texas], where the communications were not interrupted by blockade, articles of a contraband character, destined in fact to a state in rebellion, or for the use of the rebel military forces, were liable to capture though primarily destined to Matamoras'; see *The Peterhoff* (1866), 5 *J.W. Wallace's US Supreme Court Reports* at p. 59.

[181]In the opinion of the US Supreme Court: 'it makes no difference whether the destination to the rebel port was ulterior or direct; nor could the question of destination be affected by trans-shipment at Nassau, if trans-shipment was intended, for that could not break the continuity of transportation of the cargo. The interposition of a neutral port between neutral departure and belligerent destination has always been a favorite resort of contraband carriers and blockade-runners. But it never avails them when the ultimate destination is ascertained. A transportation from one point to another remains continuous, so long as intent remains unchanged, no matter what stoppages or trans-shipments intervene . . . Successive voyages, connected by a common plan and a common object, form a plural unit. They are links of the same chain, each identical in description with every other, and each essential to the continuous whole. The ships are planks of the same bridge, all of the same kind, and all necessary to the convenient passage of persons and property from one end to the other'; see *The Bermuda* (1865), 3 *J.W. Wallace's US Supreme Court Reports* at pp. 553, 555.

[182]Chief Justice Chase's pronouncement read in part: 'upon the whole case we cannot doubt that the cargo was originally shipped with intent to violate the

In 1882, the Maritime Prize Commission of the Institut de Droit International in its Wiesbaden session ardently criticized the doctrine of continuous voyage as applied in the *Springbok* case:

> que la théorie de la continuité du voyage, telle qu'elle a été admise par la Cour suprême des Etats-Unis d'Amérique, lorsqu'elle a déclaré de bonne prise le chargement du navire le *Springbok* (1867), est en opposition avec une règle reconnue par le droit coutumier de la guerre maritime, suivant laquelle la propriété neutre sur bâtiment portant pavillon neutre et expédiée d'un port neutre vers un autre port neutre, n'est pas sujette à confiscation ni à saisie par un belligérant comme prise légitime de guerre... Qu'elle doit être considérée comme une atteinte grave aux droits des nations neutres, puisqu'il en résulterait que la destination d'un bâtiment neutre à un port non ennemi ne suffirait plus pour empêcher de saisir les marchandises non contrebande de guerre qui s'y trouvent; Qu'il en résulterait en outre, quant au blocus, que tout port neutre auquel aurait été expédié un chargement neutre, à bord d'un navire neutre, deviendrait un port bloqué *par interprétation*, dès qu'il y aurait des motifs de soupçonner que le chargement, après son débarquement en port neutre, pourrait être ultérieurement rechargé sur un autre bâtiment, et expédié vers un port réellement bloqué.[183]

---

blockade; that the owners of the cargo intended that it should be trans-shipped at Nassau into some vessel more likely to succeed in reaching safely a blockaded port than the Springbok; that the voyage from London to the blockaded port was, as the cargo, both in law and in the intent of the parties, one voyage; and that the liability to condemnation, if captured during any part of that voyage, attached to the cargo from the time of sailing'; see *The Springbok* (1866), 5 *J.W. Wallace's US Supreme Court Reports* at p. 28. See also *The Pearl* (1866), *ibid.* at p. 578; *The Hart* (1865), *ibid.*, vol.3 at p. 560.

[183]See 14 *RDILC* (1882) at pp. 330–1. See also 6 *Ann.IDI* (1882–3), Torino Session at p. 101. A few years later, however, the same body of jurists recognized the soundness of the doctrine by attaching the following proviso in the Draft Rules on War Contraband: 'la destination pour l'ennemi est présumée lorsque le transport va à l'un de ses ports, ou bien à un port neutre qui, *d'après des preuves évidentes et de fait incontestable, n'est qu'une étape pour l'ennemi, comme but final de la même opération commerciale*' (emphasis added); see 15 *Ann.IDI* (1896), Venice Session at p. 231.

The doctrine was applied during the Boer War[184] by the British government which had acquiesced, though not recognized, the American practice during the Civil War, and again in 1896 by Italy during the Ethiopian campaign.[185]

The 1908–9 London Naval Conference was convened at a time when the debate concerning the legitimacy of such a practice was at its peak. The divergence of opinion was so great that at some point the controversy over the codification of the doctrine of continuous voyage threatened to result in a serious stalemate of the entire Conference. A compromise was finally reached to the effect that the theory of continuous voyage was to be retained as regards absolute contraband, but should not be applicable in matters of conditional contraband and blockade enforcement. According to Article 30 of the London Declaration, 'absolute contraband is liable to capture if it is shown to be destined to the territory belonging to or occupied by the enemy, or to the armed forces of the enemy. It is immaterial whether the carriage of the goods is direct or entails either trans-shipment or transport over land.'[186]

[184]The novel situation about the Boer War related to shipments consigned to the neutral port of Delagoa Bay, but presumably destined for a territory deprived of access to the sea. The controversy concerned three German mail steamers, the *Bundesrath*, the *Herzog* and the *General*, seized in January 1909 while bound for the Portuguese neutral port of Lourenco Marques in Delagoa Bay and suspected of carrying ammunition ultimately destined for the Transvaal and the Orange Free State. In the correspondence arising from these seizures, Great Britain argued for the principle that France had recognized in the *Frau Houwina* case, and the United States in the *Peterhoff* case. As it turned out, however, no contraband was found on board the German vessels. For more, see BRIGGS, *op. cit., supra* n.174, pp. 83–9, and MOORE, J.B., *A Digest of International Law*, vol.VII, 1906, pp. 739–44.

[185]In the case of *The Doelwick*, a Dutch merchantman bound for India with a cargo of arms and explosives was captured by an Italian warship in the Red Sea while deviating from its course in order to discharge its load at the French port of Djibouti. The contraband would then in all probability have found its way to Abyssinia. The Italian prize court sustained the legality of the capture but declined to condemn the seized property on the ground that hostilities had already ended; for more, see BRUSA, E., 'L'affaire du Doelwyk', 4 *RGDIP* (1897), p. 157*ff*.

[186]In the explicit terms of the General Report of the Drafting Committee, 'it is not, therefore, the destination of the vessel which is decisive, it is the destination of the goods. It makes no difference if these goods are on board a vessel which is to discharge them in a neutral port; as soon as the captor is able to show that the goods are to be forwarded from there by land or sea to an enemy country, that is sufficient to justify the capture and subsequent condemnation of the cargo. It is the very principle of continuous voyage, which as regards absolute contraband is thus established by Art.30. The journey made by the goods is regarded as making a unit'; see USNWC, 9 *International Law Topics* (1909) at p. 75.

In contrast, goods considered among conditional contraband when documented for discharge in a neutral port may not be considered conditional contraband even if the vessel is ultimately destined to an enemy port. In this case, as Article 35 provides, 'the ship's papers are conclusive proof both as to the voyage on which the vessel is engaged and as to the port of discharge of the goods, unless she is found clearly out of the course indicated by her papers, and unable to give adequate reasons to justify such deviation'.[187] As for blockade, the doctrine of continuous voyage was also excluded as laid down in Article 19: 'whatever may be the ulterior destination of the vessel or her cargo, the evidence of violation of blockade is not sufficiently conclusive to authorize the seizure of the vessel if she is at the time bound toward an unblockaded port'.[188]

The Continuous Voyage Rule as Applied in the First World War

By the Order-in-Council of 20 August 1914, Britain extended the doctrine to include conditional contraband. Formerly, to be liable to capture the neutral cargo had to be destined ultimately to the armed forces or a government department of the enemy state. However, under the Order of 29 October 1914, mere destination for a neutral port would be sufficient ground for capture, if the goods were consigned 'to order', or if no consignee was indicated in the ship's papers.[189] Furthermore, the burden of proof would no longer lie upon the captor but upon the aggrieved neutral. Hence, the scope of application of the continuous voyage rule was extended to include conditional contraband notwithstanding Article 35 of the London Declaration. France, Russia

[187]By Article 36, however, an exception to that rule was inserted concerning the case of conditional contraband ultimately destined to an enemy land-locked state.

[188]The General Report read as follows: 'it is the real destination of the vessel which must be considered when a violation of blockade is in question, and not the ulterior destination of the cargo. That destination proved or presumed would not then suffice to justify the capture, for violation of blockade, of a ship actually bound for an unblockaded port. But the cruiser might always prove that this destination to an unblockaded port is apparent, and that in reality the immediate destination of the vessel is really the blockaded port'; see USNWC, 9 *International Law Topics* (1909) at p. 55.

[189]See BRIGGS, *op. cit., supra* n.174, pp. 107–21.

and Germany acting in retaliation, soon adopted similar regulations.[190]

By the Order of 30 March 1916, the British government proclaimed that the distinction between absolute and conditional contraband had been rendered impracticable and should be discontinued,[191] while in July 1916 a further Order-in-Council, acknowledging the final abandonment of the London Declaration, announced that the doctrine of continuous voyage would henceforth be applicable to both the carriage of contraband and blockade running.[192] Neutrals refused to admit the legitimacy of the British claim according to which any uncommon increase of imports of neutral states adjacent to Germany could substantiate an enemy destination. The US government opposed the new belligerent pretension and noted: 'that a consignment "to order" of articles listed as conditional contraband and shipped to a neutral port raises a legal presumption of enemy destination appears to be directly contrary to the doctrines previously held by Great Britain'.[193]

The doctrine of continuous voyage was endorsed in various prize judgments the most noticeable of which was *The Kim* case

[190]See Article 5 of the French decree of 6 November 1914, in 9 *AJIL* (1915) *Sp.Suppl* at p. 26; Article 4 of the Russian Imperial Decree of 8 December 1914, *ibid.* at p. 35; Article 33 of the German ordinance of 18 April 1915, *ibid.* at p. 45.

[191]In the words of the British declaration, 'so long as these exceptional conditions continue our belligerent rights with respect to the two kinds of contraband are the same and our treatment of them must be identical'; see 10 *AJIL* (1916) *Sp.Suppl* at p. 52.

[192]On the unlimited application of the doctrine of continuous voyage during the First World War, see VERZIJL, *op. cit., supra* n.26, pp. 133–42, 767–71, 844–87, and GARNER, J.W., *International Law and the World War,* vol.II (1920), pp. 295–316, BRIGGS, *op. cit., supra* n.174, pp. 122–44, 172–212.

[193]See 9 *AJIL* (1915) *Sp.Suppl* at p. 58. In reply, Britain maintained that 'in view of the tremendous organization for war as now obtains in Germany . . . it would be absurd to give any definite pledge that in cases where the supplies can be proved to be for the use of the enemy forces they should be given complete immunity by the simple expedient of dispatching them to an agent in a neutral port'; *ibid.* at p. 80. The unprecedented extent to which supplies were reaching neutral ports was illustrated by some telling statistics: 'in 1913, during the above two months, the United States exports of lard to Denmark were nil, as compared with 22,652,598 lbs in the same two months of 1914. The corresponding figures with regard to bacon were: 1913, nil; 1914, 1,022,195 lbs; canned beef, 1913, nil; 1914, 151,200 lbs; pickled and cured beef, 1913, 42,901 lbs; 1914, 156,143 lbs; pickled pork, 1913, nil; 1914, 812,872 lbs. In the same two months the United States exported to Denmark 280,176 gallons of mineral lubricating oil in 1914 as compared with 179,952 in 1913; to Norway, 335,468 gallons in 1914, as against 151,179 gallons in 1913, to Sweden; 896,193 gallons in 1914, as against 385,476 gallons in 1913'; *ibid.* at p. 81.

brought before the British prize court in 1915. It involved four Scandinavian steamers, *The Alfred Nobel, The Bjornstjerne, The Bjornson, The Fridland,* and *The Kim,* laden with large cargoes of foodstuffs or pig products, which had left New York for Copenhagen. The President of the Prize Court found compelling evidence as to the concealed enemy destination of the shipments in the fact that 'the average annual quantity of lard imported into Denmark during the three years 1911 to 1913 from all sources was 1,459,000 lb. The quantity of lard consigned to Copenhagen on these four ships alone was 19,252,000 lb. Comparing these quantities, the result is that these vessels were carrying towards Copenhagen within less than a month more than thirteen times the quantity of lard which had been imported annually to Denmark for each of the three years before the war.'[194]

According to Allied practice, the theory of continuous voyage was elevated to an overriding pretext, the ultimate alibi for those cases of interference with neutral shipping to which established legal principles could afford no justification. Arbitrariness not only in seizure, but also in prize procedure, reached considerable heights in the name of a strict prohibition of

[194]See *The Kim* (1915), in TREHERN, E.C.M., *British and Colonial Prize Cases,* vol.I (1914–5) at p. 439. After a lengthy inquiring into the true identity and the trade record of the various companies involved in the case, he concluded that 'the cargoes claimed by the shippers as belonging to them at the time of seizure were not on their way to Denmark to be incorporated into the common stock of that country by consumption, or *bona fide* sale, or otherwise; but, on the contrary, that they were on their way not only to German territory, but also to the German Government and their forces for naval and military use as their real ultimate destination. To hold the contrary would be to allow one's eyes to be filled by the dust of theories and technicalities, and to be blinded to the realities of the case'; *ibid.* at p. 491. The evolution of the legal doctrine of continuous voyage is reviewed in *ibid.*, pp. 478–83. Since most of the seized commodities constituted conditional contraband, Sir Samuel Evans had to examine the propriety of application of the concept of continuous voyage to conditional contraband contrary to the explicit provisions of the London Declaration. In his view then, Article 35 of the Declaration introduced a mere innovation which did not reflect existing international law on the subject and, therefore, conditional contraband no less than absolute contraband should be liable to confiscation even though bound for an ostensible neutral destination; see *ibid.* at p. 485. On this last point, see also *The Louisiana* (1918), in GRANT, A.W., *British and Colonial Prize Cases,* vol.III (1917–22) at p. 67. For other prize cases of the First World War concerning the concept of continuous voyage, see *The Maracaibo* (1916), *ibid.*, vol.II (1916–17) at p. 298; *The Bonna* (1918), *ibid.*, vol.III (1917–22) at p. 168; *The Norne* (1921), *ibid.* at p. 980.

continuous voyage. As has been observed in a classical monograph dealing with the concept of continuous voyage:

> it has justly been termed 'speculative capture': a neutral vessel on a voyage between two neutral ports was seized in the hope that while it was being searched in port, or being detained awaiting search, some evidence not necessarily from the vessel itself would turn up against it . . . The abuse was in the indiscriminate and unwarranted seizure of vessels against which at the time of first detention there was no particle of evidence. The abuse was continued in the admission of extraneous evidence against the vessels improperly seized. The climax of illegality was reached in the shifting of the burden of proof to the owner of the seized goods. The captor must justify his seizure. The practical impossibility of doing so does not shift the burden to the neutral trader. Such a change in the rules of evidence is undoubtedly convenient to the belligerent but just as undoubtedly is it illegal.[195]

How to Unveil Enemy Destination: Safe Conducts and Passports

The more the deceptive practices were employed, the less belligerents accepted ordinary ship's papers as offering conclusive evidence of the ship's innocence. Most common among devious practices was the possession of a duplicate set of false papers showing a neutral destination. Fake documents were also used to 'colour' enemy goods, or convert them to neutral property. As early as the sixteenth century such devices had acquired considerable currency. It was only natural, therefore, that belligerents expressed an increasing distrust for the normal complement of papers and sought to curb fraud by tightening their prize regulations. According to a practice which met with general use by the mid-seventeenth century, neutrals could issue passports or sea-passes, to certify the free character of ship and goods, whereby neutral merchantmen would in principle be exempted from search and capture.[196]

[195]See BRIGGS, *op. cit., supra* n.174 at p. 164.

[196]The first treaty providing for neutral passports was signed by Spain and Holland in 1648. Later, Sweden sought actively and obtained the recognition of sea-passes from England. In fact, upon the model of the Anglo-Swedish treaties

The system was based on a treaty commitment agreed upon at peacetime and which provided that if one of the parties opted for neutrality in a war in which the other was engaged, the neutral's ships would be spared from all search and hindrance when in possession of a duly issued pass. This certificate, in turn, had to be delivered from some competent organ of the neutral government after having ascertained that no contraband or enemy goods were carried on board the ship. In a limited number of cases it was expressly agreed that, despite the procurement of a neutral passport, a search of the ship would be still admitted in case of reasonable suspicion. If it was proved that fraud was committed under the guise of neutral passports, the belligerent was freed from any obligation to respect them.

Indeed, in practice, abuses of the system were so common that the failure of neutral passports as a contraband control mechanism has been widely acknowledged. The real significance of that arrangement, however, lay with the fact that the supervision of trade in contraband was thus elevated to a neutral obligation. Under the sea pass system, the neutral government assumed full responsibility for something which had been traditionally seen as a purely private venture not in the least affecting public policy as such.

Rationing The idea behind this scheme was that, by allocating quotas to neutral countries neighbouring enemy territory as regards overseas imports which roughly correspond to the domestic needs of those countries, the belligerent might be relatively assured that there would be no surplus to be routed to the enemy. The logical implication of such an idea was that if the volume of a neutral country's trade in any contraband commodity was found to be greater than that suggested under the rationing system, a direct supply line to the enemy could definitely be suspected. A seizure could thus rest on mere statistical probabilities.

In the case of the *Baron Stjernblad* the British Privy Council deduced the enemy destination from simple trade statistics:

---

of 1654, 1656 and 1661, numerous other agreements were negotiated as from the second half of the seventeenth century with stipulations for passport, sea letters or *certificat de mer*; see JESSUP and DEÁK, *op. cit., supra* n.2 at pp. 191–3. See also STÖDTER, R., 'Safe-conduct and Safe Passage' in BERNHARDT, R. (ed.), *Encyclopedia of Public International Law,* instalment 4 (1982), p. 193*ff.*

> turning now to Sweden, their Lordships find that prior to the war the imports of cocoa beans into Sweden were between 1,600 and 1,700 tons only annually. There was no re-export trade to Germany. Since the outbreak of hostilities imports of cocoa beans into Sweden have increased tenfold, and a re-export trade to Germany has been developed. During the first year of the war such re-export trade amounted to over 1,200 tons, it being the regular practice to ship cocoa beans to Gothenburg in Danish steamers, and to reship them thence to Germany . . . If the shipments of cocoa beans to Sweden be considered collectively, a considerable proportion thereof must be destined for or find its way into Germany, either by the re-export to Germany of the beans themselves or by the export to Germany of the various products of the beans.[197]

Hold-Back Guarantees Under this system, first introduced in September/October 1939, a neutral vessel might be allowed on the condition that no cargo would be discharged while still under consideration by the Contraband Committee and that these items that the Committee might eventually find seizable would be promptly reshipped to an Allied port. The test case involved US ships of the Black Diamond Steamship Corporation, and thus the arrangement was also known for some time as 'black diamond' guarantees.[198] A major weakness of this device was the risk on the part of the issuing belligerent authority to order the return but never receive the neutral cargoes. As for the neutral merchants, they had to cope with the inconvenience of travelling back and forth several times since the cargo might initially be taken to a neutral port under guarantee, return to a British port if so demanded, only to be subsequently released by the Procurator-General and granted a trans-shipment licence.

[197]See *The Baron Stjernblad* (1917), in GRANT, A.W., *British and Colonial Prize Cases*, vol.III (1917–22) at pp. 20–1. In another case, it was observed with all the logical inferences which might follow that the imports of lard from the US to Scandinavian countries during the months of October and November 1914 were nearly sixty times those for the corresponding months of 1913; see *The Kim* (1915), in TREHERN, E.C.M., *British and Colonial Prize Cases*, vol.I (1914–15) at p. 439. See also *supra*, notes 194–5 and accompanying text.
[198]See MEDLICOTT, W.N., *The Economic Blockade*, vol.I (1952), pp. 87–94.

Navicerts What became known as navicerts differ essentially from the above-examined sea passes in that it fell upon a competent *belligerent* authority to deliver it. A navicert was thus a document provided by the belligerent before the departure of a given neutral consignment and certifying its innocence, or a contraband control mechanism intervening 'at the source' of neutral seaborne commerce. Neutrals were under no obligation to subject themselves to such a control. Normally, however, it would save them considerable delay and expenses since a duly issued navicert was an ample warranty to escape diversion to a belligerent port for search. Yet, it should not be assumed that unnavicerted shipments were to be automatically regarded as liable to seizure and condemnation. This so-called 'voluntary' navicert system was introduced in November 1939. The scheme was based on the idea that the British mission in an exporting country might issue a 'commercial passport' for any non-contraband consignment.[199]

By the summer of 1940, it was clear that stricter measures were necessary in order to cope with the numerous evasions. As the official historian of the British economic warfare campaign explains, 'it was impossible for the Navy, which had to patrol the seas against German raiders, submarines, and possible invasion attempts, to watch, for economic-warfare purposes, a coastline stretching from the Arctic to Equatorial Africa'.[200] The new scheme of the continental blockade, announced by the Order-in-Council of 31 July 1940, included three major innovations, namely universal and compulsory navicerting, rationing of neutral countries adjacent to enemy territories and a series of incentives to neutral shipowners such as guaranteed access to British-controlled facilities all over the world to accept tighter controls.

[199]*Ibid.*, pp. 94–101. Apart from so-called Z-navicerts which certified the innocence of freight, there was also the 'ship navicert' which was delivered when the whole cargo of the ship was covered by navicerts. A ship navicert was, in fact, the best assurance that no delays for inspection and other visit and search formalities would be experienced at sea. Documents of somewhat less exemptory power, known as 'mewcerts', were in use in the eastern Mediterranean; *ibid.* at pp. 101–2. During the First World War, a similar institution known as Letters of Assurance had been operated by British authorities at US ports. For more, see RITCHIE, H., *The Navicert System during the World War*, 1938.
[200]See MEDLICOTT, *op. cit., supra* n.198 at p. 430.

Under the *compulsory navicert* arrangement,[201] ships sailing from a neutral port to any European port as well as to certain Atlantic islands or neutral ports in North Africa should obtain navicerts for the whole cargo and in addition a ship navicert at the last port of loading. Any undocumented consignment and any ship without a ship navicert would be presumed to be carrying contraband to Europe and therefore liable to be seized as prize. Navicerts issued upon the simple initiative of British embassies, or Z-navicerts, were cancelled and all applications were treated centrally in London. Essential for the operation of the navicert system was the fixing of *quotas* as regards imports of the more important commodities by European neutrals, e.g. Spain and Portugal. When the quota-ceiling for a particular period was reached, navicerts were refused. The third feature of the new blockade enforcement policy aimed at bringing further pressure on shipping companies in order to cooperate fully and sincerely with British authorities. Any shipowner who would pledge compliance with the British regulations would have the right to a *ship warrant*.[202]

Compliance with a belligerent system of navicerts or ship warrants has been sometimes considered as betraying an act of unneutral service. For Robert Tucker, 'it seems reasonably well-established that a neutral vessel in accepting a safe-conduct pass from a belligerent subjects itself to the control of the latter and performs an act of unneutral service'.[203] Voluntary submission and acquiescence to such a mechanism, as the reasoning goes, renders the contraband control effort of the belligerent more efficient, thus allowing for an optimal use of its naval assets.

[201]See *ibid.*, pp. 436–42. On how the navicert system performed throughout the remainder of the war and especially after the US neutrality ended, see *ibid.*, vol.II, pp. 153–9, 419–27. See also MOOS, M., 'The Navicert in World War II', 38 *AJIL* (1944), p. 115*ff.*

[202]See MEDLICOTT, *op. cit., supra* n.198, vol.II, pp. 442–8. Ship warrant holders, in turn, could count on and enjoy full access to British-controlled facilities (e.g. stores, charts, dry docking, repairing) but also to British insurance and credit. The measure incited ample demand so that by the end of September 1940 it was estimated that over 50 per cent of the total ocean-going tonnage of the world consisted of British or Allied ships and of ships whose owners were warrant holders. Parallel to this 'white list' of warrant holders, the British government kept careful record and often gave the widest publicity to other lists containing suspect ships to be discriminatorily treated. The Ships' Discrimination List, a Secret Black List, and the Suspect List were all designed to convince even the unruly shippers to submit to British rules.

[203]See TUCKER, *op. cit., supra* n.3 at p. 322.

Although this would seem arguable under an extensive interpretation of the notion of 'service', it remains nonetheless impertinent as for the application of the legal principle of unneutral service.

The crucial factor which has made out of unneutral service an independent legal premise for capture is the probable identification of neutral and belligerent interests, or the fact that a neutral would be ready to yield his rights in order to offer a distinct advantage to one of the belligerents. Applying for and accepting a navicert, on the other hand, can hardly qualify as an unneutral service in the above-construed sense. In fact, by consenting to being boarded and searched while at port, neutral merchants do not violate neutrality any more than if they had received clearance on the high seas following the traditional mode of visit and search. It is notably in their own interest to have the cargo inspected before they are put to sea. Otherwise, it would be all too facile to brand practically every neutral venture in time of war as unneutral service. Pushing this logic to the extreme, the mere fact of keeping clear of prohibited war zones proclaimed by a belligerent although not reproachable in itself could still be regarded by the other belligerent as unneutral to the extent that it heeds to enemy measures presumably facilitating the enemy war effort.

3 New issues, old problems: modern developments in prize law

The Iranian Oil Shuttle Service It appears, even though information is sparse on this point, that a number of neutral vessels were used by the Iranian government in order to ferry oil from the exposed terminal of Kharg Island to safer oil installations in the south hopefully beyond the range of Iraqi bombers. In all probability, those neutral tankers engaged in the shuttle service between Kharg and Lavan or Sirri Island operated under charter arrangements with the Iranian government, while it has often been suggested that they were also regularly escorted by Iranian gunboats. According to some information published in June 1988, at the oil terminals at Kharg and Larak Island there were some seventeen supertankers serving as storage vessels for the shuttled oil. Another twenty-five chartered tankers were engaged in that shuttle service, some of which having been attacked as many as four times.[204]

To the extent that this account corresponds to reality, it would be safe to assume that the neutral ships involved in the operation should be considered as engaged in unneutral service and that under customary law principles reviewed above (see Article 46§3 of the London Declaration or World War jurisprudence) should be assimilated to enemy merchant vessels and liable to condemnation. The fact that besides being 'in the exclusive employment' of a belligerent government they were also sailing under belligerent convoy would further corroborate their being treated as enemy merchant vessels (see Article 64(a) of the Harvard Research), that is to say, as lawful prizes liable even to destruction under exceptional circumstances.[205]

The Iranian Prize Court On November 1987, Iran enacted legislation setting up a War Prize Tribunal, to be seated in Tehran, 'in order to hear complaints and disputes relating to war seizures'.[206] Neutral goods would be liable to seizure in two cases: first, if they could qualify as contraband of war in the sense of 'merchandise, means of transport and equipment which the Islamic Republic of Iran forbids from being transported to enemy territory' (Article 3d); second, if they 'could effectively contribute to increasing the combat power of the enemy [and]

[204]See DE GUTTRY and RONZITTI, *op. cit., supra* n.45, doc.2.a.37 at p. 292. It is interesting to note that when the British-registered *Burmah Endeavour*, arguably operating as ferry for Iranian oil, was attacked off Larak Island in May 1988 the British objected and recalled that 'Iraq has consistently claimed the right, *in defiance of international law*, to attack, any shipping helping to sustain Iranian economic activity'; see *ibid.*, doc.2.a.43 at p. 360.

[205]Mention should be made here of a more radical view according to which the neutral vessels, if escorted by belligerent warships, should be regarded as having forfeited all immunity, thus being liable to the same treatment as enemy warships. As one commentator pleaded along these lines, 'the Iraqi attacks on chartered shuttle tankers under neutral flags that carried Iranian oil from Kharg Island to points in the south, are justifiable on the grounds of their performing unneutral service through integration into Iran's war-sustaining effort. Of course, the same applies to neutral vessels (wherever they are located) under Iranian military convoy or escort'; see BOCZEK, *op. cit., supra* n.51 at p. 258.

[206]The Law Regarding the Settlement of Disputes Over War Prizes of 17 November 1987, was adopted by the Commission of Judicial and Legal Affairs on Jan.12, 1988, and was ratified by the Constitutional Council on 31 January 1988. The text is found in DE GUTTRY and RONZITTI, *op. cit., supra* n.45 at pp. 39–40.

their final destination, either directly or via intermediaries, is a State at war with the Islamic Republic of Iran' (Article 3b).

A few procedural rules were also enunciated in the War Prize Decree. According to Article 6, prize proceedings should follow civil procedure. All documents and collected evidence relating to seized property had to be made available to the Court within a period of two months while the latter would dispose of another two months from the moment of reception before considering the case and delivering its judgment. The claimants should appear before the Tribunal. With respect to merchandise 'susceptible to rapid deterioration, or which it is not worthwhile preserving', Article 5 stipulated that upon authorization of the Procurator of the Tribunal they could be liquidated, while the returns of the sale should be deposited in the account of the Ministry of Justice pending the prize decision.

Apparently, the Iranian War Prize Tribunal was never put to work. No pronouncements were made on numerous cases of confiscated cargoes. It is regrettable that Iran realized belatedly that judicial validation could only enhance its otherwise legitimate exercise of the rights of visit, search and capture in the Gulf. A number of obscure points in the Iranian prize enactment could thus have been elucidated, not to mention the fresh interpretation which it might have given to concepts such as continuous voyage, neutral convoys or unneutral service.

Recent UN-Mandated Maritime Embargoes Naval enforcement action authorized by the UN Security Council on three occasions in recent years,[207] would invite a few remarks concerning an analogy which could be drawn between the penalties provided against the violators of UN quasi-blockade measures and traditional rules on maritime capture. Two resolutions would be of interest in this respect. First, in the context of the UN sanctions against Iraq, Security Council Resolution 679 (1990) in para.8 called upon 'all States to detain any ships of Iraqi registry which enter their ports and which are being or have been used in violation of resolution 661, or to deny such ships entrance to their ports', except when in distress. Second, with relation to sanctions against the Federal Republic of Yugoslavia (Serbia and Montenegro), Security Council Resolution 820 (1993) speci-

[207]See *supra* notes 52–69 and accompanying text.

fied for the first time measures which may be taken against *third* ships suspected of having violated the UN trade embargo in the following terms: 'all States shall detain pending investigation all vessels . . . found in their territories and suspected of having violated or being in violation of resolutions 713 (1991), 757 (1992), 787 (1992) or the present resolution, and that, upon a determination that they have been in violation, such vessels . . . shall be impounded and, where appropriate, they and their cargoes may be forfeit to the detaining State'.

Several aspects of these provisions should be considered. To begin with, there has been a qualitative difference, in an escalatory direction, between the Gulf experience and that of the former Yugoslavia as far as the embargo enforcement is concerned. Whereas in the context of the Gulf crisis, Resolution 670 (1990) *recommended* the mere *detention* of ships of *Iraqi* registry used in violation of UN sanctions, in the case of former Yugoslavia Resolution 820 (1993) *decided* the eventual *forfeiture* of *any* vessel irrespective of its nationality. Furthermore, action had to be undertaken against vessels found anywhere within national territory rather than only those berthed in port,[208] which would imply that any ship could be ordered and escorted into port while navigating within the territorial waters of the state concerned.

Both seized and detained vessels could eventually become the property of the seizing/detaining state, if it was determined

[208]Most countries had interpreted Resolution 670 (1990) as if detention was only possible against ships which had entered a harbour; see, for instance, the Bulgarian decree of 22 October 1990, in BETHLEHEM, D.L. (ed.), *The Kuwait Crisis: Sanctions and Their Economic Consequences*, 1991, part I at p. 73; the Canadian Regulation of 1 October 1990, *ibid.* at p. 89; the Danish Executive Order of 16 November 1990, *ibid.* at p. 107; the New Zealand Regulation of 1 October 1990, *ibid.* at p. 254; the Norwegian Decree of 5 October 1990, *ibid.* at pp. 268–9; the British Order of 5 October 1990, *ibid.* at p. 370. *Cf.* the French enactment which provided for diversion to a French port of any vessel flying the Iraqi flag while navigating within the French territorial waters, *ibid.* at p. 140. At any rate, it is clear that Maritime Interception Forces could not instruct an Iraqi vessel to steer towards a given port in order to be interned. But, several aspects of such detention had been left unanswered (e.g. what would happen to Iraqi crewmen, or to ship's cargo especially if perishable, should there be any time-limit for detention, etc.). To date, the stalemate continues as to the ultimate fate of some Iraqi commercial ships and aircraft detained in foreign countries pursuant to Resolution 670 (1990). More problematic than the return of a few merchantmen detained in Yemen would appear the restoration (for want of regular maintenance) of several Iraqi aircraft still interned in some north African countries.

that they had violated the UN sanctions. With regard to the investigation and the determination as to whether or not the detained vessel had in fact violated the embargo, one can only presume that what is meant is an administrative inquiry involving agencies such as customs officials, port authorities or eventually the Foreign Trade and the Foreign Affairs Ministries. For all intents and purposes, therefore, such administrative findings would appear as the modern equivalent of the traditional judicial decision condemning a blockade-runner as lawful prize.

It is true that the Security Council in its Resolution 820 (1993) went further than ever before in filling the loopholes of its enforcement action. By providing for the seizure, detention and eventual confiscation of sanctions-busting vessels, the Security Council appears to have set up a maritime interdiction arrangement which comes closer, as far as the legal consequences for attempted breach are concerned, to classical wartime blockade than to pacific blockade.[209] Unfortunately, there has been scant information relating to the implementation of such provisos in national jurisdictions. According to UK legislation, for instance, the authority to determine whether a ship has operated in violation of the UN sanctions rests with the Secretary of State. Such determination must take the form of a certificate attesting to the conclusive evidence on the matter and following which the ship and its cargo may be forfeited and sold for the best available

[209]It will be recalled here that ships of a state under pacific blockade were only liable to sequestration, but never to confiscation, while they had to be restored at the termination of the blockade. As for ships of third states, it was never clear either in practice or theory whether the enforcing power had the right to interfere with their movement at all. The only precedent in UN practice may be found in the 1990 Draft Model Law for the Effective Enforcement of the Oil Embargo Against South Africa, prepared by Richard Lillich for the Intergovernmental Group monitoring the shipping of oil and petroleum products to South Africa and which provided in Article 5(a): 'any tanker or other ship flying the flag of Ruritania or owned or controlled, directly or indirectly, or managed or chartered, by persons subject to the jurisdiction of Ruritania, that is found to be carrying or has carried oil or petroleum products to South Africa in violation of this Act shall be subject to seizure and confiscation, together with its cargo'; see UN Doc.A/45/43 at p. 12. In the event, the UN General Assembly by Resolution 45/176 F of 19 December 1990 recommended the draft model law to member states with a view to adopting the general principles of the model law within the context of their own legal practices. See also UN Doc.A/46/43 at pp. 10–11. The embargo against South Africa was eventually lifted in May 1994; see Security Council Resolution 919 (1994) at para.1.

price.[210] In any event, up to early 1994 the Legal Department of Lloyd's Register of Shipping had no record of any ship having been confiscated for breach of Security Council Resolution 820 (1993).[211]

Current Trends in Military Manuals and Academic Works Most of the classical notions of prize law, as analysed above, have been lately reaffirmed in updated versions of national military manuals but also some influential products of scholarly reflection. In the 1989 *US Commander's Handbook on the Law of Naval Operations* prize adjudication remains a precondition for lawful capture.[212] The *Manual* endorses the concept of unneutral service, without referring to it *eo nomine*, so that neutral vessels and aircraft acquire enemy character and may be treated as enemy warships either when 'taking a direct part in the hostilities on the side of the enemy [or] acting in any capacity as a naval or military auxiliary to the enemy's armed forces', whereas they

[210]See the detailed note by FOX, H. and WICKREMASINGHE, C., 'UK Implementation of UN Economic Sanctions', 42 *ICLQ* (1993) at p. 962. The forfeiture procedure seems to be confined within the bounds of the executive. Before issuing the certificate, the Secretary of State must communicate his intention to the owner of the ship, must allow a period of three weeks for eventual representations, and must also give a hearing to the owner or any person claiming an interest in the vessel. However, the owner of the ship is ultimately given the opportunity to challenge the order of forfeiture before the English courts.

[211]A further note should be added with relation to the sanctions against Iraq. Security Council Resolution 661 (1990), although modified, has not been replaced and continues to provide the cornerstone of the ongoing sanctions against Iraq. Resolution 665 (1990) is equally in force, yet no maritime enforcement incidents have been reported for well over three years. A problem of particular concern has been the continuing interception of merchant vessels bound for or departing from the Jordanian port of Aqaba. The government of Jordan and various shipping corporations have put pressure on the multinational force in order to relax their inspection and diversion techniques since they are extremely costly, time-consuming, and even impracticable for certain types of ships. Most recently, it was rumoured that the United States was negotiating an agreement with Jordan to the effect that cargo inspection would be entrusted to civilian personnel at port – possibly employees of the Lloyd's of London. If such an arrangement was put in practice, one could speak of *navicerting* at the service of UN collective sanctions. Other interesting problems, not yet tested in practice, would involve the rules applicable in the case of capture of UN-flagged vessels, and the problem of competence of national prize courts in the case of seizures effected by a multinational naval force. These questions are briefly addressed in KATEVENIS, G., 'The Law of Maritime Warfare', 4 *Revue de Droit Pénal Militaire et de Droit de la Guerre* (1965), p. 359*ff*.

[212]See NWP9-Rev.A at para.7.9.

may be treated as enemy merchant vessels when either 'operating directly under enemy control, orders, charter, employment, or direction [or] resisting an attempt to establish identity, including visit and search'.[213]

The term 'continuous voyage' is equally avoided, yet presumptive evidence of enemy destination is accepted with relation to absolute contraband. As the relevant paragraph reads:

> when absolute contraband is involved, a destination of enemy owned or occupied territory may be presumed when: (1) the neutral vessel is to call at an enemy port before arriving at a neutral port for which the goods are documented (2) the goods are documented to a neutral port serving as a port of transit to an enemy, even though they are consigned to a neutral (3) the goods are consigned 'to order' or to an unnamed consignee, but are destined for a neutral nation in the vicinity of enemy territory. These presumptions of enemy destination of absolute contraband render the offending cargo liable to seizure by a belligerent from the time the neutral merchant vessel leaves its home or other neutral territory until it arrives again in neutral territory.[214]

Finally, the US Navy publication admits navicerting as a legitimate means of contraband control with only two remarks: first, 'the certificate is not a guarantee that the vessel or aircraft will not be subject to visit and search', and second that 'conversely, absence of a navicert or aircert is not, in itself, a valid ground for seizure of cargo'.[215]

The 1992 German *Manual* deals with prize law in a more synoptical way and basically spells out the need for judicial validation of any seizure carried out at sea. In the terms of the pertinent proviso, 'the seized ship (prize) is to be brought as safely as possible to a port of the party to the conflict or of a

[213] *Ibid.* at paras.7.5.1, 7.5.2.

[214] *Ibid.* at para.7.4.1.1. The proviso continues to specify that 'enemy destination of conditional contraband must be factually established and cannot be presumed'.

[215] *Ibid.* at para.7.4.2. As this paragraph defines, 'a certificate of noncontraband carriage is a document issued by a belligerent consular or other designated official to a neutral vessel (navicert) or neutral aircraft (aircert) certifying that the cargo being carried has been examined, usually at the initial place of departure, and has been found to be free of contraband'.

state allied with that party. In that port the permissibility of the condemnation of both ship and cargo is to be judicially reviewed by a prize court.'[216] No specific rules on unneutral service and continuous voyage are included, whereas with regard to navicerts, the Manual provides: 'to simplify such inspection, a party to the conflict may, subject to the approval of the neutral state concerned, issue an inspection document (navicert) to the neutral vessel in the port of loading. A navicert issued by one party to the conflict is not binding on the other party to the conflict. The fact that a ship carries a navicert by another party to the conflict is no permissible argument for further measures of control.'[217]

The 1994 *San Remo Manual on International Law Applicable to Armed Conflicts at Sea* contains detailed rules concerning maritime capture. Prize procedure is conceived as making part of the notion of capture, as this recurrent formulation implies: 'capture of a merchant vessel is exercised by taking such vessel as prize for adjudication'.[218] The doctrine of unneutral service is related to neutral merchant vessels that are intercepted either while on 'a voyage especially undertaken with a view to the transport of individual passengers who are embodied in the armed forces of the enemy [or] are operating directly under enemy control, orders, charter, employment or direction'.[219] As regards navicerts, the *San Remo Manual* adopts a particularly favourable position encouraging neutral states 'to enforce reasonable control measures and certification procedures in order to obviate the necessity for visit and search', and adds: 'the fact that a neutral merchant vessel has submitted to such measures of supervision as the inspection of its cargo and grant

[216]See *ZDv 15/2* at para.1145. See also para.1023 which reads: 'after the capture of an enemy merchant vessel it must be decided in a prize court procedure whether the capture was lawful. Upon confirmation by the prize court the ship becomes property of the capturing state.'

[217]*Ibid.* at para.1140.

[218]See *San Remo Manual on International Law Applicable to Armed Conflicts at Sea*, June 1994 at paras.138, 144, 146, 156.

[219]*Ibid.* at para.146(b)-(c). See also *Commentary on the Harmonised Document on International Humanitarian Law Applicable to Armed Conflicts at Sea*, March 1994, para.146.4 at p. 237. In such cases the neutral vessel is liable to capture, whereas when engaged in some other activities (e.g. belligerent acts on behalf of the enemy, acting as auxiliary to the enemy's forces, assisting the enemy's intelligence system) the neutral vessel may be attacked and destroyed as a military objective; see *ibid.* at para.67(b)-(d), and *Commentary,* paras.67.10–67.26, pp. 145–51.

of certificates of non-contraband cargo by one belligerent is not an act of unneutral service with regard to an opposing belligerent'.[220]

The latest report on Neutrality and Naval Warfare presented at the Buenos Aires Conference of the International Law Association contains similar rules on prize procedure. As a controlling principle it is provided that 'cargo constituting contraband and a ship carrying such cargo may be seized by a belligerent, brought before a prize court and condemned. Condemnation without a prize court decision is inadmissible'.[221] The doctrine of continuous voyage is upheld but only as far as absolute contraband is concerned,[222] while the navicert system is recognized only to the extent that it does not become compulsory, or that the absence of a certificate is not elevated to any sort of presumptive evidence of unneutral service; 'this navicert constitutes proof that the ship in question is not carrying contraband if controlled by the party having issued the document. The navicert is not binding on the other party, but the fact that a ship carries a navicert issued by another party may not be used to the ship's advantage'.[223]

IV Condemned at sea: the problem of destruction of merchant vessels

1 Theory and practice under the traditional rules

The question of destruction of private property at sea is perhaps the most significant point of all the *problématique* concerning the modern laws of naval warfare. In a simplified form, the legal query to be addressed here is whether the time-honoured right of capture with all its well circumscribed particulars has today been superseded by an outright faculty to destroy on sight. Be it a deplorable retrogression or not, the essence of the legal debate in the post-Second World War era in this field as in so many others comes down to whether the 'exception' has taken over the 'rule'.

[220]*Ibid.* at para.123. For similar rules applying to aircraft, see *ibid.*, paras.132–4. See also *Commentary*, para.123.1. at p. 215.
[221]See *Report on Neutrality and Naval Warfare* for ILA's Buenos Aires Conference (1994) at para.5.2.2.
[222]See *ibid.*, commentary on para.5.2.4.
[223]*Ibid.* at para.5.2.6.

Early Practice According to an early British prize tradition, neutral merchantmen enjoyed total immunity against destruction.[224] In the words of Lord Stowell:

> if impossible to bring in, their next duty is to destroy enemy's property. Where doubtful whether enemy's property, and impossible to bring in, no such obligation arises, and the safe and proper course is to dismiss. Where it is neutral, the act of destruction cannot be justified to the neutral owner, by the gravest importance of such an act to the public service of the captor's own state; to the neutral it can only be justified, under any such circumstances, by a full restitution in value. These are the rules so clear in principle and established in practice, that they require neither reasoning nor precedent to illustrate or support them.[225]

Although the view that the captor should proceed unmolested if, for any reason, unable to bring the prize to adjudication gained considerable support during the nineteenth century,[226] it clearly receded as from the Russo-Japanese war. During this conflict no less than eight neutral vessels were sunk by the Russian navy while their owners were denied any compensation. All the destroyed vessels were English, except for two German and one Danish.[227] In conformity with the Russian naval prize regulations of 1895, all passengers and as much of the cargo as possible were to be taken off before the ships be set ablaze or sunk. According to the same regulations, captured

[224]For a survey of early practice and doctrinal opinions, see GARNER, *op. cit., supra* n.28, vol.II, pp. 256–84, and 33 *AJIL* (1939) *Suppl.*, p. 559*ff.*

[225]See *The Felicity* (1819) in SCOTT, J.B. and JAEGER, W.H.E., *Cases on International Law,* 2nd edn (1937) at p. 863. And elsewhere: 'the destruction of the property by the captor may have been a meritorious act towards his own government, but still the person to whom the property belongs must not be a sufferer. As to him, it is an injury for which he is entitled to redress from the party who has inflicted it upon him; and if the captor has, by the act of destruction, conferred a benefit on the public, he must look to the government for his indemnity. The loss must not be permitted to fall on the innocent sufferer'; see *The Acteon* (1815), *ibid.* at p. 861.

[226]It is indicative that there were no losses of neutral vessels reported in the Crimean War, the American Civil War, the Franco-Prussian War, the Spanish-American War, the Boer War, the Turko-Italian War or the Balkan War; see GARNER, *op. cit., supra* n.28, vol.II at p. 257.

[227]Most incidents are reviewed in TAKAHASHI, S., *International Law Applied to the Russo-Japanese War,* 1908, pp. 310–30.

merchant vessels, regardless of their enemy or neutral character, could be destroyed in cases of unseaworthiness of the prize, of great distance from home ports, or in the presence of any other condition menacing the operations of the captor.[228]

The Legal Debate Even before the Russo-Japanese experience, the idea of an exceptional right to sink the prize instead of bringing it to adjudication had already appeared in the Projet de règlement international des prises maritimes, adopted by the Institut de Droit International in 1882. Article 55 as originally drafted by Rapporteur De Bulmerincq read as follows:

> Il sera permis au capteur de brûler ou de couler bas le navire saisi, après avoir fait passer sur le navire de guerre les personnes qui se trouvaient à bord, et déchargé autant que possible la cargaison, et après que le commandant du navire capteur aura pris à sa charge les papiers de bord et les objets importants pour l'enquête judiciaire et pour les réclamations des propriétaires de la cargaison en dommages et intérêts, dans les cas suivants:
> 1. Lorsqu'il n'est pas possible de tenir le navire à flot, à cause de son mauvais état, la mer étant houleuse;
> 2. Lorsque le navire marche si mal qu'il ne peut pas suivre le navire de guerre et pourrait facilement être repris par l'ennemi;
> 3. Lorsque l'approche d'une force ennemie supérieure fait craindre la reprise du navire saisi;
> 4. Lorsque le navire de guerre ne peut mettre sur le navire saisi un équipage suffisant sans trop diminuer celui qui est nécessaire à sa propre sûreté;

[228]In the light of these provisions, the Vladivostok prize court upheld the destruction of the *Knight Commander* by reason of the proximity of an enemy base (less than 15 miles from the Gulf of Tokyo), and the shortage of coal for the voyage to the nearest Russian port lying at an approximate distance of 750 miles; see HURST, C.J.B. and BRAY, F.E. (eds), *Russian and Japanese Prize Cases*, vol.I (1912), pp. 54–95. Likewise, in the case of the *Thea*, the prize decision referred to 'extraordinary circumstances, the proximity of the enemy's shores, the remoteness of ports to which the prize might be taken, the shortage of coal or board, and the impossibility of supplying her with coal from the cruisers owing to the high seas running'; *ibid.* at p. 98. As for the sinking of the *St. Kilda*, the Libau prize court found that 'without risk to the operations of war, and of recapture by the enemy, the captured steamer could not be taken to the nearest port, and therefore the captain of the *Dnieper* was justified in sinking her'; *ibid.* at p. 195. See also *The Oldhamia*, *ibid.* at p. 164.

5. Lorsque le port où l'on pourrait conduire le navire saisi est trop éloigné.[229]

It should be pointed out that the text fails to draw any distinction between enemy and neutral vessels. A few years later, however, at the Heidelberg session of 1888, the Institute rectified what was termed an error in Article 50 to read: 'il sera permis au capteur de brûler ou de couler bas le navire *ennemi* saisi . . .'.[230] The Institute recalled that, as had become clear from previous discussions, 'la majorité avait trouvé exorbitant qu'on put couler un navire *neutre* sans qu'il eut été condamné', and that as such it had rejected the last paragraph of Article 55, as it stood at the Wiesbaden session, which had read: 'ce même droit (celui de couler bas) est exceptionnellement reconnu au capteur, en cas de saisie d'un navire neutre condamnable'.[231]

The Second Hague Peace Conference presented the opportunity for long discussions with respect to the legality of destroying neutral vessels caught in prize.[232] The British and American delegations stood for a prohibition in absolute terms,[233] while a Russian proposal provided for an exception in circumstances of utmost necessity.[234] The main argument of the Russian delegation was that the very fact of capture transfers ownership to the captor who should thus become free to destroy

[229]See 6 *Ann.IDI* (1882–3), Torino Session at p. 114. It is important to note that there was no unanimity as to whether neutral vessels should be expressly excluded from the scope of that Article; see *ibid.* at pp. 154–5. The provision was finally adopted as Article 50 of the Draft Rules on Maritime Capture; see *ibid.* at p. 221.

[230]See 9 *Ann.IDI* (1887–8), Heidelberg Session at p. 228.

[231]*Ibid.* at pp. 200–1. See also 6 *Ann.IDI* (1882–83), Torino Session at pp. 169, 206.

[232]For a summary account on the discussions, see DUPUIS, C., *Le droit de la guerre maritime d'après les Conférences de La Haye et de Londres*, 1911, pp. 372–82, and LÉMONON, E., *La Seconde Conférence de la Paix*, 2nd edn (1912), pp. 608–15.

[233]As the proposition of the British delegation read, 'destruction of a neutral prize by the captor is prohibited. The captor must release all neutral vessels that he is unable to bring before a prize court'; see SCOTT, J.B. (ed.), *The Proceedings of the Hague Peace Conferences – The Conference of 1907*, vol.III (1921), Annex 39 at p. 1152. See also the proposition of the US delegation, *ibid.*, Annex 42 at p. 1153.

[234]According to the Russian draft proposal, 'the destruction of a neutral prize is prohibited except in cases where its preservation might endanger the safety of the capturing vessel or the success of its operations. The commanding officer of the capturing vessel may exercise the right of destruction only with the greatest discretion, and must take care to trans-ship beforehand the crew, and, in so far as possible, the cargo, and in all cases preserve all the ship's papers and all other articles that are necessary for a prize decision'; see *ibid.*, Annex 40 at p. 1152.

it as his own property. Furthermore, an absolute prohibition of destruction was believed to place those Powers not possessing distant naval bases in a greatly disadvantageous position.[235] Replying to the Russian arguments, Britain insisted that no principle authorizing destruction had as yet been established in international law.[236] The issue remained unresolved throughout the Peace Conference.

It was no great surprise that the matter surfaced again at the London Naval Conference of 1908–9.[237] The British and Japanese delegations were soon found to be isolated in supporting an outright prohibition of the destruction of merchant vessels.[238]

[235]As put by Ortchinnikow, 'it is the seizure or capture itself which transfers ownership of the seized vessel and cargo to the captor State. A judicial decision never creates a new right, it merely recognizes a right which already exists . . . This fact established, we can now see that in destroying a vessel, which is sailing under a neutral flag but which has clearly violated its neutrality, the captor is destroying his own property and not property belonging to others. He is thus acting against the interests of his own fortune, and that is why only absolutely exceptional cases will induce him to follow this procedure . . . The absolute prohibition of the destruction of prizes would give rise to a situation of marked inferiority in the case of Powers that have no colonies as compared with those that have'; *ibid.* at pp. 890, 892.

[236]In the words of Ernest Satow, 'there are perhaps reasons why there should be added in future to the rights which a belligerent possesses that of sinking neutral prizes, on condition that it is not exercised unreasonably; thus, we might invoke considerations of a military character, the necessities of the moment, the lack of ports and coaling stations, the great area of the theater of war, the vast field of commercial activities, to prove that a change is necessary; but it is not possible to hold the existence of the right we are seeking to establish has been recognized in the past . . . The adoption of a new principle giving belligerents the right to sink neutral prizes would inevitably lead to abuses and would expose every neutral vessel to the danger of being sunk whenever it met a belligerent warship, whose captain would not fail to exercise his right as he might see fit, in spite of the orders which he might have received to act with circumspection. A neutral vessel would therefore find itself in the same position as an enemy vessel'; *ibid.* at pp. 893–4. The deliberations are summarized in the General Report to the Conference Upon the Work of the Fourth Commission; see *ibid.*, vol.I (1920), pp. 257–9, and vol.III (1921), pp. 889–96, 1058–63.

[237]See DUPUIS, *op. cit., supra* n.232, pp. 382–8, and LÉMONON, *op. cit., supra* n.232, pp. 728–32.

[238]The British proposition read:

> 1. Le devoir d'un belligérant capteur est d'amener, pour qu'il soit jugé par un tribunal des prises, tout navire marchand qu'il a saisi. Lorsque c'est impossible, ce dernier, si c'est un navire ennemi, peut etre détruit après retrait de l'équipage et des papiers de bord; si la nationalité du navire est neutre, ou s'il y a un doute quelconque quant à la nationalité, il devrait être relaché, car sa destruction ne peut être justifiée, entre le propriétaire neutre et le capteur, par une nécessité quelconque de la part d'un belligérant.

Most of the memoranda submitted by other Powers admitted the possibility of a neutral ship being sunk under exceptional circumstances. Russia, for instance, maintained that 'la destruction d'un navire de nationalité neutre, saisi et sujet à confiscation, est interdite, à l'exception des cas ou sa conservation pourrait compromettre la sécurité du navire capteur ou le succès de ses opérations... le commandant du bâtiment capteur est tenu, avant de faire détruire le navire, d'en transborder les hommes et, autant que faire se pourra, la cargaison, ainsi que de prendre les mesures requises pour conserver tous les papiers de bord'.[239]

In the event, the British government surrendered to the majority view in the interest of obtaining satisfaction on some other points and arriving at an overall agreement. After all, the discrepancies were not as pronounced as they might first appear. For, as the General Report of the Drafting Committee pertinently noticed, 'it had become evident that those who declared for the right to destroy neutral prizes did not pretend to use this right wantonly and at every opportunity, but only by way of exception; and that, on the other hand, those who maintained the

---

2. Un chargement neutre licite à bord d'un navire ennemi n'étant pas saisissable, le propriétaire de ce chargement a droit à l'indemnité si le navire ennemi est détruit.

While the Japanese proposal was couched in similar terms: 'les commandants des bâtiments de guerre belligérants sont tenus d'envoyer pour être mis en jugement les navires neutres après saisie. Si, pour une raison quelconque, ils ne peuvent le faire, les dits navires doivent être relachés. En toutes circonstances les navires ne peuvent être détruits avant condamnation'; see *Proceedings of the International Naval Conference, London Dec.1908–Feb.1909, Cd.4555* at pp. 38, 49. See also the Dutch memorandum, *ibid.* at p. 52.

[239]*Ibid.* at p. 55. The submissions of Germany and France were phrased in almost identical terms; see *ibid.* at pp. 6, 30. For the United States, destruction could be envisaged in cases 'telles que l'innavigabilité, l'existence d'une maladie infectieuse, ou le manque d'un équipage de prise... Le danger imminent d'une reprise justifie la destruction, s'il n'y a aucun doute pour admettre que le navire est de bonne prise. Mais, dans tous ces cas, tous les papiers et autres témoignages doivent être envoyés à la Cour des Prises, afin qu'une décision puisse être dûment rendue'; *ibid.* at p. 16. Consider also the slightly different Spanish suggestion: 'la destruction ne serait justifiée que par des raisons résultant de l'état de la mer, des conditions des navires capteur et capturé pour naviguer ou du manque de combustible ou vivres; et non pas de la proximité de l'ennemi ou du manque d'éléments militaires suffisants pour assurer la conduction au port correspondant. Ces derniers motifs et d'autres analogues impliquent que le capteur ne possède pas assez de moyens pour mener à terme la saisie'; *ibid.* at p. 26. For the interventions of various national delegates, see *ibid.*, Annexes 86–95, pp. 268–78.

principle of prohibition of destruction admitted that the principle must give way in exceptional cases'.[240]

The destruction of neutral prizes was dealt with in chapter IV (Articles 48–54) of the unratified London Declaration. Article 48 codified the fundamental premise according to which a neutral vessel upon being seized had to be directed into an appropriate port where the validity of the capture should be judicially examined. The destruction remained, therefore, in principle prohibited. By virtue of Article 49–50, a derogation of such a principle would be exceptionally permitted if certain conditions were cumulatively satisfied. First, there had to be a valid reason for condemnation of the vessel such as an attempted breach of blockade, carriage of contraband, or an act of unneutral service. Second, there should exist a near certainty on the part of the captor that escorting the prize to port would jeopardize the safety of his ship or would hinder the accomplishment of his mission already in progress.[241] The burden of proof as to the concurrence of those circumstances lay with the captor. Failing to demonstrate so, the prize court should adjudge compensation in favour of the neutral owners.

The *Oxford Manual*, adopted by the Institut de Droit International in 1913, reaffirmed the widely shared conviction that merchant ships should not in principle be liable to destruction. Even though Article 104 of the *Manual* allowed for destruction of vessels and goods liable to confiscation, it did so in a triple-qualified way. In the first place, it confined its scope to *enemy* merchant ships so that *neutral* merchantmen appeared to enjoy an unconditional immunity against destruction. Second, a captor could only proceed under conditions of *exceptional* necessity which clearly threatened to compromise its safety. And third, human lives on board had to be imperatively protected; not simply spared but effectively saved.

[240]See USNWC, 9 *International Law Topics* (1909) at p. 113.

[241]It must be noted at this point that, according to the drafters, by 'danger' for the purposes of Article 49 should be understood a threatening situation clearly perceptible at the time of the destruction and not just any consideration of risk even remotely connected in space or in time with the act of capture. As the Commentary reads in this regard: 'it is, of course, the situation at the moment when the destruction takes place which must be considered in order to decide whether the conditions are or are not fulfilled. A danger which did not exist at the actual moment of the capture may have appeared some time afterwards'; see *ibid.* at p. 115.

The Great War and Relevant Jurisprudence Most national naval instructions and prize regulations drafted before or during the First World War followed closely the provisions of chapter IV of the London Declaration. Among those, however, some failed to draw any distinction between the destruction of enemy and neutral vessels (e.g. the Chinese, Italian, Russian or Romanian prize rules). Others contained separate provisions subjecting the destruction of neutral ships to more stringent conditions. According to Articles 94 and 96 of the 1917 *US Instructions*, for instance, an enemy ship could be destroyed in case of military necessity, whereas a neutral vessel not engaged in unneutral service could not be destroyed except in case of the 'gravest military emergency'. Likewise, the French, Japanese, German or Austro-Hungarian instructions independently treated the question of neutral prize destruction. Finally, under the English prize rules, the destruction of neutral prizes was firmly excluded.[242]

Several prize judgments dealt with the destruction of *enemy* vessels. In the first case in which a British prize court was asked for the condemnation of a vessel which had been previously sunk, it was held that 'the law is clear that in certain circumstances an enemy vessel captured at sea may be sunk instead of being brought into port to be tried in the Prize Court, and it is equally clear upon the facts of this case that in the circumstances the captain, who has made an affidavit, was justified in sinking this vessel, because he was not able to spare a prize crew in order that she might be taken into port'.[243]

French jurisprudence contains many cases which arose in the context of the blockade of Turkish coasts in the eastern Mediterranean. In the case of the *Mahrousseh*, for example, the Conseil des Prises was satisfied that 'la conservation de cette prise aurait pu compromettre le succès des opérations dans lesquelles le bâtiment capteur était engagé; qu'ainsi celui-ci a pu valablement la détruire, après en avoir fait passer le patron et l'équipage à son bord'.[244] In another case, destruction was sustained since 'il

[242]For the different national ordinances, see VERZIJL, *op. cit., supra* n.26, pp. 1236–41.

[243]See *The Stoer* (1916), in *Lloyd's Reports of Prize Cases*, vol.V (1919) at p. 19. In another case, a British armed vessel while escorting a purportedly enemy ship met with bad weather and sank it by gunfire; see *The Valeria* (1920) in GRANT, A.W, *British and Colonial Prize Cases*, vol.III at pp. 644, 834.

[244]See *The Mahrousseh* (1915), in FAUCHILLE, P., *Jurisprudence française en matière de prises maritimes*, 1916 at p. 148.

était impossible de remorquer ce voilier, vieux et mal défendu contre la mer, jusqu'au port allié le plus proche qui se trouvait à plus de 120 milles; qu'ainsi le bâtiment capteur, après avoir pris la cargaison à son bord, a pu valablement détruire le caique dont l'équipage avait fui à terre à l'approche du croiseur',[245] while in the case of the *Aghios Nikholos* reference was made to 'raisons de sécurité et des nécessités militaires'.[246]

As far as the destruction of *neutral* prizes is concerned, one has to turn to the far too numerous German and Austro-Hungarian prize decisions. Apart from repetitious references to the unique conditions of the war or to military necessity, these pronouncements are striking owing to the scarcity of legal reasoning in support of the large scale sink-on-sight campaign against neutral bottoms. As Verzijl notes in this connection, 'la jurisrpudence des prises ne présente aucune décision où l'on trouve discutée la question de savoir si et à quel point la destruction de prises neutres est compatible avec le droit des gens coutumier actuellement en vigueur'.[247]

In the case of the *William P. Frye*, sunk by a German cruiser in January 1915 after having been searched, the German government replied to American protests by referring to Article 49 of the London Declaration and by claiming that 'it was not possible for the auxiliary cruiser to take the prize into a German port without involving danger to its own security or the success of its operations'.[248] On numerous occasions, the Imperial Supreme Prize Court in Berlin reiterated the same reasoning: 'the *Maria* was seized and the commander proceeded to destroy it, because the captured vessel could not follow the warship without risk of being taken away from the latter, inasmuch as the proximity of enemy cruisers gave grounds to apprehend such recapture, and the *Karlsruhe* could not spare an adequate prize

[245]See *The Cheref* (1915), *ibid.* at p. 163.
[246]See *The Aghios Nikholos* (1916), *ibid.* at p. 197. Likewise, in the case of *The Saideh* it was upheld that 'à raison de l'état de la mer la conservation de la totalité de la cargaison aurait pu rendre la navigation dangereuse pour la gélette qui recevait l'ordre de rallier Port-Said par ses moyens; qu'ainsi le bâtiment capteur a pu valablement détruire une partie de cette cargaison'; see *The Saideh* (1915), *ibid.* at p. 172. See also *The Jabr-el-Kavater* (1915), *ibid.* at p. 169; *The Ihsan* (1915), *ibid.* at p. 199; *The Mulahat* (1916), *ibid.* at p. 247; *The Mabrouka* (1916), *ibid.* at p. 281; *The Schooner X* (1918), *ibid.* at p. 435.
[247]VERZIJL, *op. cit., supra* n.26 at p. 1249.
[248]See the note dated 5 April 1915, in 9 *AJIL* (1915) *Sp.Suppl* at p. 181.

crew and, therefore, an attempt to bring in the prize would have jeopardized the success of the warship's undertaking'.[249]

In the case of another Dutch vessel, the *Medea*, it was similarly argued that 'tenant compte, d'une part, du fait que l'ensemble de la cargaison du navire était sujet à confiscation, d'autre part de l'impossibilité manifeste, eu égard aux circonstances du moment, de conduire le navire dans un port de prise, il y a lieu de déclarer fondé l'appel interjeté par le Commissaire impérial'.[250] And elsewhere: 'la destruction de la prise fut ordonnée parce que, selon le rapport de l'officier commandant le croiseur auxiliaire, elle n'aurait pu être conduite à un port. Ce convoi aurait compromis les opérations auxquelles se livrait alors le navire de guerre; le voilier saisi n'aurait pu suivre immédiatement le croiseur auxiliaire sans qu'il y ait risque de reprise, des croiseurs britanniques se trouvant dans le voisinage.'[251]

Controversy Unresolved In the immediate aftermath of the Great War, the International Law Association initiated a re-examination of the Hague Conventions and the London Declaration with special reference to principles governing warfare at sea. Sharing the sentiment that 'the sanctioning of any exception in general terms leads to the indefinite expansion of the exception',[252] the drafters of the ILA's Laws of Naval War adopted in 1920 opted for clear-cut rules offering the least possible margin for stretched interpretation. Under Article 104, 'the destruction of unarmed enemy merchant ships and of neutral merchant ships is prohibited without exception',[253] while by Article 17§§4,6 enemy ships would be liable to destruction only in the case of forceful resistance to visit and search or escape and neutral ships only in case of blockade running, unneutral

[249]See *The Maria* (1915), in 10 *AJIL* (1916) at p. 927.
[250]See *The Medea* (1916), in FAUCHILLE, P. and DE VISSCHER, C., *Jurisprudence allemande en matière de prises maritimes*, 1924 at p. 115.
[251]See *The Semantha* (1916), *ibid.* at p. 145. In yet another context, a favourable pronouncement was delivered in the case of a submarine 'opérant loin de sa base et dans le voisinage des côtes britanniques. Il est évident, et il n'y a pas lieu d'insister davantage sur ce point, que le commandant a dû tenir pour contre-indiqué d'emmener sa prise. Il était donc autorisé à la détruire'; *ibid.* at p. 182.
[252]See 29 *Rep.ILA* (1920), Portsmouth Conference at p. 172.
[253]*Ibid.* at p. 189.

service, or active resistance to visit and search. In every case, as Article 17A stipulated, 'reasons of military or naval necessity, such as danger to the submarine's (or other warship's) own safety or to its operations, shall not be held to justify the destruction of merchantmen under the preceding Articles'.[254]

During the inter-war period, although sinking neutral vessels in exceptional circumstances had become largely accepted as solidly established in both theory and practice, a major source of controversy remained as to the exact meaning of the 'place of safety' clause. As it was observed with regard to Article 17§5 of ILA's Laws of Naval War of 1920, 'to define the term "adequate provision" is not easy. It must always be a question of fact to be determined by the circumstances peculiar to each case. Thus, on the one hand, the placing of the crew and passengers in a ship's boats in a calm sea within sight of land might be regarded as within the meaning of the term; while, on the other hand, we do not think the deck or hold of a cruiser, which within a few hours may be engaged with the enemy, can be regarded as a place of safety for non-combatants'.[255]

The point in question was answered in Article 22 of the 1930 London Treaty for the Limitation and Reduction of Naval Armaments,[256] and also in the London Protocol of 1936 on submarine warfare, which laid down that:

> the ship's boats are not regarded as a place of safety unless the safety of the passengers and crew is assured, in the existing sea and weather conditions, by the proximity of land, or the presence of another vessel which is in a position to take them on board.[257]

[254]*Ibid.* at p. 172. In subsequent draft articles, the destruction of neutral vessels was further limited to the sole cases of forcible resistance to visit and search or persistent refusal to stop; see Article 5 of the Draft Convention on Maritime Neutrality, 35 *Rep.ILA* (1928) Warsaw Conference at p. 203, and Article 9 of the Draft Convention on the Rights and Duties of Belligerents with regard to Property at Sea, 36 *Rep.ILA* (1930) New York Conference at p. 121.

[255]See 29 *Rep.ILA* (1920) Portsmouth Conference at p. 171.

[256]See 25 *AJIL* (1931) *Suppl.*, pp. 63–82. The text can also be found in SCHINDLER and TOMAN, *op. cit., supra* n.29, pp. 881–2, and RONZITTI, *op. cit., supra* n.29, pp. 347–8.

[257]See 31 *AJIL* (1937) *Suppl.*, pp. 137–9. The text can also be found in SCHINDLER and TOMAN, *op. cit., supra* n.29, pp. 883–5, RONZITTI, *op. cit., supra* n.29, pp. 349–52, and ROBERTS, A. and GUELFF, R. (eds), *Documents on the Laws of War*, 2nd edn (1989), pp. 147–51.

This principle was further sanctioned by the Nuremberg International Military Tribunal in a oft-quoted phrase:

> the Protocol is explicit. If the commander cannot rescue, then under its terms he cannot sink a merchant vessel and should allow it to pass harmless before his periscope. These orders then, prove Dönitz is guilty of a violation of the Protocol.[258]

2 The law today: unwarranted destruction in the Gulf Tanker War

Belligerent attacks on merchant shipping remained by far the most common feature of naval action throughout the eight-year war. Although estimates vary considerably, it is believed that merchant vessels came under fire in the period 1981–8 in no less than 543 incidents. Iraq was responsible for about three-fifths (or 322) of these attacks, while Iran accounted for the remaining 221. The economic warfare campaign reached its peak in 1987 with a total of 181 reported attacks; 89 and 92 for Iraq and Iran respectively. Iraqi attacks consisted exclusively of air strikes whereas Iran relied mostly on contact mines and naval shelling. Because of the means used, it has been calculated that from 1984 to 1988 Iraqi attacks resulted in the destruction or heavy damage of their targets in 20–25 per cent of the attacks, the corresponding figure for Iran being 10 per cent.[259] Ships registered under no less than 32 countries were attacked, while, according to British sources, 471 merchant seamen lost their lives as a result of those attacks.[260]

Neutral Reaction Neutral policies as regards protection of Gulf shipping underwent a major revision by the end of 1987. To

[258]See *International Military Tribunal at Nuremberg, Judgment of Oct.1, 1946,* reprinted in 41 *AJIL* (1947) at p. 305.

[259]See O'ROURKE, R., 'Gulf Ops', 115 *USNIP* (May 1989) at pp. 42–3. See also O'ROURKE, R., 'The Tanker War', 114 *USNIP* (May 1988), pp. 30–4.

[260]See Second Report of the Foreign Affairs Committee, *Current UK Policy Towards the Iran/Iraq Conflict, June 1988,* in DE GUTTRY and RONZITTI, *op. cit., supra* n.45, doc.2.a.37 at p. 292. For comprehensive data on the Tanker War up to December 1987, see 'Strategic Air Attacks in the Iran-Iraq War: The Gulf Campaign', *Middle East Military Balance* (1987–8), pp. 230–55, and HOOTON, T., 'The Tanker War in the Gulf, 1984–8', 4 *Jane's Intelligence Review* (May 1992), pp. 218–21.

Attacks on Ships in the Persian Gulf Region by Belligerent, 1981–88

Attacker	*1981*	*1982*	*1983*	*1984*	*1985*	*1986*	*1987*	*1988**	*Total*
Iraq	5	22	16	53	33	66	89	38	322
Iran	0	0	0	18	14	45	92	52	221
Total	5	22	16	71	47	111	181	90	543

Sources for 1981–87: *The Washington Post*, 13 October 1987, p. 12, and *The New York Times*, 10 January 1988, p. E3. (Data from Lloyd's Shipping Intelligence Unit for 1981–86, and Center for Defense Information for 1986 and 1987.) The two sources differ slightly on the numbers for 1986. Since the publication of last year's version of this chart (*Proceedings*, May 1988, p. 31, Table 1), the numbers for 1987 have been revised, adding one attack for each belligerent. Source for 1988: Center for Defense Information, 13 January 1989. Numbers compiled by other sources vary considerably from the numbers presented here.
*Cease-fire went into effect 20 August 1988.

Attacks on Ships in the Persian Gulf Region by Belligerent, 1988

Attacker	*Jan.*	*Feb.*	*Mar.*	*Apr.*	*May*	*June*	*July–Aug.**	*Total*
Iraq	8	5	6	0	7	1	11	38
Iran	7	7	13	7	5	3	10	52
Total	15	12	19	7	12	4	21	90

Source: Center for Defense Information, 6 July 1988 and 13 January 1989.
*Separate figures for July and August were not available. Cease-fire went into effect 20 August 1988.

Table 4 *The Tanker War in Numbers*
Source: O'ROURKE, R., 'Gulf Ops', 115 *USNIP* (May 1989) at p. 43

underscore their new active role in protecting merchant shipping, western navies hastily sent into the Persian Gulf and northern Arabian Sea an unprecedented international armada of more than eighty warships.[261] On two occasions, in December 1987 and January 1988, French warships intervened and stopped attacks on two Liberian-flagged vessels by chasing away the Iranian ships. On 20 January 1988, it was officially announced by the commander of French forces in the Gulf that French warships would henceforth be authorized to engage Iranian gunboats if, upon being duly summoned, the latter refused to discontinue attacks on neutral merchantmen irrespective of their flag.[262]

On 29 April 1988, some ten days after the US retaliatory action against Iranian objectives following the *Samuel Roberts* mine incident, the US government announced its intention to expand protection over non-US flag vessels when possible. The relevant statement of Secretary of Defense Frank Carlucci was couched in unambiguous terms of traditional neutrality law: 'aid will be provided to friendly, innocent, neutral vessels flying a non-belligerent flag outside declared war/exclusion zones that are not carrying contraband or resisting legitimate visit and search by a Persian Gulf belligerent. Following a request from the vessel under attack, assistance will be rendered by a US warship or aircraft if this unit is in the vicinity and its mission permits rendering such assistance.'[263]

The new expanded form of western naval intervention calls for two remarks. First, it is not at all clear on what legal grounds such policy could be based. Although the US policy statement referred cautiously to *assistance*, which might lead someone to think of mere search and rescue operations with a view to saving life at sea in a broad humanitarian sense, in fact neutral naval forces engaged belligerent forces in circumstances which bore no relationship to either self-defence or enforcement of national

[261]See OUDOT DE DAINVILLE, *op. cit., supra* n.100 at p. 59.

[262]See O'ROURKE, *op. cit., supra* n.259 at p. 47.

[263]See 88 *US Dept. of State Bulletin* (July 1988), no.2136 at p. 61. The new US policy of affording on-call armed protection to any unlawfully attacked merchantman was first applied in July 1988. In one incident, the *USS Elmer Montgomery* acted in response to a distress call of a Danish supertanker by firing warning shots at three Iranian speedboats as they fled the area. In another episode, US warships dispatched helicopters to defend a Panamanian-flag tanker which subsequently fired upon two Iranian gunboats; see O'ROURKE, *op. cit., supra* n.259 at p. 48.

trade rights. Indeed, it is difficult to see what the legal rationale for such a commitment might be if not to promote a trans-neutral police jurisdiction, or a sort of self-conferred guardianship of neutral rights. A second objection would relate to the real objective of the operation. One tends to forget that the new protective arrangement, as practised, was designed to repel surface, that is to say Iranian, attacks alone while it might be barely expected to have any impact on the Iraqi air-delivered missile attacks, despite the fact that these were more destructive and frequent.

In any event, the US position appears complex enough to merit analysis. It is clear that for the Reagan administration a distinction should be made between Iranian attacks against intra-neutral shipping and Iraqi attacks against neutral vessels trading with Iran. Although the former were unequivocally condemned at any opportunity, the latter were met with tolerance and understanding, even though never explicitly considered as legitimate. In May 1984, for instance, US President Ronald Reagan was reported as saying 'I think we've always recognized that in time of war, the enemy's commerce and trade is a fair target, if you can hurt them economically. So, in that sense, Iraq had not gone beyond bounds, as Iran had done.'[264]

The distinction to be drawn between Iranian and Iraqi attacks is further reflected in the manner in which US naval forces dealt with approaching Iranian or Iraqi military aircraft. As a House Committee report regarding the *Stark* incident affirmed, 'although the written rules treat both Iraqi and Iranian aircraft equally, it appears that U.S. personnel have drawn a distinction, and tend to regard Iraqis as less of a threat. For example AWACS aircraft symbolize Iraqi military aircraft as "strike support general" rather than "hostile", as presumed by the Rules of Engagement.'[265]

[264]Quoted in MENEFEE, S.P., 'Commentary on US Practice' in DE GUTTRY and RONZITTI, *op. cit., supra* n.45 at p. 112. The statement could be interpreted as recognizing the legitimacy of the Iraqi 'fire and forget' missile campaign although, literally speaking, it only concedes in unrefined terms the disruption of enemy's trade as an acceptable objective. In other words, the mere fact that the policy of striking the enemy's economic base is broadly admitted does not imply *per se* that all the means to carry out such policy should be also deemed necessarily lawful.

[265]See DE GUTTRY and RONZITTI, *op. cit., supra* n.45, doc.2.a.6 at p. 157. In the same document evidence is produced to the effect that Iraqi planes were rather

This friendly attitude, however, regarding Iraqi air force missions in the Gulf, should not be regarded as suggesting recognition of the legality of the acts in which the Iraqi planes were involved. The US partial enforcement of its own Rules of Engagement as against the Gulf belligerents, might of course raise questions of another nature, principally that of the credibility of US alleged neutrality, but it is still not conclusive as to the American position concerning the Iraqi sink-on-sight tactics. For, as the US had made clear upon advising US mariners to remain outside the belligerent proclaimed war zones, they had no intention of recognizing the legal validity of such prohibited areas or of any right belligerents might wish to claim therein.[266]

The British government, for its part, had maintained a far clearer position with reference to Iraqi practices, as the following statement reveals: 'Iraq has consistently claimed the right, *in defiance of international law,* to attack any shipping helping to sustain Iranian economic activity' (emphasis added).[267]

The Functional Approach: An Apologetic Theory Over the last few years, a number of scholars participating in the ongoing discussion concerning the modernization of the laws of war at sea have subscribed to a school of thought which maintains that *any* merchant ship could be lawfully attacked on sight if it could be established that its commercial activity is in reality promoting the war effort of the enemy. The origins of the theory can be

regularly allowed to overfly US warships on their way to attack neutral tankers calling at Iranian oil terminals. According to the experience of *USS O'Bannon,* as later reported by the MEF Commander, 'I had Iraqi airplanes flying over me in pairs at 500 feet every day, twice a day. I didn't lock on them and they didn't lock on me. But we called them up. We told them where we were. We were very clear about that. I think they knew where we were. They were headed off to do their business . . . We regarded them warily, we watched them closely, and had AWACS reporting and we monitored them with that . . .', *ibid.* Recently it has been asserted that US early warning planes were literally acting as air traffic controllers for Iraqi bombers; see BARRY, J. and CHARLES, R., 'Sea of Lies', *Newsweek,* 13 July 1992 at p. 15. See also BOYLE, F.A., 'International Crisis and Neutrality: United States Foreign Policy Toward the Iran-Iraq War', 43 *Mercer Law Review* (1992) at pp. 537–8. Given the fact, therefore, that the Iraqis were treated in every practical sense as 'virtual allies', one can logically imply that the United States also endorsed their methods; see DE GUTTRY and RONZITTI, *op. cit., supra* n.45, doc.2.a.6 at p. 153.

[266]See Defense Mapping Agency and Hydrographic Center, Special Warning No.48 of September 1980, and Special Warning No.67 of September 1985, in DE GUTTRY and RONZITTI, *op. cit., supra* n.45, doc.1.1, doc.1.9 at pp. 134, 139.

[267]See 59 *BYIL* (1988) at p. 582.

traced to Thomas Mallison's 1968 monograph on submarine warfare where he argues that 'there is no reason in either experience or logic why the Protocol [1936 London Protocol] should be interpreted as protecting neutral merchant ships which are engaged in the same functional activities that result in lack of protection for an enemy merchant ship',[268] or further back to Julius Stone's ardent advocacy that the annihilation of enemy maritime commerce should be the overriding consideration in any realistic discourse concerning the laws of war at sea.[269]

For one of the exponents of this thesis, which might be called the *functional approach*, 'legitimate belligerent attack upon a commercial merchant is driven, not by that merchant's *location* at the time of attack but its *function* relative to the ongoing hostilities (e.g., trading with a belligerent in a commodity vital to its war-sustaining effort)'.[270] Likewise, another naval expert suggests 'that the primary legal criterion for determining whether or not a merchant vessel should be a legitimate military objective should be a functional one: what task is the merchant vessel employed on at the time a targeting decision is made?'[271]

This functional definition of a military objective was chiefly used to offer a legal justification to the Iraqi indiscriminate missile attacks against ships carrying Iranian oil during the 1980–8 Gulf War. As put by one analyst, 'Iraq was within its legal rights to attack this vital source of Iran's war-sustaining economy . . . The tankers docking at Kharg could reasonably have been assured to be taking on Iranian oil for export, and such ships and their war-sustaining cargoes were legitimate objects of attack. Further, the ships carrying Iranian crude oil, whether by shuttle from Kharg to Lavan, Sirri or Larak, or from Iranian terminals destined for overseas ports, were legitimate

[268]See MALLISON, W.T., *Submarines in General and Limited Wars*, USNWC, 58 *International Law Studies* (1966) at p. 130.

[269]See STONE, J., *Legal Controls of International Conflict*, 2nd edn (1959), pp. 599–607.

[270]See RUSSO, *op. cit., supra* n.51 at p. 390.

[271]See FENRICK, W.J., 'The Merchant Vessel as Legitimate Target in the Law of Naval Warfare', in DELISSEN, A.J.M. and TANJA, G.J. (eds), *Humanitarian Law of Armed Conflict – Challenges Ahead, Essays in Honour of Frits Kalshoven*, 1991 at p. 441, and Id., 'Legal Aspects of Targeting in the Law of Naval Warfare', 29 *CYIL* (1991) at p. 274.

objects of attack by Iraqi forces, particularly since they were located either within Iranian or international waters.'[272]

A Critique However appealing the functional or war-sustaining effort theory may appear to the strategist, there is nothing *in law* to warrant the unprovoked, instant destruction of unarmed merchant vessels whether enemy or neutral for the simple reason of being engaged in enemy's commerce. There may be considerable support for this notion in political pragmatism, or economic or military strategy, but nothing in law. Even if one admits that the Iranian oil industry installations, such as the oil export terminal at Kharg Island may well have qualified as military objectives under Article 52§2 of the 1977 First Additional Protocol, it cannot be established in any legally tenable sense that this conclusion also holds true for neutral merchant vessels under the pretext that they carried Iranian crude in their tanks.[273] From a legal standpoint, one should not fail to distinguish between attacks against *enemy*, well-defended *localities* which effectively contributed to belligerent war effort (it is much less clear though whether they contributed to 'military action') and *neutral* vessels manned with innocent and unarmed *civilian crewmen*.[274]

The ill-defined criterion of contributing to an enemy's war-sustaining capacity under the functional theory has met with the suspicion of several jurists. As Louise Doswald-Beck noted,

[272]See ROACH, J.A., 'Missiles on Target: Targeting and Defense Zones in the Tanker War', 31 *VJIL* (1991) at pp. 606–7.

[273]The Kharg Island oil terminal, used for 90 per cent of Iran's oil exports, extended over 60 square miles of land and underwater pipelines, and included two main docks and a total of 14 loading piers. Given its strategic character, Kharg Island installations were protected with an array of formidable air defences including US, Soviet and British surface-to-air missiles as well as Bofors anti-aircraft guns. From mid-August 1985, when Iraq undertook a sustained campaign against Kharg Island oil facilities until the end of that year, i.e., during a period of 135 days, no less than 60 air raids had been launched, while the total number at the end of 1986 stood at 150; see *Middle East Military Balance* (1987–8) at pp. 236, 239. Similarly, the Sirri Island oil terminal came under attack for the first time in August 1986, the oil drilling platform at Rostam in October 1986, while in November 1986 the Iraqi air force bombed the oil platform at Sassan and the oil terminal at Larak Island which is situated more than 1,200 km from Basra.

[274]For some well-pointed observations on this point, see HOFFMAN, M.H., 'Les marins neutres et le droit humanitaire: un précédent en matière de protection des neutres lors des conflits armés', 74 *RICR* (mai–juin 1992), no.795, p. 285*ff*.

> the treatment of neutral merchant ships as military objectives if they help in one form or other the military 'effort' of the enemy would put a large number of ships in danger for merely continuing normal trade, which is giving too wide an interpretation of 'unneutral service'. Further, such a lack of restraint in the determination of military objectives could all too easily lead to a general sinking campaign which would probably also degrade the protection given to specially exempt vessels.[275]

As for the 1994 *San Remo Manual*, it specifies in para.67 that 'merchant vessels flying the flag of neutral states may not be attacked unless ... (f) they make an effective contribution to the enemy's military action (e.g. carrying military materials) and it is not feasible for the attacking forces to first place passengers and crew in a place of safety. Unless circumstances do not permit, they are to be given a warning, so that they can reroute, off-load, or take other precautions.' Yet, in the accompanying commentary it is explicitly provided that 'neutral merchant vessels departing from an enemy port and those carrying export cargoes such as oil were not to be considered military objectives ... [para.67(f)] would not include exports by the adverse party which might be vital for financing the war effort because the connection between the exports and military action would be too remote'.[276]

No logical construction can be stretched so far as to bridge the hiatus which separates the right to capture an adventurous

[275]See DOSWALD-BECK, L., 'Commentary No.7' in VON HEINEGG, H.W. (ed.), *The Military Objective and the Principle of Distinction in the Law of Naval Warfare – Report, Commentaries and Proceedings of the Round-Table of Experts on International Humanitarian Law Applicable to Armed Conflicts at Sea, Bochum, Nov.10–14, 1989*, 1991 at p. 79. Likewise, Frits Kalshoven observed: 'like in land and air/land warfare, contribution to the war effort is far too broad and vague a notion to serve as a determinant for the decision that a merchant vessel may be attacked as a military objective'; see KALSHOVEN, F., 'Commentary No.17', *ibid.* at p. 126. Frits Kalshoven went on to recommend caution against the often elusive language of some modern national manuals on the law of naval operations, and warned of empty restrictions which in effect 'amount to hardly any restriction at all but rather provide a licence to give prevalence to *"mission accomplishment"* over humanitarian considerations. Mission accomplishment appears to have become popular as a recent, very vague and broad version of the age-old argument of military necessity', *ibid.* at p. 127.

[276]See *Commentary on the Harmonised Document on International Humanitarian Law Applicable to Armed Conflicts at Sea*, March 1994, para.67.9 at p. 145, and para.67.27 at p. 152.

neutral from the act of sinking a defenceless civilian object without warning. In other words, a neutral activity qualifiable as sustaining the enemy's war effort can exonerate at the very most the condemnation of the neutral ship but never its instant destruction. Moreover, why should one accept that every neutral vessel plying Iranian waters operated ultimately in support of the Iranian war-fighting capacity while ships trading with Kuwait or Saudi Arabia were not considered, by analogy, as indirectly contributing to the Iraqi war machine?[277] If then one was to concede to the Iranians what had already been conceded to the Iraqis, it becomes apparent that the bulk of foreign merchant shipping upon entering the Gulf could be 'lawfully' attacked and destroyed – a rather outrageous proposition.[278]

Military Objectives: How Far Can the Definition Be Stretched? The scattered codification attempts regarding the notion of 'military objective' may throw some light in this respect. The 1922 Hague Rules of Aerial Warfare in Article 24 define a military objective as 'an objective whereof the total or partial destruction would constitute an *obvious military* advantage for the belligerent'. In the second paragraph of the same Article an exhaustive enumeration of these objectives appears, comprising 'military forces, military works, military establishments or depots, manufacturing plants constituting important and well-known centers for the production of arms, ammunition or characterized military supplies, lines of communication or transport which are use for military purposes'.

As for Article 7 of the Draft Rules for the Limitation of Dangers Incurred by the Civilian Population in Time of War, presented by the ICRC in 1956, it referred to objectives 'which, in view of their essential characteristics, are generally acknowledged to be of *military* importance'. Annexed to the Draft Rules

[277]As Christopher Greenwood put it persuasively with reference to the much discussed criterion of integration of neutral merchantmen into the war-sustaining capacity of belligerents, 'the question of what constitutes integration needs very careful discussion. If lifting Iranian oil at Kharg Island qualifies, what about lifting Iraqi oil but doing so at Kuwait?'; see GREENWOOD, C., 'Commentary No.19' in VON HEINEGG, *op.cit., supra* n.275 at p. 134.
[278]For an argument in favour of the prohibition on all destructive attack against oil-transporting platforms because of the significant environmental risk involved, see JORDAN, K.B., 'Petroleum Transport System: No Longer a Legitimate Target', 43 *US Naval War College Review* (spring 1990), p. 47*ff*.

there appeared a list of categories of military objectives which enclosed:

(1) Armed forces, including auxiliary or complementary organisations, and persons who, though not belonging to the above-mentioned formations, nevertheless take part in the fighting.
(2) Positions, installations or constructions occupied by the forces indicated in sub-paragraph 1 above, as well as combat objectives (that is to say, those objectives which are directly contested in battle between land or sea forces including airborne forces).
(3) Installations, constructions and other works of a military nature, such as barracks, fortifications, War Ministries (e.g. Ministries of Army, Navy, Air Force, National Defence, Supply) and other organs for the direction and administration of military operations.
(4) Stores of arms or military supplies, such as munition dumps, stores of equipment or fuel, vehicles parks.
(5) Airfields, rocket launching ramps and naval base installations.
(6) Those of the lines and means of communication (railway lines, roads, bridges, tunnels and canals) which are of *fundamental military importance.*
(7) The installations of broadcasting and television stations; telephone and telegraph exchanges of *fundamental military importance.*
(8) Industries of *fundamental importance* for the conduct of the war:

(a) industries for the manufacture of armaments such as weapons, munitions, rockets, armoured vehicles, military aircraft, fighting ships, including the manufacture of accessories and all other war material;
(b) industries for the manufacture of supplies and material of a military character, such as transport and communications material, equipment for the armed forces;
(c) factories or plant constituting other production and manufacturing centres of *fundamental importance for the conduct of war,* such as the metallurgical, engineering and

chemical industries, whose nature or purpose is *essentially military;*
(d) storage and transport installations whose basic function is to serve the industries referred to in (a)-(c);
(e) installations providing energy mainly for national defence, e.g., coal, other fuels, or atomic energy, and plants producing gas or electricity *mainly for military consumption.*

(9) Installations constituting experimental, research centres for experiments on and the development of weapons and war material. (emphasis added)

The Institut de Droit International in its 1969 Edinburgh session adopted a Resolution on the distinction between military objectives and non-military objects in general and particularly the problems associated with weapons of mass destruction, para.2 of which described military objectives as 'those which by their very nature or purpose or use, make an *effective contribution to military action,* or exhibit a *generally recognized military significance,* such that their total or partial destruction in the actual circumstances gives a *substantial, specific and immediate military advantage* to those who are in a position to destroy them' (emphasis added).

Article 47 of the Draft Protocol prepared by the ICRC in 1970–1, stipulated that 'attacks shall be strictly limited to military objectives, namely, to those objectives which are, by their nature, purpose or use, recognized to be of military interest and whose total or partial destruction, in the circumstances ruling at the time, offers a *distinct and substantial military advantage'* (emphasis added).[279] The 1974–7 Diplomatic Conference drew heavily upon all those earlier suggestions and finally approved the formula now appearing as Article 52§2:

[279]Para.2 of the same Article, however, provided that 'objects which are not military objectives shall not be made the object of attack, except if they are used *mainly in support of the military effort'*. The proposed amendment varied considerably in scope. For Romania, for instance, a military objective should qualify as such only if 'used directly or immediately in the conduct of military operations'. France was ready to consider as a military objective anything which 'contributes directly or indirectly to the maintenance or development of the military potential of the adverse party'. The discussions on this Article are reviewed in LEVIE, H.S., *Protection of War Victims: Protocol 1 to the 1949 Geneva Conventions*, vol.3, 1980, pp. 176–207.

> military objectives are limited to those objects which by their nature, location, purpose or use make an effective contribution to military action and whose total or partial destruction, capture or neutralization, in the circumstances ruling at the time, offers a definite military advantage.

The First Additional Protocol, therefore, is consistent with past trends in giving expression to the sentiment that an objective becomes a lawful military target only if it is linked in a marked and direct manner with the conduct or the outcome of military operations. As the official proceedings of the Conference confirm, long discussions preceded the adoption of the adjective 'definite'. The numerous other terms such as distinct, clear, immediate, obvious, specific or substantial, which were also considered demonstrate the special concern as to that necessary relationship between the object of an attack and military action.[280] If one looks at the concrete way in which Article 52§2 has been interpreted in the Commentaries on the Additional Protocol, it becomes apparent that *effective* contribution and *definite* military advantage are treated as key words in order to narrow down the scope of the notion of military objective which would otherwise risk growing unchecked.[281]

[280]See the Report to the Third Commission on the Work of the Working Group, Committee III, *CDDH/III/224,* vol.XV at p. 332, and the Report of Committee III, *CDDH/215/Rev.1*, vol.XV, §64 at p. 277. See also LEVIE, *op. cit., supra* at pp. 198, 201. Draft Article 47 was finally adopted by 79 votes to none with 7 abstentions. Most of the abstaining states including France, the Netherlands, Canada, the United States and the Federal Republic of Germany expressed their understanding that the prohibition of attack against civilian objects does not deal with the problem of collateral or incidental damage which a legitimate attack may cause.

[281]See, for instance, SANDOZ, Y., SWINARSKI, C. and ZIMMERMANN, B. (eds), *Commentary on the Additional Protocols*, 1987 at pp. 636–7, and BOTHE, M., PARTSCH, K.J. and SOLF, W.A., *New Rules for Victims of Armed Conflicts – Commentary on the Two Protocols Additional to the Geneva Conventions of 1949*, 1982 at p. 326. See also the apposite remarks on this point by DOSWALD-BECK, L., 'The Protection of Victims of Armed Conflicts at Sea', Introductory Report presented at Geneva in September 1993 for the purpose of the Round Table of Experts on International Humanitarian Law Applicable to Armed Conflicts at Sea (copy on file with author) at pp. 33–4. In the same vein, see RONZITTI, N., 'Le droit humanitaire applicable aux conflits armés en mer', 242 *RCADI* (1993), ftn.119 at p. 74. A trenchant critique of the notion of military objective as applied by coalition forces in the 1991 Gulf War against Iraq is in NORMAND, R. and JOCHNICK, C., 'The Legitimation of Violence: A Critical Analysis of the Gulf War', 35 *HILJ* (1994) at pp. 402–7. See also ROBERTS, A., 'The Laws of War in the 1990–91 Gulf Conflict', 18 *Int.Sec.* (winter 1993/94) at pp. 154–9, and GARDAM, J.G., 'Noncombatant Immunity and the Gulf Conflict', 32 *VJIL* (1992) at pp. 827–34.

One might observe, of course, that Article 52§2 of the First Protocol was not intended to apply in armed conflicts other than those on land. In fact, under the much-debated proviso of Article 49§3 the principles of international law applicable in naval and aerial warfare were not to be affected by the rules of the Protocol concerning the protection of civilian population. In that sense, for instance, Michael Bothe noted that 'ship to ship, ship to air or air to ship attacks are not covered by Protocol I, unless and to the extent they affect the civilian population on land . . . Thus, the rules of Article 52 are irrelevant for the questions whether or not an attack may be directed against a merchant vessel at sea.'[282] Be that as it may, one should not fail to notice that the definition of military objectives as laid down in Article 52§2 draws by and large on previous suggestions and draft articles not expressly limited to land warfare so that it can be safely regarded as a unitary clause of general application. There can be no objection to the view that modern laws of warfare cannot afford but a single, coherent definition of military objectives applicable in all types of military engagement.

V Concluding remarks

By way of conclusion, one may be surprised to note how little of the traditional prize law rules have changed or evolved in practice. Economic warfare is more than ever a belligerent strategy in the case of an armed conflict at sea. There is no evidence to suggest that the time-honoured right to capture enemy or, under certain conditions, neutral property at sea is now abandoned. The only possible uncertainty would concern any limitations that the UN Charter might have on the scope of the right of capture. As one expert has recently indicated, 'if the direct influence of the United Nations Charter on the law of economic warfare at sea is accepted, the legality of condemning enemy property will probably have to be reconsidered. If all measures have to meet the principles of necessity and proportionality set out in the Charter, it is doubtful whether the

[282]See BOTHE, M., 'Commentary on the 1977 Geneva Protocol I' in RONZITTI, *op. cit., supra* n.29 at p. 762. See also BOTHE, PARTSCH and SOLF, *op. cit., supra* at p. 290.

acquisition of all enemy property at sea is legally justified.'[283] The exact repercussions of the UN Charter, however, on the laws of naval warfare in general are so poorly elucidated that no significant changes in the law of capture are foreseeable.

Protected vessels such as those enunciated in the 1907 Eleventh Hague Convention are still exempted from seizure. There is much support for the view that some new categories (such as cartel vessels, vessels transporting cultural property or engaged in civilian population-relief missions) are now generally recognized, and most interestingly that passenger vessels when carrying exclusively civilian passengers, without prejudice to the right to seize, may neither be attacked nor destroyed. The US and German manuals contain explicit references to that effect,[284] while the *San Remo Manual* fully endorses this point of view.[285]

Visitation of suspect vessels, that is, halting and boarding merchantmen with a view to verifying papers and inspecting cargoes, remains an undisputed method of contraband control. Diverting and detaining a ship into a port has become today (especially for certain types of ships) an absolute necessity, although it may be contested whether diversion for the simple reason of gaining time in order to collect extrinsic evidence as to the condemnable character of the ship or cargo is a lawful procedure. Neutral convoys, such as the escort missions of Kuwaiti reflagged tankers reaffirmed, continue to enjoy immunity from belligerent visitation rights.

In the modern context, a major innovation in the law of visit and search is the increasing use of aircraft and helicopters for intercepting, challenging and even escorting merchant vessels. Maritime interdiction campaigns today appear to be a combined operation involving surface assets, patrol aircraft but also, whenever possible, the use of advanced electronics and satellite

[283]See VON HEINEGG, *op. cit., supra* n.51 at p. 134. See also VON HEINEGG, H.W., 'The Current State of International Prize Law' in POST, H.H.G. (ed.), *International Economic Law and Armed Conflict*, 1994, p. 5*ff.*

[284]See NWP9-Rev.A at para.8.2.3(6) and *Annotated Supplement* at p. 8–20, and *ZDv 15/2* at para.1034.

[285]See *San Remo Manual on International Law Applicable to Armed Conflicts at Sea*, June 1994 at para.140 and *Commentary on the Harmonised Document on International Humanitarian Law Applicable to Armed Conflicts at Sea*, March 1994, para.140.1 at p. 231. For a recent study on the question of protected vessels, see DOSWALD-BECK, L., 'Vessels, Aircraft and Persons Entitled to Protection during Armed Conflicts at Sea', 65 *BYIL* (1994), p. 211*ff.*

information. Ongoing naval enforcement action of UN sanctions underscores in a most graphic way the continued relevance of visit and search operations as well as some novel techniques.

The transformation of the traditional law of contraband solicited in chapter 5 above, however cardinal, shall not affect the validity of classical contraband control measures such as the right of visit and search and capture. For, the repeal of the neutral private right to trade in absolute contraband does not entail that the belligerent should be deprived of the means necessary to enforce such prohibition much like the legal ban on drugs trafficking, for instance, does not imply that coastguard authorities should not keep a vigilant eye against eventual violators, be it through stopping and inspecting suspect vessels or by any other means. And then there is the ever-expanding category of conditional contraband itself calling for belligerent preventive action.[286]

Prize proceedings have been rare in the post-1945 period. The Egyptian experience of the years 1949–77, however, as well as the Iranian legislative attempt to establish a prize court in the final year of the Gulf Tanker War reaffirm the conclusion that setting up a prize jurisdiction remains a current and apparently welcomed measure in protracted conflict situations for what would otherwise seem arbitrary seizures at sea. Furthermore, the doctrines of unneutral service and continuous voyage, in all likelihood, have lost nothing of their topicality as the relevant practice in the Iran-Iraq War has amply attested. Navicerting also seems a well-established procedure, although practically unused since the Second World War.

Above and beyond these prize law particulars, however, the truly interesting and vividly debated point of law concerns the conditions of lawful exercise of the right of destruction of neutral merchantmen. Recent manuals and some leading

[286]Be that as it may, an important question has still to be examined, namely what would be the practical consequences of an arms shipment of neutral origin intercepted by a belligerent navy. Should such violation of neutrality be sufficient reason to forfeit the state at fault from all neutral immunities? Moreover, could an aggrieved belligerent extend the termination of neutrality to cover all implicated, directly or indirectly, states? This hypothesis may arise, for example, in the case where the arms-producing state, the flag state of the arms-transporting vessel, or the port state where the cargo was loaded would be different ones. A further delicate point would concern the identification of the nationality of the arms manufacturer in cases of multinational consortia or of weapons systems which very frequently contain parts produced in different countries.

authorities in the field have suggested in varying terms that neutral merchantmen might be lawfully attacked and destroyed if they engage in activities that sustain the enemy's war fighting capability. The view is believed to be based on an unjustifiably broad interpretation of the definition of military objective, as codified in Article 52§2 of the 1977 First Additional Protocol, which would suffice to legitimize almost every 'sink-on-sight' type of strategy with dreadful consequences. What is more, the so-called 'functional' theory of naval targeting has failed to demonstrate how the concept of capture with all its well-circumscribed legal principles were purportedly repealed by a *right* of destruction. For, it is one thing to argue that the old right of capture has been eroded in some respects, and quite another to prove that what was previously denounced as blatantly illegal has now been transformed into accepted custom.

GENERAL CONCLUSIONS

The Finding At the outset of every work dealing with the laws of naval warfare, be it Charles Dupuis's monograph of the beginning of the century, Robert Tucker's standard reference blue-book of 1955, or Professor Ronzitti's Hague course of 1993, one is warned against the messy, chaotic, disorderly state of legal prescriptions concerning the conduct of military operations at sea. The assessment is unanimous and not a recent one: the traditional laws of naval warfare and maritime neutrality are in desperate need for deep reforms and modernization. Despite their undoubted merits, the conventional arrangements elaborated in 1907 at The Hague are ill-suited to deal with today's realities.

The problem lies not so much with treaty provisions as such, many of which may still look apposite and technically enforceable, but rather with the dramatically different combat environment, the altered socio-economic parameters of state organization, and the evolution of the concept of neutrality. The inadequacy of the Hague rules has become a cliché since the days of the two World Wars, without the precise extent to which those wars may have transformed international customary principles in the field ever becoming quite clear. On the other hand, the major naval conflicts of the last decade, i.e. the 1982 Falkland Islands campaign and the 1984–8 Persian Gulf Tanker War, delivered a final blow to the mistaken belief that post-Second World War naval engagements were somehow condemned to remain limited and thus relatively unimportant. Naval experts were forcefully reminded that the diffusion of modern weapons, both lethal and cheap, such as missiles or mines put tough new dilemmas to naval powers, while jurists became conscious of the extraordinary legal vacuum in which modern sea campaigns are conducted.

The 1907 rules governing naval hostilities, already somewhat confused and open-ended at their inception, are today, more than ever before, called into question for a variety of reasons: first, international relations operate in a different system, that of the UN Charter and, consequently, past institutions, concepts or postulates have to be reformulated in order to become compatible with the new controlling principles. Second, international armed conflicts have also experienced profound changes, particularly with regard to weapons technology. Third, state organization has evolved to the point that some of the premises of the Hague arrangements may not hold true any more. Fourth, peacetime activities at sea are now subject to such an expanded regulatory framework as the new UN Law of the Sea Convention that naval operations are inevitably affected.

Time for Action: The Guiding Principles It is certainly not for this work to indicate the most suitable forums or agencies through which the legal reform should be pursued. The author lacks the first-hand information and the experience of the practitioner, which would permit an inside view as to the optimal means of bringing about the necessary changes. Only a few thoughts can be submitted concerning the guiding principles of such an undertaking.

The controlling element and ultimate objective should be to draft a code of legal principles applicable to sea warfare which would transcend outmoded perceptions of naval operations as something juridically distinct from land or air campaigns. The continued reference to 'special usages of war at sea' is an anachronism and should find no place in a modern codification instrument. Harmonization to the fullest extent possible of the laws of naval warfare with the rules applicable to land and air warfare is a high priority. To cite but one example, the contradictory treatment of the use of false colours at sea and in the air may well find its historical explanation in the different origins and traditions of sea warfare as contrasted to air warfare (which basically comes down to the legacy of pirates roaming the seven seas versus the legacy of noblemen duelling in the skies), but has no justification whatsoever today (see Article 19 of the 1923

Hague Rules for Aerial Warfare and Article 39§3 of the 1977 First Additional Protocol).

In yet another striking contrast, belligerent aircraft are absolutely forbidden to enter neutral jurisdiction whereas belligerent warships enjoy therein various rights, such as, for instance, a right of passage, sojourn, repair and replenishment (see Articles 40, 42 of the 1923 Hague Rules and Articles 10–20 of the 1907 Hague Convention XIII). Although it might be argued rightly that warships much more than aircraft need shore-based support to complete their mission, there would still be room for harmonization between the law of naval and air operations. In this latter case, the point in question would be the uniform application of the principle of the inviolability of neutral jurisdiction, and it would be only natural that the crossing of a belligerent warship qualified – no less than the overflight of a belligerent aircraft – as an infringement upon neutral rights.

The interplay between war laws and the UN Charter has to be explored in all its perplexity. The issue is often relegated to simply gauging the effect of Article 51 on traditional rules governing the means or methods of warfare. Without doubting in principle the importance and the necessity of accommodating the self-defence concept in a modern restatement of the laws of war at sea, it would be an unpropitious, if not hopeless, exercise to measure the legality of every single belligerent act by reference to self-defence. This view seems to prevail in recent works, but is thought to prove an unfortunate suggestion. In the long term, it is submitted, neither the laws of war nor Article 51 of the Charter will be any better elucidated. It is to be expected that a great many abuses would be committed in the name of self-defence, which could only add further uncertainty and confusion.

Moreover, the focus is unjustifiably kept on the problem of self-defence while a host of other issues should also be revised in the light of the UN Charter. To give but the most telling example, the rights and duties of neutral states in an armed conflict, unpronounced upon by the UN Security Council, should be so tailored as to be compatible with the general principles of the Charter. This aspect has rarely been studied and certainly merits additional work. As argued in chapter 5, the rationale underlying some basic principles of the Charter would have a crucial role to play in constraining the neutral 'right' to trade in absolute contraband in contemporary conditions.

The influence of the peacetime law of the sea also remains to be examined. The new UN Law of the Sea Convention may have significant, yet unscrutinized, repercussions on the law of armed conflict at sea, especially on the geographical limits of naval operations. The crux of the matter relates here to the legality of belligerent operations within certain zones of neutral jurisdiction which would appear to lie half-way between the status of territorial waters and that of high seas. The question is a difficult one since the mobility of belligerent navies might be greatly restricted, yet the language of the Hague Convention XIII (references to neutral waters in Articles 1 and 4, or to neutral jurisdiction in Articles 3 and 8) would seem to favour a blanket prohibition of all belligerent action within neutral jurisdiction. It is thought that if, on the one hand, the 200-mile exclusive economic zone, or an exceptionally wide 350-mile continental shelf, is indeed a vast space to police and effectively protect against belligerent abuses, a 24-mile contiguous zone, on the other hand, is far too close to neutral shores to allow unlimited belligerent operations (one should think especially in terms of missile warfare in order to realize how exposed nearby neutral sites would be if such operations were to be authorized).

In the light of the above, two observations can be made: first, there can be no question of mechanically transposing concepts refined in the context of modern law of the sea to the sphere of naval war. The result would be unbalanced and likely to produce sustained friction between belligerents and neutrals. Second, there is nothing which would prohibit in principle, and in fact it would be more sound to envisage some new limit(s), different from the ones existing today for the purposes of peacetime sea uses, which would equitably reflect the legitimate concerns of both neutrals regarding protection of national sovereignty, and belligerents regarding mission accomplishment.

Military technology may often challenge the validity of existing legal regulations, but cannot dictate, far less establish, new rules. By reason of the secrecy in development and the enormous industrial-economic interests involved, newly invented weapons systems are extremely difficult to contain, let alone outlaw. Faced with particularly nasty novel technologies, such as laser weapons, one can feel the functional limits, or the need for reappraisal, of cardinal principles such as that of unnecessary suffering, or the one which elevates the dictates of the public conscience to an ultimate test of legitimacy.

The evolution of humanitarian law standards should be conceived as imposing a 'monodirectional' process, or a constant pursuit towards higher levels of restraint. Thus, a modern restatement of the laws of naval warfare should only promote the stringency of legal requirements. What is needed is a radical reconsideration of solutions, assumptions and compromises inherited from past times. An awakened humanitarian conscience should help to break with retrogressive ideas stemming from World War practices, such as the worrying trend of dealing with merchant seamen as if they were semi-combatants. Restraint has to be reinforced. The only recently adopted proviso of the *San Remo Manual* (Article 47e) explicitly exempting passenger ships from attack – an otherwise elementary if not self-evident principle – shows clearly the tremendous amount of progress which still has to be made.

Salutary and encouraging examples do exist. The *San Remo Manual on International Law Applicable to Armed Conflicts at Sea,* adopted in June 1994 by a group of international lawyers and naval experts, is the most serious outcome of such awareness. The *Manual* is a coherent instrument, not full of fresh ideas, but rather a careful review of the continued validity of traditional principles. Among its greatest merits, one should welcome the effort to work out as much as possible common rules for warships and aircraft, which of course underlines the ever-growing use of air power in modern naval operations. The *Manual* should also be given credit for having dispelled some ill-considered, if not dangerous, views such as the one which would allow the sink-at-sight of neutral merchantmen for carrying belligerent exportable raw materials such as oil under the label of the 'functional' or 'war-sustaining' theory. On the other hand, one can only regret the fact that the *Manual* refrained from spelling out an outright prohibition of laying drifting mines on the high seas. From the point of view of progressive development, this would have been a most positive contribution. The explanation that sowing freely floating mines could still be considered a valid option for warships under pursuit is least convincing since lacking relevance with today's means of engaging enemy targets.

Beyond Stereotypes: Suggestions for Reform As the title of this work implies, this is a selective treatment of some aspects of the laws of naval warfare and maritime neutrality among the most hotly debated in recent years. The objective was, therefore, to deal exhaustively with a limited number of issues, rather than to highlight cursorily the entire field. With regard to the issues raised in the preceding six chapters, one could recapitulate the main conclusions as follows:

Despite the often convoluted rhetoric and confusing terminology, 'war zones' is a misnomer for unrestrained attack and destruction. War zones have been condemned by courts, protested by neutrals, criticized by scholars. The tragic *Belgrano* incident, as well as that of the Iranian Airbus, have also demonstrated that the war zone device does not contribute to any containment of hostilities, nor does it solve any problem of identification. No legitimacy can thus be offered through a misleading appeal to the idea of reasonableness.

The so-called 'defensive sea areas' could be accepted to the extent they are limited to home territorial waters (or perhaps a distance beyond this to be negotiated). As regards the 'vicinity of naval operations', it is only normal that ships venturing imprudently close to the theatre of naval engagements may suffer collateral damage, but this is no compelling reason for institutionalizing the very different concept of war zones.

Naval mines pose delicate problems of indiscriminate warfare. Taking advantage of the current momentum against the reckless use of anti-personnel land-mines, the drafting of a modern instrument on naval mines appears feasible. However, in order to avoid self-nullifying clauses of the sort of the 1907 Convention VIII, states should be ready to accept more stern commitments, or meaningful limitations that would go further than the mere duty of notification 'as soon as military exigencies would permit', or a duty of cooperation in a post-war minesweeping effort (one could think of a total prohibition of drifting mines on the high seas, but also of fixing specific ceilings as to the number of anchored mines laid per square nautical mile, or as to the total area of a minefield, or as to the minimum distance between neighbouring minefields).

The undertaking might even be given a more ambitious objective, that is to regulate the use of all underwater conventional weaponry (i.e. depth charges, submarine torpedoes, dormant mine-torpedoes, and the most recently developed missile-speed torpedoes). As regards the controversial issue of minelaying in international straits, it is difficult to see why or how a state involved in an armed conflict and bordering a strait would be convinced to abstain from any belligerent action (even defensive mining) for fear of hampering the free transit passage of neutral shipping.

The distinction between permissible ruses of war and prohibited perfidy, as codified in Article 37 of the 1977 First Additional Protocol, is a salutary rule directly applicable to naval operations. The unfortunate reference, however, to generally recognized rules concerning the use of false colours at sea in Article 39§3 is without any foundation in either practice or logic. Stratagems at sea in particular, as much as deception in war in general, need urgent reassessment in the light of phenomenal developments in the electronic combat environment of today.

The arming of any ship other than commissioned warships and auxiliaries should be strictly prohibited without exception. Armaments for purely defensive purposes such as deflective devices or chaff are of limited use and could only serve, in practice, as a pretext for attack. The operation of such systems would necessitate, in any case, experienced and well-trained crews as well as sophisticated equipment, such as special radars capable to detect incoming missiles, which would tend to dilute the merchant nature of the ship.

Neutrality, as a posture of non-involvement in an armed conflict which has not been the object of any binding UN action, subsists and calls for continued legal regulation. Without any prejudice to the mechanism of collective self-defence of the Charter, non-participation in an armed conflict while maintaining trade relations with belligerents remains a question of fact and as such has to be taken care of. Neutral commerce (as the Gulf Tanker War experience proved) has to be protected – but also occasionally interfered with – by reference to a tangible set of rules and not to idle appeals to freedom of navigation, which of course emphasizes the utility of specific rules governing maritime neutrality as a live concept. Non-belligerency, meaning avowed partiality, has failed to prove its legitimacy and should continue to be treated as an occasion for sheer violation of neutral obligations.

Although most commentators agree that the export of arms today is not a private venture but belongs exclusively to the state, they fail to spell out clearly that this amounts to the abolition of what was used to be called absolute contraband, and draw the appropriate conclusions thereof. Yet, common Article 7 of Hague Conventions XIII and V is the legal anachronism *par excellence* as far as the traditional law is concerned, and modern practice has amply, though not always consistently, confirmed its abandonment. Bringing the obsolete principle into line with the philosophy of the UN Charter should lean on two crucial elements: imposing considerations of international morality and human rights law.

The bulk of prize law particulars do not seem to have lost anything of their relevance (e.g. the authority of prize jurisdiction, the exemption of neutral convoys, the doctrines of continuous voyage and unneutral service). Visit and search rights have to be redefined all the same so as to take into account the growing use of aircraft in maritime interception and inspection operations as well as the obvious necessity for diversion to port. Seizability of private property at sea remains a valid procedure as recent UN-mandated naval action has confirmed. The distance separating capture from destruction is not negligible and should not be blurred by modern concepts (e.g. the war-sustaining effort theory) which tend to deform the definition of military objective beyond recognition.

To conclude, even though there can be no doubt that the modernization of the laws of naval warfare is a topical issue – indeed a pressing necessity, and equally that with generous doses of political good will this objective could be attained, it remains doubtful whether such an undertaking will materialize in the near future. If there is a certainty, nevertheless, this is that, despite the currently re-animated discussion about the revision of the laws of naval warfare, the field still offers ample grounds for further research work. After all, it is thought that the most promising means to stimulate, nurture and eventually bring about legal reform lies with the proliferation of academic writings and initiatives which through their diversity and controversiality can give birth to the most constructive and reasonable ideas, and by this token promote the cause of international law.

SELECTED BIBLIOGRAPHY

This selected bibliography covers the legal literature up to summer 1996. It does not contain any primary sources or compilations of documents, but only monographs and leading articles in English and French related to the topics dealt with in the study. Full bibliographical indications are to be found in the text. See also the systematic bibliography by FISCHER, H. and VON HEINEGG, H.W., *The Law of Naval Warfare – A Select Bibliography*, Bochum 1989.

ABDEL FATAH, A.M., 'La jurisprudence égyptienne en matière de prise', 38 *REDI* (1982), pp. 119–52.

ADLER, S., *The Uncertain Giant 1921–1942: American Foreign Policy Between the Wars*, 1965, 340p.

AKZIN, B., 'Neutral Convoys in Law and Practice', 40 *Michigan Law Review* (1941–2), pp. 1–23.

ALFORD, N.H., *Modern Economic Warfare – Law and the Naval Participant*, USNWC, 56 *International Law Studies* (1963), 426p.

ALMOND, H.H., 'An Assessment of Economic Warfare: Developments from the Persian Gulf', 31 *VJIL* (1991), pp. 645–72.

ANDERSON, C.P., 'The Status of Armed Merchantmen', 11 *Proc.ASIL* (1917), pp. 11–19.

ANTHONY, I., *The Naval Arms Trade*, SIPRI, 1990, 221p.

—— *Arms Export Regulations*, SIPRI, 1991, 267p.

BAILEY, T.A., 'The Sinking of the Lusitania', 41 *American Historical Review* (1935–6), pp. 54–73.

BAILEY, T.A. and RYAN, P.B., *The Lusitania Disaster*, 1975, 383p.

—— *Hitler vs Roosevelt – The Undeclared War*, 1979, 303p.

BARKAS, G., *The Camouflage Story – From Aintree to Alamein*, 1952.

BARNES, W.H., 'Submarine Warfare and International Law', 2 *World Polity* (1960), pp. 121–202.

BARNETT, C., *Engage the Enemy More Closely – The Royal Navy in the Second World War*, 1991, 1052p.

BARSTON, R.P. and BIRNIE, P.W., 'The Falkland Islands/Islas Malvinas Conflict – A Question of Zones', 7 *Marine Policy* (1983), pp. 14–24.

BATY, T., 'Neglected Fundamentals of Prize Law', 30 *YLJ* (1920–1), pp. 34–47.
—— 'Continuous Voyage as Applied to Blockade and Contraband', 20 *GST* (1934), pp. 140–55.
BAUSLAUGH, R.A., *The Concept of Neutrality in Classical Greece*, 1991, 305p.
BAXTER, R.R., 'Passage of Ships Through International Waterways in Time of War', 31 *BYIL* (1954), pp. 187–216.
BEARD, C.A., *President Roosevelt and the Coming of the War 1941*, 1948, 614p.
BEHRENS, C.B.A., *Merchant Shipping and the Demands of War*, 1955, 494p.
BEKKER, C.D., *Swastika at Sea – The Struggle and Destruction of the German Navy 1939–1945*, 1953, 207p.
BELIN, J., 'La portée de la neutralité américaine', 43 *RGDIP* (1936), pp. 416–36.
BELLOT, H.H.L., 'The Right of a Belligerent Merchantman to Attack', 7 *GST* (1921), pp. 43–57.
BENTWICH, N., *The Declaration of London*, 1911, 179p.
BEST, G., *War and Law since 1945*, 1994, 434p.
BEY, A.S., 'The Egyptian Prize Court: Organization and Procedure', 5 *REDI* (1949), pp. 28–33.
BILLER, D.P., 'Policing the Persian Gulf: Protecting United States Interests and Freedom of Navigation Through Military Force', 11 *Loyola of Los Angeles International and Comparative Law Journal* (1989), pp. 171–205.
BOCZEK, B.A., 'Law of Warfare at Sea and Neutrality: Lessons from the Gulf War', 20 *ODIL* (1989), pp. 239–71.
BOOTH, K., 'The Military Implications of the Changing Law of the Sea' in Gamble, J.K. (ed.), *Law of the Sea: Neglected Issues*, 1979, pp. 328–97.
—— *Law, Force and Diplomacy at Sea*, 1985, 231p.
BORCHARD, E., 'The Arms Embargo and Neutrality', 27 *AJIL* (1933), pp. 293–98.
—— 'Sanctions Versus Neutrality', 1 *Hungarian Quarterly* (1936), pp. 254–70.
—— 'Neutrality and Unneutrality', 32 *AJIL* (1938), pp. 778–82.
—— 'Neutrality', 48 *YLJ* (1938–9), pp. 37–53.
—— 'Armed Merchantmen', 34 *AJIL* (1940), pp. 107–12.
—— 'The Attorney General's Opinion on the Exchange of Destroyers for Naval Bases', 34 *AJIL* (1940), pp. 690–7.
—— 'War, Neutrality and Non-Belligerency', 35 *AJIL* (1941), pp. 618–25.
BORCHARD, E. and LAGE, W.P., *Neutrality for the United States*, 2nd edn, 1940, 461p.
BOSMA, J.T., 'The Alternative Futures of Naval Force', 5 *ODIL* (1978), pp. 181–248.
BOTHE, M., 'Neutrality in Naval Warfare – What Is Left of Traditional International Law?' in Delissen, A.J.M. and Tanja, G.J. (eds), *Humanitarian Law of Armed Conflict – Challenges Ahead, Essays in Honour of Frits Kalshoven*, 1991, pp. 387–405.

BOTTIÉ, F., *Essai sur la genèse et l'évolution de la notion de neutralité*, 1937, 418p.

BOURDONCLE, R., 'De l'influence des ruses sur l'evolution du droit de la guerre', *Annales de l'Université de Lyon* (1958), pp. 31–133.

BOYE, T., 'Quelques aspects du développement des règles de la neutralité', 64 *RCADI* (1938), pp. 157–229.

BOYLE, F.A., 'International Crisis and Neutrality: United States Foreign Policy toward the Iran-Iraq War', 43 *Mercer Law Review* (1992), pp. 523–62.

BOZZO, L. (ed.), *Exporting Conflict – International Transfers of Conventional Arms*, 1991, 261p.

BRASSEUR, P., *La guerre de mines*, 1939, 155p.

BRIGGS, H.W., *The Doctrine of Continuous Voyage*, 1926, 226p.

—— 'Neglected Aspects of the Destroyer Deal', 34 *AJIL* (1940), pp. 569–87.

BROWN, A.C., *La guerre secrète – Le rempart des mensonges*, 1981, 2 vols.

BROWN, P.M., 'Munitions and Neutrality', 10 *Proc.ASIL* (1916), pp. 33–42.

BROWN, T.D., 'World War Prize Law Applied in a Limited War Situation: Egyptian Restrictions on Neutral Shipping with Israel', 50 *Minnesota Law Review* (1966), pp. 849–73.

BRUNEAU, J., *La ruse dans la guerre sur mer*, 1938, 223p.

BRZOSKA, M., 'Profiteering on the Iran-Iraq War', 43 *Bulletin of the Atomic Scientists* (June 1987), pp. 42–5.

BUTTE, G.C., 'The Reform of the Law of Contraband', 9 *Proc.ASIL* (1915), pp. 112–34.

CABLE, J., 'The Falklands Conflict', 108 *USNIP* (Sept.1982), pp. 70–6.

CAGLE, M.W., 'Task Force 77 in Action Off Vietnam', 98 *USNIP* (May 1972), pp. 66–109.

CAGLE, M.W. and MANSON, F.A., *The Sea War in Korea*, 1957, 555p.

CAMPBELL, G., *Mes navires mystérieux*, 1929, 260p.

CARLISLE, G.E., 'The Interrelationship of International Law and United States Naval Operations in Southeast Asia', 22 *US Judge Advocate General Journal* (July/Aug.1967), pp. 8–14.

CHAMBERLAIN, J.P., 'The Embargo Resolutions and Neutrality', 251 *Int.Con* (1929), pp. 257–340.

CHARTERIS, A.H., 'Conversion of Merchantman into War-Vessel', 18 *BYIL* (1937), pp. 199–202.

CHATTERTON, E.K., *Les bateaux-pièges (Q-ships) contre les sous-marins allemands*, 1928, 248p.

CHAUMONT, C., *La conception américaine de la neutralité – Essai sur le droit international de la neutralité aux États-Unis*, 1936, 277p.

—— 'Nations Unies et neutralité', 89 *RCADI* (1956), pp. 1–59.

CIGAR, N., 'The Soviet Navy in the Persian Gulf: Naval Diplomacy in a Combat Zone', 42 *US Naval War College Review* (1989), pp. 56–88.

COLE, S.D., 'Neutrals and Belligerents in Territorial Waters', 2 *GST* (1916), pp. 87–92.

—— 'Belligerent Merchantmen in Neutral Ports', 3 *GST* (1917), pp. 23–7.

COLOMBO, J.L., 'Falkland Operations – Super Etendard Naval Aircraft

Operations During the Malvinas War', 37 *US Naval War College Review* (1984), no.3, pp. 13–22.
COLOMBOS, C.J., *A Treatise on the Law of Prize*, 3rd edn, 1949, 421p.
Conference Report, 'The Persian/Arabian Gulf Tanker War: International Law or International Chaos?', 19 *ODIL* (1988), pp. 299–321.
Conference Report, 'L'évolution de la notion de neutralité dans les conflits armés actuels', 17 *Revue de Droit Pénal Militaire et de Droit de la Guerre* (1978), pp. 11–209.
COOGAN, J.W., *The End of Neutrality*, 1981, 284p.
COUDERT, F.R., 'Is Neutrality Consistent with International Cooperation?', 16 *Proc.APS* (Jan.1935), pp. 39–50.
COUTAU-BÉGARIE, H., *L'évolution de la pensée navale*, 1990, 231p.
COWIE, J.S., *Mines, Minelayers and Minelaying*, 1949, 216p.
CRIGHTON, V.M.S., 'The Pre-War Theory of Neutrality', 9 *BYIL* (1928), pp. 101–11.
CRUICKSHANK, C., *Deception in World War II*, 1979, 248p.
D'ASTORG, B., *La neutralité et son réveil dans la crise de la S.D.N.*, 1938, 171p.
DALYELL, T., *Thatcher's Torpedo – The Sinking of the* Belgrano, 1983, 80p.
—— *Thatcher: Patterns of Deceit*, 1986, 64p.
DAVID, E., 'La guerre du Golfe et le droit international', 20 *RBDI* (1987), pp. 153–83.
—— 'Le droit de la neutralité à l'epreuve de la guerre du Golfe (1980–1988)', 11 *Cahiers du Cedsi* (1990), pp. 43–53.
DAVIDSON, S., 'United States Protection of Reflagged Kuwaiti Vessels in the Gulf War: The Legal Implications', 4 *International Journal of Estuarine and Coastal Law* (1989), pp. 173–91.
DE BOCK, W. and DENIAU, J.C., *Des armes pour l'Iran – L'Irangate européen*, 1988, 298p.
DE MONTMORENCY, J.E.G., 'The Principles Underlying Contraband and Blockade', 2 *GST* (1916), pp. 21–30.
DE GUTTRY, A. and RONZITTI, N. (eds), *The Iran-Iraq War (1980–1988) and the Law of Naval Warfare*, 1993, 573p.
DEÁK, F., 'The Pitfalls of the New American Neutrality', 340 *Int.Con.* (May 1938), pp. 179–92.
—— 'The United States Neutrality Acts – Theory and Practice', 358 *Int.Con.* (1940), pp. 73–114.
—— 'Neutrality Revisited' in *Mélanges Phillip Jessup*, 1972, pp. 137–54.
DEHN, C.G., 'The Problem of Neutrality', 31 *GST* (1945), pp. 139–49.
DEKKER, I.F. and POST, H.H.G., 'The Gulf War from the Point of View of International Law', 17 *NYIL* (1986), pp. 75–105.
DEKKER, I.F. and POST, H.H.G. (eds), *The Gulf War of 1980–1988*, 1992, 314p.
DELBRÜCK, J., 'International Traffic in Arms – Legal and Political Aspects of a Long Neglected Problem of Arms Control and Disarmament', 24 *GYIL* (1981), pp. 114–43.
DENNIS, W.C., 'The Right of Citizens of Neutral Countries to Sell and Export Arms and Munitions of War to Belligerents', 60 *Ann.AAPSS* (1915), pp. 168–82.

DEWAR, M., *The Art of Deception in Warfare*, 1989, 224p.

DEYRA, M., *Aspects contemporains de la neutralité*, unpublished thesis, 1979, 445p.

DICKINSON, E.D., 'Neutrality and the Munitions Traffic', 29 *Proc.ASIL* (1935), pp. 45–51.

DILLON, G.M., *The Falklands, Politics and War*, 1989, 284p.

DIMITROV, G., 'Possible New Restrictions on the Use of Naval Mines' in Goldblat, J. (ed.), *Maritime Security: The Building of Confidence*, UNIDIR 1992, pp. 79–90.

DINITZ, S., 'The Legal Aspects of the Egyptian Blockade of the Suez Canal', 45 *Georgetown Law Journal* (1956–7), pp. 169–99.

DINSTEIN, Y., 'The Laws of War at Sea', 10 *IYHR* (1980), pp. 38–69.

—— 'The Laws of Neutrality', 14 *IYHR* (1984), pp. 80–110.

DIVINE, R.A., *The Illusion of Neutrality*, 1962, 370p.

—— *The Reluctant Belligerent: American Entry Into World War II*, 2nd edn, 1979, 179p.

DOSWALD-BECK, L., 'The International Law of Naval Armed Conflicts: The Need for Reform', 7 *It.YIL* (1986–7), pp. 251–82.

—— 'Vessels, Aircraft and Persons Entitled to Protection during Armed Conflicts at Sea', 65 *BYIL* (1994), pp. 211–301.

—— 'The San-Remo Manual on International Law Applicable to Armed Conflicts at Sea', 89 *AJIL* (1995), pp. 192–208.

DOSWALD-BECK, L. (ed.), *San Remo Manual on International Law Applicable to Armed Conflicts at Sea*, 1995, 250p.

DOUGLAS, L.H., 'The Submarine and the Washington Conference of 1921', USNWC, 62 *International Law Studies* (1980), pp. 477–90.

DRUMMOND, D.F., *The Passing of American Neutrality 1937–1941*, 1955, 409p.

DUKE, H., '*Mens rea* in Prize Law', 6 *GST* (1920), pp. 99–106.

DULLES, A.W., 'Cash and Carry Neutrality', 18 *Foreign Affairs* (1940), pp. 179–95.

DUMAS, J., *Les aspects économiques du droit de prise avant et depuis la guerre mondiale*, 1926, 2 vols.

DUMBAULD, E., 'Grotius on the Law of Prize', 1 *Journal of Public Law* (1952), pp. 370–89.

DUNCAN, R.C., *America's Use of Sea Mines*, 1962, 173p.

DUPUIS, C., *Le droit de la guerre maritime*, 1911, 621p.

EAGLETON, C., 'Neutrality and Neutral Rights Following the Pact of Paris for the Renunciation of War', 24 *Proc.ASIL* (1930), pp. 87–95.

—— 'The Recent Neutrality Legislation', 13 *New York University Law Quarterly Review* (1935), pp. 72–81.

—— 'Revision of the Neutrality Act', 33 *AJIL* (1939), pp. 119–26.

—— 'The Duty of Impartiality on the Part of a Neutral', 34 *AJIL* (1940), pp. 99–104.

EICHELBERGER, C.A., 'The Law and the Submarine', 77 *USNIP* (July 1951), pp. 691–9.

EL TANAMLI, A.M., 'L'exercise par l'Égypte du droit de visite, de recherches et de capture dans le canal de Suez et le golfe d'Akaba', *L'Égypte Contemporain* (avril 1955), pp. 1–40.

ELLIOTT, A.R., 'U.S. Strategic Bases in the Atlantic', 16 *Foreign Policy Reports* (Jan.1941), pp. 258–68.

ELLIOTT, C.B., 'The Doctrine of Continuous Voyages', 1 *AJIL* (1907), pp. 61–104.

ELLIOTT, P., *Allied Minesweeping in World War 2*, 1979, 201p.

FALCONBRIDGE, J.D., 'The Right of a Belligerent to Make War Upon a Neutral', 4 *GST* (1918), pp. 204–12.

FAUCHILLE, P., *Jurisprudence française en matière de prises maritimes*, 1916, 496p.

—— 'La guerre sous-marine allemande', 25 *RGDIP* (1918), pp. 75–84.

FAUCHILLE, P. and BASDEVANT, J., *Jurisprudence italienne en matière de prises maritimes*, 1918, 224p.

FENRICK, W.J., *Developments in the Law of Naval Warfare Since World War II: The Potential Emergence of a Law of Naval Warfare for Limited Conflicts*, unpublished thesis, George Washington University, 1983, 199p.

—— 'Legal Aspects of the Falklands Naval Conflict', 24 *Revue de Droit Pénal Militaire et de Droit de la Guerre* (1985), pp. 241–68.

—— 'The Exclusion Zone Device in the Law of Naval Warfare', 24 *CYIL* (1986), pp. 91–126.

—— 'The Law of War at Sea Today: A Perspective from Canada', 3 *Canadian Forces Judge Advocate General Journal* (1989), pp. 17–25.

—— 'Legal Aspects of Targeting in the Law of Naval Warfare', 29 *CYIL* (1991), pp. 238–82.

—— 'The Merchant Vessel as Legitimate Target in the Law of Naval Warfare' in Delissen, A.J.M. and Tanja, G.J. (eds), *Humanitarian Law of Armed Conflict – Challenges Ahead, Essays in Honour of Frits Kalshoven*, 1991, pp. 425–43.

FENWICK, C.G., *American Neutrality – Trial and Failure*, 1940, 190p.

—— 'Neutrality on the Defensive', 34 *AJIL* (1940), pp. 697–9.

—— 'Is Neutrality Still a Term of Present Law?', 63 *AJIL* (1969), pp. 100–2.

FIELD, J.A., *History of U.S. Naval Operations in Korea*, 1962, 499p.

FISHER, D., *The War Magician*, 1983, 315p.

FITZMAURICE, G.G., 'Some Aspects of Modern Contraband Control and the Law of Prize', 22 *BYIL* (1945), pp. 73–95.

FLECK, D., 'Ruses of War and Prohibition of Perfidy', 13 *Revue de Droit Pénal Militaire et de Droit de la Guerre* (1974), pp. 269–314.

—— 'Rules of Engagement for Maritime Forces and the Limitation of the Use of Force Under the U.N. Charter', 31 *GYIL* (1988), pp. 165–86.

—— 'Topical Approaches Towards Developing the Laws of Armed Conflict at Sea' in Delissen, A.J.M. and Tanja, G.J. (eds), *Humanitarian Law of Armed Conflict – Challenges Ahead, Essays in Honour of Frits Kalshoven*, 1991, pp. 407–23.

FRASCONÀ, J.L., *Visit, Search, and Seizure on the High Seas*, 1938, 161p.

FRAUNCES, M.G., 'The International Law of Blockade: New Guiding Principles in Contemporary State Practice', 101 *YLJ* (Jan.1992), pp. 893–918.

FREEDMAN, L., 'The War of the Falkland Islands, 1982', 61 *Foreign Affairs* (1982), pp. 196–210.

FRIEDMAN, N., 'The Falklands War: Lessons Learned and Mislearned', 26 *Orbis* (1982–3), pp. 907–40.

FROTHINGHAM, T.G., *The Naval History of the World War*, 1925, 342p.

GABRIEL, J.M., *The American Conception of Neutrality after 1941*, 1988, 289p.

GARNER, J.W., 'Some Questions of International Law in the European War – Blockades', 9 *AJIL* (1915), pp. 818–57.

—— 'Some Questions of International Law in the European War – War Zones and Submarine Warfare', 9 *AJIL* (1915), pp. 594–626.

—— 'Some Questions of International Law in the European War – The Sale and Exportation of Arms and Munitions of War to Belligerents', 10 *AJIL* (1916), pp. 749–97.

—— 'Some Questions of International Law in the European War – Destruction of Neutral Merchant Vessels', 10 *AJIL* (1916), pp. 12–41.

—— 'Some True and False Conceptions Regarding the Duty of Neutrals in Respect to the Sale and Exportation of Arms and Munitions to Belligerents', 10 *Proc.ASIL* (1916), pp. 18–32.

—— *International Law and the World War*, 1920, 2 vols.

—— *Prize Law During the World War*, 1927, 712p.

—— 'Violations of Maritime Law by the Allied Powers During the World War', 25 *AJIL* (1931), pp. 26–49.

GAVSHON, A. and RICE, D., *The Sinking of the* Belgrano, 1984, 238p.

GENET, R., *Précis de droit maritime pour le temps de guerre*, 1937, 2 vols.

GHARABACH, M.J., 'Self-Defense in International Law: Legal Aspects of IR655 Tragedy', 7 *Iranian Journal of International Affairs* (spring 1995), pp. 119–55.

GHOBASHY, O.Z., 'Egypt's Attitude Towards International Law as Expressed in the United Nations – The Egyptian-Israeli Dispute on the Freedom of Navigation in the Suez Canal', 11 *REDI* (1955), pp. 121–31.

GIBSON, R.H. and PRENDERGAST, M., *Histoire de la guerre sous-marine 1914–1918*, 1932, 448p.

GILBERT, 'Les opérations sous-marines de la marine britannique pendant la deuxième guerre mondiale', 208 *Revue Maritime* (1964), pp. 295–307.

GILLILAND, J., 'Submarines and Targets: Suggestions for New Codified Rules of Submarine Warfare', 73 *Georgetown Law Journal* (1985), pp. 975–1005.

GIOIA, A., 'Neutrality and Non-Belligerency' in Post, H.H.G. (ed.), *International Economic Law and Armed Conflict*, 1994, pp. 51–110.

GOODHART, P., *Fifty Ships that Saved the World – The Foundation of the Anglo-American Alliance*, 1965, 267p.

GORDON, E., 'La visite des convois neutres', 41 *RGDIP* (1934), pp. 566–630.

—— 'Le navire de commerce neutre sous convoi de la marine militaire d'un belligérant', 17 *RDILC* (1936), pp. 165–96.

GOY, R, 'La révision des jugements de prise après la seconde guerre mondiale', 14 *AFDI* (1968), pp. 343–68.

GRAHAM, M.W., 'Neutrality and the World War', 17 *AJIL* (1923), pp. 704–23.

—— 'The Effect of the League of Nations Covenant on the Theory and Practice of Neutrality', 15 *California Law Review* (1927), pp. 357–77.

GREEN, L.C., 'The Falklands, the Law and the War', 38 *Yearbook of World Affairs* (1984), pp. 89–119.

GREGORY, C.N., 'The Sale of Munitions of War by Neutrals to Belligerents', 60 *Ann.AAPSS* (1915), pp. 183–91.

—— 'Neutrality and the Sale of Arms', 10 *AJIL* (1916), pp. 543–55.

GRIFFITHS, M., *The Hidden Menace*, 1981, 159p.

GROSS, L., 'Passage Through the Suez Canal of Israel-Bound Cargo and Israel Ships', 51 *AJIL* (1957), pp. 530–68.

—— 'Passage Through the Strait of Tiran and in the Gulf of Aqaba', 33 *LCP* (1968), pp. 125–46.

GUICHARD, L., *The Naval Blockade 1914–1918*, 1930, 324p.

GUTTINGER, P., 'Réflexions sur la jurisprudence des prises maritimes de la seconde guerre mondiale', 79 *RGDIP* (1975), pp. 25–91.

HAGELIN, B., *Neutrality and Foreign Military Sales – Military Production and Sales Restrictions in Austria, Finland, Sweden, and Switzerland*, 1990, 158p.

HALKIOPOULOS, T., 'L'interférence des règles du nouveau droit de la mer et du droit de la guerre' in Dupuy, R.J. and Vignes, D. (eds), *Traité du nouveau droit de la mer*, 1985, pp. 1095–1104.

HALL, J.A., *The Law of Naval Warfare*, 1921, 398p.

HALL, M.T., 'False Colors and Dummy Ships: The Use of Ruse in Naval Warfare', 42 *US Naval War College Review* (1989), no.3, pp. 52–62.

HALL, S.S., 'Submarine Warfare', 5 *GST* (1919), pp. 82–94.

HAMPSHIRE, A.C., *The Phantom Fleet*, 1960, 208p.

—— *On Hazardous Service*, 1974, 256p.

HARLOW, B.A., 'The Law of Neutrality at Sea for the 80s and Beyond', 3 *Pacific Basin Law Journal* (1984), pp. 42–54.

HARTCUP, G., *Camouflage – A History of Concealment and Deception in War*, 1979, 156p.

HASTINGS, M. and JENKINS, S., *The Battle for the Falklands*, 1983, 384p.

HASWELL, J., *The Intelligence and Deception of the D-Day Landings*, 1979.

HENKIN, L., 'Force, Intervention and Neutrality in Contemporary International Law', 57 *Proc.ASIL* (1963), pp. 147–73.

HERSHEY, A.S., 'Should the Right to Establish War Zones on the High Seas Be Recognized and What, If Any, Should Be the Provisions of International Law on the Subject?', 10 *Proc.ASIL* (1916), pp. 87–92.

HERZOG, S.A., 'When Does Title to Prize Pass?', 18 *AJIL* (1924), pp. 483–506.

HEWISH, M., 'The Falklands Conflict, Part 3: Naval Operations', 15 *International Defense Review* (1982), pp. 1340–43.

HIGGINS, A.P., 'Armed Merchant Ships', 8 *AJIL* (1914), pp. 705–22.

—— 'Submarine Warfare', 1 *BYIL* (1920–1), pp. 149–65.

—— 'Ships of War as Prize', 6 *BYIL* (1925), pp. 103–10.

—— 'Visit, Search and Detention', 7 *BYIL* (1926), pp. 43–53.

—— 'Le droit de visite et de capture dans la guerre maritime', 11 *RCADI* (1926), pp. 65–170.

HILL, N.L., 'The Origin of the Law of Unneutral Service', 23 *AJIL* (1929), pp. 56–67.

HIRO, D., *The Longest War: The Iran-Iraq Military Conflict*, 1989, 312p.

HOFFMANN, R.F., 'Offensive Mine Warfare: A Forgotten Strategy?', 103 *USNIP* (May 1977), pp. 142–55.

HOLMES, W.J., *Double-Edged Secrets: U.S. Naval Intelligence Operations in the Pacific during World War II*, 1979, 231p.

HOLTZOFF, A., 'Some Phases of the Law of Blockade', 10 *AJIL* (1916), pp. 53–64.

HUDSON, M.O., 'Seizures in Land and Naval Warfare Distinguished', 16 *AJIL* (1922), pp. 375–90.

HYDE, C.C., *Maritime War*, 1918, 210p.

—— 'The Arms Traffic from the Standpoint of International Law', 16 *Proc.APS* (1935), pp. 3–11.

JACOBS, A.J., 'Neutrality', 8 *GST* (1922), pp. 39–55.

JENKINS, M., 'Air Attacks on Neutral Shipping in the Persian Gulf: The Legality of the Iraqi Exclusion Zone and Iranian Reprisals', 8 *Boston College International and Comparative Law Review* (1985), pp. 517–49.

JESSUP, P.C., *American Neutrality and International Police*, 1928, 170p.

—— 'The Birth, Death and Reincarnation of Neutrality', 26 *AJIL* (1932), pp. 789–93.

—— 'Is Neutrality Essential?', 27 *Proc.ASIL* (1933), pp. 134–42.

—— *Neutrality – Its History, Economics and Law*, vol.IV, 1936, 237p.

—— 'Planned Neutrality', 192 *Ann.AAPSS* (1937), pp. 99–106.

—— 'The Diversion of Merchantmen', 34 *AJIL* (1940), pp. 312–15.

—— 'Should International Law Recognize an Intermediate Status between Peace and War?', 48 *AJIL* (1954), pp. 98–103.

JESSUP, P.C. and DEÁK, F., 'The Early Development of the Law of Neutral Rights', 46 *Political Science Quarterly* (1931), pp. 481–508.

—— *Neutrality – Its History, Economics and Law*, vol.I, 1935, 294p.

JOHNSON, E.A. and KATCHER, D.A., *Mines Against Japan*, 1974, 313p.

JONES, T.D., 'The International Law of Maritime Blockade – A Measure of Naval Economic Interdiction', 26 *Howard Law Journal* (1983), pp. 759–79.

JOUAN, R., *La marine allemande dans la seconde guerre mondiale d'après les conférences navales du Führer*, 1949, 304p.

JOYNER, C.C. (ed.), *The Persian Gulf War – Lessons for Strategy, Law, and Diplomacy*, 1990, 256p.

KAHN, D., *Seizing the Enigma: The Race to Break the German U-boat Codes, 1939–1943*, 1991.

KARSH, E., 'Military Lessons of the Iran-Iraq War', 33 *Orbis* (1989), pp. 209–23.

KATEVENIS, G., 'The Law of Maritime Warfare – Considerations on the Law of Prize Jurisdiction Over the Enemy's Ships in Time of

War', 4 *Revue de Droit Pénal Militaire et de Droit de la Guerre* (1965), pp. 359–68.

KAUL, R., 'The Indo-Pakistani War and the Changing Balance of Power in the Indian Ocean', 99 *USNIP* (May 1973), pp. 172–95.

KENWORTHY, J.M. and YOUNG, G., *Freedom of the Seas*, 1928, 283p.

KERR, N., 'The Falklands Campaign', 35 *US Naval War College Review* (1982), no.6, pp. 14–21.

KIMBALL, W.F., *The Most Unsordid Act: Lend-Lease, 1939–1941*, 1969, 281p.

KLEEN, R., *De la contrebande de guerre et des transports interdits aux neutres d'après les principes du droit international contemporain*, 1893, 275p.

—— *Lois et usages de la neutralité*, 2 vols, 1898, 1900.

KNAUTH, A.W., 'Prize Law Reconsidered', 46 *Columbia Law Review* (1946), pp. 69–93.

KOMARNICKI, T., 'The Place of Neutrality in the Modern System of International Law', 80 *RCADI* (1952), pp. 395–510.

KOSONEN, A., 'New Legal Horizons of Neutrality and Military Export' in *Finnish Branch of ILA 1946–1986, Essays on International Law*, 1987, pp. 88–113.

KRAUSE, K., 'Transferts d'armement et gestion des conflits: le cas de la guerre Iran-Irak', *Cultures et Conflits* (1992), pp. 13–40.

KULSRUD, C.J., *Maritime Neutrality to 1780*, 1936, 351p.

KUNZ, J.L., 'The Covenant of the League of Nations and Neutrality', 29 *Proc.ASIL* (1935), pp. 36–42.

—— 'Le problème de la neutralité aux Etats-Unis 1920–1939', 47 *RGDIP* (1940), pp. 66–156.

—— 'Neutrality and the European War 1939–1940', 39 *Michigan Law Review* (1940–1), pp. 719–54.

—— 'British Prize Cases, 1939–1941', 36 *AJIL* (1942), pp. 204–28.

LAGARDERE, J.-L., 'Les modalités de conclusion d'un contrat de vente d'armes' in *Le droit international et les armes*, Proceedings of the sixteenth SFDI colloquium at Montpellier, 1983, pp. 189–203.

LALIVE, J.-F., *Le droit de la neutralité et le problème des credits consentis par les neutres aux belligérants*, 1941, 238p.

—— 'International Organization and Neutrality', 24 *BYIL* (1947), pp. 72–89.

LANGENBERG, W.H., 'Destroyers for Naval Bases: Highlights of an Unprecedented Trade', USNWC, 62 *International Law Studies* (1980), pp. 519–31.

LANGER, W.L. and GLEASON, S.E., *The Undeclared War, 1940–1941*, 1953, 963p.

LANGMAID, K., *The Approaches Are Mined!*, 1965, 256p.

LANGSTON, B. and BRINGLE, D., 'Operation Praying Mantis – The Air View', 115 *USNIP* (May 1989), pp. 54–65.

LAPIDOTH, R., 'The Reopened Suez Canal in International Law', 4 *Syracuse Journal of International Law and Commerce* (1976), pp. 1–49.

LA PRADELLE, P.G.de, 'L'évolution de la neutralité', 14 *Revue de droit international* (1934), pp. 197–221.

LARSON, D.L., 'Naval Weaponry and the Law of the Sea', 18 *ODIL* (1987), pp. 125–98.

LARSON, D.L. and ROTH, M.W., 'The Law of the Sea and Maritime Strategy', 13 *Marine Policy* (1989), pp. 193–217.

LASH, J.P., *Roosevelt and Churchill 1939–1941: The Partnership that Saved the West*, 1976, 528p.

LAURENS, A., *Le blocus et la guerre sous-marine 1914–1918*, 1924, 217p.

LAUTENSCHLAGER, K., 'Technology and the Evolution of Naval Warfare', 8 *Int.Sec.* (1983), pp. 3–51.

—— 'The Submarine in Naval Warfare, 1901–2001', 11 *Int.Sec.* (1986–87), pp. 94–140.

LAUTERPACHT, H., 'Neutrality and Collective Security', 2 *Politica* (1936–7), pp. 133–55.

LAWRENCE, T.H. and CARTER, M., 'Neutrality and War Zones', 1 *GST* (1915), pp. 33–45.

LECKOW, R., 'The Iran-Iraq Conflict in the Gulf: The Law of War Zones', 37 *ICLQ* (1988), pp. 629–44.

LEINER, F.C., 'Maritime Security Zones: Prohibited Yet Perpetuated', 24 *VJIL* (1984), pp. 967–92.

LE JEMTEL, Y., *L'assistance hostile dans les guerres maritimes modernes*, 1938, 248p.

LE MASSON, H., 'L'escadre des épouvantails', *Revue Maritime* (oct.1937), pp. 487–99.

LEROUX, C., *Le droit international pendant la guerre maritime russo-japonaise*, 1911, 268p.

LEVIE, H.S., 'The Falkland Crisis and the Laws of War' in Coll, A.R. and Arend, A.C. (eds), *The Falklands War – Lessons for Strategy, Diplomacy and International Law*, 1985, pp. 64–77.

—— *Mine Warfare at Sea*, 1992, 233p.

LEVRAN, A., 'The Iran-Iraq War and the American Naval Intervention' in Levran, A. (ed.), *The Middle East Military Balance 1987–88*, JCSS, pp. 63–92.

—— 'Strategic Air Attacks in the Iran-Iraq War: The Gulf Campaign' in Levran, A. (ed.), *The Middle East Military Balance 1987–88*, JCSS, pp. 230–55.

LINNAN, D.K., 'Iran Air Flight 655 and Beyond: Free Passage, Mistaken Self-Defense, and State Responsibility', 16 *YJIL* (1991), pp. 245–389.

LOTT, A.S., *Most Dangerous Sea – A History of Mine Warfare, and an Account of U.S. Navy Mine Warfare Operations in World War II and Korea*, 1959, 322p.

LOUVARD, J., *La guerre sous-marine au commerce*, 1934, 172p.

LOWE, A.V., 'Some Legal Problems Arising from the Use of the Seas for Military Purposes', 10 *Marine Policy* (1986), pp. 171–84.

—— 'Self-Defence at Sea' in Butler, W.E. (ed.), *The Non-Use of Force in International Law*, 1989, pp. 185–202.

LUCKNER, F.de, *Le dernier corsaire (1914–1918)*, 1929, 252p.

LUCKOW, U., 'Victory over Ignorance and Fear: The U.S. Minelaying

Attack on North Vietnam', 35 *US Naval War College Review* (Jan.–Feb.1982), pp. 17–27.
LUND, P. and LUDLAM, H., *Out Sweeps! The Story of the Minesweepers in World War II*, 1978, 192p.
MacCHESNEY, B., 'The *Altmark* Incident and Modern Warfare – Innocent Passage in Wartime and the Right of Belligerents to Use Force to Redress Neutrality Violations', 52 *Northwestern University Law Review* (1957–8), pp. 320–43.
MacDONELL, J., 'Some Notes on Blockade', 1 *GST* (1915), pp. 97–111.
MacNULTY, J.F., 'Blockade: Evolution and Expectation', USNWC, 62 *International Law Studies* (1980), pp. 172–96.
MAFFERT, S., *L'évolution de la neutralité de 1914 à la guerre de 1939*, 1942, 164p.
MALKIN, H.W., 'Blockade in Modern Conditions', 3 *BYIL* (1922–3), pp. 87–98.
—— 'The Inner History of the Declaration of Paris', 8 *BYIL* (1927), pp. 1–44.
MALLISON, W.T., *Submarines in General and Limited Wars*, USNWC, *International Law Series* (1966), 230p.
MALLISON, S.V. and MALLISON, W.T., 'A Survey of the International Law of Naval Blockade', 102 *USNIP* (Feb.1976), pp. 44–53.
MANSON, J.M., *Diplomatic Ramifications of Unrestricted Submarine Warfare, 1939–1941*, 1990, 215p.
MARTIN, C.E., 'The Legal Position of War and Neutrality During the Last Twenty-Five Years', 25 *Proc.ASIL* (1931), pp. 137–67.
MARTINEZ, J.-C., 'Le droit international et le commerce des armes' in *Le droit international et les armes*, Proceedings of the 16th SFDI Colloquium at Montpellier, 1983, pp. 93–188.
MATTHEWS, R., 'The Neutrals as Gunrunners', 35 *Orbis* (1991), pp. 41–52.
MAURER, M. and PASZEK, L.J., 'Origin of the *Laconia* Order', 109 *Journal of the Royal United Services Institution* (1964), pp. 338–44.
MAYAMA, A., 'The Influence of the Straits Transit Regime on the Law of Neutrality at Sea', 26 *ODIL* (1995), pp. 1–30.
McDONALD, W., 'Mine Warfare: A Pillar of Maritime Strategy', 111 *USNIP* (Oct.1985), pp. 46–53.
MEACHAM, J.A., 'Four Mining Campaigns: An Historical Analysis of the Decisions of the Commanders', 19 *US Naval War College Review* (June 1967), no.10, pp. 75–129.
MELIA, T.M., *Damn the Torpedoes: A Short History of US Naval Mine Countermeasures, 1775–1991*, 1992.
McDONALD, W.L., 'The Convoy Mission', 114 *USNIP* (May 1988), pp. 36–44.
McNEILL, J.H., 'Neutral Rights and Maritime Sanctions: The Effects of Two Gulf Wars', 31 *VJIL* (1991), pp. 631–43.
MEDLICOTT, W.N., *The Economic Blockade*, 2 vols, 1952, 1959.
MEYROWITZ, H., *Le principe de l'égalité des belligérants devant de droit de la guerre*, 1970, 418p.

—— 'Le protocole additionnel I aux conventions de Genève de 1949 et le droit de la guerre maritime', 89 *RGDIP* (1985), pp. 243–98.
MICHAILIDÈS, P., *La neutralité et la Société des Nations*, 1933, 252p.
MICHELSEN, A., *La guerre sous-marine 1914–1918*, 1928, 254p.
MIDDLEBROOK, M., *Operation Corporate – The Falklands War, 1982*, 1985, 430p.
—— *The Fight for the Malvinas – The Argentine Forces in the Falklands War*, 1989, 321p.
MILLER, W.O., 'Law of Naval Warfare', USNWC, 62 *International Law Studies* (1980), pp. 263–70.
MODELSKI, G. and THOMPSON, W.R., *Seapower in Global Politics, 1494–1993*, 1988, 380p.
MODJORIAN, L.A., 'Aspects juridiques de la neutralité dans le monde contemporain', 11 *Revue de Droit Contemporain* (1964), pp. 41–50.
MOHR, U., *Atlantis – The Story of a German Surface Raider*, 1955, 246p.
MOINEVILLE, H., *La guerre navale – Réflexions sur les affrontements navals et leur avenir*, 1982, 160p.
MOOS, M., 'The Navicert in World War II', 38 *AJIL* (1944), pp. 115–19.
MORABITO, R.E., 'Maritime Interdiction: Evolution of a Strategy', 22 *ODIL* (1991), pp. 301–11.
MOREY, W.C., 'The Sale of Munitions of War', 10 *AJIL* (1916), pp. 467–91.
MORI, K., *The Submarine in War*, 1931, 185p.
MORRISEY, A.M., *The American Defense of Neutral Rights 1914–1917*, 1939, 230p.
MUGGENTHALER, A.K., *German Raiders of World War II*, 1977, 308p.
MUSSINGTON, D., 'Understanding Contemporary International Arms Transfers', IISS, 291 *Adelphi Papers* (1994), 75p.
MYERS, D.P., 'The Legal Basis of the Rules of Blockade in the Declaration of London', 4 *AJIL* (1910), pp. 571–95.
NEUMAN, S.G., 'Le contrôle des transferts d'armes: utopie ou réalité?', *Cultures et Conflits* (1992), pp. 93–111.
NEUMAN, S.G. and HARKAVY, R.E. (eds), *Arms Transfers in the Modern World*, 1979, 375p.
NIELSEN, F.K., 'The Future of Belligerent Rights on the Sea', 29 *Proc.ASIL* (1935), pp. 11–19.
NORDQUIST, M.H. and WACHENFELD, M.G., 'Legal Aspects of Reflagging Kuwaiti Tankers and Laying of Mines in the Persian Gulf', 31 *GYIL* (1988), pp. 138–64.
NORTON, P.M., 'Between the Ideology and the Reality: The Shadow of the Law of Neutrality', 17 *Harvard International Law Journal* (1976), pp. 249–311.
NOTT, J., 'The Falklands Campaign', 109 *USNIP* (May 1983), pp. 118–39.
O'CONNELL, D.P., 'International Law and Contemporary Naval Operations', 44 *BYIL* (1970), pp. 19–85.
—— 'The Legality of Naval Cruise Missiles', 66 *AJIL* (1972), pp. 785–94.
—— *The Influence of Law on Sea Power*, 1975, 204p.
—— 'Limited War at Sea Since 1945' in Howard, M. (ed.), *Restraints on War*, 1979, pp. 123–34.

OGLEY, R., *The Theory and Practice of Neutrality in the Twentieth Century*, 1970, 217p.

O'ROURKE, R., 'The Tanker War', 114 *USNIP* (May 1988), pp. 29–34.

ORVIK, N., *The Decline of Neutrality 1914–1941*, 1953, 294p.

PARKINSON, F., 'Prize Law in the Seventeenth and Eighteenth Centuries' in Butler, W.E., *The Law of the Sea and International Shipping: Anglo-Soviet Post-UNCLOS Perspectives*, 1985, pp. 235–57.

PATTERSON, A., 'Mining: A Naval Strategy', 23 *US Naval War College Review* (May 1971), no.9, pp. 52–66.

PCHEDECKI, E., *Le droit international maritime et la grande guerre*, 1916, 268p.

PELLOUX, R., 'L'embargo sur les exportations d'armes et l'évolution de l'idée de neutralité', 41 *RGDIP* (1934), pp. 58–75.

PERRY, M.F., *Infernal Machines – The Story of Confederate Submarine and Mine Warfare*, 1965, 231p.

PHILLIMORE, W.G.F., 'Destruction of Merchantmen by a Belligerent', 2 *GST* (1916), pp. 175–78.

PILLET, A., 'Le libre usage du pavillon en temps de guerre maritime – Nécessité de réforme', 5 *RGDIP* (1898), pp. 444–51.

PEACE, D.L., 'Major Maritime Events in the Persian Gulf Between 1984 and 1991: A Juridical Analysis', 31 *VJIL* (1991), pp. 545–66.

PERCY, E., *Maritime Trade in War*, 1929, 114p.

PERKINS, J.B., 'Operation Praying Mantis – The Surface View', 115 *USNIP* (May 1989), pp. 66–70.

PERRINJAQUET, J., 'La guerre européenne et les relations commerciales des belligérants et des neutres: L'application des théories de la contrebande de guerre et du blocus', 22 *RGDIP* (1915), pp. 127–238.

—— 'La guerre commerciale sous-marine – Les torpillages du *Lusitania*, de l'*Arabic*, de l'*Ancona* et du *Persia* – Les protestations des États-Unis et les concessions de l'Allemagne', 23 *RGDIP* (1916), pp. 117–203, 394–423, and 24 *RGDIP* (1917), pp. 137–243, 365–436.

PHILLIMORE, G.G., 'The Future of Neutrality', 4 *GST* (1918), pp. 43–70.

PHILLIPS, W.A. and REEDE, A.H., *Neutrality – Its History, Economics and Law*, vol.II, 1936, 339p.

POLITIS, N., *La neutralité et la paix*, 1935, 228p.

PONTING, C., *The Right to Know – The Inside Story of the Belgrano Affair*, 1985, 214p.

POPPER, D.H., 'American Neutrality and Maritime Rights', 15 *Foreign Policy Reports* (1939–40), pp. 242–56.

POST, H.H.G. (ed.), *International Economic Law and Armed Conflict*, 1994, 215p.

POTTER, H., 'The Foundations of Modern Prize Law', 10 *GST* (1924), pp. 37–46.

POWERS, R.D., 'International Law and Open-Ocean Mining', 15 *US Judge Advocate General Journal* (1961), pp. 55–8.

PRESTON, A., *Sea Combat Off the Falklands*, 1982, 143p.

PREUSS, L., 'Some Effects of Governmental Controls on Neutral Duties', 31 *Proc.ASIL* (1937), pp. 108–19.

PRINCE, S., 'The Contribution of the Royal Navy to the United Nations

Forces during the Korean War', 17 *Strategic Studies* (June 1994), pp. 94–120.

PYKE, H.R., *The Law of Contraband of War*, 1915, 314p.

QUIGLEY, H.S., 'The Immunity of Private Property from Capture at Sea', 11 *AJIL* (1917), pp. 22–45.

RANFT, B., 'Restraints on War at Sea Before 1945' in Howard, M. (ed.), *Restraints on War*, 1979, pp. 39–56.

RAUCH, E., *The Protocol Additional to the Geneva Conventions for the Protection of Victims of International Armed Conflicts and the United Nations Convention on the Law of the Sea: Repercussions on the Law of Naval Warfare*, 1984, 165p.

—— 'Le droit contemporain de la guerre maritime – Quelques problèmes créés par le protocole additionnel I de 1977', 89 *RGDIP* (1985), pp. 958–76.

—— 'Military Uses of the Oceans', 28 *GYIL* (1985), pp. 229–67.

—— 'Discussion Paper on the Law of Naval Warfare', 26 *Revue de Droit Pénal Militaire et de Droit de la Guerre* (1987), pp. 31–78.

REED, J.J., 'Damn the Torpedoes!: International Standards Regarding the Use of Automatic Submarine Mines', 8 *Fordham International Law Journal* (1984–5), pp. 286–322.

REIT, S., *Masquerade – The Amazing Camouflage Deceptions of World War II*, 1978, 255p.

REUTER, P., *Étude de la règle: Toute prise doit être jugée*, 1933, 315p.

RICHARDS, H.E., 'The British Prize Courts and the War', 1 *BYIL* (1920–1), pp. 11–34.

—— 'Contraband', 3 *BYIL* (1922–3), pp. 1–16.

RICHMOND, H., 'The Value of the Right of Capture at Sea in Time of War', 9 *BYIL* (1928), pp. 50–8.

RICKOVER, H.G., 'International Law and the Submarine', 61 *USNIP* (1935), pp. 1213–27.

RITCHIE, H., *The Navicert System During the World War*, 1938, 83p.

ROACH, J.A., 'Rules of Engagement', 36 *US Naval War College Review* (1983), no.1, pp. 46–55.

—— 'Missiles on Target: Targeting and Defense Zones in the Tanker War', 31 *VJIL* (1991), pp. 593–610.

—— 'Ruses and Perfidy: Deception during Armed Conflict', 23 *University of Toledo Law Review* (1992), pp. 395–420.

ROBERTSON, H.B., 'Submarine Warfare', *US Judge Advocate General Journal* (Nov.1956), pp. 3–9.

—— 'Interdiction of Iraqi Maritime Commerce in the 1990–1991 Persian Gulf Conflict', 22 *ODIL* (1991), pp. 289–99.

RODGERS, W.L., 'Suggestions as to Changes in the International Law for Maritime War', 17 *AJIL* (1923), pp. 1–14.

ROHWER, J., 'Naval Warfare Since 1945', 104 *USNIP* (May 1978), pp. 66–83.

ROMAT, E., 'L'heureuse croisière du raider 21', *Revue Maritime* (sept.1948), pp. 1109–21.

RONZITTI, N., 'La guerre du Golfe, le déminage et la circulation des navires', 33 *AFDI* (1987), pp. 647–62.

—— 'Le droit humanitaire applicable aux conflits armés en mer', 242 *RCADI* (1993), pp. 9–196.
ROOT, E., 'The Real Significance of the Declaration of London', 6 *AJIL* (1912), pp. 583–94.
ROSCOE, E.S., *A History of the English Prize Court*, 1924, 115p.
ROTOCKI, Z., 'Aircraft and Prize Law in Sea Warfare', 4 *PYIL* (1971), pp. 187–208.
ROUCOUNAS, E., 'Some Issues Relating to War Crimes in Air and Sea Warfare', 24 *IYHR* (1994), pp. 223–40.
ROUSSOS, G., 'Le principe de la liberté de passage du canal de Suez et l'application des règles du droit de la guerre maritime', 1 *Revue de Droit International pour le Moyen-Orient* (1951–2), pp. 151–64.
ROWSON, S.W.D., 'Modern Blockade: Some Legal Aspects', 23 *BYIL* (1946), pp. 346–53.
—— 'Prize Law During the Second World War', 24 *BYIL* (1947), pp. 160–215.
ROXBURGH, R.F., 'Submarines at the Washington Conference', 3 *BYIL* (1922–3), pp. 150–8.
RUBIN, A.P., 'The Concept of Neutrality in International Law', 16 *Denver Journal of International Law and Policy* (1988), pp. 353–75.
RUGE, F., *Der Seekrieg – The German Navy's Story 1939–1945*, 1957, 440p.
—— 'L'évolution de la stratégie de la guerre des mines', *Revue Maritime* (décembre 1966), no.238, pp. 1412–26.
RUSSO, F.V., 'Neutrality at Sea in Transition: State Practice in the Gulf War as Emerging International Customary Law', 19 *ODIL* (1988), pp. 381–99.
SALWAT, A., 'Le conseil des prises égyptien: Organisation, compétence et procédure', 6 *REDI* (1950), pp. 24–32.
SANDIFORD, R., 'Évolution du droit de la guerre maritime et aérienne', 68 *RCADI* (1939), pp. 555–686.
SCHEER, R., *La flotte allemande de haute mer pendant la guerre mondiale*, 1930, 414p.
SCHEINA, R.L., 'The Malvinas Campaign', 109 *USNIP* (May 1983), pp. 98–117.
SCHILLER, T.S., 'The Gulf War and Shipping: Recent Developments' in Parritt, B.A.H. (ed.), *Violence at Sea*, 1986, pp. 109–27.
SCHINDLER, D., 'Aspects contemporains de la neutralité', 121 *RCADI* (1967), pp. 221–321.
—— 'Transformations in the Law of Neutrality Since 1945' in Delissen, A.J.M. and Tanja, G.J. (eds), *Humanitarian Law of Armed Conflict – Challenges Ahead, Essays in Honour of Frits Kalshoven*, 1991, pp. 367–86.
SCHREADLEY, R.L., 'The Naval War in Vietnam, 1950–1970', 97 *USNIP* (May 1971), pp. 186–92.
SCHWARZENBERGER, G., 'The Aid Britain Bill and the Law of Neutrality', 27 *GST* (1941), pp. 1–29.
SCOTT, J.B., 'The Neutrality of the Good Neighbor', 29 *Proc.ASIL* (1935), pp. 1–11.
—— 'Neutrality of the United States', 29 *AJIL* (1935), pp. 644–52.
SCOTT, J.B. (ed.), *The Armed Neutralities of 1780 and 1800*, 1918, 698p.

SEAMANS, A.B., 'Armed Merchantmen – A Factor in Naval Warfare', 30 *Current History* (1929), pp. 593–602.

SÉFÉRIADÈS, S., 'La conception de la neutralité dans l'ancienne Grèce', 16 *RDILC* (1935), pp. 641–62.

SEYMOUR, C., *American Neutrality 1914–1917*, 1935, 187p.

SHEARER, I.A., 'International Humanitarian Law and Naval Operations' in *Quatre études du droit international humanitaire*, 1985, pp. 17–34.

SHOTWELL, J.T., 'A Study of Neutrality Legislation', 316 *Int.Con.* (Jan.1936), pp. 5–17.

SLOUTZKY, N., *Le contrôle du commerce international des armes de guerre*, 1969, 155p.

SMITH, F., *The Destruction of Merchant Ships Under International Law*, 1917, 109p.

SMITH, H.A., 'The Future of Neutrality', 143 *Contemporary Review* (1933), pp. 314–18.

—— 'Le développement moderne des lois de la guerre maritime', 63 *RCADI* (1938), pp. 603–92.

—— *The Law and Custom of the Sea*, 3rd edn, 1959, 291p.

SMITH, R.W., 'The Q-ship, Cause and Effect', 79 *USNIP* (May 1953), pp. 533–41.

STEELE, G.C., 'Decoy as a Weapon in Naval Warfare', 68 *Journal of the Royal United Services Institution* (1923), pp. 99–108.

STETTINIUS, E.R., *Lend-Lease: Weapon for Victory*, 1944, 358p.

STIMSON, H.L., 'Neutrality and War Prevention', 29 *Proc.ASIL* (1935), pp. 121–33.

STOCKTON, C.H., 'The Declaration of Paris', 14 *AJIL* (1920), pp. 356–68.

—— 'The Use of Submarine Mines and Torpedoes in Time of War', 2 *AJIL* (1908), pp. 276–84.

STONE, W.T., 'Will Neutrality Keep U.S. Out of War?', 15 *Foreign Policy Reports* (1939–40), pp. 166–76.

STOWELL, E.C., 'The Status of Armed Merchantmen', 11 *Proc.ASIL* (1917), pp. 19–23.

STUBBS, C., 'The Position of Enemy Merchantmen', 1 *GST* (1915), pp. 9–13.

SUETER, M.F., *The Evolution of the Submarine Boat, Mine, and Torpedo from the Sixteenth Century to the Present Time*, 1907, 384p.

SWAYZE, F.B., 'Traditional Principles of Blockade in Modern Practice: United States Mining of Internal and Territorial Waters of North Vietnam', 29 *US Judge Advocate General Journal* (1977), no.2, pp. 143–73.

TÉNÉKIDÈS, C.G., 'La neutralité en son état d'évolution actuelle', 20 *RDILC* (1939), pp. 256–85.

THOMAS, E.D., 'Theory of Neutrality', 186 *Ann.AAPSS* (1936), pp. 163–68.

THOMPSON, H.K. and STRUTZ, H. (eds), *Doenitz at Nuremberg: A Reappraisal – War Crimes and the Military Professional*, 1976, 198p.

THORPE, A.G.Y., 'Mine Warfare at Sea – Some Legal Aspects of the Future', 18 *ODIL* (1987), pp. 255–78.

THORPE, F.N., 'Should the Right to Establish War Zones on the High Seas Be Recognized and What, If Any, Should Be the Provisions of International Law on the Subject?', 10 *Proc.ASIL* (1916), pp. 71–87.

TORRELLI, M., 'La neutralité en question', 96 *RGDIP* (1992), pp. 5–43.

TOUVET, G., *Les mines sous-marines automatiques de contact et la guerre de 1914–1918*, 1932, 197p.

TRAIN, H.D., 'An Analysis of the Falkland/Malvinas Islands Campaign', 41 *US Naval War College Review* (1988), no.1, pp. 33–50.

TRAPPE, J., 'On the Jurisdiction of the Egyptian Prize Court, 1948–1960', 16 *REDI* (1960), pp. 60–7.

TRÉVILY, J., *Essai sur l'histoire et la situation du sous-marin en droit international*, 1931, 251p.

TRIMBLE, E.G., 'Possible Restatement of the Law Governing the Conduct of War at Sea', 24 *Proc.ASIL* (1930), pp. 119–26.

—— 'Violations of Maritime Law by the Allied Powers During the World War', 24 *AJIL* (1930), pp. 79–99.

TUCKER, R.W., *The Law of War and Neutrality at Sea*, USNWC, 50 *International Law Studies* (1955), 1957, 448p.

TURLINGTON, E., *Neutrality – Its History, Economics and Law*, vol.III, 1936, 267p.

TURNER, S., 'The Unobvious Lessons of the Falklands War', 109 *USNIP* (April 1983), pp. 50–7.

VAN DYKE, J.M., 'Military Exclusion and Warning Zones on the High Seas', 15 *Marine Policy* (1991), pp. 147–69.

VERZIJL, J.H.W., *Le droit des prises de la Grande Guerre*, 1924, 1497p.

VINCINEAU, M., *Exportation d'armes et droit des peuples*, 1984, 315p.

—— 'Les ventes d'armes à l'Irak avant la deuxième guerre du Golfe' in Centre de Droit International – Université Libre de Bruxelles, *La guerre du Golfe et le droit international*, 1991, pp. 137–45.

VIVAUD, J., *Les navires de commerce armés pour leur défense*, 1936, 163p.

VON HEINEGG, H.W., 'Visit, Search, Diversion, and Capture in Naval Warfare: Part I, The Traditional Law', 29 *CYIL* (1991), pp. 283–329.

—— 'Visit, Search, Diversion, and Capture in Naval Warfare: Part II, Developments since 1945', 30 *CYIL* (1992), pp. 89–136.

—— 'The International Law of Mine Warfare at Sea', 23 *IYHR* (1993), pp. 53–76.

—— 'The Law of Armed Conflict at Sea' in Fleck, D. (ed.), *The Handbook of Humanitarian Law in Armed Conflicts*, 1995, pp. 405–83.

—— 'The Current State of International Prize Law' in Post, H.H.G. (ed.), *International Economic Law and Armed Conflict*, 1994, pp. 5–34.

VON HEINEGG, H.W. (ed.), *The Military Objective and the Principle of Distinction in the Law of Naval Warfare – Report, Commentaries and Proceedings of the Round Table of Experts on International Humanitarian Law Applicable to Armed Conflicts at Sea, Bochum, November 1989*, 1991.

—— *Methods and Means of Combat in Naval Warfare – Report and Commentaries of the Round Table of Experts on International Humanitarian Law Applicable to Armed Conflicts at Sea, Toulon, October 1990*, 1992.

—— *Visit, Search, Diversion and Capture – The Effect of the United Nations Charter on the Law of Naval Warfare – Reports and Commentaries of the*

Round Table of Experts on International Humanitarian Law Applicable to Armed Conflicts at Sea, Bergen, September 1991, 1995, 210p.

—— *Regions of Operations of Naval Warfare – Reports and Commentaries of the Round Table of Experts on International Humanitarian Law Applicable to Armed Conflicts at Sea, Ottawa, September 1992*, 1995, 150p.

VON MACH, E., 'An Argument Against the Exportation of Arms', 60 *Ann.AAPSS* (1915), pp. 192–4.

VON GÖSSELN, J., 'The Sinking of the *Sydney*', 79 *USNIP* (March 1953), pp. 251–5.

WARREN, C., 'Troubles of a Neutral', 12 *Foreign Affairs* (1934), pp. 377–94.

—— 'Prepare for Neutrality', 24 *Yale Review* (1934–5), pp. 467–78.

—— 'Contraband and Neutral Trade', 16 *Proc.APS* (1935), pp. 61–70.

—— 'Safeguards to Neutrality', 14 *Foreign Affairs* (1936), pp. 199–215.

—— 'Lawless Maritime Warfare', 18 *Foreign Affairs* (1940), pp. 424–41.

WEHBERG, H., *Capture in War on Land and Sea*, 1911, 210p.

WEISS, C.J., 'Problems of Submarine Warfare Under International Law', 22 *Intramural Law Review* (1967), pp. 136–51.

WHETTEN, L.L., 'Legal Aspects of the Egyptian Blockade of the Gulf of Aqaba', 45/6 *Revue de Droit International de Sciences Diplomatiques et Politiques* (1967–8), pp. 339–50.

WHITTON, J.B., 'La neutralité et la Société des Nations', 17 *RCADI* (1927), pp. 449–571.

—— 'The Changed Attitude of the Powers toward Neutrality Laws', 30 *Current History* (1929), pp. 454–60.

WILLIAMS, W.L., 'Neutrality in Modern Armed Conflicts: A Survey of the Developing Law', 90 *Military Law Review* (1980), pp. 9–48.

WILSON, G.G., 'Conversion of Merchant Ships into War Ships', 2 *AJIL* (1908), pp. 271–5.

—— 'Armed Merchant Vessels and Submarines', 24 *AJIL* (1930), pp. 337–9.

WILSON, R.R., 'Non-Belligerency in Relation to the Terminology of Neutrality', 35 *AJIL* (1941), pp. 121–3.

WISE, J.C., 'The Rights of Visit and Search, Capture, Angary and Requisition', 16 *AJIL* (1922), pp. 391–9.

WISWALL, F.L., 'Neutrality, the Rights of Shipping and the Use of Force in the Persian Gulf', 31 *VJIL* (1991), pp. 619–29.

WITSCHETZKY, F., *Le navire noir – Le croiseur auxiliaire* Wolf *1916–1918*, 1929, 249p.

WOLFRUM, R., 'Reflagging and Escort Operation in the Persian Gulf: An International Law Perspective', 29 *VJIL* (1989), pp. 387–99.

WOOD, D. and HEWISH, M., 'The Falklands Conflict, Part 1: The Air War', 15 *International Defense Review* (1982), pp. 977–80.

—— 'The Falklands Conflict, Part 2: Missile Operations', 15 *International Defense Review* (1982), pp. 1151–4.

WOODWARD, D., *The Secret Raiders – The Story of the German Armed Merchant Raiders in the Second World War*, 1955, 288p.

WOODWARD, S. and ROBINSON, P., *One Hundred Days – The Memoirs of the Falklands Battle Group Commander*, 1992, 360p.

WOOLSEY, L.H., 'Neutral Persons and Property on the High Seas in Time of War', 29 *Proc.ASIL* (1935), pp. 72–80.

—— 'Government Traffic in Contraband', 34 *AJIL* (1940), pp. 498–503.

WRIGHT, Q., 'The Future of Neutrality', 242 *Int.Con.* (1928), pp. 353–442.

—— 'Neutrality and Neutral Rights Following the Pact of Paris for the Renunciation of War', 24 *Proc.ASIL* (1930), pp. 79–87.

—— 'The Present Status of Neutrality', 34 *AJIL* (1940), pp. 391–415.

—— 'Rights and Duties Under International Law as Affected by the United States Neutrality Act and the Resolutions of Panama', 34 *AJIL* (1940), pp. 238–48.

—— 'The Transfer of Destroyers to Great Britain', 34 *AJIL* (1940), pp. 680–9.

—— 'The Lend-Lease Bill and International Law', 35 *AJIL* (1941), pp. 305–14.

YAKEMTCHOUK, R., *Les transferts internationaux d'armes de guerre*, 1980, 452p.

—— 'Le commerce des armes', 45 *Studia Diplomatica* (1992), 320p.

ZAKHEIM, D.S., 'The South Atlantic Conflict: Strategic, Military and Technological Lessons' in Coll, A.R. and Arend, A.C. (eds), *The Falklands War: Lessons for Strategy, Diplomacy and International Law*, 1985, pp. 159–88.

—— 'The South Atlantic: Evaluating the Lessons' in Brown, J. and Snyder, W.P. (eds), *The Regionalization of Warfare – The Falkland/Malvinas Islands, Lebanon and the Iran-Iraq Conflict*, 1985, pp. 37–54.

ZU DOHNA-SCHLODIEN, N., *La* Möwe – *Ses croisières et ses aventures*, 1929, 219p.

INDEX

This index refers mainly to major subject headings of the laws of war at sea; relevant international agreements, naval manuals and academic initiatives; particular naval conflicts and specific incidents/operations. It does not list case law; states; names of individuals; nor does it refer to the bibliography.

An environmentally friendly book printed and bound in England by www.printondemand-worldwide.com

PEFC Certified

This product is from sustainably managed forests and controlled sources

www.pefc.org

PEFC/16-33-415

FSC www.fsc.org

MIX

Paper from responsible sources

FSC® C004959

This book is made entirely of sustainable materials; FSC paper for the cover and PEFC paper for the text pages.

#0002 - 180815 - C0 - 216/138/37 [39] - CB - 9780710305893